THEORIES OF
PERSONALITY

TENTH EDITION

RICHARD M. RYCKMAN

University of Maine

WADSWORTH
CENGAGE Learning·

Australia • Brazil • Japan • Korea • Mexico • Singapore • Spain • United Kingdom • United States

WADSWORTH
CENGAGE Learning·

Theories of Personality, **Tenth Edition**
Richard M. Ryckman

Publisher: Linda Schreiber-Ganster

Publisher, Psychology & Helping
Professions: Jon-David Hague

Assistant Editor: Paige Leeds

Editorial Assistant: Travis Holland

Media Editor: Mary Noel

Marketing Manager: Janay Pryor

Marketing Communications Manager:
Talia Wise

Art and Cover Direction, Production
Management, and Composition:
PreMediaGlobal

Manufacturing Planner: Linda Hunt

Rights Acquisitions Specialist: Thomas
McDonough

Text Researcher: Pablo D'Stair

Cover Designer: Norman Baugher

Cover Image: © Diversphoto89|
Dreamstime.com

For product information and technology assistance, contact us at
Cengage Learning Customer & Sales Support, 1-800-354-9706.

For permission to use material from this text or product,
submit all requests online at **www.cengage.com/permissions**.
Further permissions questions can be e-mailed to
permissionrequest@cengage.com.

Library of Congress Control Number: 2011945801

Student Edition:

ISBN-13: 978-1-111-83066-3

ISBN-10: 1-111-83066-5

Loose-leaf Edition:

ISBN-13: 978-1-111-83451-7

ISBN-10: 1-111-83451-2

Wadsworth
20 Davis Drive
Belmont, CA 94002-3098
USA

Cengage Learning is a leading provider of customized learning
solutions with office locations around the globe, including Singapore,
the United Kingdom, Australia, Mexico, Brazil, and Japan. Locate your
local office at **www.cengage.com/global**.

Cengage Learning products are represented in Canada by
Nelson Education, Ltd.

To learn more about Wadsworth, visit **www.cengage.com/Wadsworth**

Purchase any of our products at your local college store or at our
preferred online store **www.cengagebrain.com**.

Printed in the United States of America
1 2 3 4 5 6 7 16 15 14 13 12

For Ralph Bogardus.
Thanks for teaching me the meaning of friendship.
You are always an important part of me.

Contents

PART THREE   Trait Perspectives

PART SIX   Social-Behavioristic Perspectives

PART SEVEN The Role of the Grand Personality Theories in Contemporary Personality Psychology

Preface

Theories of Personality serves essentially the same primary purposes in its tenth edition as in the first, published nearly 35 years ago. It reviews the basic concepts and principles of the major, grand theories of personality. These grand theories attempt to explain much of our behavior in a variety of life situations. The text is designed to assess how well each of these theories meet criteria for judging their scientific worth. It also introduces students to the many research studies that test the validity of the major concepts in the theories. In addition, this edition presents issues that currently challenge personality psychologists and discusses some of the major theoretical and research areas and ideas in contemporary personality theory and research.

The material is accessible to undergraduates who have had little or no exposure to the field of personality psychology. In this edition, I have included the latest research studies that show, in general, support for the theories. There are also many more examples from everyday life and unusual topics to stimulate interest among students of both traditional and nontraditional ages. Each major theoretical position is introduced by an overview of the theorist's basic concepts and principles; comparisons of the theories thus follow easily.

Although the goals of the text remain intact, there have been three major changes in the discipline in the past 35 years. First, there has been an explosion of individual difference research around the world because the Internet provides easy access to and the collection of data from large groups of people nationally and internationally from a variety of ages and diverse cultural backgrounds. Second, the Internet also allows researchers from all over the world to communicate with one another and to become familiar with their colleagues' research publications. Third, many of these research efforts have been conducted using the current grand personality theories and their extensions as a guide. Such efforts have generally increased the theories' validity and applicability to the solution of human problems. In this edition, I try to convey the intellectual excitement generated by the ongoing international work with these theories, and, in the final chapter, I also attempt to show how the grand theories of personality that are covered in this course continue to inspire the creative efforts of a new generation of personality psychologists, thus furthering our understanding of human personality.

Organization

The book is divided into seven parts. Part One, "An Introduction to the Discipline," notes the complex and diverse phenomena that are part of human personality. Thus, it would be impossible to create a single theory that is perfectly adequate to the task. A more reasonable goal is to increase our understanding of personality by the creation of theories that are more and more scientifically useful. Chapter 1, "Personality and the Scientific Outlook," addresses the problem of establishing an acceptable definition of personality and considers the reasons for studying individual differences from a scientific perspective. It also provides basic information about the scientific process and the interrelatedness of theory and research. This edition features extended coverage of theory construction and testing. The chapter also explains the criteria by which scientists judge the worth of a theory; students can thus evaluate the theories in succeeding chapters.

Part Two, "Psychoanalytic and Neoanalytic Perspectives," covers Freud and his psychoanalytic theory and the neoanalytic theories of Jung, Adler, Horney, Erikson, and Kohut. In the Freud chapter, his structural theory of personality is presented, along with a presentation of the various defense mechanisms that protect the individual from threat. Also, the theory of psychosexual development is described, and the latest research evidence for the character types is examined. Student interest will be stimulated by the reporting of several clinical case studies in a discussion of the primary assessment techniques. Freud used the case study procedure to better understand the personalities of his patients and to help them overcome their problems.

The chapter on Jung covers the structure and functions of the psyche and gives a presentation of his theory of psychological types. Included as well is extended coverage of the latest research that supports the validity of this theory.

In the Adlerian materials, the basic theory posits feelings of inferiority that cause people to strive for superiority in healthy or unhealthy ways. This model is presented, along with detailed descriptions of healthy and unhealthy individuals. Recent research on birth order is highlighted, and the newest theorizing and research examining the relation of birth order to intellectual achievement is presented.

In the chapter on Karen Horney, her psychoanalytic theory of self-realization is presented in detail, and her seminal views on the roles of hypercompetitiveness and competition avoidance in American society in creating neurotic individuals are examined, along with the newest, validating research evidence. There is also a focus on a more psychologically healthy competitive attitude and its positive implications for effective performance in many areas of life. The role of irrational beliefs in creating psychopathology is highlighted.

In the chapter on Erik Erikson, links are made between his theory of psychosocial development and contemporary elaborations of his position; for example, Erikson's work on identity status in adolescence is extended by the work of Marcia and Waterman. This large body of work by these researchers has been refined and extended to include the latest research on racial/ethnic identity and the emergence of a bicultural identity in minority group members. Erikson's thinking about intimacy in young adulthood is supported by the research of Orlofsky, and his ideas about generativity in middle adulthood are enriched by Bradley and Marcia. These elaborations are reviewed, together with current validating evidence. This chapter also features research tests of Erikson's theory of ego development.

The chapter on Heinz Kohut's self psychology, the latest theory to build upon classical psychoanalysis, outlines Kohut's unique interpretations of phenomena initially examined by Freud. A particular focus is Kohut's creative analysis of the long-lasting damage to the self induced by unempathic parents, who fail to provide their children with the support and understanding necessary to personal growth; such children tend to develop a pathological narcissism, characterized by an unrealistic grandiosity and exhibitionism, which results in ineffective personal functioning. The use of empathy and several new forms of transference to treat patients with various psychological disorders is considered. Finally, Kohut's imaginative account of healthy narcissistic development is presented.

Part Three, "Trait Perspectives," covers the major theories of Allport, Cattell, and Eysenck. In the Allport chapter, his devotion to constructing a humanistic theory of personality is demonstrated, and the tremendous impact of his ideas on contemporary personality psychology is explored. Also, in discussing the characteristics of maturity, there is a presentation of the positive role played by religion and values.

In the chapter on Raymond Cattell's work, the measurement principles underlying his theory of personality are clarified by means of a brief account of two forms of factor analysis—the R and P techniques. A case study demonstrates how unique individual traits can be measured. Cattell's efforts to measure the major source traits of normal and abnormal personality is presented, along with validating research evidence. Also, his attempts to account for the effects of situational variables on personality expression are given. The chapter concludes with Cattell's claim that contemporary society is generally a moral failure and that we need a new morality based on science to rectify the situation.

In the Eysenck chapter, his arousal theory is outlined, along with research evidence that validates its major hypotheses, especially in regard to behavioral differences between introverts and extraverts. There is also extended coverage of the interaction between heredity and environment as it relates to intellectual development, especially IQ. Materials also detail Eysenck's explanations of genius and the links between genius and psychopathology.

Part Four, "Cognitive Perspectives," is devoted to George Kelly's theory of personal constructs. In this edition, special emphasis is given to the ways in which the kinds of constructs individuals possess guide their personal growth. Also, attention is given to the personality assessment measure created by Kelly to map out the person's unique construct system. Finally, Kelly's views on schizophrenia are presented.

Part Five, "Humanistic/Existential Perspectives," covers Maslow, Rogers, and May. In the Maslow chapter, there is a presentation of the hierarchy of needs and a discussion of the possible dangers of B-cognizing in order to make the important point that the self-actualizing process involves the integration of both D- and B-needs. The chapter also includes a discussion of the characteristics of self-actualizing people, along with comments about their imperfections. As Maslow pointed out, all too often people believe that self-actualizers are god-like individuals with no flaws, but the truth is that they have a variety of shortcomings, as well as many strengths.

The Rogers chapter explains his view that healthy persons are those who rely on their own assessment of experiences and feelings in making moral and behavioral decisions rather than yielding to the judgments of others. This discussion leads to an analysis of his organismic-wisdom hypothesis, a central conception in his theory as well as in Maslow's. Also, a key feature of this chapter is Rogers's discussion of the functioning of the psychologically healthy person in society. Finally, there is a consideration of how Rogers's ideas apply to education and marriage. Many of these ideas are as relevant today as when they were first written in the 1960s and 1970s.

The Rollo May chapter begins with his definition of existentialism, and a survey of its roots in European philosophy. It describes the existentialists' disenchantment with our present views of science and discusses their belief that we should study issues more closely related to the major concerns of human existence. To clarify May's major concepts and principles, some similarities and dissimilarities between existentialism and psychoanalysis are examined. There is a detailed presentation of the ways in which values have decayed in contemporary society, and the resultant forms of pathology that we see among many people.

Part Six, "Social-Behavioristic Perspectives," includes Skinner, Rotter, and Bandura. The chapter on Skinner contains a careful review of basic concepts and operant conditioning principles. Recent research examples show the successful application of these concepts and principles to the treatment of behavioral disorders. The chapter on Rotter spells out the basic concepts in his social learning approach to personality and shows how these ideas may be combined to predict behavior accurately. The most recent research evidence for the locus of control construct is covered. In Bandura's social cognitive theory, the concept of self-efficacy is preeminent, and detailed discussion of its role in generating healthy and unhealthy behavior in a variety of life areas is given.

Part Seven, "The Role of the Grand Theories in Contemporary Personality Psychology," notes the important role played by the grand theories in generating new theory and research in contemporary personality psychology. The last chapter, "Theory and Research in Contemporary Personality Psychology," presents five important areas of theorizing and research in personality psychology today, all resting on a solid foundation provided by the grand theories. These areas include (1) a focus by researchers on the impact of biological factors on human development and behavior, (2) the necessity of incorporating a multicultural perspective into personality psychology, (3) the use of a trait taxonomy to increase our understanding of the role of traits within personality, (4) the emergence of a positive psychology, which will help us to better understand virtuous behavior and to identify the conditions under which such behavior in people is facilitated, and (5) the growth of our understanding of individual differences in personality that emerges through analyses of their use of the Internet.

New to this Edition

- **Chapter 3—Jung**. There is an expanded treatment of the theory of psychological types, including a new presentation of differences in the typology profiles of gifted and non-gifted adolescents.

- **Chapter 5—Horney**. Expansion of the theory and research on the central role played by neurotic competitiveness, that is, hypercompetitiveness and competition avoidance, in personality development and functioning, plus an updated treatment of the concept of personal development competition, a psychologically healthy form of competitive attitude.

- **Chapter 6—Erikson**. Extension of the concept of ego identity statuses to include theory and research on ethnic identity. There is an emphasis on the struggle by racial/ethnic minorities to reject negative stereotypes of them by the dominant White majority and to take pride in their own racial/ethnic identity. Also, as part of this struggle, there is also an eventual acceptance of the positive features of the dominant majority group as minority group members forge a new, integrated bicultural identity that maximizes their psychological health.

- **Chapter 8—Allport**. More coverage of the newest developments on the role of religion in the development of the mature human personality.

- **Chapter 10—Eysenck**. Introduction of the latest research showing that divergent and convergent thinking are both necessary for creativity. Geniuses are able to come up with many ideas when searching for a creative solution through divergent thinking and then to make a judgment by selecting the one idea from this array of possible ideas through convergent thinking. Their judgment is then deemed at some point by others in society as original and socially useful, that is, creative. Schizophrenics and other psychotics have many ideas (high divergent thinking) but do not typically engage in the convergent thinking that is necessary for creative solutions.

- **Chapter 16—Rotter**. Increased coverage of the newest research on the central role played by locus of control differences in human development and functioning.

- **Chapter 18.** The materials on behavioral genetics and evolutionary theory are updated and increased. In the section on multiculturalism, there is an increased focus on the need by clinicians to be more sensitive to the racial/ethnic and religious backgrounds of their clients in order to be more effective in their treatment of them. Increased coverage of the Big Five traits is presented. Theorizing and research in positive psychology is updated and expanded. Finally, the hottest area of development in personality psychology is presented, namely, how our understanding of people's major personality characteristics are illuminated through analyses of their differential usage of the Internet.

Helpful pedagogical features in the chapters include Evaluative Comments that assess the scientific worth of each theory; Critical Thinking Questions; a list of Suggested Readings that instructors can use in substituting or adding pertinent materials; and a Glossary, whose items are **boldfaced** in the text.

Acknowledgments

This edition has benefited immensely from the comments of many of my colleagues and from several students. I owe a debt to my colleagues and friends, Joel Gold, Jeff Hecker, Mike Robbins, Larry Smith, Bill Thornton, Geoff Thorpe, and Bart van den Borne for their encouragement. In particular, I thank Joel for the countless stimulating discussions about the various personality theories and related research over the past 40 years. Joel helped me clarify my thinking and writing about many of the topics through his highly constructive criticisms. I also would like to express my appreciation to Shawn Collier for his incisive comments on the roles played by unhealthy and healthy competitive attitudes in the differential willingness to forgive others in American culture. As always, Kathy McAuliffe handled the various tasks involved in the processing of the manuscript skillfully.

The following reviewers made many helpful recommendations that led to several substantial changes and additions in various chapters: Paul Bartoli, East Stroudsburg; Brian Lane, Ramapo College; Brian Oliveira, Santa Clara University; Lawrence Schneider, University of North Texas; Andrea Weyermann, Georgia State University.

It is also a pleasure to acknowledge the fine staff at Cengage Learning. My publisher, Jon-David Hague, and the assistant editor, Paige Leeds, were very helpful in guiding the book to completion.

Finally, I want to express my love for my darling wife, Leona, our sons, Bob and Mark, and our six grandchildren, Cailey, Laine, Maris, Jack, Matthew, and Catherine.

Richard M. Ryckman

PART 1

An Introduction to the Discipline

Personality psychology has been blessed with an array of creative thinkers, whose insights have been of immense value in helping us understand how personality originates, develops, and functions. Although all of the theories covered in this text have certain strengths, not surprisingly each of them also has its limitations. The phenomena encompassed by human personality are simply too complex and diverse for any one individual to unite them in a single, coherent theoretical framework; thus, no one theorist can ever hope to construct a completely adequate theory of personality. The goal instead is to create theories that are more and more adequate or scientifically useful. Therefore, researchers continue to test hypotheses from the various theories currently in existence in an effort to validate, extend, and improve them. Others seek to construct new theories; for them, the current theories serve to stimulate new creative efforts.

To help you understand the strengths and weaknesses of the current theories of personality, we begin by discussing the major concepts used in the construction of scientific theories, the principal research procedures used to test them, and the criteria ordinarily used by investigators to assess their worth. Exposure to this basic information in Chapter 1 should enable you to evaluate the scientific usefulness and adequacy of the theoretical positions presented in succeeding chapters. It also should help you understand better the important areas of theory and research in contemporary personality psychology that are presented in the final chapter.

Personality and the Scientific Outlook

Why Study Personality?

Virtually all of us are interested in knowing more about ourselves and others. In examining our own behavior, we wonder why we are having such difficulty in deciding on a career path, whereas some of our friends have already made their decisions many months ago. We are stymied to explain why we are sometimes rude to our romantic partner even though our love for him or her is overwhelmingly clear to us. We sometimes seek to understand why we are so competitive with others, even when we are playing a friendly game with our closest friends. Making sense of these experiences and others often can help us to make adaptive changes and to live more satisfying lives. In the process of change, our inner conflicts are confronted and resolved. We can establish and clarify the goals that serve to motivate and focus our efforts, thereby enabling us to experience personal growth within the context of making contributions to society.

We are, of course, also interested in knowing more about others. In analyzing their behavior, we wonder, for example, why one of our friends refuses to date a person we find particularly attractive. We are intrigued by the student who is fascinated by astronomy, whereas we find it difficult to listen attentively for more than 10 minutes to a lecture on the topic. On a more bizarre note, we are often at a loss to explain why a 22-year-old man would decide to attend a community gathering outside a supermarket in Tucson, Arizona, arranged so that constituents could meet and greet their local congresswoman, then shoot her in the head, kill six other innocent bystanders, including a 9-year-old girl, and wound many others.

In each of these instances, we seek to generate explanations for the actions we observe: We want to know why these individuals behaved as they did. Being able to understand the behavior of others not only satisfies our curiosity but also gives us a greater sense of control over our lives and makes the world more predictable and less threatening.

Explanations for human behavior also are sought by psychologists who work in the discipline of personality psychology. In seeking explanations for individual differences in behavior, they construct theories designed to explain and therefore help us better understand a wide variety of behavioral differences that we experience. Their efforts are aimed at understanding human motivation and behavior throughout the entire developmental process, from individual differences in activity level at birth to the different attitudes of elderly people toward dying. Clearly, the range of behavior under consideration is so great, and the phenomena examined are so complex, that no investigator, no matter how knowledgeable or creative, can study every aspect of them.

Each investigator brings to the discipline a particular perspective on the subject matter; that is, the investigator's own personality, background, values, experiences, and theoretical orientation guide his or her efforts. The upshot is that each investigator generates a particular definition of personality, along with working assumptions, regarding how personality originates, develops, and operates.

Many laypersons assume that the existence of competing theories in a scientific discipline indicates that the science is immature and has not accumulated a substantial body of knowledge about its subject matter. However, prominent thinkers in the philosophy of science contend that it is rare for any single theory to achieve unquestioned leadership in a discipline, even in the so-called mature or hard sciences, such as physics, chemistry, and biology (Mayr, 1994, p. 332). In fact, a theory's scientific usefulness in solving problems is often judged by comparison with competing theories (Kuhn, 1996, p. 23). In general, theories that are more useful and effective in solving problems tend eventually to replace those that are less useful and effective (Capaldi & Proctor, 2000, p. 448).

Defining Personality

For the layperson, personality is often defined in terms of social attractiveness. The person with a "good personality" is one who impresses others with his or her ability to get along well with people. Beauty pageant contestants are typically judged not only on their talent and physical attractiveness, but also on their "personality," here defined in terms of their popularity with judges and other contestants. Some students also talk about each other in these terms: Catherine is said to have a "great personality," meaning that she behaves in ways that the perceivers find acceptable; John is said to have "no personality," meaning that they find much of John's behavior highly objectionable. Also, personality sometimes is treated as a consolation prize: Travis encourages Matt to date an unattractive female because she has a "great personality"; Jane encourages Linda to date an unattractive male because his "personality makes up for his looks."

Personality defined in terms of social attractiveness is inadequate in two major respects. First, it limits the number and kinds of behavior considered as aspects of personality; that is, only those kinds of behaviors that the perceivers select in making judgments about the attractiveness or unattractiveness of the perceived are regarded as part of personality. Second, it carries the absurd implication that some individuals, who obviously have unique learning histories and unique, biologically based temperament traits, are devoid of personality.

Despite the many definitions of the term, investigators generally agree that **personality** is the dynamic and organized set of characteristics possessed by a person that uniquely influences his or her cognitions, motivations, and behaviors in various situations. It can also be thought of as a **psychological construct** complex abstraction that encompasses the person's unique genetic background (except in the case of identical twins) and learning history and the ways in which these factors influence his or her responses to various environments or situations. Thus, many investigators regard the study of personality as the scientific analysis of individual differences that help to account for why and how people react uniquely, and often creatively, to various environmental or situational demands. The primary focus of interest in the discipline is on the creation of theories that offer explanations for each individual's unique ways of responding to his or her physical, social, and cultural environments. These explanations then lead to predictions that are tested and buttressed by **empirical evidence**. Such theories increase our understanding of individuals and help us to predict their actions accurately.

Our ability to accurately predict an individual's behavior, because we have an adequate explanation of the factors that produce it, may prove very useful. For example, suppose that scientists learn, by verifying a theory of test anxiety about students' academic performances, that one key factor in generating high test anxiety is a lack of adequate preparation for exams. They also find that taking exams in large, crowded, hot, and stuffy classrooms of several hundred students creates severe test anxiety, an inability to concentrate, and poor performance. An instructor could use this knowledge to help improve his or her students' performances on the next test, by changing the conditions that produce poor outcomes. The instructor, for instance, could work with his or her students prior to the test to ensure that they know the materials well and could also provide, if available, separate, air-conditioned rooms for the students to take the test in small groups. These changes might well reduce their students' test anxiety and increase their chances of performing more effectively.

The Scientific Study of Personality

Personality psychologists use the scientific approach to study individual differences because they believe it is the most effective way to gather accurate information about personality functioning. They also hope that such knowledge can be used to benefit people. In the final analysis, psychologists are convinced that a scientific orientation will lead us more directly and surely to beneficial, accurate information than will orientations that rely almost exclusively on rational speculation, mysticism, intuition, or common sense. Their conviction does not mean that those alternative ways of knowing have no value and can never be used to help us understand human behavior; insights stemming from the work of philosophers, novelists, poets, and theologians certainly have contributed to the totality of human self-knowledge. The discipline of personality psychology, however, is scientific in outlook.

In general terms, science is an enterprise concerned with the description, explanation, prediction, and control of events. The outcome of all the efforts by countless investigators is the accumulation of systematized knowledge based on the observation of phenomena or events. Science is grounded in human values and concerns, from which researchers select certain problems for study. Their subjective values also may aid in the creative process in helping them to generate new thinking about problems. While their subjectivity may be helpful, especially in the early stages of research, at later points in the process, such biases may hinder psychological research by interjecting distortions into the process where disinterested objectivity on the part of the scientist is required. For example, if after analyzing his or her data, an investigator interprets them very selectively (in accordance with his or her biases), he or she may publish misleading and invalid conclusions about the study's outcomes. The beauty of science, however, is that it is self-correcting. Specifically, such distortions typically do not stand up to scrutiny from other investigators and eventually are corrected.

In conclusion, the scientific process is benefitted neither by uncompromising objectivity nor by dogmatic subjectivity. Instead there is a need to recognize that a healthy science is one that makes explicit its subjective elements as well as its objective features and recognizes the role that each one plays in the research enterprise (Bornstein, 1999, pp. 1–16; 2010, p. 147). At its best, scientific activity excites the imagination of investigators and taxes their ingenuity. It is often frustrating, for example, when one's **hypotheses** (theory-based predictions) are disconfirmed but rarely dull. Thus, even the disconfirmation of hypotheses can prove exciting in the long run as researchers strive to figure out what happened and why and then proceed to work on creating a new approach to the problem. For them, science is definitely not the passionless, automatic, and impersonal activity imagined by the uninitiated.

Scientific researchers are interested in developing adequate theories that will organize their thinking and enable them to describe, explain, predict, and control phenomena in a given domain. Thus, a **theory** is a conceptual system constructed by investigators to help make sense out of existing information and also to aid in the prediction of as yet unobserved relationships between events.

In its essence, science involves the interaction between two major processes: theory and research. A brief overview of the scientific method, including the manner in which theories are constructed and tested through empirical research, will help you to evaluate critically the theories presented later in this book.

Building Scientific Theories

Inductive versus Deductive Approaches

Inductive theories are created from a solid database of empirical observations. They consist essentially of theoretical summary statements of observed relationships among events and contain a minimum of deductive logic (Marx, 1964, p. 17–18). An example is the **law of effect**: Behaviors followed by reward or the reduction of aversive conditions tend to become more probable, whereas behaviors followed by punishers or the removal of positive reinforcers tend to become less probable (Thorndike, 1913, p. 172). This is a theoretical summary statement derived from empirical observation of the behavior of animals across many species, including humans, under reward and punishment conditions.

Advocates of the inductive approach believe that trying to create and test theories too far in advance of data collection frequently leads to useless experimentation, wasting the time and energy of researchers (Skinner, 1950, p. 194). By useless experimentation, they mean research that has little predictive accuracy or value. Such theories, they contend, contain constructs that are poorly defined and measured and that are often inaccessible to examination; thus, they generate little real knowledge. Focusing on those behaviors and performances that can be directly observed, in their view, yields substantial knowledge that increases our understanding of phenomena (Skinner, 1969, Preface). In other words, advocates like B. F. Skinner believe that such facts can eventually be related to one another in a theory that is scientifically useful.

Although the inductive approach has merit, it also has limitations. Many philosophers of science have contended that researchers using this approach actually do some intuitive theorizing *prior* to data collection, because tentative hypotheses are needed to determine what data are to be collected at a given point in an investigation (Hempel, 1966, p. 13). Also, there is no rule that can tell them when, if ever, they have collected sufficient data to justify making a theoretical generalization or summary statement (Richards, 1987, p. 50).

Most personality theorists have preferred to create and test **deductive theories**. They believe that the inductive approach is too restrictive and conservative and that theories are not simply derived from facts but are invented to account for them (Hempel, 1966, p. 13). They also contend that deductive theories can be precisely stated and tested. Theorists who rely on this strategy use their imagination and creativity to invent hypotheses as tentative answers to problems. These hypotheses must be formulated in precise terms in order to be testable. Thus, the deductive approach is to some extent inductive, in the sense that it involves the acceptance of a hypothesis on the basis of data that confirm it (Hempel, 1966, pp. 17–18).

Ideally, deductive theories consist of **postulates** and a set of interrelated and internally consistent **propositions**, from which specific hypotheses are derived logically and then tested. **Conceptual definitions** of the abstractions or constructs in the hypotheses must be stated clearly because ultimately researchers must tie their constructs or concepts to concrete entities. That is, the constructs in the hypotheses are made testable by means of **operational definitions**. In other words, the constructs in the hypotheses must be defined in terms of the specific, concrete procedures or operations used to measure them. For example, a person's characteristic level of self-esteem may be measured by scoring his or her answers to a series of items on a questionnaire. Operational definitions are important because they allow other investigators to know precisely how the characteristics were measured, thus providing an objective basis for communication among investigators who use the constructs in their own theorizing or who want to replicate the results of another investigator's efforts.

Although sometimes considered a trivial aspect of science, **replication** is critical and necessary, because the outcomes of any research effort are considered not as facts in any absolute sense but rather as probability statements. On the basis of replication findings, investigators are better able to evaluate the worth of any one hypothesis. Successful replication tends to increase confidence in the findings. Failure to replicate causes investigators to question the empirical validity of the relationship, on the assumption that the measurement procedures used to assess the constructs in the hypothesis were neither reliable nor valid. Persistent failure to replicate may force investigators to revise their theories and perhaps make new predictions.

The Establishment of Laws

The aim of scientific inquiry and of continually testing and retesting hypotheses is to establish regular, predictable relationships among variables, or **laws**. Lawful relationships are established if the hypotheses receive strong and repeated empirical support in research conducted by a variety of investigators, especially when they use multiple operational definitions of the constructs that are a part of the hypotheses. For example, if a variety of investigators repeatedly test the hypothesis that increases in people's self-esteem subsequently produce more effective performances by them on various tasks, thus finding confirming data over and over again, we would say that the relationship is lawful.

Testing the Theories: Research Methods

Various research techniques or procedures are available to investigators. We will focus on three major methods of empirical testing: the experimental method, correlational techniques, and case studies.

Experimental Method

In order to test hypotheses based on theory in a precise and rigorous manner, personality psychologists conduct laboratory experiments. In the **experimental method**, the investigator actively manipulates or systematically alters certain variables and checks their effects on other variables. The variables actively manipulated are called **independent variables**; the others are called **dependent variables**. In the traditional and strictest sense, such experiments demand the use of an **experimental group**, in which the independent variable is manipulated, and a **control group**, in which it is not; this permits a more accurate assessment of the effects of independent variable manipulation on the dependent variable.

By way of example, let us examine an experimental test of a specific theory, namely, Claude Steele's **self-affirmation theory**. Major postulates in this theory are that (1) each of us has a unique self and (2) our goal is to maintain this view of ourselves as adaptively and morally adequate, that is, as competent, good, coherent, stable, and capable of choice and control. These fundamental assumptions or postulates are presented as self-evident. They are working assumptions that focus and guide Steele's theorizing, the kinds of propositions he sets forth, the hypotheses he generates, his choice of research methods to test the hypotheses, the kinds of data analyses he uses, and his interpretations of the data. There are two major propositions in the theory: (1) any cognitions or beliefs that threaten the perceived integrity of the self, that is, its adaptive and moral adequacy, will arouse a motive to reaffirm the self, to reestablish a perception of its global adequacy; and (2) the motive for self-affirmation can be reduced by behavioral or cognitive changes that reduce the threat or the perception of the threat, thereby restoring the integrity of the self (Steele, 1988, pp. 288–295).

Adapting Steele's theoretical approach, Creswell et al. (2005, pp. 846–851) posited that self-affirmation also can buffer individuals against the adverse effects of stress. Stress is implicated in the development and progression of a variety of psychological disorders, such as depression and anxiety, as well as medical disorders, such as coronary heart disease, hypertension, and diabetes. If people affirm themselves by thinking about their most important personal values (e.g., "I am a benevolent person which means that I care about the welfare of my friends and parents"), this self-affirmation process should enhance their self-resources by making them feel more morally adequate, that is, competent, good, and in control of themselves. If they are then subjected to stress while trying to complete a challenging task, they should be able to cope with the stress better and to feel less threat in comparison to participants who have affirmed some personal values that they considered relatively unimportant in their lives (e.g., "I believe that running in road races is good exercise"). To test this hypothesis, Creswell et al. asked study participants to fill out a measure of their personal values and then to rank order them in terms of their degree of importance as guiding principles in their lives. They then randomly assigned the students to either an experimental or a control condition. In the experimental condition, study participants were asked to think about a personal value that they considered especially important in their lives (e.g., social issues like protecting the environment or helping poor people). In the control condition, they were asked to think about a personal value that they had ranked as relatively unimportant in their lives (e.g., supporting political candidates on the local level). Then all participants were asked to write a 5-minute speech on "Why I would be a good candidate for an administrative position at the university" and then to deliver it publicly, followed immediately by a mental arithmetic task (namely, counting aloud backward from 2,083 by 13s). Stress was applied when participants were performing this twofold task by asking them to "go faster" at 1-minute intervals. Physiological stress levels were assessed before the task began and showed no differences in heart, breathing, and **cortisol** levels between participants in the experimental and control conditions. During task onset during which stress was applied, participants in the experimental condition who had had their values affirmed showed lower responses to stress (lower breathing rate, heart rate, and cortisol levels) during a 45-minute interval. During task onset, control participants showed significantly higher responses to stress during the entire 45-minute interval. These results have important implications for health. Healthcare providers can utilize these value-affirmation procedures to enhance self-resources in patients. These resources could be utilized to help them reduce the levels of stress they experience during the course of serious illnesses, thereby providing tremendous benefit to them.

In this study, as in all ethically conducted research in psychology, participants took part in the research voluntarily. They did so by giving their **informed consent** to take part in the research after the experimenter had warned them about all aspects of the research that could conceivably have detrimental effects on them. They were told that they could not be informed in advance about the exact nature of the experimental manipulation because it might invalidate the results; that something might occur during the study that could make them temporarily unhappy; that they could quit the experiment at any time and not suffer any personal negative consequences (e.g., a lowering of their course grade); and that the exact nature of the manipulation and the purpose of the experiment would be explained fully during a **debriefing** session immediately following the experimental session. Thus, all participants had the option to participate or withdraw at any point. Responsible research psychologists also consider it highly important to strive to benefit study participants and to avoid doing any harm to them. They also seek to establish an excellent rapport with them through the use of informed consent and debriefing procedures, because they are committed as professional psychologists to promote the welfare of human beings and because they are convinced that data obtained in the course of their research investigations are more likely to be honest and devoid of distortion if study participants want to participate to the best of their abilities.

Correlational Method

Much of the research in personality psychology is correlational in nature; that is, it seeks to determine if there are relations between two variables. For example, is there a relation between hypercompetitiveness (striving to win in competition at any cost) and neurosis (emotional instability)? Is there a link between hypercompetitiveness and the enjoyment of mathematics? The **correlational method** expresses the direction and size of the relationship by a statistical device called the **correlation coefficient** (also known as Pearson's product-moment coefficient).

The direction of the correlation coefficient is represented by the kind of sign, positive or negative, in the computed correlation. Positive correlations indicate that that an increase in one variable is associated with an increase in another variable. For example, we know from several research studies (see Horney's views on hypercompetitiveness in Chapter 5) that individuals who strive to win in any competition with others at any cost are likely to lie and cheat to achieve their goals. They are selfish and unconcerned about the welfare of others. In short, they are not very psychologically healthy. Two investigations (Ross, Rausch, & Canada, 2003, p. 329; Ryckman, Hammer, Kaczor, & Gold, 1990, p. 635) found that the higher the study participants' scores on a hypercompetitiveness scale, the higher their scores on a **self-report** scale of neurosis, which measures their emotional instability and lack of psychological health.

Negative correlations indicate that an increase in one variable is associated with a decrease in another variable. An example of a negative correlation is Ryckman, Libby, van den Borne, Gold, and Lindner's (1997, p. 279) finding that the higher the study participants' scores on a measure of hypercompetitiveness, the lower their altruism (concern with helping others) scores. Finally, no association between two variables means that the scores on both variables are unrelated to one another. An example of two variables that are unrelated comes from the study by Ross et al. (2003, p. 329), which found that hypercompetitiveness was not associated with orderliness (being organized and neat). Thus, knowing people's hypercompetitiveness scores gives us no reliable clue concerning their level of orderliness; some hypercompetitives are orderly, others are not.

The size of a correlation indicates the degree of the relationship between two variables. A perfect positive correlation would be written as +1.00; a perfect negative relationship as −1.00; and a complete lack of association as .00. Such perfect correlations are, of course, extremely rare and are presented in Figure 1.1 for illustrative purposes only.

Correlation coefficients do not provide us with any information about which variable *causes* the other. A positive correlation between students' hypercompetitiveness and their neuroticism does not mean their higher scores on neuroticism were *caused* by their higher scores on hypercompetitiveness. The positive correlation between the two variables could have been produced by a third variable, such as greater chronic mistrust of others; increases in mistrust may cause increases in both hypercompetitiveness and neuroticism.

FIG-1.1 Scatter diagrams showing correlations that vary in direction. Each dot represents the intersection of scores for two variables for a given study participant.

A. Perfect Positive Correlation ($r = +1.00$)

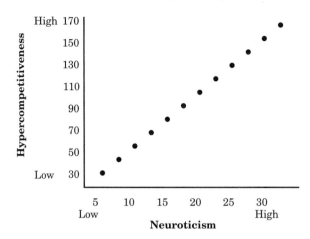

B. Perfect Negative Correlation ($r = -1.00$)

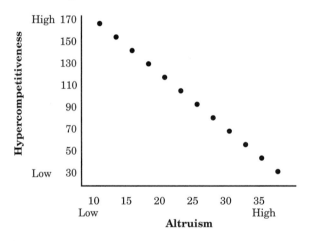

C. No Correlation ($r = .00$)

One of the primary advantages of the experimental over the correlational method is that it allows us to make causal inferences with a higher degree of confidence.

In doing correlational work, researchers want to know if a relationship between two variables that they predict is real or whether it could simply have been a chance occurrence. The concept of **statistical significance** is used to answer this question. A statistically significant result is one that has a low probability of occurring by chance alone. Traditionally, a result is considered statistically significant if the probability that it is a chance finding is 5 in 100 or less (written $p < .05$). A probability of 1 in 100 (written $p < .01$) would mean that there is even less likelihood that the result is due to chance alone. If it is unlikely that a result is due to chance, then that result must be due to factors that are not chance, but rather are systematic. Systematic factors or variables are those that are embedded in the hypothesis. For example, Kaczor, Ryckman, Thornton, and Kuehnel (1991) maintained that people higher in hypercompetitiveness tend to perceive the interactions between individuals in virtually every situation as competitive and as producing "winners" and "losers." Thus, they should see rape as involving a competitive struggle where the rapist is seen as the "winner," whereas the victim is seen as a "loser." Thus, these investigators were interested in testing the hypothesis that students higher in hypercompetitiveness would attribute more blame to a rape victim for her own victimization than would students lower in hypercompetitiveness. The correlation between the two factors or variables was .35, $p < .01$; in other words, male and female study participants higher in hypercompetitiveness assigned more blame to the rape victim for the occurrence of the crime than did participants lower in hypercompetitiveness. The likelihood that this result is due to chance is only 1 in 100; thus, this is regarded as a systematic result and not a chance finding.

Another example of correlational research in personality psychology is a study by Katz, Fromme, and D'Amico (2000, pp. 1–22) that was designed to examine the relationships, if any, between a key personality trait of undergraduates, namely, sensation-seeking and illicit drug use (e.g., smoking marijuana and pill-popping frequently), heavy drinking (five or more drinks on one occasion for males and four or more drinks on one occasion for females), and risky sexual practices (e.g., engaging in sex repeatedly without protection against socially transmitted diseases). Katz and her colleagues pointed out that these activities account for high rates of death and disease among students, and that the percentages of students reporting these risky behaviors increases dramatically during the first year in college when the influence of parents is often absent. They maintained that students higher in sensation-seeking, a trait characterized by the willingness to take risks for the sake of varied, novel, and intense experiences, would be more likely than students lower in sensation-seeking to engage in illicit drug use, heavy drinking, and risky sex. Theoretically, these predictions are based on the idea that sensation-seeking is largely a biologically based trait which makes high sensation-seekers naturally sensitive to stimuli associated with reward and relatively insensitive to punishment. Therefore, they predicted that high sensation-seekers are predisposed to expect good consequences, and not bad consequences, to occur when they engaged in these activities. For example, they should believe that heavy drinking and drug use would make them feel good, as would sex with many partners, while at the same time they were convinced they would not overdose, get HIV, or get killed while they were driving their cars while high. The data showed support for the predictions. That is, the higher the sensation-seeking tendencies of the students, the greater the amount of heavy drinking ($r = + .41$, $p < .05$), drug use ($r = + .28$, $p < .05$) and risky sexual behavior ($r = + .29$, $p < .05$). A more recent study by Yusko, Buckman, White, and Pandina (2008, pp. 1546–1556) reconfirmed several of these findings.

The results in both studies suggest that prevention programs on college campuses that are designed to reduce the occurrence of such risky behaviors could be more effective if they addressed the unique personality characteristics that influence young adults' heavy drinking, illicit drug use, and risky sexual practices (Katz et al., 2000, pp. 1–22). For example, counseling sessions could focus on creating the realization in high sensation seekers that, while their biology predisposes them to act in ways that are harmful to themselves and others, it by no means pushes them inevitably to act badly. Also, they could be told that, while it is true that engaging in such risky behaviors may feel good temporarily, the long-term consequences are disastrous, causing harm to themselves and others. They should then be encouraged to fight their natural impulses and to change them by thinking hard about the terrible consequences of acting on them.

Finally, we should note that psychologists use many other correlation techniques in their research, some of which are considerably more sophisticated than the Pearson product-moment coefficient. Examples include **partial correlation** and **multiple correlation** techniques, as well as a variety of factor analytic methods. (See Chapter 9 for the rudiments of factor analysis.)

Case-Study Method

The intensive study of an individual's life over a long period of time is called a case history, or **case study**. Such studies are frequently used in clinical and medical settings to provide descriptions and explanations of a person's actions and experiences, as well as a prescription for the treatment of the individual's problems. Personality studies using the experimental method examine average or typical differences between individuals, whereas the case-study procedure provides a rich—that is, complex and integrated—view of the uniqueness of the person. It accomplishes this goal by describing both the consistencies and the inconsistencies of the person's behavior, as well as the ways in which characteristic experiences are organized. Because it focuses on the unique characteristics of the individual, the data it yields are often, but not always, impossible to apply to people in general. The procedure also lacks the systematic control of variables inherent in laboratory experiments. This lack of control is a major source of weakness, because it makes causal inferences impossible. Yet the case-study method has considerable strength, because it can lead to serendipitous findings that, in turn, may lead to new testable hypotheses and research, and the development of more adequate theory.

A good example of the case-study method is Freud's analysis of Leonardo Da Vinci's personality, with special focus on his alleged homosexuality. The famous genius of the Renaissance had been accused and acquitted by authorities of forbidden sexual relations with other boys while he was an apprentice in the house of his master, Verrocchio. From this information and a few other biographical fragments, Freud brilliantly reconstructed much of Leonardo's unconscious life in an attempt to determine the truth or falsity of the accusation. Since Freud assumed that early childhood experiences were critical determinants of later personality development, he focused on Leonardo's only written account of his early life. As Leonardo described the flight of the vulture, he interrupted himself to discuss an early memory:

> It seems that it had been destined before that I should occupy myself so thoroughly with the vulture, for it comes to my mind as a very early memory, when I was still in the cradle, a vulture came down to me, opened my mouth with his tail and struck me many times with his tail against my lips. (cited in Freud, 1947, pp. 33–34)

Freud's interpretation was that the "tail," or "coda," is one of the most familiar symbols, as well as a substitutive designation of the male member, in Italian no less than in other languages. The situation contained in the fantasy, that a vulture opened the mouth of the child and forcefully belabored it with its tail, corresponds to the idea of fellatio, a sexual act in which the member is placed into the mouth of another person. Strangely enough, this fantasy is altogether of a passive character; it resembles certain dreams and fantasies of women and of passive homosexuals (who play the feminine part in sexual relations) (Freud, 1947, p. 381).

Freud then described this fantasy as an elaboration of another situation that he assumed everyone had experienced, namely the pleasurable sensations derived from sucking our mother's nipples during infancy. Thus, Da Vinci's fantasy suggested to Freud that Leonardo may have been a passive homosexual whose sexual life had been inhibited by an extraordinarily close relationship with his mother in the absence of his father. A *mother*, according to Freud, was depicted in Egyptian hieroglyphics by the picture of a vulture, so that Leonardo's fantasy was a memory of a time when his own mother (the vulture) held him close and kissed him passionately on the lips many times. Since the erotic feelings of the young Leonardo for his mother could not continue to develop consciously, they were repressed: In this process, Leonardo put himself in her place and then mirrored her behavior in the selection of a sexual object. Furthermore, Leonardo sublimated much of his sexual feeling by taking pretty boys into his employment as apprentices. He selected strikingly handsome boys and nursed them as his mother had protected and cared for him during his childhood.

Some people concluded Freud had proven scientifically that Leonardo Da Vinci was a homosexual because of certain early memories that the artist had reported. This conclusion is wrong. Freud has presented an interesting and ingenious but **post hoc explanation** of the dynamics of Leonardo's alleged homosexuality, based on certain information about his early life. Although Freud's intriguing formulations are intellectually stimulating, a retrospective analysis does not prove anything scientifically. Freud's own biases could have caused him to select only certain experiences from Da Vinci's life. Another investigator could analyze the same case but focus entirely on other aspects of Da Vinci's early childhood experiences and come to an entirely different conclusion.

Scientists generally prefer to conduct studies that make **a priori predictions**, that is, studies that utilize explanations to make predictions *before* the data are collected. Finally, despite the arbitrariness of Freud's retrospective explanations, not all case studies are based on retrospective reports. Often they are based on data from sources less subject to the limitations of retrospective reporting, including systematic **longitudinal studies** of the individual (Runyan, 1982, p. 442).

Criteria for Evaluating Scientific Theories

Comprehensiveness   There is general agreement among theoreticians and researchers that a theory that encompasses and accounts for a wider range and diversity of data is better and more useful than a theory that explains only a more limited range of phenomena. Thus, a good theory should meet the test of **comprehensiveness**. For example, all else being equal, a theory that explains both mature and romantic (immature) love is preferable to one that explains only romantic love. The reason is that science is generally interested in accumulating knowledge that is organized and integrated and explains the interrelationships between a variety of phenomena.

Since no theory can cover all the phenomena related to human personality, decisions must be made concerning the importance of the events to be studied. For example, is it more important that the theory adequately describes and explains eyelid conditioning or human aggression? The answer seems obvious: An understanding of aggression would allow us to account for behaviors that have important implications for human welfare, whereas an understanding of eye blinking would not seem to tell us much worth knowing. Yet, we should exercise some caution in making this judgment until we hear the other side of the argument. Many scientists maintain that in science there is no unambiguous criterion that allows us safely to exclude phenomena from the study on the basis of triviality. What may be a trivial undertaking to one investigator may be an important area of research to another. Furthermore, and more importantly, work on a seemingly trivial problem may bear fruit at some future time. In the eye blink example, an understanding of the parameters or characteristics that control eye blinking could give us information about the principles of classical conditioning, principles that can be used to explain the origins of many irrational fears and phobias in people and how to eliminate them.

As you can see, there is no clear-cut answer to this problem. One prominent personality theorist, Salvatore Maddi, has suggested that investigators can minimize the risk of triviality by relying on naturalistic observation of human behavior, that is, by studying people in their daily surroundings and, to a lesser extent, in therapeutic settings (Maddi, 1996, pp. 489–490). On this basis, we can make tentative judgments about the worth of personality theories in terms of comprehensiveness.

Precision and Testability   Besides being comprehensive, a good theory should contain constructs that are clearly and explicitly defined. Scientists want explanations that are stated in clear language. A theory that is couched in muddied language is difficult to comprehend and not very useful. It lessens the chances for clear and effective communication among scientists and hinders scientific progress. Besides having constructs that are clearly defined, a good theory should also contain **relational statements** or propositions that are consistent and logically related to one another. It is generally recognized that, in the early stages of theorizing, investigators may rely heavily on analogies and metaphors as an aid to thought, examples include Jung's "shadow," which lurks around in the darkness of the collective unconscious, and Freud's treatment of the ego as a battlefield where mortal combat takes place between the forces of the id and superego, but in the final analysis these may create inconsistencies and ambiguities that hamper understanding. An adequate scientific theory should meet the criterion of **precision**.

Not only must the constructs and relational statements in the theory be defined precisely, but the hypotheses containing them must be capable of being studied empirically; that is, they must be linked at some point with external reality. The link between conceptualization and observation is accomplished by means of operational definitions. In brief, a good theory is also judged by the **testability** of its hypotheses.

Parsimony   A good theory should be parsimonious, or economical; that is, the theory should contain only those constructs, relational statements, and assumptions necessary for the explanation of the phenomena within its domain. The inclusion of unnecessary constructs or assumptions can lead an investigator to waste great amounts of effort studying meaningless relationships. A theory that contains more constructs and assumptions than necessary fails to meet the test of **parsimony**. Conversely, however, the parsimony criterion cannot be met simply by minimizing the number of constructs and assumptions. Such a theory would be too simplistic and would not do justice to the complexity of the phenomena. Instead, a theory is parsimonious only if it adequately accounts for the complexity of the phenomena to be explained.

Empirical Validity   A good theory must have **empirical validity**; that is, it must have data that support it. This is a key function of theory. Empirical validity is determined by testing hypotheses, that is, by making observations to determine if the investigator's predictions are accurate. Of course, establishing the theory's empirical validity is far from easy. First, theories are never proven (or disproved) in any absolute sense. They are tested only indirectly, on the basis of hypotheses derived from them. Second, determining the validity of a hypothesis depends on the reliability and validity of the measures used to assess the constructs. And third, research findings obtained by testing hypotheses are always determined statistically, that is, in terms of probability.

Along with statistical significance, successful replications of findings in various studies increase our confidence in those findings. Conversely, successive failures to replicate make us even less certain that the relationship exists. When their hypotheses fail, some theorists sometimes argue that their constructs have not been measured well, and therefore, failure to confirm hypotheses should not invalidate the theory. Such claims may or may not be legitimate. On the one hand, the measurement procedures may be unreliable and error-ridden. On the other hand, a few theorists and their advocates have such strongly vested interests in their own formulations that they dismiss out of hand any evidence to the contrary, on the grounds of inadequate measurement. Such self-serving statements run counter to the ideals of science, however, and in the long run are overruled by the body of evidence accumulated by independent researchers.

Heuristic Value   A good theory has **heuristic value**, in that it stimulates and provokes investigators to do further theorizing and research. The heuristic value of theories may spring from several sources. For example, a theory may arouse researchers' intellectual curiosity; in seeking answers to the questions it raises, they pursue new paths that may prove enlightening and useful. Another theory may be so reasonable that investigators simply accept it at first blush and seek to utilize and test it. However, with the subsequent collection of large amounts of disconfirming data, researchers may seek to revise it in order to increase its predictive accuracy. Thus, new theory and research may result. Finally, investigators may examine another theory and think it inadequate, wrong, or absurd in its explanation of phenomena. Their disbelief, resistance, and even hostility may lead to a concerted effort to demonstrate its falsehood, thereby generating new conceptualizations and explanations of the same phenomena.

Applied Value   Finally, a good theory has **applied value**; that is, it leads to new approaches to the solution of people's problems (Kelly, 1955, p. 24). This criterion is not universally endorsed by scientists, especially by those who work in experimental psychology. Yet it seems particularly germane to the area of personality. There can be little question that an adequate theory of personality will focus on abnormal as well as normal development and that helping people to overcome their problems is an overriding concern of virtually all personality psychologists.

Equipped with information about the essential ingredients of the scientific process and the standards used to evaluate scientific theories, we are now in a position to examine the major theoretical approaches to personality.

CRITICAL THINKING QUESTIONS

1. Define personality from a scientific perspective. What difficulties do you see with such a definition?

2. Why is the definition of personality in terms of social attractiveness inadequate for use by psychologists?

3. What is science? In what ways does the scientific enterprise involve the use of theory and research?

4. What are the basic elements of the experimental, correlational, and case-study methods? Discuss the strengths and weaknesses of each of these methods. In studying any phenomenon, why do scientists need to rely on several methods to best understand it?

5. List and describe the six criteria commonly used by investigators for the evaluation of scientific theories. Can you think of any others?

GLOSSARY

a priori predictions   Predictions about the outcome of an investigation that are made *before* the data are collected.

applied value   Criterion or standard for judging the scientific worth of a theory: An adequate theory is capable of providing creative solutions to problems that are of interest and concern to people. For example, a theory might specify the different kinds of parental discipline that lead to the development of physically and psychologically healthy or unhealthy children. If the theory has considerable data to support it, then parents could adopt the kinds of discipline (for example, praise for their children when they exhibit helpful behavior, encouragement for cooperative behavior during play activities) that lead to healthy development and avoid or eliminate the kinds of discipline (for example, physical and verbal abuse, praise for aggressive behavior) that lead to unhealthy development. Such a theory therefore would have high applied value: It would help people to raise children who are psychologically healthy.

case study   Research technique involving the intensive study of a single person over a long period of time in order to understand his or her unique behavior.

comprehensiveness   Criterion for judging the worth of a scientific theory: Theories are judged as more adequate and useful if they encompass and account for a wide range and variety of phenomena.

conceptual definitions   The concepts in the hypotheses must be defined precisely so that accurate measures of the concepts can be devised. Vague concepts lead to faulty and ambiguous operational definitions and a poor testing of the hypotheses.

control group   In an experiment, the group that does not receive the experimental treatment. A control group is designed to provide baseline data against which the effects of the experimental manipulation on the dependent variable can be accurately judged.

correlation coefficient   A numerical index of the size and direction of an association between two variables.

correlational method   General procedure for establishing an association or relationship between events. Statistics involving correlations can vary in complexity from simple correlation coefficients to complicated factor analyses.

cortisol   An adrenal-cortex hormone that is generated by any kind of physical or psychological stress. Higher cortisol levels are indicators of greater stress.

debriefing   Informing study participants of the true nature and purpose of a study after it is completed.

deductive theories   Theories in which specific hypotheses are derived from abstract propositions and then tested by the collection of data.

dependent variables   Changes in behavior that occur as a result of the manipulation of conditions by an experimenter.

empirical evidence   Observations of phenomena made by investigators.

empirical validity   Criterion for judging the worth of a scientific theory: The theory's hypotheses are tested by the collection of data to determine whether or not they are accurate. Confirmation of the hypotheses tends to lend support to the theory; disconfirmation of the hypotheses, if repeated, tends eventually to decrease confidence in the theory.

experimental group   The group of study participants who experience the intentional alteration of factors in an experiment.

experimental method   Scientific method for studying cause-and-effect relationships between variables. It involves the manipulation of independent variables and observation of the effects of the manipulation on dependent variables.

heuristic value   Criterion for judging the scientific worth of a theory: An adequate theory should be challenging; it should stimulate new ideas and new research.

hypotheses   Tentative theoretical statements about how events are related to one another, often stated as predictions about how the operation of one set of events will affect the operation of others.

independent variables   The variables actively manipulated by the experimenter so that their effects on individual behavior can be observed.

inductive theories   Generalizations or summary statements about phenomena derived from a set of facts.

informed consent   The practice of telling study participants about the nature of their participation in a proposed experiment and then obtaining their written agreement to participate.

law of effect   The principle that a behavior becomes more likely when it is followed by a positive reinforcer or the removal of a negative stimulus, whereas it becomes less likely when it is followed by a punisher or the removal of a positive reinforcer.

laws   Systematic and highly reliable associations between variables.

longitudinal studies   Studies in which data are collected on the same individuals over time so that investigators can determine the direction and extent of changes in their behavior.

multiple correlation   Statistical technique by which it is possible to determine the relationship between one variable and a combination of two or more other variables simultaneously.

operational definitions   Procedures or operations used to define particular constructs. For example, intelligence could be operationally defined in terms of a person's scores on a verbal reasoning test.

parsimony   Criterion for judging the scientific worth of a theory: An adequate theory should be as parsimonious, or economical, as possible, while still adequately accounting for the phenomena in its domain.

partial correlation   A correlational technique that allows an investigator to assess the relationship between two events by eliminating, or *partialing out*, the influence of other variables.

personality   The term used by personality psychologists to describe the uniqueness of the individual. Personality involves judgments regarding who the person truly is and how she or he differs from other people. Particular biological tendencies and social and cultural learning experiences combine to determine the person's uniqueness.

post hoc explanation   Explanation of a phenomenon given *after* its occurrence. The explanation presumes that certain factors caused the phenomenon, but there is no evidence that they actually did so.

postulates   Fundamental or core assumptions of a theory. They are taken as self-evidently true in order to provide a clear and focused direction for theorizing and research. They specify which phenomena will be addressed by the theory and which won't be addressed. For example, one theory of aggression could postulate that aggression is learned behavior, whereas another could postulate that it is genetically based. Reliance on the assumption that it is learned would lead the theorist and investigators to focus their energies and attention on the environmental conditions that produce it and not on its instinctive origins. Reliance on the assumption that it is genetically based would focus attention on its biological roots and not on its environmental causes.

precision   Criterion for judging the scientific worth of a theory: An adequate theory should contain constructs and relational statements that are clearly and explicitly stated and measured.

propositions   General relational statements that may be true or false. They are not tested directly; instead, hypotheses are derived from them. The hypotheses, specific propositions containing constructs that are operationalized, can be tested and confirmed or disconfirmed through empirical testing.

psychological construct   A highly complex abstraction that encompasses a variety of components or dimensions. For example, intelligence is a construct that encompasses reasoning ability, spatial ability, mechanical ability, mathematical ability, and so forth.

relational statements   Theoretical propositions or hypotheses that link or relate constructs. For example, the constructs of frustration and aggression might be linked as follows: Increases in frustration lead to increases in aggressive behavior.

replication   Duplication or repetition of an experiment or study to determine whether or not the original findings are reliable.

self-affirmation theory   A theory which postulates that each of us strives to maintain a view of ourselves as morally adequate and that we respond to any threat to our self-integrity by trying to restore or reaffirm it.

self-report   A written or verbal statement given by study participants on questionnaires or in interviews concerning their personality characteristics. A self-report is sometimes limited, in that people may distort their responses to impress investigators. Participants also may be unwilling or unable to comment on some of their personality characteristics. On the other hand, a self-report allows investigators to gather large amounts of data efficiently by asking participants questions about themselves that deal with a wide variety of situations. A self-report also can be useful in yielding data that provide support for investigators' theorizing.

statistical significance   A numerical index of the probability that a particular result occurred by chance.

testability   Criterion for judging the scientific worth of a theory: An adequate theory must contain hypotheses that can be defined clearly, measured precisely, and confirmed or disconfirmed in terms of observable events.

theory   A number of interrelated conceptual statements that are created by investigators to account for a phenomenon or a set of phenomena.

SUGGESTED READINGS

Bordens, K. S., & Abbott, B. B. (2011). *Research design and methods: A process approach* (8th ed.). New York: McGraw-Hill.

Cozby, P. C. (2009). *Methods in behavioral research* (10th ed.). New York: McGraw-Hill.

PART 2

Psychoanalytic and Neoanalytic Perspectives

Only a few people in human history have generated work so creative that it shapes the course of human values, thought, and behavior. Copernicus, the eminent 16th century Polish astronomer, was one such individual; his discovery that the Earth was not the center of the universe forced us to reexamine our beliefs about our own omnipotence and omniscience. Darwin, the English naturalist of the 19th century, was another; his work forced us to realize that we too are part of the natural world and are governed to some extent by our biology.

Sigmund Freud belongs in this elite company, because he compelled us to acknowledge that we are often driven to act impulsively and irrationally by unconscious conflicts of a sexual and aggressive nature. Scholars in the humanistic tradition of Western thought, which emphasized rationality and the virtues of ethical conduct, were shocked to learn that human beings are often irrational and that they continuously engage in internal struggles to keep their sexual and aggressive impulses in check. Freud bared the baseness of the human soul for everyone to see, and some people have never forgiven him. He removed us from our pedestals and forced us to examine the dark side of our natures.

At first, he was publicly reviled and scorned. Eventually, however, investigators in many disciplines began to explore the validity of his theory. Today, Freud's influence is worldwide. Scholars in literature are fond of using psychoanalytic constructs or concepts to explain the motives of fictional characters. Psychological anthropologists focus on child-rearing practices in various cultures and often use a Freudian model to understand adult personality. Philosophers and sociologists have used the Freudian concepts of repression and anxiety in their analyses of problems confronting modern society. Freudian concepts have also been adopted by laypeople. We are all aware of the importance of Freudian slips and the ways in which the unconscious influences behavior. Sometimes we talk glibly about ego trips, denial, and Oedipal conflicts; we might speak of "getting it all out" when we are angry. In short, Freudian thinking has had a revolutionary impact on our lives. Whether we ultimately accept or reject his view of human behavior and functioning, Freud has clearly earned his place in history.

In Chapter 2, we review the basic concepts of Freud's theory. We examine his attempts to construct a theory of personality based on interpretations of self-reports by his patients. We describe the basic constructs (the unconscious, preconscious, and conscious; the life and death instincts; the id, ego, and super-ego), how they interact to produce internal conflicts, and the various defense mechanisms used to protect the ego and reduce the anxiety generated by these conflicts. We review Freud's theory of psychosexual development, with special emphasis on the origins and nature of the various character disorders. We then consider the research evidence for the theory of psychosexual development and show how Freud's theory can be applied to cases involving psychopathology. We conclude this chapter as we do each of the chapters that follow with the exception of the last chapter with an analysis of the strengths and weaknesses of the theory as reflected in the six criteria for evaluating scientific theories.

In Chapter 3, we turn to Carl Jung's theory and examine the nature of the individual psyche, all the interacting systems within the human personality that account for the mental life and behavior of the person, and the life process energy that motivates the person to action. Although both Freud and Jung used the term *libido* to describe the energy that propels the person into action, Jung's conceptualization was much broader than Freud's. Jung thought of libido not simply as sexual impulses that try to force their way into consciousness, but as forces that are generated by continuous conflicts within the psyche and that can split and move erratically through the psyche in unpredictable ways; at times these forces result in bizarre and impulsive behavior. This conceptualization adds a certain mystery to the person; if a person's behavior is determined by autonomous forces, which often operate capriciously, outside observers cannot pinpoint its causes.

Following the discussion of Jung's libido, we examine the major structures of the psyche and describe the evolution of the self as the conflicts between the various oppositional forces are resolved via transcendence. Jung believed that, in the attempt to evolve toward selfhood, people adopt different orientations or attitudes toward life and utilize different psychological processes or functions to make sense of their experiences. Eventually he combined the attitudes and functions in a theoretical scheme of psychological types and discussed the ways in which introverted and extraverted individuals try to deal with the world and their own conflicts. We present this theoretical scheme in considerable detail, review the current research evidence based on it, and then examine Jung's views of disordered behavior and therapy.

In contrast to Freud and Jung, Alfred Adler presented a simplified scheme to account for the development of personality. Adler, whose work is the subject of Chapter 4, came to believe that all individuals felt inferior and strove to overcome these feelings and to become superior. Neurotic strivings were associated with attempts to achieve personal superiority at the expense of others, whereas healthy strivings entailed a quest for reaching an ideal state of perfection or completion via efforts to improve the lot of others. Although Adler emphasized human rationality and consciousness in making decisions and the ways in which our goals inspire us to improve ourselves, his position was not totally optimistic. Never able to break completely with his Freudian origins, he concluded that our lifestyles are formed to a considerable extent by the end of our fifth year, with the implication that fundamental change is very difficult to achieve after early childhood.

Despite his adherence to this aspect of Freudian theory, however, the general tone of Adler's writings is optimistic. In Chapter 4, we see his essential humanism, his socialist political orientation, and his persistent attempts to help oppressed people. In particular, we focus on Adler's concept of social interest: his belief in an innate human need to help others and his vision of an ideal society in which cooperation, harmony, and equality would be the rule. We then outline his other major concepts and review his theory of personality development, with special emphasis on his birth-order concept and the research based upon it. Finally, we examine his view of abnormal development and the application of Adler's theory to the treatment of psychopathology.

In Chapter 5, we present the major concepts and principles of Karen Horney's revisionist view of Freudian theory. Her theory posits disturbed relationships between parents and their children as the primary cause of neurosis, not sexual trauma. Neurotics are pictured as insecure and fearful individuals with rigid, compulsive needs and strivings that are designed to reestablish the safety of their environments. Unfortunately, these strivings are almost invariably unsuccessful; for the individual, the result is conflict and pain on an unconscious level and also inefficient problem solving. According to Horney, neurotics are alienated from their real selves and from other people. They identify with a false, idealized self in order to avoid the pain of acknowledging their limitations. In Chapter 5, we chronicle the development of alienation in the early socialization process and then discuss the therapeutic procedures Horney used to reduce this alienation and to release the individual's potential for growth.

In Chapter 6, we examine the concepts and principles of Erik Erikson's psychoanalytic ego psychology. Erikson's theory systematically extends Freud's view of the role played by the ego in personality development and functioning. In contrast to Freud, Erikson saw the ego as often operating autonomously from id motivations as an entity with nondefensive functions that helps people adapt constructively to the demands of their surroundings. Our primary focus is on Erikson's dynamic theory of ego development and functioning; we pay particular attention to the crises experienced by adolescents as they try to establish their identities and by young adults who are seeking to establish intimate and long-lasting relationships. In Erikson's view, the major disturbance during adolescence is role confusion based on an inability to decide on an occupational identity. In young adulthood, the primary disturbance centers on a sense of isolation based on an inability to love and cherish another person in a personal relationship. We present considerable research support for Erikson's theorizing about these crises, as well as the rapidly accumulating evidence concerning his views about middle and late adulthood. We also consider his techniques for assessing personality, review his pioneering efforts in the psychohistorical analysis of important historical figures, and examine the application of his theory of ego development to the treatment of abnormal behavior.

Finally, in Chapter 7, we review the newest variant of psychoanalytic theory, the self psychology of Heinz Kohut. Unlike Freud, Kohut did not see human beings as driven relentlessly by sexual and aggressive instincts. Instead, he believed that pathological sexual and aggressive behavior occur as a result of damage to the self, which originally occurs early in family life. In Kohut's view, unempathic parents who fail to provide adequate nurturance, support, and understanding seriously hinder children's ability to develop a self that is realistic and capable of initiating creative action. Whereas Freud thought that the basic direction of development was set by the end of the fifth year, Kohut took a broader view: He argued that changes in the self can occur throughout the life span. However, he focused mainly on developmental changes from infancy through adolescence. In the developmental process, Kohut's emphasis is on the ways in which narcissism can give rise to either a healthy or an unhealthy adult personality. In Chapter 7, we are most concerned with his explanation of psychopathology in terms of narcissistic personality disorders. Thus, we present his views on narcissism in detail and review the research support for them. We also present Kohut's discovery of the self-object transferences, which provide a new, more in-depth understanding of the origins and cure of a variety of psychological disorders.

CHAPTER 2

Freud's Psychoanalytic Theory

Courtesy, National Library of Medicine.

Biographical Sketch

Sigmund Freud was born in 1856 in the town of Freiburg, Moravia (now Czechoslovakia), of Jewish parents. His father was a wool merchant who married twice. Sigmund, the oldest son of the second wife, had five sisters and two brothers. He was a serious boy who excelled in his studies throughout his early schooling. He could repeat verbatim a page in a book he had read and record almost the entire content of scientific lectures after he heard them. He read voraciously the works of great playwrights, poets, and philosophers, including Goethe, Shakespeare, Kant, Hegel, Schopenhauer, and Nietzsche. His love of books, in fact, led him to run up a debt at a bookstore that he had no means to settle—an indiscretion for which his father, hard-pressed for money, could find no sympathy (Puner, 1947, pp. 46–47).

Upon entering the University of Vienna, he reluctantly decided on a medical career and was graduated in 1883. He maintained that he never felt comfortable playing the doctor game, but he was impressed with the scientific attitude of people in the medical profession. Freud yearned to solve the great problems of the world and to learn all he could about human nature (Jones, 1963, pp. 3–4, 22); he perceived that science provided the means of satisfying such yearnings.

During his medical school days, Freud came under the influence of the eminent physiologist Ernst Brucke and worked as his assistant on neurological problems in lower animals. Although quite content in his work at Brucke's laboratory, Freud soon realized that his chances for advancement were poor and that the monetary rewards would always be minimal. Since he was seriously interested in a lovely young woman at the time and believed he should be earning enough money to support her before he committed himself to marriage, Freud, with Brucke's friendly encouragement, left the laboratory and entered private medical practice. Shortly afterward, in 1885, he applied for, and obtained, a postgraduate traveling stipend to work with the renowned French neurologist Jean Charcot in Paris on the treatment of nervous disorders. Elated, he wrote to his fiancée, then living in Hamburg:

> Oh, how wonderful it is going to be. I am coming with money and am staying a long while with you and am bringing something lovely for you and shall then go to Paris and become a great savant and return to Vienna with a great, great nimbus. Then we will marry soon and I will cure all the incurable nervous patients and you will keep me well and I will kiss you till you are merry and happy, and they lived happily ever after. (Jones, 1963, p. 50)

In fact, Freud and Martha Bernays were married in 1886 and remained married for more than half a century.

Upon his return to private practice, Freud developed a mentor relationship with a physician named Breuer and, under his influence, began using hypnosis. Breuer had treated a young woman, Anna O., for a group of physical symptoms including paralysis of the limbs and disturbances of sight and speech that had arisen in connection with the death of her father. Breuer found, to his astonishment, that the woman's symptoms disappeared if she talked about them while in a hypnotic trance. In this state, she would relive the terrifying experiences that gave rise to her symptoms and express the accompanying emotions fully. This physical expression of emotion he labeled a **catharsis**. Eventually Freud and Breuer severed their relationship because of Freud's insistence that the basis of such disorders was sexual (Jones, 1963, pp. 147, 165).

Freud used the cathartic method in his treatment for several years but, finding that many patients could not be hypnotized, he began asking them to concentrate on a particular symptom and to try to recall any early experiences that might explain its origins. Between 1892 and 1895, he gradually developed the method of free association, in which he asked his patients to express every thought that occurred to them, no matter how irrelevant, unimportant, or unpleasant (Jones, 1963, pp. 157–158). Although the patients' recollections seemed aimless and accidental, Freud felt intuitively that there must be some definite force controlling them. Thoroughly trained in medicine and neurology to accept the principles of **determinism** and causality, Freud could not bring himself to believe that his patients' thoughts were unrelated. In addition, Freud was impressed by the unwillingness of many patients to disclose memories that were painful to them. He labeled this opposition **resistance** and came to believe that his patients were repressing certain important memories. His job, then, was to probe their unconscious and uncover the reasons for their active resistance.

In the course of his analyses, Freud also discovered that patients insisted on tracing the origins of their traumatic experiences to early childhood. He claimed that many of these memories involved sexual experiences. Until this time, most people believed that childhood was a time of innocence, devoid of sexual urges. Freud disagreed strongly:

> We do wrong entirely to ignore the sexual life of children; in my experience children are capable of all the mental and many of the physical activities. Just as the whole sexual apparatus of man is not comprised in the external genital organs and the two reproductive glands, so his sexual life does not begin only with the onset of puberty, as to casual observation it may appear to do. (Jones, 1963, p. 172)

Freud at first believed that the early childhood seduction scenes described to him by his patients were literally true. Eventually, however, he began to have doubts. He found it difficult to believe, for example, that all his female patients' fathers were sexually perverse. He also found that literal acceptance of these accounts and subsequent suggestion to the patients of how they must deal with them did not always have therapeutic benefits. He wrote in a letter to a friend that he had to renounce his explanations of hysteria and his hopes of becoming a famous physician. But he eventually revised his **seduction theory** and concluded that the descriptions were not literally true but fantasies that were nevertheless psychically real and valid in their own right (Jones, 1963, pp. 172–173). Yet some contemporary historians of psychiatry point out that Freud, although intending to do so, never published any evidence of such repressed fantasies of sexual abuse. Instead these critics maintain that Freud inferred the existence of such memories in his patients to make them agree with his theoretical expectations (Esterson, 2001, pp. 329–352).

In any event, Freud also reported that, during analysis, patients often mentioned their dreams. He found that dreams provided the best means of unlocking the secrets of the unconscious, and could yield invaluable information about the nature of the person's conflicts and the mechanisms by which they were concealed from awareness (Jones, 1963, p. 129). In 1900, Freud published *The Interpretation of Dreams*, in which he contended that dreaming was neither an idle activity nor as chaotic as it seemed. Rather, he proposed, dreams serve as wish-fulfillment devices, and their latent content can be used to help a patient understand his or her problems.

In 1902, Freud founded the Vienna Psycho-Analytical Society, a small group of scholars from various disciplines who met in his office to discuss their work. As the membership grew, meetings were held in larger, more formal settings. The period 1905–1906 was highly productive for Freud; he published several books, including *Jokes and Their Connection with the Unconscious*, *The Psychopathology of Everyday Life*, and *Three Essays on the Theory of Sexuality*, as well as some articles. *Three Essays*, in particular, made Freud almost universally unpopular. The book was labeled "shockingly wicked," and Freud was branded as a man with an obscene and evil mind. The principal focus of the criticism was Freud's assertion that children are born with sexual urges and that their parents are selected as their first sexual objects. Freud believed that he was right, however, and that eventually his arguments would be accepted (Jones, 1963, pp. 240–243).

By 1910, Freud had gained an international reputation, but internal dissension concerning his libido theory had arisen within the Psycho-Analytical Society. The defections began with Adler and Stekel; they were followed by Jung and others. Disagreeing fundamentally with Freud, Adler minimized the importance of the sexual factor in determining behavior and elevated the concept of a struggle for power in its place. He also deemphasized or discarded the concepts of repression, the unconscious, and infantile sexuality. Such major differences led inevitably to a separation between the two men. The split with Jung was much more distressing for Freud, who had been closer personally to Jung and believed him superior to Adler in intellect and knowledge (Jones, 1963, pp. 313–314, 318).

Jung was disturbed by Freud's uncompromising and narrow view of the role played by the sexual instinct in the person's development. While he agreed with Freud that the sexual motive is important, he also thought that the person had creative urges that transcended his or her conflicts. Accordingly, Jung deemphasized the sexual factor in the development of neurosis. He considered libido, or sexual energy, as a designation of general tension and rejected Freud's belief that the Oedipal conflict involved incestuous yearnings on the part of the child. But despite the defection of some of his disciples, whose positions came to be known as the **neoanalytic perspective**, Freud's fame continued to grow, and the Psycho-Analytical Society flourished.

World War I had a profound impact on Freud's thinking and research. Acutely distressed by the mass killing and suffering, he eventually came to attribute these experiences to a universal death instinct. Despite his pessimism about the future of humankind, however, Freud continued to elaborate his ideas in a long series of books, including *Totem and Taboo* (1913), *Introductory Lectures on Psychoanalysis* (1917), *Beyond the Pleasure Principle* (1920), *The Ego and the Id* (1923), *Future of an Illusion* (1927), *Civilization and Its Discontents* (1930), *New Introductory Lectures on Psychoanalysis* (1933), and *An Outline of Psychoanalysis* (published posthumously in 1940). In the early 1930s, Hitler came to power and anti-Semitism flourished. Freud's books were burned in Berlin, and his supporters urged him to flee Vienna. With the Nazi invasion of Austria in 1938, Freud reluctantly left his home and took up residence in London. He died there on September 23, 1939. During the last few years of his life, Freud suffered from cancer of the jaw and mouth; he was addicted to nicotine, smoking more than 20 cigars each day. Despite more than 30 operations and often torturous pain, he persisted in his work until nearly the end (Edmundson, 2007, pp. 224–227).

Concepts and Principles

The Role of Conscious, Preconscious, and Unconscious Forces in Personality

Freud's fundamental assumption about our mental life was that it is divided into three parts: the **conscious**, the **preconscious**, and the **unconscious**. The conscious refers to those ideas and sensations of which we are aware. It operates on the surface of personality and plays a relatively small role in personality development and functioning. While it is true that psychologically healthy people have a greater awareness of their experiences than do unhealthy ones, still Freud believed that even relatively mature people are governed, to a degree greater than they would care to admit, by unconscious needs and conflicts.

The preconscious contains those experiences that are unconscious but that could become conscious with little effort. For example, you may have forgotten the foods you had for supper yesterday, but you could probably recall them readily if you were asked to list them for a dietician who is trying to help you lose weight. The preconscious exists just beneath the surface of awareness.

In contrast, the unconscious operates on the deepest level of personality. It consists of those experiences and memories of which we are not aware. Such mental states remain out of awareness because making them conscious would create tremendous pain and anxiety for us. The unconscious could include memories of sexual abuse that we experienced during early childhood at the hands of a parent or relative. It could consist of incestuous feelings, strong emotional reactions of anger or rage toward certain authority figures, or painful feelings of shame and humiliation growing out of competitive experiences. A key point is that such repressed memories do not simply disappear once they have been thrust from awareness; they continue to operate outside awareness, and seek expression in various defensive, disguised, and distorted ways. Unconscious ideas, memories, and experiences may continually interfere with conscious and rational behavior.

Finally, while it is impossible to make these unconscious experiences fully conscious, their existence can be clarified through the use of psychoanalytic therapeutic procedures. If therapy works, the person becomes more conscious or aware of the nature of these forces than he or she was at the beginning of therapy (Freud, 1960a, pp. 3–8).

Instincts: The Driving Forces in Personality

Rooted in the unconscious are the instincts, which, in Freud's view, largely govern our behavior. Instinctual drives are initiated when bodily needs motivate people to seek gratification, so that bodily processes can return to their prior state of equilibrium or homeostasis. Painful feelings are associated with instinctual stimulation, and pleasurable feelings are associated with a decrease in this stimulation.

Instincts have four basic characteristics: (1) a *source* in some bodily deficit; (2) an *aim* that focuses on gratification of the need; (3) an *impetus* that propels the person to act; and (4) an *object* through which the instinct achieves its aim. As Freud perceived it, many objects in the external world can provide gratification of our biological needs. That is, instincts can move from object to object in their attempt to gain maximum gratification. For example, a college man may find a new girlfriend to love if his relationship with his current companion is not satisfying; a woman who has hostile feelings toward her boss, but is unable to express them because she fears the loss of her job, may come home and behave aggressively toward her family. Instincts can even turn inward on the individual, as when a person's aggressive feelings toward others are turned toward self and result in acts of self-mutilation or even suicide. Sexual impulses can also be turned inward, as when an individual becomes self-absorbed and utilizes masturbation as the primary sexual outlet.

Life instincts Freud theorized that each person has life instincts or **eros**. These instinctive urges seek to preserve life. Each of us is motivated to satisfy our hunger, thirst, and sexual needs. Without food and water, we could not survive; the typical consequence of efforts to achieve sexual satisfaction is procreation, which helps perpetuate the species. The energy associated with these instincts he termed **libido**. Originally, Freud maintained that libido was associated only with the sexual instincts but later, revising his position, he viewed libido as the psychic and pleasurable feelings associated with gratification of the life instincts (Freud, 1952b, pp. 639–663).

Death instincts In addition to the life instincts, Freud postulated the existence of an opposing death instinct or **thanatos**. He believed that the goal of all life is death (Freud, 1952b, p. 652) that human beings strive to return to an inorganic state of balance that preceded life, in which there is no painful struggle to satisfy biological needs. The life instincts operate, however, to ensure that death is delayed as long as possible, so that human beings can obtain many other satisfactions before attaining this nirvana.

A major derivative of the death instinct is aggression, whereby individuals try to destroy others or themselves. Freud believed these aggressive impulses to be very strong; accordingly, his view of human nature was very negative. The truth is that men are not gentle, friendly creatures wishing for love, who simply defend themselves if they are attacked, but that a powerful measure of desire for aggression has to be reckoned as part of their instinctual endowment. The result is that their neighbor is to them not only a possible helper or sexual object but also a temptation to them to gratify their aggressiveness on him, to exploit his capacity for work without recompense, to use him sexually without consent, to seize his possessions, to humiliate him, to cause him pain, to torture and kill him. *Homo homini lupus* [Man is to man a wolf]; who has the courage to dispute it in the face of all the evidence in his own life and in history? (Freud, 1952a, p. 787).

Not surprisingly, Freud remained pessimistic about the future of the species. Interestingly, however, he never postulated an energy source, corresponding to libido, for the death instincts.

The individual versus society Freud recognized that society would not survive for long if its members were allowed to express all of their impulses. Stronger individuals would take advantage of weaker ones by using their superior force to gain their ends. Social instability could easily result from allowing people to mate indiscriminately whenever the urge arose. Thus, even though people may wish to act out their sexual and aggressive impulses, society does not permit them to do so and rightly so, in Freud's view. Indeed, society is often harsh in its demand that people renounce their impulses, and threatens punishment if they disobey. Eventually parents and others instill society's values so that people feel guilty if they do something wrong and become anxious if they even contemplate behaving inappropriately. Yet despite these internal checks on their behavior, people's urges continually seek expression; the result is a never-ending conflict between the individual and society. In Freud's view, individuals must eventually learn to resolve this conflict by seeking realistic ways of gratifying their impulses through behavior that is in line with the prescriptions of society.

Structural Theory of Personality and Its Dynamics

To understand the **dynamics** of an individual's conflicts, Freud postulated constructs that allowed him to describe the ways in which these parts of personality originated and interacted with one another to dynamically influence behavior. He proposed three systems of the mind: id, ego, and superego that compete for the limited amount of

FIG-2.1 Structure
of the mind. Adapted
from *The Psychology
of C. G. Jung.* by J. Jacobi,
p. 126 (1962). Courtesy
of Yale University Press,
New Haven, Connecticut.

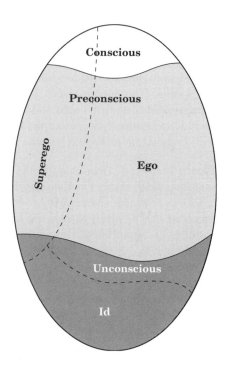

psychic energy available, energy that has its starting point in the instinctual needs of the
individual. (See Figure 2.1.)

Id Freud considered the **id** to be the original aspect of personality, rooted in the biology of the individual (Jones, 1963, p. 2), and to consist of unconscious sexual and aggressive instincts. These instincts might operate jointly in different situations to affect our
behavior. For example, we might find ourselves hating and acting aggressively toward
parents whom we dearly love, or we might feel sexually attracted to an arrogant and
obnoxious person with whom we are continually arguing.

Freud likened the id to a seething cauldron that contains powerful and primitive
urges and desires. He believed that these urges insistently and indiscriminately seek
expression in external reality. Thus, the id is amoral and unconcerned with the niceties
and conventions of society. It operates according to the pleasure principle: The aim
of these impulses is always immediate and complete discharge and satisfaction. The
pleasure principle maintains that people always strive to maximize pleasure and
minimize pain.

Ego Clearly we do not live in a social vacuum and cannot simply do whatever we wish
whenever we want something. Adults who act impulsively are called immature or childish; mature conduct demands that we control our impulses in a wide variety of situations. For Freud, this control becomes possible when the **ego** is differentiated from the
id. The ego, in his view, is the organized aspect of id, formed to provide realistic direction
for the person's id impulses. It comes into existence because the needs of the person
require appropriate transactions with the environment if they are to be satisfied. The ego,
therefore, develops partially to carry out the aims of the id. There is a dynamic interaction
between the two structures. At the same time, it functions to keep the impulses of the id in
check until a suitable object is found.

Superego   The **superego** is the construct Freud used to describe the individual's internalization of societal values. These values are instilled in the person primarily by parents, who teach which behaviors are appropriate or inappropriate in given situations. The superego thus represents a set of learned ideals. Freud eventually described the superego as having two major components, **conscience** and the **ego-ideal**. Conscience is acquired through the use of punishment by the parents; the ego-ideal is learned through the use of rewards. When we do something wrong, our conscience makes us feel guilty; when we obey our parents and win their approval by performing in socially accepted ways, we feel proud. The main functions of the superego are to inhibit the urges of the id, to persuade the ego to substitute moralistic goals for realistic ones, and to strive for perfection. Thus, the superego interacts dynamically with the id and ego.

Although the superego serves positive functions preventing the individual from expressing primitive urges publicly, encouraging the individual to set goals leading to a career as a productive citizen, it also has a negative side. The superego may be too harsh and demanding. For example, a child who incorporates parental views of sex as dirty and sinful may, in adulthood, be afraid to approach members of the other sex and be incapable of forming an intimate relationship with anyone. Adoption of such an exceedingly high standard, in Freud's opinion, inevitably creates problems for the individual.

Defense Mechanisms

The ego tries to exert control over both an id that is concerned only with gratification of its instinctual urges and a superego that constantly seeks perfection. While total, permanent control over the id and superego can never be established, there are times when the ego is able to bring these two agencies under some control, so that the individual can function effectively. To this end, the ego seeks to find realistic outlets for the person's id impulses, for example, to transform aggressive urges into more socially acceptable activities, such as competing athletically with others. Control over the superego may be established when the ego convinces the person to give up perfectionism (for example, the belief that he or she must achieve all A grades or have a perfect family) and to substitute more realistically attainable goals in these life areas.

As Freud saw it, the ego resembles a battlefield where the armies of the id and superego continually clash. Although much of the ego operates in consciousness, some of its processes are unconscious and serve to protect the person against anxiety caused by the conflicting demands of the id and superego (Freud, 1960a, p. 7). The person needs protection from **anxiety** because it is a highly unpleasant state that signals a danger to the ego (self). The danger may be that the person's instinctual impulses are out of control and are threatening to overwhelm him or her; or the danger may arise because the individual fears punishment from his or her conscience for thinking about doing something that the superego considers wrong; or the threat may come from an outside source in the environment (for example, the death of a parent, or the rejection by a boyfriend or girlfriend). In the face of these dangers, the person's ego unconsciously attempts to regain control by activating defensive processes.

These defense mechanisms can serve a useful purpose in that they protect the person against pain. They are normal and universally used reactions to pain (Freud, 1937, p. 237). However, Freud believed that defense mechanisms can be potentially pathological when they are used indiscriminately, compulsively, and in ways that continually contradict the reality of the situation (Cramer, 1991, p. 10).

The primary defenses are as follows:

Repression   **Repression** is an attempt by the ego to keep undesirable id impulses from reaching consciousness. In the course of analyzing dreams, Freud discovered that certain thoughts were blocked from consciousness repressed, because they were too painful to acknowledge, and that attempts to make patients aware of these experiences met with resistance. In Freudian terms, the battle for supremacy between the ego and the id involved an opposition between energy forces. The driving forces he called **cathexes**; the restraining forces, **anticathexes**. In other words, certain unconscious wishes or ideas were energized and strove for expression in consciousness but were met by other ideas energized by restraining forces seated in the ego. If the ego forces dominated, the wishes would be repressed—that is, forced back into the unconscious. If the id forces dominated, the person would act out his or her socially unacceptable impulses. For example, a woman who hated her father might repress her hostility and anger, and thus be totally unaware of her actual feelings. If these feelings broke through to the surface, the individual might physically attack her father or even try to kill him. The battle would be centered on her attempts to express her feelings and the ego's attempts to repress them because their expression could lead to serious problems. The ego would attempt to protect the individual by forcing her to keep her unpleasant thoughts repressed. Freud considered repression the most fundamental of all defense mechanisms. As he put it, the theory of repression is the pillar upon which the edifice of psychoanalysis rests (Freud, 1938a, p. 939).

Repression occurs entirely on an unconscious level and involves preventing unpleasant experiences that are repulsive to the ego from reaching consciousness. Repressed memories are not under the conscious control of the person.

Suppression   **Suppression** involves the individual's active and conscious attempt to stop anxiety-provoking thoughts by simply not thinking about them. If a high school student finds herself thinking sexual thoughts about her teacher, she may actively suppress them because of her moral training. The thoughts would then be stored in the preconscious and could be reactivated and made conscious by the student through an exertion of her will.

Denial   **Denial** refers to a person's refusal to perceive an unpleasant event in external reality. In adults, the use of denial may be normal during times of extreme stress. For example, we may engage in denial when we are told of the death of a loved one. Our disbelief allows us to cope with the shock and to assimilate it in a more gradual and less painful manner. If, however, we refuse to acknowledge that the loved one has died even decades after his or her death, the behavior is likely pathological.

The origins of pathological denial can be traced to early childhood where children were subjected to physical and emotional abuse by insecure parents. Such children engage in denial to defend themselves against physical pain and anger caused by these unloving caregivers. Such denial then becomes the characteristic style of reacting to pain as they age. Recent research has found that denial in adults is associated with unpredictable behavior, a flamboyant, egotistical style of behaving, and a lack of clear thinking (Cramer, 2002, pp. 111–112). Furthermore, Cramer and Kelly (2010, pp. 619–620) have found more recently that adults who were abused by their caregivers in early childhood became abusive parents themselves when they had their own children.

Displacement   **Displacement** refers to the unconscious attempt to obtain gratification for id impulses by shifting them to substitute objects if objects that would directly satisfy the impulses are not available. For example, a young boy who is insulted by a strong teenager may not be able to retaliate for fear that the adolescent might physically hurt him. Instead, he may vent his anger on someone smaller and weaker than he is. In this case, a substitute object is sought so that the impulse can be gratified, even though aggressing against the weaker child will not be as satisfying as aggressing against the teenage antagonist.

Displaced aggression can also occur against inanimate objects as well. If a man is made angry by his wife, he may not strike her, but might punch a hole in a wall or break furniture so that he can feel temporarily satisfied. Beside the costs of repair to the house, it doesn't address the source of the problem and is likely to occur again, perhaps in a stronger outburst, in the future if he becomes stressed and agitated.

Sublimation   **Sublimation** is a form of displacement in which the unacceptable id impulses themselves are transformed, rather than the object at which they aim. The unacceptable impulses are displaced by ones that are socially acceptable (Freud, 1946, p. 56). A woman with a strong need for aggression may channel her energies into activities that are socially acceptable, becoming, for example, an outstanding scientist or a world-class athlete. By so doing, she can demonstrate her dominance over others, but in a way that contributes to society. In like manner, poets and painters may satisfy some of their sexual needs through their art. Freud believed that creative sublimations of human instincts are necessary if civilized society is to survive. He also believed, unfortunately, that such creativity is available only to the few people with special gifts and talents. Furthermore, in his rather pessimistic view, even the creative elite will suffer because sublimated activities could not fully satisfy their primitive sexual and aggressive impulses (Freud, 1952a, pp. 773–774).

Regression   In **regression**, there is a movement from mature behavior to immature behavior. That is, when the ego is threatened, the person may revert to an earlier, more infantile form of behavior as a means of coping with the stress. For example, a 6-year-old boy might start sucking his thumb or clinging to his mother on the first day of school. Or a woman who learns that she has not been promoted to a higher paying job in the company may storm into her supervisor's office and have a temper tantrum.

Projection   When a person protects the ego by attributing his or her own undesirable characteristics to others, we might infer that **projection** has taken place (Freud, 1938c, p. 625). For example, a girl who hates her mother may be convinced that her mother hates her. A student who cheats on examinations may continually assert that other students received high grades because they cheated. Cramer (2002, p. 114) found that young adult males who chronically used projection as a defense were distrustful and antagonistic toward others.

Reaction formation   The conversion of an undesirable impulse into its opposite is known as **reaction formation**. Freud considered it a lower form of sublimation (Freud, 1938d, p. 625). A man who hates his wife and yet is exceedingly kind to her would be a pertinent example. He could be said to be killing her with kindness.

Rationalization   **Rationalization** is the justification of behavior through the use of plausible, but inaccurate, excuses. For example, a young athlete, dropped from the team because of lack of ability, comes to the conclusion that he did not really want to be on the team because it is going to lose so many games.

Intellectualization   **Intellectualization** is a process that allows individuals to protect themselves against unbearable pain. It involves dissociation between one's thoughts and feelings. For example, a woman may conjure up an elaborate rationale to explain the death of her young husband. By citing reasons and focusing on the logic of her argument, she may avoid, for a while at least, the tremendous pain associated with such a traumatic experience.

Undoing   Sometimes a person who thinks or acts on an undesirable impulse makes amends by performing some action that nullifies the undesirable one, a defense mechanism known as **undoing**. Such actions are typically irrational and can be seen in various superstitious rituals and some religious ceremonies. By performing the undoing act, the person is convinced that the wrong he or she committed has been rectified. For example, a boy who has continual thoughts about masturbation and believes that they are evil may wash his hands frequently as a means of cleansing himself.

Compromise formation   **Compromise formation** involves the use of contradictory behaviors to gain some satisfaction for an undesirable impulse. The barbed compliment would be an example. Jill, who really hates Kathy, comments: "My, what a pretty dress. How did *you* ever manage to select it?" Or, John, who does not like Bill, says to him during a pick-up basketball game, "Great shot! I would never have expected *you* to make it."

Other defense mechanisms postulated by Freud, including identification and fixation, will be reviewed in the section on psychosexual development.

Personality Development

The Theory of Psychosexual Development

Having reviewed the major structural components of personality, we turn now to Freud's usage of these constructs in his scheme of **psychosexual development**. The theory, it should be noted, is biological in nature; it is based on the inevitable unfolding of a series of stages in which particular behaviors occur. Normal development involves the coursing of libidinal or sexual energy through a variety of earlier stages to a final stage, aptly called the genital stage. Immediately preceding the genital stage is the latency period, in which sexual energy is considered to be dormant. Abnormal development occurs if, in early childhood, the person undergoes traumatic experiences almost invariably sexual in nature that prevent the flow of significant amounts of libidinal energy through the various stages. The result is **fixation** at a particular stage, making the person more vulnerable to crisis later in life. When subjected to stress at a later point in development, this person may then use a defense mechanism to alleviate the anxiety. For each stage at which conflict occurs, Freud postulated a corresponding adult character pattern.

Oral stage   The infant is practically all id, according to Freud, and cannot initially distinguish between the self and the environment. An infant is controlled by biological impulses and is basically selfish. The focus of pleasurable sensations or "sexual" impulses during the first pregenital stage is the mouth (Freud, 1969, p. 10); Freud labeled it the **oral stage**. Pleasurable sensations occur as the infant takes in food and water. The parents' behavior is critical in determining whether or not the infant will experience personal difficulties later in life. These difficulties may occur as a result of parental overindulgence or underindulgence of the infant's needs during the first year or so. For example, if the mother resents nursing and weans the baby abruptly, a portion of the libidinal energy available to the individual becomes fixated around this conflict, while the remaining energy flows through to the next stage.

Anal stage   During the second and third years, pleasurable sensations are focused on the anal cavity: The chief pleasures for the child involve retention or expulsion of feces (Freud, 1957, p. 324). During this **anal stage**, ego processes are being differentiated from the id and the child begins to assert his or her independence. This independence does not, however, involve rational decision making, in which the child weighs the conflicting evidence and comes to reasonable conclusions. Rather, it is a negativistic independence, in which the child rejects out of hand whatever is being offered by the parents. If the child is asked, "Will you please put on your shoes?" the answer is an immediate "No." If the child is then asked, "Do you want a candy bar?" the answer, once again, is a resounding "No" even though the child may be hungry and may have begged for candy only moments earlier. It is a period, in short, for a contest of wills and the assertion of ego control.

According to Freud, the primary contest revolves around toilet training. In this culture and others, cleanliness is a virtue, and parents typically place heavy stress on regulating defecation and urination. Children can resist these demands by retaining the waste matter or by expelling it inappropriately, for example, by wetting or soiling their pants. Conflicts during this stage precipitate particular kinds of behavioral difficulties in adolescence and adulthood.

Phallic stage   During the fourth and fifth years, sexual tension is focused on the genital area. At this **phallic stage**, both boys and girls are considered to derive pleasure from self-manipulation (Freud, 1957, p. 327). Boys, according to Freud, develop a longing for sexual contact with the mother. In the most general sense, they seek affection and love from the mother. At the same time, however, the child is increasingly aware that there is a sexual relationship between his parents and that the father is his rival. But the father is bigger and stronger physically, and the boy is fearful that he will be punished for his desires, specifically that his penis will be cut off. The child alleviates this castration anxiety by **identification** with his father. In this way, his sexual desire is shunted into more socially acceptable channels. These strong, conflicting feelings and the process by which they are more or less adequately resolved Freud named the **Oedipal complex**, a term borrowed from Sophocles' tragedy *Oedipus Rex*, in which the Greek king, Oedipus, unwittingly kills his father and commits incest with his mother. The superego is an outgrowth of the resolution of this complex, as the child takes on the values of his parents and their attitudes toward society.

Freud believed that the kinship ties and practices of various primitive societies supported his ideas about the Oedipal conflict in males (Freud, 1950, pp. 144–145). On the basis of anthropological and historical evidence, he speculated that brothers within a primitive clan banded together to kill their father, their chief rival for the affection of the women. After committing the deed, they realized that a new social organization was necessary if they were ever going to live in harmony and avoid mutual destruction in a frantic effort to possess the women. As a consequence, a law against incest was adopted. Freud theorized that all cultures had instituted two taboos: a law against incest and a law protecting the totem animal. He saw the totem animal as a symbol of the father, and worship of it as a means of allaying the clan's sense of guilt over the original patricide. In Freud's view, worship of the totem animal also symbolized a covenant between tribal members and their fathers: The father promised them protection and care, and the members promised to respect the father's life. Freud saw this covenant between tribal members and their fathers as analogous to the male child's eventual identification with his father as a means of resolving his own basic conflict over the mother.

According to Freud, the conflict process for females is very different. He postulated that a girl, lacking a penis, envies boys and seeks to obtain one. At first, girls try to compensate for this deficiency by emulating boys and by masturbation of what Freud calls their stunted penis (clitoris). Although the mother is their first love object, they come to resent her for bringing them into the world without a penis and begin to love their father because he has the desired object. They then identify with the mother as a means of vicariously obtaining the desired object (Freud, 1969, pp. 44–51). Although initially they seek the father's penis, this fantasy is then transformed into the wish to have a baby, specifically a male baby who will bring the longed-for penis with him. Since these desires can never be fulfilled, Freud considered all girls to have relatively inadequate superegos. These mutilated little creatures, as he called them, had little sense of objectivity and justice. (Some of Freud's supporters called this special conflict process in girls the Electra complex in Greek mythology; Electra induced her brother to murder their hated mother but Freud himself was reluctant to use the term, perhaps because the analogy seemed weak and at variance with his own description of the process.)

To many people, the Freudian proposal concerning the mechanisms and outcomes of the Oedipus complex, especially for girls, is patently absurd. Freud has been severely criticized for maintaining that the Oedipal conflict is biologically based and occurs universally in all human beings, and there is some cross-cultural evidence that contradicts his contentions. In some cultures at least, the resentment of the boy toward his father is based on the father's powerful position in the family and not on sexual jealousy.

Feminist scholars point to Freud's chauvinistic outlook toward women: an attitude common to the strongly patriarchal society in which he lived. Viennese women in Freud's time were second-class citizens, subject to all the degrading treatment meted out to members of minority groups. His concept of penis envy is particularly galling to women because it implies that anatomy is destiny and that constructive personal growth is virtually impossible. If you are inherently inferior, it makes little sense to expend great amounts of effort trying to improve yourself.

Karen Horney, a prominent neoanalyst, took particular issue with Freud's concept of penis envy many years ago. Her arguments are, in general, echoed by leading feminists today. Horney maintained that the Freudian position is bogged down in faulty biology. She asks why a biologically healthy female would show such psychological qualities. Further, she maintains that the Freudian interpretation does not allow for the social and cultural factors that affect the psychology of women. Penis envy is presumed to manifest itself in the behavior of the "castrating female"—ambitious, competitive, seeking to dominate and humiliate men. Tendencies toward dictatorial power and egocentric ambition, Horney noted, are characteristics of neurotic men as well as neurotic women (Horney, 1937, p. 204). These problems stem, she suggested, from an excessively competitive society in which status is conferred upon those who are achievement-oriented, dominant, and ambitious. What normal women actually envy is the status of men and the psychological and physical rewards associated with it. (Horney's position is discussed in greater detail in Chapter 5.)

Latency stage   Freud postulated a **latency stage**, from the sixth year to puberty, during which sexual development is assumed to be at a standstill (Freud, 1969, p. 10). He believed that the person's characteristic ways of behaving are established during the first five years of life and that radical personality change is extremely difficult, if not impossible, thereafter. At this point in their development, children turn to the world of school and peers and begin to learn the social and technical skills that will allow them eventually to take their place as responsible and effective citizens in their society.

Genital stage   With the advent of puberty, sexual tension increases dramatically. The reproductive organs have matured, and both sexes are now capable of procreation. Previously, the aims of the sexual instincts have been predominantly autoerotic, but now the goal is to mate with an appropriate sex object. At this **genital stage**, an adequate heterosexual adjustment depends on the amount of libidinal energy available to the person. If there have been no severe traumatic experiences in early childhood, with corresponding libido fixations, an adequate adjustment is possible. When adulthood is reached, the person typically marries and settles into family life.

For Freud, the normal person is one who makes satisfactory adjustments in two major areas—love and work. While this pronouncement appears simplistic at first blush, it becomes more profound when we realize that any person must have many outstanding qualities to attain success in these two areas. For example, to be able to love another person, one must be secure in one's own identity, generous, caring, compromising, trusting, empathic, and so forth. To be able to work productively, one must be responsible, dependable, motivated, persistent, ambitious, and so on. An inadequate adjustment, on the other hand, involves libidinal fixations and the development of specific character disorders (Freud, 1969, pp. 12–13).

Character Types

The oral character   Persons who are fixated at the oral stage have problems later in life that are related primarily to receiving or taking things from the external world. The **oral receptive character** is a result of overindulgence in infancy. The individual has become habituated to receiving support and encouragement from other people and thus is excessively dependent on others for gratification (Blum, 1953, p. 160). Such people tend to be too trusting, accepting, and gullible; they admire strength and leadership in others but make little attempt to fend for themselves. They also tend to be rather incompetent—most of their gratification is derived from what others do for them and not from what they themselves accomplish—and to be overly optimistic. This type of person inevitably experiences conflicts with others because not everyone is nurturant and supportive like a mother. How long can one expect others to remain friends if one keeps demanding all of their time, effort, and affection without reciprocating in approximate measure?

Fixation also may occur when parents underindulge or severely frustrate the needs of their infants. In this case, the person learns to exploit others and may develop sadistic attitudes (Fenichel, 1945, p. 489). This type of **oral aggressive character** tends to envy others, and their success, and to try, through the use of manipulative strategies, to dominate them. Again, it is difficult to imagine liking and supporting a person who is continually manipulative and exploitative in his or her interpersonal relations.

The anal character   **Anal eroticism** stems from difficulties during toilet training, when children are locked in a battle over power and control with their parents. If the parents are highly punitive and demanding, children may decide to defiantly keep their "prized" possessions from the parents. The **anal character**, according to Freud, is delineated by a particular constellation of traits: obstinacy, parsimony, and orderliness. Obstinacy in anal characters means that they are stubborn, defiant, and resistant to control by others. They are also overly conscientious, rigid, fiercely independent, and doggedly persistent in the performance of even the most trivial duties. Parsimony suggests that they are frugal and stingy with regard to possession, money, and time, all of which are not to be wasted. The trait of orderliness is reflected in their need to live by routine. Research by Juni and Rubenstein (1982) shows that interruptions of their routines by others cause students higher in anal characteristics to become more intensely irritable and hostile than students lower in anal characteristics. Also, students higher in anal characteristics are more meticulous, perfectionistic, and sticklers for precision than those lower in anal characteristics (Pollak, 1979, pp. 226–227).

The phallic character   The difficulties experienced by the **phallic character** stem from inadequate resolution of the Oedipus complex. In males, it is a reaction to severe castration anxiety; they behave in a reckless, resolute, and self-assured manner (Blum,

1953, pp. 163–164). Overvaluing of the penis is reflected in excessive vanity and exhibitionism. Such males have to prove that they are real men. One way of doing so is by repeated conquests of women; the Don Juan type of male fits this description. For women, the primary motive is penis envy. Consequently, they are continuously striving for superiority over men. Such women are considered to be "castrating females."

The genital character   Freud viewed the **genital character** as the ideal type. Such people are sexually mature and capable of orgasm; their libidinal energies are no longer dammed up because they have found appropriate love objects (Blum, 1953, p. 164). In Freud's view, the key to happiness is the ability to love and be loved. Sexual love is one aspect of intimacy that provides us with happiness and joy. Although establishing intimacy is central to happiness, Freud reminds us that it also makes us vulnerable to rejection by the loved one and also to the eventual loss of the loved one. Yet Freud believed that love was necessary for healthy functioning and that love had to be pursued despite the suffering that it inevitably entailed.

Genital characters are also capable of sublimating their id impulses by expressing them in the form of productive and creative work. The creative activities that bring happiness differ for each individual. Some pursue happiness by refining their intellectual skills and by seeking truth, as in the case of the scientist or university professor; others seek it through direct action, as demonstrated by the artistic grace and agility of the ballet dancer. Thus, each person has to find the course that is best for him or her (Freud, 1952a, pp. 772–776).

Research Evidence for the Theory of Psychosexual Development

We may agree that Freud created an interesting and provocative theory of human development, but the question of its empirical validity remains open and subject to examination. Even though the theory is relatively vaguely stated, hypotheses for scientific testing may still be derived from it.

The evidence for the character types   Freud's psychoanalytic theory about psychosexual development suggests that certain clusters of personality traits exist in mature adults, growing out of unresolved, unconscious conflicts originating in early childhood. Hypothesized traits in the oral receptive character, for example, include excessive optimism, dependency, talkativeness, and an intense curiosity. Traits thought to be associated with the oral aggressive character include envy, excessive pessimism, excessive manipulation of others, and hostility. For the anal character, key characteristics are an opposition to influence from others and a minute attention to detail. For the phallic character, typical traits include recklessness, excessive pride, vanity, and self-assurance (Kline, 1972, pp. 7–12). There is considerable correlational trait evidence consistent with Freud's conception of the oral receptive character, practically none for the oral aggressive character, some correlational trait support for the anal character, and no support for the phallic or genital characters. However, the relative scarcity (and in some cases the complete absence) of empirical support for Freud's ideas about some of these character types may be attributed to the absence of reliable and valid measures of such orientations and a consequent failure to test his ideas.

The oral receptive character   Researchers initially investigated Freud's classic theory by examining his ideas about the oral receptive character. Researchers maintained that, if oral receptive individuals are orally fixated and later in their development become submissive and dependent on authority figures as Freud contended, then such individuals should show greater conformity, compliance, and suggestibility to the demands of authority figures in a variety of situations.

To test this hypothesis, Tribich and Messer (1974, pp. 842–848) first measured orality in college men by administering a projective test called the Blacky Pictures. This test contains 12 cartoons depicting the adventures of a dog named Blacky. Study participants (all men) were asked to make up stories about Blacky, and their responses were then scored by trained assessors. A subject, for example, might look at one of the pictures and tell a story that involved Blacky "sucking vigorously at his mother's breast." Or he might look at another picture and say that he believed it meant that "Blacky will grow up to like eating more than anything else." (These are two actual responses of a participant in the study.)

Once the participant's level of orality was determined, he was brought individually to a laboratory where he was introduced to a high-status authority figure (a psychiatrist). Each participant was then told that, once the room was completely dark, a point of light would be shown; his task was to judge how far the point of light had moved in inches. He was told it would move between 1 and 23 inches. Before responding, however, the participant would hear the authority figure's judgment of how far it had moved. Over a series of trials, the high orals' responses were much closer to the authority figure's than were those of the low orals, thereby confirming the investigators' prediction and Freud's theory.

Freud also claimed, not only that oral receptive characters are highly dependent on others, but also that they have strong needs for contact, affiliation, and nurturance. Research has provided evidence of their needs for company and emotional support by showing that oral receptive types tend to experience aversive arousal when socially isolated (Masling, Price, Goldband, & Katkin, 1981, pp. 395–400). Specifically, these researchers found that people with oral dependency needs showed more anxiety when performing tasks alone in a soundproof chamber than when they performed them in the presence of others. Masling, O'Neill, and Katkin (1982, pp. 529–534) showed further that high-oral study participants forced to interact with a cold, impersonal individual experienced more stress than did high-oral participants who interacted with a warm, personal individual. Low-oral participants, in contrast, showed no differences in stress level between the cold and warm interaction conditions.

In terms of their needs for contact, Juni, Masling, and Brannon (1979, pp. 235–237) found that people high in orality used greater physical contact as a means of helping others solve a problem than did people low in orality. Specifically, high- and low-oral individuals participated in an experiment on problem solving. As part of the experiment, they were asked to coach (by any methods they chose) another study participant (who was blindfolded) through a maze as fast as they could. The investigators found that high-oral individuals touched the blindfolded participants more often as a means of coaching them than did low-oral participants and that the blindfolded participants tended to successfully complete the maze more quickly under the guidance of the high-oral individuals.

In these and other studies, research results have provided consistent support for the oral receptive character (Shilkret & Masling, 1981, pp. 125–129).

The anal character   There have been fewer tests of Freud's ideas concerning the anal character. Several studies, for example, have found that anal characters tend to be rigid and dogmatic and to use their time in a niggardly, thrifty, and cautious manner (Pollak, 1979, pp. 235–237). O'Neill (1984, pp. 627–628) also found that anal characters had many qualities in common with individuals high in Type A personality characteristics, who are prone to coronary heart disease (e.g., both are intensely competitive, hostile, impatient, and overly concerned with time). Tribich and Messer (1974, pp. 842–848) also found that study participants high in anality were more resistant to influence by others than were low-anal participants. In other research by Fischer and Juni (1982), study participants high or low in anality were asked to read an essay written by another student about his personal life. One of the essays was high in intimacy (i.e., the student wrote about his sex life) and the other essay was low in intimacy (i.e., the student wrote about his academic courses). Study participants high or low in anality read either an essay that was high or low in intimacy. After reading the essay, all participants were asked to write their own essay about their personal lives. (No mention was made of the kind of intimacy level they should use in writing their response.) In comparison to participants low in anality, participants high in anality who read the intimate essay chose to respond by writing an essay that was much lower in intimacy level, thereby refusing to disclose much about their personal life, despite the fact that the other student had written a very revealing essay. Apparently, high anals saw the situation as a subtle demand on them to reveal personal information; accordingly, they became defensive, and clammed up. There were no differences between high and low anals in their disclosure levels in response to the student who wrote the nonintimate essay. Both high and low anals wrote nonintimate essays. There is no current research examining the characteristics of the phallic or genital characters.

Post-classic psychoanalytic position   While the classic theory of psychosexual development claims that the etiology of the oral receptive, anal, and phallic character types can be traced to unresolved fixations growing out of the feeding process in the oral stage, unresolved fixations growing out of the toilet-training process in the anal stage, and unresolved fixations growing out of pleasurable sensations occurring in the phallic stage, there is presently little direct empirical evidence that supports this etiological position (Bornstein, 2005a, pp. 4–5). As a result, the original or classic Freudian theory about psychosexual development is largely out of favor in mainstream psychology. However, this does not mean that all Freudian ideas have been abandoned by all modern researchers. On the contrary, some contemporary researchers have adopted a **psychodynamic approach** to the study of human development (and psychotherapy), which is based on many of Freud's ideas (e.g., that unconscious conflicts originate in early childhood; that these conflicts arise between the child and an authority figure, usually the mother; that the conflicts produce anxiety and defensive maneuvers as the individual struggles to cope with the stress; and that unresolved conflicts leave an indelible imprint on the individual's subsequent development and personality functioning). Let us now examine just one of the modern psychodynamic, Freudian approaches to the study of personality development and functioning, namely, the psychodynamic perspective called the dependent personality type.

The dependent personality type   Abandoning the biologically based, oral fixation hypothesis revolving largely around breast-feeding because of the low level of empirical support, Bornstein (1992, pp. 3–23) has inserted in its place the interactional idea that highly destructive dependence in people originates in childhood experiences where parents act in an overprotective and authoritarian way toward their children. Harsh and demanding treatment and overprotection of these children creates conflict in them and may on a largely unconscious level lead them to intensely and often indiscriminately seek the guidance, help, and support of others, even in situations where they are capable of solving the problems that confront them on their own. Such a parenting style has the unfortunate consequence that it prevents the child from acquiring a sense of mastery and self-efficacy that typically follows successful learning experiences. The result is the development of a **dependent personality type** (Bornstein, 2005a, p. 17; Bornstein, Ng, Gallagher, Kloss, & Regier, 2005, p. 732). Etiological research shows that parental over protectiveness and authoritarian treatment is consistently related to later dependency in their college-aged children (Bornstein, 2005a, pp. 186–187).

Developing a more broadly based, parent-child interactional approach to the study of dependence, researchers have been able to generate some new theoretical ideas, while keeping some of Freud's ideas. For example, they now identify several core components of the dependent personality type. Specifically, there is a (1) motivational component, that is, a powerful need for support and approval from others; (2) a cognitive component, that is, a perception of oneself as powerless and ineffectual; (3) an affective component, that is, a tendency to become anxious when required to function autonomously; and (4) a behavioral component, that is, a use of self-presentational strategies to strengthen ties to potential caregivers (Bornstein, 2005b, p. 82). This new framework has generated many interesting research findings.

In the area of psychopathology, for example, people with strong dependency needs are found to be highly insecure in their personal relationships and, as a result, experience high levels of relationship conflict and disruption which is highly upsetting. Feeling ineffectual and powerless to change this aversive situation, it is not surprising that many of these individuals become depressed (Huprich, Clancy, Bornstein, and Nelson-Gray, 2004, pp. 2–16). Dozens of research studies with both clinical and nonclinical populations show consistently that people with strong dependency needs are at greater risk for depression and suicide than nondependent individuals. Research shows further that individuals with strong dependency needs tend to be obese and are more likely to develop eating disorders like bulimia and anorexia nervosa, to have elevated levels of cigarette smoking, and to become alcoholics (Bornstein, 1992, pp. 14–16; Bornstein, 1998, p. 175; Bornstein, 2001, pp. 151–162; Bornstein & Cecero, 2000, p. 324; Bornstein & O'Neill, 2000, p. 463; Perry, Silvera, & Rosenvinge, 2002, p. 412; Sprohge, Handler, Plant, & Wicker, 2002, pp. 155–158).

Contrary to the stereotypes in the minds of many clinicians and researchers that the dependent personality type is someone who is always passive and submissive, however, research now indicates that, in certain situations, such individuals actually will behave actively and assertively. Specifically, in order to achieve their goal of winning praise and approval from others, dependent personalities vary their self-presentations. In laboratory settings with no authority figure (i.e., experimenter) present, for example, they have been found to conform their opinion to those of their peers in order to win approval and praise from them. Under the same circumstances, they will also engage in self-deprecation to win favorable evaluations from their peers. In a laboratory situation with only an authority figure present, they will work hard to win his or her approval by emphasizing their competence and skill in order to impress his or her authority figure. Interestingly, when placed in a laboratory situation with both a peer and an authority figure and forced to choose between praise and approval from one or the other, they will compete hard against the peer in order to win the competition and receive praise for winning from the more prestigious authority figure (Bornstein, Riggs, Hill, & Calabrese, 1996, pp. 637–673).

Another stereotype that has recently been exploded by new research findings is the view that the dependent personality type always acts in ways that are destructive either to themselves and/or to others. Several studies in the research literature show that there are certain aspects of their personalities that make it possible for them to act sometimes in positive ways. For example, in comparison with nondependent people, high dependency individuals are found to view others as friendly and available. They believe that others are approachable and expect that others will respond to them in caring ways (Pincus & Wilson, 2001, pp. 242–243). Also, high dependency individuals are more interpersonally sensitive, and are more likely to ask teachers for guidance when confronted with difficult tasks. Since guidance from teachers usually leads to better understanding, such behavior promotes strong academic performance (Bornstein, 1992, p. 18; Bornstein, 1994, p. 629). Also, high dependency individuals' strong desire to please and win the approval of authority figures can motivate them to perform well for teachers and parents who are highly supportive. Thus, these individuals can achieve effective test performances when their need to please others exceeds their fear of rejection if they fail. In medical settings, people who have strong dependency needs are more likely to have positive attitudes toward physicians and hospitals, to develop positive relationships with physicians and other caregivers (Bornstein & Gold, 2008, pp. 154–161), and to seek medical attention more quickly when physical symptoms appear, leading to more positive prognoses for recovery (Bornstein, 1993, p. 403); also, their desire to please authority figures often results in increased compliance with medical regimens, in comparison to individuals who are nondependent (O'Neill & Bornstein, 2001, pp. 289–298; Parker & Lipscombe,1980, pp.355–363). In conclusion, dependency is neither "all good" nor "all bad." Rather, dependency can be an asset in some situations and a liability in others (Bornstein, 1993, p.404). The goal in therapy is not to eliminate all forms of dependency. Instead, it is to eliminate those forms of **unhealthy dependence**—dependence which results in maladaptive and situationally inappropriate behavior in patients—and to encourage the expression of **healthy dependence**. In healthy dependence, the person functions more autonomously, but with an ability to ask for help and support from other people when it is situationally appropriate (Bornstein, 2005a, p. 147).

Assessment Techniques

To understand the personalities of his patients, Freud relied on three major techniques: free association, dream analysis, and transference.

Free Association

Freud's technique of **free association**, as we have seen, involved the patients' self-reports of whatever thoughts and memories occurred to them without any kind of self-censorship. The patients were told to report *all* thoughts, no matter how trivial, unimportant, embarrassing, and illogical they seemed to be. Freud called this attempt at completely uncensored reporting the fundamental rule of psychoanalysis. During these sessions, Freud sat behind the patient, out of sight but in a position to watch facial expressions and gestures; in this way, he ensured that he did not elicit behavior from the patients by his own gestures and facial expressions. He wanted the patients' responses to be spontaneous and not controlled by him. Freud believed that, when resistance occurred, the analysis was definitely moving in the right direction, that is, uncovering the actual source of the patients' problems. Through the use of free association, Freud discovered that patients' problems typically stemmed from traumatic experiences in early childhood.

Freud provided an interesting nonclinical example of the use of free association to uncover an unpleasant secret (Freud, 1960b, pp. 8–11). While on vacation, Freud renewed his acquaintance with a young academician, who was familiar with some of Freud's theories but highly skeptical about their validity. The man was very depressed about the state of the world in general and about his own bleak prospects for success in academic life. Not only were few academic positions available, but his Jewish heritage virtually guaranteed his professional failure because of the anti-Semitism prevailing at the time in academic life.

The incident involved a **parapraxis**, which is basically a cognitive failure such as a slip of the tongue, a mishearing of a word, or the forgetting of an obvious word or thing. The young academician wanted to emphasize his outrage at the injustice by quoting a line from Virgil's *Aeniad*, in which the wronged Dido prays for revenge on Aeneas. The line was: *Exoriar(e) aliquis nostris ex ossibus ultor* (Let someone arise from my bones as an avenger). However, he omitted the word *aliquis* (someone). Immediately aware of his error, he tried to correct it but, even though he thought about it for a long while, he just could not remember it. Finally, he very reluctantly asked Freud to supply it, which Freud did. Feeling humiliated by his failure, the man tried to retaliate by reminding Freud of his "absurd" theory that even senseless mistakes had meaning. He then challenged Freud to prove his theory by revealing the latent meaning of the missing word, *aliquis*.

Freud promptly accepted the challenge, but only on condition that the young man report each and every thought that he had as he free-associated. The man accepted and began his free associations: "There springs to mind the ridiculous notion of dividing the word *aliquis* like this: *a* and *liquis*." Freud asked, "What occurs to you next?" The young man replied, "Reliquien [relics], liquefying, fluidity, fluid." He then asked, "Have you discovered anything yet?" Freud replied, "No. Not by any means yet. But go on." The man laughed scornfully and said, "I am [now] thinking of [Saint] Simon of Trent whose relics I saw two years ago in a church at Trent. I am thinking of the accusation of ritual blood-sacrifice which is being brought against the Jews [again today]." In the 15th century, the Jews were accused of killing Simon, a 2½-year-old child, who was subsequently declared a martyr and a saint. Only centuries later did the Catholic church exonerate the Jews and acknowledge that confessions of the crime had been extracted by torture (Erdelyi, 1985, p. 39).

The man's next association was that he had recently read an article in an Italian newspaper entitled "What Saint Augustine Thinks of Women." And then the man said that he was thinking that both Saint Augustine and Saint Januarius were calendar saints and that there was a miracle involving Saint Januarius' blood. Freud asked the man to explain the miracle of the blood, and he replied:

> They keep the blood of St. Januarius in a phial [vial] inside a church at Naples, and on a particular holy day it miraculously *liquefies*. The people attach great importance to this miracle and get very excited if it is delayed as happened once at a time when the French were occupying the town. So the general in command ... took [the priest in charge of the church] aside and gave him to understand with an unmistakeable gesture toward the soldiers posted outside that he *hoped* that the miracle would take place very soon. And in fact it did take place. (Freud, 1960b, p. 10)

Then the man paused and hesitated to go on, saying that his next thought was too intimate to report. Finally, after some prodding, he reluctantly continued: "I have suddenly thought of a lady from whom I might easily hear a piece of news that would be very awkward for both of us." Freud immediately delivered his interpretation in the form of a question: That her periods have stopped? The young man was amazed and asked, "How could you guess that?" Freud replied:

> "That's not difficult any longer; you've prepared the way sufficiently. Think of *the calendar saints, the blood that starts to flow on a particular day*, the disturbance *when the event fails to take place, the open threats that the miracle must be vouchsafed, or else*. In fact you've made use of the miracle of St. Januarius to manufacture a brilliant allusion to women's periods." (Freud, 1960b, p. 11)

The man's subdued reaction was: "I certainly was not aware of it." Freud then expanded his interpretation, explaining that the prefix *a* in *aliquis* often means no, while *liquis* means liquid. He thought the young man was trying to reject from consciousness the frightening idea "aliquis," no liquid; that is, he was trying to avoid the thought, "No menstruation, she's pregnant!" (Erdelyi, 1985, p. 41).

The young man sheepishly acknowledged that he thought his Italian girlfriend was pregnant. Freud then observed that he was also in a quandary about whether to marry her or to encourage her to have an abortion. The idea of the abortion, Freud maintained, was suggested by the young man's thoughts regarding the sacrifice of Simon as a child. Through his analysis, Freud was able to reveal, to the young man's amazement and satisfaction, the underlying meaning of his forgetting.

Dream Analysis

Another major technique used by Freud to unravel the secrets of his patients' unconscious was **dream analysis**. Freud's task, as he saw it, was to analyze and interpret the symbols present in the manifest content of their dreams, in an attempt to discover the latent or hidden meanings. As a result of his extensive clinical experiences, Freud believed that these symbols had universal meanings. Sticks, tree trunks, umbrellas, and snakes, for example, were thought to symbolize the penis; boxes, doors, and furniture chests represented the vagina. Despite their universal nature, Freud also believed that all symbols had to be judged and interpreted in terms of the unique conflicts of the individual. Also, these symbols typically had multiple meanings, which made analysis highly difficult.

In Freud's view, dreams are always disguised attempts at wish fulfillment. The wishes are unconscious motives that are unacceptable to the individual and are nearly always erotic in nature. During sleep, these impulses seek expression but are subject to censorship. As a result, they seek expression indirectly (via displacement) by taking on disguised symbolic forms. This indirect expression is seen in the manifest content of the person's dreams. Often the events in the manifest content appear totally unrelated to the actual wish. Detailed analysis by Freud, however, eventually revealed the connection, as seen in the following case study.

Freud's patient, a young woman, told him that her sister had two sons, Otto and Charles, and that, unfortunately, Otto had died recently. Otto was the patient's favorite, but she claimed that she was fond of Charles as well. She then told Freud that the evening before her appointment, she had had a dream in which she "saw Charles lying dead … in his little coffin, his hands folded; there were candles all about; and, in short, it was just as it was at the time of little Otto's death, which gave me such a shock" (Freud, 1938b, pp. 229–230). She then asked Freud what this strange dream meant. Did it mean, she asked, that she was so evil as to wish that her sister would lose the only child she had left? Or did it mean that she really wished that Charles had died instead of Otto, whom she loved so much more? Freud reassured her that neither interpretation was correct.

In the course of the analysis, Freud discovered that the young woman had been orphaned at an early age and had gone to live with her sister. A number of years later, the sister introduced her to a very attractive man. She and the man had planned to marry, but somehow the sister had intervened, and now the man no longer paid visits to the house. Although she had many other suitors, the young woman was unable to extend her affections to other men.

The object of her interest was a professor with literary talents who often gave public lectures. The young woman always managed to get tickets to hear him speak, and would sit unobserved in the audience. If she learned that her friend was going to a concert, she attended also, in the hope of seeing him. The last time she saw him was at little Otto's funeral, when he offered her and her sister his condolences. Even under those circumstances, she could not suppress her feelings of affection for the professor. The motive of her dream about little Charles then became clear: it signified nothing more than her wish to see the man again. Thus, even though the dream initially seemed strange and inexplicable, Freud was able to ferret out the hidden wish, and thus helped the woman by making her real motivation clear to her.

Transference

Besides free association and dream analysis, Freud relied heavily on **transference** to facilitate movement toward cure for his patients. In the course of treatment, Freud discovered that patients inevitably began to relive their old conflicts and interactions with authority figures (most notably, their parents) in their relationship with him. In general, he maintained, patients begin to see their therapist as a reincarnation of important figures in their past. As a result, they transfer to their therapist the kinds of feelings and behaviors previously directed toward these early authority figures.

In Freud's view, this transference phenomenon could be of inestimable value in helping therapists cure their patients. Yet it could also be a possible source of danger if the patients decided to act out their old feelings of hostility and anger toward their parents.

In general, according to Freud, the transference process is characterized by **ambivalence**; that is, patients typically have attitudes of both affection and hostility toward their parents, and these positive and negative feelings are displaced onto the therapist. Freud found that positive feelings were displaced onto him first and that negative feelings followed later. In **positive transference**, the patients developed a special affectionate interest in him. They trusted him completely and praised him lavishly. Among his female patients, some fell passionately in love with him and made sexual demands of him. Others revealed a wish that he treat them as he would a favorite daughter. In all cases, the women were highly jealous of anyone who was close to him. In his male patients, Freud also found evidence of sexual feelings toward him, although rarely in the direct form expressed by his female patients.

In his analysis of the transference process, Freud focused on the many cases where his female patients expressed their love and affection toward him. He believed that these affectionate overtures were a major sign of resistance on the part of the patients; that is, expressions of love were most likely to occur at a point in the analysis where patients had to admit or remember some particularly distressing and heavily repressed part of their past. Thus, they expressed their love for the therapist in order to avoid coming to grips with traumatic, early sexual experiences in their own lives. Freud believed that these patients unconsciously were trying to destroy his credibility as a therapist by bringing him down to the level of a lover. If they could achieve their goal, they would no longer have to listen to, or believe, his interpretations concerning the sources of their conflicts. They could, therefore, avoid the pain associated with the confrontation of their repressed memories.

But how is the therapist to react to these irrational affectionate overtures? Freud thought it made little sense for the therapist to sever the therapeutic relationship, because that would leave the repressed materials intact and the patient uncured. Nor should the therapist ever yield to the temptation of sexually consummating the relationship, for ethical reasons. Freud held the highest professional standards and argued strongly that the therapist should never violate the patient's trust. Even if the therapist had feelings of affection for the patient and was therefore experiencing a **countertransference**, he should not act on those feelings. Instead, he should continually bear in mind that his primary commitment was to the welfare of the patient and her cure. To accomplish these goals, the therapist should work patiently with her in an attempt to confront and eventually understand the reality that her feelings toward him had their origins in infantile sexual fixations. He should also make every attempt, through self-analysis, to understand the basis of his own feelings toward her. Increased self-understanding, Freud believed, helped him to understand her conflicts and wishes better and facilitated her movement toward a cure (Freud, 1958, pp. 159–171).

Under conditions of positive transference, patients typically made progress toward a cure. They were receptive to his interpretations, understood them, and were fully engrossed in the analysis. Difficulties soon arose, however, because positive transference was followed by **negative transference**. At this point, patients showed intense anger and hostility toward him, and viewed his interpretations with great distrust. Freud pointed out to his patients that their feelings did not arise from the present situation and that they were instead simply repeating negative experiences that had occurred earlier in their lives. To the extent that they accepted this explanation and explored its possibilities, they were likely to attain insight into their problems and to make progress toward the attainment of psychological health. Under these conditions, they no longer saw the therapist as an absolute authority, but rather as another suffering, striving person like themselves (Edmundson, 2007, p. 212).

Theory's Implications for Therapy

Psychopathology refers to disordered behaviors, ranging from ineffective coping with everyday problems (**neurosis**) to a serious inability to relate to other people (**psychosis**). In response to the anxiety created by the stifling of their instinctual impulses, neurotics and psychotics have resorted to various defense mechanisms. Normal growth has been arrested; as a result, their functioning is ineffective and stereotypic. To cure such individuals, it is necessary to reduce their conflicts and defenses by relieving their anxieties. The energies directed away from the maintenance of defenses then become available for constructive growth.

Through the use of free association, dream analysis, and transference, **psychoanalysis** can be made to help these individuals understand the sources of their conflicts and to see that these internal struggles have weakened the ego and prevented them from coping effectively with the demands of external reality to see that they are repeating old behaviors and using ineffective strategies in current situations. Successful therapy results in increased self-understanding and a more accurate assessment of reality. What is unconscious is made more conscious, the ego is strengthened, and the patient is then able to function more effectively in everyday life (Freud, 1969, pp. 31–35).

Evaluative Comments

We are now in a position to evaluate Freud's theory in terms of how well it meets the six criteria outlined in Chapter 1 for judging the worth of scientific theories.

Comprehensiveness   Freud was a creative thinker who constructed a highly comprehensive theory. The range and diversity of behavior and experience described and interpreted by the theory are remarkable. Freud sought to understand not only various kinds of emotional and behavioral disorders, but many other phenomena, including humor, marriage, war, death, friendship, myths and fairy tales, incest, societal mores, dreams, slips of the tongue, bungled actions, suicide, bed-wetting, creativity, competition, and absentmindedness. In short, Freud developed a theoretical system that explicitly sought to explain virtually all of human behavior. His theory remains, to the present day, the most comprehensive conceptual system ever created by a personality investigator.

Precision and testability   A major problem with Freudian theory is the relative vagueness of its concepts, the imprecision and ambiguities of its propositions or relational statements, and the difficulties it presents in deriving clear and testable hypotheses. When research is based on such loose theorizing, it is impossible to know whether the results really support the theory; when results are contrary to the theorizing, advocates can claim that the measures of the concepts and the hypotheses were not validly derived from the major theoretical propositions.

A related criticism is that much of the theory is presented in metaphors, or in terms that do not lend themselves to precise scientific testing, for example, the life and death instincts. Frequently, explanations for observations are offered after the fact. The theory "postdicts" well, but has real difficulty in predicting in advance how people will behave. Some of the evidence for it is post hoc and secured through uncontrolled case-study methods. In addition, Freud did not record the patient's observations as he heard them, thereby opening the door to criticism that his memory of these events was distorted. Finally, the universal conclusions that Freud drew about human behavior on the basis of extensive observations of a few patients seem incredible and naive. Clearly, Freud's theory does not satisfactorily meet the precision and testability criterion.

Parsimony   Freud's theory also fails to meet the parsimony criterion. Although it utilizes a number of assumptions and concepts to account for the phenomena in its domain, its proposed explanatory scheme is highly restricted in nature: sex and aggressive tendencies are the overwhelming determinants of behavior. Nowhere in the theory, for example, does Freud discuss how needs for competence, exploration, or altruism influence personal development and behavior. Thus, the motivational base of the theory is limited and does not allow for different and more adequate explanations of behavior.

Finally, Freud presented a generally pessimistic and one-sided view of human nature. People are seen as essentially irrational and controlled by amoral forces. Although he recognized fully that human beings can act rationally, he chose to focus almost entirely on the irrational side of human nature in his work.

Empirical validity   There have been literally thousands of investigations of various aspects of Freudian theorizing. These investigations can be divided generally into two categories: evidence for Freud's theory of psychotherapy and evidence for his theory of psychosexual development.

In regard to the theory of psychotherapy, Eysenck (1952) conducted an early massive review of the clinical literature to assess the effectiveness of psychoanalysis in curing people. After examining more than 7,000 case histories of patients, he concluded that psychoanalytic therapy did not significantly facilitate the recovery of neurotic patients. Although 66% of patients treated to completion by means of psychoanalysis were much improved or cured, Eysenck found that 72% of patients who were *not* treated by means of any formal therapy were also much improved or cured within two years of the onset of their illnesses. Thus, approximately two-thirds of patients recovered or improved to a marked extent whether they were treated psychoanalytically or not. Reviews during the 1980s and early 1990s indicated that Eysenck's original argument was still essentially valid (Erwin, 1980; Franks, Wilson, Kendall, & Foreyt, 1990; Grossarth-Maticek & Eysenck, 1990; Stunkard, 1991), and there are no current data today to challenge Eysenck's argument.

Besides research suggesting that psychoanalytic therapy is not very effective, Bornstein (2001) has maintained that there are two other problems with such therapy, namely, that it is too time-consuming and expensive. He proposes that analysts abandon classic psychoanalytic treatment techniques that do not work (e.g., free association, dream analysis), thereby streamlining the process and making it more efficient and less costly to patients. Thus, he implores analytic researchers to do more empirical research to test the effectiveness of such streamlined, psychodynamic approaches to treatment.

The evidence in support of Freud's theorizing on psychosexual development is, in some respects, more promising, as we have seen. That is, there are many correlational studies on the oral personality, and much of this research is consistent with Freudian theorizing, although there is little direct evidence that the origins of the orientation lie in trauma experienced by individuals surrounding the feeding situation per se. Research on the anal personality is also consistent with Freud's theorizing, but once again the specific etiology that he proposes concerning the origins of the distinctive traits in such personalities is problematic. Finally, there is no evidence in support of his phallic and genital character types, but this fact may change if researchers start to become interested in constructing individual difference measures of these character types and then testing Freudian hypotheses in these areas. There is some support for Freud's prediction that, the less adequate an individual's defenses against sexual and aggressive impulses, the greater the likelihood of psychopathology (Silverman, 1976). Also, there are data supporting the idea that sexual conflicts are present in many neurotics and that some of these disturbances arise from experiences during early childhood. It is apparent that these early experiences have a marked impact on later personality functioning in some cases. Preliminary evidence also exists for Freud's hypothesis that, under stress, study participants may fail to suppress unacceptable thoughts and thus they may show up in slips of the tongue (Baars, Cohen, Bower, & Berry, 1992, p. 311). All in all, the research evidence in support of Freud's theory of psychosexual development and the pathology engendered by failure to resolve the conflicts of early childhood is greater than some of his critics are willing to admit, but much more work testing the theory remains to be done.

Heuristic value   Freud's theory continues to have tremendous heuristic value (Shaver & Mikulincer, 2005, pp. 22–45; Westen, Gabbard, & Ortigo, 2008, pp. 78–97). As a creative scholar, he continues to serve as an inspiration to other professionals, by showing them the kinds of contributions that can be made to our knowledge of behavior through painstaking and courageous investigation. Scholars in disciplines outside of psychology, for example, in literature, art, sociology, history, anthropology, religion, philosophy, criminology, political science, and the physical sciences—all continue to make use of Freudian concepts.

Professional psychologists in a variety of specialty areas—especially cognitive, biological, developmental, clinical, and social psychology—also show an intense, ongoing interest in many of his ideas. For example, researchers in developmental psychology are still intrigued and influenced by his ideas on moral development, sex-typing, identification, parent-child relations, aggression, and dependency (Miller, 1993, p. 146). Furthermore, his once controversial ideas—(1) that unconscious states exist and influence behavior; (2) that people sometimes have conflicting feelings in situations that motivate them in opposing ways and often lead to compromise; (3) that people show resistance when threatened and then use defense mechanisms to distort information about themselves and others; (4) that frequent, compulsive, and indiscriminant use of defense mechanisms are associated with psychopathology; (5) that early experience plays an important role in subsequent development; and (6) that personality development involves not only learning to regulate sexual and aggressive feelings but also moving from an immature, socially dependent state to a more mature, interdependent one—are now generally acceptable to many psychologists; that is, there is abundant research evidence demonstrating the validity of Freud's views on these matters (Baumeister, Dale, & Sommer, 1998, pp. 1081–1124; Beutler, Moleiro, & Talebi, 2002, pp. 212–215; Cramer, 2006, pp. 18–19; Masling, 1992, p. 262; Miller, 1993, p. 146; Wakefield, 1992, p. 78; Westen, Gabbard, & Ortigo, 2008, pp. 78–97).

Much of the continuing fascination with Freud's theory lies in the unusual and complicated picture of human beings that it often paints. Men and women are not simply rational animals, but curious mixtures of the irrational and rational. They often feel constrained by society and are continually searching for acceptable ways to express their innermost feelings. In an attempt to deal with their conflicts, they use various defense mechanisms that, while temporarily protective, prove damaging in the long run. Through painful encounters with reality, they can begin to understand the limitations of their personalities, the defenses that they use to protect themselves, and the need to confront their problems directly as a means of becoming more effective human beings. It seems clear that such drama was destined to excite and interest observers of human behavior and experience. Consistent with these speculations, Bornstein (2010, pp. 133–152) has argued recently that psychoanalysis and its principles can draw upon theorizing and research from cognitive psychology, developmental psychology, social psychology, and clinical psychology to form an overarching, interpretive framework for understanding the complex, subjective experiences of individuals that culminate in the production of their unique behavior. This ability to continually stimulate thinking and debate and to inspire psychologists and psychiatrists is a major part of Freud's enduring legacy.

Applied value   In addition to his seminal contributions to therapy and the treatment of emotional disorders, Freud's insights have been applied by psychological anthropologists to cross-cultural phenomena. These investigators continue to use psychoanalytic ideas about child-rearing in their efforts to explain personality development (Haviland, 1994, pp. 379–380). Freud's ideas have also been employed by sociologists and social psychologists to help them understand the dynamics of family life and the functioning of small groups. In addition, Freudian concepts have been used fruitfully by historians, theologians, novelists, and economists. Thus, the psychoanalytic position continues to have considerable applied value.

CRITICAL THINKING QUESTIONS

1. Freud thought that the major conflict experienced by individuals was between their need to gratify their impulses and society's need to control the expression of such needs. What do you think he proposed as the best solution to this problem? Can you think of another proposal that could work better?

2. What are the primary defense mechanisms, as envisioned by Freud? Give examples of the operation of such mechanisms based on your own experiences or the experiences of other people you know.

3. What do you think might happen to a society in which id impulses were left unchecked by the superego?

4. Do you think that Freud's concept of penis envy has any merit? Why or why not?

5. Do you agree with Freud that psychologically healthy people are adjusted satisfactorily in two major areas of life—love and work? Can you think of any other areas in which satisfactory adjustments must be made if people are to be psychologically healthy? State some reasons for your answer.

GLOSSARY

ambivalence   Mixed feelings of one person toward another, characterized by alternation between love and hate.

anal character   An individual fixated at the anal stage, who derives pleasure from his/her control over retention of feces. As an adult, this person is characterized by stinginess, orderliness, stubbornness, and the hoarding of possessions.

anal eroticism   Feelings of sexual pleasure that have their source in the person's control over expulsion and retention of feces.

anal stage   Second pregenital stage of psychosexual development, in which primary gratification centers around the anal cavity.

anticathexes   Restraining forces within the personality that are designed to keep unwanted impulses from reaching consciousness or awareness.

anxiety   Painful feelings experienced when the ego is threatened.

catharsis   Reliving earlier traumatic experiences emotionally, to reduce disturbing physical symptoms.

This term derives from the Greek word meaning purification.

cathexes   Driving energy forces that attach themselves to an idea or behavior.

compromise formation   Defense mechanism that involves the use of contradictory behaviors to attain some satisfaction for an unacceptable impulse.

conscience   Punitive aspect of the superego. Once the person has incorporated societal values by forming a conscience, violation of that conscience makes the person feel guilty or ashamed. Such feelings are punishing.

conscious   A state of the mind characterized by awareness of one's experiences.

countertransference   The tendency of the therapist to react with personal feelings toward the patient on the basis of the therapist's own needs and conflicts. These feelings might involve attraction and lust, but other possibilities include dislike and even revulsion toward an aggressive and/or hostile patient because of the therapist's own insecurities. Analysis of these needs and conflicts could lead the therapist to better self-understanding, which, in turn, could lead to an increased understanding of the patient and movement toward a cure.

denial   Primitive defense mechanism in which the person protects the self against threats from the environment by refusing to recognize their existence.

dependent personality type   A personality style wherein individuals are predisposed to seek the guidance, help, and support of others, even in situations where they are capable of functioning independently and meeting challenges on their own.

determinism   Philosophical doctrine that all behavior is caused by the operation of other events and does not occur freely or at random.

displacement   Defense mechanism in which the person seeks gratification of thwarted impulses by shifting the impulses from the original, frustrating object to a substitute object.

dream analysis   Psychoanalytic technique used to probe the unconscious through interpretation of the patient's dreams.

dynamics   Complex interrelationships among the structural components of personality such that changes in one component trigger changes in the other components. For example, if id impulses (e.g., sexual urges) are activated, the superego comes into play by making the person feel guilty about his lustful feelings, while the ego searches for a more realistic and socially acceptable way of gratifying the need (e.g., by establishing a personal relationship through dating).

ego   Agency postulated by Freud to help the individual satisfy basic urges in ways deemed appropriate by society.

ego-ideal   Positive aspect of the superego, comprising the standards of perfection taught to the child by the parents.

eros   All of the instincts inherent in us that seek to maintain life.

fixation   Defensive attachment to an earlier stage of psychosexual development. Fixation prevents the learning of new behaviors, the acquisition of new interpersonal relationships, and progress in development.

free association   Therapeutic technique pioneered by Freud in which the therapist encourages patients to report, without restriction, any thoughts that occur to them.

genital character   A mature individual who is sexually developed and capable of relating to members of the other sex.

genital stage   Final stage of psychosexual development, in which an attempt is made to conduct a mature love relationship with a member of the opposite sex.

healthy dependence   A manifestation of dependence that occurs in some contexts but not others and in ways that are situationally appropriate.

id   Reservoir of unconscious forces or urges that blindly seek gratification.

identification   In Freudian theory, the defensive process whereby an individual takes on the characteristics of another person in order to relieve anxieties and reduce internal conflicts.

intellectualization   Defense mechanism in which individuals protect themselves against pain by isolating their thoughts about painful events from their feelings about them.

latency stage   Psychosexual period during which libidinal energy lies dormant and the primary focus is on the development of interests and skills through contact with childhood peers and teachers.

libido   In Freudian theory, the basic energy source contained in the id that propels behavior. Freud considered it to consist of sexual impulses; Jung conceptualized it as a more general life-energy process consisting of sexual, creative, spiritual, and self-preservative instincts.

negative transference   Phenomenon that occurs during psychoanalytic therapy in which the patient redirects toward the therapist unconscious feelings of anger and hostility retained from experiences with authority figures in childhood.

neoanalytic perspective   Theoretical positions that have their origins in Freudian psychoanalytic theory but have evolved new concepts and ways of examining and understanding human personality that are significant departures from Freud's original theory.

neurosis   Behavioral disorder characterized by underlying conflicts and anxieties that prevent the individual from coping effectively with everyday problems.

Oedipal complex   The process during the phallic stage in which the male child desires sexual contact with the mother, feels threatened by the father, and eventually resolves the conflict by identifying with the father.

oral aggressive character   An individual who becomes fixated in the oral stage because of underindulgence during feeding, when newly emerging teeth are used to bite the caregiver as a means of obtaining nourishment. As an adult, this person is characterized by envy, manipulation of others, and suspiciousness.

oral receptive character   An individual who becomes fixated in the oral stage because of overindulgence during feeding (before the emergence of teeth). As an adult, this person is characterized by gullibility, admiration for others, and excessive dependence.

oral stage   First pregenital stage of psychosexual development, in which primary gratifications center around the mouth.

parapraxis   Malfunction in language, such as a slip of the tongue, a bungled word, misreading, mishearing, or forgetting words or things, that indicates the presence of underlying conflicts.

phallic character   An individual fixated at the phallic stage who, later in life, needs to prove continually his or her sexual adequacy. The male phallic character needs to prove his adequacy through sexual conquests. This person is characterized by brashness, excessive vanity and pride, and exhibitionism. The female phallic character needs to prove her adequacy by continually ridiculing and humiliating men. This person is characterized by a domineering and contemptuous attitude toward men.

phallic stage   Third pregenital stage of psychosexual development, in which primary gratifications are derived from manipulation of the genitals.

pleasure principle   The rule by which the id operates; the id seeks to achieve pleasure and avoid pain.

positive transference   Phenomenon that occurs during therapy in which the patient redirects toward the therapist unconscious feelings of love and affection retained from experiences with authority figures (usually the parents) in early childhood.

preconscious   A state of the mind in which the person is currently unaware of some idea, memory, or event, which can, however, be made conscious with some effort.

projection   Defense mechanism in which a person attributes his or her own undesirable characteristics to others.

psychoanalysis   Theory of personality development, functioning, and change created by Freud. It places heavy emphasis on the roles of biological and unconscious factors in the determination of behavior.

psychodynamic approach   Perspective on human development and behavior based on Freudian ideas and characterized by an analysis of early childhood experiences, unconscious conflicts between children and their caregivers, and the use of defense mechanisms to cope with distress.

psychopathology   Disordered behaviors, such as neuroses or psychoses, that interfere with realistic and effective functioning or behaving.

psychosexual development   Theory devised by Freud to account for psychological and personality development in terms of individuals' attempts to come to grips with key biological impulses.

psychosis   Severe behavioral disorder characterized by an inability to relate effectively to other people.

rationalization   Defense mechanism in which individuals provide plausible but inaccurate justifications for their behavior.

reaction formation   Defense mechanism in which an impulse or behavior is converted into its opposite.

regression   Defense mechanism in which a person reverts to infantile behavior as a means of alleviating stress. Fixation and regression are concepts that are similar, but not identical. Fixation occurs very early in development and may be the underlying cause of the use of regression or other defense mechanisms by the person later in development when she is subjected to stress. A fixation can cause regression, but regression cannot cause a fixation. For example, a person who has been fixated at the oral stage by overindulgence of her feeding needs may revert defensively to thumb sucking in adolescence when she is subjected to hassles in her current life situation. It is not possible that the use of thumb-sucking for the first time in adolescence produced a fixation in the oral stage.

repression   Basic defense mechanism by which unpleasant, highly painful experiences situated in the unconscious are prevented from entering consciousness.

resistance   A patient's unwillingness to report anxiety-provoking memories and conflicts. Freud believed that resistance was a symptom of an underlying conflict.

seduction theory   Originally, the view that patients reported that they had been literally seduced by a parent of the other sex during early childhood. Later, the revised form of the theory was that patients had fantasized that they had experienced sexual abuse via seduction by a parent of the other sex.

sublimation   Form of displacement in which a socially acceptable goal replaces one that is unacceptable.

superego   Agency postulated by Freud to represent the individual's incorporation of the moral standards of society and the ways in which these internalized standards control his or her behavior via reward and punishment.

suppression   A form of defense in which threatening thoughts are removed by actively and consciously deciding not to think about them. The person can exert control over their removal and their reactivation.

thanatos   The instinct aimed at returning to an inorganic state (death).

transference   Phenomenon postulated by Freud to account for the patient's development of positive and negative feelings toward the therapist during treatment—feelings presumed to have originally been directed toward another person (usually one of the parents).

unconscious   In Freudian theory, the depository of hidden wishes, needs, and conflicts of which the person is unaware.

undoing   Defense mechanism in which a person makes amends for a socially unacceptable act by performing a related socially acceptable act that nullifies the misdeed.

unhealthy dependence   A manifestation of dependence that occurs indiscriminately and reflexively across a broad range of situations.

SUGGESTED READINGS

Freud, S. (1957). *A general introduction to psychoanalysis* (rev. ed.; Riviere, J., transalator). New York: Permabooks.

Gay, P. (Ed.). (1989). *The Freud reader*. New York: Norton.

CHAPTER 3

Jung's Analytical Psychology

Courtesy, National Library of Medicine.

Biographical Sketch

Carl Jung was born in Kesswil, Switzerland, in 1875. According to Jung, his father, a pastor in the Swiss Reformed church, was a weakling who was dominated by his wife. Jung described his mother as an insecure woman who frequently contradicted herself and treated members of the family inconsistently, sometimes in a loving and kind way, sometimes in a harsh and aloof manner. When Jung was 3 years old, his mother entered a hospital for several months, with an illness Jung attributed to marital difficulties (Storr, 1991, pp. 1–2). He reported in his autobiography that the separation from his mother had a profound impact on him: He developed an ambivalent attitude of love and hate toward her. This conflict is reflected in his later works, in which women are frequently portrayed as destroyers and dominators as well as protectors, and as unreliable and not to be trusted.

> I was deeply troubled by my mother's being away. From then on, I always felt mistrustful when the word "love" was spoken. The feeling I associated with "woman" was for a long time that of innate unreliability. That is the handicap I started off with. Later, these early impressions were revised: I have trusted men friends and been disappointed by them, and I have mistrusted women and was not disappointed. (Jung, 1963, p. 8)

During his early school days, Jung lacked companionship, probably because he was far more advanced intellectually than any of the other children. He reported that he was not athletically inclined and did not engage in typical rough-and-tumble play with his peers. Instead, he spent much of his time in solitary pursuits, in long walks during which he gloried in the mysteries of nature. Jung reported that he became fully aware of his own existence during one of his walks to school. With this awareness, he reveled in the knowledge that he was an autonomous being who controlled his own life, instead of being continually controlled by others.

> I was taking the long road to school when suddenly for a single moment I had the overwhelming impression of having just emerged from a dense cloud. I knew all at once: now I am myself! Previously I had existed, too, but everything had merely happened to me. Now I happened to myself. Now I knew, I am myself now, now I exist. Previously I had been willed to do this and that: now I willed. This experience seemed to me tremendously important and new: there was authority in me. (Jung, 1963, pp. 32–33)

In this recollection, we can see the beginnings of Jung's later focus on the importance of inner experience.

Another incident during his early school days made a marked impression on Jung and may explain his later reliance on the concept of the unconscious. In an English class, Jung was assigned a composition that interested him very much. He spent a great deal of time and effort on it, and hoped it would receive one of the highest marks in the class. Instead, his teacher accused him, in front of his classmates, of having copied it. Jung clung to his innocence, but the teacher persisted in his accusations and threatened to have Jung dismissed from school. For days afterward, Jung thought about the incident and tried to muster proof of his innocence, but there was no way of proving he had written the composition himself. At this point, his grief and rage threatened to get out of control. Suddenly, he reported, he experienced an inner silence, and something deep down inside him (his unconscious) began to speak:

> What is really going on here? All right, you are excited. Of course the teacher is an idiot who doesn't understand your nature, that is, doesn't understand it any more than you do. Therefore he is as mistrustful as you are. You distrust yourself and others, and that is why you side with those who are naive, simple, and easily seen through. One gets excited when one doesn't understand things (Jung, 1963, pp. 65–66).

The picture that emerges is that Jung was a keenly sensitive and highly intelligent boy who neither understood nor was understood by his parents, teachers, and peers. As a result, he withdrew as much as he could from people and began to rely on his own inner experiences to help him understand the world.

During his teens, Jung decided to become an archaeologist, but his family was too poor to send him to a university that included this specialty in its curriculum. Instead, he entered the nearby University of Basel and majored in medicine. He decided to specialize in psychiatry, because it seemed to provide an opportunity to reconcile two important opposing tendencies within himself: an interest in natural science and a preoccupation with religious and philosophical values. This concern with conflict between opposites became a dominant theme in his later theorizing (Storr, 1991, p. 5). In 1900, having obtained his medical degree, Jung took a position as an assistant in a Zurich mental hospital. There he became interested in the etiology of schizophrenia. He found that the fantasies and delusions of these patients were in many respects similar to the myths and fantasies that guided people in contemporary and ancient cultures. Jung believed that the materials his patients revealed to him went beyond the recollection of their personal childhood and adult experiences; he postulated the existence of a *collective unconscious* (Storr, 1991, pp. 8–9).

In 1906, he published *The Psychology of Dementia Praecox*, a psychoanalytic treatment of schizophrenia. He sent a copy of the book to Freud. A year later, he went to Vienna to meet Freud and began a collaboration that lasted until 1913. The many reasons for the final split, catalogued in Jung's *Psychology of the Unconscious*, include his basic disagreement with Freud over the importance of the sex instinct. Jung could not accept Freud's belief that such an urge was virtually the only determinant of behavior. He also grew tired of Freud's concern with the pathological side of human nature. Jung wanted to develop a psychology that dealt with human aspirations and spiritual needs; he argued that the way to self-realization was through the rediscovery of the spiritual self (Storr, 1991, pp. 12–13). In this respect, he was an important forerunner of the humanist movement.

Between 1913 and 1917, Jung went through a mental crisis in his own life that was precipitated by the break with Freud. Jung felt he could no longer rely on Freud's approach to therapy and that he needed to develop a new attitude or orientation toward treatment. He decided to let his patients tell him everything about their fantasies and dreams and tried not to interpret their self-reports in Freudian terms. Then Jung himself began to have dreams of a frightening nature. For example, he dreamed of dead bodies placed in crematory ovens, bodies that were then discovered to be alive. He also dreamed of monstrous catastrophes befalling Europe and felt vindicated when World War I broke out (Jung, 1963, pp. 170–176).

This flight into grotesque fantasies and dreams soon caused Jung to resign his lectureship at the University of Zurich. He did so consciously and deliberately because he "felt that something great was happening to me." In short, Jung began an attempt to probe the secrets of his unconscious and to unlock the mystery of his own personality. He was obsessed with understanding both sides of his personality: the inner world of subjective experience and the unconscious; and the outer world of contact with other people and material objects. Since he was already successful in his academic and writing career (his outer world), an exploration of his unconscious and inner world beckoned. In other words, Jung felt that his development was too one-sided; he was overdeveloped in terms of the outer world but underdeveloped in terms of his knowledge of the inner world. He began a quest for wholeness, for an integrated personality in which both sides of his nature would be brought into balance. Part of this journey of self-exploration also involved an acceptance of the inevitability of death and the fact that its occurrence was beyond the control of his ego. As a result, Jung eventually adopted a religious attitude toward life, in the sense that he had a greater appreciation of life and its mysteries. This inward turning and self-analysis at the middle stage of life is clearly reflected in his description of the individuation, or self-realization, process. This process is difficult and painful. In Jung's view, the person is "forged between hammer and anvil." Self-realization involves acknowledging everything you wish not to acknowledge about yourself and finding out and trying to actualize your unique potentials.

It was only toward the end of World War I that Jung emerged from his inward journey. In his opinion, the principal factor in the resolution of his crisis was that he began to understand his mandala drawings, which symbolized the self. The rest of his life was relatively uneventful, except for a period during World War II when some critics at the time accused him of being a Nazi sympathizer and an anti-Semite. Some critics (Goggin & Goggin, 2001, pp. 70–76) agree, claiming that Jung cooperated with the Nazis to help validate and make respectable the idea that Freud's psychoanalysis was a Jewish psychology that was irrelevant to the Aryans (Germanic peoples). One aspect of his own theory embraced the idea that racial differences between Aryans and Jews had their roots in the collective unconscious. Further, his belief that the potential for Aryan cultural and intellectual development was superior to the Jewish potential fit nicely with Nazi propaganda and the notion that the Germans were superior to the Jews. Jung vigorously denied that he was a Nazi sympathizer and an anti-Semite. He insisted that the primary reason for his affiliation with German psychoanalysis (as president of the newly formed, German-controlled International Society) was to assist Jewish physicians and psychologists whom the Nazis were forbidding to practice. He claimed that his interventions with German authorities included many attempts to help Jewish psychotherapists retain their memberships in the International Society and to continue their private practices. Indeed, there is some evidence that Jung did helpful work on behalf of Jewish psychotherapists with the Nazis (Bair, 2003, pp. 448–449; Noll, 1997, p. 276). Unfortunately, according to his latest biographer (Bair, 2003, pp. 431–463), this controversy cannot be resolved one way or the other until new government and/or private documentation (e.g., letters, diaries, unpublished manuscripts) surface to provide more definitive answers about his role and behavior during this historical period. Students would be wise to understand that even *if* new documentation does reveal more clearly that Jung did have these deficiencies, this does not mean that his entire theory is without merit.

During the end of his career, he spent much of his time traveling and lecturing throughout the world and died on June 6th, 1961, at the age of 85 (Fordham, 1966, p. 145).

Concepts and Principles

Jung's **analytical psychology** may be the most unusual theory in the entire body of work on personality. Although it provides numerous insights into personality functioning, it is very difficult to understand. It is complex, esoteric, and, in many respects, obscure. Part of the problem is that Jung read widely in a number of different disciplines and drew upon materials from psychology, psychiatry, literature, physics, chemistry, biology, archaeology, philosophy, theology, mythology, history, anthropology, alchemy, and astrology in his attempts to understand human functioning. Since few investigators or readers have the background necessary to evaluate the materials he utilized, it has been easier to ignore or dismiss his theorizing than to grapple with its incredible array of complex ideas. Still another difficulty lies in Jung's own failure to write clearly. He often used conventional terms in idiosyncratic ways without fully explaining the arbitrary shifts he had made in their meanings. With these difficulties clearly in mind, we present a review of the basic ideas of the theory.

The Psyche

Jung referred to the total personality as the **psyche**. He conceived of it as a nonphysical space that has its own special reality. Through the psyche, energy flows continuously in various directions—from consciousness to unconsciousness and back, and from inner to outer reality and back. Jung considered this psychic energy to be real and to be interchangeable with libido. To him, libido is a general **life process energy**, of which sexual urges are only one aspect (Jung, 1969, p. 17). Psychic energy, like physical energy, is an abstraction representing something real that cannot be touched or felt but that we know exists through its effects. Just as physical energy manifests itself in the heating and lighting of the rooms in our homes, so psychic energy manifests itself in our various feelings, thoughts, and behaviors.

Most important, psychic energy is considered an outcome of the conflict between forces within the personality. Without conflict there is no energy and no life. Love and hatred of a person can exist within a psyche, creating tension and new energy that seeks expression in behavior. Other values may also conflict, such as a desire to have premarital intercourse despite the strong disapproval of significant others. The number of potential conflicts is virtually unlimited. Jung also maintained that the various structures of the psyche are continually opposed to one another. For example, ideas in consciousness and ideas residing in the unconscious may conflict with one another. Further, the shadow— that is, the unconscious and often evil side of our nature—may conflict with the ego, while ego processes may operate to keep unpleasant memories from awareness. Thus, he conceived of the psyche as a general entity that operates according to the **principle of opposites**.

Once energy is created, it moves in a variety of directions (Progoff, 1953, p. 63). It can be dissipated in outward behavior, or it can continue to move within the psyche, first in one direction, then in another. It may split and move unsystematically through the psyche, go into the unconscious, attach itself to other energy sources, and manifest itself in bizarre psychological forms, for example, in hallucinations, delusions, or unaccountable moods. In other words, some of the libidinal energy that courses through the psyche operates autonomously, and hence unpredictably, with various results.

Libido also operates according to the principles of equivalence and entropy. These psychological formulations are based on the first and second laws of thermodynamics in physics. The **principle of equivalence** states that "for a given quantity of energy expended or consumed in bringing about a certain condition, an equal quantity of the same or another form of energy will appear elsewhere" (Jung, 1969, p. 18). In other words, an increase in some aspect of psychic functioning is met by a compensatory decrease in functioning in another part of the psyche, and a decrease in some aspect of psychic functioning is met by a compensatory increase in functioning in another area of the psyche. An increase in concern with occupational success might mean an equivalent loss of concern with one's spiritual life, and vice versa. In the area of sexuality, an erotic feeling for a person that cannot be freely expressed would be repressed but would continue to be active at the same level of intensity in the unconscious. In another person, the expression of the same feeling might be sublimated or transformed into creative work. Jung's position is similar in this respect to Freud's notion of displacement.

The **principle of entropy** refers to the process within the psyche whereby elements of unequal strength seek psychological equilibrium. If energy is concentrated in the ego, for example, tension will be generated in the psyche to move energy from the conscious to the unconscious in order to create a balance. Consider the example of an outgoing student who acts as if life consists only of beer parties and endless social activities. Suddenly, he becomes bored and restless and begins to reflect on the meaning and direction of his life. He begins to explore inner experiences that were previously unconscious. As a result of these contemplations, he may reduce his social activities and increase the time he devotes to his studies, thereby becoming a more serious student, though still not a social isolate. The critical point is that any one-sided development of the personality creates conflict, tension, and strain, whereas a more even distribution produces a more fully mature person.

The aim of individual development is self-realization, the integration of all aspects of the psyche. In such a state, there is an increased understanding and acceptance of one's unique nature. This balanced state involves the evolution of a new center (the self) to replace the old one (the ego). The ego is not useless or obsolete in the final system; it exists, but in balance with the other aspects of the psyche.

Ego Jung described the **ego** as a "complex of representations which constitutes the centrum of [the] field of consciousness and appears to possess a very high degree of continuity and identity" (Jung, 1923, p. 540). In Jung's terminology, a **complex** is a collection of thoughts that are united, often by a common feeling. Ego is a complex that is not synonymous with the psyche, but is only one aspect of it (Jung, 1969, p. 324). Nor is ego identical with consciousness. Instead, the ego, which is at the center of consciousness, is a unifying force in the psyche. It is responsible for our feelings of identity and continuity as human beings. Thus, the ego contains the conscious thoughts of our own behavior and feelings, as well as memories of our experiences.

The personal unconscious The **personal unconscious** is the region next to the ego. (See Figure 3.1.) It consists of all the forgotten experiences that have lost their intensity for some reason, possibly because of their unpleasantness. It also includes sense impressions that are too weak to be perceived consciously (Jung, 1969, p. 376). These unconscious materials are accessible to the person's consciousness under certain circumstances. For example, they could be elicited by a skillful therapist with the help of the patient.

FIG-3.1 Structural components of the psyche. (Adapted from *The Psychology of C. G. Jung.* by J. Jacobi, p. 126 (1962). Courtesy of Yale University Press, New Haven, Connecticut.)

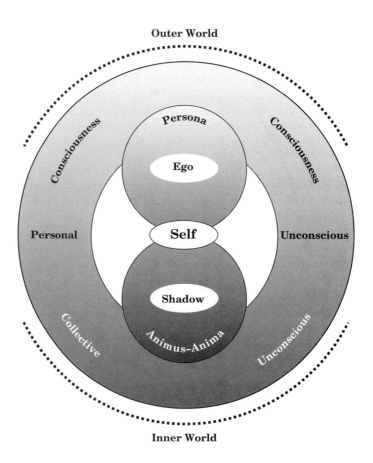

Collective unconscious   Lying still deeper within the psyche is the **collective unconscious**, characterized by Jung as "a deposit of world processes embedded in the structure of the brain and the sympathetic nervous system [which] constitutes, in its totality, a sort of timeless and eternal world-image which counterbalances our conscious momentary picture of the world" (Jung, 1969, p. 370). In other words, it is the storehouse of latent memories of our human and prehuman ancestry. It consists of instincts and archetypes that we inherit as possibilities and that often affect our behavior.

Archetypes

Archetypes are themes that have existed in all cultures throughout history. At various points in his writings, Jung referred to such themes as "imagoes" (images), primordial images, root images, dominants, and behavior patterns. According to Jung, such collective memories are universal in nature because of our common evolution and brain structure.

This concept has often been misunderstood. Writers usually refer to it as one of Jung's original contributions to psychology, although Freud had already utilized a similar concept that he called the racial unconscious. More importantly, Jung did not accept the idea, espoused by the French naturalist Lamarck, that a person's characteristics are inherited directly. Instead, he argued that we inherit pathways that carry with them a tendency or predisposition to respond to certain experiences in specific ways (Progoff, 1953, p. 70). These tendencies emerge—sometimes spontaneously and sometimes when the person is under stress—in the form of archetypal motifs or themes.

For example, Jung proposed that men and women in every culture have inherited a tendency to respond to ambiguous and threatening situations with some form of an all-powerful being that we call God. God is an absolute, necessary function of an irrational nature, which has nothing whatever to do with the question of God's existence. The human intellect can never answer this question, much less give any proof of God. Moreover, such proof is superfluous, for the idea of an all-powerful divine Being is present everywhere, unconsciously if not consciously, because it is an archetype (Jung, 1961, p. 81).

Jung contended that a person who renounces the idea of God will experience personal difficulties. Human beings must come to grips with such an idea if they are ever to achieve greater understanding of themselves. Thus, Jung would probably characterize atheists as people who have developed in a one-sided fashion and who are bound to experience difficulties eventually because they have failed to acknowledge this nonrational aspect of their nature. Searching for a rational answer in an irrational realm is a doomed quest. Jung seems to suggest that we accept the idea of an all-powerful being on faith; yet, he also seems to contradict himself by suggesting that, since the idea of God has a reality within the psyche as an archetype, it is potentially knowable. This difficulty disappears if we keep the distinction between internal and external reality clearly in view. Jung maintained that we can never offer objective proof of God's existence, that is, tangible, material proof shared by others in the external world; nevertheless, the idea of God still has validity, in a subjective or inner-reality sense, because of its roots in universal human experience.

God is a universal symbol; such symbols, though real, can never be completely understood (Jung, 1958c, p. 118). We may gain valuable information about their reality through persistent self-analysis, but we will never know them completely. They take different forms; they have a shadowy existence, a mysterious quality about them that at some point, perhaps, we must come to accept. In brief, their reality is so complex and bewildering that rational inquiry is helpful only to a point. Beyond that, movement toward a balanced psyche demands faith and an acceptance of the unknown and unknowable.

Archetypes are, essentially, thought forms or ideas that give rise to visions projected onto current experiences. For example, one of the primary archetypes is the mother-child relationship, which is characterized by the mother's protection of the child. Dissolution of this bond must ultimately occur if the person is to attain adulthood. Jung suggested that the bond is broken in many primitive cultures when young men undergo rituals of rebirth (Jung, 1961, p. 208). In our culture, if men have not undergone similar rituals (e.g., ones associated with their particular religious groups), they may never resolve their basic dependency on their mothers. In married life, they may project the mother image onto their wives by acting in childish, dependent, and submissive ways; or they may react in an opposite manner by acting in hypermasculine ways and rejecting any offers of help from their spouse.

Not all archetypes are equally developed within the psyche. Those that are well formed exert a strong influence on personality functioning; those that are not well developed exert only minimal influence. Other major archetypes in the Jungian system include the persona, shadow, anima and animus, self, and introversion/extraversion. Although introversion and extraversion are considered by many theorists not to be archetypes, Jung believed that they were. They were innate dispositions, but ones often molded by experience (Jung, 1923, p. 286).

The persona   The **persona**, in Jung's theory, is "a compromise ... between the demands of the environment and the necessities of the individual's inner constitution" (Jacobi, 1962, p. 19). It is the mask we wear in order to function adequately in our relationships with other people. This mask may take as many forms as the roles we play in our daily routines. It also aids in controlling evil forces in the collective unconscious. Presumably, the persona is an archetype because it is a universal manifestation of our attempt to deal appropriately with other people.

But the persona also has negative features. We can learn to hide our real selves behind these masks. Our personas can become split off from potentially enlightening forces in the personal and collective unconscious. We may become so committed to a particular role that we lose sight of our individuality. We all know the professor, writes Jacobi (1962), "whose individuality is exhausted in playing the professor's role; behind this mask one finds nothing but a bundle of peevishness and infantilism" (pp. 19–20). In the Jungian view, so inflexible a man needs to become more accepting of his own and other people's feelings, recognize and accept the limits of his rationality and intellect, and become more receptive to archetypes such as the wise old man—the embodiment of wisdom and understanding—who might teach him something about human fallibility. Of course, the professor might argue that such a view is sheer nonsense, that he is feeling fine and functioning well; Jungians would probably retort that the professor is simply rationalizing. The point is that, in Jung's system, excessive identification with the persona may have harmful effects on personal development.

The shadow   Jung chose the term **shadow** to indicate the dark, sinister, Mr. Hyde side of our natures. In contrast to the persona's affiliation with the ego and consciousness and its role in personal adaptation to the external world, the shadow represents the evil, unadapted, unconscious, and inferior part of our psyches. It has two main aspects—one associated with the personal unconscious, the other with the collective unconscious (Dry, 1961, p. 95). In relation to the personal unconscious, the shadow consists of all those experiences that the person rejects on moral and/or aesthetic grounds. For example, our egos may reject our sadistic impulses, or we may repress socially unacceptable sexual or aggressive impulses. Jung believed that the shadow incorporated both Freud's sexual instinct and Adler's will to power.

In terms of the collective unconscious, the shadow consists of universal personifications of evil within our psyches. The devil, in its various forms, would be a prime example. Jung maintained that we may never understand this unadapted side of our personality fully because we can never bring ourselves to confront absolute evil. Nevertheless, the shadow exists in all of us, and it manifests itself in a variety of ways—unaccountable moods, pains of unexplained origin, urges toward self-destruction, and desires to harm others. It should be clearly understood that we do not, at base, have control over these impulses. Jung believed that these repressed feelings operate independently in the unconscious, where they join forces with other impulses. The result may be a complex with sufficient force to erupt into consciousness and momentarily subdue the ego. For example, a dignified and sophisticated executive may suddenly become highly abusive toward his colleagues during an important meeting. His arguments may become totally irrational, irresponsible, and unrelated to the issue under consideration.

Finally, as with all of Jung's concepts, the shadow has positive as well as negative features. Some examples are the murderer who decides impulsively to spare his victim because the victim reminds him of a loved one; or the selfish woman who spends virtually all her time making money and then generously decides to donate a large percentage of her earnings to a local charity. More generally, the positive side of the shadow may be seen when a person feels unaccountably vital, spontaneous, and creative.

Anima and animus   Like Freud, Jung believed that all men and women have elements of the opposite sex within them. Each man has a feminine side, and each woman has unconscious masculine qualities. This concept is based, at least partially, on the fact that both men and women have varying amounts of male and female hormones. The feminine archetype in man Jung called the **anima**; the masculine archetype in woman he labeled the **animus**. Like all archetypes, the anima and animus can function in either constructive or destructive ways. Jung stated that, when the anima operates positively in man, it serves as "his inspiration": "her [anima's] intuitive capacity, often superior to man's, can give him timely warning [presumably about harmful events], and her feelings, always directed towards the personal, can show him ways which his own less personally accepted feeling would never have discovered" (Jung, 1961, p. 199). The negative aspects of the anima are seen when men act in moody, bitchy, and catty ways. The animus in women has positive manifestations when it produces arguments based on reason and logic. The negative side of the animus can be seen in these behaviors:

> In intellectual women [it] encourages a critical disputatiousness and would-be high-browism, which consists essentially in harping on some irrelevant weak point and nonsensically making it the main point. Or a perfectly lucid discussion gets tangled up in the most maddening way through the introduction of a quite different and if possible perverse point of view. Without knowing it, such women are solely intent upon exasperating the man and are, in consequence, completely at the mercy of the animus. (Jung, 1961, p. 220)

Despite Jung's claims that the anima and animus are universal phenomena, the descriptions sound suspiciously like our cultural stereotypes of the sexes. The masculine archetype includes those characteristics traditionally associated with the role of man—reason, logic, forceful argument, and social insensitivity, among others. The feminine archetype reflects traditional feminine behavior, including such attributes as emotionality, social sensitivity, intuition, vanity, moodiness, and irrationality. Although Jung did catalogue the presumed negative characteristics of the animus, his detailed arguments about the weaknesses of the anima suggest a patriarchal bias that we have already seen in the writings of Freud.

Jung noted that these archetypes may operate in dreams and fantasies, but often they are projected onto real-life objects. For example, the anima in a man could be projected onto his lover, producing a discrepancy between them that could be harmful to both parties. Perhaps he sees his lover as the universal mother, a compassionate and sensitive being who will always protect him and look out for his interests. In actuality, however, she may be an insensitive boor who is concerned only with exploiting him sexually. In a woman, the animus may take the form of the evil conqueror who, when projected onto a kindly and sensitive suitor, will inevitably produce conflicts and problems associated with her continually attempting to control and dominate him. To differentiate these universal images from their real-life counterparts is extremely difficult, but is essential if each of us is to progress toward selfhood.

The self The **self** is an archetypal potentiality in all of us. Jung saw it as an innate blueprint that, theoretically but not practically, is capable of being realized. This destiny within us involves a process that Jung called the "way of individuation" (Jacobi, 1962, p. 100) "a process by which a [person] becomes the definite, unique being that he in fact is. In doing so he does not become 'selfish' in the ordinary sense of the word, but is merely fulfilling the peculiarity of his nature, and this … is vastly different from egotism or individualism" (Jung, 1961, p. 183). Thus, the self is the final goal of our striving. The movement toward self-realization is a very difficult process, and one that can never be fully attained. After all, the self is an archetype, and archetypes can never be fully understood or realized. Jung believed that young people, in particular, would find it difficult to make much progress toward self-realization because of their youth. It takes time and a considerable variety of experience and effort to resolve the many conflicts between opposites within the psyche, so that the few people who come closest to the attainment of a more balanced self will be at least in middle age.

A distinction between the ego and the self needs to be discussed. The self refers to the total psyche or entire personality. It consists of consciousness and unconsciousness, whereas the ego is only part of the total psyche and consists of consciousness. The self can be developed if the ego is willing to listen to its messages. Specifically, the ego can illuminate the entire personality, allowing the self to become conscious and thus to be realized. For example, if you have an artistic talent of which your ego is not conscious, nothing will happen to it. If your ego, however, notices your artistic talent, you can now work to develop and realize it. Thus, the ego can help identify the hidden, unconscious potentials of the person and work to facilitate their realization.

With help from the ego, conflicts are more likely to be resolved and greater balance within personality is likely to be attained. With the attainment of balance, a new center or midpoint, the self, evolves within the personality, replacing the old one, the ego. The ego now becomes a satellite of the self, much like the earth in rotation around the sun. Consciousness does not replace unconsciousness within the psyche. Instead, the principle of opposites remains in force, with consciousness and unconsciousness contents balancing each other.

The self thus becomes a unifying force with a **transcendent function**: It provides stability and balance to the various systems of the personality. As individuals explore the unconscious aspect of their individual psyches, they learn more about this side of their nature and its functions and begin to feel more comfortable with it. A woman, for example, begins to understand how her shadow operates to make her moody or impulsive; a man begins to understand how his anima forces him to idealize his girlfriend and ignore her faults. This understanding involves a resolution, not a solution, of the individuals' conflicts. Through their new understanding, they transcend these conflicts and begin to live more productively with themselves and with others.

Much of Jung's interest in **symbols**, such as shadow and anima, stems from his search for ways in which the self has been described and expressed in various religious and occult systems, psychologies, arts, and philosophies throughout history (Progoff, 1953, p. 153). Even medieval alchemy figured in Jung's search for unique expressions of the self. He saw the alchemists' transmutation of base metals into gold as analogous to the "transformation of personality through the blending and fusion of the noble with the base components, of the differentiated with the inferior functions, of the conscious with the unconscious" (Jung, 1961, p. 232).

To Jung, the most important representations of the self were the **mandalas,** or magic circles, found in the writing and art of all cultures (see Figure 3.2). These mandalas represent the synthesis or union of opposites within the psyche that occurs when individuals attain self-realization. According to Jung, the oldest mandala is a Paleolithic sun wheel drawing based on the principle of four (Jung, 1958a, p. 326). Mandalas are also found in Buddhism, Taoism, and other Eastern religions. In these religions, the golden flower is often placed in the center of the mandala, to signify the heavenly heart, the realm of the greatest joy, and the altar upon which consciousness and life are made (Jung, 1958a, p. 320). In the Middle Ages, European mandalas often included Christ with four evangelists around him (Jacobi, 1962, pp. 128–131). According to Jung, many of his patients spontaneously reported mandalas in their dreams and also painted them during therapy sessions. Thus, drawing upon materials from an incredible variety of sources, Jung believed he had discovered a universal synthesizing phenomenon that transcended personal experience.

FIG-3.2 Mandala of awakening consciousness. (Adapted from *The Psychology of C. G. Jung.* by J. Jacobi, p. 114 (1962). Courtesy of Yale University Press, New Haven, Connecticut.)

The Theory of Psychological Types

Jung proposed that, in their attempt to evolve toward selfhood, people adopt different ways of relating to experience; that is, they adopt different attitudes toward life and utilize different psychological processes or functions to make sense out of their experiences. Jung described those basic attitudes and functions in his theory of psychological types.

Extraversion/Introversion   The two fundamental attitudes in Jung's typology are **extraversion** and **introversion**. Extraversion refers to "an outgoing, candid, and accommodating nature that adapts easily to a given situation, quickly forms attachments, and, setting aside any possible misgivings, often ventures forth with careless confidence into an unknown situation." Introversion, in contrast, signifies "a hesitant, reflective, retiring nature that keeps itself to itself, shrinks from objects, is always slightly on the defensive, and prefers to hide behind mistrustful scrutiny" (Jung, 1961, p. 54). Jung points out that people are not purely introverted or extraverted; rather, each person has both introverted and extraverted aspects. Moreover, both attitudes involve complex variations, including **dominant characteristics** (conscious) and **inferior characteristics** (unconscious). The dominant side compensates for the inferior side and vice versa. If too much libido is invested in the dominant side, for example, energy forces are set up and activated in the unconscious, typically with harmful results for the individual.

Jung's typology is based on his idea of the flow of libido within the psyche. Energy can flow outward toward life, or inward toward subjective experience. For Jung, however, extraversion and introversion are not to be simply equated with outward libidinal flow, or progression, and inward flow, or regression. Instead movement can occur in two different forms; either extraverted, when the progression is predominately influenced by objects and environmental conditions, or introverted, when it has to adapt itself to the conditions of the ego (or, more accurately, of the "subjective factor"). Similarly, regression can proceed along two lines, either as a retreat from the outside world (introversion), or as a flight into extravagant experience of the outside world (extraversion) (Jung, 1969, pp. 40–41).

Thus, extraversion and introversion each have their own special dynamics, and both attitudes have progressive and regressive properties. As with all of Jung's concepts, introversion and extraversion can have both good (healthy) and bad (unhealthy) consequences for our development. Thus, for example, introversion may have progressive effects when a person creates a unique and useful product, such as a first-rate novel. It may have regressive effects when it leads to excessive brooding and indecisiveness at a time when a person needs to make a firm judgment. Witness the student who is doing poorly in a course and who then hesitates to ask a more competent classmate or the instructor for help; failure in the course may well be the outcome. Extraversion may have progressive effects when it leads a person to make sensible decisions, for example, by asking for assistance. It may have regressive effects when it leads someone to act injudiciously, for example, by unthinkingly accepting virtually every pronouncement of authority in order to secure approval. Such a person is so committed to the object (the authority figure) as to accept his or her comments uncritically. Witness the student who changes careers on the advice of neurotic relatives.

The Four Functions   Alongside the basic attitudes of introversion and extraversion, Jung postulated four functions, or ways in which people relate to the world: sensing, thinking, feeling, and intuiting. Sensing is the initial, concrete experiencing of phenomena without the use of reason (thinking) or evaluation (feeling). Thinking proceeds from this point to help us understand events through the use of reason and logic. It gives us the meaning of events that are sensed. Feeling gives us an evaluation of events by judging whether they are good or bad, acceptable or unacceptable. Finally, in the mode of intuiting we rely on hunches whenever we have to deal with strange situations where we have no established facts (Progoff, 1953, p. 100).

Jung called thinking and feeling the **rational functions** because they involve making judgments about experiences. Sensation and intuition he labeled the **irrational functions** because they involve passively recording experiences without evaluating or interpreting them. Although many of us associate thinking with rationality and feeling with irrationality, Jung makes the point that both thinking and feeling involve assessing the worth of an experience. Thinking is primarily concerned with truth or falsity, whereas feeling measures the degree to which we like or dislike something. There is a further semantic difficulty in that Jung does not want the term *irrational* to convey the idea of excessive or mindless emotionality. Instead, he used the term to mean modes of relating to experience that are unrelated to reason. Perhaps, nonrational would have been a more suitable designation.

The rational and irrational functions are articulated, or differentiated, to varying degrees within the psyche. As Jung envisioned it, one function of the rational or irrational pair is dominant, superior or well developed, and conscious and its counterpart inferior or underdeveloped and unconscious; the members of the remaining pair exist in a kind of twilight zone, partly conscious and partly unconscious. The superior function is the most highly differentiated, followed by the auxiliary pair; the inferior function is least differentiated. For example, in a thinking person, reason and logic are well developed and conscious, and the person's feeling function is underdeveloped and unconscious. In this person, sensation and intuition are the auxiliary pair which means that each or both of them can be complementary or supportive of the thinking function. Each member of the auxiliary pair or both of them can become conscious at certain times and serve the superior function of thinking. Thus, in a highly scholarly person who relies on reason and logic to solve problems, his or her intuition can at times aid his or her thinking process by suggesting a vision of the correct solutions. Another example would be the person with strong mechanical skills who utilizes his or her sensation function to solve problems. Focus on the ways in which concrete objects can be manipulated helps the person to use his or her reasoning abilities to solve problems. In this case, one could talk about the thinking person as having a practical intellect. Inventors often tinker with mechanical things in this way for long periods of time before finally seeing the logical connections that help them reach their goals.

Finally, it should be noted that any one of the functions can be dominant; that is, there are thinking, feeling, sensing, and intuiting kinds of individuals. Of course, each of these types lacks full development. The whole or integrated person would be capable of utilizing all the functions in dealing with experiences.

The Typology   Out of the two basic attitudes and four functions, Jung fashioned an eightfold classification **theory of psychological types**. In reality, there are 16 possible personality types, if we consider that either member of the auxiliary pair can exist in a somewhat differentiated and conscious form. In his classic work on the subject, however, Jung focused his attention on eight of the possibilities—namely, introverted and extraverted thinking, feeling, sensing, and intuitive types.

The extraverted thinking type   According to Jung, the **extraverted thinking type** is characterized by a need

> to make all his life-activities dependent on intellectual conclusions, which in the last resort are always oriented by objective data. This kind of man [lives by an] intellectual formula. By this formula are good and evil measured and beauty and ugliness determined. If the formula is wide enough, this type may play a very useful role in social life, either as a reformer or a ventilator of public wrongs or as the propagator of important innovations. But the more rigid the formula, the more does he develop into a grumbler, a crafty reasoner, and a self-righteous critic. (Jung, 1923, pp. 346–347)

Such a person also has repressed feelings in his or her pursuit of ideas and ideals and tends to deny "aesthetic activities, taste, artistic sense, cultivation of friends, etc" (Jung, 1923, p. 348). Jung maintains further that a person who is developing in such a negative fashion may appear concerned about the welfare of other people but in reality is concerned only with the attainment of personal goals, for example, the self-serving activist who exploits the friendship of other people to further his or her aims.

The introverted thinking type   The **introverted thinking type**, "like his extraverted counterpart, is strongly influenced by ideas, though his ideas have their origin not in objective data but in his subjective foundation. He will follow his ideas like the extravert, but in the reverse direction: inwards and not outwards" (Jung, 1923, p. 383). The subjective foundation of the introverted thinker is the collective unconscious. Creative ideas spring from this source and not from outside sources such as traditional moral authority. As a result of this focus on internal forces, the introverted thinker appears cold, aloof, and inconsiderate of others. In addition, he or she tends to be inept socially and inarticulate in attempts to communicate ideas.

The extraverted feeling type   Jung described the **extraverted feeling type** as one who lives according to objective situations and general values (Jung, 1923, p. 356). The feelings and behavior of such individuals are controlled by social norms that is, by the expectations of others. As a consequence, their feelings change from situation to situation and from person to person. Jung believed that women were the best examples of this type. A prime example would be a college woman who breaks her engagement because her parents object to the man. Her feelings toward the young man are based on her parents' judgments. If they like him, fine; if they do not, she feels compelled to reject him. In such people, thinking is largely repressed.

On the plus side of the ledger, Jung believed that extraverted feeling women could make satisfactory marriages. "These women are good companions and excellent mothers, so long as [their] husbands and children are blessed with the conventional psychic constitution" (Jung, 1923, p. 357). By conventional psychic constitution, Jung seems to mean conformity to the traditional rules and regulations prescribed by society for the well-adjusted family.

The introverted feeling type   According to Jung, women are also the prime examples of the **introverted feeling type**. "They are mostly silent, inaccessible, and hard to understand: Often they hide behind a childish or banal mask, and their temperament is inclined to melancholy. They neither shine nor reveal themselves" (Jung, 1923, p. 389). Although they appear unfeeling toward other people, in reality they are capable of an intense emotion, originating in the collective unconscious, that can erupt in religious or poetic form.

The extraverted sensing type   Jung visualized men as the prime examples of the **extraverted sensing type**. This type is primarily reality oriented and typically shuns thinking and contemplation. Experiencing sensations becomes almost an end in itself. Each experience serves as a guide to new experience. Such people are usually outgoing and jolly and have a considerable capacity for enjoyment, some of which revolves around good food. In addition, they are often refined aesthetes, concerned with matters of good taste in painting, sculpture, and literature, as well as food and physical appearance. Such an individual who becomes overenamored of an object, for example, food or physical appearance, develops into "a crude pleasure-seeker or … unscrupulous, effete aesthete" (Jung, 1923, p. 365).

The introverted sensing type   In Jung's view, the **introverted sensing type** is an irrational type guided by the "intensity of the subjective sensation excited by the objective stimulus" (Jung, 1923, p. 395). These people seem to overreact to outside stimuli. They may take innocuous comments from others and interpret them in imaginative or bizarre ways. They may also appear rational and in complete control of their actions because they are unrelated to objects in the environment, including other people. Such types may also treat the objective world (external reality) as mere appearance, or even as a joke. Libido from primordial images affects their perception of events. Positive manifestations of libido are found in creative persons; negative manifestations are seen in psychotics.

The extraverted intuitive type   Exploiting external opportunities is the chief concern of the **extraverted intuitive type**. In Jung's words, they have a "keen nose for anything new and in the making" (Jung, 1923, p. 368). Politicians, merchants, contractors, and speculators are examples of this type; women are more likely to have such an orientation than are men (Jung, 1923, p. 369).

On the positive side, these people are the initiators and promoters of promising enterprises, and often inspire others to great accomplishments. But there are also serious dangers for people with this orientation. Although they may enliven and encourage others, they do little for themselves. And because they are impatient and always seeking new possibilities, they often do not see their actions through to completion.

The introverted intuitive type   An intensification of intuition in the **introverted intuitive type** often results in estrangement from external reality. Such people may be considered enigmatic even by close friends. On the positive side, they may become great visionaries and mystics; on the negative side, they may develop into artistic cranks who espouse idiosyncratic language and visions. Such people cannot be understood easily, and their ability to communicate effectively is further limited because their judgment functions (thinking and feeling) are relatively repressed.

Research Evidence for the Theory of Psychological Types

To assess the validity of Jung's proposed typology, investigators needed to construct a scale that measured the various concepts. The first personality inventory developed by Jungian analysts was called the Gray-Wheelwright. It has since been largely replaced by the more popular **Myers-Briggs Type Indicator** (MBTI), an inventory consisting of 166 items in a forced-choice format. Considerable work has been done to establish the reliability and validity of the MBTI (Briggs & Myers 1943, 1944, 1957, 1976).

Psychological Types and Academic Life   In academic life, research by Sak (2004, pp. 70–79), which synthesizes the results of 14 studies, shows that gifted adolescents have different typology profiles than nongifted adolescents. In general, gifted students are more introverted than extraverted, more intuitive than sensing, and slightly more thinking than feeling. Their preference for introversion means that they are more independent and idea oriented than their more normal, nongifted extraverted classmates. In addition, the gifted adolescents are much more intuitive than their normal counterparts, suggesting that gifted students are more imaginative, speculative, theoretical, and creative than their classmates. The nongifted adolescents rely more on their senses in making decisions and are, therefore, more factual in their approach to problem solving. Finally, the gifted students tended to be slightly higher than the normal students in their preferences for thinking in solving problems. These creative students also had higher SAT (Scholastic Aptitude Test) and IQ scores. In a recent study, gifted students also had higher self-esteem scores than their more normal classmates (Papazova & Pencheva, 2008, pp. 1–10).

Some implications of these results for teaching gifted students are to involve them in projects that are self-paced, less structured, and that enable them to study on their own initiative. By giving them tasks that are relatively unstructured, gifted students would have an opportunity to speculate, think about new possibilities, and to develop creative solutions to tasks that interest and challenge them.

Other research focusing on academics shows that occupational interests among college students are related in many instances to the Jungian typology. For example, introverts have strong interests in mathematics, computer programming, library science, chemistry, and engineering, whereas extraverts gravitate toward sales, public relations, acting, and restaurant and hotel management. Students who are primarily intuitive show strong interests in becoming musicians, psychologists, artists, writers, and photographers, whereas sensing types lean toward food-service work, police and detective work, and craftwork.

Thinking types prefer law, dentistry, and medicine. Feeling types are more interested in becoming preschool teachers, nurses, clergy, and counselors (Myers & McCaulley, 1985, pp. 244–248; Passmore, Holloway, & Rawle-Cope, 2010, pp. 1–16; Sandow, Jones,

& Moody, 2000, p. 32). In fact, recent research shows that most clergy in several countries are feeling rather than thinking types. Feeling types have a great desire to affiliate with others, gifts of empathy, a commitment to harmony, and a deep understanding of others (Francis, Robbins, Kaldor, & Castle, 2009, pp. 200–212).

Psychological Types and Health Care   In research on health-care providers, an investigation by Stilwell and Wallick (2000, pp. 14–20) looked at medical students' specialty choices within medicine, paying particular attention to the study participants' gender. This research shows that female feeling types chose primary care (e.g., family medicine) as their specialty. In regard to males, extraverted and thinking types opted for the surgical specialities more often than females.

> In an examination of gender differences among pharmacists, thinking males very often chose to practice in retail pharmacy, whereas female intuitives chose to practice in nontraditional environments such as nursing homes and research/teaching environments. Retail pharmacy may offer thinking males a more comfortable work environment, little patient interaction, and greater emphasis on dispensing medications. Intuitive females may prefer nontraditional sites because they require greater use of pharmacists' communication skills. (Hardigan, Cohen, & Carvajal, 2001, p. 34)

In other work in the health-care field, research by Mitchell and Shuff (1995, pp. 521–532) showed that hospice workers tended to prefer extraversion over introversion, intuition over sensing, and feeling over thinking. It seems reasonable that hospice workers would have an extraverted orientation, one which focuses their energy and attention on the outer world of human beings. Extraverted types tend to live "in and through others" with strong feelings of altruism. In regard to intuition over sensing, sensing types are conspicuously underrepresented in hospice workers. If sensing was dominant, it would be difficult for such workers to exist in a work environment with aversive stimuli like bedpans, vomiting, body odors, and physical and mental suffering. Intuition permits perceptions that go beyond the senses. Intuitive types can go beyond the immediate suffering to the significance of the lives lived and the impending death of the patients. The orientation toward feeling rather than thinking allows such workers to evidence a high level of understanding in situations of imminent death, whereas the impersonal logic of the thinking type is less likely to find reinforcement in the hospice.

Finally, in some interesting research conducted in Great Britain, Clack, Allen, Cooper, and Head (2004, pp. 177–186) examined how the personality types of physicians and their patients affected their interactions. Most patients' complaints about their doctors relate to poor communication, not to their physicians' technical incompetence. Good communication is a key determinant of patient satisfaction and willingness to cooperate with their physicians' treatment recommendations. Effective communication is likely to result when there is a "meeting of the minds" of the participants in the interactions, that is, when the personality types of the participants are compatible. Consistent with this speculation, these investigators found that much of the poor communications resulted from the fact that some of the personality types dominant in physicians were different than those of their patients. For example, doctors tended to be thinking types, whereas patients were more likely to be feeling types. Doctors tended to be technical, detached, and task-centered in their presentations, whereas patients tended to be more concerned with establishing a warm, friendly, personal relationship with their care providers. As a result, patients tended to see their doctors as uncaring, even though that was actually not the case. The data also showed that physicians tend to be intuitive types, whereas patients were more likely to be sensing types. These results mean that doctors tended to talk about the patients' illnesses in more general, speculative terms by discussing possible origins of the illness, multiple treatment options, and the long-term implications of the illness, whereas patients preferred more practical, direct, step-by-step explanations and instructions (Allen & Brock, 2000, pp. 13–15). The suggestion appears to be that patients sometimes felt that their doctors' explanations were too complicated to understand and follow.

Clack et al. (2004) conclude that doctors might benefit from education during their medical training about the concept of psychological type differences and how these differences could affect communication with their patients. Such training could result in the adoption of more flexible consultation styles that could be applied when necessary in their interactions with patients to enhance their health outcomes.

As we have seen, some complex Jungian concepts can be translated into terms that allow for empirical testing and verification and, in fact, the research provides considerable support for much of the Jungian scheme of psychological types.

Personality Development

Self-Realization

Jung conceived of personal development as a dynamic and evolving process that occurs throughout life. A person is continually developing, learning new skills, and moving toward **self-realization**. Although Jung had little to say about the developmental process in childhood, it is clear that he did not accept Freud's view that the individual's personality was relatively fixed by the end of early childhood. Neither did he accept Freud's view that only past events determine a person's behavior. For Jung, behavior was determined not only by past experiences but also by future goals. Although people can progress toward selfhood by developing differentiated psychological functions, they can also move backward. Such backward movement, however, is not necessarily detrimental; some retreats into the psyche can provide the impetus for creative growth.

The movement toward self-realization is often a difficult and painful process. It involves continual attempts by the individual to understand his or her experiences, to develop healthy attitudes, and to reconcile the opposing forces within the psyche through transcendence. The person is often beset by crises, and Jung believed that many individuals experience their most severe crises during the middle years. Adequate resolution of these crises helps move people toward a more accurate perception and a fuller understanding of themselves. The ultimate outcome is individuation; that is, the person becomes all he or she is capable of becoming as a human being.

Neurosis and Psychosis

Progress toward self-realization is not automatic. If the person grows up in an unhealthy and threatening environment, where the parents use harsh and unreasonable punishment, growth is likely to be stifled. Repressed evil forces within the psyche may also erupt without warning to produce personality dysfunction. Under these conditions, the outcome may be neurosis or psychosis.

In Jung's view, neurosis and psychosis differ primarily in the severity of their consequences. Both result from one-sided development in which repressed forces create problems in functioning. In all eight psychological types discussed earlier, intense repression of one of the four functions would probably result in a form of neurosis. For example, when thinking is repressed in the introverted feeling type, Jung argued, the thinking function may eventually project itself onto objects, thus creating problems for the person. Because the thinking function is archaic and undifferentiated, the person's judgment about the object or objects is bound to be gross and inaccurate. Such a person is unable to reason accurately about the intentions of others. As a consequence,

> other people are [assumed to be] thinking all sorts of mean things, scheming evil, contriving plots, secret intrigues, etc. In order to forestall them, she herself is obliged to start counterintrigues, to suspect others and [to] weave counterplots. Beset by rumours, she must make frantic efforts to be top dog. Endless clandestine rivalries spring up, and in these embittered struggles she will shrink from no baseness or meanness, and will even prostitute her virtues in order to play the trump card. Such a state of affairs must end in exhaustion (Jung, 1923, p. 391).

The resulting form of neurosis is neurasthenia, a disorder characterized by listlessness and fatigue.

Jung saw psychosis as an extension of neurosis that occurs when repressed and unconscious forces overpower consciousness. In his view, consciousness is a secondary phenomenon derived from unconsciousness; it is a fragile entity that can be swallowed up by unleashed forces in the unconscious. In such instances, the person collapses; the ego, attacked by elements of the collective unconscious, loses control. Jung provides an illustration of the onset of psychosis in the case of a quiet young man who imagined that a woman was in love with him. When he discovered that his love was unrequited, he

> was so desperate that he went straight to the river to drown himself. It was late at night, and the stars gleamed up at him from the dark water. It seemed to him that the stars were swimming two by two down the river, and a wonderful feeling came over him. He forgot his suicidal intentions and gazed fascinated at the strange, sweet drama, and gradually he became aware that every star was a face and that all these pairs were lovers who were carried along locked in a dreaming embrace. An entirely new understanding came to him: All had changed his fate, his disappointment, even his love receded and fell away. The memory of the girl grew distant, blurred; but instead, he felt with complete certainty that untold riches were promised him. He knew that an immense treasure lay hidden for him in the neighboring observatory. The result was that he was arrested by the police at four o'clock in the morning, attempting to break into the observatory. What had happened? His poor head had glimpsed a Dantesque picture whose loveliness he could never have grasped had he read it in a poem. For his poor turnip-head it was too much. He did not drown in the river but in an eternal image, and its beauty perished with him (Jung, 1959, p. 126).

In Jung's scheme, the collective unconscious also has its attractive elements and can sometimes lure a person into its essentially fathomless inner reality.

Assessment Techniques

Like Freud, Jung relied primarily on the case study as a personality assessment technique. He also showed his Freudian roots by utilizing dream analysis and by making use of patients' self-reports about significant early experiences. Yet, in a number of important respects, Jung's use of these techniques differed from his mentor's.

Dream Analysis

In Jung's view, dreams are involuntary and spontaneous eruptions of repressed materials that are rooted in both the personal and collective unconscious. However, their manifest content is not always a disguised attempt at wish fulfillment of sexual and/or aggressive needs. Instead, dreams are more often attempts at resolving current problems and conflicts and provide dreamers with a means of furthering their own development in a healthy direction. For example, Jung reported the case of a young man who dreamt that his father was behaving in a drunken and disorderly manner. In reality, the son stated, his father was a highly virtuous man, and he and his father had an ideal relationship. Jung interpreted the dream to mean that the son's admiration for his father prevented him from having the confidence in himself to develop his own personality. He was, in fact, too close to his father and therefore was unable to develop his own identity. It was almost as if the dream were telling the son that his father was not so virtuous after all and that there was no need for the son to feel inferior (Fordham, 1966, p. 103).

According to Jung, dreams are also compensatory in nature. They are efforts at adjustment, attempts at rectifying deficiencies in personality. People who are very shy, for example, may have dreams in which they are the life of the party. Failures in business may dream of great financial ventures and successes. Mediocre actors may dream about receiving a standing ovation for their performance in a Broadway play. Although initial research did not support the idea of compensation in dreams (Domino, 1976, pp. 658–662), more recent work is more strongly confirmatory (Cann & Donderi, 1986, pp. 1021–1030; Zadra, O'Brien, & Donderi, 1997–1998, pp. 293–311). According to Jung, individuals high in neuroticism are one-sided in their development and dissociated from their collective unconscious. Individuals low in neuroticism, in contrast, are more balanced in their development and are not dissociated from their collective unconscious. Low neurotics are able to adapt to life by keeping in touch with their collective unconscious, whereas high neurotics are not able to make this compensatory adaptation—at least not as readily as low neurotics. Thus, according to Jungian theory, high neurotics should report fewer archetypal dreams that is, dreams that are highly unusual, bizarre, and emotionally intense, than do low neurotics; this is exactly what these latter studies showed.

Cann and Donderi (1986, pp. 1021–1030) also found that intuitives recalled more archetypal dreams than did sensing types, whereas introverts recalled more dreams based on their everyday experiences than did extraverts. These findings tie in nicely with Jungian theory. Jung believed that intuitive individuals are closer to material in the collective unconscious than are sensing individuals. Intuitives, with their imaginative and creative tendencies, tolerance for complexity and change, and interest in dreams, find it easier to deal with the metaphorical characteristics of archetypal dreams. Sensing types, in contrast, have a more practical and concrete orientation that may lead them to find archetypal dreams very disturbing and difficult to process. He maintained that intuitive individuals' greater sensitivity to archetypal dreams assists their progress toward self-realization. Jung believed further that the introversion-extraversion dimension was focused more on conscious, everyday events. Extraverts focus primarily on the outer environment, whereas introverts emphasize the internal representation of these events and their storage in memory. Thus, introverts should be superior to extraverts in recalling everyday dreams. A study by Jacka (1991, pp. 27–31) using Australian students replicated the Cann and Donderi results.

Finally, two studies (Brown & Donderi, 1986, pp. 612–623; Zadra et al., 1997–1998, pp. 293–311) tested the implications of Jung's idea that dreams are attempts at resolving current conflicts and furthering personal growth. If a particular dream helps in the resolution of a problem, the dream should not recur. Conversely, if the dream does not help resolve the problem, the dream should occur again. Thus, recurrent dreams, according to Jung, indicate that the conflict has not been resolved. Recurrent dreams should, therefore, be associated with stress, anxiety, and a lack of psychological well-being. The investigators in the two aforementioned studies tested this Jungian hypothesis and found strong support for it. Study participants who reported recurrent dreams were more neurotic, anxious, stressed, and depressed than were participants who reported no recurrent dreams.

Method of Amplification

Dreams are replete with symbols that typically have multiple meanings and are very difficult to interpret. To reveal their meanings as far as was possible; Jung utilized the **method of amplification**. Unlike free association, which involves starting with a particular symbol and moving further and further away from it, the method of amplification involves adhering to a given symbol and giving numerous associations to it. In the process, the symbol's multiple meanings become clearer and provide patients with insights into their problems. These associations are given by both the patient and the analyst. Often the associations provided by the analyst determine the direction of the patient's own associations (Jacobi, 1962, p. 82). Patients usually provide the subjective or personal meanings of the symbols, whereas the therapist provides the universal meanings of the symbols as revealed in mythology, religion, alchemy, art, history, and so forth (Jacobi, 1962, p. 87).

Jung believed that analysis of a single dream could prove misleading, but analysis of a series of dreams could provide a means of achieving more accurate interpretations of the problems confronting the patient. The in-depth analysis of a series of dreams also allowed the patient and therapist to move from the personal meanings embedded in the symbols to their deeper meanings as archetypal images.

Word Association Test

In conjunction with dream analysis, Jung utilized an experimental technique called the **word association test**, in which he presented patients with stimulus words and asked them to respond with whatever words occurred to them. Jung recorded the time that elapsed between the initial presentation of the stimulus and the eventual response and used the time latency as an indicator of possible areas of resistance and conflict within the person. The longer the time interval, he assumed, the greater was the likelihood that important complexes or areas of conflict within the psyche were being tapped. In addition, areas of conflict were assumed to be present if the patient: (1) repeated the stimulus word several times as though it had been not heard; (2) misheard the word as some other word; (3) gave a response of more than one word; (4) gave a meaningless reaction (a made-up word); or (5) failed to respond at all. Jung also required his patients to recall all their responses to the word stimuli following a rest interval. Failure to reproduce the words and reporting distorted reproductions were also considered to reflect underlying conflict (Jacobi, 1962, p. 38).

Painting Therapy

Another technique used by Jung in conjunction with dream analysis was painting therapy. He relied heavily on paintings by his patients as a means of further encouraging them to express their unconscious feelings or thoughts. Pointing out that these paintings had little artistic merit, he helped patients to see that they must be expressions of their innermost selves. The painting exercises were conducted to help patients clarify the symbols seen in their dreams and to force patients to cope actively with their problems. In Jung's view, painting had real therapeutic effects. It moved patients off dead center and started them on the road to self-realization.

Theory's Implications for Therapy

Jung believed that neurosis was a severe disorder in which the person's growth toward self-realization was halted. Yet, in his view, neurosis had a positive aspect to it as well. It was a warning sign that the person's personality was desperately in need of broadening and that this could happen only if the therapist and patient utilized the correct therapeutic procedures.

Jung believed that the forms of neurosis in young and middle-aged people were radically different:

> The life of a young person is characterized by a general expansion and striving towards concrete ends; and his neurosis seems mainly to rest on his hesitation or shrinking back from this necessity. But the life of an older person is characterized by a contraction of forces, by the affirmation of what has been achieved, and by the curtailment of further growth. His neurosis comes mainly from his clinging to a youthful attitude which is now out of season. Just as the young neurotic is afraid of life, so the older one shrinks back from death. (Jung, 1954, p. 39)

Thus, in Jung's view, therapy has to be tailored to the age of the person. For the most part, Jung confined his efforts to treating the problems of the middle-aged. His analytical therapy is really a "psychology of the afternoon."

The middle-aged people who visited Jung had special problems. Unlike many neurotics who suffer because they lack a strong ego, the men and women treated by Jung were usually highly successful people, often of outstanding ability. Yet they were restless and discontented. At this stage in their development, they typically began to ask themselves whether there might not be more to life than material success. They began to search for the meaning of their existence (Storr, 1991, pp. 79–80). This search involved an exploration of the contents of their unconscious as a means of correcting an overdeveloped consciousness. In other words, they made an effort to rediscover those aspects of themselves that had been neglected. They began to realize that they must stop their relentless pursuit of success in order to rediscover the spiritual meaning of their existence. As Jung put it, people must realize that life is more than "mere getting and spending" (Jung, 1964, p. 89). They must cultivate their inner life, come to grips with its secrets, and assimilate them into consciousness. They must also come to accept the inevitability of death.

Jung viewed therapy as the process by which patients were able, through exploration of their inner lives, to broaden their personalities and to develop a spiritual or religious attitude toward their existence. It was not only patients, however, who gained insights into themselves as a result of analysis. Therapists were equally involved in the process and could derive positive benefits. Jung maintained that both analysts and patients had many limitations and that both were struggling toward self-realization. Consequently, he believed, therapists must give up all claims to superior knowledge, as well as desires to unduly influence their patients, if substantial progress toward self-realization is to be achieved.

In his view, the therapeutic process has four key stages: confession, elucidation, education, and transformation (Jung, 1954, p. 55). Confession is a necessary first step in the healing process, because it forces the individual to acknowledge his or her limitations to another. The person also becomes aware of his or her universal ties to humankind, in the sense that all men and women possess certain weaknesses. The cathartic process also leads to the patient's reliance on the therapist; that is, transference occurs. In the process of understanding this transference, the patient brings to the surface certain contents of the unconscious that the therapist clarifies; this is elucidation. During this stage, the person learns the origins of his or her problems. In the third stage, education, the person incorporates the insights into his or her personality in order to adapt to the social environment. Finally, transformation occurs when the dynamic interplay between therapist and patient leads to exciting changes that move beyond adaptation to the environment and toward self-realization.

Self-realization is an ideal state and not something to be actually attained. It is the process that is important, not the achievement of the goal. By undergoing this painful struggle to reconcile the conflicting sides of their nature, patients become more integrated, whole personalities. They do not become perfect human beings; they become, instead, what they are destined to become—individuals with unique sets of strengths and limitations. Self-realization involves the acceptance of these limitations. It is a religious experience in the sense that reconciliation of the opposites within individuals may occur when they subordinate themselves to a higher authority, who, they believe, will make all things well in the end (Storr, 1991, p. 90). However, this religious attitude does not necessarily entail allegiance to a particular orthodox creed. It may involve subordination to a set of rules or moral principles that help resolve their conflicts.

Finally, self-realization is not a state of total passivity. Rather, the person accepts the reality of each situation and adapts accordingly. He or she may work to control and change those situations in life that can be realistically shaped but knows that not every situation is controllable or should be controlled. There are some situations in which an accepting attitude is healthiest.

Evaluative Comments

At this point, let us utilize our six criteria to evaluate the scientific worth of Jung's theory.

Comprehensiveness   Jung's position comes close to matching Freud's in the sheer number and diversity of phenomena it examines. In many instances, however, it is not as detailed in its treatment of the phenomena in its domain as is Freud's. Nonetheless, Jung's theory is very comprehensive; at various points, it addresses such diverse phenomena as marriage, creativity, religion, education, and the occult.

Precision and testability   Jung's theory fails generally to meet the criterion of precision and testability. Many of its relational statements are vague and riddled with inconsistencies. Many of its concepts are also highly ambiguous. For example, archetypes are metaphysical concepts that have multiple meanings and few clear referents in external reality. As Jung himself put it:

> They can only be roughly circumscribed at best. Every attempt to focus them more sharply is immediately punished by the intangible core of meaning losing its luminosity. No archetype can be reduced to a simple formula. It is a vessel which we can never empty and never fill. It has a potential existence only, and when it takes shape in matter, it is no longer what it was. It persists throughout the ages and requires interpreting ever anew. The archetypes are the imperishable elements of the unconscious, but they change their shape continuously. (Jung, 1958b, p. 145)

Compounding this inherent vagueness, Jung argued that some of our behavior is controlled by autonomous forces in the collective unconscious forces that operate unpredictably. For instance, a man and a woman may be having an enjoyable discussion about the virtues of the sexes when they suddenly find themselves embroiled in a bitter controversy about the inherent superiority of one sex over the other. Jung might account for this unexpected shift in behavior by maintaining that the negative aspects of the anima in the man and the animus in the woman had projected themselves onto their behavior. The man might begin to argue in a womanish way and become completely irrational and emotional about the innate superiority of men, whereas the woman might become mannish and begin to argue dogmatically and in a domineering fashion about the natural superiority of women. The bitter argument might continue unabated for an hour or so and then suddenly subside. Jung would maintain that the man was anima-possessed and the woman animus-possessed. The point at which such possessions occur is completely unpredictable.

To scientists, such an assumption is totally unacceptable, because it violates their belief that all behavior is caused by previous events. Although Jung believed that determinism is a useful concept in the explanation of behavior, he also maintained that it has its limitations. In his view, people live by aims as well as by causes. Furthermore, Jung maintained that some behavior is produced according to a **principle of synchronicity** that sometimes two events occur together in time, but one event does not cause the other. For example, a man may dream of his uncle's death and then learn the next day by telephone that his uncle has just died. Clearly, dreaming about the death did not cause it. But neither was the nearly simultaneous occurrence of the events a chance happening. Instead, Jung believed that the co-occurrence was a meaningful coincidence. In his view, it is possible that an archetypal death image in some form had knowledge of the uncle's death and that it had penetrated the man's dream to make him aware of its impending occurrence. Jung believed that archetypes could readily move through and embrace the past, present, and future. Jung left unexplained the underlying mechanism and process that tell how archetypes are capable of transcending space and time boundaries, but he was convinced of the reality of this mysterious process.

Despite the ambiguity in Jung's work and his advocacy of causal explanations for some phenomena, scientists are becoming increasingly interested in testing some of Jung's complex and original ideas.

Parsimony   Jung's theory also fails to meet the parsimony criterion. There seem to be more concepts than are necessary to explain phenomena. A wide range of archetypes may be invoked to explain a specific behavior. If a person behaves aggressively, for example, it could be the result of the activation of his or her shadow, animus or anima, mother archetype, father archetype, and so forth. It could be the result of the operation of one of these archetypes, several of them, all of them, or none of them; there is no systematic explanation of why or how one takes precedence over another. Alternatively, it could be due simply to the operation of unknown and uncontrollable forces within the psyche.

Empirical validity   Although Jung's theory is difficult to test, his position has recently generated some interest, and a number of studies have been conducted. Most of these investigations have focused on his theory of psychological types, and the evidence for its validity has been consistently supportive. There is also increasing support for his theory of dreams.

Heuristic value   Jung's theory has considerable heuristic value. Although it has not been accorded high status by most scientists, it has been accepted by professionals from a variety of disciplines, including history, literature, art, anthropology, religion, music, and certain segments of the clinical psychology community. The ties with religion have been especially close because, for Jung, spiritual concerns were the highest human value. He felt that people in Western societies are too overdeveloped in the rational realm and grossly underdeveloped in the spiritual area. Accordingly, Jung believed that many of us need to turn inward and to meditate in a search for the meaning of our existence. Not too surprisingly, Jung has enjoyed considerable popular success among many idealistic middle-class students surfeited with material possessions (e.g., mall shopping until they drop, texting until their thumbs bleed) and shaken by a crisis of faith in some religious, political, and business authority figures who abuse their power. Clinical psychologists and counselors also make use of Jung's ideas about religion to help their religious clients move toward self-realization.

Applied value   Jung's theorizing about the nature of psychopathology and its treatment has had a highly positive impact on the work of many therapists. The theory has also proved useful to members of many other disciplines, including theologians, artists, photographers, and historians. The MBTI, an outgrowth of Jung's theorizing about psychological types, has also been used to good advantage by vocational counselors and by personnel managers in many businesses, as they try to place job applicants within their companies in positions that maximize performance effectiveness and personal satisfaction.

Interestingly, Jung's ideas about the need in many troubled people for a spiritual reawakening had a profound impact on Bill W., the cofounder of the Alcoholics Anonymous movement. Bill acknowledged his debt to Jung in a letter written a few years after he had cofounded the organization. According to the letter, he became convinced that he could change his own alcohol dependency after he had spoken to a former patient of Jung's. This man had given up his excessive drinking after undergoing a spiritual metamorphosis while in therapy with Jung, who had pointed out that the patient's craving for alcohol was the equivalent of his spiritual thirst for wholeness, expressed through a union with God. Jung had worked with the patient to transform his life by finding a new meaning for his existence (W., 1988, pp. 276–281). Thus, it seems clear that Jung's theory has had considerable practical impact on people from many walks of life.

CRITICAL THINKING QUESTIONS

1. What is the psyche? How does psychic energy originate, and how does it affect the person's behavior?
2. How do you define the shadow? Do you have any limitations that need changing? What are they, and how do you propose to overcome them?
3. What is the nature of the relationship between the anima and animus and our cultural gender-role

   stereotypes? In what ways are our gender-roles limiting?
4. Have you ever had a transcendent experience that helped you resolve a personal problem? Describe it as best you can, and explain how it helped you overcome the difficulty.
5. List the characteristics of the eight personality types postulated by Jung. What type(s) are you? Give reasons for your answer(s).

GLOSSARY

analytical psychology   Jung's unique brand of psychology which emphasizes the complex interplay between oppositional forces within the psyche and the ways in which these internal conflicts affect personality development.

anima   The feminine archetype in men, including both positive and negative characteristics of the transpersonal female. In a positive sense, the anima involves a sense of warmth and intuitive understanding; in a negative sense, it involves moodiness and irritability.

animus   The masculine archetype in women, including both positive and negative characteristics of the

transpersonal male. In a positive sense, the animus involves an ability to reason and use logic to solve problems; in a negative sense, it involves an uncritical and dogmatic adherence to certain ideas and an irrationality in solving problems.

archetypes   Universal themes or symbols that can be activated by forces operating in the psyche, thereby generating visions that are projected onto current experiences.

collective unconscious   The depository of instincts and archetypes that go beyond personal experience. These transpersonal experiences are the residue of human evolutionary development and can be activated under the proper conditions.

complex   Collection of thoughts united by a common feeling.

dominant characteristics   In Jung's theory, developed, differentiated, and conscious parts of the psyche.

ego   Force in the personality responsible for feelings of identity and continuity.

extraversion   One of two basic attitudes postulated by Jung, characterized by an outgoing and relatively confident approach to life.

extraverted feeling type   Individual characterized positively by an acceptance of the standards of society and negatively by a change in emotions from situation to situation, along with an indiscriminate yielding to the expectations of others.

extraverted intuitive type   Individual characterized positively by a quick grasp of the creative possibilities in various ventures and negatively by impatience and flightiness.

extraverted sensing type   Individual characterized positively by an appreciation for the arts and negatively by crude pleasure seeking.

extraverted thinking type   Individual characterized in a positive way by an ability to organize masses of facts into a coherent theory and in a negative way by a selfish and exploitative attitude toward others.

inferior characteristics   In Jung's theory, underdeveloped, undifferentiated, and unconscious parts of the psyche.

introversion   One of two basic attitudes postulated by Jung, characterized by a retiring and reflective approach to life.

introverted feeling type   Individual characterized positively by intense feelings of sympathy for others who have experienced misfortune and negatively by shyness and inaccessibility.

introverted intuitive type   Individual characterized positively by the ability to envision the future and negatively by an inability to communicate effectively with others.

introverted sensing type   Individual characterized positively by the intensity of subjective sensations and negatively by oversensitivity and obtuseness.

introverted thinking type   Individual characterized positively by imagination and an ability to think originally and boldly and negatively by social ineptness.

irrational functions   Modes of apprehending the world without evaluating it. For Jung, sensation and intuition were the irrational (nonrational) functions.

life process energy   All of the urges that are derived from conflict between forces in the psyche.

mandala   Symbolic representation of the self or of the world.

method of amplification   Therapeutic technique in which the patient and analyst continue to reassess and reinterpret the same symbols in an attempt to broaden their understanding of them.

Myers-Briggs Type Indicator (MBTI)   A paper-and-pencil test designed to measure the various psychological types postulated by Jung.

persona   Archetype consisting of the role human beings play in order to meet the demands of others. The persona also allows them to express their innermost feelings in ways acceptable to other people.

personal unconscious   In Jung's theory, the region that contains all of the personal experiences that have been blocked from awareness.

principle of entropy   In Jungian theory, the idea that energy is automatically redistributed in the psyche in order to achieve equilibrium or balance.

principle of equivalence   The idea that energy expended in one part of the psyche will be compensated for by an equal amount of energy in the same or different form in another part of the psyche. Thus, energy is neither created nor lost but simply shifted from one region of the psyche to another.

principle of opposites   The idea that the energy that propels personality and behavior is derived from the interplay between opposite forces within the psyche.

principle of synchronicity   Belief that there is an acausal order in the world that has meaning and that goes beyond causality.

psyche   A construct postulated by Jung to represent all of the interacting systems within human personality that are needed to account for the mental life and behavior of the person.

rational functions Modes of making judgments or evaluations of events in the world. For Jung, thinking and feeling were rational functions.

self In Jung's theory, an archetype that leads people to search for ways of maximizing the development of their potential.

self-realization Process that involves the healthy development of people's capabilities, enabling them to fulfill their own unique natures.

shadow The inferior, evil, and repulsive side of human nature.

symbol In Jung's psychology, a representation of a psychic fact. Each symbol was thought to have multiple meanings and to be incapable of being understood completely.

theory of psychological types Theory proposed by Jung in which people can be classified into eight types, on the basis of a combination of attitudes and functions.

transcendent function The process by which a conflict is resolved by bringing opposing forces into balance with each other through understanding.

word association test Therapeutic technique in which patients are presented with stimulus words and asked to give responses to them. Greater time latencies in responding are assumed to reflect the existence of underlying problems.

SUGGESTED READINGS

Bair, D. (2003). *Jung: A biography*. Boston: Little, Brown and Company.

Jung, C. G. (1953). *Collected works* (H. Read, M. Fordham, & G. Adler, Eds.). Princeton, NJ: Princeton University Press.

CHAPTER 4

Adler's Individual Psychology

Courtesy, The Adler School of Professional Psychology, Chicago, IL.

Biographical Sketch

Alfred Adler was born in Rudolfsheim, a suburb of Vienna in 1870, of Jewish parents (Rietveld, 2004, p. 209). His father was a grain merchant, whose work allowed the family to live an affluent, middle-class life. Adler was the third of seven children, five boys and two girls, of whom the oldest was a boy and the second a girl. As a child, he was very delicate and sickly. He had rickets and suffered from spasms of the glottis that put him in danger of suffocation whenever he screamed or cried. Other experiences made him acutely aware of the possibility of death: He was 3 years old when his younger brother died in a bed next to his; a year later, Adler himself contracted pneumonia and almost died. Upon gaining consciousness, he saw a physician standing near his bed and his parents holding down his arms and legs. He felt severe prickings on his left thigh, looked down in horror to see blood streaming out of his body as several leeches sucked blood from the wounds. He was frantic as he tried unsuccessfully to remove them. Despite the use of this relatively primitive medical procedure, Adler miraculously recovered from his pneumonia (Hoffman, 1994, p. 8). His physical weakness led his parents, especially his mother, to pamper him. Because his doctor prescribed fresh air, his parents encouraged him to play outdoors with other children. He had many pleasant memories of play experiences with his peers and showed a lifelong fondness for the company of others. He also worked extraordinarily hard, apparently in an effort to compensate for his initial weakness.

During his early schooling, he was a mediocre student; he did so poorly in mathematics that he had to repeat a grade. Adler's reaction was to work diligently on mathematical problems at home until he had mastered them. Sometime later, his mathematics teacher wrote a problem on the blackboard that no one (not even the teacher) could solve. Young Adler announced that he could solve it. Disregarding his teacher's sarcastic remark, "Of course, if no one else can, you will surely be able to," Alfred strode to the board amidst the laughter of his classmates and solved the problem. From that moment on, he was the best pupil in the class (Orgler, 1963, pp. 1–3).

Adler attended the Vienna Medical School, where he came under the influence of a famous internist who stressed that the physician must always treat the whole patient, not just the ailment. The internist was also fond of saying, "If you want to be a good doctor, you have to be a kind person." They were two lessons Adler never forgot. During his university days, he also acquired a socialist political orientation. Adler was attracted to the humanistic side of socialism—its stress on equality, cooperation, and democracy. He became an unflagging champion of the common person and fought against oppression of the masses all through his life.

Once he had received his medical degree, Adler established a private practice in a lower-middle-class Vienna neighborhood near a famous amusement park. His patients included artists and acrobats from the park shows. Some of these extraordinary physical specimens told Adler that they had achieved their powers as a reaction to weakness and illness in childhood. It was these experiences that later led Adler to focus on the concept of overcompensation.

In 1899, Adler corresponded with Freud, asking him to provide a clinical diagnosis of the difficulties being experienced by a female patient under Adler's care. Three years later, Adler was asked by Freud to join a weekly discussion group at his home, which centered on psychology and neuropathology themes and issues. In 1908, Freud's Wednesday Psychological Society changed its name to the Vienna Psychoanalytic Society. In 1910, on the basis of Freud's recommendation, the group elected Adler to succeed Freud as its president (Fiebert, 1997, pp. 241–247). However, Adler never established a warm personal relationship with Freud, nor with most of the other members of the group. He was not a person to worship at the feet of the master, and his forthright questioning and criticism of some of Freud's concepts led to his resignation from the society in 1911.

Soon after, Adler formed a group called the Society for Free Psycho-Analytic Research, a title chosen to show his obvious displeasure with what he considered Freud's dictatorial ways. In 1913, Adler changed the name of the association to the Society for Individual Psychology, to reflect his concern with understanding the whole personality—the individual as an indivisible entity. Unfortunately, the term also suggests a study of the individual as contrasted with the study of group behavior. But Adler's theory is, in many respects, social psychological in nature; for Adler, the individual can be understood only in terms of participation with other members of society.

During World War I, Adler worked as an army doctor in a Vienna hospital. Witnessing the savage effects of the war on people—effects generated by lack of trust and cooperation—he developed his concept of social interest. He returned to his writing and research with renewed purpose and focused much of his energies on disseminating information to the ordinary person about the need for cooperation, love, and respect among people. He was also instrumental in helping to establish in the Vienna school system some 30 child-guidance clinics that provided counseling for the entire family. By the early 1920s, Adler had gained international recognition and acceptance. In the late 1920s and early 1930s, he authored a number of popular books, including *The Practice and Theory of Individual Psychology* (1927), *Understanding Human Nature* (1927), *The Science of Living* (1929/1969), *The Education of Children* (1930), *The Pattern of Life* (1930), *What Life Should Mean to You* (1931), and *Social Interest: A Challenge to Mankind* (1933). During the same period, he also began accepting invitations to lecture in various European cities and, later, in the United States. He succumbed to a heart attack while on a European lecture tour in Aberdeen, Scotland, in May 1937 (Furtmuller, 1973, pp. 330–394).

Concepts and Principles

Individual psychology, according to Adler, is a science that attempts to understand the experiences and behavior of each person as an organized entity. He believed that all actions are guided by a person's fundamental attitudes toward life. True to his interest in improving the lot of humankind, he sought to correct faulty or mistaken attitudes by means of the knowledge derived from his theory. Thus, in addition to collecting basic information about human behavior, Adler was very much interested in applying such knowledge in a practical way.

The Struggle for Perfection

Out of Adler's efforts to understand "… that mysterious creative power of life—that power which expresses itself in the desire to develop, to strive and to achieve—and even to compensate for defeats in one direction by striving for success in another" came a simple, yet interesting, set of theoretical propositions (Adler, 1969, p. 1). According to Adler, an understanding of human personality was possible only in light of an understanding of the person's goals. In contrast to Freud, who was a strict determinist, Adler adopted the **teleological position** that current behavior is directed by future goals. People have a purpose in life—to attain perfection—and are motivated to strive toward attainment of this ideal. This movement toward perfection or completion, Adler proposed, is driven by feelings of inferiority—a continual struggle from "minus to plus." Thus, according to Adler, we are all engaged in a "great upward drive."

The related concept of **fictional finalism** is based on the writings of the philosopher Hans Vaihinger, who maintained in *The Philosophy of "As-If"* that people create the ideas that guide their behavior. Adopting this view, Adler believed that people strive for perceived or imagined goals that give direction to their behavior. These goals are not tangible; they are imagined ideals. In his later writings, Adler abandoned the term *fictional finalism* and instead used the term *guiding self-ideal* (Watts & Holden, 1994, pp. 161–163).

In his earliest writings, the final goal of this struggle was domination—aggressive, all-powerful control over others. Humans were seen as selfish and concerned only with self-aggrandizement. Later, Adler revised his thinking and defined the ultimate goal as **superiority.** Individuals can formulate this goal so that it guides them along either a constructive or a destructive path. The destructive path leads them to seek to dominate and exploit others. Adler talks about it as a striving for a goal of personal superiority. It is a striving that sees others as enemies or obstacles in the person's path, which must be removed, overcome, or destroyed; according to Adler, only neurotics strive for such a mistaken goal. In contrast, the constructive path leads people to relate to others with cooperation and good will; healthy people, in Adler's view, act in accordance with social interest. The striving for superiority by healthy people involves movement toward perfection or completion. In other words, Adler believed that all individuals were continually striving to improve themselves as they progressed toward perfection. He thought that such a goal could be attained only by cooperative efforts. When each of us seeks to contribute to the welfare of others, we all benefit. Through cooperation, each individual is helped to survive and to grow as a human being. (See Figure 4.1.)

Finally, Adler believed that the development of healthy or unhealthy goals is shaped to a considerable extent by experiences in the first five years of life.

Creative Evolution and Social Interest

The essence of Adler's position is that people's mental health and personal growth depends directly on their efforts to contribute to the betterment of the community. As he saw it, the species could not exist for long without sustained cooperation among its members. The life of each infant depends, for example, on the willingness of adults to extend themselves and to minister to the needs of these helpless creatures. The survival of the species also depends on the willingness of individuals to relate to one another on an intimate basis and to engage in procreative acts. In a complex society, the needs of the members can be gratified only through a division of labor and the coordination of effort among workers. Thus, without cooperative effort and good will, humanity would perish.

Adler discussed the necessity for such cooperation in the context of the evolution of the species. He proposed that there is a creative evolution in all living things that aims

FIG-4.1 Developmental paths to psychological health or neurosis.

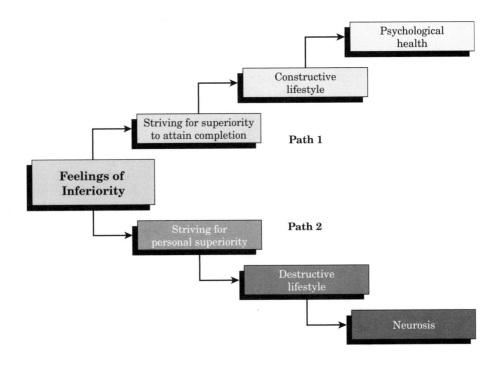

at the goal of perfection. Active, continuous movement and adaptation to the external world has always existed—a compulsion to create a better adaptation to the environment, to master it. All of us are in the midst of this creative evolution, according to Adler. We benefit tremendously from the massive efforts and contributions of our ancestors as we continue to strive in our own unique ways to improve the living conditions of all. The ultimate goal, in Adler's view, is the creation of an ideal community.

We are all born with the potential for social feeling or interest, Adler believed, but it can only come to fruition with proper guidance and training. He defined **social interest** as "a striving for a form of community which must be thought of as everlasting, as it could be thought of if mankind had reached the goal of perfection" (Adler, 1973c, pp. 34–35). By striving for others' goals, we help ourselves as well. This striving also implies respect and consideration for all human beings. "We remain open to the other and welcome him as a host would a guest, according to his own meaning, whose life is respected as equally valid as one's own" (Brennan, 1969, p. 10). Adler believed that, while we are born with the potential for social interest, it can only come to fruition by treating others with consideration and respect.

Researchers have created several useful measures of social interest and have begun to test Adler's ideas about the personality characteristics and behavior of individuals with a strong sense of social interest. Consistent with Adler's theorizing, investigators have found that people from various walks of life who achieve higher scores in social interest are more altruistic, trustworthy, socially adjusted, nurturing, and helpful than are people lower in social interest. Individuals high in social interest also report less depression, anxiety, emotional instability, loneliness, destructive narcissism, and hostility toward others (Maltby, Macaskill, Day, & Garner, 1999, pp. 197–200; Watkins, 1994, pp. 72–89). Several other studies have shown that murderers, pedophiles, and other incarcerated criminals who have committed a variety of transgressions against society are lower in social interest than noncriminals (Curlette & Kern, 2010, pp. 30–42; Daugherty, Murphy, & Paugh, 2001, pp. 465–471; McGreevy, Neubauer, & Carich, 2001, pp. 67–77; Miranda & Fiorello, 2002, pp. 62–75).

In studies with college students, those who were higher in social interest reported greater satisfaction with their lives and had emotionally closer relationships with friends and relatives than did students lower in social interest (Gilman, 2001; p. 760; Watkins & St. John, 1994, p. 167). In love relationships, research has indicated that American college students with a strong sense of social interest show more respect and consideration for their partners and do not try to manipulate them for their own selfish purposes (Leak & Gardner, 1990, p. 57). In a more recent study, unmarried Turkish university couples with greater social interest were more likely to make higher levels of sacrifice for their partners and to provide greater levels of comfort and aid to them than student couples lower in social interest (Kalkan, 2009, pp. 40–48). In mature married couples, there is a higher level of social interest where each person puts the desires of the partner ahead of his/her own and also tries to maximize the well-being of the partner (Moschetta & Moschetta, 1993, pp. 399–405).

Feelings of Inferiority and the Striving for Superiority

While he was still involved in the practice of medicine, Adler noted that individuals with defective organs typically tried to compensate for their weaknesses by intensive training. A girl with a speech impediment might try to overcome her problem by intensive and persistent practice until one day she is able to excel; perhaps she becomes a national news broadcaster. Or a boy with puny legs might strive to become an outstanding distance runner. According to Adler, it is not the defect itself that produces the striving, but the person's **attitude** toward it. The individual is free to interpret the deficiency in many ways, or even to ignore it; if it is ignored, it will not result in overwhelming striving behavior.

Adler later expanded the concept of **organ inferiority** to include exaggerated strivings caused by feelings of unmanliness. **Masculine protest** is the term he used to describe these compensation behaviors. In Adler's thinking, superiority tends to be equated with traditionally masculine behaviors such as assertiveness, independence, and dominance; inferiority tends to be equated with traditionally feminine behaviors such as passivity, submissiveness, and dependence. His thinking was presumably based on the roles enacted by males and females in Viennese society at the time. Adler himself was not a male chauvinist. In line with his egalitarian orientation, Adler abhorred the thought of treating anyone, male or female, as inferior and argued vigorously that such bias had to be eliminated (see Adler, 1927, pp. 120–148). He used the concept of masculine protest to show that women were placed in an inferior position by society and that, as a consequence, they often tried to overcome feelings of inadequacy by aping masculine behavior; he cited cases of women who spouted obscenities, swaggered, and acted tough. Lesbianism he considered to be an extreme manifestation of the masculine protest. On the other hand, compensatory behavior could also be seen in women who acted in an exaggeratedly feminine manner. These superfeminine women may have adopted this lifestyle as a means of luring men, whom they can then dominate and humiliate.

Adler applied his concept to men as well as women. Men who felt insecure could also acquire exaggerated ways of behaving to prove that they were real men. The Don Juan type engages in **overcompensation** by trying to prove his manhood by countless seductions. In either sex, such manifestations were neurotic in character.

Adler eventually broadened the concept of organ inferiority even further; he argued that all of us experience feelings of psychological and social inferiority, beginning with our earliest participation in family life. Our parents and most others are not only bigger physically than we are, but also more sophisticated and adept at solving problems. These inevitable and normal feelings of inferiority motivate individuals to strive for achievement. If individuals deceive themselves into thinking that they are not inferior in any way, then there is no basis for striving to accomplish anything. Why strive to improve if you're already perfect? In contrast, if individuals feel intensely inferior, they will become discouraged and not strive to achieve success. Why strive to achieve anything if you're convinced you're worthless? The normal perception, according to Adler, is for individuals to acknowledge some feelings of inferiority and to use these feelings as motivators to help them improve and accomplish their goals. Research by Strano and Petrocelli (2005, pp. 80–89) provides some support for Adler's theorizing. College students who reported either no feelings of inferiority or intense feelings of inferiority had lower GPAs (grade point averages) than students who reported they had some feelings of inferiority. In other words, students with normal feelings of inferiority had the highest GPAs.

Acknowledging that we all feel inferior at different points in our lives and in different areas can also serve as a basis for asking for help when we need it and giving help when others ask for it. Such cooperation can help people to overcome problems in living. But if deceive ourselves into believing that we are perfect in every way, then we are unable to acknowledge that we need help from others even when such help might be useful. Alternately, if we are convinced that we are worthless, it is pointless to reach out to others for help even though such action might prove beneficial to us. In such instances, we are likely to operate on the "useless side" of life, as Adler called it.

Style of Life and the Creative Self

Two concepts—the style of life and the creative self—are closely interrelated in Adlerian theorizing. The **style of life,** originally called the life plan or guiding image, refers to the unique ways in which people pursue their goals. An actor seeks to attain perfection through study and stage and film appearances. A scholar tries to become superior by intensive reading, studying, and thinking and by discussing ideas with her colleagues. Our unique styles of life are formed to a considerable extent during the first five years of life; later experiences are then assimilated and interpreted in accordance with these early patterns of behaving. These styles emerge as reactions to our inferiorities, real or imagined. Once established, they are difficult to modify.

The concept of the **creative self** is an outgrowth of Adler's concern with the mechanistic implications of his style-of-life construct. Adler was dissatisfied with the idea that individuals acquire unique behavior patterns strictly through a stimulus-response kind of learning, because it implies that people are passive recipients who do not interpret or act upon their experiences. The concept of the creative self implies that people create their own personalities, by actively constructing them out of their experiences and heredities. As Adler saw it, individuals are the artists of their own personalities (Adler, 1978, pp. 355–356). In the final analysis, people are responsible for their destinies. Healthy people are generally aware of the alternatives available to them in solving problems and choose to act in a rational and responsible manner. Neurotics, in contrast, may have goals that are largely unconscious and are often unaware of the alternatives available to them in a given situation.

Personality Development

Three Basic Developmental Problems of Life

There are three basic problems of life that everyone must meet in order to function in a healthy psychological way, namely, the problems of society or communal life, work, and love. In regard to communal life, Adler thought that to be fully human we must learn to affirm our fundamental connections to others and must try to build as many constructive, that is, cooperative and harmonious, relationships as we can as we journey through life. He maintained that the only security of which we can be sure is the security which originates in the good will of our fellow human beings. Unfortunately, many people do not adopt this constructive path and instead try to feel secure by isolating themselves from others. The technique of isolation, however, leads to snobbery, bigotry, hate, suspicion, jealousy, envy, and self-aggrandizement and results only in temporary feelings of security.

According to Adler, work also is necessary if the society is to function properly and prosper, and all of us need to learn how to do things, to take responsibility for our actions, and to contribute to society through our work. Criminals are those who fail to recognize the value of honest labor, as are greedy business executives who exploit the labor of others. Gamblers who do not trust their own abilities and must therefore worship "luck" also fail to fulfill the requirement of healthy work (Adler, 1930b, pp. 32–38).

Finally, the problem of love demands that we treat our loved ones with respect and dignity. Mature love involves cooperation and trust between the partners and treating one another as equals. Adler believed further that love is fulfilled in marriage. In such a union, there is intimate devotion to a partner, expressed in physical attraction, in friendship, and in the decision to have children. The outcome of this union is a cooperation, not only for the welfare of two people, but also, with the birth of offspring, for the welfare of humanity. Interestingly, Adler thought that in such a relationship, there would be no end to the partner's sexual attraction to the other because they would always be interested in one another and concerned with their partner's welfare. In his view, people who evade their marital responsibilities by engaging in sexual affairs are cowards. They lack the courage and confidence to approach the demands and inevitable conflicts of marriage directly. Commitment to the marriage partner is necessary, and patience with the partner and acceptance of him or her is the foundation upon which a successful marriage is built (Blanton, 2000, pp. 411–418).

Parental Influence in Early Childhood

Adler believed that both parents play crucial roles in the development of their children. They help shape the development of their distinctive styles of life and the goals they set (Ansbacher & Ansbacher, 1956, pp. 372–381). The mother is particularly important, because she is usually the first person to have extended, intimate contact with the child. She introduces the child to social life. If she loves the child, she is more likely to be interested in teaching him the skills necessary to secure his welfare. If she is dissatisfied with her role, she may be preoccupied with trying to prove her own personal superiority, by showing that her child is more intelligent and good-looking than all others and that she crawled, stood, and walked sooner than anyone else. Unfortunately, most children react adversely to such pressure, and the typical result is hostility and resentment.

For the father, the primary task is to prove that he is a worthwhile human being, by contributing to the welfare of his wife, his children, and his society. Furthermore, he must treat his wife as an equal and cooperate with her in meeting the problems of life. Of course, she must also value him as an equal. They must both act as constructive role models and teachers for their children. If she is afraid of losing the affection of her children and forces him to be the sole administrator of punishment for their misdeeds, she is not fulfilling her obligations as a wife and mother and is acting, instead, on the useless side of life. She is guilty of pampering her children because of her own weaknesses and of exploiting her husband. The same argument would apply to a husband who pampers his children.

Considerable research provides empirical support for Adler's views on the dynamics of family life and social interest (Amerikaner, Monks, Wolfe, & Thomas, 1994, pp. 614–623; Johnson, Smith, & Nelson, 2003, pp. 281–292; Leak & Williams, 1991, pp. 159–165; Rodd,

1994, pp. 58–68). It is only within the realm of a caring and encouraging family environment where parents are helpful and supportive of one another, are open and honest with each other, and do not handle difficulties through conflict and aggression that children begin to develop their social interest.

Birth Order

Adler believed that each child is treated uniquely by its parents, and that this special treatment is typically, but not inevitably, related to the child's order of birth within the family. Although Adler proposed that a child's order of birth in the family provided clues about the direction of his or her development, he did not believe that it was the order of birth per se that caused the behaviors associated with it. Instead, it was the unique set of experiences within the family that had important implications for development (Ansbacher & Ansbacher, 1956, p. 377). Although the child's order of birth served as a rough indicator of likely experiences, this crude assessment device could be misleading. For example, if the eldest child in a family was disadvantaged because of brain damage suffered during birth, the second child might be treated by the parents as if he or she were actually the eldest. Or, if two children were born much later than their three older siblings, the parents might treat them as if they were first- and second-borns, even though they were actually the fourth- and fifth-borns in a family of five children. Thus, the spacing of the ages of siblings may have important implications for how children are treated and how they develop.

Another factor with important consequences for development, according to Adler, is the sex of the siblings within the family. In his view, a boy brought up in a family of girls will be more likely to experience special difficulties. He may feel that he is very different and may grow up feeling isolated. As a result, he may fight to assert his difference and assume an air of masculine superiority; or he may give in and develop a more feminine orientation. Similarly, a girl raised in a family of boys is apt to develop either very masculine or very feminine qualities, depending on the kind of treatment she receives and how she interprets it (Ansbacher & Ansbacher, 1956, p. 382).

Despite this sophisticated set of arguments, simple chronological birth order, given its ease of assessment, is most often used as the measurement of choice by researchers, including the research reported here.

The eldest child tends to be the center of attention in the family before the birth of other siblings. With their births, he or she is placed in the position of the dethroned monarch, forced to share parental affection and attention with others. As a consequence, the oldest child may feel resentment and hostility toward the younger ones. Such negative feelings are likely to occur if the parents have not properly prepared the child for the arrival of a sibling or siblings. However, if they have made adequate preparations, the oldest child may adopt a protective and supportive attitude, and will often play the part of father or mother with the younger ones and feel responsible for their welfare.

According to Adler, the oldest child understands best the importance of power and authority because he or she has had to undergo their loss within the family. Consequently, the oldest child will be highly supportive of, and dependent on, authorities in later life and will be a person who tends to support the status quo. Such a person is likely to be politically conservative and conforming. The second child is likely to view the older brother or sister as a competitor to be overcome. If the older child is protective and supportive of the younger sibling's attempts to excel, healthy development is more probable; if the older child resents the second child and acts maliciously, movement toward neurosis for the younger one is more likely. Adler also suggested that the second child may set unrealistically high goals, thereby virtually ensuring ultimate failure.

The youngest child is typically regarded as the baby of the family and tends to commandeer most of the family's attention. Adler believed that parents are likely to pamper and spoil the youngest members of their families (Mairet, 1964, p. 107). The result is a person who is excessively dependent on others for support and protection, one who wants to excel in everything he or she does but often fails because of a lack of personal initiative and effort. The youngest child tends to seek easy solutions to his or her problems. Because alcoholics frequently use the bottle as a quick and easy solution to their immediate problems, we might expect the youngest members of families to be overrepresented among alcoholics. In a review of studies examining the birth-order position of alcoholics, Barry and Blane (1977, pp. 62–79) found a higher incidence of alcoholics among last-borns in 20 out of the 27 studies. This finding does not mean, of course, that every last-born will become an alcoholic. Rather, it suggests that last-born individuals in general show a higher incidence of alcoholism than do first- or middle-born children and only children.

Finally, the only child in the family, according to Adler, has no sibling rivals and is likely to be the center of attention in the family, provided his or her birth was a welcome event. If the child was unwanted, neglect or active rejection by the parents may occur. In most instances, the only child will be pampered by the parents, especially the mother. Later, the child may experience considerable interpersonal difficulty if he or she is not universally liked and admired.

Birth Order Research Evidence

It would be encouraging to report that tests of Adler's **birth-order effects** have produced strong support for his major arguments, but early reviews of the research literature have yielded data that are sometimes inconsistent with Adler's theorizing (Blake, 1989; Watkins, 1992, pp. 357–368). Also, the research results themselves can be questioned because of their correlational nature, thereby suggesting the possibility of alternative explanations of the data. Thus, caution should be exercised in interpreting these studies and their results.

Research Evidence: Intellectual Development   Adler suggested that, because of the loss of power and authority suffered with the birth of a second child, first-borns spend their lives trying to regain their lost position through outstanding achievement. First-borns, in short, want to rule over others (Ansbacher & Ansbacher, 1956, p. 379). They try to establish themselves in a position of power over others and are found to be more dominant and aggressive than later-borns (Watkins, 1992, p. 362). Thus, we would expect first-borns to excel in intellectual activities and to attain higher levels of achievement and eminence.

There is support for these predictions. Belmont and Marolla (1973), for example, found that first-borns outstripped later-borns in intellectual achievement in families of various sizes in a sample of nearly 400,000 study participants—the entire male population of The Netherlands, who attained 19 years of age during the period from 1963 to 1966. In a more recent follow-up study, Boomsma et al. (2008, pp. 630–634) found the same result for a large sample of adolescent Dutch males *and* females. Breland (1974) had also demonstrated earlier that this relationship between first-borns and high intellectual performance held true for nearly 800,000 candidates for National Merit Scholarships.

Other investigations have found that first-borns are overrepresented among college students, graduate students, university faculty, and eminent people in science and government. Wagner and Schubert (1977, pp. 78–85), for example, found that oldest sons were overrepresented among United States presidents, but not among unsuccessful presidential candidates. Zweigenhaft (1975, pp. 205–210) also found first-borns overrepresented in the U.S. Congress, and Melillo (1983, pp. 57–62) showed that first-borns were overrepresented among women with doctorates (Ph.D., Ed.D., D.S.W., or M.D.). First-born males and females also were overrepresented among world leaders, whereas middle- and last-borns were underrepresented (Hudson, 1990, pp. 583–601; Steinberg, 2001, pp. 89–110). Other data indicated that United States governors who were in office in 1988 tended disproportionately to be first-borns, as were prime ministers in Australia in this century (Newman & Taylor, 1994, pp. 435–442).

Confluence Model   Building on Adler's ideas, Zajonc has created a **confluence theory** concerned with understanding how intellectual development occurs and why first-borns are more likely to exhibit greater intellectual development than later-borns (Zajonc, 1976, pp. 227–236; Zajonc, 1983, pp. 457–480; Zajonc, 2001, pp. 490–496; Zajonc & Bargh, 1980, pp. 349–361; Zajonc & Markus, 1975, pp. 74–88; Zajonc & Mullally, 1997, pp. 685–699). His theory posits that children's intellectual growth can be enhanced or hindered by immediate family circumstances. Before the birth of other siblings, first-borns interact primarily with adults and are exposed to a fairly sophisticated language and a rich vocabulary. Just being around them gives first-borns auditory access to a large pool of words and concepts and to the process and product of abstract thought used by adults in their communications. Many of these concepts later will be incorporated into the intellectual tests that they take. Later-borns, in contrast, have less access to this linguistic pool, interact primarily with other siblings, and therefore hear a less diverse and more limited language, and witness less often the process and product of abstract thought shown in adult communications. There is now some research evidence consistent with Zajonc's theorizing. In one study, researchers found that first-born Scandinavian toddlers scored higher on vocabulary comprehension and vocabulary production than later borns (Berglund, Eriksson, & Westerlund, 2005, pp. 485–491). In the other study, Australian toddlers engaged in more symbolic play ("pretend play") than later-borns. In pretend play children make up imaginary situations and people and communicate with them. Pretend play is associated with faster cognitive and intellectual development (Kowalski, Wyver, Masselos, & DeLacey, 2004, pp. 389–400).

At the same time, first-borns who have acquired language skills faster than later-borns are thrust into the role of teacher; they are expected to tutor their less-skilled, later-born brothers and sisters in a variety of activities. As a result, they have to learn more themselves, and their intellectual development is accelerated. The demands placed on younger children are less rigorous, since younger children do not usually have the wherewithal to educate their older siblings. Consequently, the younger children's intellectual development tends not to be as great, and the youngest child in particular suffers from a lack of opportunity to tutor others.

Zajonc's theory also conjectures that twins have a poorer family environment for intellectual growth because both have an immature sibling at birth. Thus, neither one has linguistic and social skills that are superior to the other that would allow one of them to act as a tutor to the other. There are data that support Zajonc's speculation, showing that the IQ of twins is about five points less than singly born children and that of triplets is seven points less (Record, McKeown, & Edwards, 1970, pp. 61–69).

Only children are also at a distinct disadvantage, according to Zajonc. They never have the opportunity to teach other siblings and therefore are not stimulated to learn more; their intellectual prowess is therefore generally lower than those children who are in families of two.

Zajonc also maintains that single-parent families are also at a disadvantage because there is only one adult to contribute to the intellectual growth of their child(ren). This outcome can be overcome, however, if a larger number of adults, for example, uncles, aunts, grandparents, child-care persons, are available to provide a richer, more intellectually stimulating environment (Zajonc & Mullally, 1997, p. 690).

Criticisms of Zajonc's Model: First-borns　Zajonc claims that first-borns show greater intellectual development than later-borns, but some critics strongly disagree (e.g., Retherford & Sewell, 1991, pp. 141–158; Rodgers, Cleveland, van den Oord, & Rowe, 2000, pp. 599–612; Rodgers, Cleveland, van den Oord, & Rowe, 2001, pp. 523–524; Steelman, 1985, pp. 353–386; Wichman, Rodgers, & MacCallum, 2006, pp. 117–127). Rodgers et al. (2001, p. 523), for example, maintain that there are hundreds of confounding variables (e.g., parental IQ, nutrition, quality of schooling, race, region of the country, family size, or socioeconomic status) other than birth order that could explain Zajonc's results. For illustrative purposes, let us look only at socioeconomic status as a possible confounding variable, while understanding that there are many other variables that could be operating in any given situation. First, there is considerable research evidence showing that the socioeconomic status of parents is positively associated with a child's intellectual development: The higher the socioeconomic status of the family, the greater the intellectual development of the child. At the same time, higher socioeconomic status families tend to have fewer children than lower socioeconomic status families. Thus, the data showing greater intellectual development in first-borns than in later-borns may simply reflect the fact that the first-borns tested came from smaller, higher socioeconomic status families, whereas the later-borns came from larger, lower socioeconomic status families. In other words, socioeconomic status rather than birth order may have been the determining factor in intellectual development. Zajonc (1986, pp. 365–371) counters this argument by noting that there are numerous studies showing that first-borns have greater intellectual growth than later-borns no matter what the socioeconomic status of their families.

Despite the fact that the relationship between birth order and intellectual development is still found even after controlling for socioeconomic status, there are, of course, many other variables, including parental educational level, quality of school, and parental resource allocation that can account for the relation between birth order and intellectual development and achievement. In fact, recent research by de Haan (2010, pp. 576–588) shows that parents tend to invest more money in the schooling of their first-born child, less in their second-born child, and even less in their third-born child, and so forth. It should not be surprising, therefore, that first-borns are most successful in their level of educational achievement, followed by less educational achievement by second-borns, and even less by third-borns.

Finally, Wichman et al. (2006) suggested that, since the birth order effect claimed by Zajonc is in doubt because of the hundreds of uncontrolled confounding variables still untested, perhaps parents and family members might, as a practical matter, be wise to focus on supporting and encouraging the intellectual development of *all* the children within their families instead of concentrating primarily on the development of later-borns as suggested by the birth order effect hypothesis promulgated by Zajonc. Nevertheless, Wichman et al. also realize that there is also a great need for scientific research that controls for possible confounding variables before the birth order effect claim offered by Zajonc can finally be put to rest.

Criticisms of Zajonc's Model: Only Child　Other critics like Falbo take issue with other aspects of Zajonc's confluence model. She strongly disagrees with Zajonc's conjecture that only children are lower in intellectual development than children in families with siblings because they have no opportunity to tutor brothers and sisters. She maintains that, while only children do not have siblings to tutor, they nevertheless have the undivided attention of their parents, who may spend large amounts of time instructing them. In support of this argument, Falbo and Cooper (1980, pp. 299–300) have found that mothers with a single child of preschool age do spend more time with them during a typical week than do mothers with more children. Also, Lewis and Feiring (1982, pp. 115–145) found that, during mealtimes, one-child families engaged in more parent-child conversations, with a greater exchange of information, than did families with two or three children. More recent research also indicates that only borns themselves report feeling very close to their parents and being treated as "small adults" and discussing many different topics with their parents and other adults (Roberts & Blanton, 2001, pp. 125–140). Finally, other research has shown very clearly that only children are more intellectually advanced than later-borns from large families, and are as advanced as first-borns from small families (Falbo, 1977, pp. 47–61; Falbo & Polit, 1986, pp. 176–189).

Research reviewed by Falbo and Polit (1986, pp. 176–189) with samples consisting primarily of American children and a study by Falbo and Poston (1993, pp. 18–35) with Chinese children indicated further that only children are as sociable and as psychologically well adjusted as children from other types of families. These findings call into question Adler's assertion that only children tend to be socially maladjusted because they do not have an opportunity to learn adequate social skills through frequent interactions with brothers and sisters (Adler, 1937, pp. 211–227).

Finally, other critics like Steelman (1986, pp. 373–377) point out that there are still other limitations of Zajonc's model. She notes, for example, that children interact with other adults who are nonfamily members (teachers, clergy, friends of the family); they also read books, watch television, play games on the Internet, and have "virtual friends" on the Internet. All of these interactions may have implications for the intellectual development of first-borns, later-borns, and only children. Thus, research that examines all these types of interaction, not just the interactions between parents and first-borns and between siblings and first-borns, is needed. Such research, she thinks, may well lead to the development of a more adequate theory about birth order and intellectual development and increase our understanding of the relationship even more.

Development of a Destructive Lifestyle

Out of this incredible welter of family experience and the person's interpretation of it emerges a guiding goal and a distinctive style of life. As hinted earlier, the three major sets of environmental factors that may give rise to severely destructive or neurotic life goals are: (1) organ inferiority; (2) neglect or rejection; and (3) pampering.

A destructive life goal can be established in families where either parent (but especially the mother) is emotionally detached from the children or authoritarian (harsh and rejecting) in their disciplinary practices (Johnson et al., 2003, p. 282). It also can occur where parents pamper their children. Adler believed that pampering of children by parents was especially damaging. Pampering occurs whenever parents overindulge their children by persistently gratifying every wish they have without requiring them to make any effort to reciprocate. Research shows that such children are likely to grow into young adulthood with feelings of entitlement and narcissism. They have little sense of social interest and at base feel incompetent and inferior (Capron, 2004, pp 76–93).

Neurotic individuals who grow up in destructive family environments are those who feel very acutely their own inferiority when threatened and who compensate for these feelings by establishing unrealistically high goals that they believe will enable them to demonstrate personal superiority over others. Neurotics are grossly inaccurate in their self-evaluations. They are continually tense and fearful, especially of decisions, tests, and defeats. In the final analysis, they are terrified of being unmasked and recognized by others as inferior. Such people do not act in accordance with social interest; they are not courageous. Instead, they continually adopt safeguarding or defensive strategies to protect themselves.

Development of a Constructive Lifestyle

People who develop a healthy or constructive style of life, according to Adler, have experienced a family life in which there is little fighting, bickering, arguing, and blaming (Johnson et al., 2003, p. 286). In such a family, parents treat their children with respect and consideration. Under such conditions, Adler believed, individuals are likely to feel secure and accepted and to learn the importance of equality and cooperation between people and to develop goals in accord with social interest. Adler left the nature of these goals unspecified: They could range from principles such as "honesty is the best policy" and "do unto others as you would have them do unto you" to specific occupational goals such as professor, doctor, computer technician, auto mechanic, book sales representative, or television repair person. Adler believed that individuals could fill any of these roles in accordance with social interest—that is, by expending maximum effort and utilizing their abilities to the maximum for the welfare of society. Thus, auto mechanics are as worthwhile as physicians, if each is maximizing the use of his or her abilities and making the best efforts within the context of behaving in accordance with social interest.

Adler also maintained that the healthy person could change his or her fictional finalisms or guiding self-ideals if circumstances demanded it. Would such a person act dishonestly and steal a loaf of bread to feed a starving child? Adler would probably answer, "Yes, but only if the individual had exhausted every other avenue in trying to solve the problem." The healthy person lives by principles, but is realistic enough to modify them under exceptional circumstances.

Adler's Four Major Lifestyle Types

Adler employed a simple classification scheme to help people understand the nature of destructive and constructive lifestyles more fully. He provided this typology reluctantly, because he did not consider human beings as types but believed each person had a unique style of life (Ansbacher & Ansbacher, 1956, p. 166). Nevertheless, he believed that such a typology had some educational value, and he presented it with that disclaimer.

Ruling, getting, and avoiding types all have destructive lifestyles, whereas socially useful types have constructive lifestyles.

The ruling type   Individuals of the **ruling type,** according to Adler, lack social interest and courage. When threatened, they try to reduce feelings of anxiety by acting in antisocial ways. Their striving for personal superiority is so intense that they typically exploit and harm others; they need to control others in order to feel powerful and significant. As children, ruling types want to exclude stronger children and play only with weaker children, so that they can dominate. When they fail to get their way, they throw themselves on the floor, hold their breath, or scream, kick, or yell in the hope that their parents will succumb.

When they become adults, ruling types want to be conquerors; they want to lord it over their spouses. They expect their spouses to cater to their every need and to pay constant attention to them. As parents, they order their children to obey "because I said so!" As leaders of teenage gangs, they are arrogant and vain; they like to threaten their followers: "If you don't steal that CD, I'll break your arm!" Ruling types may also try to control people through the use of money, in the belief that everyone has a price (Mosak, 1977, pp. 218–219). Adler cited juvenile delinquents, suicidal individuals, and drug addicts as prime examples of the ruling type.

The getting type   Individuals of the **getting type** are relatively passive and make little effort to solve their own problems. Instead, they rely on others to take care of them.

Children of many affluent, permissive parents are given whatever they demand; growing up in such an environment, they have little need to do things for themselves, and little awareness of their own abilities to be productive or to give to others. Lacking confidence in themselves, they attempt to surround themselves with people who are willing to accede to their requests. Getting types frequently use charm to persuade others to help them (Mosak, 1977, p. 78).

The avoiding type   People of the **avoiding type** lack the confidence necessary for solving crises. Instead of struggling with their problems, they typically try to sidestep them, thereby avoiding defeat. Such individuals are often self-absorbed; they are inclined to daydream and create fantasies in which they are always superior (Adler, 1930a, pp. 142–143).

The socially useful type   People of the **socially useful type** grow up in families where the members are helpful and supportive of each other, treat each other with respect and consideration, and are disinclined to handle stress and problems through conflict and aggression (Leak & Williams, 1991, pp. 159–165). Instead they have the courage to face their problems directly as a means of solving them. As adults, their orientation to family members is based on respect, affection, and friendship and not on manipulation and game playing (Leak & Gardner, 1990, p. 57).

Socially useful people are psychologically healthy. They face life confidently and are prepared to cooperate with others, contribute to the welfare of others, and build a better community. They see a life goal of "making a lot of money" as unimportant. In short, they act in accordance with social interest (Crandall, 1980, pp. 484–487; Leak, Millard, Perry, & Williams, 1985, pp. 197–207).

Assessment Techniques

Like Freud, Adler sought to understand the individual's personality by focusing on early childhood experiences. He used three major techniques: early recollections, dream analysis, and birth-order analysis.

Early Recollections

Adler believed that reports by patients of their earliest memories provided valuable insights into their unique styles of life. He maintained that patients were very willing to discuss these memories. Often the memories were based on actual experiences, but sometimes they were fanciful. Whether real or imaginary, Adler thought they still revealed important meanings, and gave glimpses into the person's strivings for superiority (Ansbacher & Ansbacher, 1956, pp. 351–352).

To illustrate the importance of these memories, Adler reported the recollections of a woman whose father gave her a pony when she was 3 years old. He also gave her older sister a pony on the same occasion. Mounted on her own pony, the sister took the reins of the patient's pony from her father and proceeded triumphantly down the street. However, the patient's pony, hurrying after the other, went so fast that the patient fell down in the dirt. Later in life, she told Adler, she surpassed her sister as a horsewoman, but she never forgot this early humiliating experience (Ansbacher & Ansbacher, 1956, pp. 354–355).

Adler first noted that the woman mentioned her father and not her mother in recalling this incident. He interpreted this to mean that, as a child, the woman was not particularly satisfied with her home life and that perhaps her mother favored her older sister. This information could prove useful in her treatment.

Next Adler observed that the older sister appeared to triumph in the incident; this implied an unhealthy competition between the two sisters. The younger sister (the patient) believed that she was continually being humiliated in the relationship. When she reported that she later surpassed her sister as a horsewoman, Adler concluded that she felt the need to triumph over her. However, her victory did not in the least diminish her feelings about the original experience. Thus, the patient's memory simply reinforced her attitude: "If anyone is ahead of me, I am endangered. I must always be the first." In Adler's view, such striving is typical of second children, who are always trying to overtake the pace-maker, the oldest child. This unhealthy attitude toward life, along with others, was causing the patient needless pain. By revealing to the patient her basic attitude, Adler enabled her to begin making changes that would lead to a more satisfying outlook on life.

Besides therapists' use of case studies to illustrate the importance of early recollections in exploring people's striving for superiority, researchers have begun to examine how early recollections can reveal facets of individuals' personality traits and self-concept. For example, Chaplin and Orlofsky (1991) analyzed the contents of the earliest memories reported by alcoholics and nonalcoholics. They found that the earliest recollections of alcoholics reflected less social interest, a more passive and powerless orientation to life, greater depressive feelings, and a more negative self-concept. Their memories were also more rife with beatings, abandonment by one or both parents, and emotional deprivation. After undergoing Adlerian therapy for their substance abuse, these alcoholics began to realize that they could produce positive changes and could gain control over their drinking (Chaplin & Orlofsky, 1991, pp. 365–367).

Dream Analysis

Adler also utilized dream analysis as a major technique for understanding each patient's personality. Unlike Freud, however, he did not focus on sexual interpretations of manifest dream content. Instead, he believed that a person's dreams are determined by his or her goal of superiority. More specifically, dreams reflect the individual's unconscious attempts to achieve personal goals in accordance with his or her unique style of life. The student who is courageous and unafraid of examinations, for example, may dream of climbing a mountain and enjoying the view from the top, whereas the student who is a quitter and wants to postpone examinations may dream of falling off the mountain (Adler, 1969, p. 70). Each student's dreams are controlled by his or her unique style of life.

For Adler, dreams also provide glimpses of the future, and thus suggest potential solutions to the person's problems. For example, Adler cites the case of a man who was very disappointed in his wife. His primary complaint was that she did not take adequate care of their two children. Adler saw the complaint as a symptom of a deeper, underlying hostility toward her because he believed she had not married him out of love.

In the course of analysis, the man reported a dream in which he had three children, the youngest of whom got lost and could not be found. The man interpreted his dream as a warning not to have more children because his wife would neglect them. While acknowledging the plausibility of this interpretation, Adler pointed out that the dream about a third child might suggest instead a desire to reconcile with his wife and develop a more satisfying relationship with her (Mairet, 1964, pp. 164–166).

Birth-Order Analysis

Adler's third technique for understanding the patient's personality was birth-order analysis. Adler believed that a correct analysis of the effects of patients' birth positions on their subsequent behavior would help win their confidence. This emphasis on unavoidable childhood circumstances also helps patients to stop blaming themselves for developing a faulty style of life (Forer, 1977, p. 110). Reducing self-blame and resistance, in turn, enables patients to adopt more constructive goals and behavior.

Theory's Implications for Therapy

Neurotics and psychotics, according to Adler, are individuals who have developed faulty styles of life, usually as a result of parental pampering, neglect, or rejection during early childhood. In many instances, parental behavior was erratic, mixing pampering and rejection. As a consequence of such treatment, Adler believed, children become highly anxious and insecure. To cope with their feelings of inferiority, they begin to develop protective devices—most often, a strong striving for personal superiority. Neurotic individuals begin to believe that they actually are superior to others and to act in ways consistent with that belief. They strive to be perfect, to avoid failure at all costs. They belittle others, and perceive them as competitors who must be defeated in order to achieve personal satisfaction. Psychotics, too, view others with suspicion, but they validate their worth not so much through comparison with others as through the use of private logic and reasoning and delusions of grandeur.

According to Adler, the goal of therapy is the reorganization of patients' mistaken beliefs about themselves and others, the elimination of faulty goals, and the implementation of new goals that will help them realize their potential as human beings. "The patient must be guided away from himself, toward productivity for others; he must be educated toward social interest; he must be brought to the only correct insight, that he is as important to the community as anyone else; he must get to feel at home on this earth" (Adler, 1973d, p. 200).

The therapist acts as the patient's guide to facilitate movement toward these ends. He or she believes that a good therapeutic relationship is a friendly one, between equals (Sprouse, Ogletree, Comsudes, Granville, & Kern, 2005, pp. 137–148). Accordingly, they first jointly seek to understand the childhood origins of the patient's difficulties to understand why the patient feels the need to be superior to others. Encouraged by the therapist, the patient moves away from competitive self-centeredness and comes to realize that psychological health is contingent on developing a cooperative attitude toward others and seeking to contribute to the welfare of society. The patient begins to see that he or she is a worthwhile part of the community and to appreciate the joy of accepting responsibility for one's actions. As a result, the person is no longer a taker but a giver. Slowly, the patient moves toward a reorganization of perceptions and begins to behave differently toward others.

Evaluative Comments

We turn now to an assessment of the scientific worth of Adler's theory in terms of our six criteria.

Comprehensiveness   Adler addressed himself to a wide range of phenomena involving disordered behavior. He discusses at length the etiology and cure of many different kinds of neurosis and psychosis. But Adler also sought to understand the ways in which political, educational, and religious institutions affect personality development. He tried not only to assess the impact of the destructive elements of these institutions on the individual but also to outline the ways in which they could be restructured to promote psychological health and well-being. In general, then, Adler's theory is comprehensive in nature, although, like Freud's theory, it has a very limited motivational base.

Precision and testability   Generally, the concepts in Adler's theory are global in nature and poorly defined. He postulated, for example, a proof complex that is "found in many people who want to prove that they also have a right to exist or that they have no faults" (Adler, 1973b, p. 75). How would one go about measuring this proof complex? The same difficulty arises in seeking to operationalize such Adlerian concepts as redeemer complex, exclusion complex, predestination complex, and creative power.

The relational statements of the theory also are vaguely stated. Witness a hypothesis such as this: "The law of movement and its direction originate from the creative power of the individual and use, in free choice, one's experiences of one's body and of external effects, within the limits of human capacity" (Adler, 1973a, p. 51). How much creative power is needed to affect the person's unique movements? How much movement occurs if the creative power of the person is utilized? How do you define movement? Creative power? It is interesting to note that Adler believed that this hypothesis had already been empirically validated.

Parsimony   Adler made a diligent effort to construct a scientific theory that was understandable to the ordinary person. The result was a commonsense psychology that utilizes only a few constructs. But although parsimony of explanation is considered a virtue in scientific psychology, the set of constructs must be adequate to the task of accounting for human behavior in all its complexity. Because Adler postulated a master motive—the striving for superiority—his position has a reductionist quality that fails to do justice to the great diversity of reinforcers that motivate us. Also, because there are only a few constructs in the theory, they must be applied in highly general and imprecise ways. As we have seen, constructs are defined so loosely that it is often unclear what dimensions they encompass and how they are related to everyday situations.

Empirical validity   Empirical support for Adler's theory is generally not very strong. However, this situation may well change in the near future, now that investigators have begun to construct reliable and valid measures of some of his key constructs most notably, social interest (Crandall, 1975; Greever, Tseng, & Friedland, 1973; Leak et al., 1985). Other researchers have tried to construct and validate a measure of Adler's typology of the lifestyles of healthy and unhealthy children and adults (Kannarkat & Bayton, 1979; Stiles & Wilborn, 1992; Wheeler, Kern, & Curlette, 1986). The current interest in operationalizing such key concepts and establishing their reliability augurs well for eventual hypothesis testing.

Heuristic value   Clearly the chief contribution of Adler's theory is the number of subsequent investigators of human personality who have been influenced by it. Adler's position has contributed to theory in the areas of existential psychology and psychiatry, neo-Freudian psychoanalysis, personality diagnosis including dream interpretation, the practice of psychotherapy, and the theory of positive mental health (Ansbacher & Ansbacher, 1973, p. 3). Adler has directly influenced such prominent psychologists and psychiatrists as Albert Ellis, Carl Rogers, Abraham Maslow, and Rollo May (Ansbacher, 1990, pp. 45–53; Ellis, 1973, pp. 111–127) and has had considerable impact on the experimental work of Julian Rotter. (See Chapter 16.)

Applied value   In addition to its considerable heuristic value, Adler's theory focuses on phenomena like feelings of inferiority and striving for superiority that are of particular relevance in a highly competitive and achievement-oriented society. In short, it is a theory that addresses itself to problems and issues that matter in a culture such as ours. His theory has had considerable applied usefulness in the areas of psychopathology, psychotherapy, education, and family life.

CRITICAL THINKING QUESTIONS

1. Adler maintained that we all have had feelings of inferiority. Do you agree? If so, what were the primary sources of these feelings for you and/or your friends? If you disagree, why do you think he's wrong?

2. Do you agree with Adler that much of our behavior is guided by goals? What are some of your major goals? What are some of the major goals of college students today? Do your goals differ from theirs?

3. Adler's view of the healthy society is based on his concept of social interest. What is it? Does the concept differ in any way from the concept of enlightened self-interest? What are you doing currently, if anything, to improve your contributions to others?

4. One of Adler's most interesting concepts is that of birth order. Do you agree with him that a person's order of birth can have a dramatic impact on his or her personality development? How many children are there in your family? Have your parents (or guardians) treated you and your siblings differently? If you are an only child, do you think that fact has made any difference in the way your parents treated you?

5. Is it possible to treat each other as equals in a largely capitalistic society such as ours?

GLOSSARY

attitude   Learned tendency to respond to an object in a consistently favorable or unfavorable way.

avoiding type   An unhealthy person who lacks the confidence to confront problems and avoids or ignores them.

birth-order effects   Adler's belief that how each child is treated by parents depends on the child's order of birth within the family and that, in consequence, birth order is an important correlate of personality development.

confluence theory   Theory which maintains the intellectual maturities of children growing up in the same families flow together over time in their influence on each other, changing most profoundly when new offspring join the sibship.

creative self   Term used by Adler to reflect his belief that people have the ability to create actively their own destinies and personalities.

fictional finalism   Imagined goal that guides a person's behavior; also called the guiding self-ideal by Adler in his later writings.

getting type   An unhealthy person who attains personal goals by relying indiscriminately on others for help.

individual psychology   Theory advanced by Adler that seeks to understand the behavior of each person as a complex, organized entity.

masculine protest   Attempt by an individual, male or female, to compensate for feelings of inferiority by acting as though superior to others.

organ inferiority   Biologically based defect that gives rise to feelings of inadequacy.

overcompensation   Exaggerated attempts by individuals to overcome their feelings of inferiority by acting as though they are personally superior to others.

ruling type   An unhealthy person who strives for personal superiority by trying to exploit and control others.

social interest   Innate tendency in human beings to help and cooperate with one another as a means of establishing a harmonious and productive society.

socially useful type   A healthy person who actively and courageously confronts and solves his or her problems in accordance with social interest.

style of life   The individual's distinctive personality pattern, which is basically shaped by the end of early childhood.

superiority   The striving to attain perfection. Adler categorized superiority into two types: (1) personal superiority, which he considered harmful because it implies seeking satisfaction at the expense of others; and (2) strivings for superiority in the sense of perfection, which he considered healthy because they imply a striving for fulfillment of individual potential through helping others and being helped by them.

teleological position   The belief that goals determine behavior, or, more generally, that behavior is directed and shaped by a designing force.

SUGGESTED READINGS

Adler, A. (1927). *The practice and theory of individual psychology.* New York: Harcourt, Brace & World.

Adler, A. (1969). *The science of living.* Garden City, NY: Doubleday Anchor. (Original work published 1929.)

Ansbacher, H. L., & Ansbacher, R. R. (Eds.). (1956). *The individual psychology of Alfred Adler.* New York: Basic Books.

CHAPTER 5

Horney's Social and Cultural Psychoanalysis

Bettmann/Corbis

Biographical Sketch

Karen Horney (pronounced *horn-eye*) was born in 1885 in Blankenese, a village on the north bank of the Elbe River approximately 12 miles west of Hamburg, Germany. Her father, Berndt Wackels, was a sea captain employed by one of the large shipping lines located in Hamburg. Horney's mother, Clotilde van Ronzelen, was a member of a prominent Dutch-German family. Captain Wackels, 18 years her senior, had four children from a previous marriage. Their first child was a son, Berndt, followed four years later by Karen.

As a child, Karen had ambivalent feelings toward her father. He took her on several boat trips with him throughout the world and instilled in her a love of the sea and of travel and a cosmopolitan outlook on life. She loved him deeply but felt intimidated by his stern, self-righteous manner. Wackels was a god-fearing, religious fundamentalist who strongly believed that women were inferior to men. He restricted Karen's activities, while granting freedoms and privileges to her brother. He vehemently opposed her ambitions, especially her educational goals. For example, Karen decided at age 13 that she wanted to study medicine, but her father said he would not pay for her education. Bitter at her father's opposition, she complained, "He, who has flung out thousands for my stepbrother, who is both stupid and bad, first turns every penny he is to spend for me 10 times in his fingers" (Paris, 1994, p. 7). But fortunately her mother was more encouraging and protected her from her father's authoritarianism, so that Karen was able to pursue her goal of medicine. Apparently, though, neither parent gave Karen much affection. Thus, wracked by doubts about her self-worth, she uncritically accepted the protection of her mother and became a clinging, highly compliant daughter, presumably as a means of feeling safe and wanted. Horney's feelings of inadequacy were heightened by her perception that she was physically unattractive, although others did not see her that way. She reacted strongly to this negative self-image by investing all of her energies in her studies. Looking back many years later, she said, "If I couldn't be beautiful, I decided I would be smart." An excellent student, Horney entered medical school in Freiburg in 1906; she was the only woman in her class. In this male-dominated atmosphere, she sometimes felt that she had to prove she was as competent as, if not more competent than, her male friends and associates. Yet her social life during this period was full, exciting, and rewarding. She was introduced to Oskar Horney, a student majoring in economics, and she married him while still in medical training. After finishing his studies, Oskar went to work in an investment firm and was promoted rapidly to manager of company operations. In the meantime, Karen was finishing her medical studies, while trying simultaneously to fulfill the roles of homemaker and mother to a newly born daughter (the first of three daughters).

The conflicts inherent in these activities, coupled with the death of her mother and emerging difficulties in her marriage, plunged Horney into depression, and she entered therapy with psychoanalyst Dr. Karl Abraham. Disappointed with the results of her therapy, Horney began to question the basic tenets of psychoanalysis. For several years, she participated in weekly evening sessions with other analysts at Dr. Abraham's home, to discuss psychoanalytic concepts, principles, and therapeutic practices. These informal sessions led to the formation of the Berlin Psychoanalytic Institute, of which Horney remained an active member from 1918 until 1932.

During this period, she also became more outspoken about the limitations of orthodox psychoanalysis. She believed strongly that Freud had placed too much stress on the role played by the sexual instincts in the development of neurosis and not enough on the cultural and social conditions that fostered pathology. For Freud, neurosis was essentially an outgrowth of the person's inability to cope with sexual impulses and strivings; for Horney, neurosis was primarily the result of disturbed human relationships. In her view, neurosis and sexual disturbance were often, but not inevitably, intertwined. When they were, it was the neurosis, based upon faulty character structure, which produced impaired sexual functioning; for Freud, it was impaired sexual functioning that was the primary cause of neurosis. Horney believed further that each culture generates its own unique set of fears in its members. In one culture, fears might be created by nature—for instance, living at the base of an unpredictable volcano or in the scorching desert; in another, by war-like neighbors. In our culture, the heavy emphasis on competition and the achievement of individual success sometimes leads to a fear of failure or of being inferior to others. The normal person, according to Horney, is capable of adjusting to these threatening conditions and of making the best use of what the culture has to offer. The neurotic, in contrast, is unable to adjust and uses defenses rigidly and indiscriminately to lessen his or her fears and to feel safe.

Interwoven with the problems generated by living in a particular culture are the problems and fears created by the unique social or interpersonal conditions of a person's life. Mistreatment by parents, siblings, peers, authority figures, and others may all contribute in complicated fashion to maladjusted functioning. Thus, in Horney's judgment, sociocultural conditions have a tremendous impact on the individual's development and functioning. Emphasizing the role of the socialization process in the onset of neuroses, and deemphasizing (but not eliminating) the role of biology, Horney began to reinterpret much of Freud's thinking, including his libido theory, his theory of psychosexual development, and his theory of therapy. Her new theory germinated under the stimulation of debates with her colleagues and students at the Berlin Psychoanalytic Institute and can be seen in its evolutionary form by reading her books in chronological order: *The Neurotic Personality of Our Time* (1937), *New Ways in Psychoanalysis* (1939), *Self-Analysis* (1942), *Our Inner Conflicts* (1945), *Neurosis and Human Growth* (1950), and the posthumous *Feminine Psychology* (1967).

In 1932, Horney left the Berlin Psychoanalytic Institute and came to the United States, where she became associate director of the Chicago Psychoanalytic Institute. Two years later, she moved to New York to establish a private practice and to work and teach courses at the New York Psychoanalytic Institute. While in New York, she had many opportunities to meet and exchange ideas with prominent social scientists, including Erich Fromm, Clara Thompson, Margaret Mead, H. S. Sullivan, Ruth Benedict, and John Dollard. It was also here, in 1937, that she divorced her husband. She continued to refine her theories, to write books and journal articles, and to give lectures on her ideas to various professional societies. Her ideas, unfortunately, rankled some of her more orthodox Freudian colleagues at the New York Psychoanalytic Institute, and eventually she felt obligated to resign. Several other members resigned in sympathy with her. Shortly afterwards, she helped found the American Institute for Psychoanalysis as a vehicle for promoting her own theories. She succumbed to cancer in 1952 after a lengthy illness (Rubins, 1978).

Concepts and Principles

Hypercompetitiveness: A Major Form of Neurotic Competitiveness

According to Horney (1937, pp. 188–206), **hypercompetitiveness** is an indiscriminate need to compete and win and to avoid losing at any cost as a means of maintaining or enhancing one's feelings of self-worth. It also includes feelings and thoughts of manipulation, aggressiveness, exploitation, and derogation of others across a myriad of situations. Horney maintained that such an exaggerated competitive attitude was a central feature of American culture and had a highly detrimental impact on the individual's development and functioning.

> Our modern culture is based on the principle of individual competition, [and] the … individual has to fight with other individuals of the same group, has to surpass them and, frequently, [to] thrust them aside. The advantage of the one is frequently the disadvantage of the other. The psychic result … is a diffuse hostile tension between individuals. [This] competitiveness, and the … hostility that accompanies it, pervades all human relationships. Competitive stimuli are active from the cradle to the grave [and present] a fertile ground for the development of neurosis. (Horney, 1937, pp. 284–287)

While Horney's views about our culture were expressed nearly 75 years ago, such neurotic competitiveness remains a key feature of American life today (Duina, 2011, pp. 5–6; Stewart, 2010, pp. 189–195). According to Horney, hypercompetitive individuals have typically grown up in families where they were verbally and physically abused by their parents. As a result, they feel powerless and insignificant; these feelings are largely unconscious. To overcome their self-perceptions of inadequacy and inferiority and the feelings of anxiety attendant upon them, they begin to fantasize about attaining unlimited success and power. An incessant and indiscriminate striving for personal superiority permeates virtually every area of their lives. These individuals are possessed by a grandiose sense of self-importance and an exhibitionism designed to win attention, recognition, and admiration. They seek self-aggrandizement through indiscriminate competition. Ruthlessly single-minded, they come to perceive others as malevolent and believe that their best chance for survival is to regard everyone with distrust. In their self-defeating quest for superiority, they become hostile, dogmatic, arrogant, aggressive, and derisive toward others. Their sexual life consists largely of attempts to subdue and humiliate their partners, as further proof of their own superiority (Horney, 1937, pp. 195–197).

To assess the validity of Horney's theorizing about hypercompetitiveness, investigators needed to construct a scale that measures it, and to establish its reliability and validity (Ryckman, Hammer, Kaczor, & Gold, 1990, pp. 630–639). Sample items and the scoring procedure for the scale appear in Table 5.1.

Using this instrument, researchers found strong empirical support for Horney's ideas. College men and women who scored higher in hypercompetitiveness were generally less psychologically healthy than were college men and women lower in hypercompetitiveness. Ross and Rausch (2001, pp. 471–480), for example, found that hypercompetitives are characterized by **primary psychopathy**, but not **secondary psychopathy**. Primary psychopaths have an inclination to lie when it suits their purposes, to lack remorse when they have wronged others, and to be manipulative. In essence, they are morally

TABLE 5.1   SAMPLE ITEMS FROM THE HYPERCOMPETITIVE ATTITUDE SCALE

1. If I can disturb my opponent in some way in order to get the edge in competition, I will do so.

2. I can't stand to lose an argument.

3. I find myself being competitive even in situations which do not call for competition.

4. I compete with others even if they are not competing with me.

5. Winning in competition makes me feel more powerful as a person.

Note: Study participants respond to each item on a 5-point scale: never true of me (1), seldom true of me (2), sometimes true of me (3), often true of me (4), and always true of me (5). Higher scores indicate greater hypercompetitiveness.

Source: Adapted from Ryckman, Hammer, Kaczor, & Gold, 1990, pp. 630–639.

barren. Secondary psychopaths, in contrast, tend to be more guilt-ridden and to be less clear in their life goals. Watson, Morris, and Miller (2001, pp. 346–349) showed further that hypercompetitives are characterized by irrational beliefs (e.g., "It's better to ignore personal problems than try to solve them"), making catastrophic statements in stressful situations (e.g., "If I don't get this job, my life is over"), and making extreme, either-or-statements ("I absolutely must perform well at important tasks or else I am an inadequate, worthless person"). Individuals higher in hypercompetitiveness are also more likely to have stronger needs for power and control over others, to be lower in altruism, social concern, and forgiveness of others and higher in narcissism, exhibitionism, neuroticism, mistrust, dogmatism, anger, hostility, and anxiety than are people lower in hypercompetitiveness (Collier, Ryckman, Thornton, & Gold, 2010, pp. 535–543; Fletcher & Nusbaum, 2008, pp. 312–317; Ross, Rausch, & Canada, 2003, pp. 323–337; Ryckman, Hammer, Kaczor, & Gold, 1990, pp. 630–639; Ryckman, Libby, van den Borne, Gold, & Lindner, 1997, pp. 271–283; Ryckman, Thornton, & Butler, 1994, pp. 84–94).

Consistent with these findings, Houston, Harris, and Norman (2003, pp. 269–278) found that hypercompetitive men and women undergraduates also reported high levels of aggressive driving, endorsing strongly statements such as "I make rude gestures at other drivers when they do something I don't like"; "I flash my high beams at slower drivers so they will get out of my way"; "I follow a slower car at less than a car length"; and "I pass in front of a car at less than a car length."

Hypercompetitives also are indiscriminate in their pursuit of success, but do they actually experience any success in various settings? The answer to that question is yes, but they nevertheless report seeing themselves as intellectual phonies in academic and work settings and are wracked with doubts about their own accomplishments (Ross, Stewart, Mugge, & Fultz, 2001, pp. 1347–1355). For example, Bing (1999, pp. 80–99) found that their intense competitive striving was related positively to higher grade point averages. However, while striving for this success, they reported feeling hostile toward their fellow students, anxious, stressed, and socially isolated. Hypercompetitives report that they lie, cheat, and manipulate others to attain their goals generally. Thus, their academic success may have been accomplished, at least in part, by plagiarism and cheating on their exams.

Hypercompetitives not only experience social distance from their classmates, they also experience considerable difficulties in their romantic relationships. Given their basic mistrust of others and their almost constant efforts to compensate for low self-esteem and feelings of inadequacy by trying to prove themselves superior to others, including their romantic partners, it is not surprising that their relationships are characterized by conflict, jealousy, and dishonesty. They also try to prove their superiority by manipulating and deceiving their partner, for example, by trying to keep them uncertain about the strength of their commitment and/or by lying to them to keep them from knowing about other lovers (Ryckman, Thornton, Gold, & Burckle, 2002, pp. 517–530). Based on these research findings, it would be fair to say that hypercompetitives are characterized by alienation from other human beings and that this social disconnectedness creates psychological difficulties (e.g., doubts, stress, anxiety, and loneliness) for them.

Competition Avoidance: The Other Major Form of Neurotic Competitiveness

Besides hypercompetitiveness, Horney discussed another major form of neurotic competitiveness, namely, **competition avoidance**. She defined it as the need by individuals to check their ruthless ambition and excessive competitive strivings because of an extreme fear of losing the affection and approval of others as a consequence of either being successful in competition with others or through failure in such competition (Ryckman, Thornton, & Gold, 2009). In particular, such individuals fear that success in competition will cause others to dislike and resent them. As a consequence, they try hard to avoid competing whenever they can. If they must compete, they are so afraid of succeeding that they may minimize their efforts as they near victory, making it unlikely for them to win. Also, they may minimize their chances for success by belittling themselves. For instance, when competing against less intelligent opponents, they may try to appear even less intelligent than they actually are.

Competition avoiders not only fear success, but also failure as well. They fear others who defeat them will denigrate them by calling them names such as stupid and slow. Thus, competition avoiders tend to feel embarrassed or humiliated by competitive defeat. They think that failure in competition will cause others to dislike and ridicule them.

Horney believed that competition avoidance had its origins in early childhood where competition avoiders grew up in the shadow of a parent who was generally adored by outsiders, that is, a beautiful, but neurotic, mother or a benevolently despotic, highly successful father. Such parents are incapable of giving genuine warmth and affection to their children—the warmth and affection that they desperately need in order to feel loved and secure (Horney, 1937, p. 80). Consequently, the children finally conclude that affection of a kind (i.e., approval) was attainable at a price, namely, that of self-subordinating devotion. Horney believed further that such children eventually stop rebelling, repress their hostility, and become compliant. Their needs for ambition and personal success are checked for the benefit of approval from their parents and later others. They perceive that the approval of others can be lost as a consequence of either being successful in competition with others or through failure in such competition (Horney, 1950, pp. 221–223).

To assess the validity of Horney's theorizing about competition avoidance, researchers have constructed a scale that measures it, and to establish its reliability and validity (Ryckman, Thornton, & Gold, 2009). Sample items and the scoring procedure for the scale appear in Table 5.2.

Using this scale, researchers have found very strong support for Horney's theorizing. University students who were higher in competition avoidance scored higher in neuroticism, had greater fears of both success and failure, a lower desire to prove themselves in competitive situations, higher levels of **self-handicapping**, and were more maladaptive. They also were more modest and willing to conform to group standards than were those lower in competition avoidance. These findings suggest that competition avoiders will have a great deal of difficulty competing realistically and constructively in various achievement situations.

TABLE 5.2   SAMPLE ITEMS FROM THE COMPETITION AVOIDANCE SCALE

1. There's nothing so great about winning in competition, especially when it causes others to dislike you.

2. I avoid competition because losing in competition is humiliating.

3. When I'm close to victory in competition, I find that something holds me back and makes it impossible for me to win.

4. I usually perform beneath my capabilities.

5. Despite how they may act, people really resent those who win in competition.

Note: Study participants respond to each item on a 5-point scale: strongly disagree (1), slightly disagree (2), neither disagree nor agree (3), slightly agree (4), and strongly agree (5). Higher scores indicate greater competition avoidance.

Source: Adapted from Ryckman, Thornton, & Gold, 2009, pp. 175–192.

Personal Development Competitiveness: Competing in a Psychologically Healthy Way

Finally, while hypercompetitiveness and competition avoidance are clearly maladaptive, Horney did not think that all forms of competitive orientations are bad. She speculated that each person is born with a set of potentials that can be realized under the right familial conditions (Horney, 1950, p. 18). These family conditions include experiences where children are raised in a democratic environment and given warmth and affection by their parents. Because their parents are trustworthy and enhance feelings of security in them, children in such families should be more likely to develop trusting, affectionate, and constructive relations with others. Thus, they should be able to focus on the development of their real self, that is, on the development of their potentials for constructive growth.

In fact, Ryckman, Libby, van den Borne, Gold, and Lindner (1997, pp. 271–283) have constructed a reliable and valid psychometric instrument that assesses individual differences in such competitors. They defined **personal development competitiveness** as an attitude in which the primary focus is not primarily on the outcome (i.e., winning), but rather more on the enjoyment and mastery of the task. Individuals with such attitudes are more concerned with self-discovery, self-improvement, and task mastery than with comparisons with others. The focus is also not on the denigration of others in order to enhance the self. Others are not seen as obstacles standing in the person's way, but rather as competitors who provide the individual with personal discovery and learning opportunities. **Personal development competitors** want strongly to win and be successful, but not at the expense of other people (Ryckman, Hammer, Kaczor, & Gold, 1996, p. 375).

Sample items and the scoring procedure for the scale appear in Table 5.3.

TABLE 5.3   SAMPLE ITEMS FROM THE PERSONAL DEVELOPMENT COMPETITIVE ATTITUDE SCALE

1. I value competition because it helps me to be the best that I can be.

2. I enjoy competition because it gives me a chance to discover my abilities.

3. I like competition because it teaches me a lot about myself.

4. I enjoy competition because it brings me and my competitors closer together as human beings.

5. Without the challenge of competition I might never discover that I had certain potentials or abilities.

Note: Study participants respond to each item on a 5-point scale: strongly disagree (1), slightly disagree (2), neither disagree nor agree (3), slightly agree (4), and strongly agree (5). Higher scores indicate greater personal development competitive attitudes.

Source: Adapted from Ryckman, Hammer, Kaczor, & Gold, 1996, pp. 374–385.

Using this instrument, researchers have found preliminary support for Horney's theorizing. That is, college students who score higher in personal development competitiveness have lower scores on neuroticism and higher scores on self-esteem and optimal psychological health. They are also more achievement oriented, altruistic, and concerned about the welfare of others than those who score lower on the dimension. In contrast to hypercompetitives, personal development competitors are associated positively with the forgiveness of others who have transgressed against them (Collier et al., 2010, pp. 535–543). Finally, personal development competitors treat others with respect and as equals (Ryckman Hammer, Kaczor, & Gold, 1996; Ryckman, Libby, van den Borne, Gold, & Lindner, 1997; Ryska, 2002).

The Etiology of Neuroses in the Family

In Horney's view, because parents generally adopt the values of society, their relationships with their children are often implicitly hypercompetitive and give rise to neuroses. Attitudes and behaviors of hypercompetitive parents that cause disturbed relationships include "direct or indirect domination, indifference, erratic behavior, lack of respect for the child's individual needs, lack of real guidance, disparaging attitudes, lack of reliable warmth, having to take sides in parental disagreements, isolation from other children, injustice, discrimination, unkept promises, hostile atmosphere, and so on" (Horney, 1945, p. 41). Rarely, if ever, does only one of these factors operate to produce pathology in a particular person; behavior is invariably multidetermined, with several factors operating jointly to produce disturbance.

The operation of these negative factors creates **basic anxiety** in children—a feeling of being isolated and helpless in a potentially hostile world. They dread their social environment, which they perceive as unfair, unpredictable, begrudging, and merciless. These children also feel that their freedom is being taken away, and happiness prevented, by parents and other adult authority figures. Thus, their self-esteem and self-reliance are continually being undermined. Fear is instilled in them by intimidation and isolation, and their natural exuberance and curiosity is stifled by brutality or overprotective love (Horney, 1939, p. 75).

The Use of Neurotic Strategies to Cope with Feelings of Basic Anxiety

To cope with the feelings of insecurity, isolation, and hostility that accompany basic anxiety, children often resort to certain defensive attitudes. These protective devices provide a temporary alleviation of pain and make them feel safe (Horney, 1942, p. 45). Horney discussed these defenses as neurotic needs or strivings designed to reestablish the safety of their environments. They are distinguished from normal needs by their compulsiveness, rigidity, and indiscriminate usage and by the fact that they are unconscious (Horney, 1945, pp. 30–31). Horney outlined and described 10 neurotic needs (Horney, 1942, pp. 54–60).

The neurotic need for affection and approval   Although we all wish to be liked and appreciated by people of whom we are fond, neurotics show an indiscriminate hunger for affection, regardless of whether they care for the person concerned or whether the person has any positive feelings toward them. They are overly sensitive to any criticism or indication that the attention they want and need from others is not forthcoming. They will sever a budding relationship with someone who does not accept an invitation for dinner, even if the person is unable to attend for reasons beyond his or her control. They may also terminate a relationship if someone disagrees with them about some trivial issue. Such individuals also have strong inhibitions about expressing their wishes or asking for favors, and they are incapable of saying no to the demands of others. Salespeople can readily convince them to buy household appliances that they really do not need; on a date, they can be persuaded to have premarital sex even if it is a violation of their moral principles and causes them considerable anguish afterward (Horney, 1937, pp. 35–38).

The neurotic need for a partner who will take over one's life   Many neurotics are excessively dependent on others. They feel very lonely and inadequate without the presence, benevolence, love, and friendship of a partner. Driven by the strong need for a partner, they select one without much prior reflection and consequently discover that he or she does not meet their expectations. Whereas a genuine and mature partnership involves mutual caring, sharing, and love, neurotics are incapable of such behavior and typically become associated with others who are bound by the same limitations. Thus, their relationships are disturbed and unsatisfying (Horney, 1939, p. 251).

The neurotic need to restrict one's life within narrow borders   Neurotics are generally not risk takers. They are afraid of expressing their wishes for fear of disapproval and ridicule. Even in situations where spontaneity and expansiveness are valued and accepted (for example, parties or athletic contests), neurotics may be unable to assert themselves. Therefore, they may avoid such situations by claiming that they are boring and not worthwhile. They may avoid accepting jobs as teachers or as business executives because they are afraid that they will fail and face public humiliation. As a result, many neurotics feel safe only by living a highly circumscribed life in which routine and orderliness are paramount. Safety is also achieved through compulsive modesty and submission to the will of others.

The neurotic need for power   In normal individuals, the need for power manifests itself in the realistic realization of their physical strength, reasoning capacities, maturity, and wisdom. Their striving for power is typically associated with a worthy cause, such as the betterment of their family, professional group, or country. In power-oriented neurotics, however, striving springs not from strength, but from anxiety, weakness, and feelings of inferiority. Neurotic striving for power serves as a protection against helplessness, one of the key elements of basic anxiety. Because neurotics hate any appearance of weakness, they avoid situations where they would have to ask for help or where they would be expected to yield to the wishes of others. Their feelings of insignificance cause them to conjure up a rigid ideal image of themselves that makes them believe they should immediately, and with little effort, be able to master any situation, no matter how objectively difficult. Their belief in their own superiority implies that they should control the direction and outcomes of their relationships. These tendencies to control, however, may be masked or repressed to such a degree that they (and others) are unaware of them. The neurotic may appear to be highly generous and supportive of others' freedom, while in fact unconsciously striving to control others' lives in very subtle ways. If control is not possible, such neurotics may experience depression, severe headaches, or stomach upsets.

Power-oriented neurotics want to be right all the time; they become irritated at being proven wrong, even in trivial matters. Also, they need to be able to predict what will happen in the future and exhibit a strong aversion to any situation involving uncontrollable factors. Power-oriented neurotics see self-control as a virtue and feel contempt for anyone who cannot control his or her emotions. Thus, their own relationships are severely impaired, both because they must control their emotions at all times and because they view signs of affection from their partners as indications of weakness.

Furthermore, their relationships are permeated by conflict, because they must always be right and must never give in (Horney, 1937, pp. 160–171).

The neurotic need to exploit others   Exploitative neurotics are hostile, distrustful individuals who need to exploit others in order to feel safe. They may steal other people's ideas, jobs, or partners to obtain relief from their feelings of insecurity. They lead a parasitic kind of existence; they expect others to do favors for them and to lend them money. They live as though they had a right to expect good things to happen to them and to blame others for bad things.

A frequent correlate of their need to exploit others is the fear that others will cheat or exploit them. As a consequence, such neurotics live in constant fear that others will take advantage of them. They may react with anger that borders on rage if there is the slightest delay in getting back work tools lent to a neighbor or if a cashier makes an honest mistake and overcharges them slightly (Horney, 1937, pp. 183–186).

The neurotic need for social recognition and prestige   Normal individuals take pride in being popular and in being recognized by others for their accomplishments. Yet their lives do not revolve totally around these events, nor do they devote virtually all of their energies to the attainment of recognition and prestige. Pathological individuals, however, are often driven by the need to be admired and respected by others. They evaluate all things—ideas, people, possessions, groups, in terms of their prestige value. To them, it is imperative that they have prominent friends, belong to prestigious groups, read the latest books, see the latest plays and films, and have spouses who enhance their prestige (Horney, 1937, p. 172). Their primary fear is loss of status.

The neurotic need for personal admiration   Neurotic individuals are filled with self-contempt and loathing. As a means of avoiding these painful feelings, they are driven to create an idealized image of themselves. This essentially unrealistic image operates largely on an unconscious level and varies depending upon the neurotic's prior experiences and character structure. Some neurotics unconsciously strive to be exquisite human beings, devoid of flaws and limitations. They act as though they were paragons of virtue or intelligence and are thereby forced to deny the fact that they are not always generous, loving, caring, or brilliant. Such neurotics are not concerned primarily with recognition of their status and material possessions, but with having others admire their idealized selves; they want to be seen as saints or geniuses (Horney, 1945, pp. 96–99).

The neurotic ambition for personal achievement   Related to the needs for prestige, social recognition, and personal admiration is the neurotic's need for personal achievement. Although it is perfectly normal for people to want to be best in their chosen occupation, neurotics are characterized by indiscriminate ambition and striving to be best in too many areas. This type of neurotic may want to be simultaneously a great painter, an outstanding physician, a prominent musician, and a world-renowned architect. Because they expect too much and are obligated to divide their energies, they are doomed to failure and are inevitably disappointed. Moreover, their indiscriminate strivings force them to seek not only their own superior achievement but also the defeat of others. Such neurotics have the hostile attitude that "no one but I shall be beautiful, capable, [and] successful" (Horney, 1937, p. 192). Indeed, ambitious neurotics act as if it were more important for them to defeat others than to succeed themselves. In reality, their own success is of the utmost importance to them but, because they are not very likely to be highly successful, they must at least feel superior by tearing others down (Horney, 1937, pp. 188–194).

The neurotic need for self-sufficiency and independence   At times, we all have a need for privacy and solitude. When the stresses associated with our daily interpersonal interactions become too overwhelming, we sometimes retire to the privacy of our rooms, or take a vacation, or distract ourselves by engaging in a variety of constructive solitary activities—perhaps jogging, reading, or woodworking. When we are refreshed, we rejoin the fray and are usually better able to cope with the situation. In contrast, many neurotics are permanently estranged from others. They are afraid to express emotional feelings toward others lest they be placed in a vulnerable position and learn negative things about themselves, which would be shattering. Consequently, they avoid long-term obligations such as marriage.

By remaining distant from others, neurotics also maintain their illusion of personal superiority. In their fantasies, they are clearly superior to others, and they jealously guard this illusion by avoiding interpersonal comparisons and especially competition. They are convinced that others should simply recognize their greatness. Thus, their imagined superiority over others is unlikely to be tested against reality by actual performance (Horney, 1945, pp. 73–80).

The neurotic need for perfection and unassailability   The need for perfection, Horney believed, typically has its origins in early childhood. Perfectionistic neurotics often have self-righteous, authoritarian parents who exercised unquestioned control over their lives and who instilled in them the need to attain lofty goals and to apply excessively high standards to their actions. Such individuals were often criticized and ridiculed for failure to measure up to these unrealistic standards. Unfortunately, these neurotics adopt their parents' values and spend much of their lives trying to act in ways that leave them beyond reproach and criticism. Obviously, no human being can be completely moral and virtuous in every respect, and so there is a tendency for them to maintain an appearance of perfection and virtue (Horney, 1939, pp. 215–219). In their minds, they equate knowing about moral ideals with being a good person (Horney, 1950, p. 196). Seeing themselves as fair, just, and responsible (although they often are not), they demand respect from others and are hypersensitive to any suggestion that they may have flaws and limitations.

The Three Basic Neurotic Trends

Although Horney believed that her descriptions of the 10 needs were valid, she also perceived certain similarities and commonalities among them. As a result, she classified them into three basic types: compliant, aggressive, and detached.

Compliant types   All the traits and needs associated with **moving toward people** are manifested by **compliant types**. They have neurotic needs for affection and approval, for a partner to control their lives, and for a life contained within restricted borders. These types, as Horney saw it, need to be liked, wanted, loved, appreciated, protected, and guided by others (Horney, 1945, p. 51). As a result, they tend to be self-effacing and submissive and to devalue their own talents and abilities. Compliant types try desperately to live up to the expectations of others as a means of receiving approval. Any criticism, rejection, or desertion by others is terrifying, and they will make the most pitiable efforts to win back the positive regard of the person threatening them (Horney, 1945, p. 54). Consistent with Horney's theorizing, research by Coolidge, Moor, Yamazaki, Stewart, and Segal (2001, p. 1391) shows that compliant types tend to be highly dependent on others.

Aggressive types   People who have neurotic needs for power, exploitation, social recognition and prestige, personal admiration, and personal achievement are **aggressive**

types. These needs are all associated with **moving against people**. Whereas compliant types assume everyone is nice, aggressive types believe that others are essentially hostile and untrustworthy. Aggressive types believe, in the Darwinian sense, that only the fittest survive and that the strong annihilate the weak. Thus their primary aim is to be tough, or at least to appear tough. They regard all feelings, their own as well as others', as "sloppy sentimentality" (Horney, 1945, pp. 64–65). They make especially poor marriage partners because their prime concern is not the expression of positive and joyous feelings toward the partner but the acquisition of a mate who can enhance their own prestige, wealth, or position.

Aggressive neurotics are driven to demonstrate continually that they are the strongest, the smartest, or the shrewdest. Research by Coolidge et al. (2001, p. 1391) indicates that aggressive types are antisocial, sadistic, and narcissistic. They are also highly competitive and extremely hardworking; they invest all of their intelligence and zest in their work and its success. Yet their apparent interest in their work may be misleading because, for them, work is only a means to an end—enhancing their prestige and wealth.

Detached types   Indiscriminate needs for self-sufficiency and perfection characterize **detached types**. These needs are associated with **moving away from people**. Detached types tend to shroud themselves in secrecy. They are reluctant to divulge even the most trivial details of their lives, even where they were born or how many siblings they have, and most of their activities are solitary. They prefer to work, eat, and sleep alone in order to prevent being disturbed by others. In their favor, detached types are not conforming automatons. They will fight for their beliefs and to maintain their integrity. Unfortunately, their independence has a negative aspect to it: It is aimed at *never* being influenced or obligated (Horney, 1945, p. 77). Coolidge et al. (2001) found that detached types are highly avoidant of others and self-defeating.

The Basic Conflict in Neurosis

The three basic neurotic trends in Horney's scheme are not mutually exclusive. Neurotics have within them all three elements, although one typically predominates. Each neurotic trend has a set of needs associated with it. As mentioned earlier, people characterized by moving toward people have excessively strong needs for approval and affection; people characterized by moving against people crave recognition and admiration from others; and those characterized by moving away from others have an inordinate desire to be independent and self-sufficient. In each neurotic individual, one trend typically predominates, and the gratification of the associated needs is pursued relentlessly and endlessly; the other two trends and their associated needs are repressed. Although repressed, however, these needs continue to exist. Since they are not being gratified, the person is in continual turmoil. For example, an individual who moves toward people in virtually every situation, in an attempt to obtain love and approval, will find it virtually impossible to satisfy personal needs for independence and recognition. An individual who moves indiscriminately against people, in order to obtain recognition and prestige, will find it nearly impossible to receive affection and love from others. After all, a person can't systematically exploit people and expect to be showered with love and approval in return. And an individual who moves indiscriminately away from people will be very unlikely to win their love and approval or to satisfy personal needs for recognition. Isolation and secrecy are incompatible with social approval and recognition.

In Horney's view, the three fundamental attitudes and their associated needs are present to some degree in every neurotic individual. The tension created because these attitudes and their associated needs are incompatible and create contradictory tendencies within the person constitutes the **basic conflict** of neurosis. These contradictory attitudes create turmoil and conflict on an unconscious level, sap the person's energies, and result in fatigue and inefficiency in solving problems. In normal persons, the three trends are also present, but they complement each other and make for inner harmony. People low in neurosis are much more flexible: They can alternatively give in to others, fight others, or keep to themselves, as appropriate. In contrast, neurotic individuals are driven to fight, to comply, to be aloof, regardless of whether or not their behavior is appropriate to the circumstances (Horney, 1945, pp. 34–47).

To illustrate how the three contradictory attitudes operate on an unconscious level to create basic conflict in the neurotic, let us examine the case of one of Horney's patients, a woman named Clare.

Clare, a 30-year-old magazine editor, entered therapy because she was easily overcome by a paralyzing fatigue that interfered with her work and social life. She could do routine work but could not finish any difficult tasks. Clare had been married when she was 23; her husband died three years later. Since his death, she had established a relationship with another man, which continued throughout the period of psychoanalysis. According to Clare, both relationships were satisfying sexually, as well as otherwise.

In the course of the analysis, Horney discovered that Clare had a compulsive modesty, a need to force others to recognize her superiority, and a compulsive dependence upon her partner. Clare was unaware of any of these trends in herself at the outset of therapy.

Horney made the diagnosis of compulsive modesty by listening carefully to Clare's reports about herself. She continually described herself as not very intelligent, attractive, or gifted and tended to dismiss any evidence to the contrary. She claimed that others were clearly superior to her. If others disagreed with her, she automatically assumed that they were right. She recalled that, when her husband started an affair with another woman, she said nothing in opposition, although the experience was deeply painful. She even managed to consider his behavior justified, on the grounds that the other woman was more attractive and affectionate. Clare also found it impossible to spend money on herself. She could not bring herself to buy dresses or books or to take trips. And even though she was an executive, it was impossible for her to give orders. If she was forced to do so, she did so in a very apologetic way.

The consequences of this self-effacing trend were discontent and a general lowering of self-confidence. Clare was basically unaware of her discontent and was truly surprised when she had crying spells. Eventually, she began to realize that intense anxiety lurked behind her facade of modesty. The realization came when she was about to offer other company executives a suggestion for improving her magazine. About to make her recommendation, she experienced intense panic. When she made the suggestion anyway, a sudden attack of diarrhea forced her to leave the room during discussion of the idea. When she returned, she found the discussion moving in her favor, and her panic subsided. When her plan was finally accepted, she felt elated.

The next day, she came to Horney's office for a session and told the therapist of her experience. When Horney remarked that the adoption of the suggestion was a triumph, Clare became annoyed and rejected her congratulations. It had been presumptuous of her to offer such a plan; who was she to know better than the others? But gradually Clare began to realize that, by suggesting a plan, she had ventured forth from her narrow lifestyle and taken a risk. She also realized that she was ambitious and did have a strong desire for social recognition and success. These needs had been repressed, but they were continually operating on an unconscious level and striving for expression. The facade of modesty was a means of making her feel safe. It prevented her from having to test her ideas and abilities in direct competition with others and, most importantly, from having to cope with anticipated failure or rejection. The result of these insights was that Clare began to have more confidence in herself.

Clare also was highly dependent on men, although she did not realize it initially and claimed that there was nothing wrong in her relationships. Analysis revealed that she was totally devoted to her current male friend; her thoughts centered around a call or letter or visit from him. Hours spent without him she considered boring and empty, and she felt totally miserable about incidents that she interpreted as utter neglect by him. She had fantasies about him, in which he was a great and masterful man and she was his slave. In her dreams, he gave her anything she wanted and made her into a famous writer.

The main feature of her compulsive dependence was an entirely repressed parasitic attitude, an unconscious wish to have the partner supply the content of her life, take responsibility for her, solve all her problems, and make her into a great person without any effort on her part. This neurotic striving alienated her from him because the inevitable disappointments she felt when he could not fulfill her unrealistic expectations prompted her to become deeply irritated and angry with him. For fear of losing him, much of this anger was repressed, but some of it emerged in occasional explosions. Eventually, through analysis, Clare began to understand her deep dependency on her friend and the reasons for her hostility and anger. Her fatigue appeared only occasionally, rather than continually, as it had before. She also became more capable of productive writing, although she still suffered occasionally from writer's block. Her relationship with her partner became more spontaneous and honest. Her behavior became less compulsive and defensive, and both she and Horney were pleased with the substantial progress she had made at the time the analysis was terminated (Horney, 1942, pp. 75–88).

Personality Development

Horney's Critique of Freud

Horney agreed with Freud that adult personality structure and functioning are influenced tremendously by early childhood experiences. Like him, she also believed that unconscious processes play an important role in the formation of character and that the use of defenses is an inevitable outgrowth of people's attempts to cope with inner conflicts and anxiety. She also agreed that the removal of these defenses is essential for adequate and effective functioning. Despite this common ground, Horney disagreed with Freud that the inherited set of sexual and aggressive strivings is more important than the environment, that the important experiences in the formation of character are primarily sexual in nature, and that, in adulthood, people are doomed to repeat compulsively ways of behaving learned in childhood (Horney, 1939, p. 33). Finally, Horney believed that Freud's theory of psychosexual development was essentially invalid. In particular, she strongly criticized Freud's explanations of the role played by the Oedipal conflict and penis envy in the formation of female character and his theory of **female masochism**.

Do Women Really Want to Be Men?

According to Freud, many abnormalities seen in women grow out of their frustrated wishes to be men. He maintained that the most upsetting event in the development of girls is their discovery that boys have penises and they do not. They react to this discovery with what Freud called **penis envy**, the wish to have a penis, too, and envy toward the more fortunate male sex. Since their supposed deficiency is an unalterable fact, they transfer the wish for a penis to a wish for a child, particularly a male child who will bring the penis with him. They then identify with their mothers, hoping to become mothers themselves some day, as a means of indirectly obtaining the desired object.

In Freud's view, women's most significant attitudes and wishes derive their energy from penis envy. Thus, happiness during pregnancy results from symbolic possession of the penis (the male child in the womb). Menstrual cramps are caused by fantasies in which the father's penis has been swallowed. Women who try to surpass men or to disparage them are characterized as castrating females. Defloration during sex may arouse hostility toward the partner because it is experienced as castration. Women's physical modesty is seen ultimately as a wish to hide the deficiency of her genitals (Horney, 1939, pp. 101–104).

In sum, the Freudian view of development leads to the unequivocal conclusion that women are inferior creatures. Feminine inferiority feelings are simply an expression of contempt for their own sex because of their lack of a penis. Furthermore, little can be done to eliminate this self-loathing because the perceived defect is biologically based and cannot be altered. Anatomy is destiny, according to Freud.

Horney's criticism of Freud's view was a complicated one. She considered Freud a genius who had identified an important phenomenon in women, but she questioned his attribution of the phenomenon completely to instinctual sources. She thought that penis envy did derive to some extent from anatomical differences between the sexes, but that more important sources were the cultural and social forces in a patriarchal society that indoctrinates both sexes with the assumption of male superiority and female inferiority.

Anatomically, she maintained that penis envy has its origins in the girl's desire to urinate like a boy. She believed that fantasies of omnipotence are more easily associated with the jet of urine passed by the male. As evidence, she cited a game played by European boys, in which they would stand at right angles to each other and urinate to make a cross, concentrating their thoughts simultaneously on a particular person and wishing he or she would die. This experience is laden with feelings of magic and power. The significance of the cross is heightened by its religious connotation and the idea that X marks the spot. In addition, males are able to look at themselves in the act of urinating, thereby satisfying their sexual curiosity, whereas females are unable to see or perform in the same way because their genitals are hidden. Thus women, according to Horney, may actively envy males because of the ready visibility of their genitals. Finally, a male derives pleasure from holding his penis while urinating, and this may be construed as permission to masturbate. Females, in contrast, are often forbidden to touch or manipulate their vaginas and clitorises (Horney, 1967, pp. 39–41).

Socially and culturally, Horney maintained, our whole civilization is essentially masculine. Its laws, religion, morality, science, art, and business are the creation of men. Men are clearly in the dominant or superior position, while women occupy an inferior place. Unfortunately, in Horney's judgment, women have adapted themselves to the inferior status assigned to them by men and judge themselves as inferior (Horney, 1967, pp. 55–57). This perverse adaptation results not only in self-hatred, but in contempt for other women and resentment and hostility toward men. Thus, they lack faith in women's capacity for any real achievement and minimize success whenever it occurs. Even motherhood appears as an unfair burden to women who have adopted the masculine disregard and disrespect for the accomplishments of women. Feeling that they have been discriminated against by fate, women also make unconscious claims for compensation. In their fantasies, they reject the feminine role and wish for all the qualities and privileges that in our culture are regarded as masculine: strength, courage, success, sexual freedom, and independence (Horney, 1939, p. 108).

Thus, Horney saw penis envy not as a castration complex—felt loss of the penis and fantasies of its symbolic replacement—but rather as a justifiable envy of qualities associated with masculinity in our culture. According to Horney, women must realize that their inferiority feelings are based upon unconscious acceptance of an ideology of male superiority, and that their feelings about themselves can only be changed if efforts are made to make society itself more democratic and egalitarian. Anatomy is not necessarily destiny, in Horney's opinion, although it does play a part.

Horney's Humanistic View of Development

As we have seen, Horney believed that the unique social and cultural experiences of children are crucial in determining their adult personalities, and that harsh and arbitrary treatment of children by parents lays the foundation for neurosis. Healthy development, she believed, was predicated on warm, fair, considerate, supportive, and respectful treatment by the parents (Horney, 1942, p. 43). In her **humanistic view of development**, Horney maintained that everyone was special and had a unique set of potentials that would flourish under wise parental guidance. These intrinsic potentialities she called the **real self**. With proper support, she believed, everyone could develop toward self-realization; that is, they could develop the depth and clarity of their own feelings, thoughts, wishes, and interests, the ability to tap their own resources and gifts, the faculty to express themselves, and the ability to relate to others spontaneously (Horney, 1950, p. 17). Unfortunately, however, many people do not receive proper guidance. Instead they are treated arbitrarily and with a lack of respect, and the result is alienation from the real self.

Alienation and the idealized self   Horney maintained that unfavorable environmental conditions impair the realistic inner confidence of people and force them to evolve defenses. Because their energies are directed toward the development of defenses in order to feel safe, attempts to develop their real selves are overridden. To the extent that safety is paramount, people's innermost feelings and thoughts recede in importance and become blurred. They are no longer the masters of their destiny but are driven by their neurotic needs. Alienation from their real selves causes people to seek a sense of stability and identity, a sense that they are significant and worthwhile.

The answer for neurotics is to create an **idealized image** of themselves. Such an image endows them with unlimited abilities and powers. In their imaginations, they become heroes, geniuses, supreme lovers, saints, and gods. These images provide an avenue for dealing with their basic conflicts. According to Horney, neurotics eventually try to actualize the **idealized self** by achieving success, glory, and triumph in the outside world. They are relentlessly and painfully driven to be perfect; they believe that they should be able to do everything, know everything, and like everyone. Horney calls this compulsive need the **tyranny of the shoulds**:

> He should be the [epitome] of honesty, generosity, considerateness, justice, dignity, courage, unselfishness. He should be the perfect lover, husband, teacher. He should be able to endure everything, should like everybody, should love his parents, his wife, his country; or, he should not be attached to anything or anybody, nothing should matter to him, he should never feel hurt, and he should always be serene and unruffled. He should always enjoy life; or, he should be above pleasure and enjoyment. He should be spontaneous; he should always control his feelings. He should know, understand, and foresee everything. He should be able to solve every problem of his own, or of others, in no time. He should be able to overcome every difficulty of his as soon as he sees it. He should never be tired or fall ill. He should always be able to find a job. He should be able to do things in one hour which can only be done in two to three hours. (Horney, 1950, p. 65)

Neurotics cling to these impossible standards because their attainment promises to satisfy all their inner conflicts and to eliminate all pain and anxiety. Unfortunately, self-idealization does not work. When neurotics compare the **actual self** (the self as it is at the moment) against the measuring rod of the idealized self, the actual self inevitably falls short. Poor performance during lovemaking, for example, belies the belief that they are great lovers. Hesitation and stammering while asking the boss for a promotion is clearly at variance with their view of themselves as articulate speakers. Working at a menial job is a constant reminder that they have not achieved high occupational status and success. As a result of the discrepancies that they experience between their actual and idealized selves, neurotics are filled with self-contempt and hatred. Although they are aware of the results—feeling inferior, tormented, guilty— they are completely unaware that they themselves have brought about these painful feelings and self-evaluations (Horney, 1950, p. 116). Thus, self-hate is essentially an unconscious process. Rather than examine themselves critically, neurotics are prone to externalize their hatred and to see it as emanating from other people or institutions or from fate.

Externalization: Trying to keep the idealized self intact

The tendency of neurotics to experience internal processes as if they occurred outside the self and to hold external factors responsible for their difficulties is called **externalization**. In part, externalization involves projection, that is, the tendency to attribute one's own failings and shortcomings to others. It also involves perceiving feelings in others rather than in oneself. Thus, neurotics tend to believe that others are angry with them when actually they are angry with themselves. They attribute good feelings in themselves to outside forces such as the weather or to fate, successes to good luck, and so forth. Most importantly, the neurotic's self-contempt is externalized. In the aggressive type, the tendency is to despise others. Aggressive neurotics feel superior to others and reinforce their feelings of superiority by seeing others as inferior and worthy of contempt. In the compliant type, the tendency is to see others as filled with contempt for them. Horney believed that this projection is particularly damaging; it makes the compliant type of neurotic shy, inhibited, and withdrawn (Horney, 1945, p. 118).

In effect, externalization consists of the obliteration of the actual and real selves. It is designed to ensure survival of the idealized self. It does not work very well, however, and neurotics are forced to rely on other defenses for support.

Auxiliary approaches to artificial harmony

Horney described seven defenses used by neurotics to help them cope with their inner conflicts and with disturbances in their interpersonal relationships (Horney, 1945, pp. 131–140).

Blind spots   Many laypeople have wondered how neurotics are unable to perceive the overwhelmingly blatant discrepancies between their actual and idealized selves. Neurotics seem to have **blind spots**, areas in which obvious contradictions are blotted out or ignored. The reason, according to Horney, is that neurotics are often inordinately numb to their own experiences (Horney, 1945, p. 133).

Compartmentalization   The defense called **compartmentalization** involves the separation of beliefs or actions into categories (compartments), so that they do not appear inconsistent with one another. For example, a Ku Klux Klan member may convince himself that he is a Christian by maintaining that his Christian beliefs of love and tolerance extend only to humans; since, in his view, Black people are clearly animals and, therefore, inhuman, he can continue to hate and persecute them without feeling the conflict between his actions and his beliefs.

Rationalization   The form of self-deception called **rationalization** uses plausible excuses to justify one's perceived weaknesses or failures. For example, aggressive neurotics view feelings of remorse and sympathy for others as weakness. Therefore, an aggressive neurotic who sends flowers to his longtime colleague's widow as an expression of sympathy might justify his action by claiming that he sent them only because it was his duty as a fellow employee.

Excessive self-control The neurotic's compulsive need to restrict expression of emotions is termed **excessive self-control**.

> Persons who exert such control will not allow themselves to be carried away, whether by enthusiasm, sexual excitement, self-pity, or rage. In analysis they have the greatest difficulty in associating freely; they will not permit alcohol to lift their spirits and frequently prefer to endure pain rather than undergo anesthesia. In short, they seek to check all spontaneity. (Horney, 1945, p. 136)

Because the most destructive actions are violent ones prompted by rage, most of the neurotic's energy is directed toward controlling rage. However, the suppression of rage leads to an unconscious buildup of even more rage, which, in turn, requires even more self-control to choke it off.

Arbitrary rightness Doubt and indecision characterize the neurotic. Because these feelings are intolerable, neurotics employ **arbitrary rightness**; that is, they attempt to settle all disputes by declaring dogmatically that they are correct.

Elusiveness Neurotics who use **elusiveness** as a means of protection can never be pinned down to any statement; they deny ever having made the statement or claim that the other person misinterpreted their meaning. Elusive neurotics are continually equivocating and are unable to give a concrete report of any incident. As a result, the listener is confused as to what really did happen.

Horney maintained that this same confusion of truth reigns in the lives of neurotics. At times they are overly considerate; at others, ruthlessly inconsiderate. They can be highly domineering in some respects, self-effacing in others. Because of these inconsistencies, it is sometimes difficult for an analyst to guide them to an accurate identification of their underlying conflicts.

Cynicism The protective device of **cynicism** involves a denying and deriding of moral values. Neurotics tend to be Machiavellian in their outlook. They believe that people are not to be trusted, and that they can do whatever they please as long as they are not caught. They are people of expedience, not principle.

In summary, all of these irrational defenses help (at least temporarily) to maintain the neurotics' idealized conception; in so doing, they make healthy growth virtually impossible.

Empirical Evidence: Irrational Beliefs and Psychopathology

A common theme in Horney's theorizing about neurosis is that abnormal people have numerous irrational beliefs about themselves and others that create and increase their suffering and encourage ineffective ways of behaving in relationships with others. Thus, neurotics believe that they are paragons of virtue, brilliant thinkers, and great lovers; blame other people, fate, or institutions for their failures; claim to be invariably right; and convince themselves that no one can be trusted. They are driven by moral absolutes (the tyranny of the shoulds) that require them to act as though they were completely honest, courageous, and unselfish.

Horney's assertions concerning the link between irrational beliefs and psychopathology are supported by considerable correlational evidence. Studies have found that, the greater the number of irrational beliefs held by individuals, the more likely they are to be pessimistic and depressed (e.g., Chang & Bridewell, 1998, pp. 137–142;

Halamandaris & Power, 1997, pp. 93–104; Macavei, 2005, pp. 73–81; Moller, Rabe, & Nortje, 2001, pp. 259–270). Westphal and Wagner (1993, pp. 151–158) also found that pregnant adolescents held a greater number of irrational beliefs specific to sex, dating, and birth control and fewer beliefs that might deter pregnancy, compared to adolescents who had never been pregnant. Pregnant adolescents were more likely to believe before they became pregnant, for example, that: (1) "if a girl doesn't have a boyfriend, there is something wrong with her"; (2) "pregnancy can never happen to me"; and (3) "having a baby makes me an adult." Finally, Lamontagne, Boyer, Hetu, and Lacerte-Lamontagne (2000, pp. 63–65) showed that shoplifters tended to be depressed and often used irrational beliefs as a prelude to engaging in criminal behavior (e.g., "I am careful and smart; I will not get caught"; "Even if I do get caught, I will not be turned in and prosecuted").

Many studies have shown that marriages experiencing higher levels of distress are characterized by greater numbers of irrational beliefs. A study by Goodwin and Gaines (2004, pp. 267–279), for example, of married manual workers, students, and small business owners in three post-Communist countries (Georgia, Russia, and Hungary) found that the greater the number of dysfunctional beliefs, the greater the level of marital dissatisfaction reported by the couple.

In an earlier study comparing couples in therapy with couples not in therapy, Eidelson and Epstein (1982, pp. 715–720) found that those experiencing marital difficulties held a variety of dysfunctional beliefs. They believed, for instance, that disagreement with their spouses was destructive and indicative of a lack of love or even imminent divorce, even though conflicts based upon interpersonal differences are an inevitable part of any relationship. Unhappy couples also believed that partners who truly know and care about each other should be able to sense each other's needs and preferences without explicit, direct communication; as a result, they put less effort into clear communication, and so suffered disappointment and escalation of conflict. Unhappy couples believed that they could not change themselves, nor could their partners change. Such an extreme belief led to feelings of helplessness and diminished satisfaction with the relationship. Finally, unhappy couples believed that they must be perfect sex partners (recall Horney's point that many neurotics believe that they are great lovers), and, accordingly, experienced anxiety and inhibition in the sexual sphere.

To change these irrational thoughts and move toward improved mental health, Horney maintained, therapists need to actively challenge the irrational beliefs and to replace them with more realistic thoughts and feelings. Cognitive therapists generally agree with Horney's contention, although they do not adopt much of Horney's psychoanalytic and humanistic approach to therapy (e.g., the emphasis on the role of unconscious factors in personality functioning, and the use of free association and dream analysis to uncover the source of the client's difficulties as a means of recognizing and accepting his or her real self), as we shall see. To bring about constructive change in distressed couples, modern cognitive therapists teach their clients that disagreements are part of any healthy relationship, and that it is realistic to voice these disagreements, as long as it is done in a respectful way and with the aim of finding constructive resolutions and improving the relationship. In the course of therapy, cognitive therapists also typically challenge their clients to examine the evidence they are using to maintain and strengthen any irrational beliefs they might have as a means of getting them to reconsider their positions and make constructive changes that would help their marriage. They also help their clients to change dysfunctional beliefs (e.g., "It's all his (her) fault" or "It's all my fault") by redistributing responsibility more realistically. Therapists also work with their clients to stop their absolutistic thinking whenever it occurs (e.g., "He (she) will never change, so what's the use of trying?" and "Once a slob, always a slob") by pointing out instances where the partner has acted in ways that run contrary to the spouse's absolutistic beliefs.

Therapists also help their clients to stop making negative comments continually about their spouses. They know that such negative thoughts and comments have a way of snowballing and being very hard to stop. Clients can be trained to picture a stop sign, or picture a wall, whenever they begin to become too critical, thereby stopping the destructive thought process. In addition, they can also be taught to give more praise to the partner where it is deserved and realistic to do so. By using these techniques and others, therapists can help eliminate much of the distress in these marriages (Freeman & Oster, 1998, pp. 111–115).

Assessment Techniques

Horney agreed with Freud that free association and dream analysis could help therapists identify the sources of neurotics' problems; she disagreed with him, however, in interpreting what they revealed. Whereas Freud continually interpreted patients' free associations and dream reports in terms of thwarted sexual or aggressive strivings, Horney's interpretations focused on the disturbances her patients experienced in their interpersonal relationships and on the neurotic trends they used to cope with their basic anxieties and fears.

Horney also saw the personal relationship between analyst and patient differently than did Freud. Freud believed strongly that psychoanalysis was a science. He perceived himself as an objective observer whose role was to collect data and present them to the patients for their consideration and use. Accordingly, the analyst must refrain from making value judgments about the patients' personal qualities and experiences, so as to allay patients' fears of condemnation and encourage freer expression of their thoughts and feelings. Horney, however, thought it impossible for an analyst to refrain from making value judgments during the course of therapy. In her opinion, patients could sense that the analyst was indeed making such judgments and trying to hide the fact only served to make the relationship worse. Instead, the analyst should be more honest and open with patients and more active and directive in offering suggestions. Such an approach, she believed, would facilitate the growth of the relationship and lead more readily to a cure.

Theory's Implications for Therapy

Neurotics are alienated from their real selves and from others. They have identified with an idealized self and so have become pretenders who are afraid of having their limitations exposed by others. Horney believed that they will only have a chance to realize their potential when they are able to relinquish their illusions about themselves and their illusory goals. Removing the obstructions to growth, however, is a long and difficult process, for neurotics are strongly committed to defending their illusions. Aggressive types, for example, hope that analysis will remove all impediments to their achieving unqualified triumphs and unquestioned sainthood. Thus, they think only of perfecting their idealized selves, whereas the analyst seeks to help remove their idealized selves and to promote the growth of their real selves.

For Horney, therapy is a human relationship, and all the difficulties that neurotics have in their relationships with other people operate during the therapeutic process. Patients may become argumentative, sarcastic, or assaultive. They may be evasive, refuse to discuss a subject, or talk with emotionless intelligence about their problems, as if such problems were unimportant. They may react with rage and become abusive toward the analyst. Yet many of these behaviors are signposts directing the therapist's inquiries; that is, they provide clues that point to the presence of underlying conflicts. Patients tend to be highly threatened by the therapist's inquiries and to experience considerable anxiety. For the patients, this anxiety is terribly painful, but for the therapist it may also have a positive meaning. It may indicate that the patients are now strong enough to take the risk of confronting their problems more directly. According to Horney, the therapist's inquiries help patients become more aware of all the obstructive forces operating within them. She believed, however, that this self-knowledge must not remain at an intellectual level only; it must become an emotional experience as well. In her view, intellectual insight is important, but it does not have sufficient impact on the patient to promote change. Only when patients feel the intensity of the unconscious forces operating within them are they motivated to relinquish their illusions.

Once patients have given up their illusions, the therapist focuses on helping them find their real selves. Through free association and dream analysis, their real selves may begin to emerge. Patients are reinforced for any sign of greater independence in their thinking, of assuming responsibility for themselves, and of being interested in the truth about themselves. They are also encouraged to seek their own identities through self-analysis outside of the therapeutic setting. The analyst takes care to point out any signs of progress made by patients in their human relationships. These glimpses of growth have a highly positive impact on patients, who experience a sense of fulfillment that is different from anything they have known before. This acts as the best incentive for them to work harder at their own growth, toward greater self-realization. As they grow, they begin to realize that there are other problems in the world besides their own. They begin to extend themselves to others—their family, community, nation, and world. They become more willing to accept responsibility not only for themselves, but for others as well. They begin to find the inner certainty that comes from a feeling of belonging through active and unselfish participation (Horney, 1950, pp. 333–365).

Evaluative Comments

We turn now to an evaluation of Horney's theory in terms of our six criteria.

Comprehensiveness   Because of its primary focus on abnormal rather than normal phenomena, Horney's theory is limited in its comprehensiveness. In discussing the etiology and cure for different types of abnormal phenomena such as neurosis, however, she devotes considerable attention to the impact of complicated social and cultural forces on their development and maintenance. Thus, the explanatory base for her theory of abnormal behavior is much richer than Freud's. Possibly the most original aspect of her theory is the concept of the idealized self and the discrepancy between this idealized self and the real self. Here we see her humanistic interest in understanding not only the forces that produce and maintain neurosis, but the prerequisites of positive growth and optimal personality functioning.

Precision and testability   Many of Horney's concepts are abstract and difficult to define precisely. To her credit, Horney made a strenuous effort to define her terms; nonetheless, some of them remain relatively imprecise and unclear. Given these definitional ambiguities, it is very difficult to design adequate tests of the theory.

Parsimony   Horney's theory is clearly not overly simple. Her explanations of the origins and development of neurosis are rich and complicated and seem generally adequate to the task. Thus, her theory seems parsimonious.

Empirical validity   Research interest in Horney's theory has been almost nonexistent until recently. There have been few attempts to test her theory primarily because psychometrically sound measures of her theoretical concepts have not been available. However, the creation of a hypercompetitiveness scale (and very recently a competition avoidance scale) has generated some interest in testing parts of her theory. Also, the development of a new instrument to measure Horney's ideas about the three neurotic trends promises to generate more research tests of her theory of neurosis (Coolidge et al., 2001, pp. 1387–1400).

Heuristic value   Horney's ideas about the tyranny of the shoulds are highly original and are utilized by Ellis in dealing with the sources of depression (Ellis, 1987, p. 123). Although cognitive therapists and researchers use many kinds of therapeutic procedures that cannot be directly traced to Horney's theory of psychotherapy, Ellis's **rational emotive behavior therapy** is in many respects an outgrowth of Horney's recommendations concerning the treatment of patients (Ellis, 1995, pp. 162–163). In rational emotive behavior therapy, patients are seen as possessing a number of irrational beliefs that lead to various kinds of self-destructive behavior. Therapists then challenge these beliefs as a way of changing them and subsequently patients substitute more rational, reality-based beliefs. If these changes occur, people will be more likely act in more constructive ways. For example, patients may hold the irrational beliefs: "Everybody must love me," and "I must love everybody." The possession of such beliefs is likely to produce anger, resentment, and eventually depression when patients learn that not only do certain people not love them but even dislike them. Also, they may come to realize that, despite all their efforts to the contrary, there are some people they cannot love. When more rational beliefs are implemented (e.g., "I am worthwhile even if I don't love everyone," and "It might be nice to have everyone love me, but I know that such a situation is an impossibility so I am not going to worry about it continuously"), more realistic and adaptive behaviors are likely to follow.

Also Horney's theorizing about human growth and self-realization mark her as an important early contributor to the development of humanistic psychology.

Applied value   In addition to its heuristic value, Horney's theory has had an important impact on the work of cognitive-behavioral therapists, who help to alleviate the suffering of many clinical clients.

CRITICAL THINKING QUESTIONS

1. Name and define three kinds of competitive attitude. How are they differentially related to psychological health? In your opinion, what is the predominant competitive attitude in America today? Give reasons for your answer. What kind of competitive attitude do you and your friends have?

2. How are Horney's ideas on the development of women consistent with the teachings of feminists today?

3. Why are the spontaneity and expansiveness that characterize the healthy person missing in the neurotic?

4. Is it always unhealthy or inappropriate to blame others for your failures, as suggested by Horney? Can you think of any instances when you and/or a friend failed at something, and it was not your fault and/or the fault of your friend?

5. Horney thought that each person had a real self consisting of worthwhile, intrinsic potentialities that awaited further development. Have you been able to identify such potential strengths in yourself? What are they and what have you done to facilitate their development?

GLOSSARY

actual self   The self as it is at the moment, including all of the person's actual strengths and weaknesses.

aggressive types   Neurotic individuals who protect themselves against feelings of insecurity by exploiting others in order to feel superior.

arbitrary rightness   A protective device in which people are convinced that they are invariably correct in all their judgments.

basic anxiety   The painful psychological state in which a person feels isolated and helpless in a potentially hostile world.

basic conflict   The turmoil created within neurotics because the three major trends are incompatible with one another. As the person indiscriminately pursues the predominant trend and the fulfillment of the needs associated with it, he or she is unable to satisfy the needs associated with the two trends that are repressed.

blind spots   Defense mechanism in which painful experiences are denied or ignored because they are at variance with the idealized self.

compartmentalization   Defense mechanism by which neurotics alleviate tensions by separating beliefs and actions within themselves.

competition avoidance   Need by individuals to check their ruthless competitive ambition because of excessive fear of losing the affection and approval of others. The terms neurotic competitiveness and competition avoidance appear antithetical, but are not. Horney was a neo-Freudian so she believed that competition avoiders would consciously avoid competition, but unconsciously they would still be intensely and irrationally competitive. They can not show their hypercompetitiveness to others for fear of losing their affection and approval, so they repress their intense competitive feelings. These feelings, however, continue to operate on an unconscious level.

compliant types   Neurotic individuals who cope with feelings of basic anxiety by indiscriminately seeking the approval and affection of others through excessive conformity.

cynicism   Defense mechanism in which the person claims to believe in nothing so that he or she cannot be hurt or disappointed by others.

detached types   Neurotic individuals who protect themselves by continual avoidance of others.

elusiveness   Defense mechanism whereby a person refuses to take a position on anything so that he or she can never be proven wrong and criticized or ridiculed by others.

excessive self-control   Defense mechanism whereby a person exercises willpower, consciously or unconsciously, to keep emotional impulses under control.

externalization   Defense mechanism whereby a person experiences inner emotions externally and blames others for his or her own weaknesses and failings.

female masochism   For Freud, a perversion in which women experience a blending of pleasure and pain during certain activities and fantasies. He believed that male masochism occurred only in males with feminine (passive) natures.

humanistic view of development   An optimistic view of development that sees each person as having intrinsic and unique potential for constructive growth.

hypercompetitiveness   An attitude in which a person is driven to attain personal success at any cost.

idealized image   Fantasies of neurotic individuals in which they visualize themselves as perfect beings.

idealized self   The defensive identification of neurotics with their idealized images.

moving against people   A major neurotic trend that seeks to control basic anxiety through domination and exploitation of others.

moving away from people   A major neurotic trend that protects the person against basic anxiety by utter detachment and extreme self-sufficiency.

moving toward people   A major neurotic trend that protects the person against basic anxiety by self-effacement and obliteration.

personal development competitiveness   An attitude in which the primary focus is not on the outcome but on the enjoyment and mastery of the task.

penis envy   In Horney's view, essentially a sociocultural phenomenon in which women are indoctrinated to see themselves as inferior and men as superior. As a result, they unconsciously strive to emulate masculine goals and values and to obtain the advantages and privileges that accrue to members of the male sex.

personal development competitor Healthy competitor characterized by wanting to win, but not at all costs. Such a person is oriented primarily toward self-improvement and task mastery and sees his or her opponents as helping him or her to attain these goals.

primary psychopathy Disorder characterized by aggressiveness, callousness, and a lack of remorse for transgressions.

rational emotive behavior therapy A cognitive-restructuring therapy in which the faulty beliefs of neurotics that lead to emotional disturbance are identified, challenged, and then replaced with more constructive, rational ways of thinking and behaving.

rationalization A defense in which people ward off anxiety by offering plausible, but inaccurate, excuses for their conduct.

real self The unique set of potentials for constructive growth within each person.

secondary psychopathy Disorder characterized by excessive guilt and by a lack of clarity about life goals.

self-handicapping Giving plausible excuses for poor performance in order to protect the individual's self-esteem. (I failed that test because my friends forced me to go out partying with them the night before the test.)

tyranny of the shoulds Concept used by Horney to describe the moral imperatives that relentlessly drive neurotics to accept nothing less than perfection from themselves.

SUGGESTED READINGS

Horney, K. (1937). *The neurotic personality of our time.* New York: Norton.

Horney, K. (1945). *Our inner conflicts.* New York: Norton.

Horney, K. (1950). *Neurosis and human growth.* New York: Norton.

CHAPTER 6

Erikson's Psychoanalytic Ego Psychology

Courtesy of Jon Erikson

Biographical Sketch

Erik Homburger Erikson was born in 1902 near Frankfurt, Germany. His parents were Danish. Erikson never knew his natural father, who abandoned Erik and his mother before Erik was born. Although Erikson (1975, p. 27) maintained that his parents were legally married at the time of their separation, one prominent biographer thinks they were not and that Erik was probably an illegitimate child (Roazen, 1976, p. 96). In any event, soon after the abandonment, his mother left Denmark for Germany to be near friends and to await the birth of her child.

A few years after Erik's birth, she took him to a local Jewish pediatrician, Dr. Theodor Homburger, for treatment of a minor illness. The mother and doctor soon became friends, eventually fell in love, and were married. Erik was given his stepfather's name and taken to live in the doctor's home. To ensure that Erik would be comfortable in his new life, his mother and stepfather decided not to tell him his natural father had abandoned him. Still, he quickly developed an acute sense that something was wrong: Although his mother and stepfather were Jewish, his own physical appearance was clearly Scandinavian—tall, with blue eyes and blond hair. Adding to his confusion about his identity, he was called *goy* (non-Jew) by members of his parents' temple, but identified as a Jew by his classmates. Later, when he found out the truth about his heritage, his identity crisis worsened. Although he kept his stepfather's surname until well into adulthood, he eventually took the surname Erikson, for reasons that remain obscure—perhaps to affirm his Scandinavian heritage and establish his identification with the Danish father who had abandoned him (Roazen, 1976, pp. 98–99).

His early life was apparently serene in most other respects. Erik attended primary school from age 6 to 10 and a humanistic gymnasium (roughly equivalent to high school) until he was 18. He did not take well, however, to the strict and formal academic atmosphere, and he was not a good student (Coles, 1970, p. 14). His aversion to formal education continued throughout his life; he never earned a university degree.

Rejecting his stepfather's pleas to become a physician, Erikson left home after graduation and wandered through Europe, where he was free of attempts by his family and friends to convince him to make something of himself. During this moratorium, Erikson was wracked by doubts concerning his choice of an occupation. A year later, he returned home and enrolled in an art school to prepare for a career as an artist. He stayed for approximately a year, became restless again, and traveled to Munich, where he enrolled in another art school. After two years in Munich, he moved to Florence, a city he loved. There, he completely gave up sketching and simply wandered about the city; he was eager to learn about its culture and history. It should be noted that during this period he was not considered odd or sick by his family or friends, but simply as a wandering artist engaged in a natural struggle to find himself (Coles, 1970, pp. 14–15).

After his stay in Florence, he returned home and, at 25, prepared to settle down to study and teach art for a living. At that point, however, fate intervened. Erikson was asked by a former high school friend, Peter Blos, to join him as a teacher at a small, experimental American nursery school in Vienna. While at the school, Erikson met Anna Freud and her famous father, Sigmund, and was introduced into their circle of friends. Anna Freud was trying to convert a psychoanalytic interest in the childhood experiences of adults into a concern with understanding the dynamics of childhood itself (Coles, 1970). Erikson shared her pioneering interest and was eventually trained by her as a child analyst.

Though fully accepted by the psychoanalytic group surrounding Freud, Erikson was still unsure that he wanted to earn his living as a psychoanalyst. He still wanted to paint and draw. As his clinical experience with children grew, however, he began to see a connection between psychoanalysis and art. He observed that children's dreams and play involve important visual images that only later are translated into words in therapy (Coles, 1970, pp. 22–23). Also, Freud himself was becoming increasingly interested in the application of psychoanalysis to art, and this fact made a deep impression on Erikson (Coles, 1970, p. 24). Finally, Erikson began to think seriously about a career as an analyst, because he had acquired a new set of responsibilities. At a party he had met a young woman of mixed Canadian-American background, Joan Serson, and promptly fallen in love with her. A few months later, they were married. He finished his training at the Vienna Psycho-Analytical Society over the next four years and was elected a member in 1933.

Later that year Erikson, his wife, and their two young sons emigrated to the United States and settled in Boston. The first child analyst in Massachusetts, Erikson held positions at Harvard Medical School, Massachusetts General Hospital, and the Harvard Psychological Clinic. His thinking and his professional development were profoundly influenced by the Harvard intellectual community, most notably by anthropologists Margaret Mead, Gregory Bateson, Ruth Benedict, and Scudder Mekeel and psychologists Kurt Lewin, Henry Murray, and Lawrence Frank. In 1936, Erikson left Cambridge for New Haven, where he accepted a position at the Yale University Institute of Human Relations. In 1938, his third child, a daughter named Sue, was born. That same year, stimulated by conversations with his anthropologist colleagues, Erikson left New Haven to observe the behavior of Sioux children living on the Pine Ridge Reservation in South Dakota.

In 1939, Erikson moved to California, where he became affiliated with the Institute of Child Welfare at the University of California at Berkeley. Continuing his analytic work with children, Erikson devised "experimental play situations" designed to demonstrate the hopes, fears, struggles, defeats, and victories of growing children, as he sought to understand the crucial events in the life process. During this period, he also went north to observe the children of another Native American people, the Yurok. His anthropological work convinced him that the members of these cultures were not savages or sick simply because they utilized rituals and ceremonies to express their underlying needs; their rituals and ceremonies simply differed from the ones used in our own culture. He also refused to label their behavior neurotic or anal, as some analysts were prone to do; he rejected the idea that their unusual ritualistic behavior could be explained only by reference to unresolved conflicts surrounding toilet training during early childhood. Instead, he began to see that the Yurok and Sioux went through a series of developmental crises similar to the ones that people in our own society experienced and that successful resolution of these crises strengthened the members and moved them toward psychological health (Evans, 1967, p. 62). Thus, Erikson's anthropological experiences led him to recognize the limitations of Freud's theory of infantile sexuality and to replace it with a more general lifespan theory of ego development, in which he posited that the development of the person is marked by the unfolding of a series of stages that are universal to humankind.

In 1950, Erikson published *Childhood and Society*, a text that soon brought him international recognition as a leading spokesman of ego psychology. In it he presented the details of his theory of human development, which was based on his many years of cross-cultural research and clinical experience. He showed convincingly how various developmental stages unfold and how the ego changes, grows, and synthesizes a myriad of experiences. He also expanded on Freud's theory of infantile sexuality by placing and analyzing its basic propositions within a broader historical and sociocultural context. In brief, Erikson for the first time integrated psychoanalysis with history and anthropology.

While the *Childhood and Society* manuscript was in press, Erikson became involved in a political struggle between the University of California faculty and Regents. In the anti-Communist hysteria of the McCarthy era, the Regents passed a requirement that all faculty members sign a loyalty oath swearing that they were not members of the Communist party and did not support any party or organization that advocated the violent overthrow of the government. Erikson courageously refused to sign the oath. Instead, he resigned his university position and wrote an explanatory statement that was read to the members of the American Psychoanalytic Association. The letter read in part:

Dear Sirs:

I deeply appreciate the privilege of a free hearing before a committee of colleagues. With you I shall not play hide-and-seek regarding a question which must be implicit in what you wish to ask me and which must be explicit in what I shall have to say: I am not and have never been a Communist, inside "the party" or outside, in this country or abroad. One may say, then, why not acquiesce in an empty gesture if it saves the faces of very important personages, helps to allay public hysteria, and hurts nobody? My answer is that of a psychologist. I do believe that this gesture, which now saves face for some important people, will, in the long run, hurt people who are much more important: the students. Too much has been said of academic freedom for the faculty; I am concerned about certain dangers to the spirit of the student body, dangers which may emanate from such "compromises" as we have been asked to accept. For many students, their years of study represent their contact with thought and theory, their only contact with men who teach them how to see two sides of a question and yet to be decisive in their conclusions, how to understand and yet to act with conviction. Young people are rightfully suspicious and embarrassingly discerning. I do not believe they can remain unimpressed by the fact that the men who are to teach them to think and to act judiciously and spontaneously must undergo a political test; must sign a statement which implicitly questions the validity of their own oath of office; must abrogate "commitments" so undefined that they must forever suspect themselves and one another; and must confess to an "objective truth" which they know only too well is elusive. Older people like ourselves can laugh this off; in younger people, however, and especially in those more important students who are motivated to go into teaching, a dangerous rift may well occur between the "official truth" and those deep and often radical doubts which are the necessary condition for the development of thought.

In this sense, I may say that my conscience did not permit me to sign the contract after having sworn that I would do my job to the best of my ability. (Coles, 1970, pp. 157–158)

In 1951, Erikson moved east once more and worked at the Austen Riggs Center in Stockbridge, Massachusetts, an institute for psychoanalytic training and research.

In 1958, he published a psychohistorical account of the life of theologian Martin Luther, *Young Man Luther: A Study in Psychoanalysis and History*. His work became increasingly popular among psychologists, historians, psychiatrists, anthropologists, philosophers, theologians, and biologists, as well as among students, and he was invited to lecture in colleges and universities all over the world (Coles, 1970, p. 255).

In 1960, Erikson returned to Harvard, where he taught an extremely popular undergraduate course entitled "The Human Life Cycle." (According to Erikson, his students irreverently dubbed it "From Womb to Tomb.") Erikson remained at Harvard until his retirement in 1970. Among the noteworthy texts he authored during this period were *Insight and Responsibility* (1964), *Identity: Youth and Crisis* (1968), and *Gandhi's Truth* (1969), a brilliant account of the life of India's nonviolent political leader, Mahatma Gandhi, which earned Erikson both the National Book Award and a Pulitzer Prize. He also published *In Search of Common Ground* (1973), *Dimensions of a New Identity: The 1973 Jefferson Lectures in the Humanities* (1974), *Life History and the Historical Moment* (1975), *Toys and Reasons: Stages in the Ritualization of Experience* (1977), *Identity and the Life Cycle: A Reissue* (1979), *The Life Cycle Completed* (1982), and *Vital Involvement in Old Age* (1986).

In 1978, Harvard awarded Erikson an honorary doctorate, and in 1982 he established the Erik H. and Joan M. Erikson Center to provide a forum for interdisciplinary studies of the life cycle. He continued his professional contributions through writing and consulting with various groups across the United States until shortly before his death in 1994 (Kroger, 1989, p. 12). His final days were spent in a nursing home in Harwich, Massachusetts, on Cape Cod. Following his death, Mrs. Erikson received letters of condolence from people throughout the world. Among them was a very warm and personal letter from the President of the United States at that time, Bill Clinton, who praised Erikson's many professional contributions and concluded that Erikson had clearly "made a tremendous difference in our world" (Wallerstein, 1995, p. 174).

Concepts and Principles

Ego Psychology: Liberalizing the Psychoanalytic Position

Erikson's position represents a systematic extension and liberalization of Freud's view of the role of the ego in personality functioning. Freud saw the ego as a relatively weak agency that operated in the service of the powerful id. In his judgment, ego functioning was primarily concerned with satisfying the person's biological needs by seeking realistic outlets that did not offend the moral prescriptions of a largely punitive superego, or inhibiting the id's urges when suitable objects for impulse gratification were not available.

In contrast to this traditional view, Erikson proposed that the ego often operates independently of id emotions and motivations. In his view, portions of the ego are neither defensive in nature nor concerned with the control of biological urges. Instead, the ego often functions to help individuals adapt constructively to the challenges presented by their surroundings. This new perspective examines ego function in relation to society. It provides a more positive view of personality, in which the ego has organizing and synthesizing functions that help people resolve inner conflicts as well as environmental challenges. Within this elaborated framework, the ego is a powerful agency that typically operates to promote health.

Ego psychology thus emphasizes the integration of biological and psychosocial forces in the determination of personality functioning. It gives special attention to the unique interpersonal, cultural, and historical context within which people face a common series of developmental crises. Each culture, in Erikson's view, has evolved unique ways of helping individuals resolve their crises so that their egos can be strengthened. Thus, the focus in Erikson's psychology is on the emergence of a strong ego identity as individuals resolve the crises inherent in the developmental process.

The Epigenetic Principle

Like Freud, Erikson postulated that human development is governed by the **epigenetic principle** that development occurs in a series of stages, universal to humankind, that unfold in a predetermined sequence. Unlike Freud, however, he placed much greater emphasis on the growth and positive functioning of the ego. He posited further that ego development occurs throughout the lifetime, not just in early childhood. Erikson believed that, at critical points in the maturational process, people everywhere have "a readiness to be driven toward, to be aware of, and to interact with a widening social radius and ... that society, in principle, tends to be so constituted as to meet and invite this succession of potentialities for interaction and attempts to safeguard and to encourage the proper rate and the proper sequence of their unfolding" (Erikson, 1963, p. 270).

Each stage, according to Erikson, is marked by a particular psychosocial **crisis**, or turning point—a crucial period in which a decisive turn one way or another is unavoidable (Erikson, 1964, pp. 138–139). Crises are moments of decision between progress or regression in development. Erikson optimistically believed that the general tendency in human nature is toward the resolution of crises in a way that moves people toward a strong self-identity. He maintained that "such developmental and normative crises differ from imposed, traumatic, and neurotic crises in that the very process of growth provides new energy even as society offers new and specific opportunities according to its dominant conception of the phases of life" (Erikson, 1968b, pp. 162–163). Whether these crises are resolved satisfactorily depends to a considerable degree on the quality of the individual's psychosocial experiences. It also depends on the person's active attempts to analyze and integrate experiences and to utilize emerging abilities and skills. Thus, Erikson did not see people as passively buffeted around by outside forces. Rather, he saw them as actively seeking to deal with their experiences in a constructive, growth-promoting way.

Positive resolution of each crisis contributes to a progressive strengthening of the ego, whereas negative resolution results in the ego's weakening. A positive resolution at one stage also increases the chances that individuals will be able to resolve the crises at later stages. Conversely, an inability to resolve a crisis at a given stage reduces the chances of successful adaptation during succeeding stages. Thus, the stages are interrelated and interdependent (Erikson, 1963, p. 272); each one builds on the stages that precede it. Also, once a crisis has been successfully resolved during the stage at which it first emerged, it does not mean that individuals have moved totally beyond it forever as they continue movement through the life-span. The ego strengths that they have acquired can continue to be present in later stages and to influence the individual's behavior in constructive ways. Or the same issues can reemerge during later stages and be readdressed by individuals, with even stronger, more positive resolutions occurring. On the negative side, issues that have been resolved earlier can reemerge during later stages as individuals confront new problems. A failure to resolve them adequately could result in a decline in ego strength (cf. Cramer, 2004, p. 281).

In describing ego strength, Erikson used the term **virtue**, meaning "inherent strength or active quality." Virtues are human qualities or strengths that emerge from successful resolution of the crises associated with various developmental stages (Erikson, 1964, p. 113). In Erikson's view, each stage provides the opportunity for the establishment of a unique strength or virtue. The establishment of each virtue, however, is not an irreversible achievement, nor does it make the individual impervious to new conflicts later in the developmental process (Erikson, 1963, pp. 273–274). Finally, crisis resolution is never completely positive or negative (Evans, 1967, p. 15); rather, each conflict resolution carries with it both positive and negative learning about events and people. Positive crisis resolution occurs when the ratio of positive to negative learning is weighted in favor of the positive.

Personality Development

The Stages of Ego Development

Erikson postulated eight stages of ego development. The first four are closely wedded to Freud's oral, anal, phallic, and latency stages, although Erikson placed less emphasis than did Freud on the sexual bases of the conflicts in these stages, and more on the individual's social experiences. The remaining four stages show little reliance on Freud's theorizing.

Table 6.1 presents a schema of the various stages.

Oral-sensory stage: Basic trust versus mistrust The first stage corresponds closely to Freud's oral stage and occurs during the first year of life. Pleasurable sensations center around the mouth, and the focal activity is feeding. The infant lives and loves through its mouth. The mother is the one who typically ministers to the infant's needs, and healthy development in the infant depends on the quality of her care. The mother's attitude toward her child-care function is shaped by the society in which she lives. If the society downgrades the status of motherhood, the result will likely be a caretaker who resents her role; if society praises and extols the virtues of motherhood, her attitude is likely to be healthy and constructive.

In Erikson's view, if the mother acts in a loving and consistent way, the infant is likely to develop a sense of **basic trust**. As they interact, the infant comes to recognize the mother by sight, her touch, the sound of her voice, and even her smell. All of the senses are part of the interaction process between the two. The infant's first social achievement is his or her eventual willingness to let the mother out of sight without becoming unduly anxious, on the basis of an inner certainty that she will return to feed and care for the infant. Such certainty provides the rudiments of an ego identity because it depends on the infant's recognition that people are dependable (Erikson, 1963, p. 247). The basic trust that develops between mother and child is not totally one-sided; it is truly an interpersonal experience. Not only does the mother's dependability foster trust in the infant;

TABLE 6.1 THE EIGHT STAGES OF EGO DEVELOPMENT

Stage	Estimated Age	Ego Crisis	Ego Strength
1. Oral-sensory	Birth–1	Basic trust vs. mistrust	Hope
2. Muscular-anal	2–3	Autonomy vs. shame and doubt	Will
3. Locomotor-genital	4–5	Initiative vs. guilt	Purpose
4. Latency	6–12	Industry vs. inferiority	Competence
5. Adolescence	13–19	Identity vs. role confusion	Fidelity
6. Young adulthood	20–24	Intimacy vs. isolation	Love
7. Middle adulthood	25–64	Generativity vs. stagnation	Care
8. Late adulthood	65–death	Ego integrity vs. despair	Wisdom

Source: Adapted from Erikson, 1950, 1963.

the infant, too, begins to act in a trustworthy way. As the infant develops teeth, he or she is driven to bite. The infant must learn not to engage in this behavior, however, lest the mother withdraw in anger and pain. If the infant learns properly, the mother will come to trust her child, and both parties can engage in a relaxed and mutually gratifying set of experiences.

In contrast, a sense of **basic mistrust** is created if the mother acts in an unreliable, aloof, and rejecting way. The mother's lack of dependability and care is likely to frustrate, anger, and enrage the infant, who becomes more demanding and unpredictable. The feeling of being deprived also leaves a residue of mistrust that continues to have effects later in the developmental process. If the interpersonal experiences with the mother are generally more positive than negative, the child develops an attitude toward others that is more trusting than mistrusting. The healthy person is not completely trusting, however; such a person would be too naive, gullible, and easily hurt by others. A certain amount of mistrust is healthy. Some people are dangerous, and precautions must be taken to ensure survival.

If this stage has a positive resolution, in which more trust than mistrust emerges, the outcome is a sense of confidence and **hope**. The beginnings of hope established during the first stage of life can be dashed later if new pressures or conflicts arise, or they can be strengthened substantially by subsequent positive experience. Society, in Erikson's judgment, provides an opportunity for the perpetuation and strengthening of trust through its religious institutions. Trust, in his view, becomes the capacity for faith. Whereas Freud viewed religious beliefs as unhealthy delusions that prevented people from dealing constructively with reality, Erikson saw religious institutions as "giving concerted expression to adults' need to provide the young and the weak with a world-image sustaining hope" (Erikson, 1964, p. 153). Erikson's view of organized religion, however, was not entirely positive. He did recognize that, all too often, the church has exploited the most infantile strivings in human beings, for its own self-aggrandizement (Erikson, 1964, p. 153).

Muscular-anal stage: Autonomy versus shame and doubt Erikson's second stage is closely related to Freud's anal stage and occurs during the second and third years of life. During this period, the child's muscles begin to mature, and he or she starts to learn how to exercise control over them. This is the period during which toilet training occurs in our society. Youngsters must learn to control their anal sphincter muscles so that elimination of waste materials can be accomplished in a manner deemed appropriate by society. Erikson pointed out that intense conflicts over whether to hold on or let go do not arise in all societies. In many agrarian cultures, for example, parents ignore anal behavior and leave it to older children to take toddlers out to the bushes so that they can perform the elimination function. The toddlers learn by imitating the behavior of the older children. In our society, however, the scene is set for intense conflict, according to Erikson, because we have as our ideal the always clean, punctual, and deodorized body (Erikson, 1968b, pp. 107–108). Thus, children must be trained to obey, and this leads to a conflict of wills and a power struggle between parents and children. Ironically, just as children have learned to trust their parents and the world, they must now learn how to assert their independence. They must become self-willed and take chances with their trust in order to establish what they can do by themselves (Evans, 1967, p. 19).

A sense of **autonomy** and self-control is engendered if parents guide their children's behavior gradually and firmly. When this is the predominant treatment, children experience an increased sense of pride in their accomplishments and good feelings toward others. The virtue that emerges is **will**, defined as "the unbroken determination to exercise free choice as well as self-restraint" (Erikson, 1964, p. 119), a gradual increase in the power to exercise judgment and decision.

If parents are either too permissive or too harsh and demanding during this stage, children experience a sense of defeat that can lead to **shame and doubt** concerning their ability to make effective judgments and to exercise control over their lives. One result may be the neurotic attempt to regain control by compulsive action (Erikson, 1963, p. 252).

Individuals who develop a sense of control over their lives tend later to support society's legal institutions to the extent that they are equitable in the administration of the law. They see that only through adherence to the law can they and others preserve their own freedom, independence, and sense of rightful dignity (Erikson, 1963, p. 254).

Locomotor-genital stage: Initiative versus guilt   The third stage, ages 4 and 5, bears some resemblance to Freud's phallic stage. If the resolution of conflict in the previous stage has been successful, children feel that they are now individuals in their own right. During the third stage, their **initiative** is sparked, and they must find out what kind of people they may become (Erikson, 1968b, p. 115). Children at this stage become curious about their parents, their friends, and their surroundings. Now that their developing bodies allow them to locomote more freely, they independently seek out more contact with others beyond the family circle. They engage in play and other experimental activities with their peers. Their language becomes refined, and they ask incessant questions about innumerable things. Their imaginations are very active, and they fantasize about being adults. There is also a great deal of playacting, as children start trying out a variety of adult roles (Erikson, 1968b, p. 115).

At this age, children are intrusive. Like Freud, Erikson believed that, besides exploring their environments and trying out new roles, children show an over concern with sexual matters. They attempt (largely in fantasy) to possess the parent of the opposite sex, with an accompanying feeling of rivalry toward the parent of the same sex. If children are punished severely for these advances, they develop a sense of **guilt**. If, on the other hand, the parents act in an understanding way and guide the children's motives and desires into socially acceptable activities, they develop a sense of **purpose**. This virtue involves thinking big, identifying with parents, and beginning to set major life goals.

Play activities greatly affect the development of these goals. Children playact being mothers or fathers and achieving success as doctors, nurses, teachers, astronauts, firefighters, and so forth. These activities are not merely recreational, according to Erikson. Rather they often involve conflict and purpose. To understand something, children must construct it and reconstruct it themselves. In the process of "working through" these roles, they begin to make preliminary judgments about their future (Erikson, 1977, pp. 34–46).

Latency stage: Industry versus inferiority   Erikson's fourth stage loosely parallels Freud's latency period and occurs from ages 6 to 12. During this period, there is a lull in sexual desires and feelings, and children turn from home to school life, whether school is classroom or jungle or field (Erikson, 1963, p. 258). It is a period of learning new skills and of making things. Children develop a sense of **industry**, which means that they are busy learning how to complete jobs (Evans, 1967, p. 28). Teachers become important in their lives; by introducing them to the technology of the culture, teachers prepare children for the future and for careers.

The danger in this period is that children may fail to learn new things and, as a result, develop feelings of **inferiority**. Failure to learn may be caused by an insufficient resolution of the conflicts in the preceding stage. Children may still want their mothers more than they want knowledge; or they may still compare themselves to their bigger and better-skilled fathers, and experience acute feelings of inadequacy. In Erikson's view, parents can help to minimize these feelings by gradually preparing children for the rigors of the school environment and by encouraging them to trust their prospective mentors. Erikson believed that a positive identification with their teachers is necessary if children are to develop a strong ego. Society needs teachers who are trustworthy and encouraging and who know how to emphasize what children can do (Erikson, 1968b, p. 125). The positive outcome of such sensitive treatment by teachers is that children develop the virtue of **competence**, giving them a healthy preparation for their roles as workers in later life.

Adolescence: Identity versus role confusion   The fifth stage of development occurs from ages 13 through 19. Individuals who have adequately resolved the conflicts inherent in the prior stages bring into adolescence a growing sense of self-identity. The parents have made their child feel that he or she is *somebody*. Young people know that they are an integral part of the family, and yet they also have a budding sense of independence and personal efficacy. They recognize their own competence, can take initiative, and are able to see a variety of tasks through to completion. Thus, they enter adolescence with a variety of loosely related segments of identity based on experiences in the earlier stages. Mixed in with the individual's sense of positive identity, according to Erikson, is a negative identity consisting of all the things the individual has done for which he or she has been punished and for which the individual feels guilty or ashamed. It also includes feelings of incompetence and inadequacy based on past failures (Evans, 1967, pp. 35–36).

During adolescence, these prior identifications are questioned and then restructured by an ego that seeks to integrate them with strong, emerging sexual feelings and the social roles that are available to the individual. The integration now taking place in the form of ego identity is more than the sum of the childhood identifications. It is the accrued experience of the ego's ability to integrate all identifications with the vicissitudes of the libido and with the opportunities offered in social roles. The sense of ego identity, then, is the accrued confidence that the inner sameness and continuity prepared in the past are matched by the sameness and continuity of one's meaning for others, as evidenced in the tangible promise of a "career" (Erikson, 1963, pp. 261–262).

Identity is a multifaceted concept. At base, however, it refers to a conscious sense of uniqueness and direction, derived from a variety of psychosocial experiences that are integrated by the ego—including all our previous identifications learned as a participant in a variety of groups (family, church, school, and peer) and all our self-images (Evans, 1967, p. 36). It involves the sense that we have made an adequate sexual choice and have found a suitable partner to love. It also encompasses our connection with the future when we opt for specific careers and become recognized by others as responsible members of society. A large part of our identity rests on what we do for a living, on the support we receive from society, and on our internalization of the ideals of our class, our nation, and our culture (Erikson, 1964, p. 93). Identity consists, therefore, of the things we are, the things we want to become, and the things we are supposed to become. It also consists of the "things which we do not want to be or which we know we are not supposed to be" (Evans, 1967, p. 32).

Identity is not achieved once and for all during adolescence. However, adolescence is the period during which an **identity crisis** is normative. It is a **moratorium** between childhood and adulthood in which individuals attempt to solve special problems. If these problems are not resolved satisfactorily, a frantic search for identity may be started anew, even in old age.

In Erikson's judgment, the identity crises experienced by youths stem from **role confusion** concerning who they are and what they will become. For many youths, adolescence is a period of torturous self-consciousness characterized by awakening sexual drives and rapid growth of the body, by doubts and shame over what they are already sure they are and what they might become.

The most disturbing part of life during this period, according to Erikson, is youths' inability to decide on an occupational identity. Empirical support for his contention is provided by a survey of adolescents' opinions conducted by Violato and Holden (1988). The investigators asked a large sample of adolescents to indicate how often they worried about a variety of topics, including their careers, alcohol use, smoking, grades, sexual impulses, personal appearance, and their interactions with family, parents, and friends. The areas of greatest concern and worry were careers and grades, followed by personal appearance, then interactions with family, friends, and parents, sexual impulses, and lastly, alcohol use and smoking behavior (Violato & Holden, 1988, p. 106).

Although they have a strong need to commit themselves to a set of goals and principles that would give direction and meaning to their lives, many adolescents find it extremely difficult to make satisfactory choices. Erikson maintains that in such an unsettled period, confused youths try to establish their identities by overidentifying with an assortment of heroes.

> To keep themselves together, they temporarily overidentify with the heroes of cliques and crowds. On the other hand, they become remarkably clannish, intolerant, and cruel in their exclusion of others who are "different," in skin color, cultural background and often in entirely petty aspects of dress and gesture arbitrarily selected as *the* sign of an in-grouper or out-grouper. It is important to understand ... such intolerance as the necessary *defense against a sense of identity diffusion*, which is unavoidable at a time of life when the body changes its proportions radically and when life lies before one with a variety of conflicting possibilities and choices. Adolescents temporarily help one another through such discomfort by forming cliques and by stereotyping themselves, their ideals, and their enemies.... It is difficult to be tolerant if deep down you are not quite sure that you are a man (or a woman), that you will ever grow together again and be attractive, that you will be able to master your drives, that you really know who you are, that you know what you want to be ... and that you will know how to make the right decision without, once [and] for all, committing yourself to the wrong friend, sexual partner, leaders, or career. (Erikson, 1968a, p. 200)

The behavior of many young people, according to Erikson, is characterized by **totalism**, a setting of absolute boundaries in one's values, beliefs, and interpersonal relationships (Erikson, 1964, p. 92). Adolescents embrace simplistic ideologies and follow them with little questioning; they may accept, for example, the values mouthed by celebrities in the drug culture, by delinquent gangs and fanatic religious cults, and by political groups that seem to provide simple answers to difficult and threatening problems. Erikson cautioned against simply labeling such behavior as pathological; instead, we should try to understand it as an alternative way of dealing with experience. Although such behavior has destructive outcomes that cannot be condoned, it also has survival value for many young people (Erikson, 1964, p. 93).

Erikson's view of young people and their development is generally optimistic. He believed that some of their confusion and failure to act constructively is not their fault; rather, rapid political, cultural, and technological changes lead to the questioning of established values that no longer seem to work. Adolescent confusion can also be traced to adults, who are unclear about their own values and, therefore, cannot provide proper guidance. Lastly, young people rightfully protest when adults behave in corrupt and evil ways and are themselves not worthy of emulation. Erikson stressed that adults need young people as much as young people need adults. Young people are the caretakers of the future; through their protests, they also force the older generation to restructure its own value system.

The successful resolution of the crisis of adolescence leads to a sense of **fidelity**, which Erikson called "the ability to sustain loyalties freely pledged in spite of the inevitable contradictions of value systems" (Erikson, 1964, p. 125). Young people are now much more honest with themselves and with significant others. They select friends, mates, and coworkers and commit themselves to these people. They develop a loyalty to a vision of the future, and they move to meet it (Erikson, 1975, p. 209). They are ready to take their place in a technological society not just as guardians of traditions and customs but as rejuvenators and innovators of the culture. Youths who have not adequately resolved their conflicts may develop a **negative identity**, in which they act in scornful and hostile ways toward roles offered as proper and desirable by the community (Erikson, 1968b, pp. 172–173). Their loyalties are to groups, people, and ideologies that are destructive to themselves and to society.

Young adulthood: Intimacy versus isolation   The sixth stage spans the ages of 20 to 24. Having established a stable self-identity during adolescence, healthy young adults are able to enter into intimate relationships with others (Beyers & Seiffge-Krenke, 2010, pp. 387–415). They are now eager and ready to strengthen their personal identity. They seek to commit themselves to partnerships, and they have the strength to abide by such commitments even when significant compromises and sacrifices are necessary (Erikson, 1963, p. 263).

Erikson pointed out that the establishment of intimate relationships is not to be confused with "intimacies" (Roazen, 1976, p. 103); that is, the intimacies involved in sexual intercourse are not to be mistaken for true **intimacy**, the ability to establish close relationships with others. Erikson believed that a truly intimate relationship is possible only between partners who have clearly established identities and loyalties. Because adolescents are still struggling to establish their identities, it follows that they cannot love (be intimate) in the truest sense. Mature love, for the young adult, involves "mutuality of mates and partners in a shared identity, for the mutual verification through an experience of finding oneself … in another" (Erikson, 1964, p. 128).

Healthy intimate relationships are beneficial to both the person and society. According to Erikson, such relationships meet the following standards:

1. A mutuality of orgasm
2. with a loved partner
3. of the opposite sex
4. with whom one is able and willing to share a mutual trust
5. and with whom one is able and willing to regulate the cycles of
   a. work
   b. procreation
   c. recreation
6. so as to secure to the offspring, too, all the stages of a satisfactory development (Erikson, 1963, p. 266).

At this point, it must be noted that, when Erikson referred to a healthy intimate relationship, he meant one that is heterosexual and normative. As we shall see, many of the researchers who followed in Erikson's footsteps, conducting research on ego identity statuses and the various intimacy statuses, have adopted Erikson's viewpoint. Erikson was, at base, a Freudian, and like Freud, he thought that homosexuality was an aberration. Today, there are various authority figures in psychology who would disagree with Erikson (and with Freud for that matter). They maintain that homosexuality is not an aberration and that the adoption of a homosexual identity and the choice of a same-sex partner can be a healthy one (Cross & Epting, 2005, pp. 53–63; Halbertal & Koren, 2006, p. 37).

Moreover, they contend that members of the dominant, heterosexual majority need to abandon their restrictive view of what constitutes a healthy sexual orientation because it often leads to persecution and discrimination of homosexuals and can create serious psychological difficulties for them, for example, depression and suicide (Watzlawik, 2004, pp. 172–173).

To return to Erikson's normative model, young heterosexual adults who cannot develop a capacity for intimacy and productive work experience a sense of **isolation**. Isolation is the inability to take chances with one's identity by sharing true intimacy (Erikson, 1968b, p. 137). Such individuals are self-absorbed and engage in interpersonal relationships on a very superficial level. In young adults who develop their capacity for intimacy more than their sense of isolation, the result is the emergence of the virtue of **love**.

Middle adulthood: Generativity versus stagnation

The seventh stage spans the middle years, from ages 25 to 64. Healthy adults have a strong ego identity and mature relationships with others. At this stage, **generativity** involves the process of establishing and/or enhancing a creative and productive career and of being concerned with ensuring the well-being of the next generation. As they advance in their careers and are successful, they contribute to the development and perpetuation of their society and hence indirectly to the welfare of the next generation. They can also contribute in many ways more directly to the well-being of the young who are more immediately present. The crisis centers on the question of whether adults are going to be productive and creative and helpful to the younger generation or whether they are going to stagnate. **Stagnation** involves a lack of productivity, boredom, and interpersonal impoverishment (Erikson, 1968b, p. 138). If the capacity of adults for generativity exceeds their sense of stagnation, the virtue of **care** emerges. The older generation is thus concerned, not only with its own personal development, but with helping the younger generation to develop in constructive ways. Although it is clear that generativity includes having children as a means of ensuring the survival of society, Erikson stressed that people can be generative even if they do not have children. Childless individuals can contribute to the higher development of society through productive work and through active demonstration of concern with the betterment of young people. Being teachers and mentors to the young also shows a sense of concern (McAdams, Hart, & Maruna, 1998, p. 10).

Late adulthood: Ego integrity versus despair

The final stage lasts from the age of 65 to death. It is primarily a time of intense reflection, involving reminiscence, the recollection of memories and dreams, and attempts to reconstrue the meaning of life while coming to terms with impending death (Walaskay, Whitbourne, & Nehrke, 1983/1984, p. 62). Healthy people are those who have adapted to the triumphs and disappointments of their lives, who have been the originators of others or the generators of products and ideas. They are able to look back at their lives and conclude that they were special and had meaning. They are also able to accept the inevitability of death as a necessary part of the life cycle and not fear it. In brief, elderly people who are functioning well see a unity and meaning in their lives. They have **ego integrity**.

In contrast, individuals who are unable to accept the inevitable failures in their lives and who have led selfish, uncaring lives experience **despair**, because they realize life is now short and there is no time to start a new life or try out new paths to integrity (Erikson, 1963, p. 269).

Finally, the virtue of **wisdom** is associated with a meaningful old age. According to Erikson, "wisdom is detached concern with life itself in the face of death itself" (1964, p. 133). It involves overcoming one's self-centeredness, gaining a deeper insight into one's own and other people's motives and behavior, and developing feelings of genuine empathy, sympathy, and compassion for others (Ardelt, 2000, p. 361). Wisdom affirms the integrity of experience despite a decline in bodily functioning. It allows the person to envisage human problems in their entirety and to communicate to the younger generation a constructive living example of the final period in the life of a unique human being (Erikson, 1964, pp. 133–134).

Research Support for the Theory of Ego Development

Empirical verification of Erikson's complicated theorizing about ego development requires extensive longitudinal studies in order to assess changes in development as people proceed through the life cycle. Such research is costly and difficult. Consequently, there has been relatively little research to date aimed at verifying Erikson's elaborate explanations of the ways in which the eight stages of development influence one another. In addition, empirical verification of the theory is difficult, because the hypotheses are often not clearly stated and many of its constructs are highly abstract and difficult to measure adequately. Despite these difficulties, researchers have been able to create acceptable measures of some of the stages of ego development and have conducted important research based on extensions and refinements of Erikson's theorizing.

Industry in the latency stage   There is very little research examining Erikson's ideas about the first three stages, and investigators are just beginning to test Erikson's ideas about children's learning to be industrious through school experiences. Kowaz and Marcia (1991, pp. 390–397), for example, have created an individual differences measure of industriousness and examined how scores on this factor are related to several aspects of children's cognitive, motivational, and behavioral functioning in the classroom. They found that highly industrious children were more motivated to succeed in school and obtained higher grades than children who were low in industriousness. Furthermore, these results showed that highly industrious children had stronger preferences to make and do things rather than to engage in fantasy by making things up. They also were more content with their school experiences than were their less industrious peers. These results are generally supportive of Erikson's astute observations.

Ego identity in adolescence   Approximately 45 years ago, Marcia (1966, pp. 551–558) identified four distinct positions, or identity statuses, implicit in Erikson's theorizing about identity development in adolescence: (l) identity diffusion, (2) foreclosure, (3) moratorium, and (4) identity achievement. These statuses are defined in terms of the two dimensions of crisis and commitment. *Crisis* refers to an active period of struggle that individuals experience as they seek to resolve questions that arise in the selection of a career, a partner, and a set of values or principles to follow. *Commitment* involves making firm decisions in these areas and then pursuing goals consistent with those decisions.

Individuals with **identity diffusion** lack firm commitments and are not actively in crisis. They may never have experienced crisis, or they may have experienced a period of struggle in the past and been unable to resolve it by making a decision. Lacking a clear sense of identity, such people may exhibit a range of negative emotional states, including pessimism, boredom, unfocused anger, personal confusion, and feelings of helplessness and hopelessness (Waterman, 1985, p. 13).

Individuals in **foreclosure** have never experienced a crisis but have nevertheless made firm commitments to certain goals, beliefs, and values. A good example is the first-year college student who is uncritically following his or her parents' wishes and is pursuing a degree in medicine without examining whether this goal is actually the best in terms of his or her needs and abilities. Individuals in **moratorium** are currently in a state of crisis and are actively considering alternatives in an attempt to arrive at a decision. Finally, individuals with a status of **identity achievement** have undergone a period of crisis and, as a consequence, have developed firm commitments.

In addition to clarifying and making explicit Erikson's four phases of ego-identity development in adolescence, Marcia (1966, pp. 551–558) created an elaborate interview procedure to measure them. This instrument allows investigators to identify the interpersonal relationships of individuals who occupy particular identity statuses and to assess the implications of each status for personality functioning and performance. It has also spurred the construction of several other, less complicated measures of the ego-identity construct (Bourne, 1978, pp. 223–251; Rosenthal, Gurney, & Moore, 1981, pp. 87–99). The research on identity status generally assumes that a progressive strengthening in the sense of identity occurs during adolescence and into adulthood. Marcia (1966, pp. 551–558) posits a progression from low to high ego maturity as follows: diffusion, foreclosure, moratorium, and identity achievement. Within this overall progression, however, different people follow different sequential patterns. While one person in the moratorium phase moves progressively toward identity achievement, another person may move regressively from moratorium status to ego diffusion. Or an adolescent in a foreclosure state may simply remain there into adulthood. Some possible developmental pathways are illustrated in Figure 6.1.

Most studies in this research literature suggest that men and women undergo similar patterns of identity development (Kroger, 2007, p. 65). The sexes do differ, however, in the psychological meanings they attach to their emerging identities. For example, both males and females high in identity achievement characterize themselves as assertive and adequate. However, for males, perceptions of their assertiveness are based on their productivity (getting things done) and power over others. For females, their assertiveness is expressed in the social realm-giving advice to help others, being talkative, socially poised, and personally charming (Cramer, 2000, pp. 58–60). These different meanings are probably dependent on the particular goals sought by males and females. Specifically, male identity centers primarily on the attainment of a career, whereas female identity has a multiple and varying base, which revolves around career and/or marriage and/or child-bearing. Females also engage in more active reflection regarding an identity based on personal relationships than do males (Waterman, 1993, p. 62).

Many studies have examined the kinds of family relationships reported by university men and women who have different ego identity statuses. A summary of these data (Adams, Berzonsky, & Keating, 2006, pp. 81–91; Kroger, 2007, p. 107) showed that the parents of foreclosures do not emphasize the learning of autonomy by their children. Instead, they encourage their children to strongly follow their rules and values, so it is not surprising that foreclosures learn to endorse parental authority, values, and norms.

FIG-6.1 Possible sequential development patterns. **D**, identity diffusion; **M**, moratorium; **F**, foreclosure; **A**, identity achievement. (Adapted from Waterman, 1982, p. 343.)

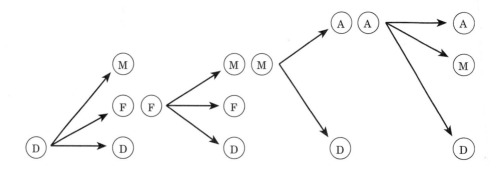

Like their parents, foreclosures tend to be authoritarian, that is, rigid and prejudiced toward others (Fulton, 1997, p. 9). Thus, they do not actively explore alternatives and exhibit a lower ego identity. Instead, they tend to be rigid in their thinking. In contrast, identity diffusers report the most distance between themselves and their parents. They have the lowest level of emotional attachment to their parents (Arseth, Kroger, Marinussen, & Marcia, 2009, pp. 1–32; Kroger, 2007, p. 107), and perceive them as indifferent and rejecting. Moratorium adolescents have ambivalent feelings toward their parents, which stem from differences in opinion concerning the goals and values considered worthy and appropriate for pursuit by teenagers. In times of crisis, these young people are unlikely to turn to their parents for support and advice. Once the crisis has been resolved and identity achieved, however, warmer relationships are typically established, and the parents of identity-achieved adolescents show respect for their children's opinions and needs for independence (Adams et al., 2006, p. 83; Kroger, 2007, p. 108; Marcia, 1993, p. 33; Waterman, 1982, pp. 351–352). Identity achievers show the highest levels of emotional attachment to their parents (Arseth et al., 2009, pp. 1–32).

Researchers also have devoted considerable attention to the information-processing and problem-solving strategies and abilities of college students in each of the four identity statuses. This research area is also concerned with the academic motivation, goals, and achievements of these students. Several studies have shown, for example, that identity achievers and moratorium individuals tend to construe most personal problems as manageable and solvable. Accordingly, they confront their problems directly, by actively seeking out relevant information and considering alternatives when attempting to deal with them. They also process greater amounts of information and report feeling more certain of their ideas. In making decisions, identity achievers are more reflective and rational, as are moratorium individuals. Foreclosures, in contrast, focus their attention so narrowly when trying to solve their problems that they fail to attend to relevant information. Their rigidity keeps them from assimilating novel information and/or from considering alternative courses of action that could help successfully resolve personal difficulties. Foreclosures are intolerant of ambiguity and tend to rely on others for help when they are confronted by stressful problems (Schwartz, Adamson, Ferrer-Wreden, Dillon, & Berman, 2006, p. 62).

Finally, identity diffusers characteristically avoid dealing with their problems, possibly to reduce painful ambiguity. Thus, they tend to procrastinate and to delay making decisions for as long as possible (Shanahan & Pychyl, 2007, pp. 901–911). Under stress, they are rather disorganized in their thinking (Berzonsky, 1992, pp. 771–788; Berzonsky & Neimeyer, 1988, pp. 195–204; Blustein & Phillips, 1990, pp. 160–168; Marcia, 1994, pp. 59–103; Read, Adams, & Dobson, 1984, pp. 169–177). Identity diffusers also tend to handle stress by engaging in risky behavior, for example, excessive drinking, drug use, unprotected sex with many partners (Bishop, Weisgram, Holleque, Lund, & Wheeler-Anderson, 2005, pp. 523–533; Dunkel & Papini, 2005, pp. 489–501).

In research on academic motivation, Adams and Fitch (1983, pp. 1266–1275) have shown that identity achievers are more attracted to scholastic or academically oriented departments than to departments that emphasize social activities and the material benefits of pursuing degrees (such as high-paying jobs upon graduation). Identity achievers also are cognitively complex, are low in procrastination (e.g., they do not delay writing term papers or studying for exams), and attain higher grades than do college students of other statuses (Marcia, 1993, p. 27; Schwartz et al., 2006, p. 62; Shanahan & Pychyl, 2007, pp. 901–911).

In terms of their job performances after they graduate from college, identity achievers show less burnout (or emotional exhaustion) from their work. Instead, they show high levels of energy on the job, persistence, and a willingness to pursue their goals until they accomplish them (Luyckx, Duriez, Klimstra, & De Witte, 2010, pp. 339–349).

In terms of their psychological health, Schwartz (2004, p. 480) found that identity achievers were better adjusted than identity diffusers, having greater ego strength, a greater perceived control over their outcomes, and a clearer purpose in life. Cramer (1998, p. 156) found further that identity achievers made less use of defense mechanisms in dealing with their problems and had higher self-esteem and pride in their accomplishments than students in the less advanced statuses.

Identity achievers also showed greater cultural sophistication and tolerance for out-groups, a greater level of closeness to their friends, as well as higher levels of logical and moral reasoning, than did members of the other statuses (Cote & Levine, 1983, pp. 43–53; Rowe & Marcia, 1980, pp. 87–99; Schwartz et al., 2006, p. 62; Waterman, 1982, pp. 341–358). They also manifested a greater openness to the opinions of other group members, presumably because of their secure sense of self and their highly flexible cognitive systems (Slugoski, Marcia, & Koopman, 1984, p. 658).

Erikson's idea that adolescence is characterized by psychosocial growth is supported by research. Adams, Ryan, and Keating (2000, p. 116) found that university students tended to gain in ego strength as they proceeded from their first-year to their second-year. They begin to think more analytically about their beliefs, values, and goals, especially those students who took courses in departments that emphasized the development of academic and intellectual qualities, societal concerns, and personal commitments to occupations. Other research showed that the number of students who achieved identity for both occupation and ideology, that is, a set of values and principles to guide one's life—increased significantly from the first year to the senior year of college (Adams & Fitch, 1982, pp. 574–583; Waterman, Geary, & Waterman, 1974). By the second half of their senior year, most students had achieved strong identities.

Finally, a longitudinal study by Stein and Newcomb (1999, pp. 39–65) showed that individuals who achieved strong identities or ego strength in adolescence experienced enhanced psychosocial growth as they grew older, reporting favorable outcomes in their love relationships, in caring for the younger generation, and life satisfaction in mid-adulthood.

Extensions and refinements of Marcia's ego identity statuses   While Marcia's ego identity status scheme has increased our understanding of the identity process in adolescence tremendously, most of the research based on it has been conducted with White university samples. Accordingly, such an orientation means that current research tends to ignore studying minority populations in countries such as the United States, Great Britain, France, and the Netherlands despite the fact that there are millions of minority group members and that minorities are increasing at a rapid rate. This emerging non-White population has unique **ethnic identity** concerns that need to be addressed (Schwartz, 2005, p. 297). As Phinney (1990, p. 502) sees it, the formation of ethnic identity may be thought of as a process of ego identity formation that takes place over time, with the same ego identity statuses as Marcia proposes being involved. That is, minority group members typically move from identity diffusion where they initially show a lack of interest (no exploration or commitment) with ethnicity, to a foreclosure status where their views of their own ethnicity is simply based on the views of authority figures in their lives (usually their parents), to a moratorium status where they begin actively exploring their own ethnicity, to identity achievement where they have evolved a clear, confident sense of their own ethnicity.

Through this entire ego identity process, ethnic groups (e.g., Blacks, Hispanics, Asians, Native Americans) face the unique burden of struggling to form an identity in relation to a majority White culture which often discriminates against them and disparages them. When they are confronted with negative stereotypes and attitudes (e.g., name-calling) and internalize them, it can lead to negative consequences for their psychological and behavioral development. In contrast, it is possible for minority group members to reject the negative stereotypes and attitudes of the dominant group and to establish a sense of pride in their own ethnicity/race. Under these conditions, they are able to adjust well in school and to perform well academically. In a study by Shrake and Rhee (2004, pp. 601–622), for example, it was found that Korean American adolescents who had more positive views of their own ethnicity were able to adjust better socially in school and to achieve higher grade point averages (GPAs) than their counterparts who had more negative views of their own ethnicity.

While a positive sense of their ethnic identity is generally helpful to minority group members, it is still true that they need to consider their identity in relation to the dominant culture. A strong, positive sense of ethnic identity accompanied by active hostility and rejection of the majority culture is associated generally with negative and rebellious attitudes toward the dominant society and poor social and academic performance (cf. Shrake & Rhee, 2004, p. 606). In contrast, research has indicated that a strong sense of ethnic belonging accompanied by positive attitudes toward the majority culture, which is indicative of integration, contributes to healthy psychological adjustment and development. Thus, the development of a **bicultural identity** in minority individuals is associated with the highest levels of mental health and productive performance. Such an identity requires high levels of competence and flexibility and is very difficult to attain. Research is now underway to illuminate more precisely how some individuals are able to achieve this goal, whereas others fail. (See Chapter 18 for additional materials on ethnic identity.)

Intimacy in early adulthood   On the basis of Erikson's writings, Orlofsky and his colleagues have identified six distinct statuses associated with intimacy issues during early adulthood (Orlofsky, 1976, pp. 73–88; Orlofsky, Marcia, & Lesser, 1973, pp. 211–219). Individuals are interviewed and their responses classified according to three criteria: (1) the presence or absence of relationships with same- and other-sex friends; (2) the presence or absence of enduring, committed sexual-love relationships; and (3) the depth (emotional closeness) or superficiality of their relationships.

Intimate individuals have deep relationships with male and female friends and are involved in enduring, committed heterosexual relationships.

Preintimate individuals also have close emotional ties to others but are ambivalent about committing themselves to enduring love relationships.

Stereotyped individuals have many relationships, but they are superficial and utilitarian and lacking in closeness and commitment.

Pseudointimate individuals, like stereotyped people, form relationships that lack depth; unlike stereotyped people, however, they have entered into enduring heterosexual commitments.

Isolated individuals are completely, or nearly completely, withdrawn from social situations and relationships with peers (Orlofsky et al., 1973, p. 213).

Merger individuals are those who have committed themselves to enduring relationships or those who are uncommitted but are seeking committed relationships. Merger individuals in committed relationships have become absorbed in their relationships at the expense of their own autonomy and sense of self. Such relationships are characterized by excessive dependency and **enmeshment**. Merger individuals in uncommitted relationships are insecure and tend to seek out dependency relationships (Levitz-Jones & Orlofsky, 1985, p. 158; Levitz-Jones & Orlofsky, 1993, pp. 127–128).

Research has shown that intimates work at developing mutual personal relationships and have several close friends with whom they discuss personal matters (Orlofsky et al., 1973, p. 213). Although they will disclose personal information to their close friends, they will not discuss personal matters with casual acquaintances. Thus, they are selectively self-revealing, in contrast to individuals in the lower intimacy statuses (Prager, 1986, p. 91). Intimates are warm, candid people who have a genuine interest in and concern for others. Their sexual relationships are mutually satisfactory, and they are able to make lasting commitments without overly compromising their own independence (Orlofsky et al., 1973, p. 213; Orlofsky, 1978, p. 436). According to Prager (1986, p. 96), they also have a strong internal locus of control over their lives. In other research, Prager (1989, p. 448) found that unmarried and married couples who had attained intimacy status had a history of greater self-disclosure over a broad range of topics with their partners than did pseudointimate-status couples. Intimacy-status couples also reported the highest levels of satisfaction with their relationships.

Preintimates have had some dating experience, but are in conflict regarding commitment and are ambivalent about the risk of failure involved in intimate sexuality. Their values, however, are similar to those held by intimates—namely, respect for the integrity of others, openness, a sense of responsibility, and mutuality—and it is possible that they can resolve their ambivalence and move into the highest intimacy status.

Stereotyped individuals have superficial relationships. They date regularly and will sometimes see the other person for months but do not become further involved. They enjoy sex and tend to be continually searching for new conquests. They treat others as sexual objects and are only interested in satisfying their own needs. They tend to be shallow and exploitative and have limited self-awareness.

Pseudointimates resemble stereotyped individuals, with one major exception: They have made a lasting commitment to one person. In this sense, they resemble intimate individuals, but they are self-absorbed and not genuinely concerned about others.

Isolates are characterized by the absence of any enduring relationships. They rarely initiate social contacts and date very rarely. The anxiety that accompanies close personal contacts forces them to withdraw from others. Isolates are nonassertive and lack social skills. They may present themselves as bitter and mistrustful or as smug and self-satisfied. Their interpersonal difficulties may be traced to a lack of trust in themselves and others (Orlofsky et al., 1973, p. 213).

Orlofsky's research has shown further that high-intimacy men are almost invariably identity achievers; preintimates are most frequently in the moratorium status; stereotyped and pseudointimate men tend to be foreclosures; and isolates tend toward identity diffusion (Orlofsky et al., 1973, p. 217).

Research on the newest status, mergers, shows that women in this group are excessively dependent on their male partners. To achieve their goals, such women may employ subtle manipulation such as acting seductively, using flattery, or dropping hints, while their male partners rely on domineering and bullying tactics such as threatening, ridiculing, and insulting their partners (Howard, Blumstein, & Schwartz, 1986, p. 107). In such relationships, the woman loses her own sense of autonomy and fails to see her partner as a separate individual. The result is excessive possessiveness, jealousy, and a belief that she is unable to get along or find any happiness without her partner. Merger women frequently disclosed that they bickered continually with their boyfriends as a means of delineating a sense of separateness. One merger woman said, "I broke up with my boyfriend because he won't argue with me and I *need* someone to argue with" (Levitz-Jones & Orlofsky, 1985, p. 167). Although these couples cling to each other, they are actually low in mutuality, trust, and openness and, therefore, low in intimacy. One outcome is that, as compared with high-intimacy women, merger women are more likely to become depressed.

Generativity in middle adulthood　Initial research in this area focused on individuals who were low or high in generativity. First, we will review some of the earlier research using this classification scheme, and afterward, we will present the newest categorization model and accompanying research.

In terms of the earlier research, Vandewater and McAdams (1989, pp. 435–449) assessed the generativity of study participants by asking them to identify three creative products or projects in which they were currently involved. They were told that creativity was broadly defined and included such activities as making *things* (such as building a model airplane or making a delicious dinner), coming up with good *ideas* (providing useful advice, telling a good story), or doing things for *people* (raising children, teaching students, serving as an example to others). Finally, they were asked to give their reasons for getting involved in the activities. Judges rated the participants' descriptions in terms of their degree of generativity. In the judges' opinion, the first of the following examples of the participants' responses shows no generativity, while the second shows considerable generativity.

> [Participant 1] Made several dresses for myself recently. I think sewing saves me money (which makes me feel good) and … results in a wardrobe that looks and fits better than store-bought clothing. It is basically a self-satisfying endeavor. (Vandewater & McAdams, 1989, p. 440)
>
> [Participant 2] Successful business career. Attained management objective. [I am a] good example for women to follow. [I helped to] expand [the] role of women in free enterprise. (Vandewater & McAdams, 1989, p. 441)

Following this assessment of the participants' level of generativity, all participants filled out a series of self-report scales designed to assess their belief in the species, their trust in human beings, and their tendencies toward nurturance or self-absorption. In line with Erikson's ideas, generative participants exhibited a basic belief in the goodness and worthwhileness of human life. They trusted in the future advancement of human life, even in the face of compelling evidence of human destructiveness, and were more committed to helping others reach their goals than were individuals suffering from stagnation in their lives. Generative participants were not self-absorbed, but oriented toward helping others (Vandewater & McAdams, 1989, pp. 437–438). Not surprisingly, participants high in generativity report greater happiness and satisfaction with their lives than do participants low in generativity (McAdams, de St. Aubin, & Logan, 1993, p. 225).

Another investigation also showed that good fathers, those who were caring and active in their children's physical, social, and intellectual development, were also happier in their marriages than were uninvolved fathers. Also, contrary to speculation in the print media that greater involvement in family life would hinder men's careers, their more active participation with their families was associated with greater occupational success (Snarey, 1993, pp. 349–353).

Other research by Snarey and his colleagues has focused on the relationship between male infertility in early adulthood and its implications for the subsequent attainment of generativity in middle adulthood (Snarey, Son, Kuehne, Hauser, & Vaillant, 1987, pp. 593–603). Although there are many possible ways to achieve generativity, a primary way for many males is to guide the development of their biological offspring. Thus, men who learn that they are infertile are likely to experience a sense of shock, disbelief, and helplessness, a feeling that their ability to choose their destiny has been denied. There are various styles of coping with this difficulty, and the investigators sought to determine which were most successful in helping such men resolve their anxieties and move toward the attainment of a sense of generativity in middle adulthood.

The study found that men who used parent-like substitute activities, by encouraging the development of other people's children (for example, by leading a youth group, teaching Sunday school, or becoming a Big Brother to a neighborhood boy), were the most likely to adopt a child and the least likely to divorce. They were also the most likely to experience a strong sense of generativity in middle adulthood. Conversely, men who exhibited self-centered substitute behavior were least likely to adopt a child, most likely to divorce, and least likely to achieve generativity in later life. Self-centered substitution styles included treating themselves as if they were their only child, becoming preoccupied with body building and health foods, and treating nonhuman objects (such as pets or cars) as if they were their babies. Thus, this study showed clearly that generativity is not tied exclusively to the biological act of becoming a father. It can also be achieved through the substitution of altruistic, parent-like activities with other children or the adoption of children (Snarey et al., 1987, pp. 593–603).

Generative statuses   In the past few years, Bradley and Marcia (1998, pp. 39–64) have provided a more sophisticated model of generativity-stagnation that increases our understanding of the generativity process beyond that of the two-level model that has just been presented. It encompasses five different status levels or styles of generativity which are based on two criteria: involvement and inclusivity. *Involvement* reflects the degree of active concern for the creative and productive growth of oneself and others. It encompasses the development of one's skills and knowledge and the sharing of those skills and knowledge with others, as well as the ability to follow through on one's commitments. *Inclusivity* refers to the scope of one's caregiving, in terms of who or what is to be included or excluded.

Individuals with a **generative style** represent the highest level of generativity. Such individuals are highly involved and committed to their work and to the growth of young people. They work extremely hard to develop their skills and to benefit society and the younger generation. Research by Bradley and Marcia (1998, p. 51) shows that they are open to experience, warm, friendly, and tolerant of different ideas, values, and traditions. Their caregiving, therefore, encompasses all youth, not just those who agree with them. An example might be the college advisor who is trying very hard to increase his or her counseling skills to be of maximum service to all of the advisees, irrespective of their race, age, gender, or physical appearance.

The next three styles represent more moderate levels of generativity. People with a **conventional style** are extremely hardworking and conscientious, creative and productive, but are nevertheless low in inclusivity (Bradley & Marcia, 1998, pp. 43–51). They feel that young people need firm guidance and have difficulty accepting deviations from their established lifestyles, values, and goals. They are threatened when young people disagree with them and tend to reject them. The highly productive teacher who is supportive of the aspirations of only those students whose values and goals mirror his or her own would be a good example. Individuals with an **agentic style** are very productive and contribute to society but are low in inclusivity. They are more concerned with their own self-interests and are generally unsympathetic to the young. It should be noted that Bradley and Marcia (1998, p. 59) think that some of the self-interest associated with the agentic style is healthy and conducive to personal growth. An example might be the actor who is only concerned with his or her career and the number of Oscars he or she can amass who pays no attention to the legion of young fans unless it can further his or her own career. People with a **communal style** are not committed as much to their own personal growth, but instead are almost obsessively concerned with the welfare of the younger generation. They are very sympathetic and caring (Bradley & Marcia, 1998, p. 53), but often at the expense of developing their own personal skills and relationships. Self-sacrificing parents who devote themselves to their children and other youngsters at the expense of the development and utilization of their own creative abilities would be an example.

Finally, individuals with a **stagnant style** show the lowest level of generativity. They show little self-satisfaction and a lack of concern with helping the younger generation. An example might be the highly intelligent clerk in a bureaucratic institution who is unchallenged and bored by the routine of the job and who lives a life isolated from others, including members of the younger generation.

Ego integrity in late adulthood   Focusing on the crisis experienced by individuals during the final stage of life, Walaskay et al. (1983/1984, pp. 61–72) used an interview procedure to classify elderly men and women (of average age 75) as characterized by ego integrity or despair. Following the interview, all of the study participants responded to several personality questionnaires designed to assess their anxieties about death, their memories of earlier life stages, and their current levels of psychological well-being. As expected on the basis of Erikson's theory, the investigators found that despairing individuals had more negative memories, experienced greater death anxiety, and were more dissatisfied and maladjusted as compared to individuals high in ego integrity. In a subsequent study by Taft and Nehrke (1990, pp. 191–193), elderly people with a strong sense of ego integrity reported that they had reminisced about their past in order to resolve troubling experiences and arrive at a better understanding of their lives, whereas individuals filled with despair had not engaged in such life reviews. The attempt to resolve troubling past experiences by high ego integrity people who achieved self-acceptance involved the very difficult process of self-forgiveness. Elderly people who had achieved ego integrity reported that, during the self-forgiveness process, they had to acknowledge their limitations, accept responsibility for their transgressions, promise themselves that they would never make those mistakes again, and apologize to the people they had offended. If it was not possible to apologize to the offended (e.g., if they had committed transgressions against their spouse, and he or she had died), they said they believed that they must make reparations by doing good works (Ingersoll-Dayton & Krause, 2005, pp. 267–289). Other research by Santor and Zuroff (1994, pp. 294–312) showed that elderly people with a strong sense of ego integrity who had forgiven themselves and accepted their past experienced fewer feelings of hostility, resentment, and depression than did those who were less accepting. In brief, elderly individuals who accepted their past were more psychologically healthy than were those who did not (Santor & Zuroff, 1994, pp. 297–309).

In thinking about psychologically healthy older adults, we should not form the impression that such individuals are just waiting to die. Many older adults can and do continue to contribute to society and to younger generations in the eighth stage of life. Erikson says that old age can involve a **grand-generativity**. Specifically, elderly people, especially those who are physically healthy, can continue to contribute to the welfare of younger people and to their own personal growth in their roles as aging parents (e.g., as financial helpers to their middle-aged children), old friends, consultants, mentors, grandparents, and foster grandparents (Erikson, Erikson, & Kivnick, 1986, p. 74; Winefield & Air, 2010, pp. 277–283). Thus, the active developmental work they have done during middle-age can carry into the eighth stage as well and be an integral part of successful aging. As several foster grandparents noted:

Grandparent 1: It's given me a new outlook on life. These children are our future. They need us to teach them … to point them in the right direction.

Grandparent 2: It beats sitting around and doing nothing. It's motivating to do things for others. I'm doing something worthwhile.

Grandparent 3: It gave me a new lease on life. I have something to look forward to. Children can teach you a lot. (Fisher, 1995, pp. 247–248)

Thus, many psychologically healthy elderly strike a balance between a relatively passive reflection on their past lives and a continued vital involvement in the world and other people.

In conclusion, although research on the crises during on the first four stages is still relatively sparse, research on the last four stages is more plentiful, and it shows support that is highly consistent with Erikson's ideas.

Assessment Techniques

Erikson always identified himself as a psychoanalyst and paid homage to Freud's insights and techniques. At the same time, he extended and modified many of Freud's concepts and methods and forged new ones of his own.

One basic difference in technique involves Erikson's view of the relationship between therapist and patient. He adopted a more egalitarian and personal stance toward his patients than did Freud. Whereas Freud tried to foster an impersonal, objective atmosphere by requiring his patients to recline on a couch while he remained seated in a chair out of sight, Erikson asked many of his patients to sit across from him in an easy chair. Freud was guided by his view of the consulting room as primarily a scientific laboratory, and only secondarily as a healing sanctuary. Erikson, however, believed that such neutrality on the part of the therapist can prove harmful to patients, because it may induce fears of losing their identity. In his view, patients can be helped only to the extent that the therapist becomes actual or real to them (Roazen, 1976, pp. 67–69). Thus, Erikson advocated a stance of "disciplined subjectivity," in which the therapist seeks to analyze and understand the patient's problems through empathy, as well as by examining historical events that have affected the patient's life.

Erikson used the Freudian concepts and procedures of transference, free association, and dream analysis in his work, but his usage differs in a number of respects from his mentor's. Especially different is his view of dreams and their meanings. Whereas Freud interpreted dreams as wish fulfillment of sexual needs, Erikson typically interpreted them in psychosocial terms as attempts to preserve and enhance identity. He agreed with Freud that dreams can be indicators of people's struggles to understand prior developmental crises; in Erikson's view, however, they are more likely to revolve around questions of identity than of sexuality. Erikson also differed from Freud in that he attached considerable importance to understanding the manifest content of dreams, rather than delving into the depths of dreamers' psyches to get at latent contents and their meanings. In Erikson's view, a dream's manifest content can reveal important information about current life problems and about the dreamer's view of his or her relationship with the therapist. Although Erikson acknowledged that analysis of latent content can lead to the discovery of important information about the sources of prior conflicts, he believed that dreams also have a healing function; they provide suggestions about how to cope with the future as well as the past (Roazen, 1976, p. 56).

Freud worked primarily with neurotic adults; Erikson was essentially a child analyst and, as such, he had to use techniques appropriate to that age group. Thus, Erikson utilized a variety of play-therapy techniques to increase his understanding of the unique problems of his young patients. For example, he encouraged his patients to use toys to construct exciting scenes from their own imaginations. He found that these play constructions provide important clues to the sources of the child's problems. They also provide an opportunity for the child to create ideal situations and to master reality through experiment and planning (Erikson, 1963, p. 222). Thus, play enables youngsters to relive their past, to redeem their failures, and to strengthen their hopes for the future. As mentioned earlier, play is not primarily a recreational activity, but a work activity designed to enhance mastery.

Finally, Erikson was a pioneer in the use of **psychohistorical analysis** to increase our understanding of the lives of important historical figures. Erikson developed the procedure because he was interested in building a bridge between psychoanalysis and history. All too often, he maintained, historians have ignored the role of individual development in their attempts to explain historical events, while analysts have focused too narrowly on early personal development and have deemphasized the role of broader historical processes in their efforts to explain the behavior of individuals. Psychohistorical analysis was Erikson's attempt to overcome such myopia by applying his theory of ego development and its various crises throughout the life cycle to the biographies of prominent individuals, including Thomas Jefferson, George Bernard Shaw, Martin Luther, Mahatma Gandhi, and Adolf Hitler. At the same time, the analyst seeks to understand their lives by judging them in terms of the unique historical periods in which they lived and wrote. Psychohistorical analysis takes a broad perspective that includes an appreciation of the tremendous impact of political, economic, social, and cultural forces on the development and personalities of historical figures. It also seeks to recognize and take into account the subtle ways in which the analysts' own values and experiences, and their own historical period, guide their interpretations of these people's lives (Erikson, 1974, pp. 14–15).

Theory's Implications for Therapy

For Erikson, neurotics and psychotics are people with confused identities who lack a sense of mastery over their experiences. Their egos are fragmented and weak, and they are unable to relate well to others or to take their place in society. These difficulties are an outgrowth of their failure to resolve successfully one or more of the crises inherent in their life cycles.

Failure to develop a sense of basic trust in the first stage of life, Erikson believed, can lead to serious pathology in later life, including schizophrenia. In this case, failure to establish trust in others eventually leads the person to break with external reality. To help such a person, Erikson maintained, the therapist must teach the patient to trust the world again (Evans, 1967, p. 55).

In the case of paranoia, Erikson saw a fixation in development "somewhere between the hope and will state" (Evans, 1967, p. 56). Paranoids are unable to overcome the suspicion that the adults who tried to train their will during the anal stage were really trying to break it. If confronted later in life with restricted opportunities (such as not being able to find a job), they are likely to believe that others are out to get them—to stop them from demonstrating their ability to succeed independently (Evans, 1967, pp. 56–57).

Erikson believed that obsessive-compulsive neuroses also result from fixations at the anal stage, which stem from parental over harshness in their training procedures. Obsessive-compulsives are given to stubbornness, procrastination, and ritualistic repetitions as means of regaining control of their lives (Erikson, 1968b, p. 111). Treatment requires not only identification of the sources of the conflict with parents, but also encouragement by the therapist of the patient's own capabilities and freedom to exercise will without feelings of shame and doubt (Evans, 1967, p. 58).

Major adjustment problems in adolescence typically center on the lack of clear occupational goals. This difficulty may be traced, in part, to a failure to develop a sense of self-control over one's choices or to a lack of imagination and direction concerning one's ideals and goals during the muscular-anal and locomotor-genital stages.

These problems may be compounded by a strong sense of inferiority about one's competence to perform tasks well, as a result of failure to grow during the latency period. Under these circumstances, confused adolescents faced with the tremendous pressures of making a decision may react badly. They may drop out of school, leave jobs, stay out all night, turn to destructive acts such as vandalism and robbery, or withdraw into bizarre and horrible moods.

Erikson believed that adolescents' only salvation in this situation is for friends, family, therapist, and judiciary personnel to avoid typing them with diagnostic labels, such as borderline psychotic or schizoid, and to accept the fact that there are special social and cultural conditions that trigger such behavior (Erikson, 1968b, p. 132). The use of labels may force young people to embrace a negative identity more strongly, thereby exacerbating their problems; what they need from the therapist is sympathetic treatment and encouragement. At the core of therapeutic treatment is the patient's need to rebuild a personal identity. This is an extremely difficult task and, because it is so painful, patients typically engage in resistive behavior; usually, they try to convince the therapist that their negative identities are real and necessary. Erikson believed that the therapist should acknowledge the validity of this contention, but not let the patient conclude that this negative identity is "all there is to me." The therapist should treat such patients with understanding and affection, but not permissively; it is important to point out firmly the patients' strengths and to indicate directions for positive growth (Erikson, 1968b, pp. 212–216). The therapist should encourage patients to develop their talents through social experimentation; such activities typically result in increased ego strength.

A major contributing factor to the development of neurosis in young adults is their failure to relate intimately to others. Neurotics are often lonely, isolated people who have been unable to accept the risks and responsibilities associated with the establishment of truly intimate relationships. They lack the ability to love and to establish deep, enduring friendships. Because sexual relations are part of the expression of mature love, we might expect such individuals to experience difficulties in the form of impotence, premature ejaculation, or frigidity. These problems can be overcome only when these disturbed and distressed individuals have undergone therapeutic experiences that strengthen their sense of identity. Erikson believed that only people with strong egos are capable of coping with the disappointments, hurts, and possibilities of rejection associated with opening oneself up to another.

Neurosis during middle adulthood is associated with an inability to experience satisfaction in guiding and helping the next generation. Such self-absorbed individuals feel strongly that life should have greater meaning and joy, yet they experience boredom and stagnation. Treatment of these individuals focuses on the early childhood origins of their excessive self-love and lack of trust, which now prevent them from extending themselves to others.

Finally, pathology in late adulthood is correlated with fragmentation of the ego. Elderly neurotics are still unable to adapt themselves to earlier defeats and to integrate these experiences into their self-concepts. They are likely to feel that they have not accomplished all their goals and that there is not enough time to rectify the situation. They fear death. Treatment is aimed at helping the patient see that each life cycle is unique, that it permits no substitutions, and that death is an inevitable part of it (Erikson, 1968b, p. 139).

Evaluative Comments

We now examine the scientific worth of Erikson's theory.

Comprehensiveness   An imaginative and original thinker, Erikson created a theory that is indeed comprehensive. It addresses itself to a wide variety of phenomena, both normal and abnormal, and seeks to account for the biological, social, cultural, and historical factors that jointly determine personality development and functioning. The range of phenomena explored includes race relations, mythology, national identity, play activities, marriage, divorce, incest, sexual relations, occupational choice, academic success and failure, love, womanhood, and cross-cultural rituals. In addition to its focus on different types of psychopathology, it also makes an effort to describe and explain healthy personality functioning.

Precision and testability   Erikson's theory fails to meet the criterion of precision and testability. It is populated by highly abstract concepts that have few clear referents. The identity concept is particularly nebulous. At one point, Erikson described it as "wholeheartedness, wholemindedness, wholesomeness, and the like. As a Gestalt, then, wholeness emphasizes a sound, organic, progressive mutuality between diversified functions and parts within an entirety, the boundaries of which are open and fluent" (Erikson, 1964, p. 92). At another, he defined it as "the capacity of the ego to sustain sameness and continuity in the face of changing fate" (Erikson, 1964, p. 96). In another context, it refers to the "things which we want to become, and we know we are supposed to be, and which ... we can fulfill" (Evans, 1967, p. 32). Evidently, the concept is extremely complex and does not lend itself readily to precise measurement. As a result, the theory is difficult to test.

Difficulties in testing also arise because the theory's general propositions and the specific hypotheses associated with them are often stated rather vaguely. For example, Erikson maintained that fixations that occur during specific stages influence later character development in specific ways. This would suggest a number of distinct character types, each with a unique set of personality characteristics or traits, but nowhere has Erikson had much to say about these implications of his theorizing. In fairness to Erikson, however, he tackled an enormously difficult task—namely, the description and explanation of the eight stages of ego development as they are influenced by complicated biological, social, cultural, and historical forces. Nor does the ambiguity of his concepts mean that they are useless. We have seen, for example, how his ideas about ego identity in adolescence, intimacy in young adulthood, generativity in middle adulthood, and ego integrity in late adulthood have been refined by various investigators and utilized successfully in testing aspects of the theory.

Parsimony   Although we can admire the scope of Erikson's theory, its explanatory base is rather limited. Most phenomena are explained in terms of identity formation, disintegration, or integration, often in post hoc fashion. The identity concept seems to carry too heavy a burden, and thus the theory is not parsimonious.

Empirical validity   Not enough research has been conducted to test the Erikson's theorizing on the first four stages, perhaps because they are too similar to familiar Freudian theorizing and therefore not exciting enough to capture researchers' attention. Most of the current research has focused instead on the last four stages. Empirical research on these stages has produced findings that are highly consistent with Erikson's theory, yet there is clearly a need for additional research that: (1) focuses on domains like friendship, dating, and sex roles; (2) identifies the conditions that produce arrested development and a lack of clear and stable identity; (3) examines in even greater detail the process of identity development for gender, racial, and ethnic groups other than Caucasian; (4) uses longitudinal procedures to test Erikson's theorizing about the interrelatedness of the stages and their mutual influence; and (5) uses what is known about identity to help youth make their way in a society that has become increasingly complex and unstructured (Schwartz, 2001, pp. 49–50).

Heuristic value Erikson's theory has had strong heuristic value; it has generated interest among scholars in many disciplines. His ethical concerns, expressed in his discussions of the various virtues associated with development, have stimulated thinking among theologians and moral philosophers. His extensive analysis of the meaning of rituals in various societies has influenced cultural anthropologists. His use of psychohistorical analysis to study political, religious, and literary figures has had a considerable impact on historians. Within psychology, Erikson's work has also contributed greatly to lifespan psychology and the development of adult psychology. Perhaps the most significant impact of his ego psychology is that it has served to broaden the theoretical base of psychoanalysis and has influenced the thinking of colleagues within the psychoanalytic community.

Applied value Erikson's work has had tremendous practical impact in the areas of child psychology and psychiatry, vocational counseling, marriage counseling, education, social work, and business. His ideas about the stages of ego development and their inherent conflicts have stimulated clinicians to develop treatment programs for children, adolescents, and older adults. Vocational counselors make use of Erikson's provocative thinking in advising young people about occupational goals. Mental health consultants conduct workshops with business employees to discuss ways of overcoming the sense of stagnation that many of them experience midway through their careers and use Erikson's ideas to help them achieve increased feelings of generativity.

Erikson's work also has been popular with students and other members of the general public; it helps to increase their understanding of the kinds of stresses they are likely to experience at a given stage in their lives and provides recommendations for alleviating these stresses so that positive growth can be achieved.

CRITICAL THINKING QUESTIONS

1. What is an identity crisis? Is it a typical experience for adolescents, as Erikson claimed? Have you ever experienced (or are you currently experiencing) an identity crisis? In what area of your life? What happened?

2. Erikson emphasized the role of the mother in creating a sense of basic trust or mistrust in children. What is the role of the father in child care? Is it as important as the mother's? Is it different and, if so, in what ways?

3. In Erikson's view, the ability to love someone presupposes a strong identity. Since many adolescents have confused identities, they cannot truly love anyone. Do you agree or disagree with this conclusion? Why?

4. Since Erikson took the position that healthy, intimate relationships involve a mutuality of orgasm with a loved partner of the opposite sex, what was his view of homosexual relationships? Do you agree or disagree with him? Why or why not?

5. Do you agree with Erikson's belief that the most disturbing part of adolescence centers on the inability to decide on an occupational identity? Is this the major problem for you or any of your friends?

GLOSSARY

agentic style   Highly productive and creative middle-aged adults who contribute indirectly to successive generations through their work. They do not, however, show much direct concern for the welfare of the young people in their immediate surroundings.

autonomy   Sense of independence that individuals experience if they successfully resolve conflicts during the second stage of life.

basic mistrust   Belief that others cannot be trusted; it results from the mother's failure to act in a consistent and affectionate manner toward her infant.

basic trust   Belief that others are reliable; it stems from the receipt of consistent and affectionate treatment by mothers during the first stage of development.

bicultural identity   A sense of identity in which minority group members are characterized by positive attitudes toward their own ethnic group *and* toward the majority group. Such an integrative identity is associated with high levels of mental health.

care   Virtue in healthy middle-aged people that leads them to feel a concern for the welfare of the younger generation.

communal style   Middle-aged adults who neglect their own personal development as they indiscriminately sacrifice themselves for the younger generation.

competence   Strength in healthy children involving the ability to make things and complete tasks.

conventional style   Middle-aged adults who contribute to their society and to successive generations through their creative work. However, their concern for the development of the younger generation is selective because they seek to guide and nurture only those young people who mirror their values and goals.

crisis   Turning point in individual development in which conflicts can be resolved positively, thereby strengthening the ego, or negatively, thereby weakening it.

despair   Negative outcome in the last stage of life for individuals who have been unable to resolve their conflicts constructively; it includes the fear of death and the belief that their lives have been failures and that they are unable to rectify the situation.

ego integrity   Feeling by the elderly that, on balance, their lives have had positive meaning and have been worth living.

ego psychology   Theory that the ego is not always controlled by id impulses, but often functions independently of these urges, thereby providing the individual with an opportunity for creative action and positive growth.

enmeshment   Fusion with another person, in which one's own sense of self and identity is lost.

epigenetic principle   Principle that there is a genetically determined sequence to human growth and that each stage in the sequence unfolds in an invariant order.

ethnic identity   A sense of belonging and commitment to a group because the individual shares a common heritage, knowledge, attitudes, and values with other members.

fidelity   Sense of loyalty and commitment to friends and coworkers and to a value system; fidelity results from the positive resolution of conflicts during adolescence.

foreclosure   Identity status within adolescence in which individuals who have never experienced a crisis concerning their goals have nevertheless made firm commitments concerning them.

generative style   Middle-aged adults who contribute to their society and to the development of the younger generation through their sustained productive and creative work. They are concerned with fostering the personal growth of all youth, not just those with similar outlooks and values.

generativity   In middle-aged adults, the sustained effort to develop into creative and productive human beings who use their skills and knowledge to help develop and maintain societal institutions without which successive generations would be unable to survive. Generativity also involves direct attempts on the part of this older generation to guide and nurture the younger generation.

grand-generativity   Individuals in old age who continue to develop their talents and to contribute to individuals of all ages. In these relationships, they seek to integrate outward-looking care for others with inward concern for the self and its development.

guilt   Feeling of wrongdoing experienced by youngsters when they show inappropriate behavior and are punished for it.

hope   Optimistic belief that persistent wishes and goals can be attained.

identity   Multifaceted concept that involves knowing who you are and where you are going, as well as what you are not and do not want to be; the unified sense of self as uniquely different from others.

identity achievement   Identity status within adolescence in which individuals have undergone a period of crisis and, as a result, have developed firm commitments concerning their life goals.

identity crisis   A developmental turning point, associated primarily with adolescence, in which basic choices need to be made by the person in various life areas. For example, primary decisions and commitments need to be made about a career, a mate, and an ideology to live by.

identity diffusion   Identity status within adolescence in which individuals are not actively in crisis about their life goals and have not made any commitments concerning them.

industry   Sense of satisfaction that accrues to children as a result of being actively engaged in learning new skills and completing tasks.

inferiority   Negative outcome of the fourth stage of development; in this state, children feel that they are incompetent failures.

initiative   Feeling that one has control over one's outcomes and can therefore be the source of ideas and action.

intimacy   Ability of people with mature egos to become one with their partners without losing their separate sense of identity.

intimate individuals   Individuals whose relationships are characterized by depth and commitment.

isolated individuals   Individuals who have withdrawn from social relationships.

isolation   Inability to take chances with one's identity by sharing true intimacy.

love   Ability to trust and share one's experiences and identity with a partner so that both parties are enhanced.

merger individuals   People who have lost their sense of identity and who live through their partners.

moratorium   Time of exploration during adolescence in which individuals are experiencing a crisis concerning their life goals and are actively considering alternatives in an attempt to arrive at decisions.

negative identity   Commitment to values and roles that are unacceptable to society.

preintimate individuals   Individuals who have deep relationships, but are reluctant to commit themselves to enduring relationships.

pseudointimate individuals   People who have enduring relationships, but whose relationships lack depth.

psychohistorical analysis   Erikson's technique for analyzing the lives of historical figures on the basis of his theory of ego development.

purpose   Virtue that emerges when parents guide their children into socially desirable activities and, as a result, the children set (in a preliminary fashion) life goals.

role confusion   State in adolescence in which young people cannot decide on their proper life roles.

shame and doubt   Negative state in which youngsters feel unable to make their own judgments or to exercise control over their lives, as a result of faulty parenting in the anal stage.

stagnant style   Middle-aged adults who make little or no effort to develop their skills or to nurture the younger generation. They are bored, apathetic, and dissatisfied with themselves and do not contribute much either to society or to the younger generation.

stagnation   Feeling of being unproductive and useless that stems from an inability to care for something or someone.

stereotyped individuals   Individuals whose relationships are shallow and exploitative.

totalism   Premature, unquestioning commitment by adolescents to simplistic ideologies and ideas as a means of reducing their own painful feelings of confusion.

virtue Strengthening of the ego that emerges following the successful resolution of a crisis associated with one of the developmental stages.

will Virtue that involves youngsters' determination to exercise free choice in making decisions and not be controlled by others.

wisdom Virtue that emerges following successful resolution of the crisis of old age; the ability to put one's life experiences into a life-cycle perspective, to accept that one's life, in general, had unity and meaning and that it was worth living.

SUGGESTED READINGS

Erikson, E. H. (1963). *Childhood and society* (2nd ed.). New York: Norton.

Erikson, E. H. (1968). *Identity: Youth and crisis*. New York: Norton.

CHAPTER 7

Kohut's Self Psychology

Chicago Institute of Psychoanalysis.

Biographical Sketch

Heinz Kohut was born in Vienna, Austria, on May 3, 1913. His father, Felix, was a highly successful businessman and an erudite and cultured person. A gifted pianist, Felix was preparing for a career in music when World War I broke out. Like the countless men who went off to war in those turbulent times, Kohut's father was absent during his son's first five years. Perhaps distracted and haunted by the war when he returned, Felix remained a rather distant figure in his son's life. Heinz had ambivalent feelings toward his parents. An only child, Heinz felt his mother, Else Lampl, was oppressively close at times, but distant at others.

Kohut's education was remarkable. As a member of one of Vienna's elite families, Heinz was provided with an education in the classics while he was in high school. He studied French and then, as a young man, spent a full year in Paris perfecting his skills. He was also exposed to eight years of Latin and six of Greek. He spent time studying literature, music, art, and history. From the time he was 8 until he was 14, his parents hired a tutor to stimulate him intellectually. Heinz and the tutor would go to the opera and to art museums; they also talked and played intellectual games as they strolled the streets of beautiful Vienna. At the time of his graduation from high school, Heinz was at or near the top of his class academically and was also active in athletics; he was good at track and he boxed well.

At 19, Kohut entered the University of Vienna and eventually earned an M.D. degree in 1938; he received his principal training in neurology. He also became highly interested in psychoanalysis during this period. Kohut never knew or met Freud, but he admired him tremendously and consciously tried to model himself after his idol. In fact, Kohut showed up at the train station in Vienna when Freud and his family began their journey to England to escape the Nazis, in 1938. Kohut fondly recalled, in later years, that Freud looked out of the train window and saw Kohut and a friend standing on the platform. Kohut tipped his hat, and Freud tipped his hat in return as the train rolled out of the station. Already, it was clear that Kohut was on a mission to follow in Freud's footsteps and to promote psychoanalysis as a science and therapy.

In 1940, Kohut left Vienna and came to the United States. He settled in Chicago, grew to love the city with its rich and diverse cultural life, and lived there until his death. He was a lecturer in the Department of Psychiatry at the University of Chicago and a faculty member and training and supervising analyst at the Chicago Institute for Psychoanalysis. During his professional life, he worked tirelessly as an administrator promoting psychoanalysis, had a full clinical practice, and taught classes in psychoanalytic theory. In the classroom, Dr. Kohut made an indelible impact on his students. He was a brilliant teacher and could weave an entire lecture from just about any comment or question. Taking every question seriously, he tried to put himself in the questioner's shoes.

Eventually, Kohut decided to publish his ideas. They were the product of his intense, lifelong concern with the task of understanding another human being. His major theoretical works, *The Analysis of the Self* (1971) and *The Restoration of the Self* (1977), emphasize his new perspective on narcissism and emphasize the importance of the role of an empathic environment on personality development and mental health. Published posthumously, *How Does Analysis Cure?* (1984) presents an elaboration of his ideas about the nature of psychoanalytic cure, a further elaboration of the concept of empathy, a clarification of the status and meaning of the Oedipal complex within self psychology, a presentation of his ideas on the nature of defenses and resistances, and a revision of his ideas about the alter-ego transference. Finally, *Self Psychology and the Humanities* (1985) details how the humanities—particularly history, literature, and art—inspired and provided affirmation of his neoanalytic views.

Kohut received many honors and awards in his life, from being elected as president of the American Psychoanalytic Association to being awarded the Heinz Hartmann prize of the New York Psychoanalytic Association. As he grew older, he turned down many other awards and ceremonies, so that he could devote all of his energies to his work. He had a single-minded purpose to advance psychoanalysis as a science and as a therapy through the addition of his ideas on the self. His single-mindedness often led to conflicts with some of his colleagues, who accused him of failing to recognize the contributions of his peers in the discipline and sometimes even appropriating and publishing others' ideas as his own. His original ideas were also highly controversial, however, and he faced an unrelenting barrage of criticism from within the analytic community. Many analysts, especially those with orthodox orientations, rejected his views. He lost many of his valued colleagues and friends, primarily because he dared to express ideas that deviated from the classical psychoanalytic position. Kohut died on October 8, 1981 (Goldberg, 1982, pp. 257–258; Strozier, 1985, pp. 3–12).

Concepts and Principles

Self Psychology: The Newest Development in Classical Psychoanalysis

Kohut's **self psychology** focuses primarily on understanding and explaining the development of the self and its impact on the person's mental health within a context of human interaction. Kohut strongly criticized classical psychoanalytic theory in many respects and saw his own work as more accurately recognizing the role of narcissism in normal adult psychology. As Kohut's ideas developed, they involved reinterpretations of many of the phenomena originally examined by Freud. For example, Kohut criticized Freud's libido theory, which maintained that individuals are driven by sexual and aggressive instincts to gratify their urges on various targets, usually other people. In Kohut's theory, individuals do not seek relationships with other people primarily to gratify these instinctual needs. Instead, satisfaction of sexual and aggressive needs is secondary to people's basic needs for human relatedness. Whereas Freud believed that the frustration and repression of sexual and aggressive instincts caused pathological behavior, Kohut believed that it was threats and damage to the self that produced aberrant sexual and aggressive behavior.

Kohut also thought that Freud's preoccupation with instinctual needs in personality development caused him to obscure the needs that all individuals have for contact and affiliation with others. Indeed, there is scientific evidence that the development of affectionate bonds between parents and their children is not usually an outgrowth of libidinal aims, but rather is a critical, independent aspect of development that expresses biological propensities to establish links to people (Eagle, 1984, pp. 15–16).

Kohut believed that his theory modifies and extends not only classical psychoanalytic theory but also important aspects of **ego psychology**. You may recall that Erikson's psychology focuses on the emergence of a strong ego identity as individuals resolve the crises inherent in the developmental process. For Erikson, the ego was the key theoretical concept. It acts, when healthy, to unify and direct personality functioning. In Kohut's theory, this unifying and directing role is attributed to the self and not to the ego. But aren't these two concepts interchangeable synonyms? In Kohut's opinion, the answer is no. He believed that there are important distinctions between the self and the ego, and that the self is the more fundamental concept. In this view, it might be said that the id, ego, and superego are all facets and agencies of an underlying self; their actions are controlled and directed by the self when it is functioning in a healthy way. Coherent functioning of the self structure leads to feelings of well-being and also secondarily to an increase in the strength and dominance of the ego. The ego then provides the individual with the means to solve his or her problems realistically and creatively. When the self is damaged psychologically, it becomes fragmented and enfeebled, the ego fails to function properly, and the individual is unable to cope with his or her problems in an adaptive and satisfying way (Kohut, 1971, p. 119). Thus, Kohut postulated that many of the insights achieved by an ego psychology like Erikson's complement his own theory (Kohut, 1984, p. 65).

Self Psychology as Object-Relations Theory

Psychoanalytic models of personality development may be divided into several categories. One kind is called **object-relations theory**. A fundamental premise of object-relations models is that **object relations** are central to psychoanalytic thinking and treatment. However, the meanings associated with the term *object relations* vary considerably from theory to theory. It is important to clarify these meanings so that we can better understand the various models. For example, in classical psychoanalysis, an object refers to a target of the instincts, that is, of sexual or aggressive drives. Thus, in the Freudian sense, an object could be another person (for example, one's husband or wife), a part or parts of the person (for example, breasts or a penis), or a thing (for example, in the discharge of aggressive impulses by destroying a chair).

For object-relations theorists like Kohut, however, objects are defined as other people. These people may be internal or external to the individual and may be real or imagined. External objects are real people. Internal objects are mental representations of people or things that exist within the self. They are called **self-objects** because the individual experiences them as an integral part of the self. Self-objects generally denote psychologically important people who support the cohesion of the self. They help individuals regulate tensions and stresses that confront them and that they are incapable of handling. For infants, these self-objects are the parents, who minister to their infants' needs by feeding, bathing, clothing, and comforting them. By doing so, the parents are able to reduce the infants' tensions and stresses. Later in childhood, as children actively interact with relatives, siblings, friends, teachers, and so forth, these individuals have the potential to become self-objects. In adulthood, the range of potential self-objects is expanded even further and may include boyfriends or girlfriends, spouses, and political, religious, military, and academic leaders. Thus, Kohut maintained that the need for self-objects does not fade with maturity. Self-objects are required throughout the lifespan to help us cope with the particular problems and issues that confront us (Leider, 1995, pp. 26–27). While self-objects are required to help us cope with our own difficulties, we need to transform them gradually and integrate them into our personalities so that we can act in psychologically healthy ways.

Personality Development

Pre-Oedipal Development of the Nuclear Self

Kohut maintained that, strictly speaking, the neonate has no self (Kohut & Wolf, 1978, p. 416). However, the social environment into which the child is born also includes the primary caregivers, who treat the child as if he or she had a self, by giving the child a name, getting him or her to sense that he or she is distinct from others, and by taking care of his or her bodily needs. Through those interactions, a rudimentary self begins to crystallize. As reliably as they can, the parents care for the child's needs, laugh and talk to the child, play with the child, and comfort and console the child when he or she is distressed. Thus, there is often an immediate and strong bond between the child and his or her parents. This positive interactive process between the child and the parents contributes to the development of a core or **nuclear self** within the first two or three years of life. Without their general care, support, and love, the infant would soon perish.

The mother is usually the primary self-object, the one who ministers to the infant's needs, although Kohut pointed out that the father and other adults can respond adequately to the baby's needs (Kohut, 1985, p. 167). Initially the infant exists in a state of **primary narcissism**—in a state of self-love that is perfect and blissful; all of the child's needs are fulfilled by the mother. Inevitably, however, the equilibrium of this primary narcissism is disturbed by the unavoidable delays and shortcomings of the mother's care (Kohut, 1971, p. 64). For example, she may not always respond to the infant's cries for food or drink immediately because of an emergency elsewhere in the home, or she may not always return the infant's smile because she is tired at the end of a long day of household chores. She may neglect to comfort the child when in distress, to put the appropriate winter clothing on the child for an outing on a snowy, windy day, and so forth. Kohut maintained that, under these conditions, the infant tries to remove the disequilibrium, but this requires the responsiveness of the self-object. If the mother is not sufficiently responsive, a traumatic state ensues; the infant then tries to restore the original state of perfection by the establishment of a **grandiose self**.

The grandiose self involves the unconscious belief of the child that he or she is great and perfect. The child also has a need to be mirrored, that is, a yearning for parental feedback that he or she is admired and has an impact on others. According to Kohut, it is usually the mother who does the **mirroring** for both sexes. She mirrors the child by reflecting, echoing, approving, and confirming his or her innate sense of greatness (Kohut & Wolf, 1978, p. 414). By her mirroring, she makes it possible for the child to internalize others' approval and admiration. The child now feels worthwhile. This process is facilitated further by the mother's **empathy**. She must be able to put herself in the child's place, to recognize and understand the child's exhibitionistic needs to be admired, and to try to meet them. Such mirroring and empathizing are necessary if the child is going to start developing in a healthy way.

However, continued healthy development also depends on the mother's efforts to support realistic change in the child's grandiose self by setting limits on the expressions of his or her strongly unrealistic exhibitionistic needs and by helping the child to accept the realistic limits of his or her actual abilities and talents. Kohut said that such discipline involves **optimal frustration**, which means that the mother handles the immature, exhibitionistic needs of her child by adopting a calming, soothing, and loving attitude as she makes clear the unrealistic nature of the child's strivings rather than by acting aggressively toward the child (Kohut & Seitz, 1963, pp. 138–139). In other words, the child's unrealistic grandiosity and exhibitionism must be modified by gradual frustrations accompanied by loving support (Kohut, 1966, p. 253). As a result of these phase-appropriate optimal frustrations, the child undergoes **transmuting internalization**, which means that he or she can now decathect (disengage) some of the primitive narcissistic libido from the grandiose self and invest it in an emerging new psychic structure—a more realistic and independent nuclear self. In other words, optimal frustrations in parental responsiveness can facilitate maturation because, when self-object support is phase-appropriate and gradually limited, the child can learn to do without assistance what previously had been done for him or her by the parents (Watson, Biderman, & Sawrie, 1994, p. 701). For example, consider a boy with the grandiose belief that he is so special that his parents should only pay attention to him and should cater to his every need and demand. Such a boy could demand that his parents wash, feed, and dress him each morning. While such a grandiose wish and related parental behavior is developmentally appropriate during infancy, it is clearly inappropriate once the boy is 3 or 4 years old. At this point, the parents would have to begin gently frustrating him by firmly insisting that he learn how to wash, feed, and dress himself. If their encouragement and insistence is successful, the boy will eventually begin to learn a set of skills that allow him to see himself more realistically as an initiator of action and as competent.

Failure of the mother to empathize with her child and her inability to appropriately mirror the child because of her own pathology produces a lowering of his or her self-esteem; then, in a defensive attempt to ward off feelings of inadequacy, the child fixates on the grandiose self and, as a result, behaviors associated with an unbridled, primitive, grandiose, exhibitionistic self are enhanced and displayed. Consider the inadequate boy who protects himself by acting as though everyone is his slave and under his control. He may become bossy, throw frequent temper tantrums when he doesn't get his way, and even hit his parents or others when they oppose him. A mother with strong dependency needs of her own may fail to point out to him, in a loving and yet firm way, that his behavior is wrong and will not be permitted. Instead, she may overindulge him. She may laugh and comply with his demands when he becomes bossy, consider his temper tantrums cute, and ignore his hitting behavior because of her fear of losing his approval or love. Given her own pathological needs, she doesn't dare to frustrate him and so he fails to recognize and learn that there are limits on his behavior. The formation of a more realistic nuclear self is precluded, and consequently his narcissistic libido remains invested in a primitive, unmodified grandiose and exhibitionistic self.

Or consider the case of a girl who does not receive appropriate mirroring from her mother. She may fantasize in a grandiose way that she is precious. She may insist that her parents buy her the most fashionable clothes and jewelry, no matter what the financial income of the family. Instead of calmly pointing out to her that she cannot have her own way all the time and refusing her unreasonable demands, the mother may simply comply. Later, the girl may become almost totally self-absorbed and concerned with clothes and her physical appearance. As a result, she may be unable to maintain relationships with other females, because she sees herself as superior to them. Her male admirers may also grow tired of worshipping at her feet and suffering her demands for continual praise.

The nuclear self is based on interactions not only with the mother, but importantly with the father as well. When unavoidable shortcomings in parenting disturb the balanced state of primary narcissism, the child unconsciously attempts to restore equilibrium by identifying and associating with an admired, omnipotent, self-object, the

idealized parent imago. This idealization occurs because the child has an innate **need to idealize**. According to Kohut, it is principally the father who is idealized by the male. For the female, it is usually the mother who is idealized (Kohut, 1977, p. 185). The infant now cathects (invests or attaches) his or her libido (for example, love, affection, admiration) to this idealized structure. This idealized parent imago involves an unconscious merger with those people that the child can admire, with those who present an image of calmness, infallibility, and omnipotence (Kohut & Wolf, 1978, p. 414). Initially, these positive feelings toward the revered parent accompany the relief of the infant's distress on being picked up, soothed, and rocked in the powerful embrace of the parent. Later, in early childhood, children often express unbridled admiration for a parent because they are cognitively immature and unable to make appropriate discriminations. They often imitate the parent's mannerisms, speech, and activities; because they have a massive narcissistic investment in the parent, they experience tremendous gratification through such imitative expressions (Kohut, 1971, p. 139). In such situations, children are not separate initially from their parents but are simply merged with them. They are living through their parents and are highly dependent on them.

Kohut believed that such unrealistic idealization is necessary initially, if children are to begin growing in a healthy way. Thus, empathic parents allow their children to glorify them initially, so that their children can vicariously experience feelings of being worthwhile (Kohut, 1971, p. 139). However, Kohut maintained that, soon afterward, these parents must gradually support the process of taming this unabashed admiration through the effective use of optimal frustrations; that is, they must teach them about the realistic imperfections and limitations of the idealized parent imago. For example, the father may allow his son to learn that he is not invincible, that there are times when others beat him fairly in athletic or business competitions. Or the mother may allow her daughter to learn that she sometimes feels resentful and hostile and acts harshly toward others when they fail to agree with her viewpoint. The healthy parent is one who is optimally failing. An effective father must not lose all credibility by complaining constantly to his son that he is an abject failure totally unworthy of admiration, nor should the father pose as a superman without faults or flaws. Instead, the father must gradually reveal some of his limitations to his son when he considers it helpful to the son's personal growth.

This new learning process enables the children to see their parents more realistically and to engage in the transmuting internalizations that result in the consolidation of a cohesive self structure, that is, in the formation of the nuclear self. If the parents fail to empathize properly with their children, the idealized parent imago remains primitive and largely unrealistic. In a clinical case cited by Kohut, a patient's attempt to idealize his father was rejected; the father responded by criticizing and belittling his son. Analysis revealed that the father was unable to accept this idealizing role because he had low self-esteem. As a result, the son tried to enhance his self-esteem by reinstating the old grandiosity and exhibitionism that had been fostered by his mother (Kohut, 1971, pp. 139–140).

In summary, the nuclear self evolves during the first two or three years of life and is therefore pre-Oedipal (Okun, 1992, p. 32). It is also bipolar, because it represents the outgrowth of efforts to recognize and to come to grips with the imperfections and limitations of two poles of the self: the grandiose self and the idealizing self (as represented mentally by the idealized parent imago). As a result of these efforts, the domain and power of the child's infantile fantasies are diminished, and a core or nuclear self encompassing a rudimentary and more realistic set of skills and talents is established. This nuclear self then serves as a solid foundation upon which a more organized and integrated **cohesive self** can be built. Formation of the cohesive self is not distinct from the formation of the nuclear self. Rather, the cohesive self is simply a quality of the nuclear self; specifically, it refers to the degree of integration, coherence, and vitality of the nuclear self (Tolpin, 1980, p. 310). If the cohesive self is developing properly, it helps the individual make even more progress toward the attainment of optimal mental health.

Pre-Oedipal Development: The Oral and Anal Stages

Kohut did not abandon Freud's theory of psychosexual development completely. He agreed with Freud that the child may develop oral or anal fixations during this early period, but he explained their etiology differently than did Freud. In general, Kohut saw these fixations as the result of the child's defensive efforts to cope with damage to the nuclear self that has been caused by unempathic caretaking and not as the result of frustration of the child's sexual aims.

Oral stage For Freud, the focus during this stage is on the feeding process itself and on frustrations experienced when the mother either underindulges the child by premature weaning or overindulges the child, who consequently feels frustrated at finally having to give up the breast or bottle. The result is oral fixations that have a negative impact on later personality functioning. Thus, for Freud, frustration of the child's pleasure-seeking (sexual) needs leads to disordered functioning.

In contrast, Kohut believed that, during this period, the child demands an emotionally supportive, food-giving self-object (the mother) to empathically minister to his or her needs. If the mother is unempathic—for example, indifferent or rejecting—there is damage to the child's self-esteem. The self then fragments; the child regresses to pleasure-seeking (sexual) oral stimulation and becomes orally fixated. Thus, it is damage to the self that produces pleasure-seeking, sexualized drive fixations (Kohut, 1977, p. 81).

Anal stage Freud claimed that the child may become anally fixated in response to frustration of the pleasure-seeking impulses associated with the retention or expulsion of feces. The anal retentive individual may be characterized later in life as obstinate and stingy, whereas the anal expulsive individual may become very messy or, through reaction formation, a person with compulsive needs for orderliness and cleanliness.

Kohut, on the other hand, believed that the mother is not only responding to the child's pleasure-seeking (libidinal) impulses, but also to the child's self-object needs. Again, her attitude plays a critical role in the child's development. More specifically, she can respond to her child's giving and offering feces by mirroring her approval, thereby confirming the child's self. The child would then feel pride. Conversely, if she rejects the "gift" of the feces, she is rejecting a self that is just beginning to assert itself as a center of creative-productive initiative. In reaction, the child could easily become preoccupied with his or her feces and the pleasures associated with their retention. In brief, the child would experience a fragmentation of the self, that is, excessive concern with a body part (Kohut, 1977, pp. 75–76).

Oedipal Development: The Phallic Stage

In Kohut's view, the Oedipal complex is a basic and important phenomenon discovered by Freud. However, Kohut believed that Freud's explanation of its operation is limited and needs amplification (Kohut, 1977, p. 223).

Phallic stage You may recall Freud's description of the Oedipal process in 4- and 5-year-old boys and girls. Boys, according to Freud, develop a longing for sexual contact with the mother, but fear that they will be punished by their fathers for their desires.

They experience castration anxiety and identify with their fathers to alleviate it. The resolution of their conflict is accompanied by the formation of the superego, as boys take on the values and ideals of their fathers. In girls, the process is considerably different. Upon discovery that they lack a penis, they experience penis envy. According to Freud, they resent the mother for bringing them into the world without a penis and begin to love their father because he has the desired object. They then identify with the mother as a means of vicariously obtaining it. Their fantasies revolve around the wish to have sexual intercourse with the father and to have his baby. Specifically, they long for a male baby who will bring the longed-for penis with him.

Kohut reinterpreted the Freudian explanation of the Oedipal process. He believed that the only children able to adequately resolve Oedipal conflicts are those with cohesive nuclear selves, formed during the pre-Oedipal years by associations with empathic parents. Unless they see themselves as independent centers of initiative, they are unable to experience the instinctual desires for the parent of the opposite sex that initiate the Oedipal conflicts and their eventual resolution (Kohut, 1977, p. 227). For example, if the mother's responses to her son during the pre-Oedipal period were grossly unempathic and unreliable, he would be very likely to cling to an infantile grandiose self. As a result, he would be unable to engage in the transmuting internalizations that are necessary for the establishment of a stable and clear nuclear self separate from his mother. Thus, the Oedipal conflict would remain unresolved, because his libidinal energies would remain focused on his grandiose self rather than on the mother (Kohut, 1971, pp. 64–65).

Kohut's interpretation of an unresolved Oedipal conflict in girls is also very different from Freud's. He described his analysis of an artist in her forties who was experiencing low self-esteem and feelings of hopelessness. She had previously been to another analyst, who had interpreted her difficulties in classical psychoanalytic terms. The analyst had pointed out to her that her present depressive feelings stemmed from her inability to accept her femaleness; that is, her problems were the result of penis envy. Kohut noted that the woman did have bathroom dreams about wanting to have a penis and to urinate standing up like a man. She had also dreamed that, as a little girl, she had yearned to see her father's body, especially his genitals. Kohut reassured her that these dreams were not primarily related to sexual matters. Instead they were based on her need to extricate herself from her relationship with her emotionally shallow and unempathic mother and to turn toward her emotionally more responsive (empathic) and loving father. He arrived at this insight when the patient reported the memory that her mother had repeatedly and harshly warned her never to sit down on a toilet outside their own house because the seats were contaminated with dirt, bacteria, infections, and so forth. This fear was inculcated in the daughter because of the mother's own hidden paranoid outlook on the world. And the daughter's healthy attempts to move toward the world were made impossible by the infiltration of the mother's paranoid beliefs into the child's psyche. Her wish to see the father's penis was her sexualized attempt to turn toward him for a positive, healthy, nonparanoid view of the world. She needed his support to overcome her mother's influence over her, so that she could, metaphorically, sit down on the toilet; that is, she needed to gain his support in order to rebuild her weakened self, so that she could be joyful and alive in her sexual and nonsexual experiences, not empty and suspicious like her mother (Kohut, 1977, pp. 221–222).

In conclusion, Kohut believed that a successful resolution of the Oedipal conflict takes place only when the child already possesses a firm nuclear self. The successful resolution of the conflict makes the person more definitely a male or female self on moving into the latency period (Kohut, 1977, pp. 239–240).

Post-Oedipal Development: The Latency and Genital Stages

Latency stage   For Freud, the sexual instinct lies dormant during the latency stage, from about the sixth year to puberty. He believed that the fundamental personality was established during the first five years of life and drastic changes were extremely difficult, if not impossible, to make thereafter. Freud also thought that, during this period, children turned to the world of school and peers and became motivated to learn a variety of physical, social, and academic skills that would increase their sense of competence and ability to function more effectively in their daily living.

Kohut, in contrast, believed that the person's personality is still subject to considerable changes after age five. He asserted, for example, that the superego is fragile, and subject to change, not only during the latency period but in adolescence as well. Under the impact of a traumatic experience, such as his father's decision to sever all ties with the family following divorce, an adolescent boy may reject the uncertain superego, which was based largely on the internalization of his father's values and seek another external object to idealize. In that search, the boy may attach his narcissistic libido to an antisocial group, for example, a teenage gang or an extremist religious cult. In Kohut's view, gradual disappointments in the father that lead to a more realistic view of him have healthy repercussions for the child's development, whereas severely negative experiences such as abandonment by the father are likely to do lasting damage to the nuclear self (Kohut, 1971, pp. 44–48).

Genital stage   With puberty, sexual tension in the adolescent increases greatly. The reproductive organs have matured, and both sexes are now capable of reproduction. In the earlier stages, the aims of the sexual instincts have been predominantly autoerotic, but now the goal is to mate with a heterosexual object. In Freud's view, an adequate heterosexual adjustment depends on the amount of sexual energy or libido available to the person during this period. If the conflicts in the prior stages have been resolved adequately, so that there are no libidinal fixations on infantile objects, an adequate adjustment is possible. For Freud, when the person reaches adulthood, he or she typically marries and settles into family life. Careers are pursued to provide support for the family. Thus, normal development involves satisfactory adjustments in two areas: love and work. The normal or psychologically healthy person is called the genital character. Conversely, an inadequate adjustment in these areas because of libidinal fixations leads to the development of various character disorders.

Kohut's view of adolescence is much different. In discussing sexual fixations during this stage, he noted that they are almost always an outgrowth of damage to the self caused by unresponsive and unempathic parents. The parents' pathology causes the teenagers to feel unloved, alone, and vulnerable. To overcome these feelings, they may become intensely exhibitionistic and commit destructive acts that win them the recognition, admiration, and approval of their peers—for example, stealing cars and taking their friends for a joyride; drinking excessively and damaging other people's private property while in a stupor; or attacking and beating the elderly. These acts are expressions of narcissistic rage and aggression; they temporarily relieve the adolescents' lethargy and depression, resulting from the unavailability of a mirroring object and of an idealizable self-object (Kohut, 1977, p. 272).

Kohut believed that healthy development occurs when individuals have acquired a firm and vigorous self within the context of having emotionally close and loving relationships with others. Empathic treatment by parents ensures that children will be encouraged to develop a firm and realistic sense of self. Such a sense of self is characterized by feelings of autonomy, for example, individuals direct their own thoughts, make and respect their own judgments, and assume responsibility for their own actions. A vigorous self is associated with a strong ego that utilizes its skills and talents to solve love and work problems (Kohut, 1977, p. 284). If the parenting has been largely unempathic, a firm sense of self will typically be lacking, and people will be unlikely to develop the skills that are necessary to cope with problems. Instead they may, for example, seek to establish a relationship with an unempathic parent in which he or she either provides mirroring for their primitive sense of grandiosity or a sense of security, esteem, and direction. Thus, they may rely too heavily on their parents for support and guidance. Under such conditions, there is a blurring of boundaries between family members. For example, teenage daughters and their mothers may become too dependent on each other, and they may seek and even demand love and approval from one another (and criticize the other for not providing it). They may continually overact emotionally to one another, leaving them with little energy to seek to establish self-determined goals or values (Perosa & Perosa, 1997, pp. 144–146).

Finally, healthy development is not achieved once and for all at a particular time in the lifespan. Rather, the individual continually attempts to strengthen his or her autonomous self by overcoming problems and conflicts that can occur at any time. Kohut asserted, for example, that people in late middle age (approximately 58–64) are especially prone to crisis. Such people are experiencing an "ultimate decline" and are wracked with anxiety and concern about whether they have lived up to their potentials. This is the time, according to Kohut, when many individuals who think they are failures feel completely hopeless and depressed. He believed that suicides committed in late middle age are a remedial act; they express a wish to wipe out the mortification and shame experienced by a fragmented and inadequate self (Kohut, 1977, p. 241). People in this age group can be helped to recover from their sense of shame and to reconcile themselves with impending death.

Disturbances to the Self

According to Kohut, disturbances to the self can be classified into several subgroups depending on the nature and severity of the problem. In many of these disturbances, parental pathology (e.g., depression, paranoia) plays a major role in the etiology of disturbances to the self. He also thinks that some of these disturbances have a biological basis.

In the event of extremely serious permanent or protracted damage to the self, when few defense mechanisms are available to effectively cover the defect, the resulting pathological state is called a **psychosis**. In schizophrenia, for example, the nuclear self is disorganized and chaotic because of a confluence of biological and constitutional factors; a lack of joyful and empathic responses by the parents to the child's existence and assertiveness may also play a role. In addition, at a critical point, the child may have been deprived of an opportunity to merge with an idealized self-object (Kohut & Wolf, 1978, p. 415; Wolf, 1988, pp. 67–68). Kohut believed that, in such major disorders, the parents may fail to meet both needs—the need to be mirrored and the need to idealize the parents. The severe damage to the self results in a disorder characterized by delusions of greatness and disorganized speech and behavior (American Psychiatric Association, 2000, p. 297).

The second subgroup of important disorders consists of the **borderline states**. Here, too, the nuclear self is in a state of functional chaos, and the damage to the self is either permanent or protracted. The major difference between these disorders and the psychoses is that the people suffering from borderline states are able to cover the defects in the self by the use of complex defense mechanisms (Kohut & Wolf, 1978, p. 415; Wolf, 1988, pp. 68–69). Borderline states are psychotic-like conditions that typically do not collapse into the mass deterioration of a psychosis because the individual employs various protective defenses (Leider, 1995, pp. 3–6; Tolpin, 1980, p. 302).

Included among the borderline states we find the schizoid and paranoid personality disorders. Individuals with **schizoid personality disorders** achieve emotional distance from others by showing emotional coldness and flatness. This maneuver protects them from serious breakup or distortion of the self. Such individuals appear to lack a desire for intimacy, seem indifferent to opportunities to develop close relationships, and do not derive much satisfaction from being part of a family or other social groups. They prefer being alone and engage most often in solitary activities or hobbies (American Psychiatric Association, 2000, pp. 694–695).

Individuals suffering from **paranoid personality disorders**, in contrast, distance themselves from others by being hostile and suspicious. They assume that other people will exploit, harm, or deceive them, even if there is no evidence to support their belief. Such individuals are also reluctant to confide in others, or to become close to them, because they fear that any information they share will be used against them. Also, they read hidden meanings that are demeaning and threatening into innocuous remarks. For example, individuals with this disorder will see an honest mistake by a store clerk as an attempt to cheat them. They also tend to bear grudges and are unwilling to forgive any slights or insults they think they have received (American Psychiatric Association, 2000, pp. 690–691).

The third subgroup consists of the narcissistic personality and behavior disorders. Kohut's term **narcissistic personality disorders** refers to individuals with grandiose styles of thinking, hypersensitivity to criticism, and overreactions to failure that interfere with effective interpersonal functioning, whereas his term **narcissistic behavior disorders** refers to individuals who act out their grandiose fantasies by engaging in perversions and delinquent behavior. In general, people with narcissistic disorders routinely have problems with self-esteem. They may overestimate their abilities and inflate their accomplishments, and will often appear boastful and pretentious. Alternately, they may be self-deprecating and minimize their abilities and accomplishments. They are often preoccupied with fantasies of unlimited success, power, brilliance, or beauty, or with fears of failure and deficiency. They may ruminate about long-overdue admiration and privilege and compare themselves favorably with famous people (American Psychiatric Association, 2000, pp. 714–715). These disorders are pathological, but many of them are not necessarily severely pathological; that is, many of them operate within the normal range of thinking and behavior. Therefore, aspects of them are quite common among normal individuals.

Much of Kohut's personality theory is concerned with the impact of narcissistic disorders on human development and functioning. While the origins and course of the development of these disorders are complex, Kohut offered a simpler typology of their operation in order to clarify our understanding of them.

Typology for Narcissistic Personality and Behavior Disorders

Narcissistic personality disorders   Kohut and his colleague Wolf listed four types of narcissistic personality disorders: the understimulated self, the fragmented self, the over-stimulated self, and the overburdened self (Kohut & Wolf, 1978, pp. 118–122; Wolf, 1988, pp. 70–76).

The understimulated self   The first disordered type is the **understimulated self**. It results from prolonged lack of stimulating responsiveness on the part of the parents. Kohut saw this lack of parental responsiveness to the child's mirroring and idealizing needs as the most dangerous threat to the psychological survival of the individual in Western culture. He argued that many children today have fewer and fewer opportunities to participate emotionally in their parents' lives, given the high rates of divorce and separation and the need for both parents to work long hours at several jobs if the family is to survive economically. Although children may have an opportunity to participate with the parents in play and leisure activities, they do not usually have opportunities to get to know their parents more personally in their other life activities, particularly in regard to parental ambitions, ideals, and goals. Kohut believed that children should have an opportunity to learn not only about their parents' hopes and dreams, but also about their nontraumatic limitations, failures, and disappointments. Only through such revelations can children undergo the transmuting internalizations that are necessary for the establishment of independent nuclear selves (Kohut, 1977, pp. 269–270).

As a result of lack of parental stimulation, these individuals experience themselves as boring and apathetic and will resort to any kind of stimulation in their attempts to ward off feelings of lethargy and deadness. According to Kohut, toddlers may try to alleviate apathy and lethargy by engaging in head-banging, older children by engaging in compulsive masturbation, and adolescents by engaging in various daredevil activities. Adults try to alleviate their boredom and deadness by engaging in promiscuous sexual activities and various perversions, gambling, drug and alcohol abuse, and hypersociability (Kohut & Wolf, 1978, p. 418; Wolf, 1988, pp. 70–71).

The fragmenting self Kohut's second type of narcissistic personality disorder is the **fragmenting self**. It too results from a lack of parental responsiveness. But here the inability to respond adequately may focus on a single aspect of the child's total self. For example, consider a son whose mother is generally loving and empathic. One day he comes home from school and tells his mother exuberantly about the great grades he received on his report card. Suddenly, she remarks critically that he should stop waving his arms around when he's talking because everyone knows he's a klutz and he may hit her in the face or knock something over. This rejection of his emotional outpouring and his feelings of pride, his exhibitionism may shift his attention to a part of his body (his wildly waving arms) just at the most vulnerable moment, when he was offering his total self to her for approval (Kohut, 1971, p. 121). Later in life, he may feel physically uncoordinated and inexplicably dejected after receiving recognition of his academic accomplishments from his teachers. Kohut would say there has been damage to the total self, so that the person feels fragmented whenever the traumatic experience is reactivated.

The overstimulated self The third type of narcissistic personality disorder is the **overstimulated self**. It occurs as a result of excessive responsiveness to the child's grandiose and idealizing needs. The child's grandiose fantasies of greatness and unrealistic goals are constantly reinforced by the parents, who reward the exhibitionistic behavior with constant admiration, attention, and approval. Such parents do not provide the optimal frustration of the child's grandiose and idealizing fantasies; that is, they do not demonstrate the realistic limitations of the child's fantasies or of his or her talents and abilities and, as a result, the child does not begin to establish a strong nuclear self that is separate from the primitive grandiose self and its unrealistic counterpart, the primitive idealized parent imago. Such a child then moves into adulthood with only a weak separation between the fantasy selves and the realistic, but weak, nuclear self. Because the child is now subject to being flooded by unrealistic, archaic greatness fantasies, which produce painful tension and anxiety because they are at variance with his or her weak, realistic, nuclear self, the child may try to avoid becoming the center of attention. Thus, the child will shy away from creative and productive activities for fear of being overwhelmed by an uncontrollable grandiosity (Kohut & Wolf, 1978, p. 419; Wolf, 1988, pp. 71–72).

The overburdened self The last type of narcissistic personality disorder is the **overburdened self**. People of this type view the world as hostile and dangerous. They quickly respond with irritability and hostility to even minor frustrations. However, these reactions rapidly subside once the frustrating event has passed. The disorder can be traced to early childhood and the lack of an opportunity for children to merge with the calmness of omnipotent self-objects (parents). In other words, idealized parents have failed to teach their children how to handle interference with their goals calmly and with composure. Consequently, they become quickly overburdened when threatened and react emotionally and irrationally.

Narcissistic behavioral disorders Listed among the narcissistic behavioral disorders are mirror-hungry personalities, ideal-hungry personalities, alter-ego personalities, merger-hungry personalities, and contact-shunning personalities. While the first three disorders are relatively mild and occur within the normal range of functioning, the last two are much more severe types of psychopathology (Wolf, 1988, pp. 72–74).

Mirror-hungry personalities **Mirror-hungry personalities** are continually searching for self-objects who will admire and nurture their famished selves. Such individuals typically were raised in families where the parents gave them insufficient mirroring attention. There are, however, mirror-hungry individuals who were given sufficient mirroring attention by their parents, usually their mother, but the attention focused not on meeting their needs but on the mother's needs. In other words, such a mother might continually praise her son's beautiful physical appearance, an area of intense concern to her, but not his physical strength, an area of strong concern to the son. Mirror-hungry individuals are impelled to display themselves, to show off, to evoke the attention of others as a means of counteracting their own lack of self-esteem. In adolescence, they may eventually find an admiring boyfriend or girlfriend who will fulfill their needs for a while, but most mirror-hungry personalities will soon become bored and seek new self-objects whose attention and recognition they hope to cultivate (Kohut & Wolf, 1978, p. 421; Wolf, 1988, p. 73).

Ideal-hungry personalities **Ideal-hungry personalities** had their needs to idealize and admire various self-objects frustrated in childhood. As a result, they are continually searching for others whom they can admire for their intelligence, power, beauty, or moral stature. They experience themselves as worthwhile only for as long as they can continue their admiration of these idealized figures. Eventually, ideal-hungry people find defects in these figures, become disillusioned, and begin the search for the next great person to admire. They invest their libido in this figure until he or she disappoints them (Wolf, 1988, p. 73).

Alter-ego-hungry personalities **Alter-ego-hungry personalities** can only experience themselves as real and worthwhile when they are in relationships with self-objects who will conform to their opinions, beliefs, values, and behavior. This disorder probably stems from severe frustration of their mirroring and idealizing needs during early childhood. Inevitably, such individuals discover that the other person is different from themselves and has his or her own separate and distinct personality. The estrangement that follows almost always leads to a breakup of the relationship. Like the mirror- and ideal-hungry personalities, alter-ego-hungry personalities are prone to look restlessly for one replacement after the other (Kohut & Wolf, 1978, p. 422; Wolf, 1988, p. 73).

Merger-hungry personalities People with **merger-hungry personalities** have self structures that are seriously defective. According to Kohut, all children have a need to idealize. They attempt to fulfill this need by merging initially with an all-powerful and admired figure. However, if such a figure is not available in the family for any reason, for example, because of the early death of a parent or because of parental separation or divorce, merging is prevented. Consequently, under these conditions the idealizing needs of these children are not met. Also, they cannot learn about the limitations of the idealized figure through optimal frustration, nor can they develop an independent sense of self through transmuting internalizations. Merger-hungry personalities then continue to seek primitive self-objects to fulfill their desperate need for self structure. They incorporate such idealized figures and unfortunately blur the boundaries between themselves and the others. This blurring interferes with their ability to discriminate their own thoughts, feelings, wishes, and intentions from those of the idealized figures. One negative result of such blurring of boundaries is that merger-hungry personalities feel intolerant of the actual idealized figure's independence. They are very sensitive to separations from the self-object and demand his or her continual presence (Kohut & Wolf, 1978, p. 422; Wolf, 1988, p. 74).

Contact-shunning personalities   **Contact-shunning personalities** are also seriously disturbed individuals. They too were prevented from merging with admired figures in early childhood. As a result, they have a tremendous yearning for an all-encompassing union with idealized figures. However, unlike the merger-hungry individuals, the contact-shunning personalities avoid social contact and become isolated. They avoid others not because of disinterest, but because their need of them is so great. They fear rejection by the adored figures, and there is also the apprehension that their weakened self structure would be completely swallowed up by these figures if their union occurred (Kohut & Wolf, 1978, p. 422; Wolf, 1988, p. 74).

The Role of Narcissism in the Development of the Self

In thinking about the role of narcissism in personality development, it would be easy to consider only the negative aspects of the construct. In popular usage of the term, people who are narcissistic are considered to be selfish and psychologically unhealthy. But Kohut maintained that narcissism has positive as well as negative implications for personality development. He believed that narcissism can contribute either to health or to mental illness, depending on the degree to which the two major narcissistic constellations or structures, the grandiose self and the idealized parent imago, can be transformed into more realistic structures. In families where parents are unempathic, the two major structures remain unrealistic and unchanged. The result is development of an unhealthy self (See Figure 7.1).

Research by Otway and Vignoles (2006, p. 113) found support consistent with Kohut's theorizing. British adults who recalled being raised by unempathic parents reported high levels of **unhealthy narcissism**. Threats to this damaged self often elicit narcissistic rage and pathological aggression. Newer research by Trumpeter, Watson, O'Leary, and Weathington (2008, pp. 51–71) is consistent with the work of Otway and Vignoles (2006), showing that American university students who recalled being raised by unempathic and unloving parents had higher levels of unhealthy narcissism and depression and lower levels of self-esteem.

In contrast, where the parents are empathic and provide their children with adequate opportunity and encouragement to learn, the two structures, the grandiose self and the idealized parent imago, are modified and become more realistic. Out of this learning process, children invest their narcissism in a more independent core or nuclear self. (See Figure 7.2.)

This **healthy narcissism** serves as the mainspring in their struggle for human creativity and meaningful human exploration (Goldberg, C., 1980, p. 12). They can now

FIG-7.1 Kohut's model for the role of primary narcissism in unhealthy development.

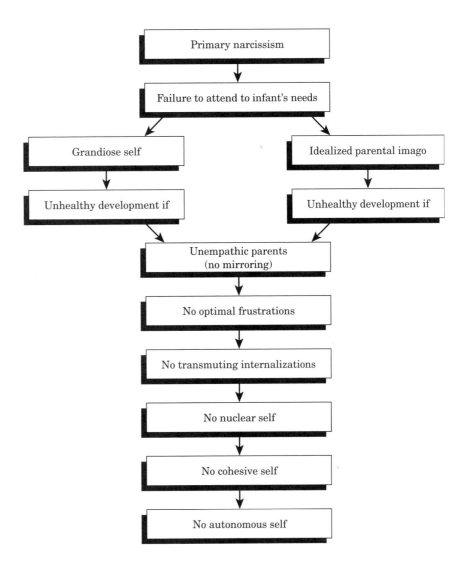

transform innate aggressive tendencies into healthy, mature self-assertiveness. The nuclear self then exercises its assertiveness by initiating action and serves as the organizer of the ego's activities. This realistic and strong ego then works toward the attainment of the self's goals. In Kohut's view, the nuclear self aims at the unfolding of the person's intrinsic patterns for creative action, as expressed through the workings of its realistic ego. In short, an empathic and supportive family environment provides an opportunity for the establishment of a core nuclear self, its growth into a more cohesive self, and the movement of this more unified self toward the attainment of a cohesive and relatively **autonomous self**.

In Kohut's view, the autonomous self is the epitome of mental health. The development of this independent self does not mean that the individual has no further need of others. People are always with us; they listen to us, applaud us, challenge us, help us, or ignore us. Kohut believed that we all have a continuing need for relatedness to self-objects. But the person who has evolved into an autonomous self now has a less urgent need to follow the expectations and demands of others and a greater flexibility in their interactions with them (Goldberg, 1988, p. 72).

FIG-7.2 Kohut's model for the role of primary narcissism in healthy development.

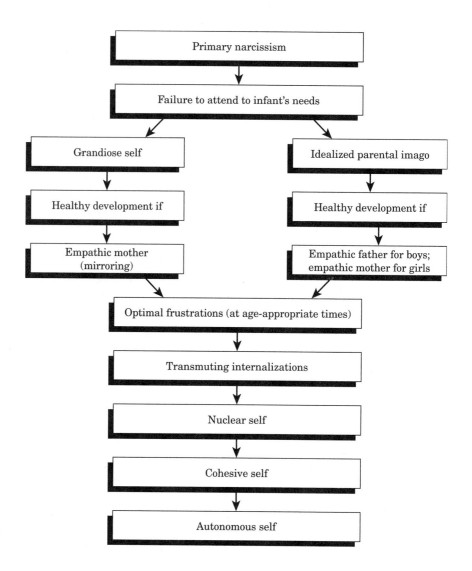

Also, as people move toward the attainment of this ideal state, they become increasingly liberated from unrealistic narcissistic needs and experience instead the joy of creative maturity (Kohut, 1977, p. 285). The transformed narcissistic energies of mature people allow them to experience pleasure in living, to feel realistic pride in their accomplishments, to love others as well as themselves, and to be successful at their work. They are also able to accept the limitations of their physical, intellectual, and emotional powers and the inevitability of their death (Kohut, 1966, p. 268).

Research Support for the Theory of Self Development

There is ample longitudinal research showing that the quality of the interactions between infants and their caretakers has a decided impact on their cognitive and emotional development. Moreover, infants who are exposed to unempathic and unresponsive parents do tend to be at risk for the development of psychological disorders later in life (Lichtenberg, 1991, p. 19). These findings are clearly consistent with Kohut's views. However, Kohut overemphasized the role of the mother in producing subsequent psychopathology in her child. Although Kohut recognized differences between infants in regard to their needs, drives, and anxiety tolerance, he nevertheless minimized the infants' influence on their environment (Silverman, 1986, p. 54). In fact, abundant research evidence shows that infants are very active in controlling interactions with their caregivers. For example, infants use gaze, smiling, crying, and head-turning to arouse maternal responsiveness. By virtue of their individual differences, some infants appear to enjoy cuddling and holding, whereas others react negatively, by kicking and thrashing (Lichtenberg, 1991, pp. 19–20). This limitation in Kohut's theorizing remains to be addressed by self psychology researchers.

There is greater difficulty in trying to validate Kohut's ideas about self-objects. He believed that infants use self-objects to regulate tensions but that eventually these self-objects must be transformed and gradually integrated into the personality, so that the individuals can act in psychologically healthy ways. Researchers are uncertain about when and how this modification process occurs (Lichtenberg, 1991, p. 31). Of course, the range of self-objects increases throughout childhood, as children establish relationships with relatives, friends, siblings, teachers, and others. In adulthood, the range of self-objects is expanded even further and may include romantic partners, spouses, and religious, military, and academic leaders. Kohut believed that self-objects are required throughout the lifespan. From a research standpoint, however, we know very little about how, when, and why certain self-objects are utilized and/or modified by individuals as they struggle toward self-realization. There is clearly a need for more research to determine whether Kohut's complicated theorizing has any validity in this respect and to assess longitudinal changes in self-objects as people proceed through the lifespan. Unfortunately, when we move beyond infancy research, we find that there are only a few longitudinal studies in existence, and these are based on adults' retrospective reports of their childhood experiences. Such reports must be viewed with caution because they are subject to memory bias and because it is impossible to establish cause-and-effect relationships among the variables. In addition, empirical validation of the theory is difficult, because many of the hypotheses are not clearly stated and many of the constructs are highly abstract and difficult to measure adequately. Despite these problems, investigators have begun to make some inroads in testing the theory, by developing reliable and valid measures of key constructs like narcissism, empathy, self-esteem, and mental health. Using these new measures, investigators have conducted important research by testing certain aspects of Kohut's theorizing.

For example, a study by Zamostny, Slyter, and Rios (1993, pp. 501–510) found that male and female students who reported having had many narcissistic injuries in childhood were the ones who were most academically and socially maladjusted during their college careers. These traumatic experiences included parental loss, serious personal illness, physical and/or sexual abuse within the family, severe financial problems, and serious psychological disorders in parents. More recent research by Lapsley and Aalsma (2006, pp. 53–71) is consistent with the research of Zamostny et al. (1993), showing that unhealthy narcissists reported many more adjustment problems in college and were higher in anxiety, depression, and lower in self-esteem than healthy narcissists who, in contrast, reported very few problems within their family life or in their friendships.

Wink (1991, 1992) also examined the early life of college students. In particular, he examined reports by college female narcissists of their early childhood relations with parents. He found that the unhealthy narcissists, that is, those characterized by overt grandeur, exhibitionism, and poor impulse control, reported very negative and troubled relations with their parents, and especially their mother. Both parents were seen as cold and uncaring (unempathic), but only the mother was perceived as distrusted and disliked. These women also reported a lack of enjoyment of childhood activities. In contrast, healthy narcissists, that is, those characterized by an independent sense of self and high, but realistic, achievement aspirations, reported that their relations with parents were untroubled. They also stated that they had engaged in many positive activities during childhood, including writing poems and stories, painting, and going on hikes.

Wink also collected additional data twice on these college women approximately 20 years after their graduation, when they were in their early or mid-40s and then again in their early 50s. These data showed that unhealthy narcissists were even more unempathic, irresponsible, hypersensitive, and moody than they had been in college. Most importantly, there was a decrease in their feelings of well-being, increased boredom with their lives, and a growing pessimism about their health and the future. Unhealthy narcissists also experienced less satisfaction in their marriages and in their occupations and reported that they were unable to put their lives together effectively. In a related study, Wink (1991) found that these same women also reported drug use and conflicts in their friendships. Healthy narcissists, on the other hand, showed personal discomfort only in their 20s, when they were first trying to juggle the demands of family and career. By the time they reached their 40s, these problems were resolved. Healthy narcissists in their 40s and their 50s showed a tremendous growth in self-confidence, social poise, understanding of self and others, an increased level of effective functioning, and a continued commitment to a high-status career. These women also reported less drug dependence and had good marriages and careers. They were also satisfied with their roles as mothers (Wink, 1991, pp. 769–785; Wink, 1992, pp. 7–30; Wink, 1996, pp. 64–67).

There are also several investigations that have focused on Kohut's ideas concerning the relationships between narcissism and grandiose thinking. This research provides consistent support for Kohut's theorizing. In one study, Gabriel, Critelli, and Ee (1994) showed that there are elements of grandiose thinking in highly narcissistic students. They found that male and female college students higher in unhealthy narcissism had stronger tendencies to overestimate their physical attractiveness than did students lower in unhealthy narcissism; that is, highly unhealthy narcissists rated themselves as far more attractive than they were actually rated by a group of independent observers. The ratings of students low in unhealthy narcissism did not differ from those provided by the observers. Also, in comparison to their actual performances on tests designed to measure their intelligence, students higher in unhealthy narcissism more strongly overestimated their intelligence than did students lower in unhealthy narcissism (Gabriel et al., 1994, pp. 151–153).

This tendency toward overinflation, which stems from perceptions of their own inadequacies and insecurities, is associated with poor experiences in their romantic relationships. Unhealthy narcissists continually seek admiration from their partners, are easily hurt by criticism, show little understanding of their partner's needs, and are often willing to exploit or take advantage of them. In the beginnings of their relationships, unhealthy narcissists idealize their partners. But soon they come to see them as flawed, tire of them, and search for new partners that will give them anew the admiration they so desperately crave. It is not surprising, then, that the romantic relationships of unhealthy narcissists are characterized by a lack of commitment and dissatisfaction and that they are continually searching for new partners (Campbell & Foster, 2002, pp. 484–495).

Finally, some research focuses directly on the association between unhealthy narcissism and self-esteem. Kohut maintained, for example, that the activation of the grandiose self reflects an attempt to ward off feelings of worthlessness and low self-esteem. According to him, such individuals are constantly seeking confirmation of their worth through unrealistic displays of grandiosity. Research by Raskin, Novacek, and Hogan (1991, pp. 19–38), using four different samples of college students, provides support for Kohut's theorizing. They found that unhealthy male and female narcissists in all four samples tried to bolster and enhance their feelings of self-esteem by engaging in grandiose and exhibitionistic behavior.

Kohut also believed that, if other people threatened their self-esteem by outperforming them in competitive situations, narcissists would react with rage, anger, and hostility and would then proceed to derogate them. Several investigations provide confirmation for these ideas (Corbitt, 1994, pp. 199–203; Emmons, 1984, pp. 291–300; Morf & Rhodewalt, 1993, pp. 668–676; Smalley & Stake, 1996, pp. 483–485). In the research by Morf and Rhodewalt (1993, pp. 668–676), for example, it was found that unhealthy narcissists react strongly to ego threats by derogating their opponents. They had study participants perform a competitive task that ostensibly measured their level of social sensitivity. They were then given feedback by the experimenter concerning the quality of their performance. In the high-threat condition, participants were told that their opponents had much higher scores and thus were much more socially sensitive; in the low-threat condition, participants were told that their opponents had about the same scores. Study participants were later given an opportunity to rate their opponents' personalities. The investigators found that participants higher in unhealthy narcissism gave a much more negative rating to their opponents than did participants lower in unhealthy narcissism, but only under the high-threat condition. Under the low-threat condition, unhealthy high- and low-narcissistic participants did not differ in their evaluations of their opponents' personalities (Morf & Rhodewalt, 1993, pp. 668–676).

Assessment Techniques

Kohut agreed with Freud that free association, dream analysis, and analyses of transference were techniques that could be used to probe the unconscious of patients, to help in understanding their problems, and to facilitate their cure. However, Kohut disagreed in many respects with Freud's interpretations of the psychological data gathered through the use of these techniques. In addition, Kohut elevated the concept of empathy to primary status as an assessment tool and believed that the other techniques were all auxiliaries of it.

Empathy as the Primary Data Collection Tool

Kohut defined psychoanalysis as the scientific study of complex mental states. In order to study these mental states, he thought, analysts must get as close to the immediate subjective experiences of their patients as they could. Consequently, Kohut advocated the use of empathy or, as he sometimes called it, vicarious introspection- as the primary tool of inquiry. For him, empathy meant our ability to put ourselves in the place of others, to think about their experiences, and to feel them as though they were our own. Only then can we understand them.

> Let us consider a simple example. We see a person who is unusually tall. It is not to be disputed that this person's unusual size is an important fact for our psychological assessment—without introspection and empathy, however, his size remains simply a physical attribute. Only when we think ourselves into his place, only when we, by vicarious introspection, begin to feel his unusual size as if it were our own and thus revive inner experiences in which we had been unusual or conspicuous, only then do we begin to appreciate the meaning that the unusual size may have for this person and only then have we observed a psychological fact. (Kohut, 1959, p. 207)

Once therapists have collected these psychological facts or data, they could interpret their meanings for the patients. For Kohut, empathy was, in its essence, neutral and objective. It was a technique used by therapists to collect accurate, objective data about the inner subjective state of another person. This point, Kohut felt, was misunderstood by many professionals and laypersons, who confused empathy with either sympathy or compassion. But these terms are not equivalent. Rather, empathy serves as a prerequisite for our ability to experience compassion. Compassion, in other words, grows out of our ability to accurately assess another's needs. However, empathy can also be used in the service of people's destructive acts. In order to hurt our enemies, for example, we must have accurate knowledge of their weaknesses: Our destructive actions are most effective when they are based on an empathic understanding of victims' sensitivities (Kohut, 1980, p. 483). Of course, analysts do view their patients with compassion, warmth, and sympathy, but that must be distinguished from the empathy used to collect accurate data about the patients' inner experience.

Free Association

Kohut maintained that the use of free association by patients facilitated therapists' ability to empathize with their patients' experiences. The patients' associations reveal areas of resistance that, once recognized, show the activities, vulnerabilities, and defenses of the archaic or immature self. This primitive self does not want to reexpose itself to the devastating, traumatizing narcissistic injury of finding that the parents do not respond to its basic mirroring and idealizing needs; that is, the resistances are a means of protecting patients from the anxiety associated with a disintegrating self (Kohut, 1977, p. 136). Freud, in contrast, believed that these resistances were attempts by his patients to protect themselves against the anxiety associated with early traumatic sexual or aggressive fantasies or experiences.

Dream Analysis

For Kohut, there are two types of dreams. The first follows Freud's analysis of the meaning of dreams very closely; that is, these dreams have both a manifest and latent content. The analyst's task is to interpret the associations to, and the symbols present in, the manifest content in an attempt to discover the latent meaning. Such dreams are unconscious attempts at wish fulfillment. The wishes are unacceptable to the person and are nearly always sexual in nature. The aim of the therapist is to follow the patient's free associations into the depths of the psyche until the unconscious meaning has been uncovered.

In the second type of dreams, free associations do not lead to unconscious hidden layers of the psyche. Instead, the free associations provide the therapist with further imagery on the same level as the manifest content. An examination of this content reveals that the healthy parts of the person's psyche are reacting to a disturbing change in the condition of the self. Kohut calls these dreams **self-state dreams**. Associations to these dreams do not lead to any deeper, underlying meaning (Kohut, 1977, pp. 109–110).

Kohut provides an interesting case study to illustrate the second type of dreams, that is, dreams in which the problem originates in a defect in the self. It involved a man whose mother provided him with grossly inadequate mirroring in his childhood and whose father provided a poor example of the needed, idealized father image. He recalled that, as a child, he drew people with large heads supported by bodies consisting of pencil-thin trunk and legs. Throughout his life, he had dreams in which he experienced himself as a brain at the top of a lifeless body. As the analysis progressed, he became able to describe the sexual fantasy he had whenever he became depressed, that is, whenever he experienced his self as empty and lifeless. In this fantasy, he imagined himself using his brains to subdue a powerful male figure; he then chained his adversary up to a wall, and performed oral sex on the male figure in order to deplete the giant's strength. In conjunction with these fantasies, he masturbated to orgasm. From early in his life, the patient had felt unreal: He experienced his body-self as fragmented and powerless, because of the lack of empathic responses from both of his parents. Only one fragment of his grandiose-exhibitionistic self had remained somewhat firm, namely, his thinking processes (his brains). His fantasy expressed the attempt to use the last remnant of his grandiose self (his omnipotent thought) in order to regain possession of the idealized omnipotent self-object (his father), that is, to exert absolute control over it and to internalize it via fellatio. Although the masturbatory act gave the patient a feeling of strength and increased self-esteem, it was unable to fill the structural defect in the self (absence of the idealized parent imago) and therefore had to be repeated again and again. In the course of therapy, the patient was able to fill the void by transmuting internalizations of idealized goals, which provided narcissistic sustenance to the self (Kohut, 1977, pp. 125–127).

Transference

In classical psychoanalysis, transference refers to the process in which the patient relives feelings, attitudes, desires, and fears from childhood in his relationships with people in the present. These feelings and attitudes almost always revolve around unresolved sexual and aggressive conflicts with the patient's parents. In treatment, these feelings are remobilized in relation to the therapist. The patient faces the traumatic memories again and reexperiences and slowly relinquishes the infantile wishes. This process is called *working through*. It has been compared with the work performed in the psyche of an individual who is in mourning. While the bereaved has to give up a love object of the present, the patient must give up the hope of fulfilling unmodified sexual wishes and must relinquish the objects of the past (Kohut & Seitz, 1963, p. 129).

Transference is also recognized in self psychology, but the disturbances that are relived are usually not sexual in nature. Instead, the disturbances are caused by damage to the self in early childhood. There has been developmental stunting of personal growth, because of the severe frustration of children's three basic needs. First, infants need to be mirrored, that is, to have their innate sense of greatness validated and approved. Later, as the grandiose self is modified, children's need to be mirrored is modified to a need to have their competent performances validated and approved. Second, infants need to idealize others, that is, to admire those who can protect them during times of stress that are beyond their competence to manage satisfactorily. At first, this admiration is unbridled, but later in childhood, as we mature and learn gradually about the imperfections in the admired figure, our admiration becomes more realistic and disillusionment less disturbing. Third, children need to be acknowledged by their kin as a fellow human being (for example, to feel a sense of acceptance and belonging). Initially, Kohut saw this last as a part of the mirroring process, but he later drew a distinction between the two needs (Kohut, 1984, pp. 192–194), on the grounds that there are situations in everyday life when the self is strengthened not because mirroring attests to the person's competence and achievement but because the person feels quietly sustained by another in whose presence he or she feels accepted (Basch, 1989, pp. 14–15).

The original childhood experiences that created these unmet needs can be reactivated in the therapeutic relationship if the analyst is able to respond properly, which requires that the analyst recognize and work through his or her own **countertransference** needs; that is, the analyst must recognize and work through his or her own unresolved narcissistic disturbances so as not to interfere with the developing transference. To accomplish this goal, the therapist must not become annoyed or irritated with the patient's attempts to glorify him or her. Second, the therapist must not respond to any of the patient's bizarre fantasies by becoming critical, moralistic, or judgmental. Third, the therapist must not deal with his or her own tensions or anxieties about the patient's experiences by responding with faulty interpretations or premature conclusions. Instead the therapist must adopt an attentive, but unobtrusive and noninterfering, attitude toward the patient. Under these circumstances, transference can take place, as the patient tentatively and gradually gives voice to the underlying fears and longings.

In **mirror transference**, patients relive early experiences in which their mother or father failed to mirror them and seek to be validated by the therapist's approval; in **idealizing transference**, patients relive early experiences in which their father or mother failed to fulfill their needs for a comforting protective figure and see the therapist as an admired and powerful figure who will protect and help them; and, in **alter-ego transference**, they seek from the therapist the comfort and acceptance that their own parents failed to provide (Basch, 1989, p. 14). If these transferences are successful, the therapist will be drawn into these narcissistically pathological situations, will gain better empathic understanding of the patients, and will be able to offer explanatory interpretations about the origin of the pathologies (Kohut, 1971, pp. 28–29; Kohut, 1984, pp. 104–108).

Finally, note that not all of the patient's self structure is defective. If it were, the patient would be psychotic and unanalyzable (Kohut, 1971, p. 31). Substantial portions of the self are healthy and cohesive and are utilized in the formation of a realistic bond and alliance between the patient and the therapist. On the basis of this realistic, trusting bond, the patient can now begin to work through the early, harmful experiences and to bring them under the increased control of his or her ego with the aid of the therapist's insight-providing interpretations.

Theory's Implications for Therapy

The patient with a narcissistic personality disorder has suffered a stunting of personal growth because of disturbances in his or her relationships with parents during early childhood. The patient remains fixated on an archaic grandiose self and/or on an archaic idealized parent imago. These unrealistic structures were not modified and then integrated with the rest of the person's personality in the normal course of development. Thus, there is a defensive **splitting** between aspects of the deprived nuclear self and the two primitive, fixated self-structures. The person's ego is hampered in its attempts to function in a mature and realistic way (Kohut, 1971, p. 3). The goal of therapy, therefore, is to redirect narcissistic energies (libido) from these unrealistic structures to the nuclear self and its ego. The therapist uses the major psychoanalytic techniques to gather information about the defects in the patient's self and then provides understanding and interpretations that facilitate and make possible positive change. If these interpretations are accepted by the patient, transmuting internalizations (new learning) occur and lead to a revitalized nuclear self with an ego that is stronger, more cohesive, and more resilient. The person is now more free to continue moving toward the realization of his or her potentials (Paul, 1989, p. 126).

To understand this therapeutic process more fully, let us examine one of Kohut's case studies, involving a patient diagnosed with a narcissistic disorder (Kohut, 1977, pp. 6–54).

The patient was a professional writer in his early thirties when his wife left him, after six years of marriage. He sought help because he suffered from low self-esteem and a deep sense of inner emptiness. In other words, he manifested a primary structural defect in his self. His apathy and lack of initiative made him feel only half alive, and he attempted to overcome this sense of emptiness with the aid of emotionally highly charged sexual-aggressive fantasies. The fantasies involved exercising sadistic control over women by tying them up. He actually had acted out this fantasy with his wife, who regarded his behavior as sick. Kohut said these fantasies and enactments were attempts to cover a primary defect with the aid of defensive structures.

The man also complained about having a writing block and, though he still had a job, was not performing in a satisfactory way; that is, while writing, he often became tense and excited and then had to either suppress his imagination or stop writing.

Within a mirror transference, the therapist learned that the patient's difficulties were based partly on his mother's failure to mirror him appropriately when he was a child. Also, his idealizing transference revealed that his father had provided him with a poor idealized image. In regard to his mother, the patient recalled that he had experienced his mother's responsiveness to him as insufficient and faulty. He recalled how many times during his childhood he tried to look at her suddenly so that she could not have time to cover over her indifference to him by showing a falsely friendly and interested facial expression. He also remembered a situation when he had injured himself and some of his blood had stained his brother's clothes. His mother did not accurately discern that he was the injured party. Instead, she immediately grabbed his brother and rushed to the hospital; she left the patient at home.

One result of the mother's inadequate empathic responsiveness was a maldevelopment in the grandiose-exhibitionistic sector of the patient's personality. Because of her indifference, he did not learn that his real abilities might gain recognition. Thus, he was traumatically frustrated and remained fixated on archaic (primitive and unrealistic) forms of exhibitionism. This exhibitionism occasionally broke through in frantic activity and wild sexualized fantasies in which the mirroring object (always a woman) was under his complete, sadistically enforced control; she was a slave who had to comply with his every wish.

The patient's tenseness and feelings of fear when he was writing were due to deficiencies in the tension-regulating structures of his self, combined with fixations in his grandiose-exhibitionistic sector caused by his mother's failure to help him learn how to modulate his unrealistic feelings of grandiosity. Because he lacked sufficient self structure to curb and neutralize his grandiose and exhibitionistic impulses and to regulate tension, the activation of his imagination while writing resulted in extreme overstimulation; to defend himself against this terrifying experience, he stopped writing.

In part, the patient's writer's block could also be attributed to his father's lack of empathic responsiveness. To overcome the harm he had experienced as a result of his mother's chronic indifference, the patient turned toward his father for closeness, approval, and affirmation. The patient had tried to acquire and to integrate into his personality certain of his father's admired strengths and abilities; because his father loved language and writing, the patient throughout adolescence tried to come close to him through writing. The tragedy was that the father also failed him as the mother had before: The father could not allow himself to be idealized by his son; he did not foster, through the appropriate empathic responsiveness, the development of the idealizing relationship for which the son yearned. After his mother died, the patient tried, yet again, to lay claim to his father's attention. However, he was disappointed by his father's lack of interest in him and by his father's remarriage.

By reliving these painful experiences and working through them in many therapeutic sessions with the aid of the therapist, the patient began to make progress toward the development of a more realistic and cohesive self. He told the therapist that he had begun to formulate his own ideals and more healthy ways of gaining recognition from others. He said that he now realized that the possession of his own independent goals and ideals was essential to his emotional health. He returned to his writing and was no longer frightened when his imagination was activated. His writing resulted in some creative products and he found considerable satisfaction in his accomplishments. In addition, the patient came to realize that his sexual fantasies were mobilized in reaction to narcissistic injuries he had suffered. Some analytic gains were made in this area, but Kohut pointed out that more work remained to be done. As a result, the patient returned for further analysis in this area and eventually abandoned his fruitless attempts to strengthen his enfeebled self with the aid of sadistic sexual fantasies.

Finally, Kohut emphasized that successful analysis does not mean that patients who acquire a strong cohesive center to their personality will thereafter unfailingly be able to deal with others and their environment in accordance with their highest ideals. He maintained that patients who have undergone therapy will not undergo miraculous changes. Instead, when therapy is successful, individuals will show considerable improvement in various areas of their lives. On the whole, good analysis means that patients are able to experience the joy of existence more keenly and consider their life more worthwhile (Kohut, 1977, pp. 283–285; Kohut, 1984, p. 209).

Evaluative Comments

We turn now to an evaluation of the scientific worth of Kohut's theory.

Comprehensiveness   Kohut was a controversial thinker who created a comprehensive theory of personality. His theory addresses both normal and abnormal phenomena, not only on the level of the individual but also on the group level. Kohut used his theoretical ideas to explain a variety of phenomena, including sex, aggression, dreams, fantasies, perversions, anxiety, vandalism, gambling, depression, hypochondriasis, masturbation, art, creativity, family development, independence, love, and group and political behavior. Not only did he focus on normal and abnormal behavior, but he made an effort to describe and explain states of optimal psychological health.

Precision and testability   Like classical psychoanalysis, Kohut's self psychology is dotted with imprecise concepts. The concept of the self-object, for example, is confusing. Self-objects are mental representations of external objects, such as our parents or other members of our family. They are conceptualized as a part of the self because functionally they fill in for deficient self structure. Sometimes they are merged with the individual's concept of himself; at other times, they are seen as having a separate existence within the self. If self-objects refer to other people, then why not simply talk about the person (self) and other people, each with their own separate existences? Although not all analysts would agree, a possible answer is that Kohut wanted to maintain the intrapsychic (within the person) orientation of psychoanalysis. Analysis is an in-depth exploration of the inner workings of a person's mind. It is not interpersonally oriented; it does not try to understand the interactions between two separate individuals. By discussing the self in terms of self-objects, Kohut is able to maintain the intrapsychic orientation characteristic of psychoanalytic theory. Nevertheless, some analysts still have difficulty understanding and accepting the concept (Goldberg, A. I., 1980, p. 2).

Narcissism, too, is a fuzzy concept for several reasons: first, because it is an abstract psychoanalytic concept with multiple meanings; second, because, in the popular mind, it is tinged with negative connotations such as selfishness and excessive self-absorption. In fairness to Kohut, he noted this problem and made considerable efforts to inform people that narcissism can take many forms, some psychologically unhealthy and some healthy. Despite his efforts, it is not always clear which meaning of the term he has in mind when he discusses the role of narcissism in the person's development.

While it is easy to confuse the concept of empathy with sympathy and compassion, Kohut does take pains to give it a very precise meaning that distinguishes it from other emotional states. The problem here, therefore, is not with his conceptual definition but more with his ability to precisely measure it. Kohut claims that it is a neutral assessment tool whose use allows him to collect psychological data objectively. Here the analyst acts as the assessment instrument, that is, as a scientific observer who becomes immersed in the subjective experiences of the patient. If the analyst can adopt the perspective of the other without allowing his or her preconceptions and feelings to interfere with the process, that is, if the analyst can be neutral and objective, then he or she can gather psychological facts accurately. Of course, there is no direct proof possible that the analyst has indeed been able to become immersed in the experiences of the patient without distorting them via his or her own theoretical preconceptions, attitudes, biases, needs, and so forth. Thus, we are simply left with the analyst's word that he or she has tried to proceed in an objective way. Perhaps the analyst simply found what he or she was looking for (Akhtar, 1989, p. 353). Thus, there is a need to collect other corroborating data both inside and outside of the analytic setting before confidence in the therapist's findings can be established (Goldberg, 1988, p. 56).

Besides these problems, difficulties in testing also arise because many of the theory's hypotheses are stated vaguely. For example, Kohut maintains that children growing up with an unempathic mother will cling to a vaguely delimited image of absolute perfection and, as a consequence, will show a wide variety of pathological behaviors. These behaviors are dependent on the extent and severity of the mother's faulty response (Kohut, 1971, p. 65). Unfortunately, Kohut does not spell out very precisely what he means by a response that varies in extent and severity or what the specific behaviors might be.

Parsimony While Kohut's theory is complicated and comprehensive, it nevertheless has a restricted explanatory base. While, to a large extent, he does incorporate key Freudian concepts to explain a variety of phenomena, he still relegates many of these concepts to a secondary status. In much of his hypothesizing and theoretical explanations, he relies heavily on a few concepts, such as empathy, narcissism, and self-objects. Empathy, in particular, seems to be an overworked concept in his theory (Akhtar, 1989, p. 353). Failures in mental health are almost invariably attributed to the influence of unempathic parents. Yet it is clear that sometimes psychologically healthy people have grown up in relatively unempathic environments. Also, it is possible that pathological development may occur even where the child has had the benefits of empathic parenting (Goldberg, 1988, p. 112). Kohut's theory is too reductionistic and, therefore, fails to meet the parsimony criterion.

Empirical validity Data collection within the therapeutic situation has not established much empirical support for Kohut's theory. Many psychoanalysts continue to endorse Freud's views that pathology is the result of unresolved conflicts of a sexual and aggressive nature and reject Kohut's view that pathology stems from unresolved narcissistic disturbances and damage to the self. As a result, these analysts report that they see no disorders of the self in their therapy sessions with patients. Conversely, analysts who accept Kohut's view tend to overestimate the incidence of self-psychopathology (Kohut, 1977, p. 278). Thus, these two opposing camps are collecting two different sets of psychological data. Adherents of the classical or orthodox analytic perspective find data supportive of Freud's theory, but not Kohut's; self psychologists find data more supportive of Kohut's theory than of Freud's classical theory.

There is also considerable controversy as to whether mirroring and idealizing transferences are necessary for a therapeutic cure.

Data collection outside of the therapeutic situation has yielded much more evidence consistent with Kohut's theorizing. Unhealthy narcissism, for example, is associated with various kinds of adjustment difficulties and low self-esteem, whereas healthy narcissism is linked consistently with positive mental health outcomes. However, as yet, there is no research that examines the links between the level of transmuting internalizations experienced by individuals and their level of mental health. Finally, detailed study of the role played by self-objects in the mental health of individuals over the lifespan is sorely needed.

Heuristic value   Kohut's theory is highly heuristic. In place of the traditional psychoanalytic focus on instincts operating within a mental apparatus, Kohut introduced a concept of self that is inherently assertive and oriented toward development of its potentials. This dramatic shift in theoretical focus generated tremendous controversy and led to a reexamination of many of the concepts of classical psychoanalytic theory and therapy. Even today, debate continues to rage over a number of changes advocated by Kohut. For example, there are still arguments between analysts concerning Kohut's assertion that damage to the self plays the key role in unhealthy personality development. Many analysts continue to argue that frustration of individuals' sexual and aggressive needs accounts for unhealthy development. Others disagree with Kohut's view that damage to the self due to faulty child-rearing practices can explain all kinds of psychopathology. Moreover, many analysts continue to maintain that narcissism is basically pathological (Akhtar, 1989, p. 349); they strongly reject Kohut's idea that narcissism can be associated positively with creativity and mental health. In the history of science, such conflicts between new theories and their predecessors are not unusual or necessarily destructive. In fact, they often result in scientific progress. Thus, these stimulating conflicts between advocates of classical psychoanalysis and self psychology may well eventually lead to an increased understanding of personality functioning (Goldberg, A. I., 1980, p. 2).

Finally, there is growing recognition that Kohut made substantial contributions to psychoanalysis, on both theoretical and therapeutic levels. He is credited with postulating a set of developmental needs in children, for example, needs to be mirrored, to idealize powerful figures, and to be accepted by others, that had been neglected by analysts in their clinical practices. He postulated that these needs, if unmet, result in pathology. He also broadened the concept of transference in original ways, by discussing how mirroring, idealizing, and alter-ego transferences help patients relive early experiences with significant self-objects in which these developmental needs were not met. Under empathic therapeutic conditions, therapists at different times serve as significant self-objects, so that patients can resume the thwarted developmental process, work through it, and experience a restoration of the self (Baker & Baker, 1987, p. 7).

Applied value   Kohut's writings and clinical observations of patients have stimulated considerable research on the narcissistic personality. His work on narcissism has also been at least partially responsible for increasing therapists' interest in understanding and trying to help patients suffering from narcissistic personality disorders. It also seems likely that, as a result of exposure to Kohut's ideas, many therapists are now more inclined to refocus their attention on the use of empathy and self-object transferences as therapeutic tools. Thus, Kohut's theory may have some applied value, although convincing demonstration of the usefulness of his views on therapy awaits the publication of more clinical data. Finally, there is a need to subject Kohut's hypotheses to experimental test.

CRITICAL THINKING QUESTIONS

1. Why did Kohut think that it is necessary and healthy for the mother to mirror her child during infancy?
2. In what ways are children grandiose in their behavior? How would a parent modify children's unrealistic beliefs and behavior as they grow older without permanently damaging their views of themselves? Give some pertinent examples from your own upbringing.
3. What are unempathic parents? List some behaviors of such parents and explain why you think they would have a negative effect on their children's development.
4. Do you agree with Kohut that the chief problem in today's society is that children grow up with understimulated selves? How do such children cope with their feelings of emptiness and depression? What will you do, if you have children, to ensure that they will not develop along the same lines? If you already have children, do they have understimulated selves or are they more vibrant, cohesive, and productive? What did you do to facilitate these outcomes?
5. Most of us think of narcissistic people as psychologically unhealthy? However, Kohut maintained that certain forms of narcissism are healthy. Can you think of any examples of your own narcissistically healthy behavior in personal relationships?

GLOSSARY

alter-ego-hungry personalities   Individuals who feel worthwhile only if they have a relationship with a self-object who looks and dresses like them and has similar opinions and values.

alter-ego transference   The process in which a patient whose needs for belonging as a member of the group have not been met by family members relives these experiences with an accepting therapist. This acceptance serves as a means of reassuring the patient that he or she shares a common humanity with others. The strengthening of the patient's self feeling does not derive from having his or her accomplishments mirrored, but from quietly being sustained by another in whose presence the patient feels accepted, irrespective of his or her level of accomplishment.

autonomous self   The self of an individual who has achieved optimal mental health and, with it, a freedom from inhibitions that interfere with his or her ability to act productively. The autonomous self is seen as the initiator of action and is able to avail itself of the talents and skills at its disposal; as a result, the person is able to love and work successfully.

borderline states   Primary disorders of the self in which damage to the self is permanent or protracted. In contrast to the psychoses, the central defect is better covered by major defenses.

cohesive self   A personality that is organized and resistant to fragmentation. It is healthy and functions effectively, because its narcissistic energies are primarily invested in the pursuit of realistic goals.

contact-shunning personalities   A common narcissistic character type. Because of their intense longing to merge with self-objects, such individuals are highly sensitive to rejection. To avoid this pain, they avoid social contact.

countertransference   The therapist's tendency to react to the patient on the basis of his or her own narcissistic needs and conflicts. Working through these conflicts can increase the therapist's self-understanding and facilitate movement toward the patient's cure.

ego psychology   Theory that postulates that the ego often operates independently of id impulses and, as a result, the individual has considerable opportunity for personal growth.

empathy   The ability to assume the perspective of another person, to know and understand his or her experiences.

fragmenting self   Pathological condition in which the person feels uncoordinated. In less severe cases, an individual may feel tired, mentally slow, and/or awkward following several minor experiences of failure. In more severe cases, a person may show hypochondriacal worry over his or her physical health.

grandiose self A primitive view of oneself as great; this condition is expressed in unrealistic exhibitionism.

healthy narcissism A kind of narcissism in which the person sheds excessive parental dependencies, starts to exercise autonomy, develops skills, and becomes a creative, empathic, and achievement-oriented person within a context of enduring interpersonal commitments.

ideal-hungry personalities Individuals who experience themselves as worthwhile as long as they can relate to people they can admire for reasons of intelligence, beauty, power, or moral stature.

idealized parent imago Children's initial view of their parents as perfect, that is, as all-knowing and all-powerful.

idealizing transference The process in which a patient whose needs to be protected by an admired, powerful parent in early childhood were frustrated relives these experiences. During this reliving, he or she is given an opportunity to work through these negative experiences with an idealized therapist in order to overcome the developmental defect.

merger-hungry personalities Individuals who experience others as their own self. It does not matter to these individuals whether the merger is with mirroring, idealized, or alter-ego self-objects. The key to understanding them is to note that the self-objects are used as substitutes for their own self deficiencies and that the fluidity of the boundaries between them and others interferes with their ability to discriminate their own thoughts, feelings, wishes, and intentions from the self-objects'.

mirroring Process whereby a person sees himself or herself in the face of the other (usually the mother). It is the process of being shown and knowing oneself through interactions with others. From a developmental perspective, it begins when mothers reflect to the infant what they see in him or her. When parents are empathic, they mirror generally a highly positive representation of the infant and start him or her toward healthy self-development. When they fail to mirror, the infant becomes confused and alienated from others and starts on the path toward unhealthy self-development.

mirror-hungry personalities Individuals who crave self-objects whose confirming and admiring responses will increase their feelings of self-worth.

mirror transference A transference in which a person who had not been adequately mirrored—that is, confirmed and given approval—by his mother relives these experiences with the therapist. When such a transference develops, the patient has the opportunity to work through those negative experiences with the therapist and hence to overcome his or her feelings of worthlessness.

narcissistic behavior disorders Self disorders characterized by individuals' attempts to shore up their fragile self-esteem by engaging in addictive, perverse, or delinquent behavior.

narcissistic personality disorders Self disorders characterized by grandiose thinking, hypersensitivity to slights and perceived failures, inability to forgive, lack of zest, impaired personal relationships, and fragile self-esteem.

need to idealize A fundamental, biologically based need to seek protection and security by identifying with an all-powerful and all-knowing person, usually the parent (idealized parent imago).

nuclear self The foundation of an individual's personality. It is established through a learning process initiated by parents, in which individuals modify their unrealistic beliefs about themselves and their caretakers. The result of this learning process is the firm establishment and comfortable utilization of skills and the ability to see oneself as a center of initiative and productivity.

object relations Relationships between individuals and other people. In self psychology, object relations are usually discussed in terms of mental representations of real external people that exist within the individual or self.

object-relations theory The theory that the course of human development depends on the quality of the relationships established between individuals, particularly between parents and their children.

optimal frustration An ideal, nontraumatic frustration of a person's needs that fosters new learning and personal growth. Parents who are too severe or too lenient with their children adversely affect their development.

overburdened self Pathological condition in which the person has not had an opportunity to merge with the calmness of an omnipotent self-object, usually a parent. The result is lack of the self-soothing capacity that could have been learned through such contact. Thus, individuals without a capacity to soothe themselves in times of stress may overreact emotionally when confronted by threatening situations.

overstimulated self   Pathological condition in which individuals exposed to excessive stimulation in childhood, because their fantasies of greatness were continually reinforced by unempathic (nonunderstanding) caregivers, may later be frightened by their unmodified grandiose fantasies to the point of avoiding situations in which they are the center of attention.

paranoid personality disorders   Borderline states in which deficiencies in self structures are shielded against further damage by using hostility and suspicion to keep potentially injurious objects at a safe distance.

primary narcissism   An initial state of well-being and satisfaction in which all of the infant's needs are gratified and the infant feels an oceanic perfection and bliss.

psychosis   A primary disturbance of the self in which defenses do not cover major defects in the self.

schizoid personality disorders   Borderline states in which defective self structures are protected against further damage by aloofness and superficial involvement in relationships.

self-objects   Mental representations of other people which are used by the person to regulate tensions within himself or herself and are experienced as part of the self. Self-objects are used by the person to exercise control over his or her own body. For example, a boy might admire his father's calmness in stressful situations. The boy might form a mental representation of his father and then use this self-object as a means of regulating his own aggressive impulses when he is insulted by other boys at school. Use of the self-object (the calmness of his father) under threatening conditions allows the boy to exercise control over his own mind and body instead of acting upon his aggressive feelings and fighting.

self psychology   Theory that the self (and its needs), and not the instincts, is the center of psychological motivation, organization, and change in personality. It also assumes that psychological damage to the self, not frustration of the sexual and aggressive instincts, produces psychopathology.

self-state dreams   Dreams that are not disguised attempts at wish fulfillment but rather straightforward depictions of the current state of the self. These dreams are analyzed for insight into the diffuse feelings of anxiety that the patient has about a fragmenting self. The analysis is in terms of the manifest content of the dreams. Attempts to find a latent content with underlying sexual meaning are believed to be unsuccessful.

splitting   A defense in which individuals disavow (split off) feelings of emptiness, depression, and deprivation in one sector of personality by acting out various grandiose ideas or by engaging in perverse, but exciting, activities under the control of another sector of the personality.

transmuting internalizations   The process whereby individuals learn more realistic and effective ways of thinking, feeling, and behaving as a consequence of interactions with empathic parents.

understimulated self   Pathological condition in which individuals feel empty, bored, and depressed because their parents have failed to respond empathically to their mirroring and idealizing needs. To overcome these aversive feelings, the individuals engage in various exciting but counterproductive activities, such as gambling, sexual perversions, excessive drinking, and drug abuse.

unhealthy narcissism   A form of narcissism characterized by unrealistic feelings of grandeur, exhibitionism, poor impulse control, and impoverished relationships with their parents.

working through   The emotional process that patients go through in an attempt to resolve traumatic conflicts so they can developmentally move beyond being governed by infantile wishes.

SUGGESTED READINGS

Kohut, H. (1971). *The analysis of the self.* New York: International Universities Press.

Kohut, H. (1977). *The restoration of the self.* New York: International Universities Press.

Kohut, H. (1984). *How does analysis cure?* Chicago: The University of Chicago Press.

PART 3

Trait Perspectives

The earliest attempts to explain human behavior involved the use of typologies, in which behavior was classified into discrete, all-or-nothing categories. For example, Hippocrates (and later Galen) classified individuals as melancholic, choleric, phlegmatic, or sanguine and explained the behavior of each of these mutually exclusive types by positing the operation of bodily humors, or internal fluids. Specifically, he proposed that a predominance of black bile caused people to be melancholic and depressed; an excess of yellow bile made them irritable and short-tempered; too much phlegm made them slow and lethargic; and disproportionate amounts of blood caused them to be hopeful and sanguine. Hippocrates also believed that body type was related to physical disease. On the basis of his many observations of patients, he concluded that people with short, thick bodies were prone to stroke (*habitus apoplecticus*), and those with tall, thin bodies to tuberculosis (*habitus phthisicus*).

The inadequacies of such typologies are painfully clear. They involve unsophisticated and oversimplified theoretical and empirical treatments of differences in behavior along with medical explanations that are obsolete in light of current knowledge. But useful vestiges of Hippocrates' legacy to the medical profession and to behavioral science can still be seen in research on hormonal therapy and the effects of various hormones on performance in humans and lower animals.

The assessment of personality traits based on facial features also had its origins in antiquity and, throughout history, has commanded the attention of theologians, poets, philosophers, artists, writers, and scientists. Before the 19th century, devotees of physiognomy tended to make their judgments about personality on artistic grounds; they offered lyrical descriptions of the beauties of various aspects of the face and sometimes presented their version of truth in aphorisms, such as:

> A beard on a woman is a sign of little honesty.
> Bright eyes are the sign of wantonness.
> The smallness of the forehead indicates a choleric man.
> Men with curved noses are magnanimous. (Mantegazza, 1899, p. 13)

Interest in the subject seems to have reached a peak in the late 19th century, but even today there are occasional books and studies on the topic.

The primary orientation of typological studies in the 19th century was scientific, with attempts to measure facial features and relate those measurements to psychological characteristics. Unfortunately, virtually all these findings are meaningless in a scientific sense, because they are based on the biased and subjective impressions of the investigators and on woefully inadequate methodologies. Yet, scientific research that examines the effects of physical attractiveness on behavior is extremely popular today. Cross-cultural evidence shows that standards of beauty vary from country to country, and most contemporary researchers in this area assume that standards of beauty are learned and not biologically based. Their work also shows that physically attractive people are better liked by others than are unattractive people. Among college students, the physically attractive are seen as possessing more socially desirable traits than unattractive people. Beautiful people are seen as more poised, interesting, sociable, independent, dominant, exciting, sexy, well adjusted, socially skilled, and successful than the unattractive (Baron & Byrne, 2003, pp. 271–273). It does seem, then, that people who are seen as beautiful are also generally seen as good, a finding that was accurately predicted by a number of early physiognomists.

Phrenology was still another attempt to use physical traits to relate constitutional factors to individual differences in traits. This system purports to assess personality traits from the shape and contours of the skull. Popularly known as the study of bumps on the head, phrenology originated in the 19th century as a serious attempt to relate knowledge about brain structure and function to behavior (Davies, 1955, p. 3). Its foremost proponent was Franz Gall (1758–1828), a German anatomist and physician who believed that the mind was composed of approximately 40 independent faculties. These faculties were catalogued by him, and later by various disciples, under such headings as combativeness, benevolence, amativeness, language, secretiveness, self-esteem, destructiveness, and hope (Davies, 1955, p. 6). Gall claimed that these faculties were located in various organs, or regions, of the brain and that the development or lack of development of these organs affected the size and shape of the skull. To judge a person's character or personality, therefore, he believed it was necessary only to study these contours. A person with a well-developed benevolence region, for example, would be judged as having a kindly character; one with an underdeveloped region would be characterized as cruel.

Gall had a single-minded passion for scientific inquiry about brain structure and function; his pupil and colleague Johann Spurzheim did not. Spurzheim's view of phrenology was based on religious and philosophical speculations as well as on scientific research. He sought to popularize phrenology and discussed, in public lectures, its applications to education, medicine, mental health, and penology (Davies, 1955, p. 8). These efforts and those by other disciples proved very successful, and phrenology flourished. During the last half of the 19th century, however, phrenology was attacked by numerous critics on religious and philosophical as well as scientific grounds (Davies, 1955, pp. 65–75).

Opponents attacked phrenology as atheistic and immoral, because it attributed behavior to natural, not divine, causes and because its acceptance implied an endorsement of fatalism. Fatalism, however, was not consistent with the aims of phrenology, whose proponents linked it directly to social reform. Phrenologists considered the diseased brains of the insane to have resulted from violations of natural laws. To overcome their deficiencies, these people should once again follow natural law; they should get plenty of fresh air and physical exercise, eat bland foods, and avoid liquor and tobacco. In the crudest sense, phrenologists were arguing for the establishment of a warm, supportive environment for the insane, an idea still acceptable to the contemporary mental health movement.

Despite the irrational nature of the attacks on phrenology, its critics were effective in damaging the movement. Scientific evidence also took its toll. Pierre Flourens demonstrated in his experiments with pigeon brains in 1845 that large portions of the brain could be destroyed without impairment of function. In 1861, Paul Broca showed conclusively that the faculty of speech was located not near the eyeballs, as Gall maintained, but in the temporal region (Davies, 1955, p. 142). Despite these overwhelming criticisms, phrenology is credited with having an important impact on the field of neurology, in that it directed the attention of researchers to cerebral structure and function. Sporadic interest in the topic still exists, not within the scientific community but among people who also embrace pseudosciences such as astrology and palmistry.

Although there have been numerous other investigators of the relationships between body build and behavior since Hippocrates, the leading researcher in this area in modern times is William Sheldon. Sheldon's typology links body type and personality traits by using a more sophisticated measurement system than his predecessors'. He and his associates examined the physiques of thousands of college students—by photographing them in the nude from the front, side, and rear—in an attempt to determine whether there were any basic regularities among them. After careful examination, Sheldon concluded that there were three extreme components of body builds: endomorphy, mesomorphy, and ectomorphy. Endomorphy is the relative predominance of soft roundness throughout the various regions of the body; mesomorphy is the relative predominance of muscle, bone, and connective tissue; ectomorphy is the relative predominance of linearity and fragility. Positing each of these as a continuous dimension that varied along a seven-point scale, he assigned each person a set of three numerals from 1 to 7. The resulting pattern was the person's somatotype. Thus, a 711 is an extreme endomorph, a 171 an extreme mesomorph, and a 117 an extreme ectomorph.

Sheldon maintained that the person's somatotype is genetically determined and causes people to develop and express personality traits consistent with their body builds. For example, he hypothesized that endomorphs (high in fatty tissue) would be sociable, complacent, and capable of easy communication of feelings. He thought mesomorphs (high in muscle tissue) would be adventurous, bold, competitive, aggressive, and energetic, whereas ectomorphs (low in fatty and muscle tissue) would be inhibited, introverted, hypersensitive to pain, and secretive. He tested these hypotheses by having observers rate individuals on these trait dimensions and found empirical support for his ideas (Sheldon, Hartl, & McDermott, 1949, pp. 26–27). Although this study has been strongly criticized on methodological grounds (Sheldon himself made both the physical and psychological ratings), more methodologically sound studies—in which investigator bias was minimized by having one investigator rate the somatotypes and having the study participants independently rate their own personality traits—have also produced supportive evidence for Sheldon's position (Child, 1950; Cortes & Gatti, 1965; Yates & Taylor, 1978). Despite these findings, however, there is no direct proof that the correlations were caused by biological factors. As an alternative to Sheldon's genetic position, social-learning theorists propose that the relation between body build and traits is the result of learning; that is, people have certain stereotypes about the kinds of traits that are associated with specific physiques—stereotypes that are perpetuated through books, films, magazines, and television, as well as through contact with other people. Adults often transmit these stereotypes to their children, who learn to incorporate the expected traits into their own body concepts, so that these traits eventually become a central part of their own self-concept.

Although Sheldon's measurement system is superior to his predecessors', it is still far too subjective and imprecise when compared to the procedures used by researchers such as Cattell and Eysenck to assess traits and types. Yet the fundamental ideas underlying the modern view of typologies, as exemplified by both Cattell and Eysenck, are found in Sheldon. Thus, these typologies do not classify behavior (from which traits are inferred) into discrete, mutually exclusive categories; instead, types are continuous, higher order concepts that encompass a group of correlated traits. The difference between traits and types lies in the greater inclusiveness and abstractness of the type concept. Both traits and types, in the modern view, involve the use of graduated dimensions along which individual differences can be quantitatively arranged. For example, neuroticism is a major type, and people can and do differ in the degree of neuroticism. Neuroticism, in turn, is the outgrowth of a number of traits that are correlated with each other, including (low) self-esteem, (high) depression, and (high) emotionality. Again, people can and do vary, from low to high, on each of these component traits.

In Part 3, we review and evaluate the positions of three of the most prominent trait theorists: Gordon Allport, Raymond Cattell, and Hans Eysenck. Gordon Allport, whose theory is discussed in Chapter 8, set out to correct Freud's pessimistic view of human nature by establishing the broad outlines of a humanistic psychology; he focused on the uniqueness of the individual and on the creative and rational aspirations of most people to realize their potentials. An important forerunner of the humanistic movement popular in psychology today, Allport, and his work, would fit quite readily in Part 5, where we discuss the humanistic/existential positions. Because he believed the trait concept to be central to an adequate theory of personality, however, Allport belongs firmly within the trait perspective framework.

After tracing Allport's humanistic roots, we detail his attempts to create an adequate definition of personality or self and outline his theory of traits. We review his theorizing about the developmental process of "becoming," the role of traits in this emergent process, and his conception of the mature personality. According to Allport, the development of maturity takes considerable time, so that only adults are capable of coming close to self-actualization. Moreover, the process involves abrupt shifts, so that mature individuals are qualitatively different from abnormal or immature ones. Mature people have been able to free themselves from excessive reliance on the immediate gratification of basic impulses and drives; they are emotionally secure, self-accepting, and tolerant toward others. In Chapter 8, we also cover the many techniques Allport used to assess personality, the major differences between idiographic and nomothetic approaches to data collection, and the application of Allport's theory to the treatment of people with behavioral disorders.

In Chapter 9, we focus on Raymond Cattell, who believed that an adequate theory of personality must rest on solid measurement and statistical procedures. The chapter also provides an introduction to the complex factor-analytic methods he used to identify the basic traits of personality. Cattell proposed 16 source traits that could be used to explain personality functioning. Through extensive research, however, he later discovered 12 abnormal factors. The 12 psychopathology factors are assessed through his Clinical Analysis Questionnaire (CAQ). Cattell believed that he had uncovered the major source traits found in normal and abnormal people.

In Chapter 9, we also present Cattell's econetic model, which describes the influence of the physical, social, and cultural environments on individuals and their subsequent behavior, and his specification equations, through which he sought to combine traits and situations as a means of accurately predicting behavior. This multidimensional model includes a complex representation of how traits are dynamically interrelated and how they operate across a variety of situations. Next, we examine Cattell's views on the role of heredity and the role of learning in personality development, in which he went beyond classical and instrumental conditioning to propose a more complex form of integration learning. We also discuss the use of precise measurement procedures in personality diagnosis, to identify disordered behavior and put the clinician in a better position to help clients. According to Cattell, the P technique, which involves testing the client repeatedly on a large number of personality dimensions over a long period of time, can provide an accurate assessment of changes occurring in the client during therapy. Finally, we present Cattell's ideas on the need for a new morality based on scientific data, a position he called Beyondism.

In Chapter 10, we review the major contributions to personality theory and the research of Hans Eysenck, who made concerted efforts to gather factual support for his concepts through rigorous experimental research. We describe his typology, with its major dimensions of introversion/extraversion, stability/neuroticism, and impulse control/psychoticism, and the Eysenck Personality Questionnaire used to assess them. We review the limitations of his earlier inhibition theory and present his improved arousal theory, along with the latest evidence in its support. This theory seeks to explain behavioral differences among various types of individuals on the basis of an interaction between inherited arousal levels and levels of environmental stimulation. In discussing the development of personality types, Eysenck emphasized their genetic basis and the implications for human functioning of genetic research on animals lower on the phylogenetic scale. We then discuss the socialization process and its impact on introverts, extraverts, neurotics, and psychotics, and outline Eysenck's use of numerous assessment techniques. Finally, we present Eysenck's views on the development and treatment of disordered behavior, with special attention to two major behavior-therapy techniques, flooding and systematic desensitization.

Courtesy of the Harvard University Archives.

CHAPTER 8

Allport's Trait Theory

Biographical Sketch

Gordon Allport was born in 1897 in Montezuma, Indiana, the son of a country doctor and the youngest of four boys. He characterized his family life as marked by trust and affection, along with a strong emphasis on the virtue of hard work. Allport was scholarly from an early age; he was good with words but poor at sports. He did not get along very well with his peers. In a show of utter contempt, one of his classmates even said of the young scholar, "Aw, that guy swallowed a dictionary" (Allport, 1968, p. 378).

Although academically he finished second in his high school class of 100 students, Allport insisted that he was "a good routine student, but definitely uninspired about anything beyond the usual adolescent concerns" (Allport, 1968, p. 379). Following his older brother Floyd, who had graduated from Harvard, Allport squeezed through the entrance tests and matriculated there in 1915. The years at Harvard were stimulating and enlightening, according to Allport. He was overwhelmed by the intellectual atmosphere and the strict adherence to the highest academic standards; it was a real intellectual awakening for the small-town boy from the Midwest. Allport followed the example of his older brother and majored in psychology. Besides enrolling in courses taught by prominent psychology professors, he also participated in a number of volunteer service projects (Allport, 1968, p. 381).

After receiving his baccalaureate in 1919, Allport took an opportunity to teach English and sociology at Robert College in Constantinople, Turkey. The following year he won a fellowship for graduate study at Harvard. Before returning to Cambridge, however, he decided to visit a brother who was working in Vienna at the time. He also decided to see if he could arrange a private meeting with Sigmund Freud. With the audacity of youth, he wrote a letter to Freud announcing that he was in Vienna and implying that Freud would no doubt be glad to meet him. To his great surprise, Freud replied in his own handwriting and invited Allport to visit him at his office.

When Allport arrived, Freud ushered him into his famous inner office and sat staring at him expectantly. Not expecting the silence and not knowing what to say, Allport thought fast and told him of an episode on a streetcar on his way to the office. He reported that he had seen a 4-year-old boy who displayed a conspicuous dirt phobia. The boy kept saying to his mother "I don't want to sit there-don't let that dirty man sit beside me." Since the mother was so clean and dominant looking, Allport assumed Freud would quickly see the point of the story, that the boy's abhorrence of dirt was a result of his mother's obsession with cleanliness. Instead, when he had finished the story, Freud hesitated and asked kindly, "And was that little boy you?" (Allport, 1968, p. 383). Allport, flabbergasted, realized that Freud was so accustomed to thinking in terms of neurotic defenses that Allport's

187

manifest motivation had completely escaped him. Allport reported that the experience taught him that depth psychology often plunged too deeply into the psyche and that psychologists might understand people better if they paid more attention to their manifest, conscious motives before probing into their unconscious natures.

Allport entered graduate school in psychology and finished the work for his doctorate in two years. He received his Ph.D. in 1922, at the age of 24 (Allport, 1968, p. 384). He was interested in developing a psychology of personality, but practically no one else in academic life had similar interests; he reported that his thesis was perhaps the first one devoted to an examination of personality traits. Immediately after receiving the degree, Allport had a shattering experience that, he later claimed, was a turning point in his life and career. He was invited to attend a meeting of experimental psychologists at Clark University to discuss current problems and issues in sensory psychology. After two days of such discussions, the eminent psychologist Titchener allotted three minutes to each graduate student to describe his own investigations. Allport reported his work on personality traits and was punished by total silence and stares. Titchener strongly disapproved of his presentation and demanded of Allport's major professor, "Why did you let him work on that problem?" Allport was mortified, but later, when they had returned to Harvard, his professor consoled him by saying, "You don't care what Titchener thinks." And Allport found that in fact he did not (Allport, 1968, p. 385). The experience taught him another lesson—not to be unnecessarily bothered by rebukes or professional slights and to pursue his own interests. From that point on, Allport remained a maverick in psychology, a person who thought deeply and originally about issues and who stated his views candidly, no matter how controversial they were in the eyes of others.

Except for a brief stint at Dartmouth, Allport spent most of his professional life at Harvard. During this period, from 1930 to his death in 1967, he wrote many scholarly theoretical and research articles on topics that included prejudice, expressive movements, rumor, and attitudes and values. He also published a number of books, including *Personality: A Psychological Interpretation* (1937), *The Individual and His Religion: A Psychological Interpretation* (1950), *Becoming: Basic Considerations for a Psychology of Personality* (1955), *The Nature of Prejudice* (1958), and *Pattern and Growth in Personality* (1961). Fittingly, his work was recognized by his colleagues, and he was awarded many honors. He was elected president of the American Psychological Association in 1939 and received the Distinguished Scientific Contribution Award in 1964. He said, though, that he valued one honor above all others: At the 17th International Congress of Psychology in Washington, DC, in 1963, 55 of his former Ph.D. students presented him with two handsomely bound volumes of their own writings with the dedicatory inscription, "From his students in appreciation of his respect for their individuality" (Allport, 1968, p. 407).

Concepts and Principles

A Humanistic View of Personality

Allport, like many investigators in the discipline, commented on the virtual impossibility of defining personality in precise terms. After reviewing definitions offered by theologians, philosophers, lawyers, poets, sociologists, and psychologists, Allport proposed his own version in his first book. For him, personality was "what a man really is." But this definition was still too brief and vague; accordingly, he offered a more precise one: "Personality is the dynamic organization within the individual of those psychophysical systems that determine his characteristic behavior and thought" (Allport, 1961, p. 28).

Allport referred to personality or self as a dynamic organization because he believed that personality cannot usefully be regarded as a collection of fragmented components acting independently of one another. Allport saw personality as striving toward unity and as continually evolving and changing. The person is in a state of **becoming**. Although situational influences have an effect, it is the individual's own perception of these influences that determines his or her behavior. Thus, in Allport's view, even behavior that seems to be controlled by external forces is really controlled by internal forces. For example, "if a child is a hellion at home, and an angel outside, he obviously has two contradictory tendencies in his nature or perhaps a deeper genotype that would explain the opposing phenotypes" (Allport, 1968, p. 46). A situationist would simply predict that the child would behave differently depending on which situation is salient. Allport contended that the differences in behavior are caused by opposing tendencies or traits in the person's nature—for example, by learned predispositions to act differently in two different situations.

Allport became more Freudian in his suggestion that a unifying **genotype** actually may be responsible for the two **phenotypes** (behaving like a hellion at home and an angel outside). For example, the underlying tendency, or genotype, might be expedience—the tendency to perform behaviors advantageous to oneself. Behaving like a hellion at home might maximize parental attention, whereas behaving like an angel outside might win the approval of teachers. As you can readily see, such trait explanations can be invoked on a post hoc basis and made to fit virtually any data. The point here is that, although situations play a role in behavior, Allport's primary focus is on traits and other internal characteristics as determinants of behavior. Moreover, he refers to these internal factors as **psychophysical systems**; this term implies that personality consists of both mind and body elements organized into a complex, inextricable unity.

Finally, Allport's definition of personality refers to the individual's characteristic, or unique, behavior and thought. Allport maintained that all the traits we apparently share with others are, at base, idiosyncratic. He acknowledged that this aspect of the definition is very broad, but he wanted to take into account the fact that we not only adjust to our environment by behaving in certain ways, but we also reflect on it. By so doing, we ensure not only survival but growth.

Allport's view of personality emphasizes the uniqueness of the individual and the internal cognitive and motivational processes that influence behavior. These internal processes and structures include the person's physique, intelligence, temperament, reflexes, drives, habits, skills, beliefs, intentions, attitudes, values, and traits. Allport sees personality as jointly determined by biology and the environment. The physique and intelligence level of the individual are largely inherited and set limits on the person's ability to adapt to his or her environment. Temperament, too, is inherited. It is the emotional facet of personality and is defined as "the characteristic phenomena of an individual's emotional nature, including his susceptibility to emotional stimulation, his customary strength and speed of response, the quality of his prevailing mood, and all [the] peculiarities of fluctuation and intensity in mood" (Allport, 1961, p. 34). These inherited structures and processes are shaped by the person's environmental experiences. For example, a child with an excitable and active nature may have it altered by a family environment where his parents are extraordinarily harsh and controlling (Allport, 1937, p. 125).

Allport believed that at birth the infant is almost entirely a creature of heredity. Yet not every inherited tendency is observable at birth; throughout life, there is a subtle biological influence upon development. As the person matures, however, changes also occur through interactions with the environment and the accompanying learning process. In general, Allport believed that, with growing maturity, we become increasingly active, creative, self-reliant, and characteristically rational, largely as a result of learning experiences. We become increasingly capable of making conscious and deliberate choices among alternative behaviors. Allport chose this positive and optimistic approach in reaction to the more pessimistic views current at the time, which he believed were too static, reductionistic, and mechanistic and placed too much emphasis on the unconscious and irrational side of human personality. Allport's **humanistic theory** was an attempt to provide a much needed corrective for this one-sided view.

The Theory of Traits

The major concepts in Allport's **trait theory** revolve around the different kinds of traits that are contained in the **proprium**, or self, and how they are shaped as the self continues to develop as the person proceeds through the life span. In Allport's theory, it is difficult to understand the links between the concept of traits and the concept of the self. It is clear, however, that the self is the broader, more encompassing term. Within the self we find, not only the person's traits, but his or her habits, needs, interests, skills, and so forth. For Allport, it is traits that are central in helping us understand the uniqueness of the person's style, expressiveness, and behavior. Thus, traits are the key structures within the self; traits initiate and direct the individual's behavior in unique ways. Knowledge of their operation increases our understanding of the individual immensely. The self acts as a unifying force, striving to bring a sense of coherence to the various characteristics and abilities of the person.

What Is a Trait?

For Allport, a trait is "a generalized and focalized neuropsychic system (peculiar to the individual) with the capacity to render many stimuli functionally equivalent and to initiate and guide consistent (equivalent) forms of adaptive and expressive behavior" (Allport, 1937, p. 295). Thus, a trait is something that actually exists but is invisible. It is located in certain parts of the nervous system. Although we do not see it, we infer its existence by observing the consistencies in a person's behavior. Dissimilar stimuli are all capable of arousing a trait readiness within the person. The trait then manifests itself through a variety of responses. All these different responses are equivalent, however, in the sense that they serve the same function—that is, expression of the trait. Figure 8.1 illustrates the manner in which a trait operates. In this example, a college man's shyness is inferred from his inability to establish friendships with other students, his avoidance of social gatherings, his enjoyment of solitary recreational activities such as reading and stamp collecting, and his hesitancy in participating in seminar discussions.

Cardinal, central, and secondary traits   Allport also made a number of distinctions among various kinds of traits. Characteristics that are pervasive and dominant in a person's life he called **cardinal traits**. These are master motives, ruling passions, eminent traits (Allport, 1961, p. 365). For example, a person may have an overwhelming need to be powerful, a need for power that can be inferred from virtually all his behavior. Such a person would not only strive to attain a position of power within society but would also interact with his golf partner, his mail carrier, his children, and his

FIG-8.1 The trait in action. Dissimilar stimuli arouse the trait, which manifests itself in a variety of functionally equivalent responses.

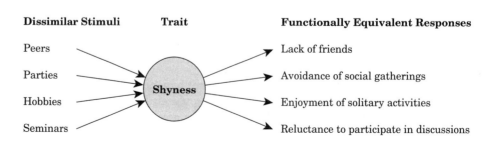

Dissimilar Stimuli	Trait	Functionally Equivalent Responses
Peers		Lack of friends
Parties	**Shyness**	Avoidance of social gatherings
Hobbies		Enjoyment of solitary activities
Seminars		Reluctance to participate in discussions

marriage partner in a similar fashion. He would try to dominate his spouse and would even try desperately to win a game of Ping-Pong with his 5-year-old daughter. A casual conversation with an acquaintance might lead to a bitter struggle on his part to win on some trivial issue.

Characteristics that control less of a person's behavior but are nevertheless important are called **central traits**. Such traits are the ones people mention when asked to describe another person or to write a letter of recommendation. For example, we may say that someone is intelligent, sincere, kind, possessive, competitive, ambitious, funny, and honest. These are major characteristics that control the person's behavior in a variety of situations, but they do not possess the generality of a cardinal trait. Characteristics that are peripheral to the person—preferences, for example, are called **secondary traits**. A person might love banana cream pie or prefer to vacation in Maine or Hawaii. Such traits re generally less important, less conspicuous, less generalized, and less often called into play than central traits (Allport, 1937, p. 338).

Common traits versus personal dispositions   Allport made yet another distinction among traits. **Common traits** are categories for classifying groups of people on a particular dimension (Allport, 1961, p. 349). We might say, for example, that some people are more dominant than others or that some people are more polite than others. Such generalized dispositions are, in Allport's view, of limited usefulness in a science of personality.

Much more to his liking is the concept of **personal dispositions**. In contrast to the common or generalized trait, the personal disposition is a unique characteristic of the person, a trait not shared with others (Allport, 1961, p. 358). Allport urged psychologists to stop paying so much attention to the role of common traits and focus instead on those characteristics unique to the individual. He believed that common traits were categories into which the individual is forced, whereas personal dispositions more accurately reflect the individual's own personality structure.

> By common trait methods, we find that Peter stands high in *aesthetic interest* and *anxiety*, but low in *leadership* and *need-achievement*. The truth is that all these common traits have a special coloring in his life, and—still more important—they interact with one another. Thus, it might be more accurate to say that his personal disposition is a kind of *artistic and self-sufficient solitude*. (Allport, 1961, p. 359)

By and large, investigators have claimed that unique or individual constructs are impossible to imagine. If we used constructs that were unique to the individual, there would be no words in the language for them. We would continually have to invent new terms to describe each individual's motives and behavior—a hopeless undertaking (Holt, 1962, pp. 377–402). But Allport argues that we can talk about personal dispositions if we focus on the unique configurations or patterns of traits within an individual's personality. In his view, only by focusing on the uniqueness of the individual can we hope to make substantial advances in our understanding of personality.

Personality Development

In Allport's theory, personality development centers on the concept of the self. He acknowledged that it is a slippery concept and has been used by different investigators in different ways. It has also encountered vigorous opposition from many psychologists. Wundt, the eminent 19th century structuralist, thought the concept of self or ego or soul was hindering progress in psychology and declared that he favored a "psychology without a soul" (Allport, 1955, p. 36). Wundt's objection, which was shared by many behaviorists who came after him, was that some investigators assign a primary, reified role to the term self, treating it as an actual entity which can direct behavior. An example of such reification might be: "Her strong sense of self caused her to give up smoking." Her behavior is explained in terms of her strong self. Allport agreed that such reification is damaging to psychology because there is no actual entity within the person called the self which caused behavior, but he maintained that we must use the term because the one certain criterion we have of our identity and existence is our sense of self. It is a fundamental experience; if we discard it, we discard the essence of personality.

The Proprium, or Self

Substituting the term *proprium* for self, Allport used it to mean a sense of what is "peculiarly ours," including "all aspects of personality that make for inward unity" (Allport, 1955, p. 40). In his view, the proprium, or self, develops continuously from infancy to death and moves through a series of stages.

The bodily self   The first aspect of selfhood, the **bodily self**, becomes salient in infancy. As infants, we are continually receiving sensory information from our internal organs, muscles, joints, and tendons. These sensations become particularly acute when we are hungry, when we are frustrated, and when we bump into things. In such situations, we learn the limits of our own bodies. As we mature, these recurrent bodily sensations provide information that confirms our own existence. In Allport's view, these sensations provide an anchor for our self-awareness. When we are healthy, we hardly notice the sensations; when we are ill, we are keenly aware of our bodies (Allport, 1961, p. 114). How intimate these sensations are is suggested by Allport in an interesting example:

> Think first of swallowing the saliva in your mouth, or do so. Then imagine expectorating it into a tumbler and drinking it! What seemed natural and "mine" suddenly becomes disgusting and alien. Or picture yourself sucking blood from a prick in your finger; then imagine sucking blood from a bandage around your finger! What I perceive as belonging intimately to my body is warm and welcome; what I perceive as separate from my body becomes in the twinkling of an eye, cold and foreign. (Allport, 1955, p. 43)

Later in the developmental process, we experience sensations from our bodily growth. In adolescence, when these changes are abrupt, some people feel puny, ugly, and awkward; others feel strong, beautiful, and graceful. Some girls may test their ability to attract boys by accentuating female physical attributes. Some boys may test their prowess in physical games and exaggerate their sexual exploits. Allport believed strongly that this bodily sense forms the core of the self and remains an important aspect of selfhood throughout life.

Self-identity   The second aspect of the proprium, **self-identity**, also develops during the first 18 months of life. Despite the vast changes that occur in the course of our lives, there is a certain continuity and sameness in the way we perceive ourselves. "Today I remember some of my thoughts of yesterday; and tomorrow I shall remember some of my thoughts of both yesterday and today; and I am certain that they are the thoughts of the same person of myself" (Allport, 1961, p. 114). Although this concept of self-identity may seem obvious and even trite, recall Erik Erikson's description of the crises faced by people, especially adolescents, who doubt or are confused about their identities.

Self-esteem The third aspect of the proprium, which emerges during the second and third years of life, is **self-esteem**. At this point, children have become more familiar with their environment; they experience pride when they master available tasks and humiliation when they fail. One symptom of their growing self-awareness is the outpouring of opposition to virtually any suggestion from the parents. It is a time for testing the limits of the environment and for refusing to take orders from others. Children are typically very negativistic at this stage. These oppositional tendencies often reappear in adolescence, when the perceived enemies typically are parents and other authority figures.

Self-extension From approximately 4 to 6 years of age, children are primarily concerned with possessions. At this age, children are typically very egocentric. Allport offers an amusing and informative example of egocentricity in a 5-year-old:

> Tommy.... entered a church with his mother and noticed the cross upon the altar. "What's that?" he inquired. "A cross," whispered his mother. "Red Cross?" he asked. "No, just a cross." "Oh, I know," said the boy, "T for Tommy." It will be many years before Tommy will be capable of understanding the reverse interpretation of the symbol that it represents "the I, crossed out." (Allport, 1950, p. 33)

As people mature, they extend their loyalties to family, church, nation, and career group. They no longer see these groups from a selfish perspective ("What can they do for me?") but become more concerned with benefiting other people on the basis of moral principles and ideals (Allport, 1955, p. 45). Thus, **self-extension** in the earliest phases of development is selfish; in the later phases, it is unselfish.

Self-image Along with self-extension, children begin to develop a **self-image**. According to Allport, the self-image has two components: (1) learned expectations of the roles we are required to enact; and (2) aspirations for the future we seek to attain (Allport, 1955, p. 47). The self-image evolves slowly in conjunction with the conscience. Children learn to do things that others expect of them and to avoid behaviors that will bring disapproval. They begin to formulate plans for the future and to make tentative decisions about careers and the values they will embrace.

The self-as-rational-coper During the period between 6 and 12, children begin to engage in reflective thought. They devise strategies to cope with problems and delight in testing their skills, particularly intellectual ones. At the same time, they are capable of distortion and defense. Nevertheless, the thrust of Allport's argument is that children at this stage are beginning to sense their rational powers and to exercise them (Allport, 1955, p. 46). Allport calls this aspect of the proprium the **self-as-rational-coper**, or sometimes simply the rational agent.

Propriate striving From the beginning of adolescence at age 13, people begin to develop the facet of the self that Allport called **propriate striving**. Allport distinguished between two kinds of motives: peripheral and propriate. Peripheral motives are impulses and drives, the striving toward the immediate gratification of needs and reduction of tension. We are hungry; we eat. We are thirsty; we drink. We are cold; we put on clothing. We are fatigued; we go to sleep. These are simple and automatic acts aimed at reducing tensions. Propriate motives, in contrast, involve the deliberate increase or maintenance of tensions in the service of important goals. During adolescence, we strive to attain a college degree, sometimes at tremendous personal cost; we may try to become the best athlete in a given sport; we may yearn to be a great artist or novelist. Propriate striving is ego-involved behavior, characterized by the unification of personality in pursuit of major life goals. "The possession of long-range goals, regarded as central to one's personal existence, distinguishes the human being from the animal, the adult from the child, and in many cases the healthy from the sick" (Allport, 1955, p. 51).

The emergence of propriate striving is closely related to the development of conscience. In the child, the evolving conscience is a "must" conscience, which is similar to Freud's conscience concept. It is a conscience based on fear of punishment. Children begin to internalize their parents' values and standards and feel guilty if they violate the rules. As people mature, however, there is a marked change in their perception of the world and other people. They begin to develop an "ought" conscience. At this stage, obedience to the external standards of authority gives way to internal, or self-generated, rules. Conduct is guided by the person's own values and self-image.

The shift from a "must" to an "ought" conscience is not automatic. Many chronological adults are still children in conduct. They continue to react in terms of parental prohibitions; they suffer from unresolved guilt feelings and rehash old conflicts with authority figures (Allport, 1955, p. 74). They have not learned to rely on their own judgment and to orient themselves toward the attainment of challenging goals.

The self-as-knower In adulthood, we begin the development of the **self-as-knower**. We now are capable of integrating all the prior aspects of the proprium into a unified whole. As Allport put it:

> We (now) not only know things, but we know the empirical features of our own proprium. It is I who have bodily sensations, I who recognize my self-identity from day to day; I who note and reflect upon my self-assertion, self-extension, my own rationalizations, as well as upon my interests and strivings. When I thus think about my own propriate functions I am likely to perceive their essential togetherness, and feel them intimately bound in some way to the knowing function itself. (Allport, 1955, p. 53)

Finally, although the various aspects of the proprium may first emerge at different stages of life, in Allport's view they all continue to develop and do not function separately. Several or even all of them can operate simultaneously in a given situation:

> Suppose that you are facing a difficult and critical examination. No doubt you are aware of the butterflies in your stomach (bodily self); also of the significance of the exam in terms of your past and future (self-identity); of your prideful involvement (self-esteem); of what success or failure may mean to your family (self-extension); of your hopes and aspirations (self-image); of your role as the solver of problems on the examination (rational agent); and of the relevance of the whole situation to your long-range goals (propriate striving). In actual life, then, a fusion of propriate states is the rule. (Allport, 1961, p. 137)

Development of the Mature Personality

Allport described the developmental process as one of "becoming." The development of the mature personality takes time, he believed, so that only the adult is capable of coming close to self-realization. These shifts in development are not always smooth and even; they are, instead, often abrupt and discontinuous. The normal or mature person is qualitatively different from the abnormal or immature one.

> Initially, the infant is an unsocialized being: Even at the age of two the child is, when measured by standards applied to adults, an unsocialized horror. Picture, if you can, an adult who is extremely destructive of property, insistent and demanding that every

desire be instantly gratified, helpless and dependent on others, unable to share his possessions, violent and uninhibited in the display of all his feelings. Such behavior, normal to a two year old, would be monstrous in a man. Unless these qualities are markedly altered in the process of becoming, we have on our hands an infantile and potentially evil personality. (Allport, 1955, pp. 28–29)

During this early stage of development, not only are children dependent on others, but most of their behavior is designed to help them survive. They perform those behaviors that will reduce hunger and thirst, for example. They also learn what Allport called our "tribal conformities," for example, the wearing of clothes or brushing of teeth (Allport, 1955, p. 63).

As their propriums develop, children also learn to protect themselves against threats through the use of various defensive strategies. In this regard, Allport accepted the validity of Freud's ego defense mechanisms, but he held that excessive and indiscriminate use of these strategies is indicative of an abnormal or immature personality. The mature personality, in his view, is relatively free of these debilitating tactics. Granting that adult behavior is sometimes motivated by sexual and aggressive needs, Allport once again maintained that such motivations play a relatively small part in the functioning of the mature person, which is directed more by current motives and events. Thus, a student who eats too little, for example, may not be fixated at the oral stage but, rather, may have a contract to eat in the university dining hall, where the food is relatively unappetizing.

Functional Autonomy

The early development of the person, then, is characterized by the presence of peripheral motives. Later, as the proprium develops, there is a shift from this type of motivation and learning toward propriate strivings—the use of creative and spontaneous energies to move toward full maturity. The key question is how we free ourselves from our infantile motives so that we can function as mature adults. The answer, according to Allport, is found in his general law of motivation called **functional autonomy**.

"Functional autonomy regards adult motives as varied and as self-sustaining, contemporary systems growing out of antecedent systems but functionally independent of them" (Allport, 1961, p. 227). As persons mature, their bonds with the past are broken. Mature individuals no longer depend on parents; their behavior is independent of their parents' wishes. Nor do they need to use defensive tactics to protect their self-esteem from attacks by others; they are now capable of judging their conduct by self-generated rules. A few examples may clarify the concept:

> An ex-sailor has a craving for the sea, a musician longs to return to his instrument after an enforced absence, a miser continues to build up his useless pile. Now the sailor may have first acquired his love for the sea as an incident in his struggle to earn a living. The sea was "secondary reinforcement" for his hunger drive. But now the ex-sailor is perhaps a wealthy banker; the original motive is destroyed and yet the hunger for the sea persists and even increases in intensity. The musician may first have been stung by a slur on his inferior performance into mastering his instrument; but now he is safely beyond these taunts, and finds that he loves his instrument more than anything else in the world. The miser perhaps learned his habit of thrift in dire necessity, but the miserliness persists and becomes stronger with the years even after the necessity has been relieved. (Allport, 1961, p. 227)

Thus, Allport's concept of functional autonomy serves as a bridge between the phase of development controlled by immature strivings and that characterized by mature motives.

It should be noted that Allport's concept provides a description of shifts in the developmental process, not an explanation of why the shift occurs. Allport struggled mightily to provide an adequate explanation of the phenomenon. He saw its basic roots as biological but concluded that we lack knowledge of the specific neurological mechanisms that may be involved (Allport, 1961, pp. 244–245). Speculating further, he proposed that each person has a creative energy level that must be satisfied. If it is not, then new interests and motives must develop. These new developments are qualitatively different from motives that operate simply to satisfy basic hunger, thirst, and sex needs. In Allport's view, people are innately curious; they seek to understand themselves, others, and their environments. They are continually trying to discover their place in the world, to establish their unique identities. This creative quest for growth, meaning, and selfhood is part of human nature (Evans, 1970, p. 32). It underlies the phenomenon of functional autonomy and helps explain the radical shift in motives as people move toward maturity. To be sure, this creative urge for meaning is influenced and modified by experiences with others and the environment. For example, a person has no fully formed, innate need to be a physician, but acquires an interest in medicine through reading, friends, teachers, and parents. The creative urge simply provides the impetus to do something that is challenging and capable of fulfilling his or her potential.

Characteristics of Maturity

To Allport, then, mature individuals are those who are able to free themselves from excessive reliance on earlier motives. On this basis, he developed six criteria for judging whether or not a person is mature (Allport, 1961, p. 283).

Extension of the sense of self   Truly mature persons, according to Allport, are able to participate in activities that go beyond themselves. They are concerned not only about their own welfare but also about the welfare of others, a view advocated by the major religions of the world as well.

> True participation gives direction to life. Maturity advances in proportion as lives are decentered from the clamorous immediacy of the body and of ego-centeredness. Self-love is a prominent and inescapable factor in every life, but it need not dominate. Everyone has self-love, but only self-extension is the earmark of maturity. (Allport, 1961, p. 285)

Warm relatedness to others   The mature individual is also capable of relating warmly to others. Allport distinguished between two kinds of warmth. The first is intimacy—the capacity for love, whether of family or friends. The second kind is compassion. Allport believed that mature persons have a certain detachment in their dealings with others that allows them to be respectful and appreciative of individual differences in behavior and thought. Thus, they are not constantly complaining, criticizing, sarcastic, possessive, gossipy, or intrusive on the privacy or rights of others. In short, the mature person follows the rule, "Do not poison the air that other people have to breathe," and realizes that all mortals are in the same human situation: They did not ask to come into the world; they are saddled with an urge to survive and are buffeted by drives and passions; they encounter failure, suffer, but somehow carry on. No one knows for sure the meaning of life; everyone is growing older as he sails to an unknown destination. (Allport, 1961, p. 285)

Self-acceptance   Mature persons are emotionally secure. They avoid overreacting in matters that are beyond their control. They have a high tolerance level for frustration because they have reached the point of **self-acceptance**. Immature persons, in contrast, tend to act impulsively and to blame others for their own mistakes. Unlike mature persons, they do not bide their time or make plans to circumvent obstacles in their path. In brief, they lack the kind of self-control that characterizes the mature person.

Realistic perception of reality   Mature persons are accurate in their perception of events. They do not continually distort reality. They have the knowledge and skills necessary for effective performance and living, and the capacity to lose themselves in their work. In short, they are problem-centered, not ego-centered.

Self-objectification   Mature persons know themselves. They are blessed with **self-objectification**—insight into their own abilities and limitations. Correlated with their insight is a sense of humor. Mature individuals have the ability to see the absurdity in life and not be overwhelmed by it. They can be amused by their own mistakes and not deceived by their own pretentiousness.

Unifying philosophy of life   Finally, mature individuals have developed "a clear comprehension of life's purpose in terms of an intelligible theory" (Allport, 1961, p. 294). They have a sense of directedness and a set of life goals. Although adolescents have ideals, they are typically vague. When young people seek to implement their ideals and fall short, they experience disappointment. In their late 20s, people begin to learn that they must compromise with reality. They find that their jobs are not as challenging or rewarding as they had hoped, that their marriages or living arrangements fall short of their desires, and that they have not been able to overcome some of their personal limitations (Allport, 1961, p. 295). They find that their goals and values are changing and a revised and clearer set of principles is beginning to emerge. Mature persons have a fairly clear self-image and have evolved a set of standards that guide their conduct. This set of principles need not be religious in nature, but it can be.

The Role of Religion as a Unifying Philosophy of Life

According to Allport, religion can play an important part in helping individuals become more mature. He believed that commitment to religious beliefs can help organize and give constructive meaning to our lives. He also understood that many individuals would reject his suggestion completely by arguing that religion has done tremendous harm to human beings throughout history. Allport acknowledged that millions of people have maimed and killed each other in the name of religious conviction throughout the ages and that they continue to do so today, but he cautioned us to remember that, on the other side of the coin, many people throughout the world have been taught by religious leaders to accept others as equals and to treat each human being with kindness, compassion, dignity, and respect, and they do (Allport & Ross, 1967, p. 433). Thus, Allport embraced a more differentiated view of the importance of religion in each person's life, distinguishing between immature ("bad") and mature ("good") religious orientations. He associated what he termed **extrinsic religious orientations** with immaturity, and **intrinsic religious orientations** with maturity. Extrinsically oriented people, Allport maintained, use their religion as a means to an end. Such people tend to use their religion primarily for self-serving, ulterior motives such as security, comfort, status, or social support (Allport & Ross, 1967, p. 441). For example, they attend their house of worship primarily to establish business contacts and/or to attain status in the community. Or they call on God primarily in times of need or crisis, for example, when they fail on examinations or when they experience serious illness. They also tend to see their church as superior to other churches and believe that God prefers them to individuals who belong to other faiths (Allport, 1961, p. 300). There is initial empirical support for Allport's argument in newer research (Hall, Matz, & Wood, 2010, pp. 126–139) which shows that, when extrinsically oriented church members band together with other church members to affirm their values, they may then treat nonchurch members as outsiders, devalue them, and become prejudiced against them.

Intrinsically oriented people, in contrast, consider their religious beliefs as ends in themselves, in Allport's opinion. Such individuals do not bargain with God or use God as a "security blanket." They do not feel smug and superior to others. In fact, they are very motivated to help others in need. They take their religious beliefs seriously and organize their lives in terms of them. Their religious beliefs help integrate their personalities and produce a consistent morality. Such a religiosity is based on a faith, but a faith that is open to change and correction (Ventis, 1995, p. 35). Allport and Ross (1967, p. 434) summarize the difference between the two orientations by saying that "the extrinsically motivated person uses his religion, whereas the intrinsically motivated lives his religion."

Over a period of more than 40 years, researchers have used the Religious Orientation Scale (Allport & Ross, 1967, pp. 432–443), a measure of intrinsic and extrinsic religiosity based on Allport's original conceptualization, to study a variety of personality issues, and the results generally have been consistent. Research has shown that intrinsically oriented individuals tend to be more compassionate, personally competent, emotionally secure, more flexible in their reactions to crises and more capable of overcoming them than their extrinsically oriented counterparts. Intrinsically oriented people are generally less prejudiced, anxious, fearful, and obsessed with their death than extrinsically oriented individuals (Blaine & Crocker, 1995, p. 1031; Donahue, 1985, pp. 400–419; Hill & Pargament, 2003, pp. 64–74; Lesniak, Rudman, Rector, & Elkin, 2006, p. 22; Maltby & Day, 2000, p. 122; McFarland, 1989, pp. 324–336; Park, Cohen, & Murch, 1996, pp. 75–96; Ponton & Gorsuch, 1988, pp. 260–271; Steffen & Masters, 2005, pp. 217–224; Ventis, 1995, pp. 39–41). Chinese university students who are intrinsically religious are also less fearful and anxious, not only about their own eventual death, but about the death of people who are close to them (Hui & Fung, 2009, pp. 30–50). In short, intrinsically oriented individuals are, on average, more psychologically healthy than their extrinsically oriented counterparts (Dezutter, Soenens, & Hutsebaut, 2006, p. 807).

Limitations of Allport's Views on Religiosity Differences

Finally, it is clear that Allport's conceptualization of individual differences in intrinsic and extrinsic religiosity has assigned a more psychologically healthy orientation in personality development and functioning to those individuals who embrace a more individual and personal orientation to religion and God (intrinsically oriented people) than to those who embrace a more social inclination to religion and God (extrinsically oriented people). Yet, recently there have been some researchers who criticize Allport's distinctions as being overly simplistic.

First, they point out that even intrinsically oriented individuals can feel superior about their own religious views and subsequently harbor prejudice against the members of outgroups whom they consider inferior to themselves. While they may report on personality tests that they are open and treat members of other groups fairly, particularly the poor, these direct, easy-to-fake self-reports may be guided by their need to say socially approved things. This result is not found with testing that is more indirect and less subject to **social desirability biases** (Hall et al., 2010, p. 129).

Second, his critics argue that Allport was perhaps correct in assuming that people who go to their house of worship *primarily* oriented toward making friendships, developing business contacts, and/or acquiring status in the community are more likely to be prejudiced toward members of other religious out-groups and less psychologically mature than those who go to services primarily to worship God. Nevertheless, they argue that he seems to have thrown the "baby out with the bathwater" by assuming that *all* social motives for attending religious services are bad. Cohen, Hall, Koenig, and Meador (2005, pp. 48–61) argue that, while Allport's position has had much value in increasing our understanding of the role of religion in personality functioning, by condemning all social motives for religiousness, his position is limited and biased in some respects. They maintain that Allport's position is most strongly related to American Protestant religions of the early 20th century, which embrace an extreme individualistic orientation to life and worship that focuses on a private, pietistic relationship to God, faith, and salvation. Such a religious viewpoint meshes well with Allport's theory of personality, which places such an extraordinary emphasis on human individuality. These scholars maintain that, as a result of Allport's extreme focus on private motives, he simplistically downgrades the role of all social motives in religious worship. In contrast to Allport, they think there is much value in the worship we see in Christian churches, Jewish synagogues, Muslim mosques, and in other houses of worship which center on community values and rituals which bind individuals together in their worship of God. For example, singing together in praise of God promotes solidarity among adherents within Christianity. Children in Judaism who undergo a Bar Mitzvah (boys) or Bat Mitzvah (girls) are now seen by members of the synagogue as adults having moral responsibility. They can now lead religious services. Their entry into adulthood through the ceremony increases the sense of community and is celebrated by the membership. In Islam, social courtesy and cooperation are part of worship practice outcomes which bind believers to other worshippers and to humanity in general.

In conclusion, his critics argue that the strong American individualism that Allport embraced remains a powerful and ubiquitous force even today, but that it unfortunately obscures our understanding of the more collectivistic or social motives of religious motivations that often create a social solidarity that is healthy (Cohen & Hill, 2007, pp. 709–742). These scholars urge researchers in this area to take another look at Allport's original conceptualization and scales as a means of seeing that they are useful only in limited ways. They maintain that there is a need to expand our theorizing and scale construction in this important area as a means of being able to conduct research that will increase our understanding of the positive role played by some social religious motives in our lives as we move through the 21st century.

Study of Values

Besides his studies of religion, Allport also focused on values as guides to a person's behavior. He and his colleagues devised a scale to assess the extent to which a person holds six major values (Allport, Vernon, & Lindzey, 1960):

1. *Theoretical*: Focus on the discovery of truth, and interests that are empirical, critical, and rational.
2. *Economic*: Focus on usefulness and being practical.
3. *Aesthetic*: Focus on form and harmony, and interests in the artistic side of life.
4. *Social*: Focus on the altruistic love of others, and a tendency to be kind, sympathetic, and unselfish.
5. *Political*: Focus on power over others, dominance, influence, and social recognition.
6. *Religious*: Focus on unity, and a tendency to seek to comprehend the cosmos as a whole (Lubinski, Schmidt, & Benbow, 1996, p. 445).

Across several studies, male adolescents and young adults scored higher on the Theoretical, Economic, and Political values than females, whereas females scored higher on the Aesthetic, Social, and Religious values. In terms of their occupational interests, adolescents and adults who had strong theoretical orientations gravitated toward science (physics and chemistry) and mathematics, those who scored highest on the economic value had strongest interest in business management, those highest on the political value preferred the military and law, those who scored highest on the aesthetic value were most positive toward careers in music, art, writing, and teaching. Those who valued the social highest had strongest interest in social work and business sales, and those who scored highest on religious orientation saw themselves with careers involving religious activities (e.g., pastoral counselors, ministers) (Lubinski et al., 1996, pp. 444–449; Schmidt, Lubinski, & Benbow, 1998, pp. 436–453).

Although there has been only a smattering of research over the last four decades since the creation of the scale by Allport and his colleagues, recently personality psychologists have been focusing more and more on the study of values, as we shall see in the last chapter, and we can expect a resurgence of interest in Allport's ideas about values.

Assessment Techniques

Idiographic versus Nomothetic Approach

Because Allport considered personality to be a dynamic and interrelated entity, he thought it pointless to focus on only one or two of its facets. Its complexity, he believed, meant that investigators must employ every legitimate method to study it (Allport, 1961, p. 395). By legitimate methods he meant reliable and valid assessment procedures based on objective and systematic observations of given phenomena. Illegitimate methods, according to Allport, include "gossip, prejudiced inference, the exaggerated single instance, unverified anecdote [and] "character reading" (Allport, 1961, pp. 395–396).

Among the legitimate methods used to study personality are (1) constitutional and physiological diagnosis; (2) studies of sociocultural membership, status, and roles; (3) personal documents and case studies; (4) self-appraisal techniques, such as self-ratings and Q-sorts (see Chapter 13); (5) conduct samplings, such as behavior assessments in everyday situations; (6) observer ratings; (7) personality tests and scales; (8) projective tests; (9) depth analysis, such as free association and dream analysis; (10) expressive behavior measures; and (11) synaptic procedures (Allport, 1961, p. 458). Synaptic procedures involve combining the outcomes of a variety of assessment techniques to produce a general picture or profile of the individual's personality (Allport, 1961, p. 445).

Although some of these techniques seek to define the typical case or average person, Allport's own focus was on the uniqueness of the individual. "Each person is an idiom unto himself, an apparent violation of the syntax of the species" (Allport, 1955, p. 19). Thus, he fought an uphill battle against the prevailing view in American psychology that a science of personality should seek to establish universal laws of human functioning—to understand the behavior and experience of people in general. Such an approach Allport labeled **nomothetic**. His own approach, in which the primary goal is to understand the functioning of a specific individual, he labeled **idiographic**.

These two views generate different kinds of information about people. The nomothetic approach relies heavily on the use of statistics in the analysis of human behavior. For example, it can tell us that, in comparison to Bill or Jane, John has a lower need for achievement because he scored only at the 10th percentile on a paper-and-pencil test designed to measure this characteristic, whereas the other two people scored well above the 95th percentile. Further testing could tell us that John is above average in intelligence as compared to other adolescents of the same age. Allport asserted that this sort of information about John, though useful, is limited, because it does not tell us anything about

John's uniqueness. The idiographic approach, in contrast, would provide us with information about the ways in which these and many other characteristics interact within John's personality. It would give us a view of the dynamic and organized personality that is peculiar to John. Thus, Allport would seek to establish the lawfulness in John's behavior and experiences through the use of such techniques as personal records, pattern analysis of expressive movements, graphology, and case studies (Allport, 1937, pp. 369–399).

An Idiographic Analysis

A prime example of the use of personal documents to facilitate understanding of an individual's personality and life is Allport's pioneering analysis of the correspondence of Jenny Gove Masterson. Between the ages of 58 and 70, she wrote a series of 301 letters to two friends of her son, Ross, which provide insight into her personality and her strange, tempestuous relationship with Ross.

The case of Jenny Gove Masterson As a young woman, Jenny married a railway inspector named Henry Masterson. Before her marriage, she had earned her own living, and now she found it very irritating to remain at home idle all day. She complained often to her husband about her situation, but to no avail. Like most men in the early 1900s, he was vehemently opposed to his wife's seeking employment. Before the issue was resolved, her husband died. A month later, her son was born.

Shortly afterward, Jenny went to work as a telegrapher to support herself and her infant son. She did not complain about widowhood but was very happy to have a child to whom she could give her undivided attention. Jenny was so content with this arrangement that she rejected several desirable offers of marriage. She lavished affection on Ross and was his constant companion. Several of her relatives claimed that she spoiled him, but she replied that she would gladly scrub floors to buy him the things he said he wanted. After several quarrels with her relatives about her pampering of Ross, she severed her relationship with them for 25 years.

When Ross reached puberty, Jenny sent him to an expensive boarding school. In order to afford his educational expenses, she took a position as a librarian and lived chiefly on cereal and milk in a small, windowless room. For several years after, she remained Ross's closest companion. This overprotectiveness continued for several more years until finally he rebelled. He began to see other women, and quarrels with Jenny about them were frequent and very bitter. Eventually Ross married but kept it a secret from his mother. She soon discovered the deception, however, and was furious. She drove him out of her home with violent denunciations and threatened to have him arrested if he tried to see her again. A few years later, she relented and began to see and correspond with him until his untimely death.

Let us now examine a sample of four letters that Jenny wrote to Ross's two friends, Glenn and Isabel, over this stormy period of more than a decade.

At the time the first letter was written, in 1928, Ross had abandoned his wife and had begun a relationship with another woman. Jenny was despondent and turned to his friends, Glenn and Isabel, for support; in the letter, she explained the reasons for her unhappiness with Ross and the antagonism between them.

> It isn't money that stands between Ross and me, not by any means, it's *women*, more women. (My writing is awful, I'm all nerves.) Sometimes I wonder if Ross is a trifle off balance-sex mad. At first he talked lovely about saving money, building up a character in business and that sort of thing, and I was in the 7th Heaven. He has saved money, it's in our joint names in a bank, several hundred dollars. That's why I skimped so. But all the time he was carrying on an affair with a woman, … a very bad affair, and before he got out of it, he wasn't so far from the Pen. I helped him out

of that. Now, it's Marie, the Butcher's daughter from Toledo. When Ross ditched his wife he wrote to Marie. [Now] Marie [speaks] of coming to N.Y. this winter and renting a room. Ross and I had a scrap, I refuse to do it. Marie will never enter any house that I am in … I did not intend to say so much, but I'm heartsore, and sick, and truly discouraged. Ross cares *absolutely nothing at all for me*—I am a great drawback and burden to him. (Allport, 1965, pp. 51–53)

In the second letter, written in 1929, Jenny mentions Ross's poor health. He suffered from an infected ear and, when they operated, the doctors found a large mastoid on the inner ear and an abscess on the outer covering of the brain. She also mentions her resentment of Ross's girlfriend, whom she calls a chip (whore).

Ross called to see me last week, he is still in the Dr.'s hands. He looks very poorly. I invited him to have luncheon with me, and he did … It was a swell luncheon, and he seemed to enjoy it. You know the way to bring Ross to his senses is *to give him what he wants* and then leave him alone. I wish now that I had left him last May when he moved the Chip to the Bronx. But even if he marries her now (she may force him into it) he will not remain with her long. And that is where I come in, and why I invited him to luncheon so that he may not be *quite* alone until he finds a new chip. Right well I know that he hasn't a bit of use for me, is ashamed of me, and despises me, but still the tie of blood is there, and I cannot believe that he is altogether insensible to it. (Allport, 1965, p. 70)

Unfortunately, Ross did not recover from his illness and died shortly afterward. In the third letter, written at the end of 1929, Jenny's hostility toward Ross's girlfriend erupts, and she blames her for Ross's death.

My affairs. Oh, they are all in a turmoil. The chip lady [although] all dissolved in tears, and of course heartbroken, is not too liquid to forget that material things count in this mundane sphere, and lo! she claimed Ross's clothes, and Ross's car. [She claims to be Ross's closest relative.] If she is Ross's nearest relative it is she who will receive the [Veteran Administration's] compensation, and that would be tragic enough to make one die of laughter. She has only known him *6 months*. February was the beginning of their "Great Romance"—dirty and low as they are made—the low contemptible street dog. She killed Ross, morally and physically. (Allport, 1965, pp. 73–74)

Following Ross's death, Jenny entered into a series of legal entanglements with his girlfriend over his estate, from which Jenny emerged victorious. In the fourth letter, written in 1930, Jenny recalls the happy time she and Ross had shared on his last birthday.

This month has been pretty hard on me. I had to move, it cost a lot, then came Ross's birthday, October 16. Last October 16 Ross spent with me. I watched for him all morning, my heart in my mouth. Then early in the afternoon he came, carrying a lovely bunch of red roses, my favorites, he always got red roses for me. I was in Heaven. He had not forgotten me, he chose to have dinner with me, not with the Chip. He took me to a nice place … on Broadway, and then to a show, a splendid show, he came to my room on the roof, and kissed[me] goodnight under the stars, how little we dreamed of what the next year would bring! I am always thinking of him, always wishing that I had done something I did not do, or left something undone, or unsaid, that I did do, and said. (Allport, 1965, p. 88)

In 1931 Jenny entered a home for women—she described it as similar to a good hotel—where she lived until her death in 1937. The superintendent of the home reported that she had become unbearably difficult during the year before her death. She had taken to sweeping her dinner onto the floor if it displeased her and had even attacked one of the other boarders; Jenny hit her over the head with a pail. The boarders were afraid of her, and the superintendent had been considering her removal to an institution for the insane just before her death.

Analyzing the correspondence   Allport asked 36 judges to read Jenny's letters and then to characterize her in trait terms. The judges assigned a total of 198 trait names, which were subsequently reduced to eight major, central traits. In order of importance for understanding her personality, they were: quarrelsome/suspicious, self-centered, independent, dramatic, aesthetic/artistic, aggressive, cynical/morbid, and sentimental. Allport believed that these results provided some insights into Jenny's personality that went beyond a commonsense interpretation of the letters but cautioned that the judges' assessments were nevertheless still primarily intuitive.

Allport then reported a follow-up study in which content analysis was used to assess the structure of Jenny's personality. Content analysis is a research technique for the objective, systematic, and quantitative description of communications (Allport, 1965, p. 197). First, the content of her letters was coded; that is, what she said was classified into a number of distinct categories, such as hostility, art appreciation, and affection. Then, for each category, a frequency count was recorded, for example, the number of times she made a hostile remark, mentioned her love of art, or commented on her affection for people. These data were then subjected to a complex statistical procedure called factor analysis (see Chapter 9) to discover the major traits of Jenny's personality. The results obtained by means of this relatively objective analysis were quite similar to the findings produced by the more intuitive judges' ratings.

Allport was careful to point out that, although these two approaches offer some valid insight into the uniqueness of Jenny's personality, they by no means provide all the answers about her.

Theory's Implications for Therapy

For Allport, the healthy or mature person is continually in a state of becoming; the unhealthy or immature person is one whose growth has been stifled. He believed, like Freud, that development could be arrested as a result of faulty relationships with parents, especially the mother, in early childhood. Allport believed that people need to feel secure and protected and that deprivations of love and affection can have a lasting and harmful impact on growth.

> All in all a generous minimum of security seems required in early years for a start toward a productive lifestyle. Without it the individual develops a pathological craving for security, and is less able than others to tolerate setbacks in maturity. Through his insistent demanding, jealousy, depredation, and egoism, he betrays the craving that still haunts him. By contrast, the child who receives adequate gratification of his infant needs is more likely to be prepared to give up his habits of demanding and to learn tolerance for his later frustrations. Having completed successfully one stage of development, he is free to abandon the habits appropriate to this stage and to enter the mature reaches of becoming. (Allport, 1955, p. 32)

To overcome these deprivations, Allport believed that the person must come to feel "accepted and wanted by therapist, family, and associates." The person must feel loved and must learn to love. "Love received and love given comprise the best form of therapy" (Allport, 1955, p. 33).

But this is only one side of the picture. Many people who have had secure and loving backgrounds later become neurotic. Although their secure backgrounds make them free to grow, other problems arise. Society exerts pressures on individuals to adjust to its norms, and often these adjustments preclude positive growth.

> Society itself is sick. Why … make a patient content with its injustices, hypocrisies, and wars? And to what society shall we adjust the patient? To his social class, thus making him provincial and depriving him of aspiration? To his nation, thus giving him no vision of mankind as a whole? It is doubtful that we can accept society (any society) as a standard for a healthy personality. A head-hunter society demands well-adjusted head-hunters as citizens, but is the deviant in this group who questions the value of decapitation necessarily an immature human being? (Allport, 1961, p. 305)

Indiscriminate acceptance of society's demands restricts self-extension, distorts the self-image, produces a defensive self, and stunts propriate striving. Loyalties become restricted; correspondingly, there is a growing intolerance of other people and groups. People come to see themselves and their goals in terms of the values established by others. For example, a person may see himself as a lawyer and pursue that goal because his parents demand that he do so; in the process, important goals that he actually desires to pursue are shunted aside. As a result, the person experiences considerable conflict and uses defensive maneuvers to alleviate the suffering. Movement toward self-realization is hindered. The task of the therapist, in Allport's view, is to help such individuals become aware of the sources of their distorted goals and to assist them in the attainment of maturity and well-being.

Evaluative Comments

We now consider the scientific worth of Allport's theory.

Comprehensiveness   Allport's theory is comprehensive in the sense that it is incredibly eclectic; it borrows concepts from learning theory, psychoanalysis, and existentialism. Its focus, however, is largely limited to healthy development. Moreover, it describes the developmental stages of the proprium only in general terms, with little attempt to specify precisely the variables that control the occurrence, maintenance, or modification of self-phenomena. Finally, the theory is restricted in that, although it recognizes the influence of the situation, it does not specify in enough detail how the social environment affects the development of personality.

Precision and testability   Allport's theory is populated with vague and ill-defined concepts and propositions. Terms such as propriate striving and the self-as-rational-coper do not lend themselves readily to operational definitions. Nor was Allport explicit in stating the relationship between his trait concepts and his theory of the development of the proprium. Given these problems, it would be difficult to design adequate tests of his theory.

Parsimony   Allport's theory fails to meet the parsimony criterion not because it is surfeited with excess concepts but because it has too few concepts to account for the phenomena within its domain. It is doubtful that the complexities of the developmental process can be described adequately in terms of his seven major aspects of the self.

Empirical validity   Very few attempts have been made to determine the validity of Allport's theory of traits and self-development, presumably because the theory is primarily descriptive and lacks specific propositions from which researchers might derive testable hypotheses. As a result, empirical support for these aspects of his theory is weak. However, Allport's distinction between intrinsic and extrinsic religiosity has generated considerable research over the past six decades, and the findings are generally consistent with his theorizing.

Heuristic value   Although Allport's theory, in general, has not generated much research, his insistence on the role of individual traits (personal dispositions) in an adequate theory of personality remains highly relevant and provocative to the present day for personality psychologists (Funder, 1991).

> Psychology is truly itself only when it can deal with individuality. It is vain to plead that other sciences do not do so, that they are allowed to brush off the bothersome issue of uniqueness. The truth is that psychology is assigned the task of being curious about human persons, and persons exist only in concrete and unique patterns. We study the human person most fully when we take him as an individual. He is more than a bundle of habits, more than a point of intersection of abstract dimensions. He is more than a representative of his species, more than a citizen of the state, more than an incident in the movements of mankind. He transcends them all. The individual, striving ever for integrity and fulfillment, has existed under all forms of social lifeforms as varied as the nomadic and feudal, capitalist and communist. No society holds together for long without the respect man shows to man. The individual today struggles on even under oppression, always hoping and planning for a more perfect democracy where the dignity and growth of each personality will be prized above all else. (Allport, 1961, p. 573)

Thus, Allport remains the champion of the idiographic approach to the study of personality. Many investigators have been forced by Allport's clear voice to reconsider their acceptance of the tenets of a nomothetic science and to concede with him that any worthwhile theory of personality must take into account the uniqueness of the individual.

Applied value   Allport's theory has not had much impact on disciplines outside psychology, with the exception of his ideas about religiosity, which have influenced people in pastoral psychology. Within psychology, his theory of self-development has proved highly useful to clinical psychologists in their treatment of patients.

CRITICAL THINKING QUESTIONS

1. What is a trait? What kinds of traits are there, according to Allport? Give examples of each kind in yourself and in two other people you know.

2. Do you agree with Allport that children are "unsocialized horrors"? What are the implications of his view for the disciplining of children?

3. Describe the criteria used by Allport to characterize the mature person. Can you think of any others? In terms of Allport's criteria, how mature are you and your friends?

4. In Allport's opinion, religion can be a force for good or evil in a person's life? How do you see it? What are the consequences for your daily life of your beliefs about religion? If you are an atheist, what elements of Allport's views on religion do you accept or reject, and why?

5. Is it always healthy to live by your own standards and values and not by the standards and values of other people? Have you have been in situations where the standards and values you embrace were wrong and those of others morally right? Give some examples, if possible.

GLOSSARY

becoming   Developmental process involving movement toward self-realization.

bodily self   Feelings about oneself based on feedback from one's physical senses.

cardinal traits   Characteristics that serve as the motivating force for virtually all of an individual's behavior.

central traits   Characteristics that control an individual's behavior in many situations but are less comprehensive than cardinal traits.

common traits   Dispositions shared with others.

extrinsic religious orientations   According to Allport orientations that are used by people for self-serving purposes. The primary orientation is a narcissistic focus on having their needs met.

functional autonomy   Process whereby a behavior that was once controlled by a basic motive comes to operate independently of that motive.

genotype   Inherited characteristic that may or may not be reflected in the phenotype, or outward appearance, of the individual.

humanistic theory   A theory that emphasizes the dignity and worth of the person. It optimistically assumes the creativity of the individual and movement toward psychological health.

idiographic   Scientific approach to the study of behavior that seeks to understand the uniqueness of a specific individual through intensive investigation.

intrinsic religious orientations   According to Allport, orientations that are adopted by people to help them make sense of their experiences and to surrender themselves to a power higher than themselves. They are oriented toward helping others and are not narcissistic.

nomothetic   Scientific approach to the study of behavior that seeks to establish laws by specifying the general relationships between variables.

personal dispositions   Traits unique to the individual.

phenotype   Outward appearance of a particular characteristic that may or may not reflect the underlying inherited genotype.

propriate striving   Motive that propels the individual toward the attainment of important, long-range goals. These drives involve an increase, rather than a decrease, in tension.

proprium   Term used by Allport to signify all the various aspects of the person that make him or her unique; the self.

psychophysical systems   Components of personality, as defined by Allport, on the basis of his belief that psychological concepts represent actual underlying states in the nervous system.

secondary traits   Peripheral characteristics, such as preferences, that exert little control over a person's behavior.

self-acceptance   Acknowledgement and understanding of one's own limitations, along with recognition of one's strengths.

self-as-rational-coper   Awareness of oneself as someone capable of rationally formulating and utilizing strategies in order to solve problems and attain personal goals.

self-esteem   Feelings about one's worth.

self-extension   Sense of identity with one's possessions, family, home, and country. In the immature person, self-extension involves egocentricity—a view of other objects, such as family or other people, only in terms of their contributions to one's own welfare and security. In the mature person, it involves the need to contribute to the well-being of individuals and groups that are central to one's existence.

self-identity   The feeling that one is an established human being with a unique past that guides one's present and future judgments.

self-image   Role played in order to win the approval of others; also, plans and behavioral strategies for the future that help people attain their goals.

self-as-knower.   The different aspects of the proprium or self (the bodily self, self-identity, self-esteem, self-extension, self-image, self-as-rational coper, and propriate strivings) are unified by the final aspect of the proprium, the self-as-knower. The self-as-knower is the integrative totality of the person in the process of growth; an entity that is becoming or moving toward self-realization.

self-objectification   Ability to perceive accurately one's own abilities and limitations.

social desirability biases   Habitual ways of responding to personality tests that respondents use to win the approval of others by endorsing statements that are socially desirable (some examples: I am always courteous to others; I never lie; I am never prejudiced against others).

trait theory   Conception of personality that postulates the existence of underlying dispositions or characteristics that direct behavior.

SUGGESTED READINGS

Allport, G. W. (1937). *Personality: A psychological interpretation*. New York: Holt.

Allport, G. W. (1955). *Becoming: Basic considerations for a psychology of personality*. New Haven, CT: Yale University Press.

Allport, G. W. (1961). *Pattern and growth in personality*. New York: Holt, Rinehart & Winston.

CHAPTER 9

Cattell's Structure-Based Systems Theory

Courtesy of University of Illinois.

Biographical Sketch

Raymond Bernard Cattell was born in Staffordshire, England, in 1905. His father was an engineer designer who owned his own business. He recalled that his father provided much of the intellectual stimulation in his childhood, often by leading discussions around the family dinner table in which he extolled the virtues of liberalism in national and international politics. While young Raymond was impressed greatly by his father's intellectual prowess initially, he became slightly disappointed later in his life when he learned that his liberal father's IQ was only 120, whereas his more politically conservative mother's IQ was a more impressive 150. He also noted that his mother's relatives had higher occupational status than the relatives of his father.

In any event, Cattell's childhood generally was idyllic, and he spent much of his time on the beach, learned to sail at age seven, and spent much of his time with his friends engaging in mock battles in boats, and in exploring the coast with his friends, as he put it, in "sun and rain." His closest companions were boys who helped him build boats and joined him in making gunpowder in his "chemistry shed" for their mock battles. By the time he reached college age, Cattell had decided that he wanted to be a scientist and to use science to help humanity get beyond its irrationalities, including the senseless slaughter of millions of civilians and military personnel in World War I (Cattell, 1974, pp. 61–63).

Cattell received a Bachelor of Science degree in chemistry from the University of London when he was 19 and his Ph.D. in psychology from the same institution in 1929 when he was only 24 years of age. While at the university, he served as a research assistant to the famous psychologist/mathematician Charles Spearman. Spearman devised the method known as factor analysis, and Cattell relied heavily on the technique in developing his own theory of personality.

Through Spearman and his intellectual predecessors, British scientist Sir Francis Galton and statistician Karl Pearson, Cattell was introduced to the statistical study of personality and ability functioning. Galton, in his pioneering work on the origins of genius, used statistical analyses of biological data to show associations between phenomena. Pearson later developed a formal mathematical technique, known as the Pearson product-moment correlation coefficient, to measure the size and direction of the association between two events. This procedure was later used in the creation of the factor-analytic method.

Following his graduation, Cattell served as director of a psychology clinic in England, and then went to New York to become a research associate of learning theorist Thorndike, E. L. at Columbia University. Following his brief stay at Columbia, he held positions at Clark University, Harvard, and Duke before accepting a post at the University of Illinois in 1944. He remained at Illinois until 1973, when he retired and left to establish the Institute for Research on Morality and Self-Realization in Boulder, Colorado. In 1977, Professor Cattell became affiliated with the department of psychology at the University of Hawaii at Manoa. He was professor of psychology at the Forrest Institute of Professional Psychology in Honolulu, where he worked to spread an appreciation of the principles of Beyondism (a new morality based on scientific research) among social scientists and educated laypeople.

Two other influences on Cattell's thinking should be mentioned. First, his clinical experience led him to accept many of the psychoanalytic formulations, so that his theory is an interesting blend of rigorous experimental work and clinical observation. Second, Cattell was influenced greatly by British social psychologist William McDougall, who espoused an instinct doctrine of social behavior. McDougall sought to explain social behavior by postulating seven basic instincts: repulsion, curiosity, flight, pugnacity, self-abasement, self-assertion, and parenting. Through extensive factor-analytic research, Cattell identified 10 **ergs** (innate motives that influence behavior): food seeking, mating, gregariousness, parental protectiveness, exploration, escape to security, self-assertion, narcissistic sex, pugnacity, and acquisitiveness. He tentatively identified several others but waited for more confirmatory research before assigning them independent status. As we shall see, Cattell also relied heavily on McDougall's concept of sentiment.

Over a period of 70 years, Cattell published approximately 40 books and well over 500 research articles. He was also the author or coauthor of numerous personality tests, including the Culture Fair Intelligence Tests, the Eight State Questionnaire, the Motivation Analysis Test, the Object-Analytic (O-A) Personality Test Battery, the Institute for Personality and Ability Testing (IPAT) Anxiety Scale Questionnaire, the Clinical Analysis Questionnaire (CAQ), and the popular Sixteen Personality Factor Questionnaire (16 PF).

Among his more notable books, *Description and Measurement of Personality* (1946) was an early attempt to encourage good, solid, empirical research in the area of personality by presenting the basic concepts of his theory and attendant research findings. In *Personality: A Systematic Theoretical and Factual Study* (1950), he sought to build on this foundation and, in addition, to evaluate data and theories from other fields, including psychoanalysis, cultural and physical anthropology, and sociology. His next book, *Personality and Motivation: Structure and Measurement* (1957), offered the most comprehensive treatment of his position to date. In 1965, he published a popular version of his theory, *The Scientific Analysis of Personality* (updated with colleague Kline, P. as *The Scientific Analysis of Personality and Motivation* in 1977). The *Handbook of Multivariate Experimental Psychology* (1966), edited by Cattell (and updated with colleague Nesselroade, J. R. in 1988), included some of his views on the multivariate approach to the study of personality. He coauthored (with Child, D.) *Motivation and Dynamic Structure* (1975) and coedited (with Dreger, R. M.) the *Handbook of Modern Personality Theory* (1977). Shortly thereafter, Cattell published *Personality and Learning Theory* in two volumes: Volume 1, *The Structure of Personality in Its Environment* (1979), and Volume 2, *A Systems Theory of Maturation and Structured Learning* (1980). This impressive work represented Cattell's monumental attempt to integrate his earlier theoretical and research efforts and to present an expanded theory of personality development that took into account both biological and environmental influences. In 1982, he published *The Inheritance of Personality and Ability,* which sought to demonstrate the importance of genetic factors in the determination of personality and features newer methodologies for assessing that role. Finally, Cattell published two books in which he sought to derive a code of ethics and spiritual values from science, *A New Morality from Science: Beyondism* (1972) and *Beyondism: Religion from Science* (1987).

Finally, the American Psychological Association (APA) announced just 6 months before Professor Cattell died that he had been selected to receive the American Psychological Foundation Gold Medal Award for Life Achievements in Psychological Science for his many contributions to the discipline. However, just two days before the presentation of the award, the presentation was abruptly suspended by the foundation's board of trustees after it received a letter from a humanities professor who was the executive director of the Institute for the Study of Academic Racism, an organization that monitored campus racism. The humanities professor charged that Cattell had a lifetime commitment to fascist and eugenics causes and should not be given the award. Shortly afterward, the national director of the Anti-Defamation League echoed that sentiment, arguing that APA should not give its "seal of approval to a man who has, whatever his other accomplishments, exhibited a lifelong commitment to racial supremacy theories." In response, APA formed a blue-ribbon panel to evaluate the accusation and review Cattell's work. Cattell protested that he was not a racist and had never been one. Moreover, he claimed that his work had always stemmed from his belief that important policy decisions in all walks of life should be based on scientific information and knowledge rather than on prejudice, superstition, or political pressure. However, as his health worsened (and before the panel rendered its judgment about his work), Cattell decided to be done with the controversy. He wrote a letter to the APA withdrawing his name from consideration. A few weeks later, Professor Cattell died from cancer at his home in Honolulu, Hawaii, on February 2, 1998 (Paul, 2004, pp. 195–197).

Concepts and Principles

Approach to Theory Building

Cattell's **structure-based systems theory** considers personality as a system in relation to the environment and seeks to explain the complicated transactions between them as they produce change and sometimes growth in the person. Structure-based learning implies that there are sets of traits within the person that can initiate and direct behavior. These traits are often genetically based but subject to modification by learning experiences. Cattell was convinced that an adequate theory of personality must examine and explain the goal-directed motivation of individuals, which goes beyond simple conditioning principles and involves individual cognitive activity. According to Cattell, we must focus on the complicated kinds of cognitive and motivational learning that guide people's actions. In addition, an adequate theory of personality must consider the ways in which the culture and various groups within it influence individuals and are, in turn, influenced by them.

To accomplish these goals, Cattell believed, the structure and process concepts (concepts that assess stability and change in personality functioning) of the theory must be grounded in multivariate research, analysis, and precise measurement. Disdaining "armchair speculation," Cattell believed strongly that all scientific advances depend on exact measurement (Cattell, 1950, p. 4). In his view, measurement provided the foundation from which theories spring, and not the reverse.

Cattell's approach to theory building was to begin with empirical observation and description and, on this basis, to generate a tentative rough hypothesis. From this hypothesis is derived an experiment for testing it empirically. The resulting observations, or experimental data, are used to generate a more precise hypothesis, from which the investigator deduces a new experiment to test it. New data are collected, and the process begins again. Cattell called this process the **inductive-hypothetico-deductive spiral**. (See Figure 9.1.)

FIG-9.1

The inductive-
hypothetico-deductive
spiral. (Adapted from
Nesselroade, J. R. &
Cattell, R. B. (Eds.) 1988,
*Handbook of Multivari-
ate Experimental
Psychology* 2nd ed., p. 17.
Used with kind permis-
sion from Springer
Science and Business
Media.)

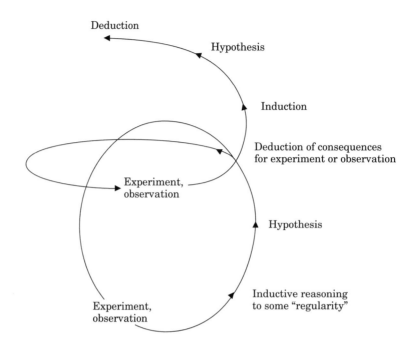

Cattell's inductive theory-building technique was in contrast to the hypothetico-deductive model presented in Chapter 1, in which the investigator begins with a set of general propositions, deduces a hypothesis, and then tests it through the collection of data. Although the hypothetico-deductive model is the one generally employed in the social sciences, Cattell criticized it on several grounds. He thought that all too often it demands that the investigator have a fully developed hypothesis before starting research. Thus, it fails to teach neophyte investigators about research as an exploratory process and may lead them to believe that confirmation of the hypothesis rests on some single measurement difference. According to Cattell, this belief was particularly misleading because it encouraged the researcher to conclude that the behavior under consideration was caused by a single event, when, in fact, it had multiple origins. Of course, Cattell may have been knocking down a straw man: Few investigators in contemporary psychology are naive enough to believe that behavior is usually caused by a single event. Cattell's point, however, was that excessive reliance on **bivariate experiments** can led to oversimplified interpretations of the way events operate in reality and that only **multivariate experiments** allow investigators to analyze and interpret complex behavior adequately.

In making his case for the use of multivariate experiments in psychology, Cattell argued that the bivariate method, that is, manipulating an independent variable and assessing its impact on a dependent variable, artificially considers "bits" of human behavior and ignored the "total organism" (Cattell, 1965, p. 20). In contrast, the multivariate experimenter considers the "whole person" and the complexity of human behavior. The investigator "actually measures all the variables and then set[s] an electronic computer to abstract the regularities which exist" (Cattell, 1965, p. 22). Cattell did not consider bivariate experimentation worthless. He simply believed that a far more rewarding and scientifically useful strategy was to utilize multivariate techniques in initial, exploratory research to identify key variables and generate hypotheses that could then be tested using bivariate and manipulative experimental designs (Cattell, 1979, p. 7).

Methodology: Factor Analysis

To study multiple-variable problems, Cattell relied heavily on **factor analysis**, a highly complicated statistical procedure used to isolate and identify a limited number of factors that underlie a larger group of observed, interrelated variables. Factor analysis has a number of forms, but most of Cattell's work relied on two of them: the R technique and the P technique.

R technique   The most common form of factor analysis is the **R technique**. It usually involves giving large groups of study participants a variety of personality tests and then intercorrelating their scores. If, for example, we administered to a large introductory psychology class a series of tests measuring indecisiveness, tendency to brood, depression, aggressiveness, competitiveness, and conceit, scored each of them, and then intercorrelated all of the participants' scores, we might obtain the series of correlations shown in Table 9.1. From these correlations, we can see that participants who scored high in indecisiveness also had high scores on the brooding and depression tests; that is, these three tests are highly intercorrelated. The remaining three tests (aggressiveness, competitiveness, and conceit) are also highly intercorrelated but are essentially unrelated (very low correlations) to the first three. High intercorrelations, or clustering, among variables suggest the presence of some underlying factor or factors that caused participants to respond in the way they did on the tests that cluster together.

Thus, the investigator starts with a large number of surface variables (**surface traits**) and seeks to reduce them to a few common source factors (**source traits**) that can be used to predict the variation in the original surface-variable measures. Variables that are strongly intercorrelated are considered to be measuring, to a great extent, the same entity or factor. The problem facing investigators is that they must eventually label the underlying factors. Because these subjectively based interpretations have important implications for future theorizing and research, considerable skill and care must be exercised in the labeling process. Inaccurate interpretations can be costly.

Once the intercorrelations have been determined, further factor-analytic computations are employed to derive a factor matrix such as the one shown in Table 9.2. The degree of association between each surface variable and its underlying factor is called the **factor loading**. Loadings of .30 and above are usually considered substantial and significant. In Table 9.2 we can see that indecisiveness, brooding, and depression all load significantly on factor 1, which we can tentatively label "guilt-proneness." Aggressiveness, competitiveness, and conceit load significantly on factor 2, which we can tentatively label "dominance."

Once the factors have been tentatively identified, researchers usually seek to refine them using other samples and to cross-validate them by using study participants of different ages, ethnic and cultural backgrounds, and so forth. They may also place more

TABLE 9.1   INTERCORRELATIONS BETWEEN SIX TEST VARIABLES

Test	*A*	*B*	*C*	*D*	*E*	*F*
A Indecisiveness	—					
B Brooding	.72	—				
C Depression	.85	.67	—			
D Aggressiveness	.02	.04	.07	—		
E Competitiveness	.08	.18	.00	.83	—	
F Conceit	.16	.04	.10	.92	.68	—

TABLE 9.2   LOADING OF SIX TESTS ON TWO FACTORS

Test	Guilt-proneness (factor 1)	Dominance (factor 2)
A Indecisiveness	.68	.14
B Brooding	.76	.08
C Depression	.86	.04
D Aggressiveness	.11	.88
E Competitiveness	.03	.69
F Conceit	.15	.52

tests into the analysis in an effort to discover new variables that load significantly on the same factor.

P technique   The R technique allows investigators to assess the existence of common traits in large populations; the **P technique** is designed to discover the unique trait structure of a single individual (Cattell, 1961, p. 415; Cattell, 1965, p. 372). It involves testing the individual repeatedly over a period of time on a number of personality traits. Figure 9.2 shows the outcome of a P technique study of a 24-year-old graduate student in drama. This study measured eight traits in a series of 80 sessions over a 40-day period. During the same period, the student also kept a diary. The baseline in Figure 9.2 indicates a few of the major experiences he reported: rehearsals for a play in which he had a starring role; a cold he had during rehearsals; the play itself; an accident that happened to his father; reproach from an aunt for not helping his family enough; and worry over apparent hostility from his academic advisor. Closer examination of the figure indicates that fatigue mounted continuously during the strenuous month before the play and subsided somewhat afterward. His anxiety level was generally higher during the rehearsal period, when he reported falling further and further behind in his college work because of the time spent in rehearsals. His prayers to God to help him through this trying period (as seen in the activation of the appeal erg) also increased dramatically during the rehearsal period. His father's serious accident (fractured pelvis) on March 20th caused a sharp rise in his protective instinct toward his parent. There was also a rise in his sexual (mating) urges after the 57th session, which was connected with increased time spent in dating. On the crucial nights of the performance, there was a great temporary increase in his feelings of narcissism (self-absorption) and self-regard (self-sentiment), and a sharp relapse and recovery in self-assertion. Finally, his fear and anxiety levels started to rise as he worried about his advisor's apparent hostility because he was behind in his courses (Cattell, 1957, pp. 552–554). Using the P technique, Cattell could assess the process of change in an individual's motivation.

Defining Personality

Cattell defined personality as "that which tells what [a person] will do when placed in a given situation" (Cattell, 1965, pp. 117–118). Consistent with his mathematical analysis of personality, Cattell then presented the definition as a formula:

$$R = f(S, P)$$

In other words, the behavioral response (R) of a person is a function (f) of the situation (S) confronted and the individual's personality (P). Although most trait theorists deemphasize the role of situational parameters in influencing behavior, Cattell expanded

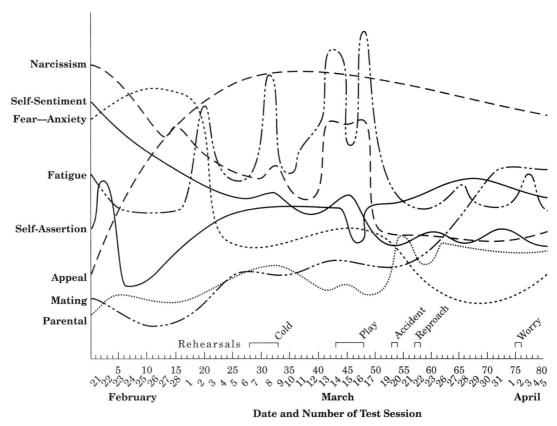

FIG-9.2 Use of the P technique to track changes in the intensity levels of various traits over time. (Adapted from Cattell, 1957.)

his theorizing to include the ways in which situations, in conjunction with personality traits, influence behavior (Cattell, 1979, 1980). To account for situational influences, he constructed a model for classifying situations and assessing their impact on the individual. Before examining this model in more detail, however, we turn to Cattell's treatment of the major personality factors, including ergs, sentiments, attitudes, interests, emotional states, and especially traits.

Classifying Traits

According to Cattell, **traits** are relatively permanent and broad reaction tendencies and serve as the building blocks of personality. He distinguishes between constitutional and environmental-mold traits; ability, temperament, and dynamic traits; and surface and source traits. Let us consider each of these major distinctions in turn.

Constitutional traits and environmental-mold traits **Constitutional traits** are determined by biology, whereas **environmental-mold traits** are determined by experience, that is, by interactions with the environment. In other words, some traits are determined by nature, whereas others are determined by nurture.

Cattell created a complicated statistical procedure called **multiple abstract variance analysis (MAVA)** to assess the degree to which various traits are determined genetically or environmentally. The method is based upon complex comparisons among people of the same family who were raised together and those who were raised apart, as well as members of different families (that is, unrelated people) who were raised together and those who were raised apart. Specifically, a test designed to assess a particular trait is administered to identical twins raised together, identical twins raised apart, fraternal twins raised together, fraternal twins raised apart, siblings raised together, siblings raised apart, unrelated children raised together, and unrelated children raised apart (Cattell, 1982, p. 90). The degree of genetic similarity is, of course, greatest in identical twins and least in unrelated children. The test scores of the individuals in each of these groupings are then correlated with each other, through a technique known as intraclass correlations. Whereas ordinary correlations (see Chapter 1) are obtained by examining the same individual's scores on different tests, intraclass correlations result from comparing the scores of different individuals on the same test. By using a number of complex mathematical equations, researchers can then determine the relative contributions of genetic and environmental factors in the development of a particular trait.

For example, a researcher interested in determining the contributions of genetic and environmental factors to the development of intelligence would administer an intelligence test to members of the various groupings (or classes) just described. Because identical twins have the same genes, any differences in intelligence between them are presumably due (primarily) to differences in their environments. Thus, the correlation between identical twins, even those raised in radically different environments, for a trait based entirely on heredity should theoretically be +1.00. (In reality, the correlation will be slightly lower, because of errors in measurement; the test will not be perfectly reliable.) In contrast, fraternal twins have only 50% of their genes in common; therefore, the correlation for a trait that is totally genetically determined would be lower for fraternal than for identical twins.

If the correlation between the scores on the intelligence test for identical twins raised together is +.86 and the correlation for identical twins raised apart is +.72, these results, correlations that are high and similar in magnitude, would suggest that intelligence is largely hereditary. However, if the correlation for identical twins raised together is +.86 and that for identical twins raised apart is only +.22, these radically different correlations would suggest that environment has a much greater impact than heredity.

Pursuing the same problem from another perspective, if the correlation is +.86 for identical twins raised together, +.60 for fraternal twins raised together, +.47 for siblings raised together, and +.32 for unrelated individuals raised together, these data would suggest that intelligence is largely hereditary. This conclusion is based on the principle that, for a genetically determined trait, the further away we get from genetic similarity, the smaller the correlations should be. As it happens, these decreasing correlations are based upon actual data and have led investigators to conclude that approximately 70% of the variation in intelligence among individuals is due to genetic factors and the remaining 30% to environmental factors and errors of measurement (McGee & Wilson, 1984, p. 320).

An important feature of MAVA is that it allows researchers to make more precise determinations of the contributions of genetic and environmental factors to the development of traits than do other methods. This information can then be used to help clinicians make decisions about the kinds of treatment that should be used to maximize the chances of patient recovery. Cattell pointed out that clinicians only ask for trouble if they try to change a largely genetic trait; instead, they should shrewdly use the trait as a fulcrum for levering some other trait that *is* susceptible to change, that is, an environmentally based trait. For example, a clinician who knows that a client has an IQ of 140 can use that fact to facilitate insights into the person's emotional problems. The same clinician would pursue a different strategy if the client's IQ were only 80 (Cattell, 1982, p. 396).

Ability traits, temperament traits, and dynamic traits   Traits can be further subdivided into ability, temperament, and dynamic traits. **Ability traits** refer to the person's skill in dealing with the complexity of a given situation. Thus, intelligence is an ability trait in Cattell's scheme. **Temperament traits** refer to stylistic tendencies, being, for example, chronically irritable, excitable, moody, easygoing, or bold. **Dynamic traits** refer to the person's motivation and interests. An individual may be characterized, for example, as ambitious, power-seeking, or sports-oriented (Cattell, 1965, p. 28).

In addition to these distinctions, Cattell, like Allport, found it useful to categorize traits as either common or unique. Common traits refer to characteristics shared by many people, for example, intelligence, confidence, powerlessness. Unique traits are those specific to one person; for example, Bill is the only person with an interest in collecting 1898 census records for the cities of Baltimore and Los Angeles. Virtually all of Cattell's work focuses on common traits, but his incorporation of the concept of unique traits enabled him to emphasize that personalities are unique. The organization of common traits within a given personality, Cattell pointed out, is always unique.

Surface versus source traits   The distinction between surface and source traits is perhaps the most important that Cattell made. Surface traits are "simply a collection of trait elements, of greater or lesser width of representation which obviously 'go together' in many different individuals and circumstances" (Cattell, 1950, p. 21). When intercorrelated, these variables cluster together to form surface traits. A source trait, in contrast, is the underlying factor that controls the variation in the surface cluster. Surface and source traits, as we have seen, are measured by the methods of factor analysis. Once we have accurately identified the major source traits controlling behavior, we should be in a better position to predict behavior accurately, on the assumption, of course, that we have sufficient information about the person's ways of reacting in a given situation.

Major Source Traits or Primary Factors

According to Cattell, any attempt to discover the major source traits or **primary factors** of personality must begin with an adequate inventory of all the personality traits that can be used to describe individuals. He called this total domain of personality traits the **personality sphere** and suggested that the only practical source for such a listing is language. Cattell argued that, over the centuries, every aspect of behavior whereby one human being is likely to affect another has been assigned some verbal symbol, that is, a trait name (Cattell, 1957, p. 71). Therefore, Cattell began by examining the 4,500 trait names found in the English language by Allport and Odbert (1936). By eliminating synonyms, he reduced the total to 171. Utilizing observer ratings of individuals on these traits, he then identified 36 clusters of correlations, or surface traits. Subsequently, he added 10 more surface traits, a few from the psychiatric literature, and some that emerged in experiments over the years. These 46 surface traits, Cattell maintained, comprise the whole personality sphere (Cattell & Kline, 1977, pp. 30–31).

Later, Cattell and his coworkers constructed personality questionnaires on the basis of items that incorporated the surface traits, administered these questionnaires to study participants, scored them, and factor-analyzed the results to yield the underlying source traits of personality. Using these and other data collection techniques, they were able to identify 16 primary factors or major source traits (Cattell, 1965, p. 64). These were initially labeled factors A, B, C, D, E, and so on, but later, as more and more supportive evidence accumulated, they were more clearly identified and given labels. These 16 basic traits were then used in the construction of the **Sixteen Personality Factor (16 PF) Questionnaire**. The traits are assumed to control a person's behavior, starting with factor A and ending with factor Q.

To measure the traits, study participants are given hundreds, even thousands, of items. Then their scores are factor-analyzed. Once the factors begin to emerge, other items are added and given to additional large groups of normal study participants in order to refine the factors. The items that load most heavily on each factor are retained; the ones that do not are eliminated.

Using this statistical procedure, individuals can score low or high on the following 16 factors: warmth (A), reasoning ability (B), emotional stability (C), dominance (E), liveliness (F), rule consciousness (G), social boldness (H), sensitivity (I), vigilance (L), abstractedness (M), privateness (N), apprehension (O), openness to change (Q1), self-reliance (Q2), perfectionism (Q3), and tension (Q4).

Some of the traits predict a person's behavior better than others. For example, information about a person's reasoning ability (factor B) would enable an investigator to predict that person's performance on a history exam more effectively than would knowledge about the person's liveliness (factor F).

Low or high factor scores and their implications for personality functioning
Low scores on a factor do not necessarily mean that the implications for an individual's personality functioning are negative nor do high scores necessarily mean that the implications for personality functioning are positive. Whether low or high scores have positive or negative implications for personality functioning depends on the nature of the situation that confronts the individual and the extremity of their scores on the dimensions (factors) being assessed. For example, people low in warmth may be reserved and have a strong capacity to be objective, practical, and independent in their decision-making in many situations (e.g., in business and political settings) where such qualities may be constructive. Those extremely low on warmth, however, may well have difficulty in maintaining close relationships. They may be unable to express much affection and support for their spouses, and research shows they often end up in marital therapy (Cattell, H. E. P. & Schuerger, 2003, p. 46). In contrast, individuals high on warmth have the capacity to form and maintain rewarding personal relationships. However, those with extremely high scores on warmth may experience feelings of loneliness, if they are not continuously in personal relationships. Research indicates that students with such extreme scores on warmth tend to have poor grades because they may continuously seek out other students for long sessions of partying, leaving them little time to study (Cattell, H. E. P. & Schuerger, 2003, pp. 44–47).

Factor A: Warmth   Individuals low on factor A tend to be reserved and cautious about involvement with others. They tend to like solitude and often focus their attention on mechanical, intellectual, or artistic activities, where they can often operate effectively. Low scorers can be uncomfortable in situations that call for intimacy or extensive social interaction. High scorers on factor A have a strong interest in people and seek interactions that call for closeness with them. Extremely high scorers on this factor may be uncomfortable in situations where close relationships are unavailable, for example, in jobs which often involve solitary tasks like forest ranger.

Factor B: Reasoning ability   Low scorers have lower intellectual ability, whereas high scorers often have high intellectual ability (educational level).

Cattell distinguished between two kinds of intellectual ability: crystallized and fluid. **Crystallized intelligence** refers to "abilities [that are] distinct from fluid intelligence and considered [to be] due to investment of fluid intelligence in cultural learning" (Cattell, 1982, p. 432). **Fluid intelligence** is defined as abilities "which appear most purely in unlearned performances with new data" (Cattell, 1982, p. 432). In other words, fluid intelligence refers to innate abilities, whereas crystallized intelligence refers to abilities that are the product of cultural learning and schooling, based on the application of innate intelligence to problems.

Cattell believed that, too often, we equate intelligence with crystallized intelligence, which is what traditional IQ tests measure. To help overcome this simplistic view, Cattell developed the **Culture Fair Intelligence Test**, which is designed to measure fluid or innate intelligence independent of cultural learning and training. See Figure 9.3 for some sample items from the test.

From a lifespan perspective, Cattell suggested that fluid intelligence increases from birth to about 18 years of age and then begins a slow decline to old age. Crystallized intelligence, representing an accumulation of learning *through* fluid intelligence, shows a slight, steady growth throughout life, despite the weakening of fluid intelligence (Cattell, 1987, p. 118).

Factor C: Emotional stability   Low scorers feel powerless to control life's challenges. They have low ego strength and tend to be unable to adapt to life stresses. High scorers take life in stride and cope with stresses and challenges in an adaptive way. Their ego strength is high. Research in many different laboratories in North America and Great Britain shows that people who are neurotic or highly anxious also tend to have low ego strength. Cattell observed that alcoholics, narcotics addicts, juvenile delinquents, and

FIG-9.3 Sample items from the Culture Fair Intelligence Test. (From Cattell, R. B., *The Scientific Analysis of Personality* p. 302–303. Copyright © 1965 by Aldine Publishers. Reprinted by permission of Aldine Transaction, a division of Transaction Publishers.)

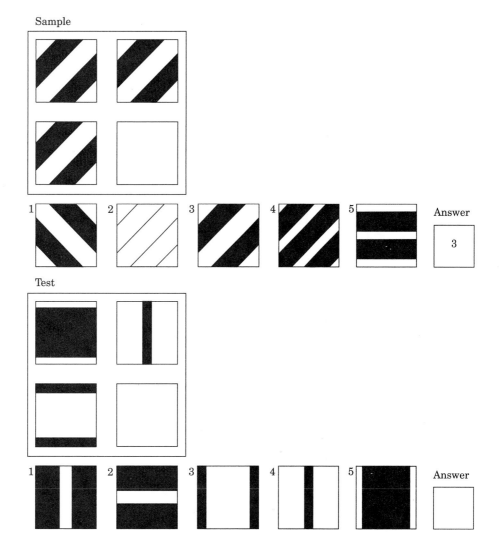

school dropouts are abnormally low in ego strength. The essence of the factor is an inability to control one's impulses or to deal realistically with problems (Cattell, 1965, p. 73–74).

Factor E: Dominance   Low scorers are cooperative and agreeable and tend to accommodate others' wishes. They are willing to set aside their own feelings in order to avoid conflict. Extreme deference can disappoint those who wish for a more forceful participating response. High scorers, Cattell maintained, are vocal in expressing their opinions and wishes and have a commanding, take-charge presence. Cattell mentioned that men and boys score higher on dominance than women and girls; so do firefighters, Olympic champions, and pilots. But extremely high scorers, however, are overbearing, stubborn, and argumentative and can alienate people. Such excessive dominance is prevalent in psychopaths, including con artists and incorrigible criminals (Cattell, 1965, p. 92).

Some of Cattell's ideas about dominance have been corroborated by current research (Grant, 2005, p. 5). Specifically, many studies have shown support for Cattell's idea that there is a biological basis for dominance, namely, that high levels of testosterone can produce dominance behavior in both men and women, although men have 10 times more testosterone, on average, than women. Also, there is support for Cattell's belief that the level of testosterone and the dominance behavior that follow from it can be influenced by environmental conditions.

Factor F: Liveliness   The quiet attentiveness of low scorers can make them reliable and mature, though they are not the life of the party. Extremely low scorers can inhibit their spontaneity so that they appear constricted. High scorers are high spirited and stimulating and drawn to lively social situations. Extremely high scorers may be impulsive, unreliable, and immature. They may find it difficult to restrain their enthusiasm in situations that call for decorum.

Factor G: Rule consciousness   This factor is similar in many respects to Freud's concept of the superego (Cattell, 1965, p. 94). Low scorers tend to avoid following rules and regulations, either because they lack internalized values and standards or simply because they hold unconventional values. High scorers conform to conventional cultural standards. Extremely high scorers can be perceived as inflexible and moralistic.

Factor H: Social boldness   Low scoring individuals may be afraid to speak in front of groups and may experience stress when facing difficult situations. High scorers initiate social contacts and can be fearless in the face of intimidating social situations. Extremely high scorers may be thin-skinned or exhibitionistic. This primary trait has a moderate degree of inheritance—approximately 40%—according to the cumulative findings of several investigations that used a variety of statistical techniques to assess genetic and environmental contributions to trait development (Cattell, 1982, p. 341).

Factor I: Sensitivity   Low scorers may be tough minded, that is, so concerned with being objective and practical that they exclude taking feelings into account. Extremely low scorers may have trouble in situations that demand an awareness of feelings. High scorers are tender minded, refined, and empathic. They tend to be aware of the feelings of others and are more attuned to people's feelings. Extremely high scorers may be so focused on their subjective feelings in situations that they ignore their practical aspects. High scores are associated with parental overprotection and indulgence, whereas tough-mindedness is related to strict parental disciplining (Cattell, 1965, pp. 96–98).

Factor L: Vigilance   People who score low expect fair treatment from others and have trusting relationships. However, extremely low scorers often are exploited by others because they do not give enough thought to others' motivations. At the extreme, high scorers tend to be suspicious and distrustful of others. They may be unable to relax their vigilance.

Factor M: Abstractedness   Low scorers tend to focus on specific, observable data and are good at implementing concrete solutions to problems. Extremely low scorers may be so concrete that they "miss the forest for the trees." High scorers are more preoccupied with thinking, imagination, and fantasy and are often creative. Extremely high scorers can be so absorbed in thought that they can be absentminded and impractical.

Factor N: Privateness   Low scorers are open and willing to talk readily about themselves. They are genuine and unguarded. At the extreme, low scorers may be forthright in situations where it might be better to be tactful. High scorers are tactful, diplomatic, and insightful regarding others' motives. At the extreme, high scorers often maintain their privacy at the expense of developing close relationships with others. The N factor is probably acquired in childhood under conditions of intense competitiveness where children have to learn to fend for themselves (Cattell, 1979, p. 68).

Factor O: Apprehension   Low scorers tend to be untroubled by self-doubt. They are self-confident, resilient, and placid. The self-confidence of extreme low scorers often cannot be shaken, even in situations that call for reevaluation and change. High scorers are insecure, anxious, and guilt-prone. According to Cattell, excessive guilt-proneness is a trait found in pathological individuals, including alcoholics, criminals, and patients with bipolar affective disorders. Such people have few friends and are often critical of group life and standards (Cattell & Kline, 1977, p. 116).

Factor Q1: Openness to change   Low scorers adhere to traditional ways of behaving. They prefer the status quo and doing things in a predictable way. Among extremely low scorers, there is little or no attempt to initiate change, even in situations that call for it. High scorers think about ways they can change the status quo. They tend to think critically, enjoy experimenting, and like to challenge authority. At the extreme, high scorers find it hard to "leave well enough alone."

Factor Q2: Self-reliance   Low scorers prefer being around others and like to work in groups. Extremely low scorers, however, often fail to work independently. High scorers enjoy spending time alone and prefer to rely on their own thinking when making decisions. Extremely high scorers may have trouble working collaboratively.

Factor Q3: Perfectionism   Low scorers are unstructured and prefer to leave their decisions to chance. They usually "go with the flow." While they may seem spontaneous, extremely low scorers may also be disorganized, unprepared, and undisciplined. High scorers are organized and plan ahead. They are most comfortable in structured situations. At the extreme, high scorers may be compulsive.

Factor Q4: Tension   Low scoring individuals are "laid back" and slow to become frustrated. At the extreme, they are unmotivated. High scorers have considerable drive and tend to be fidgety when they have to wait. Extremely high scorers tend to be highly impatient and irritable (Cattell, H. E. P. 2001, pp. 189–191).

Primary factor patterns   While an examination of each primary factor independently of the others yields important personality information, it is also possible to increase our understanding of the personalities of individuals by looking at each primary factor in combination with one other or several other factors. Thus, a score on one scale (factor) may interact with a score on another scale to modify the meaning of both (Cattell, H. E. P. & Schuerger, 2003, pp. 125–136). For example, consider the personalities of two students, Reva and Nick. Reva is low on warmth and very high in dominance, whereas Nick is low on warmth and very low on dominance. Based on her scores, Reva would be characterized as stubborn, argumentative, and domineering and indifferent to the needs of others. Nick, in contrast, would be submissive, that is, low in dominance, and low in warmth—he would be avoidant of others.

Research with the 16 PF

The 16 PF test has been put to excellent use in the occupational realm. Individuals fill out the test and then have the profile of their test scores, that is, their standing on the 16 source traits, compared with the personality profiles of large numbers of people who are in particular occupations and performing well. The major assumption of this matching procedure is that, the more similar a person is to others on a job, the more comfortable and satisfied the person would be once he begins employment in the job. People then can be counseled to seriously consider seeking a job that matches up well with their personality. People who do not match up well in a particular job can be encouraged to consider alternative jobs that might be more suitable and satisfying (Schuerger, 1992, p. 238).

Profiles for some occupations include actress, teacher, musician, police officer, and physician. In a study by McKenzie and DaCosta (1999, pp. 215–225), student actresses were higher on factor E (dominance), factor F (liveliness), factor M (abstractedness, which includes imaginativeness), and much lower on factor G (rule consciousness) and factor Q3 (perfectionism) than student teachers. Interestingly, performing musicians were found across several studies to be higher in factor B (reasoning), factor I (sensitivity), and lower in factor A (warmth) than nonmusicians (Buttsworth & Smith, 1995, p. 595). That is, musicians were more intelligent, sensitive, and reserved. They spent less time interacting with other people; possibly, as a result, they had more free time for creative pursuits. As you might expect, police officers were higher in factor C (emotional stability, adaptiveness, maturity), factor E (dominance, forcefulness, assertiveness), factor G (rule consciousness, dutifulness), factor H (social boldness), and factor Q3 (perfectionism, self-discipline) (Austin, Hofer, Deary, & Eber, 2000, p. 411; Cattell, H. E. P. & Mead, 2008, pp. 150–151). Finally, a recent study by Taber, Hartung, and Borges (2011, pp. 202-209) found that first-year medical students had different profiles depending on whether they were in person-oriented specialties (family medicine, internal medicine, pediatrics, physical medicine, and rehabilitation) or technique-oriented specialties (anesthesiology, emergency medicine, radiology, surgery). People-oriented medical students were higher than technique-oriented students in factor A (warmth), factor G (rule consciousness), factor I (sensitivity), and factor O (apprehensiveness). In contrast, technique-oriented medical students were higher than people-oriented students in factor E (dominance), factor L (vigilance), and factor Q4 (tension).

The 16 PF test has been used to good advantage by counselors to identify specific areas of conflict within marriages based on the personality characteristics of the partners. Research on married couples, for example, has indicated that in marriages where either partner is too high in factor Q3 (too inflexible and compulsive) and too low on factor F (too serious and silent), the partners were very dissatisfied with the relationship. Also, considerable dissatisfaction was experienced when either party was too high on factor A (too gullible) and too low on factor Q_3 (too undisciplined). Scores that were too high on factor E (too argumentative) in either partner was also a major source of dissatisfaction with the relationship (Schuerger, 1992, p. 242).

The 16 PF test also has been used to study the personality characteristics of heroin addicts. Narayan, Shams, Jain, and Gupta (1997, pp. 125–127) compared the personality characteristics of heroin addicts to non-heroin addicts in India. They found that the addicts were lower in factor B (reasoning ability), factor C (emotional stability), factor G (rules consciousness), and higher in factor O (apprehension) and factor Q4 (tension) than nonaddicts. These results were found after controlling for the influence of age, amount of income, and education levels in the two groups.

Finally, Yang, Choe, Baity, Lee, and Cho (2005, pp. 407–414) studied the personality characteristics of Korean adolescents who were addicted to the Internet, that is, adolescents who reported using the Internet, on average, more than 2.3 hours each weekday (Monday–Friday). They also reported feeling a compulsion to use the Internet and experiencing withdrawal symptoms (e.g., sleep problems, difficulties concentrating in school) when they were unable to do so. These adolescents were compared to those youngsters who reported minimal use, that is, an average of less than one hour per day, had no compulsion to use it, and had no withdrawal symptoms. The investigators found that, in comparison to nonaddicts, Internet addicts were lower in factor C (emotional stability), that is, these adolescents were more irritable, hostile, and anxious. Addicts were also higher in factor M (imagination and abstract thinking). Other characteristics, however, of people higher in factor M include being self-absorbed and oblivious of particular people and physical realities. In general, the investigators found that Internet addicts had a personality profile that predisposed them to derive most of their satisfaction from Internet activities (mostly playing virtual games) rather than from conventional social activities or friendships. These results tied in with prior research which showed that Internet addicts were introverted, socially isolated, lacked friends, and had poor self-esteem.

Given the correlational nature of the Internet study, it remains unclear whether the personality traits of the adolescents preceded their overuse of the Internet and caused them to use it to excess, or whether the personality traits were formed as a consequence of excessive Internet use. Future research should address this problem and identify the causal sequence.

Major Global or Second-Order Factors

While looking at factor patterns yields a more refined view of the individual's personality, sometimes a test administrator wants a more general or bird's eye view of the person's personality. In that case, the primary factors or source traits can be analyzed further via factor analysis to yield what Cattell called global or **second-order factors**. In general, such an analysis yields five global factors and their meanings: (1) introversion/extraversion (low scorers on this dimension tend to value time spent alone or in solitary pursuits, whereas high scorers tend to be people-oriented and to value time spent with others in social pursuits); (2) low anxiety/high anxiety (low scorers tend to be unperturbed by most events and less easily upset than most people; high scorers tend to be more easily upset by events); (3) receptivity/tough-mindedness (low scorers tend to be open to people, feelings, and new ideas; high scorers tend to prefer known, concrete, familiar territory); (4) accommodation/independence (low scorers tend to accommodate others' wishes often at their own expense, whereas high scorers tend to "take charge"—people who influence rather than being influenced); and (5) lack of restraint/self-control (low scorers tend to be impulsive and have fewer resources for controlling their behavior; high scorers tend to have many resources for controlling their behavior). Once the test administrator has developed a sense of the big picture painted by the test-taker's global or second-order factor scores, he or she can examine the primary factor scores and their interactions to fill in the "fine grain" specifics or uniqueness of the individual's personality (Cattell, H. E. P. 2001, p. 201).

The Major Abnormal Traits

The source traits or primary factors utilized in the 16 PF focus primarily on normal personality, but extreme scores can suggest the presence of some personality maladjustment. In any event, the 16 PF does not measure all aspects of deviant behavior and does not assess the characteristics of psychotics. Applying factor analysis to surface traits in the normal and abnormal personality spheres, Cattell derived 12 further factors that measure psychopathology. These 12 factors, listed in Table 9.3, have been combined with those previously included in the 16 PF in the construction of a new test, the **Clinical Analysis**

TABLE 9.3   MAJOR ABNORMAL SOURCE TRAITS ASSESSED BY THE CLINICAL ANALYSIS QUESTIONNAIRE

Factor	Normal source trait	Abnormal source trait
D_1	**Low hypochondriasis** Is happy, mind works well, does not find ill health frightening	**High hypochondriasis** Shows overconcern with bodily functions, health, or disabilities
D_2	**Zestfulness** Is contented about life and surroundings, has no death wishes	**Suicidal disgust** Is disgusted with life, harbors thoughts or acts of self-destruction
D_3	**Low brooding discontent** Avoids dangerous and adventurous undertakings, has little need for excitement	**High brooding discontent** Seeks excitement, is restless, takes risks, tries new things
D_4	**Low anxious depression** Is calm in emergency, confident about surroundings, poised	**High anxious depression** Has disturbing dreams, is clumsy in handling things, tense, easily upset
D_5	**High energy euphoria** Shows enthusiasm for work, is energetic, sleeps soundly	**Low energy depression** Has feelings of weariness, worries, lacks energy to cope
D_6	**Low guilt and resentment** Is not troubled by guilt feelings, can sleep no matter what is left undone	**High guilt and resentment** Has feelings of guilt, blames self for everything that goes wrong, is critical of self
D_7	**Low bored depression** Is relaxed, considerate, cheerful with people	**High bored depression** Avoids contact and involvement with people, seeks isolation, shows discomfort with people
P_a	**Low paranoia** Is trusting, not bothered by jealousy or envy	**High paranoia** Believes he or she is being persecuted, poisoned, controlled, spied on, mistreated
P_p	**Low psychopathic deviation** Avoids engagement in illegal acts or breaking rules, sensitive	**High psychopathic deviation** Has complacent attitude towards own or others' antisocial behavior, is not hurt by criticism, likes crowds
S_c	**Low schizophrenia** Makes realistic appraisals of self and others, shows emotional harmony and absence of regressive behavior	**High schizophrenia** Hears voices or sounds without apparent source outside self, retreats from reality, has uncontrolled and sudden impulses
A_s	**Low psychasthenia** Is not bothered by unwelcome thoughts or ideas or compulsive habits	**High psychasthenia** Suffers insistent, repetitive ideas and impulses to perform certain acts
P_s	**Low general psychosis** Considers self as good, as dependable, and as smart as most others	**High general psychosis** Has feelings of inferiority and unworthiness, timid, loses control easily

Source: Reproduced by special permission of the Institute for Personality and Ability Testing, Inc.

Questionnaire, which should be of considerable interest and use to clinical psychologists. Thus, Cattell believed that he had identified the major source traits of both normal and abnormal personality.

Dynamic Traits and the Dynamic Lattice

Cattell subdivided dynamic traits into attitudes, sentiments, and ergs. He defined attitudes as specific interests in particular courses of action toward certain objects in a given situation (Cattell, 1965, p. 175). Cattell viewed them as hypothetical constructs that intervene between environmental stimuli and eventual external responses. For example, a student might have the attitude, "I want very much to kiss this handsome guy the next time we go out together." The student shows an intense interest (I want very much) in a particular course of action (to kiss) toward a specific object (this handsome guy) in a given situation (the next time we go out together). Ergs and sentiments are inferred from the factor-analytic study of attitudes. For example, a man may have a timid disposition that is based on an underlying fear erg (Cattell, 1950, p. 84).

Sentiments are large, complex attitudes. They incorporate a host of interests, opinions, and minor attitudes. For instance, a man's sentiment about his home may be seen in his attitudes about his wife, his children, and marriage in general, as well as in his interests in home repairs, landscaping, and the like (Cattell, 1950, pp. 161–162). Such a sentiment would be learned over a long period of time. Cattell characterized sentiments as environmental-mold traits, that is, traits learned through experience with people.

An *erg* is "an innate psychophysical disposition which permits its possessor to acquire reactivity (attention, recognition) to certain classes of objects more readily than others, to experience a specific emotion in regard to them, and to start on a course of action which ceases more completely at a certain specific goal activity than at any other" (Cattell, 1950, p. 199). In short, an erg is an innate drive triggered by stimuli in the environment that ceases when its goal is reached. For example, the parental erg is released by cries of distress from children and satisfied when they are out of danger. Other basic drives (see Biographical Sketch) include food seeking, mating, exploration, and acquisitiveness.

Why did Cattell think these drives are innate? He based his judgment on both naturalistic and clinical studies. Naturalistic studies involve observation of behavior analogous to human behavior in mammals lower in the phylogenetic scale, as well as general observations of human behavior in a wide variety of situations and cultures (Cattell, 1979, p. 155). It was inconceivable to Cattell that human beings, who are clearly related structurally and functionally to primates and other mammals, could lack the instinctual equipment that those animals possess.

Cattell believed that we must seek not only to describe and measure a person's traits but also to show how they are interconnected (Cattell, 1950, p. 156). Thus, he postulated that the dynamic traits are organized in complex ways within the cognitive and motivational structure of the organism and form a **dynamic lattice**. To explain how the traits are intertwined, he relied heavily on the concept of **subsidiation**, the process whereby certain dynamic traits are subsidiary to (or dependent on) other traits. Thus, sentiments are dependent on ergs, and attitudes depend on sentiments. For example, a high-school student may spend large amounts of time watching the stars (positive attitude or interest in such behavior) because of his great love of science (positive sentiment). His love of science is turn rests on the fact that involvement in science satisfies his strong curiosity about the ways in which the universe operates (positive erg satisfaction).

The dynamic lattice describes a complicated and often bewildering intertwining of interests, attitudes, sentiments, goals, and drives. Figure 9.4 presents only a fragment of a dynamic lattice for a hypothetical person, involving attitudes, sentiments, and innate goals. At the right of the diagram, we see the ergs; in the middle are the various sentiments; and at the left are a variety of attitudes. We can see that numerous ergs give expression to various sentiments, that the sentiments are related to one another, that several attitudes converge on the same sentiment, and that a few attitudes are common to different sentiments. We might speculate that this person's love for his wife is based on her satisfaction of his needs for sex, protection, and companionship. In addition, he knows that he must maintain a healthy bank account to ensure his security and to secure the material goods his wife needs to be happy. When all these facts are registered on a conscious level, the person may perceive a need to change his dynamic lattice. He may

FIG-9.4 Fragment of a dynamic lattice, showing interrelationships among attitudes, sentiments, and ergic goals. (Adapted from Cattell, R. B. (1950) *Personality: A Systematic Theoretical and Factual Study*, p. 158. Reprinted by permission of the Estate of R. B. Cattell.)

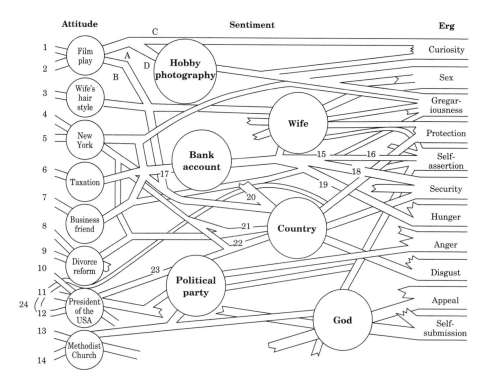

decide to discontinue his frequent recreational trips to New York for fear they will deplete his bank account and create unhappiness for himself. Alternatively, he may wish to talk to his business friend as a means of securing a higher income and thereby ensuring maximum satisfaction for both his wife and himself.

Changes in the dynamic lattice can also occur as a result of the person's mood or emotional state; that is, a person's traits, attitudes, sentiments, interests, and even goals can be modified by such states as fatigue, guilt, anxiety, depression, arousal, extraversion, stress, and regression. (e.g., a person who feels confused may therefore act impulsively.) These states can be measured by the **Eight State Questionnaire** (Cattell & Kline, 1977, p. 22). Changes in the dynamic lattice can also be produced by changes in the person's environment. (e.g., a serious setback in business will force a drastic change in the person's lifestyle.)

Sentiments are less susceptible to change than are attitudes, according to Cattell, because sentiments are the deeper, underlying structures in personality. Occasionally, though, changes in personality can occur. A person may lose his family in a catastrophe, for instance, and this traumatic event will trigger major changes in personality functioning (Cattell, 1950, p. 160).

Finally, Cattell integrated all the attitudes, interests, ergs, and sentiments that continually interplay within the personality by postulating a master motive called the **self-sentiment**. The self-sentiment coordinates the various attitudes, sentiments, and interests of the person and also regulates expression of the ergs.

The Econetic Model

A major criticism of trait theories has been that they neglect the role of the environment in predicting behavior. The **econetic model** represented Cattell's efforts to remedy this deficiency. It postulates that human behavior is the result of a complex and subtle interplay between traits and situations. As a first step in trying to understand this complicated interaction, Cattell proposed the construction of a taxonomy of situations or environments. To map this vast **environmental sphere**, he began sampling situations mentioned on every 10th page of encyclopedias of a given culture. (This procedure is similar to his efforts to map the traits in the personality sphere.) This approach yielded some encouraging consistencies in the kinds of situations found, but so far investigators have not followed up on these pioneering efforts (Cattell, 1979, p. 218). Nevertheless, Cattell believed that econetics (the study of the ecology) is likely to develop rapidly in the future, with the cooperation of investigators from various disciplines in the social sciences, and that eventually a reliable and objective taxonomic scheme will be constructed.

The next step, according to Cattell, is to assess the impact of these situations on the individual. Some situations have relevance for the individual; others do not. Of the situations that do play a role in the person's life, some have tremendous impact; others have only minimal impact. Some objects in situations are accessible to the individual; others are not. What these situations mean to the individual also depends on the person's moods. In brief, once the classification task is complete, the unique psychological meaning of various situations for the individual must be established (Cattell, 1979, p. 220). Obviously, these assessments of environmental effects on the individual are complex. They involve measuring the effects of other people and of the physical, social, and cultural environments on the individual. Each of these components may be weighted differently and contribute differentially to the modulation of the person's traits and subsequent behavior. Finally, the relative contributions of these factors change over time.

Dynamic Calculus

All these complexities, according to Cattell, can be integrated into the prediction of behavior by means of the **dynamic calculus**. It consists of a set of **specification equations** that take into account the multiple traits that influence behavior as well as the impact of the environment. They are called specification equations because they specify the ways in which traits and situations are to be combined to predict performance. In actuality, specification equations are highly complicated and take into account a number of factors not discussed in our treatment of Cattell's theory. (For a detailed discussion of the basic equations and their derivations, see Cattell, 1979, 1980.) The general form of the equation, however, is

$$
\begin{aligned}
R = {} & (b_1A_1 + b_2A_2 \ldots + b_nA_n) \\
& + (b_1B_1 + b_2B_2 \ldots + b_nB_n) \\
& + (b_1C_1 + b_2C_2 \ldots + b_nC_n) \\
& + (b_1K_1 + b_2K_2 \ldots + b_nK_n)
\end{aligned}
$$

In this formula, R is the performance or response of the individual in a given situation. It is determined by a weighted combination of (1) the person's source traits (A_1, A_2, ..., A_n); (2) the person's states and moods (B_1, B_2, ..., B_n); and (3) the social and cultural meanings (C_1, C_2, ..., C_n) of the situation for this person. It could also include the weighted combination of any other factors that have not yet been specified (K_1, K_2, ..., K_n).

In the formula, b_1, b_2, ..., b_n are weights. They are unique to each factor and show the degree to which each is involved in the person's performance in the situation under consideration (Cattell, 1965, pp. 78–80). Weights for traits are generated by experiments in which the performances of large groups of comparable individuals are assessed and the relative importance of the traits is determined by factor analysis. These weights are then used in the general equation, along with the person's own scores, as a means of predicting performance. Other statistical procedures, for example, the P technique, are used to establish the weights for states and the unique meaning of the situation for the individual.

By way of example, suppose that we are interested in predicting a student's performance on a math test. Let us assume that we know that intelligence (A_1) is the most important source trait in predicting success on the test, followed by conscientiousness (A_2) and self-sufficiency (A_3). Let us also assume that we have been able to establish the weights for states (e.g., anxiety and fatigue levels) and the unique meaning of the situation, that is, its relevance and importance, to this student.

If the weights on these factors can vary from .00 to 1.00 (with a weight of 1.00 signifying maximum loading, or highest importance), and if scores can vary between 0 and 100, then we might find a distribution of weights and scores as follows

$$R = [.8(90) + .6(80) + .3(30)] + [.6(90) + .8(100)] \\ + [.9(70) + .8(100)]$$

In this equation, high scores of 100 indicate maximum intelligence, conscientiousness, and self-sufficiency; minimum anxiety and fatigue; and high relevance and importance of success on math tests. Working through the equation gives us an expected performance as follows:

$$R = [.8(90) + .6(80) + .3(30)] + [.6(90) + .8(100)] + [.9(70) + .8(100)]$$
$$R = [72 + 48 + 9] + [54 + 80] + [63 + 80]$$
$$R = 129 + 134 + 143$$
$$R = 406$$

Maximum performance on the test would be predicted as follows:

$$R = [.8(100) + .6(100) + .3(100)] + [.6(100) + .8(100)] + [.9(100) + .8(100)]$$
$$R = [80 + 60 + 30] + [60 + 80] + [90 + 80]$$
$$R = 170 + 140 + 170$$
$$R = 480$$

Thus, our hypothetical student scores 406, as compared to a maximum score of 480. Our prediction is that the student will perform well.

The combination model just presented is linear in nature. Cattell said that we should use it if it helps us predict behavior accurately, and we should modify or even abandon it if it does not. At this point, however, Cattell thought that a linear model and not a curvilinear one is adequate for the prediction of much of our behavior (Cattell, 1965, p. 252). We could use it to predict academic performance or job success, for example. This multidimensional model includes a complex representation of the ways in which traits and situations are dynamically interrelated.

Personality Development

The Role of Heredity and Environment

Unlike any of the other theorists reviewed in this text, Cattell discussed prenatal influences on personality in detail. It is known, for example, that children born with Down's syndrome, a chromosomal abnormality, have limited intelligence and severely restricted behavior patterns. Metabolic abnormalities can also lead to mental retardation. Injuries to the head at birth can produce deficiencies in intelligence and motor coordination, or even paralysis. Temperament, Cattell believed, is related to the mother's endocrine condition during the gestation period, although the nature of the relationship is unclear. Thus, the physiological condition of the mother affects the normal process of nervous system maturation in utero (Cattell, 1950, pp. 557–559).

In addition to biological influences on personality, Cattell discussed the tremendous impact of the environment, especially at later stages of development. At first, biological and maturational influences are paramount. Research has shown that, in both motor and verbal learning, untaught twins achieve the same levels of performance as those who have been thoroughly trained (Cattell, 1950, p. 561); that is, untrained children learn certain skills very rapidly once they are mature enough to do so and quickly achieve levels of proficiency equal to those of their well-trained counterparts. As the person grows older, however, the environment has an increasing impact on personality formation.

The Role of Learning

Cattell distinguished among three kinds of learning that are involved in personality formation: classical conditioning, instrumental conditioning (reward learning), and integration learning. **Classical conditioning** involves pairing a neutral stimulus with a stimulus that provokes a particular response until the presentation of the neutral stimulus itself is capable of evoking the response. A classical-conditioning interpretation has been used to account for the acquisition of many fears and phobias. Cattell believed that it plays a role in unconscious learning, in the formation of phobias, and in the acquisition of deep and powerful emotional attachments (Cattell, 1965, p. 268).

Much more of our personality learning, according to Cattell, occurs through reward learning, or **instrumental conditioning**. We perform a certain action in order to reach a goal. A rat in a Skinner box presses a bar and receives food pellets; it quickly learns to press the bar. Bar pressing is instrumental to the attainment of the goal. Under other conditions, the animal presses the bar and is shocked; it quickly learns to avoid pressing the bar. Similarly, a person learns to diet because weight loss will bring approval from his friends and from his doctor. Or a child takes a cookie without her parents' permission and is spanked. She rapidly learns not to take cookies from the cookie jar, at least not when her parents are in the vicinity.

Cattell believed that reward learning is paramount in the formation of dynamic lattices (Cattell, 1965, p. 269). A student may have a sentiment about her athletic prowess, for instance, and train hard and long. Such training may prove highly rewarding if she subsequently performs at a track meet and wins a race. As a consequence, her sentiment toward athletic prowess is satisfied, and so is her erg for self-assertion, that is, her innate need to feel proud. The formation and maintenance of the dynamic lattice depends on **confluence learning**, that is, the acquisition of behaviors and attitudes that simultaneously contribute to the satisfaction of two or more different goals (Cattell, 1965, p. 270). For example, the student athlete may develop a positive attitude toward dieting and physical exercise because they satisfy her need for pride (self-assertion erg) and her need to do something different (curiosity erg). Thus, learning may involve the satisfaction of a number of goals within the person's dynamic lattice. The sentiments themselves are learned via reward learning, as when the student's interest in proving her athletic prowess was reinforced by successful performance.

Cattell also postulated a complex form of learning called **integration learning**. It appears to be a form of cognitive and instrumental learning in which the developing person uses ego and superego processes to maximize long-term satisfactions. The person learns to seek realistic satisfactions (Cattell, 1965, p. 276). Cattell agreed with Freud that the development of the ego and superego occurs during the second through the fifth years of life, that this period is marked by conflicts, and that it is critical in the development of personality (Cattell, 1950, pp. 573–575).

Cattell saw ages 6 through 13 as a carefree period in which children continue to strengthen their egos and extend love beyond themselves and their parents to others. It is a period of consolidation. Adolescence brings rapid physical changes and increases in emotional instability, social awkwardness, and sex interests, along with augmented concerns about being altruistic and contributing to society. The primary sources of conflict during this period are "(a) the task of gaining independence from the parents; (b) the task of gaining status in an occupation, preparing for that occupation, and achieving economic self-support; (c) achieving satisfactory sex expression by winning a mate; and (d) achieving a stable, integrated personality and satisfactory self-concept" (Cattell, 1950, p. 594). These conflicts are due, in Cattell's opinion, to both biological and environmental influences.

Maturity, the period from 25 to 55, is a time of little basic personality change. Although there is a slight decline in biological efficiency (for example, increased problems with hearing and vision and a slowing of metabolism), Cattell believed that, through learning and experience, increases in creativity are possible. Emotional stability increases for both sexes (Cattell, 1950, pp. 610–613). Maturity is also a period in which adjustments need to be made, as people discover that adolescent dreams and aspirations are, in many respects, unrealistic. Near the end of this period, increased leisure time brings a tendency to revive romantic interests. Cattell cited the finding in the Kinsey report that men at this age tend to show revived interest in extramarital affairs. In women, with the approach of the menopause, there is a wistful longing for romance (Cattell, 1950, p. 616).

Old age brings a more rapid decline in physical power. Performance on tasks demanding ingenuity suffers, whereas performance on tasks requiring experience remains steady or increases only slightly. Cattell thought the following characteristics are typical of people in old age (Cattell, 1950, pp. 618–619): worry over finances; worry over health; feeling unwanted, isolated, or lonely; feeling suspicious; loss of memory; mental rigidity; hoarding (often of trivial things); feelings of inadequacy and, as a result, feelings of insecurity and anxiety; feelings of guilt; irritability; reduction of sexual activity but increased sexual interest, especially in the male; untidiness, uncleanliness; inability to adjust to changed conditions; and decreased social contacts.

Although it is true that decline in physical health and competence is associated with old age and that this deterioration may manifest itself in lessened performance, some research casts doubt on the accuracy of the negative characteristics frequently attributed to the elderly (Field & Millsap, 1991). Older people do not necessarily lack confidence or feel powerless, and they are not necessarily wracked by guilt and anxiety. Indeed, many older people are highly competent, satisfied with their situations, and actively engaged in meaningful activities. Furthermore, research indicates that the elderly are generally less lonely than adolescents and young adults (Taylor, Peplau, & Sears, 2000, p. 237). Thus, it is time for a more realistic appraisal of both the strengths and limitations associated with old age. We need to move away from the concept of the elderly as doddering old codgers who cannot tie their shoelaces and also from the glorification of the period as the golden years when senior citizens flower and prosper without a care in the world.

Theory of Abnormal Development

Accepting the clinical notion that neurosis and psychosis are based on unresolved conflicts within the person, Cattell sought to develop quantitative techniques to aid the therapist in diagnosis and treatment. He envisioned the conflicts in Freudian terms, as involving struggles among id, ego, and superego, and calls for the development of a "quantitative psychoanalysis" (Cattell, 1965, p. 230). For example, a man's interest in marrying one of two women is based on the operation of a number of ergs and other personality factors. Cattell gave a simplified version of the formulas that could be used by a clinician to predict how the man might resolve his conflict

$$I_{Jane} = 0.6E_{sex} + 0.5E_{greg} + 0.3M_{superego}$$
$$I_{Sally} = 0.6E_{sex} + 0.3E_{greg} + 0.3M_{superego}$$

In this example, the man is in real conflict because the various ergs and the superego sentiment are approximately equal in strength. But because the gregariousness erg is slightly stronger for Jane, the decision will be in her favor. In ordinary language, the two women are approximately equal in their satisfaction of his sexual needs and their respectability in the eyes of others, but Jane is a more pleasing companion socially than Sally, so he decides to marry Jane (Cattell, 1965, p. 232). This example is only illustrative, of course, and was presented by Cattell to enhance understanding. He knew that it over-simplified the clinical situation.

Cattell also proposed that clinicians rely on diagnostic tools that have been empirically validated in trying to understand their clients' conflicts. These tools, including the 16 PF and the CAQ, provide a means of assessing the major factors in personality, not only the Freudian structures of id, ego, and superego, but also the attitudes, interests, and sentiments of the client (Cattell, 1961, chap. 14).

Neurosis Neurosis, according to Cattell, is the "pattern of behavior shown by those individuals who come to a clinic for aid because they feel themselves to be in emotional difficulties (and who do not have that kind of disorder that a psychiatrist recognizes as psychosis)" (Cattell, 1965, p. 209). He used such an operational definition because he was convinced that an understanding of neurosis must begin by identifying those measurements that differentiate this group from normal members of the general population. Using this initial criterion, he found that neurotics do indeed differ from both psychotics and normals on a number of personality dimensions. Thus, neuroticism and psychoticism do not just differ in degree; they are different kinds of illness (Cattell, 1965, p. 210).

Antecedents of neurosis, according to Cattell, are a childhood family characterized by conflict, inconsistent discipline, and insufficient affection; parental demands to adhere to excessively high moral standards; and genetically based lower than average emotional stability (Cattell, 1950, p. 497).

Countless factor-analytic studies by Cattell and scores of other investigators have found neurotics to be low in ego strength or emotional stability, high on abstractedness and tendermindedness, and low on dominance. High abstractedness means that neurotics tend to disregard external facts and social necessities and refuse to change their ideas to bring them into line with acknowledged facts; very high sensitivity means that they show too much emotional sensitivity to others and considerable capricious behavior. In addition, neurotics are shy and generally inhibited. Finally, their low ego strength means that they are easily overcome by their emotions, are subject to moods, and cannot adjust their behavior to the realities of a given situation (Cattell, 1965, pp. 211–212; Meyer, 1993, p. 96).

Above all, neurotics tend to be highly anxious (Meyer, 1993, p. 96). Cattell traced their anxiety to a number of sources. It may arise because the ergic tension of the person is unsatisfied. True to his Freudian roots, Cattell noted that ergic drives for sex and pugnacity (aggression) are more frequently punished in our society and, as a consequence, can give rise to high levels of anxiety. Also consistent with the orthodox Freudian position was Cattell's belief that anxiety can arise as a result of low ego strength and a highly punitive superego. In original fashion, however, Cattell suggested that high levels of anxiety may result in part from a constitutional proneness to threat reactivity; in other words, neurotics may be biologically more sensitive to threats than are normals. Another cause of high anxiety may be a very broad self-sentiment; that is, a person who is committed to a great variety of activities is more vulnerable to threats than is one who does not have such a broad range of pursuits. Finally, high levels of anxiety can arise if the individual is forced to deal with many trivial details in life in order to achieve ergic and self-sentiment satisfactions (Cattell, 1961, pp. 18–22).

Psychosis Psychosis, according to Cattell, is "a form of mental disorder different from neurosis, in which the individual loses contact with reality and needs hospitalization for his own protection and that of others" (Cattell, 1965, p. 373). In contrast to neurotics, psychotics lack insight into their problems, are unable to take care of themselves, and may be a threat to others.

Bipolar affective disorder (formerly called manic-depressive psychosis) and schizophrenia are highly inheritable (Cattell, 1982, p. 28), but differences in family environments contribute to the onset of the two types of psychosis. Parents of bipolar disorder patients are warmer and much more overprotective of their children than are the parents of schizophrenics; parents of schizophrenics have been found to be much more ambivalent in their attitudes toward their children (Cattell, 1950, p. 542). Using the 16 PF, investigators have found that schizophrenics are lacking in ego strength and are pessimistic, seclusive, retiring, subdued, shy, aloof, introverted and conceited, and motivated strongly by unresolved sexual and aggressive urges (high in drive tension) (Meyer, 1993, pp. 46–47). In the manic phase, patients with bipolar disorder tend to be highly energetic, talkative, extremely cheerful, joyous, and humorous, whereas in the depressive phase they tend to become absorbed in their own thoughts, are guilt-prone, and lack confidence (Meyer, 1993, pp. 77–80).

Assessment Techniques

Cattell rightfully can be called a "psychometrist of personality," because he placed such heavy emphasis on the use of testing and statistical techniques. We have already seen how he used factor analysis to derive personality traits. To apply the factor-analytic procedures, however, investigators must first collect masses of data from large numbers of people. Cattell relied on three major procedures to obtain such data: the L-data, Q-data, and T-data methods.

L-data, or life-record data, refers to the measurement of behavior in actual, everyday situations. Such data might include records that show the number of automobile accidents the person has had over the past 20 years, her marks in school, the number of civic organizations of which she is or has been a member, and so forth. Because some L-data might be very difficult to obtain, the investigator may be forced to take second-hand data, in the form of ratings by someone who knows the person well. Thus, different aspects of the person's behavior, such as her dependability on the job, her level of dissatisfaction with the job, her friendliness to coworkers, might be assessed by means of trait ratings (on 10-point scales, for example) by coworkers and friends.

The second source of information is called **Q-data**, or questionnaire data. Such information is often gathered in an interview situation, in which respondents fill out paper-and-pencil tests from which trait scores can be derived. The 16 PF is an excellent source of Q-data.

The third type of data, called **T-data**, is based on objective tests. Information is gathered by an observer in a standard test situation and is then scored. Whereas Q-data are based on self-reports that can be faked by the subject, T-data are essentially unfakeable. For example, if a person is asked on a questionnaire whether or not he ever cheats on examinations, he may report that he never does so, even though he does. If he is asked to respond to a Rorschach test, however, the inkblots are ambiguous and the subject does not know the dimensions on which his responses will eventually be scored (Cattell, 1965, pp. 60–62).

Theory's Implications for therapy

Skillful treatment of mental disorders, according to Cattell, depends on personality-factor assessments that provide not only a profile for diagnosis but also a statement about the kinds of constitutional factors that influence behavior (Cattell, 1965, p. 288). The availability of reliable and valid measuring instruments, moreover, can help the clinician make better judgments about the efficacy of treatment procedures; that is, the clinician can assess the client's personality before and after therapeutic intervention and note the changes in behavior (Cattell, 1961, p. 413). Cattell recommended the P technique, repeated testing over time on a number of personality dimensions, as the procedure best able to provide an accurate assessment of the complex changes occurring in clients as they move through therapy (Cattell, 1961, p. 415; Cattell, 1965, p. 372).

Cattell believed that all therapy should rest on precise measurement, but that astute clinical observation also has merit and should be used in conjunction with testing procedures. In this regard, as in others, he was an eclectic. He appreciated and accepted many of Freud's clinical insights, but he maintained that a therapy built on pronouncements and not on measurement can, in the long run, do serious harm to society. In general, he was contemptuous of the "fanciful and presumptuous theorizing of premetric, pre-experimental" theorists (Cattell, 1965, p. 333).

Cattell believed that a Freudian search for the causes of a disorder in early traumatic experiences may be beneficial to the client. By reliving the experiences, the client is in a better position to reevaluate his or her own emotional reactions and eventually to change destructive behavior. Some of these changes can be effected, in Cattell's view, through behavior therapy in which the person is taught new responses to threatening stimuli. Thus, to a limited degree, he accepted as valid therapeutic approaches that utilize historical analysis (e.g., psychoanalysis) or a direct reconditioning approach (behavior therapy).

In the final analysis, however, Cattell opted for a view of therapy that recognizes that people with severe disorders are defective throughout their whole personality functioning (Cattell, 1965, p. 335). We cannot simply focus on traumatic experiences involving sex and aggression, nor can we focus only on certain limited and specific areas of behavior change. Rather, we must address ourselves to the full range of constitutional personality factors that set limits on the person's performance and to the complex interweaving of traits and sentiments that influence behavior patterns. In short, we need complex measurement procedures to assess complex underlying structures. On the basis of this assessment, we will be able to conclude that some kinds of therapy will prove more effective than others, depending on the kinds of factors that are causing the specific neurosis or psychosis. For example, in psychoses based largely on constitutional factors, therapy might involve the use of drugs, electric shock, or lobotomy (Cattell, 1950, p. 543). In certain neuroses, therapy might start with dream analysis and the reliving of traumatic experiences (Cattell, 1961, p. 415). Where the problem is of a minor and relatively restricted nature, in the sense that it does not involve deep-rooted trauma, behavior therapy might be effective. Thus, Cattell was eclectic in his attitude toward the kinds of treatment to be used in therapy, but he was single-minded in his determination that all therapy should be based on solid measurement procedures.

Beyondism: A New Morality Based on Science

Throughout his long scientific career, Cattell wrote about the possibility of erecting ethical values on the firm foundation of science. Specifically, he thought that only science could provide solutions to the problems that plague the various nations of the world. He sought to convince the public that they should fund psychology more generously because he believed that advances in psychology are vital to humankind.

Cattell began by arguing that scientific research and data should be used to identify the type of person who can help produce a more successfully surviving society (Cattell, 1972, p. 158). Such data could also be used to generate a moral code that will, when put into action, help solve the major problems that plague society. Cattell argued strongly that the survival of any society depends on sound ethical values and that, the more solid these values, the happier the future of the society (Cattell, 1987, p. 146).

For Cattell, the supreme value is survival of the group, not the individual. Whereas nonsurvival of a society is easy to document because it simply fails and ceases to exist, survival, in Cattell's view, is judged not simply by its continued existence, but rather in terms of graded levels of functioning along a dimension of success. Cattell used several indices to identify more successfully surviving societies: (1) a population size per unit area that can be maintained at a standard of living adequate for effective citizenship; (2) a degree of control of the physical environment to protect the population against famine, volcanic eruptions, earthquakes, floods, and pollution; (3) creativity demonstrated by adaptability to even wider sections of the environment—for example, colonizing climatically difficult regions or exploring outer space; and (4) movement in a direction aimed at solving problems that historically have plagued, and continue to plague, society (Cattell, 1972, p. 115).

Cattell's examination of American society led him to the pessimistic conclusion that it is declining and moving slowly toward extinction, because current values are not working. He noted increases in drug abuse and crimes of violence, millions of people unemployed, high rates of divorce and out-of-wedlock births to teenagers, decreases in the educational accomplishments of young people, overpopulation, poverty, and pollution of the environment. A new morality is needed, Cattell believed, because the current morality is not working.

Beyondism is Cattell's proposed system for discovering and clarifying ethical goals based on scientific knowledge and investigation (Cattell, 1987, p. 1). Beyondism refers not to an afterlife, such as that espoused by various religions, but to providing a better life for people by going beyond the present situation. According to Cattell, social-scientific research can generate knowledge that will enable us reach that goal by helping us adapt to evolutionary requirements.

Interestingly, Beyondism contains strong elements of faith, and thus can be characterized as a religion, even though it rests (or will rest eventually) on an empirical foundation. Its two major elements of faith are that the universe exists and that evolution exists within the universe (Cattell, 1987, p. 4). According to Cattell, the basic requirements of biological evolution are: (1) there must be natural variation; therefore, groups (nations) must agree to take separate paths, both culturally and racially; (2) individuals and groups must experience natural selection, under which some forms of life survive better than others through better adaptations to the environment (Cattell, 1987, pp. 5–8). Cattell maintained that natural selection occurs simultaneously between and within nations (Cattell, 1987, p. 6).

Cattell believed that, to ensure diversity in the human gene pool, nations should agree to compete against each other as they struggle to survive. In his view, increased interdependence tends to result in excessive imitation and uniformity; nations fail to branch out into more divergent cultural and genetic types (Cattell, 1972, p. 224). To make certain that nations develop separately, Cattell opposed immigration and the interbreeding of national groups. Critics point out that opposition to immigration in the belief that it would contaminate the genetic purity of the nation has served to justify bigotry in the past. The scientific IQ test was used early in the 20th century by U.S. citizens who felt threatened economically by the influx of immigrants. Their interpretation of the IQ test results was that members of immigrant groups (predominantly Italians, Russians, Poles, Slavs, and Jews) were genetically inferior and biologically prone to feeblemindedness. On the basis of this interpretation, the U.S. government severely restricted immigration by these groups (Bruinius, 2006, p. 256; Duster, 1990, p. 11).

To Cattell, the evolutionary advantages of competition among nations outweigh the accompanying danger of war; to eliminate war by eliminating competition, he maintains, would be the supreme example of throwing the baby out with the bathwater (Cattell, 1972, p. 198). In Cattell's view, it would not work anyway, because a nation that lays down its arms would quickly be overthrown by another invading nation (Cattell, 1972, pp. 198–199); his solution was that each nation must create a defense so powerful that the costs of aggression would be prohibitive to other countries (Cattell, 1972, pp. 204–205). Critics might argue that such a strategy simply accelerates the arms race and thereby increases international tensions and the prospects of war.

Genetic diversity and group survival are also promoted by competition within nations, according to Cattell. To further the evolutionary process within nations, he maintained, we need to encourage development of a population with higher intelligence and emotional stability, because populations with these qualities are more likely to survive (Cattell, 1987, p. 213). Toward this end, Cattell favored implementation of a program with two aspects: restrictive eugenics and creative eugenics.

Restrictive eugenics is a policy aimed at reducing the number of mentally defective individuals through voluntary or forced sterilization (Cattell, 1972, p. 349). In nature, Cattell argued, defective individuals face early death; therefore, reducing the birth rate of such people would spare parents much pain and suffering. Thus, Cattell saw selection by birth rate as more humane than selection by death rate. He also pointed to new scientific techniques that can identify defects shortly after conception so that the embryo can be aborted (Cattell, 1972, p. 160). In a less controversial vein, Cattell foresaw the use of genetic engineering to reduce the incidence of disabilities such as diabetes and phenylketonuria mental retardation (Cattell, 1972, p. 147).

Cattell's call for the sterilization of individuals viewed as mentally defective is essentially a replay of the views of a number of prominent biologists, mathematicians, psychologists, politicians, and writers associated with the eugenics movement early in the 20th century. These professionals recommended sterilization as a means of ridding society of heritable disorders. However, critics argued that involuntary sterilization was an unconstitutional violation of people's rights. Although the U.S. Supreme Court agreed, several states still have sterilization laws (Bruinius, 2006, pp. 317–321; Duster, 1990, p. 30). Opponents also maintained that the eugenics movement consisted largely of middle-class and upper middle-class people, who used the results of flawed scientific research compatible with their own class bias to rationalize sterilization of lower class individuals (Kevles, 1985, p. 167). The same class bias was also used to argue for reducing the birth rate among poor people and increasing it among the rich (Kevles, 1985, pp. 182–184).

Cattell argued not only for restricted eugenics but also for a program of **creative eugenics**. This program, like its predecessors in the early 1900s, would encourage more intelligent people to have more children, while discouraging the less intelligent from reproducing. According to Cattell, there is a slight positive correlation between intelligence and socioeconomic status, as defined by education and income (Cattell, 1987, pp. 206–207). Although the correlation is not strong, Cattell thought it offers the best available guide to a general policy aimed at producing the best (most intelligent) citizens. Specifically, he believed that socially successful individuals should be encouraged to have more children, and poorer people fewer. Toward this end, he advocated providing tax relief or cash to those with above-average incomes to encourage childbearing, while eliminating the current tax deductions for children in families earning less than the average income. Taxes paid by middle- and upper-class people legitimately can be given to poor people, in Cattell's view, only if they are capable of being reformed and rehabilitated (Cattell, 1972, p. 360). He considered such transfers illegitimate in the case of those who are, in his words, "inherently inadequate," those marked by low reasoning ability (extemely low B factor scores), emotional instability (extremely low C factor scores), poor superego development (very low G factor scores), self-absorption and a disregard for practical planning (very high M factor scores), and conceit and egotism (extremely high E factor scores) (Cattell, 1987, p. 57). Such people, according to Cattell, are highly irresponsible and deliberately evade their work responsibilities (Cattell, 1987, p. 57).

In Cattell's view, democracy offers the form of government best suited to implement Beyondism and bring about progress, because it provides a more favorable climate for scientific thought and research than other political systems. Above all, it is one of the few systems in which violent revolution is unnecessary for progress (Cattell, 1972, pp. 340–341).

Finally, Cattell believed that, if a government spends unrealistically on welfare for the poor and/or too little on defense, research, and education, it is likely to collapse economically or be defeated in war. Beyondists would establish national and international research centers to collect data relevant to evolutionary progress. They advocate a greatly increased commitment to education, with a focus on furthering the intellectual and moral growth of those born with higher intelligence (Cattell, 1987, p. 84). The chief challenge to education in the future, according to Cattell, is to teach students the fundamentals of genetics and social-scientific research, along with the art of analyzing arguments, so as to ensure that society will profit from their knowledge and expertise (Cattell, 1972, p. 380).

Cattell's ideas have been criticized on several grounds. Gorsuch (1984, p. 217), for example, points out that most people in the world could not hold the Beyondism philosophy because they don't have an understanding of scientific method; so the philosophy is restricted to an elite few. Also, Jahoda (1989) suggests that Cattell's postulated link between higher intelligence and sound moral values is dubious. Leaders of organized crime or producers of pornography do not seem to suffer from below-average intelligence, neither did Hitler. Although Cattell maintained that Beyondism is rooted in science, most of the arguments he mustered have little or no empirical basis; rather, they were based on his own value system and conservative philosophy.

Finally, Cattell's policy of providing higher education primarily for children from affluent families, on the grounds of their higher native intelligence, has little empirical support. Distributions of intelligence scores for richer and poorer people, in fact, show considerable overlap; many poor people can and do benefit from higher education. To limit their opportunities for advancement and a better standard of living by focusing our resources primarily on the children of the well-to-do seems shortsighted, uncaring, and contrary to the democratic ideal of equal opportunity.

Evaluative Comments

We turn now to an examination of the scientific worth of Cattell's theory.

Comprehensiveness   There is little doubt that Cattell devised a comprehensive theory of personality. His theory addresses a wide range of diverse phenomena, both normal and abnormal, and seeks to account for both the biological and sociocultural factors that influence behavior. The range of his interests and efforts in pursuing this formidable task was indeed impressive.

Cattell fully recognized the complexity of the motives that determine behavior and the need for measurement procedures equal to the task. It is from this perspective that he criticized the overreliance of researchers on the bivariate experiment. However, he did not take an either/or position on the merits of the multivariate approach and the deficiencies of the controlled experiment, nor did he suggest that investigators abandon the bivariate approach altogether. Instead, he recognized that both approaches have unique assets.

Thus, Cattell recognized the complexity of personality; he developed a theory that seeks to approximate that reality; and he sought to utilize measurement procedures commensurate with the task.

Precision and testability   Of all the theorists in this text, Cattell demonstrated the most concern with constructing a theory based on precise measurement. He steadfastly worked to define and refine his concepts through the use of sophisticated and elaborate factor-analytic procedures. Despite this emphasis, critics have argued that his data are fraught with ambiguities and subjectivity. They maintain that he himself made the decision to include only certain traits in his factor analyses; therefore, it should not surprise anyone that he got out of the analyses the traits that he put in. In response, Cattell cited his painstaking efforts initially to include virtually all the traits known to human beings in his factor analyses. Recall that his construction of the personality sphere was an attempt to examine all the traits that could be used to describe behavior. It is a good bet that he has covered most of them.

Another criticism of the factor-analytic approach concerns the subjectivity involved in labeling factors. Despite the emphasis on objectivity in his measurement procedures, Cattell still had to use subjective judgment in interpreting the meaning of the factors and labeling them. Recognizing this problem, Cattell proceeded cautiously and labeled factors only after several replications provided supportive evidence. He also sought cross-validation of factors through research with different populations. Through this continual process of refinement, the labeling of factors becomes more readily apparent, and less subjective.

Parsimony   Cattell attempted to construct a theory that is parsimonious by using factor-analytic techniques to uncover the major source traits of normal and abnormal behavior. He also took the person's abilities and mood fluctuations into account in creating his theory. In addition, his econetic model provides a number of concepts that help explain the impact of environment on behavior. Thus, Cattell's theory seems economical without being overly simplistic.

Empirical validity   Cattell spent most of his research career establishing the reliability and validity of his trait concepts. Thus, there is considerable empirical support for these basic concepts, as well as some support for various hypotheses based on them. However, there is still only minimal support for his econetic model.

Heuristic value   Many psychologists agree that there is a great deal to admire about Cattell and his efforts as a scientific investigator. He is seen as a first-rate scholar with wide-ranging interests and expertise in many areas. There is little question that he was incredibly productive as a researcher and prolific as a writer, and he had the kind of curiosity, intelligence, and boldness necessary in a pioneering investigator. Despite all this, the theory itself has generated relatively little research. Why? First, as with Jung, Cattell's work is difficult to understand. The language of the theory is often technical and forbidding. Second, although factor analysis is a relatively objective and precise statistical technique, some investigators believe that the investigator's own biases can influence the outcomes, and they look askance at the research results compiled by Cattell and his associates. Finally, and perhaps most importantly, for much of his career Cattell made little effort to expand his theory so as to include environmental factors in the prediction of behavior. To experimentalists wedded to a strong environmentalism, his emphasis on the primacy of inner traits was unappealing. Hopefully, Cattell's later work on the econetic model will arouse investigators' interest in his theory and stimulate more research.

While there has been little research on the theory itself, Cattell's pioneering ideas have stimulated new thinking and research in contemporary personality psychology. In particular, personality psychologists acknowledge Cattell's seminal contributions to behavioral genetics, his creativity in devising new methods to study the complexity of traits, and the importance of his long-standing call for a new taxonomy of traits to focus research in their attempts to understand the influence of traits on behavior. (See Chapter 18 for more details.)

Finally, it should be noted that Cattell's philosophical views on the need for a new morality based on science (Beyondism) have not met with a positive reception from personality psychologists. Rather than criticize these speculations, his colleagues have tended to ignore them; it seems likely that his views will suffer the same ignominious fate as those of his predecessors in the 1920s and 1930s.

Applied value   Cattell's work has had considerable influence in the clinical diagnosis of psychopathology and in the assessment of therapeutic growth; it has had an even greater impact on occupational psychology. It has provided vocational counselors with reliable personality testing procedures that have been used to provide information to young people and adults concerning the kinds of occupations that might be compatible with their interests and abilities. Management supervisors in business and industry have also used Cattell's tests in making decisions about the placement of workers in jobs suited to their talents and personalities.

CRITICAL THINKING QUESTIONS

1. What is the inductive-hypothetico-deductive spiral? How does this approach to the construction of personality theory differ from the hypothetico-deductive model used by most researchers?

2. What is factor analysis? What are some of its strengths and weaknesses as a personality assessment procedure?

3. From Cattell's perspective, what is a trait? What are the primary source traits in personality? Do

you think Cattell has identified all of them? Which ones, if any, has he missed?

4. Is there necessarily a decrease in physical and mental powers with the onset of old age? Are the elderly people you know powerless and helpless?

5. Are you a Beyondist? What are some of the strengths and weaknesses of Cattell's moral philosophy?

GLOSSARY

ability traits   Skills that enable individuals to cope effectively with problems posed by the environment.

beyondism   A new morality Cattell claimed was based on scientific research and data. He believed this new set

of ethics would help society progress beyond the current state of instability, confusion, and crisis.

bivariate experiments   Investigations designed to assess the impact of one variable on another. Cattell thought that such experiments are limited in their usefulness because they did not do justice to human behavior, which is typically determined by many variables.

classical conditioning   Type of learning in which a stimulus that is originally incapable of evoking a response becomes capable of evoking it after continued pairing of this stimulus with one that naturally produces the response.

Clinical Analysis Questionnaire   Personality test designed to measure normal and deviant personality traits. It includes the 16 PF traits and 12 other psychopathological traits.

confluence learning   Acquisition of attitudes and behaviors that contribute simultaneously to the satisfaction of two or more goals.

constitutional traits   Characteristics that are rooted in biology and are very resistant to change.

creative eugenics   A program advocated by Cattell to increase the birth rate of more intelligent people in the belief that such individuals will develop sounder ethical values and contribute more to society's well-being.

crystallized intelligence   Abilities that are the result of cultural learning—for example, verbal and mathematical skills.

Culture Fair Intelligence Test   Test developed by Cattell that assesses innate abilities or fluid intelligence. It assesses abilities rooted in the genetic makeup of the person and is independent of cultural learning.

dynamic calculus   A set of mathematical formulas (specification equations) that integrate traits, environment, and motivational factors in the prediction of behavior.

dynamic lattice   Complicated and organized system of traits within the human personality.

dynamic traits   Characteristics that embrace people's motives and interests.

econetic model   Model that postulates a complex interaction between traits and the physical, social, and cultural environments in the prediction of behavior.

Eight State Questionnaire   Personality test that measures basic moods and emotional states.

environmental-mold traits   Characteristics learned through experiences with the environment.

environmental sphere   Listing of all the terms used in a culture to designate situations or environments.

ergs   Innate drives that control behavior.

factor analysis   Statistical technique designed to simplify a complex set of data by accounting for them in terms of underlying factors, usually fewer in number than the original number of variables in the original data set.

factor loading   The degree of association between a specific variable and a general factor.

fluid intelligence   Abilities that are innately based.

inductive-hypothetico-deductive spiral   Approach to theory construction and validation in which facts are collected first and then generalized into hypotheses, which lead to deductions that can be tested empirically.

instrumental conditioning   Type of learning in which the presentation of a rewarding or punishing stimulus is made contingent on the occurrence of a response or behavior; also known as operant conditioning.

integration learning   Type of learning proposed by Cattell in which people utilize their reasoning abilities and value systems to maximize the attainment of long-range goals.

L-data   Information about a person's life based on the actual observance of the person's behavior or on records of the person's behavior. For example, a high-school student's absences from class can actually be recorded by a truant officer who actually sits in the student's classes for a month; alternatively, finding this procedure too time-consuming, the truant officer may simply use the teacher's record of the student's class attendance.

multiple abstract variance analysis (MAVA)   Statistical procedure used to determine the precise contributions of genetic and environmental factors to the development of traits.

multivariate experiments   Investigations designed to assess the impact of several variables on a given behavior.

P technique   Form of factor analysis that permits assessment of the unique trait structure of an individual.

personality sphere   Listing of all the traits used to describe behavior in a culture.

primary factors Source factors or traits that emerge from an analysis of the correlations among a number of surface variables.

Q-data Information about a subject's behavior obtained through self-ratings on a questionnaire.

R technique Form of factor analysis used to infer underlying source traits in large subject populations.

restrictive eugenics A program to reduce the birth rate of the mentally handicapped; Cattell advocated this program in the belief that such individuals are a costly burden to society and slow its evolutionary growth.

second-order factors Global or higher order factors that emerge after an analysis of the associations among a number of primary factors or source traits.

self-sentiment Master motive that integrates the various attitudes, sentiments, and interests of the person.

Sixteen Personality Factor (16 PF) Questionnaire Factor-analytically derived questionnaire created by Cattell to measure the primary or basic underlying traits of personality.

source trait An underlying characteristic inferred from the intercorrelations among a number of measured variables or surface traits.

specification equations Formulas that specify the ways in which traits are weighted in relation to given situations and then combined to predict behavior.

structure-based systems theory Theory that seeks to explain the complicated, dynamic interactions between goal-oriented people and their environments.

subsidiation Process involving the interrelatedness of traits within the dynamic lattice or organizational structure of personality. Attitudes are subsidiated to, or dependent on, sentiments; sentiments are dependent on ergs.

surface trait An observable trait that is controlled by an underlying source trait.

T-data Objective test information based on an observer's judgments of how a subject reacts to the environment; the data are collected in situations that do not permit the subject to know what aspect of his or her behavior is being evaluated.

temperament traits Innate tendencies to react to the environment in particular ways. Temperament includes such variables as the person's moodiness, excitability, activity level, and speed of response to stimuli.

traits Relatively permanent and broad reaction tendencies that serve as the building blocks of personality.

SUGGESTED READINGS

Cattell, R. B. (1965). *The scientific analysis of personality.* Baltimore, MD: Penguin.

Cattell, R. B. (1979/1980). *Personality and learning theory* (Vols. 1 and 2). New York: Springer.

Cattell, R. B. (1987). *Beyondism: Religion from science.* New York: Praeger.

CHAPTER 10

Eysenck's Biological Typology

Courtesy of the University of London, British Postgraduate Medical Federation.

Biographical Sketch

Hans Eysenck was born in Berlin on March 4, 1916. His parents, both well-known actors, divorced when Eysenck was only 2 years old, and he went to live with his maternal grandmother. Like his parents, she had a deep fondness for the theater, but her own acting career had been cut short when she was crippled by a fall. Not surprisingly, Eysenck was also drawn to acting, and at the age of 5 or 6, he played in a film in which his mother was the star. His father wanted him to pursue a career in acting, but his mother, whom Eysenck calls the more sensible, opposed it, and he turned away from acting as a profession.

Eysenck's father was Catholic, his mother Protestant. Although he was christened and confirmed in the Lutheran faith, Eysenck was not particularly religious. In fact, he had to be bribed by the promise of a bicycle to attend the classes preparing him for confirmation.

Eysenck reported that as a youngster he was rather wild. On one occasion, he bet one of his friends that he could swing himself near the top of the roof in the inside of the gym on some rings, then let go, and land on his feet. Unfortunately, someone left some barbells lying on the floor. He landed right on them, fell on his right arm, and broke every available bone. Around the same time, he almost lost his right eye when he and some other boys were shooting paper arrows at each other from rubber bands. One boy shot a metal staple instead of a paper arrow and it lodged in Eysenck's eye and had to be removed by an ophthalmologist. As he grew older, the eye grew increasingly weak, so that after age 60 he was reduced to having sight in only one eye.

During his youth Eysenck also engaged in his share of schoolyard fights, vowing never to seek out a fight, or to force one on anyone weaker, but also never to shun one, and if forced into one to do his darnedest to win it. He also was a very good athlete, participating in many sports, including soccer, ice-hockey, field hockey, rowing, and tennis (Eysenck, 1997b, pp. 18–21).

Living as a young man in Germany between the wars, when economic and political turmoil culminated in the rise of Nazism, Eysenck took a great interest in politics and read widely. He embraced socialism, in which he saw the promise of a better world, free from war, prejudice, and poverty; as he matured, however, he began to see its problems and limitations. He summarizes this political maturation process as follows: One who is not a socialist in his or her youth has no heart; one who remains a socialist in middle age has no head. Although he is no longer a socialist, neither is he a conservative; he eschews all party labels and doctrines. Nevertheless, Eysenck has published numerous research papers on political matters, as well as two books: *The Psychology of Politics* (1954) and, with Glenn Wilson, *The Psychological Basis of Ideology* (1978).

In 1934, one year after Hitler assumed power, Eysenck left Germany; he had been told that he would not be allowed to enter the university unless he joined the SS (the Nazi secret police). His mother had married a Jewish film producer and moved to France, and they prevailed upon Eysenck to join them. He spent some time at the University of Dijon studying French literature and history, but eventually he settled in London. There, after studying for the matriculation examination for a year at Pitman's Commercial College, he enrolled at the University of London.

At the University of London, Eysenck had to select a major area for study. Although he had read widely in the classics of German, French, and English literature and loved music, painting, and poetry, he believed that the arts were primarily for fun and emotional experiences. He decided that his life's work would be in science and declared physics as his major. However, university officials told him that he lacked the prerequisites to study physics and, rather than spend another year taking the required subjects, he asked if there was any science he could declare as a major. He was told, "There's always psychology." Eysenck asked, in ignorance, "What on earth is that?" "You'll like it," was the reply, and he became a psychology major!

Eysenck entered a department populated by a number of eminent faculty, including psychometricians Cyril Burt and Charles Spearman. He also studied genetics with J. B. S. Haldane and L. Penrose and took a statistics course from Egon Pearson. His first research article appeared in 1939, just after he earned his B.A. degree, and he obtained a Ph.D. from the University of London in 1940.

By this time, Eysenck was married to Margaret Davies, a Canadian mathematician. The couple had one son, Michael, now a well-known psychologist in his own right. The marriage subsequently ended in divorce, and Eysenck later married Sybil Rostal, a psychologist and daughter of a famous violinist. Their marriage produced three sons and a daughter.

With England at war with Nazi Germany, Eysenck tried to enlist in the Royal Air Force but he was turned down as an "enemy alien." Employment opportunities were scarce for the same reason. Unable to secure a university position, Eysenck eventually obtained a research position at Mill Hill Emergency Hospital, where he began studies on suggestibility in hysterics. He also worked on such topics as parotid-gland secretion in affective mental disorders, screening tests for neurotics, memory tests, and the effects of motivation on intelligence. In addition, he completed a large-scale factor analysis of patients' symptoms, from which he derived the theory that there are two major personality factors: neuroticism and extraversion/introversion. These ideas led to the publication of his first book, *Dimensions of Personality* (1947). In his second book, *The Scientific Study of Personality* (1952), he added psychoticism as the third major dimension.

After the war, Eysenck began work at the Maudsley Hospital, the best-known psychiatric hospital and teaching unit in England. Appointed as director of the psychology department, he was encouraged by officials to establish a training program for clinical psychologists. Toward this end, Eysenck traveled in 1949 to the United States to examine and evaluate clinical psychology programs at various universities.

On the basis of his trip to the United States, Eysenck came to three major conclusions about the shortcomings of clinical training and practice: First, clinical psychologists were subordinate to psychiatrists; second, many clinical psychologists slavishly utilized psychoanalytic concepts in their therapeutic work; third, clinicians depended too heavily on projective tests, even though they were unreliable and invalid. Eysenck resolved, upon his return to England, to forge an independent department of psychology, to move away from psychoanalysis, and to develop a program of study that was strongly scientific in orientation, with a focus on the interdependence of clinical and experimental work. To his credit, Eysenck was able to create such a department, which is flourishing;

his colleagues and students are carrying out research in behavior therapy (Eysenck, 1980, pp. 153–157).

A prolific writer, Eysenck produced approximately 80 books, countless chapters in edited books, and approximately 1,100 research articles, many of them coauthored with colleagues. Among his more notable books are *Uses and Abuses of Psychology* (1953), *The Dynamics of Anxiety and Hysteria* (1957), *Sense and Nonsense in Psychology* (1962), *Smoking, Health, and Personality* (1965), *The Causes and Cures of Neurosis* (with Stanley Rachman, 1965), *Personality Structure and Measurement* (with S. B. G. Eysenck, 1969), *The Structure of Human Personality* (1970), *The IQ Argument* (1971), *The Experimental Study of Freudian Theories* (with Glenn Wilson, 1973), *The Inequality of Man* (1975), *Psychoticism as a Dimension of Personality* (1977), *The Intelligence Controversy* (with Leon Kamin, 1981), *Personality and Individual Differences: A Natural Science Approach* (with Michael Eysenck, 1985), *The Causes and Cures of Criminality* (with Gisli Gudjonsson, 1989), *Rebel with a Cause: The Autobiography of Hans Eysenck* (1990), *Smoking, Personality, and Stress: Psychological Factors in the Prevention of Cancer, and Coronary Heart Disease* (1991), and *Genius: The Natural History of Creativity* (1995). An expanded and revised version of his autobiography was published in 1997, shortly before his death. He had been suffering from a malignant brain tumor for about a year and finally succumbed on September 4, 1997, at a hospice in London. A final book, *Intelligence: A New Look* (1998), was published posthumously.

Concepts and Principles

Eysenck observed that psychology has two major orientations—personality psychology and experimental psychology—and that, unfortunately, theoreticians and researchers in the two areas tend to ignore each other's work; that is, experimental psychologists show little concern with individual differences, and personality theorists ignore the need for empirical evidence. As a result of this mutual indifference, nonscientific or prescientific theorists and practitioners abound in the field of personality. We are left with dozens of theories of personality, but very little in the way of factual support for them. What is required is a more theoretical approach seeking causal connections and using experimental tests of the deductions from the theories in question. As an integral part of this approach, investigators also need to account for the role of personality factors in their experimental work.

To accomplish this goal, Eysenck suggested that we must integrate the two approaches by: (1) identifying the main dimensions of personality; (2) devising means of measuring them; and (3) linking them with experimental, quantitative procedures. Only in this way, Eysenck believed, can we claim to be testing theories using a scientific perspective (Eysenck, 1947, pp. 1–2; Eysenck, 1997a, p. 1234).

Identifying and Measuring the Main Dimensions of Personality

Eysenck defined personality as a more or less stable and enduring organization of a person's character, temperament, intellect, and physique, which determines his unique adjustment to the environment. *Character* denotes a person's more or less stable and enduring system of conative behavior (*will*); *temperament*, his more or less stable and enduring system of affective behavior (*emotion*); *intellect*, his more or less stable and enduring system of cognitive behavior (*intelligence*); *physique*, his more or less stable and enduring system of bodily configuration and neuroendocrine endowment. (Eysenck, 1970, p. 2) Thus, his definition emphasized traits (stable and enduring characteristics), which, when clustered together, are organized as types.

Eysenck's **typology** is hierarchically organized and consists of types, traits, and habits. Types are most abstract, followed by traits, and then habits. Specifically, each of the type concepts is based on a set of observed intercorrelations among various traits. Each trait, in turn, is inferred from intercorrelations among habitual responses. Habitual responses, in turn, are based on specific observable responses. (See Figure 10.1.) For example, extraversion

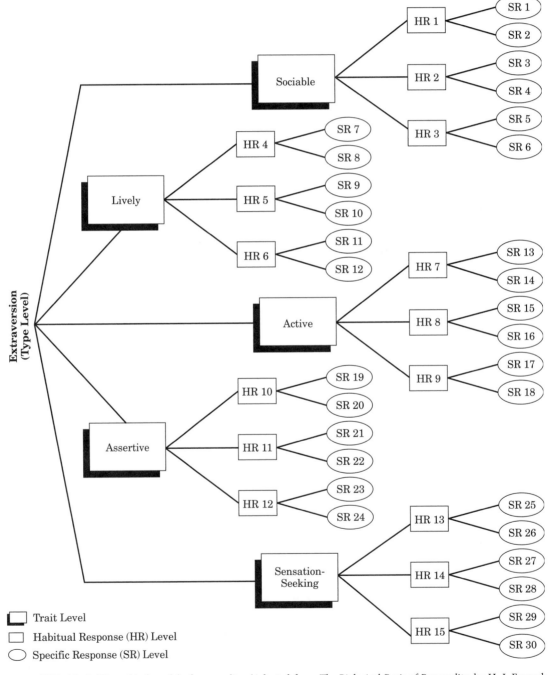

FIG-10.1 Hierarchical model of personality. (Adapted from *The Biological Basis of Personality,* by H. J. Eysenck, 1967, p. 36. Courtesy of Charles C. Thomas, Publisher, Ltd., Springfield, Illinois.)

is based on observed intercorrelations among traits such as sociability, impulsivity, activity, liveliness, and excitability. Each of these traits is inferred from intercorrelated habitual responses such as going to parties, liking to talk to people, going to films on the spur of the moment, and so forth. These habits are themselves inferred from observable specific responses—actual occasions when the person went to a party, talked to people, and so forth.

On the basis of numerous factor analyses of personality data gathered from different study participant populations all over the world, Eysenck derived two factors that could readily be labeled introversion/extraversion and stability/neuroticism. Later, on the basis of other statistical analyses, he postulated a third dimension, impulse control/psychoticism (Eysenck, 1982, p. 9). These three dimensions, according to Eysenck, are the major individual difference types most useful in describing personality functioning.

Once he had identified the three primary dimensions, Eysenck proceeded to construct a paper-and-pencil test to measure them. The original test is the **Eysenck Personality Questionnaire (EPQ)** (Eysenck & Eysenck, 1975). However, the psychoticism dimension in this test was found to have poor reliability, so a revised version was constructed to address this problem (Eysenck, Eysenck, & Barrett, 1985, pp. 21–29). Some sample items for each dimension in the revised scale are listed in Table 10.1. It should be noted that study participants who score high on the neuroticism or psychoticism scales for the revised, shortened version of the test are not necessarily neurotic or psychotic, but are at risk for developing the disorders.

Figures 10.2, 10.3, and 10.4 present the particular traits that define the type concepts, or primary dimensions, of extraversion, neuroticism, and psychoticism. **Extraverts** are sociable and impulsive individuals who like excitement and who are oriented toward external reality; **introverts** are quiet, introspective individuals who are oriented toward inner reality and who prefer a well-ordered life. Although these definitions are similar to those used by Jung (see Chapter 3), Eysenck did not accept Jung's account of the origins of these attitudes nor the manner in which they operate in the subterranean psyche of the individual (Eysenck & Eysenck, 1985, p. 48).

Neurotics, in Eysenck's view, are emotionally unstable individuals. Some have unreasonable fears of certain objects, places, persons, animals, open spaces, or heights

---

TABLE 10.1   SAMPLE ITEMS FROM THE EYSENCK PERSONALITY QUESTIONNAIRE-REVISED*

Extraversion

1. Are you a talkative person?
2. Are you rather lively?
3. Do you enjoy meeting new people?

Neuroticism

1. Does your mood often go up and down?
2. Are your feelings easily hurt?
3. Are you an irritable person?

Psychoticism

1. Do you take much notice of what people think?
2. Do you try not to be rude to people?
3. Do good manners and cleanliness matter much to you?

---

*Yes responses to the extraversion and neuroticism items indicate extraverted and neurotic tendencies, respectively; *No* responses to the psychoticism items indicate a psychotic tendency.
Source: Adapted from Eysenck, Eysenck, & Barrett, 1985.

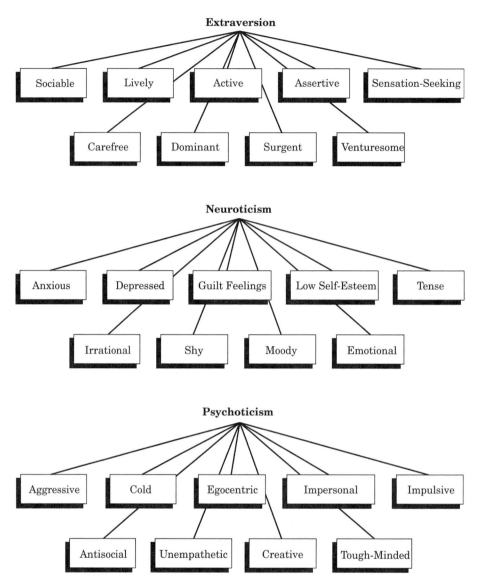

FIG-10.2 Traits making up the type concept of extraversion. (Adapted from Eysenck, H. J. & Eysenck, M. W., *Personality and Individual Differences: A Natural Science Approach,* p. 15. Copyright © 1985 by Plenum Press. Used with kind permission from Springer Science and Business Media.)

FIG-10.3 Traits making up the type concept of neuroticism. (Adapted from Eysenck, H. J. & Eysenck, M. W., *Personality and Individual Differences: A Natural Science Approach,* p. 15. Copyright © 1985 by Plenum Press. Used with kind permission from Springer Science and Business Media.)

FIG-10.4 Traits making up the type concept of psychoticism. (Adapted from Eysenck, H. J. & Eysenck, M. W., *Personality and Individual Differences: A Natural Science Approach,* p. 14. Copyright © 1985 by Plenum Press. Used with kind permission from Springer Science and Business Media.)

(Eysenck, H. J., 1965, p. 97); others may exhibit obsessional or impulsive symptoms. The hallmark of the disorder for most neurotics is an anxiety level disproportionate to the realities of the situation (Eysenck, H. J., 1965, pp. 97–98). Yet some neurotics are free from the burden of anxiety and fear. In this grouping, we find the psychopaths—individuals who seem unable to assess the consequences of their actions and who behave in an asocial or antisocial manner regardless of the punishment meted out by others (Eysenck, H. J., 1965, p. 100).

Psychotics differ generally from neurotics in the severity of their disorders. Showing the most severe type of **psychopathology**, psychotics may be insensitive to others, hostile, cruel, and inhumane, with a strong need to make fools of people and to upset them. While psychotics often show very severe psychopathology like **schizophrenia**, the fact that they can act in antisocial ways by being hostile, cruel, and inhumane toward others, violating the ordinary rules that govern social behavior, means that are likely to also manifest conduct disorders, a less severe form of psychopathology than schizophrenia. People characterized by conduct orders are cruel, unempathic, hostile, egocentric, and do not comply with social rules, traits that they hold in common with psychotics. Thus, we would expect on conceptual grounds that people who are high on the psychoticism dimension would be identified as likely to have character disorders. In a survey of the research literature, Center and Kemp (2003, pp. 75–88) found very strong support (18 out of 20 studies) for a positive link between psychoticism and conduct disorder in children and adolescents.

Despite all these socially undesirable traits, however, Eysenck believed that psychotics tend to be creative, *but* only in the limited sense that they can give original responses to various stimuli (Eysenck, 1993, pp. 152–153; Eysenck & Eysenck, 1985, p. 14).

What is the basis for his contention that there is a link between genius and psychosis? First, he pointed out that, throughout history, geniuses—that is, those who demonstrate supreme creative achievement—have tended to show episodes of various forms of psychopathological behavior. (See Table 10.2.) Thus, creativity is linked to abnormality. Second, many of the traits associated with high scores on the psychoticism dimension are conducive to the pursuit of a creative career. Geniuses must buck tradition to strike out on their own. They cannot be concerned about pleasing others; instead they must be self-centered, aggressive, tough-minded, and persistent to overcome the many obstacles placed in their path (Simonton, 1994, p. 292).

Examples of the insensitivity, cruelty, and heartlessness of highly creative individuals abound. For instance, the mathematician Gauss was working on a particularly difficult problem when a servant came into his room to inform him that his sick wife was about to breathe her last. Gauss could only mutter, "Tell her to wait a moment till I'm through." Or there is the example of Cavendish, the notable physicist and chemist, who was so eccentric that, when he was about to be introduced to some scientific celebrities, he abandoned all amenities and ran down the hall, squealing like a bat. Cavendish ordinarily said no more than a few words to a man and refused to talk to any woman. At home, he communicated via written memos to his female servants and fired instantly any servant who crossed his path (Simonton, 1994, p. 269).

Third, Eysenck noted that the hallmark of the creative genius is his or her ability to think in unusual, almost bizarre ways. Many psychotic individuals, especially those diagnosed with schizophrenia, also have concepts that are diffuse and overinclusive and, in consequence, are able to connect ideas that others would see as unrelated (Simonton, 1994, p. 292). Eysenck cited considerable evidence that schizophrenics perform very well on tests of **divergent thinking**, which shows their ability to think in unusual and original ways. For example, an item on such a test might be:

"How many uses can you think of for a brick?" More normal people might reply that it can be used to build houses, to repair walkways, and to repair chimneys. People high on the psychoticism dimension, as well as schizophrenics, might give the same responses and quickly add the following: it could be used also as a doorstop, as a paperweight, as a thing to make water in a pond splash, as a weapon of aggression, as a walnut crusher, and as a substitute barbell to do bicep curls. Thus, people higher on psychoticism give more unusual responses, thereby showing greater originality and fluency of ideas (Eysenck, 1995, pp. 236–245).

Eysenck claimed that the originality of both geniuses and psychotics is based on a cognitive style that is overinclusive—that allows them to interpret all kinds of ideas as relevant to any problem under consideration. He thought further that this overinclusiveness may be due to a failure of cognitive inhibition caused by high levels of **dopamine** and a lack of **serotonin** in the brain (Eysenck, 1995, pp. 264–265). Specifically, Eysenck maintained that normal people process incoming information by narrowing it down—by deciding which information is relevant to the solution of a problem and which information is irrelevant. Normal individuals then include in their thinking the information that

TABLE 10.2 EMINENT PERSONALITIES WITH SUPPOSED MENTAL ILLNESSES

Schizophrenic disorders (and other cognitive psychoses):

Scientists: T. Brahe, Cantor, Copernicus, Descartes, Faraday, W. R. Hamilton, Kepler, Lagrange, Linnaeus, Newton, Pascal, Semmelweis, Weierstrass, H. Wells.

Thinkers: Kant, Nietzsche, Swedenborg.

Writers: Baudelaire, Lewis Carroll, Hawthorne, Hölderlin, S. Johnson, Pound, Rimbaud, Strindberg, Swift.

Artists: Bosch, Cellini, Dürer, Goya, El Greco, Kandinsky, Leonardo da Vinci, Rembrandt, Toulouse-Lautrec.

Composers: Donizetti, MacDowell, F. Mendelssohn, Rimsky-Korsakov, Saint-Saëns.

Others: M. Barrymore, de Sade, Goebbels, Herod the Great, Joan of Arc, Nero, Nijinsky, Shaka.

Affective disorders (depression, mania, or bipolar):

Scientists: Boltwood, Boltzmann, Carothers, C. Darwin, L. De Forest, J. F. W. Herschel, Julian Huxley, T. H. Huxley, Jung, Kammerer, J. R. von Mayer, V. Meyer, H. J. Muller, J. P. Müller, B. V. Schmidt, J. B. Watson.

Thinkers: W. James, J. S. Mill, Rousseau, Sabbatai Zevi, Schopenhauer.

Writers: Balzac, Barrie, Berryman, Blake, Boswell, V. W. Brooks, Byron, Chatterton, J. Clare, Coleridge, William Collins, Conrad, Cowper, H. Crane, Dickens, T. Dreiser, R. Fergusson, F. S. Fitzgerald, Frost, Goethe, G. Greene, Hemingway, Jarrell, Kafka, C. Lamb, J. London, R. Lowell, de Maupassant, E. O'Neill, Plath, Poe, Quiroga, Roethke, D. G. Rossetti, Saroyan, Schiller, Sexton, P. B. Shelley, C. Smart, T. Tasso, V. Woolf.

Artists: Michelangelo, Modigliani, Pollock, Raphael, Rothko, R. Soyer, Van Gogh.

Composers: Berlioz, Chopin, Elgar, Gershwin, Handel, Mahler, Rachmaninoff, Rossini, R. Schumann, Scriabin, Smetana, Tchaikovsky, Wolf.

Others: C. Borgia, Clive, O. Cromwell, A. Davis, J. Garland.

Personality disorders (including severe neuroses):

Scientists: Ampère, Cavendish, A. S. Couper, Diesel, Einstein, Frege, S. Freud, Galton, Heaviside, Huygens, Marconi, Mendel.

Thinkers: J. Austin, Beccaria, Comte, Descartes, Hegel, Hobbes, Hume, Kierkegaard, B. Russell, Spencer, Voltaire, Wittgenstein.

Writers: H. C. Andersen, E. B. Browning, R. Browning, Bunyan, Carlyle, Dickinson, Dostoevski, T. S. Eliot, Emerson, Flaubert, García Lorea, Gide, Allen Ginsberg, Gogol, Heine, G. M. Hopkins, A. Huxley, W. M. Inge, Melville, Pavese, Proust, S. Richardson, Rimbaud, Ruskin, Tennyson, de Tocqueville, Tolstoy, Verlaine, T. Williams, Zola.

Artists: Borromini, Bramante, Caravaggio, Cézanne, C. Chanel, Munch, Romney.

Composers: Beethoven, Bruckner, O. de Lasso, Schubert, Wagner.

Performers: S. Bernhardt, J. Dean, W. C. Fields, C. Gable, C. Grant, J. Joplin, M. Monroe, B. Powell.

Leaders: C. Barton, Bismarck, W. Churchill, M. B. Eddy, Göring, A. Gramsci, A. Hamilton, Hitler, H. Hughes, A. Krupp, H. Lee, R. E. Lee, Lincoln, Luther, Mussolini, Napoleon, Nightingale, Nixon, T. Roosevelt, W. Wilson, M. Wollstonecraft.

Note: Because almost all of these diagnoses are not based on objective clinical assessments, most are highly tentative.
Source: From Simonton D. K., *Greatness: Who Makes History and Why*, p. 287. Copyright © 1994 Guilford Press. Reprinted with permission.

they consider will help them solve the problem and exclude the rest because of its perceived irrelevance. Eysenck argued that schizophrenics and geniuses, in contrast, are characterized by a breakdown in this inhibitory process caused by very high levels of dopamine. Thus, the failure to inhibit ideas produces an overinclusiveness (a wide range of concept associations) that is associated with one important facet of creativity, namely, originality (Eysenck, 1995, pp. 249–279). There is substantial empirical support for Eysenck's ideas that schizophrenia and psychoticism are associated with very high levels of dopamine (Colzato, Slagter, van den Wildenberg, & Hommel, 2009, pp. 377–380).

If psychotics and geniuses are both characterized by originality, why do geniuses produce outstanding creative works that contribute greatly to society, whereas most psychotics spend much of their lives in institutions and fail to achieve greatness? For the answer, Eysenck thought that we had to understand that originality was a necessary, but not sufficient, condition for creative work. The other condition involved in creative work besides originality is social usefulness. Works are creative if they are original *and* useful to society. Geniuses embody both conditions because they have the right *combinations* of personality traits, whereas psychotics do not. Specifically, geniuses are generally characterized by high ego strength and confidence, extraordinarily high persistence motivation, and very high (although not extraordinarily high) intelligence. These traits interact with originality to generate creative products of social usefulness in eminent men and women. These same traits are not, however, typical in institutionalized psychotics (Eysenck, 1995, pp. 114–123).

Also, empirical support for Eysenck's position holds for people who are normal but who score high on the psychoticism scale. Abraham, Windmann, Daum, and Gunturkun (2005, pp. 520–534) found that men and women university students and adults with no university education who scored high on the psychoticism scale had elevated levels of originality, but there was no relation between their psychoticism scores and the practical usefulness of their ideas, that is, their creativity.

An Update on the Association Between Dopamine Levels and Creativity

Recent research by Chermahini and Hommel (2010, pp. 458–465) provides a more differentiated view of the role played by dopamine levels in creative brain processes and outcomes. In support of Eysenck, these researchers found that higher levels of dopamine were associated positively with higher levels of divergent thinking in Dutch university students. But Eysenck never examined the role of dopamine and its association with **convergent thinking**, whereas these researchers did. They found that lower levels of dopamine were associated with greater convergent thinking. Such thinking involves focusing on one idea from an array of possible ideas in coming up with a creative solution. Thus, divergent and convergent thinking are *both* necessary for creativity. Geniuses are able to come up with many ideas when searching for a creative solution through divergent thinking and then to make a judgment by selecting the one idea from this array of possible ideas through convergent thinking. Their judgment is then deemed at some point by others in society as original and socially useful (creative). Schizophrenics and other psychotics have many ideas (high divergent thinking) but do not typically engage in the convergent thinking that is necessary for creative solutions.

Inhibition Theory

Once Eysenck had described the major dimensions of personality to his satisfaction and devised a psychometrically sound test to measure them, it remained for him to develop a theory that would explain *why* people who differed along the dimensions should behave differently from one another. After developing such a theory, he needed to provide empirical evidence that different types of people did indeed differ in their actions. To achieve these goals, Eysenck began to construct a theory that had a strong physiological base but did not ignore environmental influences.

Eysenck began by postulating that individual differences along the introversion/extraversion dimension are strongly determined by heredity and have their origins in the cerebral cortex of the central nervous system. Information from the environment is transmitted from the sense organs along neural pathways to the brain, where excitatory and inhibitory cortical processes result in either the facilitation or inhibition of behavioral and cognitive responses (Eysenck, H. J., 1965, p. 70). Drawing upon the work of Teplov (1964) and Pavlov (1927), Eysenck maintained that extraverts have relatively strong inhibitory processes and weak excitatory processes. In addition, their nervous systems are strong, which means that they have a large capacity to tolerate stimulation. Introverts, in contrast, have strong excitatory processes and weak inhibitory processes. Also, their nervous systems are weak, which means that they have only a small capacity to tolerate stimulation. Thus, the brains of extraverts react more slowly and weakly to stimuli, thereby creating a *stimulus hunger*, or desire for strong sensory stimulation, which causes them to seek excitement by approaching the environment, attending parties, making friends, taking risks, and so forth. Conversely, introverts are inherently more cortically aroused, have brains that react more quickly and strongly to stimuli, and can tolerate only relatively small amounts of stimulation. As a result, they tend to find strong stimulation from the environment aversive and spend more time in contemplative activities such as reading, writing, and playing chess.

This **inhibition theory**, with its differential neurological underpinnings for introversion and extraversion, leads to a host of behavioral predictions that have generally received empirical confirmation. For example, in comparison to introverts, extraverts are fonder of loud music, bright colors, and jazz (perhaps because it is more complex and unusual, and therefore more interesting and stimulating). They are also more likely to use alcohol and other drugs, to smoke, and to engage in various types of sexual activity (Eysenck, H. J., 1965, pp. 84–85; Harakeh, Scholte, deVries, & Engels, 2006, pp. 232–245; Martsh & Miller, 1997, p. 153). More specifically, Eysenck's research has shown that, compared to introverts, extraverts have sexual intercourse at an earlier age, more frequently, with more partners, and in a wider range of positions (Eysenck & Eysenck, 1985, pp. 317–319). More recent research shows that extraverts seek social contact at an early age and their social skills become well developed. These social skills help extraverts in communicating with others and encourage them to engage in more social activities. Possibly as a result of their sociability and the social support attending it, extraverts tend to be better able to adapt to experiences of adversity or trauma than introverts (Campbell-Sills, Cohan, & Stein, 2006, pp. 585–599) Finally, Eysenck added the concept of **reactive inhibition** to his theorizing about introverts and extraverts. He borrowed the term from Hull's (1951) learning theory. Hull proposed that every repetition of an action creates reactive inhibition—a neural fatigue that builds to the point where the individual can no longer respond. Eysenck maintained that extraverts are more susceptible to reactive inhibition than are introverts and, as a result, are more likely to tire of a given activity sooner and turn to another. According to Eysenck, this changeableness of extraverts affects their behavior in many ways. When they are first hired and start to work on the job, they show high levels of involvement, but they soon tire of the job and are more likely to change jobs or careers. They are also more likely to change their romantic partners when they become unhappy (Eysenck, H. J., 1965, p. 81; Langelaan, Bakker, van Doornen, & Schaufeli, 2006, pp. 521–532).

Arousal Theory

Although inhibition and excitation were useful concepts in helping to predict behavioral differences between introverts and extraverts, they were extremely difficult to measure. Eysenck turned to the concept of **cortical arousal** because it can be more precisely assessed and can generate predictions across a wider variety of tasks and in a wider range of situations. Finally, **arousal theory** has the advantage of identifying the physiological systems underlying individual differences in introversion/extraversion and stability/neuroticism, whereas the earlier inhibition theory was not able to identify precisely the physiological systems underlying inhibition (Eysenck & Eysenck, 1985, pp. 196–199).

Arousal theory and introversion/extraversion In the latest version of his theory, Eysenck traced the differences in behavior between introverts and extraverts to various parts of the **ascending reticular activating system (ARAS)**. The ARAS is a network of fibers traveling upward from the lower brain stem to the thalamus and cortex. Stimulation of the ARAS results in increases in alertness and arousal of the cortex. Other fibers descend from the lower brain stem and, thereby, influence bodily musculature and the **autonomic nervous system** (Cofer & Appley, 1964, pp. 399–400). At the same time, fibers descending from the cortex can modulate the activity of the brain stem. Thus, the relation between the ARAS and the cortex is reciprocal: The ARAS can activate the cortex, and the cortex in turn can influence the ARAS, either increasing its excitability or inhibiting it.

In Eysenck's theory, introverts are assumed to have innately higher levels of arousal than do extraverts and, consequently, to be more sensitive to stimulation. Eysenck explained the relation between arousal and sensitivity to stimulation as follows:

> If sensory stimulation is registered in the cortex to a degree which is a joint function of the objective level of intensity of the stimulation and of the arousal existing in the cortex at the time of arrival of the neural message, then identical intensities of input will be experienced as stronger by introverts than by extraverts. (Eysenck, 1976, p. 113)

Thus, any given level of incoming stimulation is amplified by the high cortical arousability of introverts. To date, however, research shows little support for the idea that introverts' levels of arousal are innately higher, although a good deal of scientific evidence indicates that introverts are indeed more sensitive to stimulation (Stelmack, 1990, p. 293).

Eysenck further assumed that very low and very high levels of stimulation produce negative **hedonic tone**, negative feelings, and negative evaluation of the experience; whereas positive hedonic tone, positive feelings, and positive evaluation of the experience, occurs only at intermediate levels of sensory stimulation. Thus, it follows that the preferred level of stimulation should be lower for introverts than for extraverts (Eysenck & Eysenck, 1985, p. 248). Figure 10.5 illustrates this relationship between levels of stimulation and hedonic tone for introverts and extraverts.

Using this new theoretical formulation, Eysenck could make and verify the same predictions concerning the behavior of introverts and extraverts in sensory-deprivation and pain-tolerance conditions that he had made using his earlier inhibition theory.

FIG-10.5 Theoretical relationship between level of stimulation and hedonic tone as a function of extraversion. (Adapted from Eysenck, H. J. & Eysenck, M. W., *Personality and Individual Differences: A Natural Science Approach*, p. 249. Copyright © 1985 by Plenum Press. Used with kind permission from Springer Science and Business Media.)

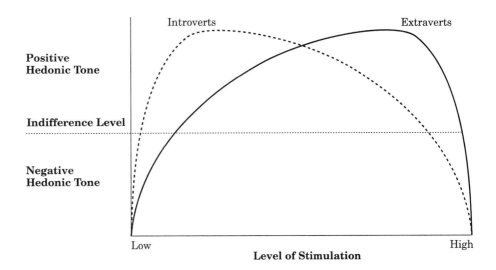

In addition, the revised theory has been tested in several new and interesting areas, including students' performances on a variety of academic tasks, their study habits, and their need for closure under time pressures. We now consider those findings.

A study by Furnham and Bradley (1997) examined the impact of playing music on the performances of introverts and extraverts. They reasoned that introverts would show poorer performances on a reading comprehension test than extraverts when pop music was being played as they worked, but not when they took the test with no music being played. Playing music provides extra-stimulation and pushes the introverts quickly beyond their optimal level, whereas extraverts need the extra-stimulation provided by the music to help them approach their optimal level of functioning. The results confirmed the hypotheses. Introverts and extraverts did not differ in their performances when they took the test in silence. However, introverts performed more poorly than extraverts in the presence of music. Also, in the same study, participants were asked to examine 20 pictures of various objects for 2 minutes and memorize as many of them as they could. They were then asked to recall them. Introverts had poorer recall than extraverts when music was playing while they were trying to memorize the items, whereas they did not differ when the task was performed in silence. The extra-stimulation appeared to serve as a distractor, thereby restricting their memory and recall. Introverts and extraverts did not differ in recall levels when they did the task under no music conditions (Furnham & Bradley, 1997, pp. 452–454). In a related study by Furnham and his colleagues, it was found that introverts performed more poorly than extraverts on a reading comprehension task while watching a TV drama. No differences in the performances of introverts and extraverts occurred when they took the test with no TV on (Furnham, Gunter, & Peterson, 1994, pp. 709–710).

The findings in the two studies by Furnham and his colleagues have important implications for students who are trying to maximize their academic potential. Introverts should avoid studying and/or doing homework in settings where external stimuli are present, which can distract them from working with full attention on their academic tasks, whereas extraverts should do their studying and/or homework in settings where there is sufficient external stimulation to facilitate movement toward their optimal level of arousal.

Campbell and Hawley (1982, pp. 139–146) also made use of Eysenck's arousal theory to predict differences in the study habits of introverts and extraverts. Specifically, they noted the study locations of students in the campus library and then obtained their consent for an interview about their study habits. They also asked students to fill out the EPQ (Eysenck & Eysenck, 1975). In the interview, study participants were asked to indicate, on a scale from 0 to 10, the number of times per hour that they took study breaks. They were also asked to indicate, on a scale from 1 (low) to 6 (high), what levels of noise, crowdedness, and socializing opportunities they preferred while they studied in the library. They were also asked to indicate, on a scale from 1 (not at all) to 6 (highly), how important socializing activities were to them in choosing a study location.

On the basis of Eysenck's theory, Campbell and Hawley predicted that introverts would prefer study locations that minimized intense external stimulation, such as individual study carrels where talking was not permitted, whereas extraverts would prefer seating arrangements that provided stimulation, such as a large reading area with sofas and lounge chairs, where socializing was permitted and where auditory and visual stimulation was high. This prediction was based on Eysenck's argument that introverts have a lower threshold for arousal of the reticular activating system than do extraverts. As a consequence, introverts should experience greater levels of arousal at lower intensities of stimulation. In addition, Eysenck's theory postulates that introverts would be more likely to experience negative hedonic tone and increased aversion to stimulation above an optimal level of stimulus intensity and that this optimal stimulus intensity would be lower for introverts than for extraverts. These predictions were strongly confirmed. Introverts tended to study in quiet areas and to use individual study carrels; extraverts studied in areas where they could socialize and where the level of auditory and visual stimulation was relatively high. Extraverts also reported that they preferred to study in noisier, more crowded areas, where they would have more opportunities to socialize. Such opportunities were highly important to them, and not as important to introverts.

Campbell and Hawley (1982) also predicted that extraverts would report taking more study breaks—looking around the room, walking around—than did introverts. Eysenck argues that, when performing long tasks, extraverts generate reactive inhibition (fatigue) more quickly and at greater levels than do introverts, and this rapid accumulation of reactive inhibition produces rest pauses. Since extraverts are more susceptible to inhibition, the monotony of studying should prompt extraverts to experience more rest pauses and consequently to take more study breaks. This prediction was also strongly confirmed. Furthermore, Davies and Parasuraman (1982) found that, on tasks that require vigilance, extraverts tire more easily than do introverts and are more likely, as a result, to make errors. One important practical implication of this finding for employers is to hire introverts rather than extraverts as quality-control workers, air traffic controllers, or security personnel at airport check points (Cox-Fuenzalida, Angie, Holloway, & Sohl, 2006, pp. 432–439).

In a completely different avenue of programmatic research, studies have found that, on average, extraverts experience more positive emotions, that is, happiness and a greater sense of well-being than introverts. Extraverts more than introverts seek out situations where they can interact with others, and the nature of these interactions generally produces enjoyment and happiness for them. These results were found in a study by Srivastava, Angelo, and Vallereau (2008, pp. 1613–1618) based on records kept by introverts and extraverts on the number of social interactions they recalled experiencing the previous day from the time they woke up until they went to sleep at night. Since social interactions generally produce positive affect (enjoyment and happiness) for both introverts and extraverts, the fact that extraverts had *more* social interactions than introverts means that extraverts are happier than introverts.

But why did extraverts have more social interactions? One possibility is that extraverts are more assertive and confident than introverts. Another possibility is that the greater number of social interactions makes extraverts feel more socially connected to others (more trusting and emotionally secure) which, in turn, means that they have higher self-esteem and fewer anxiety and depressive symptoms, with the consequence that they are happier than introverts (Lee, Dean, & Jung, 2008, pp. 414–419). In related fashion, extraverts tend to experience, not only more positive emotions, but fewer negative emotions. Thus, they have fewer thoughts about suicide, fewer attempts at committing suicide, and fewer actual suicides than introverts (Brezo, Paris, & Turecki, 2006, pp. 180–206). Lastly, research by Romero, Villar, Luengo, and Gomez-Fraguela (2009, pp. 535–546) suggests that extraverts are happier because they are more optimistic about achieving success in the pursuit of their goals, including ones that grow out of social interactions (e.g., friendship).

Finally, Landrum (1992, pp. 151–155) has found that college student extraverts tend to consume more chocolate, coffee, tea, and soft drinks like Coca-Cola and Dr. Pepper than do introverts. All of these contain caffeine, which has strong arousal effects. Many studies have shown that caffeine has a differential impact on the performances of introverts and extraverts—specifically, that increases in arousal induced by larger and larger doses of caffeine typically serve to improve extraverts' academic performance, whereas introverts' performance improves only to a point and then significantly declines at the highest doses (Bullock & Gilliland, 1993, pp. 113–123). In other words, the performance of both introverts and extraverts increases with moderate levels of caffeinated coffee drunk prior to the test (approximately one and one-half cups for a person weighing 150 pounds), but the performance of introverts declines considerably with higher levels of caffeinated coffee (three or more cups), whereas the performance of extraverts continues to improve.

Autonomic activation and neuroticism   In his arousal theory, Eysenck located the seat of neuroticism in the **visceral brain**, or limbic system. The structures of the visceral brain—the hippocampus, amygdala, cingulum, septum, and hypothalamus—are involved in generating emotionality. The visceral brain and the ARAS are only partially independent of each other; thus, cortical and autonomic arousal can also be produced by activity in the visceral brain. In particular, such activity produces arousal of the sympathetic branch of the autonomic nervous system, thereby preparing individuals for fight (anger) or flight (fear). It stops digestion, makes the heart beat faster, and increases breathing rates. People high in neuroticism have lower thresholds for activity in the visceral brain and greater responsivity of the **sympathetic nervous system** (Eysenck & Eysenck, 1985, p. 206). Thus, neurotics are innately more reactive; they overreact to even mild forms of stimulation. Figure 10.6 illustrates the physiological systems involved in generating behavioral differences among individuals who vary along the stability/neuroticism and introversion/extraversion dimensions.

Eysenck proposed that the greater responsivity of the sympathetic nervous system in neurotics is most obvious under relatively stressful conditions (Eysenck & Eysenck, 1985, p. 206), when the emotional reaction engendered by stress may interfere with performance. Most researchers have not directly investigated the effects of neuroticism on performance but have opted to study the strongly related dimension of anxiety. (Study participants' anxiety scores typically correlate positively with their neuroticism scores in the +.60 to +.70 range.) Anxiety consists of two components: emotionality and worry. Emotionality refers to physiological changes and the accompanying unpleasant feelings of uneasiness, nervousness, and tension. Worry is the cognitive component of anxiety;

FIG-10.6 Diagrammatic representation of the mutual interactions among the reticular formation, visceral brain, and cortex. VB, visceral brain; ARAS, ascending reticular activating system; AAP, ascending afferent pathways. (Adapted from the *Biological Basis of Personality*, by H. J. Eysenck, 1967, p. 231. Courtesy of Charles C Thomas, Publisher, Ltd., Springfield, Illinois.)

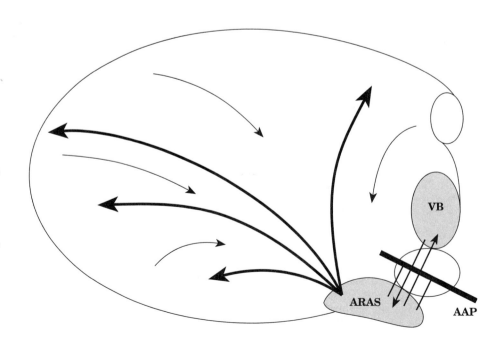

it includes persistent concern about one's performance and its consequences, negative self-evaluations, and negative task expectations (Eysenck & Eysenck, 1985, p. 292).

According to Eysenck, the adverse effects of anxiety on performance are attributable to task-irrelevant processing activities such as worry. Students who report high levels of worry generally do poorly on exams and have lower grade-point averages (Eysenck & Eysenck, 1985, pp. 293–294). When highly anxious people do perform as well as those low in anxiety on certain tasks, they expend much more effort and experience much more distress. Thus, anxious people may perform as efficiently at times as nonanxious people, but at a greater cost to their physical well-being (Eysenck & Eysenck, 1985, pp. 298–299).

Because neurotics possess labile and overactive autonomic nervous systems, they are very likely to experience high levels of fear and anxiety in stressful situations. Among such situations are those that involve intimacy between individuals; therefore, we would expect neurotics to attempt to reduce levels of intimacy. Research has shown that this is indeed the case. In a study by Campbell and Rushton (1978), for example, study participants high in neuroticism showed higher levels of gaze aversion than did participants low in neuroticism when talking to an experimenter.

Hormones and Psychoticism Eysenck worked hard at developing a causal theory of psychoticism, but the theory remains at a rudimentary stage. However, a number of related facts—that males as a group invariably score much higher on the Psychoticism (*P*) scale of the EPQ than females, that criminals and psychopaths (with high *P* scores) tend to be male rather than female, and that women (at least premenopausal women) become schizophrenic less readily than do men—suggested to Eysenck that psychoticism is perhaps related to maleness. In particular, maleness is linked very closely to the secretion of **androgens** (Eysenck, 1982, p. 19). In addition, high *P* scorers, like schizophrenics, show a relative lack of serotonin and the presence of certain **antigens** in their bodies. This fact suggests a strong relation between *P* and schizophrenia and, according to Eysenck, may hold the key to a biological explanation of psychoticism (Eysenck, 1982, p. 20). At the present time, however, there is only rudimentary research evidence to support Eysenck's speculations about the association between hormones and psychoticism.

Personality Development

In Eysenck's view, human beings are biosocial creatures; that is, people are born with certain innate predispositions to respond in particular ways to the environment, but these predispositions (or traits) can be altered to some extent by socialization demands. Thus, the environment and our genes interact to produce behavior; biological factors typically play the stronger role.

The Role of Heredity

Eysenck found the strong genetic basis of the primary personality types confirmed in three ways: (1) the same three personality orientations are found universally, despite the unique social and cultural factors that pressure individuals in different national groups to behave in ways consistent with their national affiliations; (2) these traits show stability within given individuals over long periods of time, during which a variety of experiences occur without appreciably modifying basic responses; (3) the evidence provided by twin studies is consistent with the genetic hypothesis.

Carefully translated versions of the EPQ have been administered to large samples of people in a variety of nations and then factor-analyzed using a special method designed to show whether or not the same factors or different factors appear in all the cultures. If environment or culture played the major part in determining personality, we would expect to find different numbers and kinds of factors; if genetics played the major role, we would expect to find the same three factors despite cultural variations. Eysenck reported support for the genetic hypothesis: The same three factors emerge from the analysis despite cultural variations—or variations in age and sex, for that matter. These primary factors have been found in both males and females in 35 nations, including Greece, France, Spain, Hungary, Japan, Egypt, Iran, Iceland, Sri Lanka, Uganda, the Commonwealth of Independent States (formerly the Soviet Union), and the United States (Eysenck, 1990, pp. 245–246). Studies utilizing the **Junior Eysenck Personality Question-naire** (Eysenck, S. B. G., 1965) to measure extraversion, neuroticism, and psychoticism in children within different cultures—including Hungary, Spain, Japan, Singapore, and Greece—have found results similar to those obtained with adults (Eysenck & Eysenck, 1985, pp. 102–107).

Other studies have found the same three dimensions—introversion/extraversion, stability/neuroticism, and impulse control/psychoticism—in children as well as adults (Rachman, 1969, pp. 253–254). Numerous longitudinal studies have shown, moreover, that these three traits are stable from childhood to adulthood. Individuals who are introverted in childhood, for example, tend to be introverted in adulthood (Eysenck & Eysenck, 1985, pp. 113–114). In other words, study participants respond consistently to the trait questionnaires, despite the many experiences that have occurred during the long intervals between testing.

Finally, Eysenck reviewed a number of studies using identical and fraternal twins, raised together or apart, who were given the same tests to assess extraversion and neuroticism. These studies allow investigators to make relatively precise determinations of the contributions made by genetic and environmental factors to the development of these traits. (To review the logic and rationale of twin studies, see Chapter 9.) One study showed that, for extraversion, the intraclass correlation for **monozygotic twins** (MZ twins) brought up together was .42; for MZ twins raised apart, it was .61; and for **dizygotic twins** (DZ twins), it was −.17. Thus, MZ twins, whether raised apart or together, were more alike in extraversion than were DZ twins (Eysenck & Eysenck, 1985, pp. 93–95). For neuroticism, the corresponding correlations were .38, .53, and .11, respectively; these results again support the genetic hypothesis, even though the correlations for MZ twins raised apart are higher than the correlations for MZ twins raised together and seem counterintuitive. Furthermore, twin studies focusing on the biological basis of various psychoses, such as schizophrenia and manic-depression, also suggest that heredity plays an important part in the development of these disorders (Eysenck, 1967, p. 222).

The Role of Socialization

According to Eysenck, socialized conduct is mediated by conscience, which he defines as the sum total of an individual's learned or conditioned responses (CRs). Individuals learn behaviors that run counter to their own wishes in order to avoid being punished by authority figures such as parents, teachers, and clergy. For example, they must learn to be clean, not to defecate or urinate whenever and wherever they please, and to control their sexual and aggressive impulses. They also must learn not to lie, not to fight with others who disagree with them, and not to steal. Any performance of these behaviors meets with punishment. Eventually, the mere thought of performing the behavior produces an unpleasant emotional reaction, and the act is avoided. Later, these unpleasant emotional reactions occur in the presence of similar activities and lead to an avoidance of these secondary activities as well. For instance, a child may be punished severely for stealing from a particular playmate. Later he may experience unpleasant feelings if he even thinks about stealing from *any* of his peers. Thus, through conditioning, individuals learn to desist from performing behaviors that society deems harmful. The members of society also reward individuals for exhibiting certain behaviors, and thereby shape their behavior in ways that society considers acceptable.

Individuals differ in the degree to which they learn the rules of society. Specifically, Eysenck proposed that introverts learn the rules more quickly and efficiently than do extraverts. He believes that the basis for these differences is genetic: Introverts have chronically higher cortical arousal than do extraverts; arousal tends to facilitate learning; therefore, introverts learn more readily than extraverts (Eysenck & Eysenck, 1985, p. 241). Because it is more difficult for extraverts to learn societal rules, they tend to be undersocialized, whereas extreme introverts tend to be oversocialized. Extraverts are less mature generally than introverts; that is, introverts learn how to behave appropriately (in line with societal demands) at a much earlier age. For extraverts to learn the appropriate behaviors, it takes many more instances of pairing the lying—or stealing or other behavior—with punishments before the lessons are learned. Thus, extraverts are older by the time they finally learn appropriate behaviors, if they ever learn them well.

Because they are less readily conditioned, extraverts experience less inhibition with respect to antisocial behavior. Thus, criminals tend to be extraverted. Extraversion in combination with neuroticism, Eysenck noted, facilitates the development of criminality, because neurotics are relatively anxious, and anxiety drives people who have acquired antisocial responses (extreme extraverts) to express those responses. Research has also shown that it is primarily the impulsivity rather than the sociability component that is related to criminality.

Introverts, in contrast, are characterized by an overreadiness to form very strong consciences; they tend to be wracked by guilt and anxiety whenever they think about violating the rules of society. As a result, they are unlikely to turn to crime. Eysenck believed that, under stressful conditions, extreme introversion may lead to obsessive-compulsive, phobic, or depressive behavior (Eysenck, H. J., 1965, p. 267). Eysenck also explained the shyness of neurotic introverts in terms of their innate arousal levels. Shyness is likely to occur in social situations characterized by stress, such as meeting new people or facing the possibility of criticism or disapproval by authority figures. Because introverts are chronically aroused, and neurotic people are innately more susceptible to stress, social situational stress is likely to produce withdrawal in people who combine these traits (Eysenck & Eysenck, 1985, pp. 316–317).

Psychoticism and intelligence level have also been linked to antisocial and criminal behavior (Eysenck & Eysenck, 1985, pp. 330–332; Eysenck & Gudjonsson, 1989, pp. 49–55). Criminals tend to have low IQs, according to Eysenck. One possible explanation, he suggested, is that people whose intelligence is low enough to prove a handicap in achieving educational success will find it difficult to earn a satisfactory living along conventional lines and, therefore, may turn to crime. Critics argue that it is not low intelligence that causes criminality, but rather the criminals' socioeconomic background. More specifically, they argue that the criminals' poverty deprives them of opportunities to increase their IQs through education, so that eventually they are motivated to engage in illegal activities. But Eysenck maintained that the scientific evidence shows that IQ has an effect on criminal behavior *independent* of social class (and race, for that matter). He admitted that all the data used to reach this conclusion are based on offenders who have been caught, and the possibility exists that the more intelligent lawbreakers, whether violent or white-collar criminals, simply never get caught. But he maintained that the number of such criminals is relatively small and would not appreciably change his basic conclusion.

Despite the genetic basis of personality, Eysenck was most emphatic in pointing out that personality development can and does respond to socialization. He rejected the view that, if heredity is so important, modification of behavior is impossible. Predispositions for a person to behave in a certain manner are genetically determined, but these tendencies to respond can be modified by environmental influences (Eysenck, 1982, p. 29). For example, even though extraverts generally condition poorly, they can learn societal rules well if they are subjected to rigorous and prolonged training by parents and others, and so can be prevented from engaging in antisocial acts. Conversely, introverts may eventually engage in criminal acts if their parents neglect to provide them with appropriate training.

Intelligence, Heredity, and Social Policy

Although Eysenck did not formally incorporate intelligence into his tripartite typology, he did argue strongly that, as a major aspect of personality, intelligence must be considered in any discussion of the socialization process.

Eysenck believed that, as with the three primary types, intelligence has strong genetic roots, but its development can be altered by environmental influences. On the basis of considerable research, Eysenck concluded that approximately 80% of human intelligence is inherited, whereas 20% can be attributed to the influence of the environment (Eysenck, 1975, p. 244). Like Cattell, he used research data based on twin studies as evidence of its strong biological base. (See Chapter 9.) Eysenck also cited IQ comparisons between various other blood relatives: Generally speaking, the closer the degree of kinship between two individuals—that is, the more genes they share in common—the more similar are their IQs. For example, brothers resemble each other in IQ more than do first cousins (Eysenck & Kamin, 1981, p. 51).

To Eysenck, it was abundantly clear that human beings are genetically unequal in traits and intellectual abilities. Yet many modern sociologists and psychologists continue to insist that we are all genetically equal, out of a concern that recognition of genetic inequalities would lead to unequal treatment before the law, inequality of opportunity, and political inequality (Eysenck, 1975, p. 22). Eysenck readily acknowledged that their fears have a solid basis in fact, as evidenced by the crude eugenics programs advocated by proponents of the genetic position in the early 1900s (and today by Cattell); those programs gave rise to laws that restricted the immigration of groups considered inferior into the United States and provided for sterilization of all individuals labeled as feebleminded.

While sympathizing with the concerns of professionals who seek to protect the rights of all citizens, Eysenck strongly opposed the distortion or denial of scientific facts.

> [What I am] trying to point out is that equality before the law, equality of opportunity, and equality as a citizen, are not dependent on *identity* of genetic endowment; *these are human rights, of universal validity, which are independent of biological findings.* Indeed, it would be extremely dangerous to argue … that people are universally entitled to these equal rights *because* they are genetically equal; if science should prove that such genetic equality was a myth … the whole case for equality as a human right would fall to the ground. [S]cience does indeed show that genetic equality is a myth. [However], this does not in any way lead to an argument favoring inequality before the law, inequality of opportunity, or inequality of political rights. (Eysenck, 1975, p. 22)

Rejecting the crude eugenics position, Eysenck did favor a meritocracy. People with the highest ability levels should be selected for access to higher educational and career opportunities, without regard for their race, sex, age, religion, ethnic background, or social class. He noted that many people oppose a meritocracy on the grounds that it leads to elitism. However, Eysenck said that such people seldom consider the alternative, namely, allowing access to these positions to anyone, irrespective of ability levels. He asked, "If your child needed the services of a brain surgeon to remove a tumor to save his life, would you prefer a brain surgeon of the highest ability, or just any third-rate medical student?" Again, "If your plane had engines that began sputtering, would you prefer a pilot of the highest ability or would just anyone do?" (Eysenck, 1975, p. 222). For Eysenck, the answer was clear: A meritocracy is preferable to a "mediocracy" (Eysenck, 1975, p. 223).

Finally, Eysenck recognized the difficulty of devising an IQ test free of social-class bias in order to make these selections fairly. There is reason to believe that traditional IQ tests discriminate against lower-class individuals by asking for information based on experiences to which they are unlikely to have been exposed. Thus, certain questions may have different meanings for middle-class and lower-class children and adults. One popular IQ test, for example, asks children: "What's the thing for you to do if another boy hits you without meaning to do it?" The correct answer is "Walk away." But for a ghetto child, whose survival depends on being tough, the logical answer is "Hit him back." This answer is considered incorrect and receives a score of zero on the test (Morris, 1982, p. 334).

Eysenck admitted that no IQ test is ever completely culture-free or culture-fair. However, he argued that a revolution now occurring in the IQ testing area will solve the problem. Direct physiological measures of biologically based intelligence are now available. Electrodes placed on the skull measure changes in the electrical activity of the cerebral cortex. The resulting **electroencephalogram (EEG)** can be used to assess **evoked potentials**. If an experimenter presents a visual or auditory stimulus and records the subsequent activity in the brain, the stimulus evokes a series of waves. In highly intelligent people, the waves are complex; in less intelligent individuals, the waves are simpler. (See Figures 10.7 and 10.8.) The differences between high- and low-IQ individuals in the form of the evoked potentials are apparently related to the number of errors made in transmission of the incoming visual and auditory information. Low rates of error are associated with more complex evoked potentials, whereas high error rates are associated with simpler forms. Eysenck believed that the use of such procedures in the future will help ensure fairness in selection procedures (Eysenck & Eysenck, 1985, pp. 167–175). It should be noted, however, that one prominent critic, Leon Kamin, has called into

FIG-10.7 Evoked potential waveforms for six high-IQ and six low-IQ study participants: auditory stimulation. (Adapted from Eysenck, H. J. & Eysenck, M. W., *Personality and Individual Differences: A Natural Science Approach*, p. 170. Copyright © 1985 by Plenum Press. Used with kind permission from Springer Science and Business Media.)

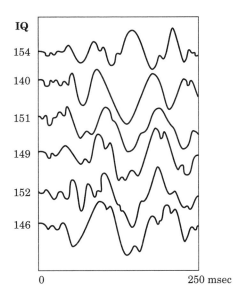

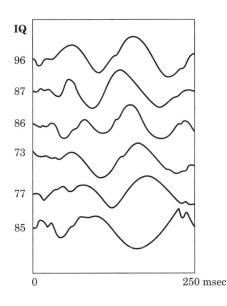

FIG-10.8 Evoked potential waveforms for six high-IQ and six low-IQ study participants: visual stimulation. (Adapted from Eysenck, H. J. & Eysenck, M. W., *Personality and Individual Differences: A Natural Science Approach*, p. 171. Copyright © 1985 by Plenum Press. Used with kind permission from Springer Science and Business Media.)

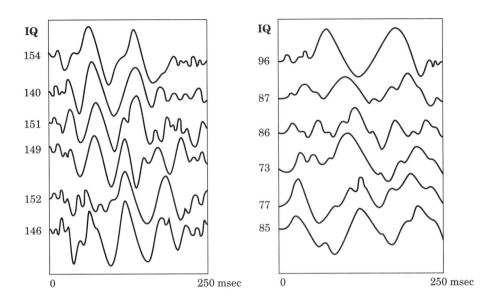

question Eysenck's assertion that psychophysiological response measures are highly correlated with IQ. Kamin maintains that it has been impossible to replicate the results showing more highly complex waves in high-IQ people and simpler waves in low-IQ people (Eysenck & Kamin, 1981, pp. 180–181).

Assessment Techniques

Like Cattell, Eysenck can be considered a psychometrist of personality, because of his insistence on the need for rigorous measurement in studying personality structure and functioning. Seeking to develop reliable and valid measures to assess personality, Eysenck relied heavily on factor analysis and other statistical techniques. Having identified the major dimensions of personality through factor analysis, Eysenck constructed tests to assess them. He then administered the tests to identical and fraternal twins to assess the contribution of genetics to the major dimensions of personality. He also sought to validate his theoretical ideas through a variety of experimental procedures.

To test his hypothesis that introverts condition more quickly and with fewer errors than do extraverts, for example, Eysenck employed a host of experimental techniques, including eye-blink conditioning and vigilance tasks. In the eye-blink paradigm, a tone or other neutral stimulus is used as the conditioned stimulus (CS), and a puff of air to the eye is the unconditioned stimulus (UCS). Conditioning occurs when the CS alone is sufficient to produce the eye-blink response. In general, introverts tend to learn the eye-blink response to the tone more quickly than do extraverts (Eysenck & Eysenck, 1985, pp. 241–248). A typical vigilance task requires study participants to detect sequences of three odd digits in a very long series of digits presented by tape recorder at a rate of one digit per second. For example, in the sequence 1, 4, 8, 2, 5, 4, 1, 3, 9, 4, 2, 6, study participants would have to pick out the sequence 1, 3, 9 (Eysenck, H. J., 1965, p. 42). Introverts are expected to perform better because they are more aroused, and in fact they generally do outperform extraverts on such tasks (Eysenck, H. J., 1965, p. 431).

In testing various aspects of his arousal theory, Eysenck relied on a variety of physiological measures to assess arousal, including heart rate, electroencephalogram,

electrodermal response, and **pupillary response**. Although these physiological measures typically show only modest positive intercorrelations (the typical range is +.20 to +.30), it has been shown quite consistently that introverts manifest greater physiological responsiveness to stimulation than extraverts; the most consistent results are obtained on electrodermal measures (Eysenck & Eysenck, 1985, pp. 205–231). According to Eysenck, not only do introverts demonstrate greater emotional responsiveness, but they also exhibit higher chronic levels of arousal than do extraverts (Eysenck & Eysenck, 1985, pp. 223–224).

Finally, Eysenck used research on lower animals to draw implications about the behavior of humans. For example, he reported exposing rats in a confined space to bright lights and loud noise and then recording their defecation and urination behavior. Animals that showed greater defecation and urination were assumed to be more emotional and reactive to stimuli than were those that showed less of these behaviors. Reactive, emotional rats were then bred with one another, and the nonreactive animals were also interbred. Over several generations, distinct reactive and nonreactive strains developed. Animals in both groups were trained to approach a goal box for food reward by running down an alleyway. Then, as they approached the goal box, all of them were shocked. The animals were then considered to be in conflict: They wanted to approach the goal box to obtain food but feared receiving shock if they did so. The hypothesis was that the reactive strain of animals, being more emotional than the nonreactive strain, would experience more stress in anticipating the electric shock, and correspondingly their goal-box approach responses would be slower. This hypothesis was supported. Eysenck saw clear implications for the behavior of neurotic (high innate emotionality) and nonneurotic (low innate emotionality) humans who are subjected to stress; that is, neurotics experience greater conflict under stress and perform less efficiently than non-neurotics (Eysenck & Eysenck, 1985, pp. 99–100).

Theory's Implications for Therapy

In Eysenck's view, neurotic behavior is most likely to be learned under certain environmental conditions, especially in those individuals who have inherited labile autonomic nervous systems. The acquisition of disordered behavior by such individuals obeys the laws of learning, and these same conditioning principles can be used to eliminate the undesirable behaviors and to teach new, desirable ones. Eysenck called the application of learning theory and principles to the treatment of disordered behavior **behavior therapy**.

Learning theory postulates that neurotic behavior is unadaptive behavior, harmful to the individual or others. People with an extreme dread of spiders, for example, are forced to live circumscribed lives. They may be unable to sleep at night for fear of being bitten. Their inability to sleep peacefully or for long periods of time may make them restless, irritable, and easily fatigued, and thus have a negative effect on their performance at home and their relationships with others. They may avoid social invitations to others' homes because of the possible presence of the feared creatures. They may avoid picnics outdoors, walks in the woods, and a variety of other recreational activities that might result in contact with spiders.

Acquisition of Neurotic Behavior Through Classical Conditioning

In Pavlov's prototypical experiment on **classical conditioning**, a hungry dog who naturally salivated to the sight of food learned to associate a bell—originally a neutral stimulus that did not evoke salivation—with food, so that eventually, after several pairings, the sound of the bell alone acted as a CS to produce salivation. (See Figure 10.9.)

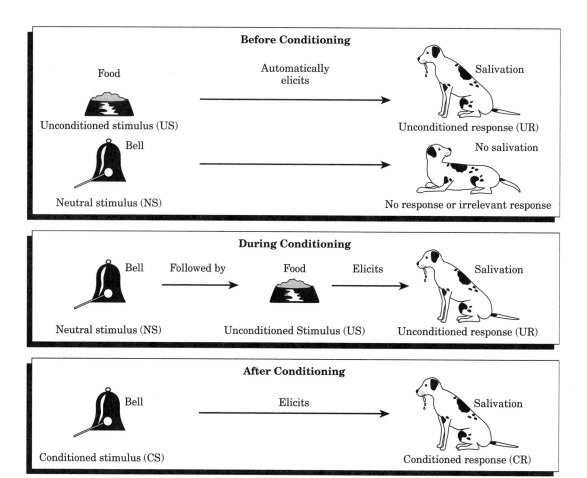

FIG-10.9 Classical conditioning procedure.

In the acquisition of neurotic behavior, Watson's famous (but, by current research standards, ethically questionable) experiment with little Albert provides the classic illustration of the process. Albert was an infant of 11 months who was fond of white rats. He loved playing with them and showed no fear whatsoever. Using classical conditioning, Watson created a phobia for white rats in Albert. Watson stood behind Albert with an iron bar and hammer and, whenever the boy reached for the animal, made an extremely loud noise. In this experiment, the animal was the CS, and the loud, fear-producing noise was the unconditioned stimulus(UCS). As expected, the unconditioned response (UCR), fear, became conditioned to the sight of the rat (the CS), and Albert developed an intense fear of the rat. He would whimper and cry and try to crawl away from it (Eysenck, 1982, pp. 125–126; Watson & Rayner, 1920). Figure 10.10 illustrates this process of phobic conditioning.

Elimination of Neurotic Behavior Through Counterconditioning

Once neurotic behavior has been acquired, one major way to reduce or eliminate it, in Eysenck's view, is through **counterconditioning**. In counterconditioning, the person must learn to make a new response to a CS that elicits maladaptive behavior. The new response is one that is antagonistic to the old one. We know that the autonomic nervous system, which mediates emotional reactions, is divided into two portions, sympathetic and

FIG-10.10 Phobia acquisition via classical conditioning.

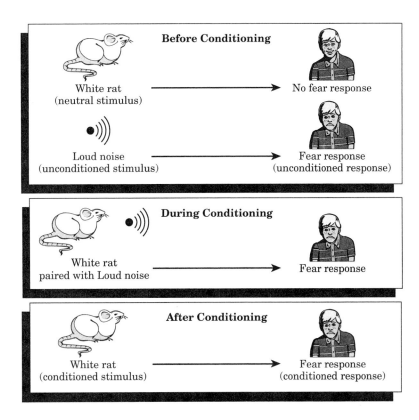

parasympathetic. As we have seen, the sympathetic nervous system prepares the individual for fight (anger) or flight (fear) by slowing down the digestive process and increasing heart and breathing rates. The **parasympathetic nervous system** acts antagonistically: It speeds up the digestive process and slows heart and breathing rates when the person is relaxed.

Watson intended to eliminate the rat phobia in little Albert, but the boy's mother removed him from the hospital before the counterconditioning experiment could be started. Instead, Watson's associate, Mary Jones, conducted a related experiment in which she used counterconditioning to eliminate a fear of rabbits in Peter, a boy about the same age as Albert.

Jones began by offering Peter some chocolate when he was fairly hungry. As he began to eat, she brought the feared object into the room and placed it next to him. The basic idea was to eliminate Peter's phobia about rabbits by counterconditioning him to associate the sight of the rabbit not with fear, but with the pleasant sensations engendered by eating chocolate. A difficulty arose immediately, however, when the experimenter placed the rabbit next to the child. She found that the fear response was so strong that the boy cried despite the chocolate. The experimenter then moved the rabbit to a corner of the room 20 feet away, and the child stopped crying and resumed eating. Gradually, she brought the rabbit closer to Peter until the boy could play with it happily. The sympathetic conditioning of fear was completely eliminated by the parasympathetic conditioning of pleasantness associated with eating chocolate (Eysenck, H. J., 1965, pp. 132–135; Jones, 1924). This counterconditioning process is illustrated in Figure 10.11.

Use of Behavior Therapy to Eliminate Disorders

Eysenck advocated three major behavior techniques that have been used successfully to treat a variety of phobias—fears of the dark, heights, closed spaces, snakes, spiders, dogs, hospitals, and dentists—as well as enuresis (bedwetting), obsessions, compulsions, test

FIG-10.11 Reduction of phobia through counterconditioning.

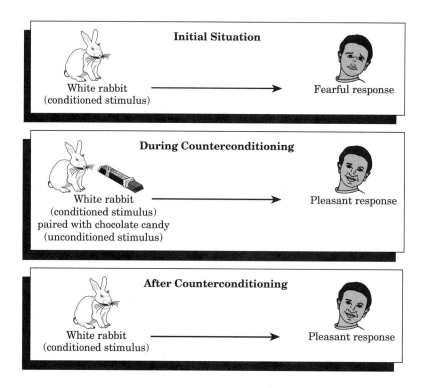

anxiety, and public speaking anxiety. These three techniques are modeling, flooding, and systematic desensitization.

In **modeling**, phobic people watch nonphobics cope successfully with dreaded objects or situations. Clients later confronted with these objects show a reduction or elimination of their fears. (See Chapter 17 for a more detailed presentation of modeling techniques used to treat phobias by social cognitive theorist Albert Bandura.)

In **flooding**, clients are exposed to dreaded objects or situations for prolonged periods of time in order to extinguish their fear. Prolonged rather than brief exposure is generally more effective in reducing or eliminating fear (Hecker & Thorpe, 1987, p. 220). The rationale is that presentation of the feared stimulus initially elicits a strong, negative emotional reaction but that prolonged exposure results in a rapid decline in fearfulness (O'Leary & Wilson, 1987, pp. 166–167). Once the fear is reduced, the person can begin to reappraise the situation and learn that nothing dreadful will happen (Marshall, 1985, p. 132). To ensure full exposure to the dreaded object or situation, the client is prevented from making an avoidance or escape response.

A classic study by Marshall (1985) illustrates phobia reduction in people who are afraid of heights. Before therapy began, clients who reported a fear of heights were given a behavioral test requiring them to walk as far as they could up a flight of fire-escape stairs. The top step was approximately 30 feet above the ground. Clients generally became very upset when they were only 6.5 feet above the ground. At this point, they stopped and would go no further. They were then brought to the flat roof of a six-storey building that was surrounded by a guardrail 3 feet from the edge. The therapist instructed the clients to walk to the railing and look down at the street below. They were told to remain there, no matter how anxious they felt, until the therapist signaled the end of the session. Some of the clients were exposed only briefly (approximately 9 minutes) to the dreaded situation; others were exposed to it for a longer period (approximately 30 minutes). All clients were then retested by having them walk up the fire-escape stairs. Most of the clients who were exposed for long periods were able to walk up to the 20-foot level; a few walked up the entire 30 feet. Clients exposed for brief periods improved only slightly (walked up 7 or 8 feet), and a few actually worsened. A follow-up study one month later showed that the long-exposure clients maintained their gains, whereas the brief-exposure clients showed no improvement.

There have been dozens of exposure-based, flooding studies, and the results indicate that the treatment procedure is highly effective in eliminating a variety of phobias (Olatunji, Deacon, & Abramowitz, 2009, pp. 172–180). However, Olatunji et al. argue that, since exposure to feared objects creates extremely high levels of fear in clients initially, such research should be conducted only by well-trained and experienced therapists who scrupulously follow ethical standards, including obtainment of Informed Consent from patients as soon as possible in treatment. (See Chapter 1 for information on Informed Consent.)

In contrast to flooding, **systematic desensitization** involves a gradual, client-controlled exposure to the anxiety-eliciting object or situation. Systematic desensitization involves counterconditioning by having the client make a response antagonistic to anxiety in the presence of the anxiety-evoking stimuli, so that the anxiety is suppressed. Typically, clients are trained in muscle relaxation, which results in lowered physiological arousal and feelings of calmness. The clients construct a hierarchy of anxiety-eliciting situations, ranging from mildly stressful to very stressful. Then, while deeply relaxed, clients are asked to imagine the mildest situation. If they experience great anxiety, they are instructed to stop visualizing the scene and to restore bodily relaxation. The scene is then repeated until they can visualize it without anxiety, and then the next item in the hierarchy is presented. Clients proceed through the hierarchy until they can be exposed to even the most threatening stimuli without distress. Then they are given a behavioral test to determine if the fear has been eliminated.

Systematic desensitization procedures can be used effectively in actual situations. For example, Redd (1980) reports that a cancer patient who had undergone successful gastrointestinal surgery for the removal of a tumor could not retain solid foods. Even though the cancer had been removed, the patient reported that, as she began to eat, she experienced discomfort, believed that it was caused by her cancer, became anxious, and vomited. As a result, she had lost 25 pounds and was readmitted to the hospital because of her weakened condition. The patient was trained to relax and then given small amounts of food while relaxed. She consumed a cup of soup without gagging or regurgitating. She was then given a spoonful of egg, gagged on it, and regurgitated the second spoonful. She began to cry and said she knew she would never be able to eat again. The therapist reassured her that she would. During the next session, she experienced some anxiety, but completed the relaxation exercises. She was then able to consume one egg. After 14 sessions, she was able to eat all the foods presented to her. During the next 10 days the therapist met with her and praised her lavishly for her progress in putting on weight. When she regained her strength, she left the hospital and returned home. A nine-month follow-up showed no new problems or symptoms.

Evaluative Comments

We can now examine the scientific worth of Eysenck's theory.

Comprehensiveness   Eysenck's theory is clearly comprehensive; it addresses a broad range of normal and abnormal phenomena. Thus, Eysenck sought to understand a wide variety of normal and abnormal behaviors, including student study behavior, coffee drinking, smoking, alcoholism and other drug use, sexual practices, phobias, criminal behavior, the creative behavior of normal people as well as geniuses and psychotics, physical diseases, and neurotic and psychotic behavior.

Precision and testability   Eysenck, like Cattell, worked diligently to construct precise measures of his theoretical concepts. However, most of his efforts centered on the construction of tests to assess the major dimensions of personality. There are measurement problems with the concept of arousal, as Eysenck acknowledged, but work to rectify these difficulties continues. In comparison to the Freudian viewpoint and its variants, Eysenck's theory is much more precisely stated and testable.

Parsimony   Eysenck's theory fails to meet the parsimony criterion. For example, he himself acknowledged that the three major types, extraversion, neuroticism, and psychoticism, cannot adequately describe personality functioning. Some of the traits that make up the types appear to describe aspects of personality functioning independently of the three types. According to Eysenck, however, these traits could not be measured as reliably as the three types, nor could they be linked as easily to other physiological measures and other types of laboratory measures. Thus, Eysenck advocated focusing first on the three types before utilizing the more specific traits (Eysenck & Eysenck, 1985, p. 74). In this respect, he clearly differed from Cattell, who now conducts research with approximately 35 normal and abnormal primary traits. As a result, Eysenck's theory appears to be too economical, although one can appreciate the rationale for his decision.

The fact that Eysenck's theory lacks an explicit and independent situational taxonomy also makes it simplistic. He focuses primarily on the biological end of personality and does not fully address the differential impact of various situations on people. Instead of extending the theory to include an independent assessment of the impact of these situational influences, Eysenck argued that his type and trait approach implicitly acknowledges the role of the situation. He maintained that people with particular personality traits *choose* the situations in which they find themselves: An interest in books takes the introverted person to the library and bookstores; an interest in sports takes the athletic person to the athletic field and the gym; an interest in opera takes the person to the theatre, and so forth. Eysenck maintained, therefore, that the kind of situations in which these people operate is not primary; instead, it is the kinds of previously existing systems of likes and dislikes—that is, traits, that rule their behavior (Eysenck & Eysenck, 1985, p. 35).

Although Eysenck's contention has some validity, it does not address the many involuntary situations that do have an independent and differential impact on specific kinds of people. The athlete finds himself or herself in academic situations like classes on astronomy or physics; the bookworm finds himself or herself assigned by the campus administration to a small room with two other roommates even though he or she prefers living in a room by himself or herself; or the extraverted student who prefers a large triple is assigned to a single room. This problem was not addressed by Eysenck.

Eysenck also argued that the names of given traits usually imply the situations in which they can be demonstrated and measured. Thus, he maintained, a trait theory indirectly implies a taxonomy of situations (Eysenck & Eysenck, 1985, pp. 38–39). For example, the trait of sociability can only refer to situations involving relatively free interactions between people; the trait of athleticism implies situations where one can test one's athletic skills. Yet Eysenck seemed to be treating the concept of situations much too globally. Situations involving sociability, for example, can be distinguished one from another— office parties, business meetings, home parties, receiving lines at the opera, or dorm parties—and it is doubtful that these specific kinds of situations would all have the same impact on the sociable person.

Empirical validity   There is considerable empirical support for Eysenck's arousal theory, especially as it applies to the differential behaviors of introverts and extraverts. However, much more research is required to test Eysenck's ideas about the differential behavior of neurotics and psychotics. Also, Eysenck's interesting and provocative theory of genius, which shows its links to biology and psychopathology, needs much research (Eysenck, 1995, p. 9).

Heuristic value   There is much to be admired in Eysenck's prodigious efforts as a scientist. He was seen by many psychologists as an excellent scholar, highly creative, and incredibly productive. Although much of his influence has been in Great Britain, many American psychologists are familiar with his work. Because the language of Eysenck's theory is less forbidding, it is more appealing to researchers than is Cattell's approach. In fact, the popularity of Eysenck's theory is growing rapidly in the United States and is likely to increase even more as his colleagues continue to work to refine and extend it.

Applied value   Eysenck was one of the pioneers in creating the behavior therapy movement. His views on the acquisition and elimination of behavioral disorders has had a positive impact on behavior therapists. Thus, his theory has strong applied value in helping people cope successfully with a variety of behavioral disorders.

CRITICAL THINKING QUESTIONS

1. Do you think that Eysenck's use of only three types to describe personality functioning is an over-simplification? Why or why not?
2. Why are extraverts more likely to engage in a wider variety of sexual activities than introverts?
3. Are you primarily introverted or extraverted? How does your personality orientation influence your study behavior and your personal relationships?
4. Do you see any problems with Eysenck's proposed meritocracy in selecting individuals for higher educational opportunities? How would you ensure equal treatment for everyone, yet still make sure that society had the most competent people in the various occupations?
5. What principles of learning do behavior therapists rely on to eliminate phobias? Are the procedures they use to eliminate fears effective, in your opinion?

GLOSSARY

androgens   Male sex hormones; in mammals, the principal one is testosterone.

antigens   Protein or carbohydrate substances (such as toxins or enzymes) that, when introduced into the body, stimulate the production of antibodies.

arousal theory   Explanation of behavioral differences in terms of the interactions between inherited levels of nervous system arousal and levels of environmental stimulation.

ascending reticular activating system (ARAS)   The part of the central nervous system located in the lower brain stem; it is involved in the arousal of the cerebral cortex.

autonomic nervous system   The part of the peripheral nervous system—usually not under the individual's voluntary control—that regulates the operation of internal organs and glands; it consists of sympathetic and parasympathetic subsystems.

behavior therapy   Multifaceted approach to the treatment of disorders based on the principles of conditioning, counterconditioning, extinction, and reinforcement.

classical conditioning   Association learning whereby a neutral stimulus ispaired with an unconditioned stimulus (UCS) that naturally evokes an unconditioned response (UCR). Through pairing with the UCS, the neutral stimulus becomes a conditioned stimulus (CS), which, when presented in the absence of the UCS, evokes a conditioned response (CR) that is similar to the UCR.

Convergent thinking   A type of critical thinking which involves focusing in on one idea from an array of ideas in arriving at a solution that society later sees as, not only original, but as socially useful.

cortical arousal   State of the cortex during periods of perceptual or cognitive activity.

counterconditioning   Procedure often utilized for therapeutic purposes, in which a conditioned response (CR) is weakened by associating the stimulus (CS) that evokes it with a new response that is antagonistic (incompatible) with the CR.

divergent thinking   The ability to think along many different paths, to consider alternatives not ordinarily considered in trying to solve problems.

dizygotic twins   Twins that develop simultaneously from two separate fertilized eggs (also called fraternal twins).

dopamine   A neurotransmitter or chemical in the brain that, in excessive amounts, can reduce cognitive inhibitions.

electrodermal response   Changes in the electrical conductance of the skin that are associated with arousal.

electroencephalogram (EEG)   Recording of electrical activity in the cerebral cortex obtained by means of electrodes placed on the skull.

evoked potentials   Patterns of waves that occur in the brain following its stimulation.

extraverts   Individuals who have an outgoing and sociable approach to life.

Eysenck Personality Questionnaire (EPQ)   An inventory designed to measure the major personality types in adults.

flooding   Form of behavior therapy in which the client is exposed to the most intense stimuli that evoke fear, typically for prolonged periods of time, in an effort to extinguish it.

hedonic tone   Positive or negative feelings and evaluations associated with various levels of arousal.

inhibition theory   Explanation of behavioral differences on the basis of inhibitory cortical processes that hinder nervous-system arousal.

introverts   Individuals who have a shy and retiring approach to life.

Junior Eysenck Personality Questionnaire   Inventory designed to measure the major personality types in children.

modeling   Demonstration of behavior by one person so that another person can imitate it.

monozygotic twins   Twins who develop from the splitting of a single fertilized egg (also called identical twins).

neurotics   Individuals who are emotionally unstable and overly reactive to stimuli.

parasympathetic nervous system   Division of the autonomic nervous system that conserves bodily energies by slowing heart and breathing rates.

psychopathology   Various forms of disordered behavior that vary in terms of the severity of impairment.

psychotics   Individuals who are aloof, inhumane, aggressive, and insensitive to the needs of others, but also creative.

pupillary response   Changes in dilation of the pupils of the eyes associated with arousal.

reactive inhibition   Each time a person responds, a small increment of neural fatigue is built up. Over many responses, fatigue builds to the point where the person stops responding.

schizophrenia   Severe psychotic disorder characterized by flat or inappropriate emotion and by withdrawal from external reality and other people. Schizophrenics are also characterized by thought disorder. While their lack of cognitive inhibition may sometimes result in creative test performances because it allows them to think in unusual ways, sometimes their inability to control the running together of ideas produces gibberish.

serotonin   A chemical neurotransmitter in the brain believed to be associated with psychoticism and schizophrenic thinking.

sympathetic nervous system   Division of the autonomic nervous system that mobilizes the body's resources for action, speeding up heart and breathing rates and slowing the digestive process.

systematic desensitization   Behavior therapy designed to reduce the strong anxieties associated with various stimuli; the client is gradually exposed to them and, at each level in the anxiety hierarchy, learns new responses through counterconditioning.

typology A means of classifying behavior through the use of continuous, highly abstract concepts (types) that encompass clusters of correlated traits.

visceral brain Parts of the brain that underlie emotional feelings and expression; also known as the limbic system.

SUGGESTED READINGS

Eysenck, H. J. (1967). *The biological basis of personality.* Springfield, IL: Charles C Thomas.

Eysenck, H. J. (1970). *The structure of human personality* (3rd ed.). London: Methuen.

Eysenck, H. J. (1995). *Genius: The natural history of creativity.* New York: Cambridge University Press.

Eysenck, H. J., & Eysenck, M. W. (1985). *Personality and individual differences: A natural science approach.* New York: Plenum Press.

PART 4

Quiz 4

Cognitive Perspectives

To understand the role of cognition in current theories of personality, we must first examine the meaning of the term. In ordinary language, *cognition* refers to the thoughts or ideas we have about the world around us. Thus, in the broadest sense, we are talking about symbols that occur inside us and that help us make sense of the world. Technically, theories of cognition are concerned with how we gather information about events and how we process this information in order to act on the environment.

If cognition involves internal ideas or thoughts, it could be argued that the various psychodynamic and trait theories considered so far are all cognitive. After all, Freud's concept of the ego deals, in large measure, with our attempts to understand external reality and to perform those behaviors that will maximize our pleasure. The conflicts between id and superego also involve the use of internalized rules to restrict the expression of inappropriate id impulses. These rules, which we use frequently in decision making, can be construed as primarily cognitive in nature.

The trait concept employed by Allport, Cattell, and Eysenck to account for personality functioning is also a cognitive construct. Traits are beliefs assumed to guide behaviors and influence judgments about the environment. Allport goes beyond Cattell in postulating a developmental process of becoming that is largely cognitive: For Allport, the mature person is one who is capable of making use of information in a rational way. The self-actualization theories created by Maslow and Rogers can also be construed as cognitive, as we shall see in Part 5; so can the work of some of the social-learning theorists reviewed in Part 6. These positions incorporate cognitive constructs such as expectancy, imitation, verbal and pictorial imagery, and memory.

Why, then, is this section of the text limited to Kelly's theory? The answer is that, although many other theories have elements of cognition, Kelly's stands alone as a comprehensive and pure cognitive theory of personality, focused solely on the ways in which we process information as a means of increasing our understanding of the world. His is a largely intellectualized view of personality that sees all of us acting as scientists in order to predict and control events. In Kelly's view, we are all continually trying to make sense of our world by forming hypotheses about how it works, testing them in the real world, and then revising them if they do not fit or work. Our aim, according to him, is to maximize our predictive accuracy about the ways in which the world operates.

To present this view, Kelly built a theory with a brand new terminology and changed or did away with many of the traditional concepts used in psychology to explain the actions of individuals. For example, Kelly did away with the concept of need as it was used by traditional learning theorists. In their view, individuals in a quiescent state start to experience bodily needs for food, water, and sex. These needs then motivate them to seek objects that reduce their tensions so that they can once again exist in a homeostatic state. Kelly also did away with the concept of incentive, whereby people are motivated to work toward the attainment of certain goals for reinforcement. Kelly did not like the conceptualization of human beings as inert objects who have to be prodded into action by internal needs or by external incentives and reinforcements. Instead, he postulated that human beings are born in process; they continually seek to predict accurately events in the world around them (Kelly, 1955, pp. 35–49). For Kelly, people are not passive pawns controlled by cyclic internal urges or external demands. Instead, they are very often active, curious, and creative beings who are continually seeking to increase their understanding of the world. Kelly clearly believed that human beings are motivated, but the focus is on cognitive motivation and not on biological drives rooted in tissue needs.

Kelly also had little use for the concept of reinforcement as it is traditionally used by learning theorists. For example, he rejected the empirical law of effect, which states that behavior is more likely to occur again if it has been followed by a positive reinforcer and less likely to occur again if it has been followed by a punishing stimulus, because this law suggests that our behavior is under the control of external influences. Instead, he believed that our actions are controlled more by cognitive processes: What is important is our anticipation of events and the subsequent validation of our predictions.

In Chapter 11, we take a close look at Kelly's unique and clearly stated theory. We begin by examining the fundamental assumption underlying the theory—the philosophical stance called *constructive alternativism*. After outlining the basic terms of the theory, we present the fundamental postulate and numerous corollaries of his personal-construct position. Next, we examine Kelly's Role Construct Repertory Test (RCRT), which is designed to measure individuals' personal-construct systems. We then discuss Kelly's view of psychotherapy and the roles of therapist and client. An actual case history illustrates how Kelly's theory is applied to psychopathology. Finally, a review of the research shows how investigators have used variants of Kelly's RCRT to study the cognitive functioning and behavior of schizophrenic patients.

CHAPTER 11

Kelly's Theory of Personal Constructs

Robert D. Farber University Archives & Special Collections Department, Brandeis University Libraries.

Biographical Sketch

George Alexander Kelly was born in a small town in Kansas in 1905, the only child of a Presbyterian minister and his wife. He attended high school in Wichita, Kansas, and then Friends University, where he enrolled in courses in music and public debating. He graduated from Park College in 1926 with a degree in mathematics and physics. He flirted with the idea of becoming an aeronautical engineer but eventually committed himself to education. He held a variety of jobs; for instance, he taught speech-making to students in a labor college and taught an Americanization class for recent immigrants.

In 1929, he was awarded an exchange scholarship and spent a year at the University of Edinburgh, where he earned a bachelor's degree in education. He returned to the United States with a developing interest in psychology and entered the graduate program in that field at the University of Iowa. In 1931, he was awarded his Ph.D. for a dissertation in the area of speech and reading disabilities.

Kelly's professional career in psychology began with his acceptance of a position at Fort Hays State College in Kansas. Soon afterward, he began developing psychological services for the State of Kansas; he established a network of traveling clinics throughout the state. It was during this period that Kelly largely abandoned the psychoanalytic approach to human personality. He reported that his clinical experiences had taught him that people in the Midwest were paralyzed by prolonged drought, dust storms, and economic concerns, rather than by overflowing libidinal forces. He began to develop his own theory, which he based partly on his observation of a friend who took a part in a dramatic production in college, lived it for the two or three weeks the play was in rehearsal, and was profoundly influenced by it. Kelly noted that, although many people would dismiss his friend's efforts as sheer affectation, in fact his behavior was not false or without substance. It eventually expressed his real self. This experience led Kelly to formulate a fixed-role therapy technique designed to help people overcome their own limitations.

The crux of Kelly's theory of personal **constructs** arose from his observation that "people tended to have the symptoms they had read about or had seen in other people" (Kelly, 1955, Vol. 1, p. 366). When the terms, or constructs, *inferiority complex* and *anxiety* were popular in the 1920s and 1930s, people began to describe themselves as having inferiority complexes or anxieties. These self-descriptions were subsequently used in their interpretations of reality. Kelly's preoccupation with the structure of language and the impact of language and roles on behavior led him to read the works of the eminent linguist Korzybski and the role-playing theorist Jacob Moreno; on the basis of his reading, he was able to refine his theory (Kelly, 1955, Vol. 1, pp. 360–366).

After a stint in the navy as an aviation psychologist during World War II, Kelly was appointed associate professor at the University of Maryland. He left Maryland in 1946 to become professor of psychology and director of clinical psychology at Ohio State University. During the following two decades, Kelly continued conducting research and formulating his theory. He also taught a number of courses for graduate students who were training to become clinical psychologists. Some of his students disliked and feared him. There were several reasons for their feelings. First, he could be very formal in his interactions with them. He insisted, for example, that students call him "Professor Kelly" and on his calling them "Mister" "Miss," or "Mrs.," right up to the acceptance of their Ph.D. dissertation. Then he told them to call him "George" and he called them by their first names. Second, students who did not measure up to his (and the department's) high standards could well find themselves face-to-face with Kelly in his office where he would dismiss them rather quickly from the program. Third, a few students found some of his behavior hurtful. For example, when one of his students asked Kelly to autograph one of his books, Kelly wrote:

To a promising student,
who, while I'm not sure
what he actually promises,
will certainly produce
something worth-while for
those whom he touches. (Fransella, 1995, p. 25)

The student felt insulted because he thought that, while the first line was complimentary, the second two were hostile, whereas the last three were merely polite. Despite the fact that he was disliked by some students for his sometimes abrasive behavior, the majority of the students liked him and respected his brilliant intellect. In addition, many of his students agreed that he was a fine teacher. As one of his ex-students, Brendan Maher, put it:

He was undoubtedly one of the small number of true teachers that I have met. He was delighted to hear the student's ideas, to encourage and help the student to bring them to a successful completion. This is the kind of thing that does not make students into mechanical imitators, nor indeed into disciples, in the narrow sense of the word. What it did do was to make many of us feel that he respected us, was willing to have us disagree with him and that he always had at the back of his own head the possibility that he might be wrong; it made us into lifelong friends, admirers of Kelly the man, aware of the possibility of error in our own convictions, and free to pursue our ideas as we saw fit, and know that we were honoring his teaching in doing so. (Fransella, 1995, p. 26)

It should also be noted that many of his former students have become prominent figures in psychology.

Finally, during his tenure at Ohio State University, he produced his major theoretical work, *The Psychology of Personal Constructs*. He also traveled widely and lectured at many universities throughout the world. In 1965, he accepted the Riklis Chair of Behavioral Science at Brandeis University. He died in 1967.

Concepts and Principles

Constructive Alternativism

The concept of **constructive alternativism** underlies Kelly's theory of cognition. Quite simply, it is the assumption that all of us are capable of changing or replacing our present interpretation of events (Kelly, 1955, Vol. 1, p. 15). In colloquial terms, we can always change our minds. The assumption also implies that our behavior is never completely determined; we are always free to some extent to reinterpret our experiences. Thus, Kelly believed in the primacy of individuals as responsible agents who make their own choices and decisions. We don't just react to our experiences; we act upon them by interpreting and reinterpreting them in our own idiosyncratic ways (Fransella & Dalton, 1990, p. 1). Yet Kelly also believed that some of our thoughts and behavior are determined by other phenomena. In other words, his theory is constructed on a joint base of freedom and determinism. "Determinism and freedom are inseparable, for that which determines another is, by the same token, free of the other" (Kelly, 1955, Vol. 1, p. 21).

Thus, if a student decides that the attainment of a college degree summa cum laude is important to him or her, this subjective fact will then determine certain other behaviors: For example, he or she will curtail his or her social activities and spend more time studying in the library or the dormitory room. In brief, he or she was free to choose his or her goal but, once chosen, the goal determines certain related behaviors. Translating this example into Kelly's terminology, we can say that the **superordinate construct**, attainment of the college degree, was freely chosen. It then acted to control other **subordinate constructs**—the number of social activities and the number of hours spent studying.

> The relation established by a construct or a construction system over its subordinate elements is deterministic. In this sense the tendency to subordinate constitutes determinism. The natural events themselves do not subordinate our constructions of them, we can look at them in any way we like. The structure we erect is what rules us. (Kelly, 1955, Vol. 1, p. 20)

Theorists who adopt a behavioral stance, in contrast, maintain that all behavior is determined. They disagree with Kelly on the free choice of goals, which, they argue, are also determined by prior experiences.

Every Person as Scientist

Kelly believed that each of us, like the scientist, attempts to predict and control events. We are continually in the process of evaluating and reevaluating our experiences and trying to use our interpretations to understand and control the world around us. We have our own theories about human behavior. We test hypotheses based on the theories, and we weigh the experimental evidence (Kelly, 1955, Vol. 1, p. 5). On the basis of this evidence, the world becomes more predictable, or we come to understand that we must change our concepts or constructs about it if we are to function effectively.

As scientists in this sense, we use our own highly personalized view of reality in making judgments, which are rarely open to the scrutiny of others. Our constructs are not as objectively defined as those used by research scientists, and our theories rarely meet the rigorous criteria set by conventional science. In short, we have rather common-sense views of ourselves and reality, and the possibilities for distortion and error are great. Moreover, many of us continually shift our view of reality to fit the data. No matter how distorted our views of reality are, however, they are still real to us, and we operate accordingly. "A person may misrepresent a real phenomenon, such as his income or his ills, and yet his misrepresentation will itself be entirely real. This applies even to the badly deluded patient: what he perceives may not exist, but his perception does" (Kelly, 1955, Vol. 1, p. 8).

Thus, Kelly embraced the phenomenologist position of the humanist theorists reviewed in Part 5. Like the humanists, Kelly believed we are not passive organisms; we relate actively to the environment, often in creative ways.

The Nature of Constructs and Construing

In building our systems of personal constructs, we place interpretations on events; that is, we construe them. We construe the meaning of events for ourselves through an abstraction process, by placing constructions upon our experiences (Kelly, 1955, Vol. 1, p. 50). We then utilize our constructions to deal with new information from the environment. These interpretations are reality for us and determine how we act. They are also highly personalized: We may have the same experiences as others do, but we often interpret them differently.

The constructs that we form and then use to deal with new experiences are based on our previous experiences. For Kelly, constructs are ways of organizing experiences in terms of similarities and contrasts: "In its minimum context, a construct is a way in which at least two elements are similar and contrast with a third" (Kelly, 1955, Vol. 1, p. 61). Thus, constructs must contain at least three elements and may contain many more. At the same time, they are bipolar; they involve contrasts as well as similarities. To say that an object is a chair implies that it is not also a table. To say that bearded men tend to be virile is to imply that clean-shaven men are impotent.

Because constructs are personal, people may apply different labels to the same experiences. For example, an individual may believe that she is being "pleasant" in interpersonal relationships, while others may see her willingness to yield indiscriminately to their wishes as "excessive dependence." Even when two people label an experience similarly, the contrast end of the dimension may differ. For example, Bill and Jim may both label certain behaviors as "sincere." However, Bill may see behavior at the opposite end of the spectrum as "insincere," whereas Jim may label it "morally degenerate." Thus, Bill might react to these contrast behaviors with mild disapproval, whereas Jim would probably become angry and upset under the same circumstances. Their subsequent behavior toward the person exhibiting the contrast behavior may also differ. Bill might try to reason with the insincere person; Jim might attack or avoid the moral degenerate.

Finally, Kelly believed that constructs are not identical to the verbal labels used to express them. Constructs are actual discriminations people make on an experiential level between varieties of experiences (Bannister, 1977, p. 33). Sometimes people formulate constructs before they can verbalize them. This is particularly true of children, who, for example, may be capable of showing affection toward loved ones but incapable of verbalizing their feelings. People who are disturbed often repress or distort certain experiences and are unable or unwilling to deal with them on a verbal level; therapy with an expert may help them deal with the limitations inherent in their construct systems.

Additional Characteristics of Constructs

Kelly refers to constructs that are highly important in people's lives as **core constructs**. These are beliefs that reflect their personal identity, structures that help maintain their existence. Core constructs are very resistant to change, whereas **peripheral constructs** are relatively easy to change. For many people, a belief in God is a core construct central to their existence. For these same people, their belief that baseball great Ted Williams of the Boston Red Sox hit .401 during the 1941 season is a peripheral belief, which would change readily should they learn that Williams actually hit .406 during the 1941 season. Peripheral constructs, according to Kelly, can be altered without serious modifications in the core structure. In the previous example, changes in the individuals' beliefs about Williams's batting average would not produce any modification in their beliefs about God (Kelly, 1955, Vol. 1, pp. 482–483).

Constructs are arranged hierarchically within a particular person's cognitive world; that is, one construct may subsume one or more other constructs (Kelly, 1955, Vol. 1,

p. 57). For example, a person seen by others as a moralizer may actually use a superordinate construct of good versus bad to control many other concepts: A good person might be intelligent, cooperative, kind, ambitious, and sincere; a bad person might be stupid, competitive, cruel, unambitious, and insincere.

Constructs also vary in their **range of convenience**—the number of other constructs to which they are related; that is, a given construct has relevance for some constructs but not for others (Kelly, 1955, Vol. 1, p. 68). The good/bad dichotomy probably has a wide range of convenience for many people, although they still would not apply it to every construct. Other constructs—fat/thin, for example—are much more limited. We may think of fat people versus thin people, or fat lions versus thin lions, but we do not ordinarily think of fat weather versus thin weather, or fat crying versus thin crying.

Related to a construct's range of convenience is its **permeability**. A construct is considered permeable if it will allow new elements—that is, constructs currently excluded from its range of convenience, to be construed within its framework (Kelly, 1955, Vol. 1, p. 79). For instance, the construct of right versus wrong may allow people to include new ideas and behavior as right or wrong. They may be prepared to make a judgment concerning the moral validity of euthanasia, for example, a topic about which they had previously been ignorant. If the construct were impermeable, they would be incapable of making such a moral evaluation. Of course, it is rare that a construct is completely impermeable; usually, there are varying degrees of permeability. By introducing the notion of permeability, Kelly made allowances for change in the system. Other ways of talking about change would include growth, personal development, and realization of the self.

In short, Kelly has posited a complicated, hierarchical system of cognition populated by personal constructs derived from experience that now control or determine the ways in which the person will react to incoming stimuli or information. Although much of the person's behavior is determined by such constructs, there is also room within the system for change because the superordinate concepts are free and often permeable. Change in these permeable constructs would then produce changes in the subordinate construct system.

In addition, Kelly proposed that constructs could be characterized as preemptive, constellatory, and propositional. A construct that includes only its own elements and precludes these elements from being part of other constructs is called a **preemptive construct**. For instance, a person may argue that "anything which is a ball can be nothing but a ball"; thus, balls cannot be "pellets," "spheres," or "shots" (Kelly, 1955, Vol. 1, p. 153). Such black-or-white thinking sometimes characterizes interpersonal relationships as well, as when someone argues that "capitalism is nothing but exploitation of the masses by big business," or "the health-care bill endorsed by Obama is nothing but an attempt by big government to control every aspect of our lives."

A **constellatory construct** "permits its elements to belong to other realms concurrently, but fixes their realm memberships" (Kelly, 1955, Vol. 1, p. 155). Stereotypes belong to this category; that is, once we identify persons or objects as members of a given category, we then attribute to them a cluster, or constellation, of other characteristics or traits. Although we are fully aware that we tend to stereotype people in terms of ethnic and cultural backgrounds, we also have reliable stereotypes of people (that may have harmful consequences) on the basis of other, seemingly insignificant characteristics, such as hair color. For example, Lawson (1971) asked college men and women to rate fictitious people with different hair colors on a variety of personality characteristics. He found that men tended to see blonde women as more beautiful, delicate, and feminine than either brunettes or redheads. Both men and women rated brunette women most favorably, and artificial or bleached blondes most unfavorably. Brunettes were seen as intelligent, ambitious, sincere, strong, safe, valuable, and effective. Both men and women also gave their highest rating to dark-haired men, who were seen as more handsome, intelligent, ambitious, sincere, strong, rugged, valuable, effective, and masculine than were men with blond or red hair. Men with blond hair were generally rated more favorably than were redheads. Thus, people with certain genetic traits may become victims of other people's constellatory constructs, or stereotypes.

Finally, a construct whose elements are open to construction in every respect is called a **propositional construct**. "Any round object can be considered, among other things, to be a ball." Under this construct, a ball can also be elliptical, worn, or small. Propositional thinking is flexible thinking. The person is continuously open to new experience and is capable of modifying existing constructs. In Kelly's view, the person best equipped to deal with the environment is one who knows the circumstances under which propositional or preemptive thinking is appropriate. If we relied exclusively on propositional thinking, we would be immobilized; because we were continually reevaluating and reconstruing our experiences, we would be unable to act. A star receiver on a professional football team, for instance, needs to consider the object being hurled at him as a football and nothing else; in this case, preemptive thinking is appropriate and effective. But sole reliance on preemptive thinking leads people to make dogmatic and unyielding judgments, often to their own detriment.

The Fundamental Postulate and Its Corollaries

The basic assumption underlying Kelly's theory is that "a person's processes are psychologically channelized by the ways in which he anticipates events" (Kelly, 1955, Vol. 1, p. 46). Kelly believed that people are behaving, changing organisms who operate in terms of their expectations about events. In short, expectations direct actions. They provide the motivation for behavior. In terms of Kelly's scientist analogy, people seek to predict and verify their views of events. They generate a construct system by construing events and then act on the basis of those constructs. From this basic postulate, Kelly derived a number of corollaries or propositions.

Individuality corollary   People anticipate events in different ways. According to Kelly, this **individuality corollary** lays the groundwork for the study of individual differences. People differ because they have had different experiences and also because they take different approaches to anticipation of the same event (Kelly, 1955, Vol. 1, p. 55). Thus, the construct systems people generate are idiosyncratic in many respects. But there are also commonalities among people in the way they construe events; people can and do interpret experiences in the same ways.

Organization corollary   Kelly's **organization corollary** proposes that "each person characteristically evolves, for his convenience in anticipating events, a construction system embracing ordinal relationships between constructs" (Kelly, 1955, Vol. 1, p. 56). People differ not only in their constructs but also in the way in which they organize them. Organization of constructs also serves to reduce conflict for the person. If a married man knows that his wife and family come first, even before his mother, then potential conflicts can be minimized. Doubt as to which construct is superordinate can be painful, as many husbands have learned.

Choice corollary   Kelly assumed that all of us are continually making choices between the poles of our constructs. In proposing the **choice corollary**, he assumed further that we tend to make choices that will allow us to deal most effectively with ensuing events. Should we be cautious or risk-taking in a given situation? Should we marry or not marry? Should we pursue a college degree or drop out? Kelly maintained that people tend, in general, to make choices that define and elaborate the system; that is, we choose alternatives designed to increase our confidence in our interpretations of the world, as well as alternatives that increase our understanding of it through personal growth. Kelly believed that we are biologically predisposed to make the elaborative choice; that is, we are predisposed to take risk, to try out new constructs, so that we can increase our understanding of more and more of our worlds.

Fragmentation corollary   According to Kelly, our construct systems are in a continual state of flux. Within these systems, we may successively use a variety of subsystems that are inferentially incompatible with one another (Kelly, 1955, Vol. 1, p. 104). In other words, our construct subsystems are not always mutually consistent, and we may sometimes show behaviors that are inconsistent with our most recent experiences. Kelly calls this the **fragmentation corollary**.

Suppose, for example, that a young woman decides that she loves a man and declares to friends that she has agreed to marry him. The following day, however, instead of showing affection toward him, she begins to criticize him harshly in front of friends, pointing out his moral flaws, and declares that the marriage is off. Kelly might explain the inconsistency in her behavior by pointing out that, although she loves him, she also knows that he is very selfish and inconsiderate in his treatment of others and will eventually hurt her. Thus, the construct "fiancé" subsumes the construct "love" and also the construct "despising his personal characteristics." Such fragmented and inconsistent construct systems can exist side by side within a person's cognitive world and show up in successive behaviors when other constructs in the larger system trigger them. In this case, the incompatible systems may have been triggered by the superordinate construct "mother" if it was her mother who brought the man's many shortcomings to her attention.

In trying to predict behavior, according to Kelly, we have to discover such ruling constructs and show how, in the final analysis, they control the person's behavior. Kelly is taking issue here with some of the early learning theorists, who held that behavior is determined by its immediate antecedents. What Kelly is saying is that the prediction of behavior is much more complicated, that it involves an assessment of the meanderings of the individual's cognitive world, and that this world is not always composed of logical and consistent subsystems.

Commonality corollary   Kelly's individuality corollary states that people who differ in their construction of events will behave differently; his **commonality corollary** states that those who interpret events similarly will behave alike. The underlying assumption is that "to the extent that one person employs a construction of experience which is similar to that employed by another, his psychological processes are similar to those of the other person" (Kelly, 1955, Vol. 1, p. 90). Thus, if their constructs are similar, people may act alike, even though they have been exposed to different stimuli. For example, two students may enroll in the same philosophy course on existentialism even if one has previously attended a philosophy course on formal logic and the other has attended one on the philosophy of art. Even though they have been exposed to different stimuli (the materials on formal logic, in one case, and the materials on the philosophy of art, in the other), they may act alike (enroll in the course on existentialism) if they construe their experiences in these two courses similarly, that is, if they both conclude that courses in philosophy are good. If courses in philosophy are good, then it is likely that the course in existentialism will be good, and therefore they will enroll in it.

Sociality corollary   Finally, Kelly proposed that, "to the extent that one person construes the construction processes of another, he may play a role in a social process involving the other person" (Kelly, 1955, Vol. 1, p. 95). In other words, insofar as we can understand another person's construct system, we can predict accurately what the other person will do and adjust our behavior accordingly. Much of our behavior, Kelly maintained, consists of such mutual adjustment. In this way, the **sociality corollary** enables us to function effectively in society and in our interpersonal relationships.

In healthy marriages, for example, there is a mutual understanding of the roles each partner is seeking to enact; each partner validates the image the other person is trying to project (Neimeyer & Hall, 1988, p. 297). Kelly referred to these images as **core role constructs**—the important, ongoing pattern of behaviors that follow from each partner's understanding of how the other person thinks (Kelly, 1955, Vol. 1, pp. 97–98). In unhealthy marriages, the partners repeatedly invalidate each other's images. The role relationships become strained, because each partner can no longer predict with accuracy what the other person is going to do. For example, if a woman believes that a loving relationship between husband and wife is characterized by kindness and affection, insensitive or abusive behavior on the part of her husband is likely to weaken her beliefs about the relationship, thereby reducing the predictive power of her construct system, until she experiences chaos in the relationship (Kelly, 1955, Vol. 1, p. 501; Neimeyer & Hall, 1988, p. 298).

Personality Development

Kelly assumed that the development of each person revolves around attempts to maximize understanding of the world through the continuing definition and elaboration of his or her construct system. Like other major humanistic psychologists, Kelly simply assumed that this tendency was innate. Certainly he did not believe it was learned, although he assumed that the person's interaction with the environment plays the major role in helping to move the individual toward personal growth. He rejected outright the mechanistic learning view that behavior was determined solely by the operation of environmental events. Individuals do not simply react to the environment. Instead, they actively, uniquely, and systematically construe it and then utilize these constructions to anticipate events. They use previous experiences to create hypotheses about possible new outcomes. In Kelly's view, people do not respond to the environment in order to maximize pleasure and avoid pain, as reinforcement theorists assume. Instead, they actively seek to maximize the accuracy of their views.

Kelly developed several models of the ways in which the individual utilizes information from the environment in deciding on a course of action. One of the more important ones he termed the circumspection-preemption-control (C-P-C) cycle. The cycle begins, according to Kelly, when the person circumspects by considering all the possible ways of construing a given situation; that is, the person considers a series of propositional constructs that might help in dealing with the situation at hand. Next comes the preemption phase, when the person reduces the number of available constructs and seriously considers only those that will help solve the problem. Finally, in the control phase, the person decides on a course of action by choosing the single construct that he or she believes to be most useful in solving the problem (Kelly, 1955, Vol. 1, pp. 516–517). As an illustration, consider the case of a young woman who wants to become a world-renowned violinist. She could construe herself in many different ways—as a future tennis great, a lazy person, or a popular local actress. Until she rejects these self-constructs and settles on one that paints her as a dedicated student of music, she is unlikely ever to become successful and to realize her ambition. By making that choice, she exercises control over her behavior and anticipates the extension of her construct system.

In Kelly's view, people are continually acting in this way; that is, they consider the alternatives in a given situation, reduce the possibilities to those that they think will work, and then act in accordance with their choices. Thus, he saw the developmental process as a creative and dynamic interchange between individual and environment, with constructions and reconstructions in the light of new experiences. Its aim is to maximize the person's understanding and, therefore, his or her control over the environment. The healthy person, then, is one who has an accurate and valid construct system and a flexible view of the world.

Assessment Techniques

Kelly used many different techniques to assess personality and promote positive growth in his clients. Some of these procedures he devised himself; others he borrowed and adapted from the works of other major personality theorists.

Kelly noted two general approaches to the appraisal of clients' experiences—one focusing on the past, and the other tending to deemphasize the past and to concentrate instead on the present. Kelly agreed that therapists should not dwell exclusively on the past, but he did think clinicians should make use of case histories. As he saw it,

> the past is important because its events are the validational evidence against which [the client] won and lost his wagers, against which he tested his personal constructs. They are the checkpoints he had to use in charting the course of his life. To understand what they actually were is to get some notion of the ranges of convenience of the client's constructs, what the system was designed to deal with, one way or another. Moreover, many of these events will have to be given some stabilizing interpretation in the new construct system produced under therapeutic intervention. (Kelly, 1955, Vol. 2, p. 688)

Moreover, case histories provide evidence of how people's culture affects their lives. Kelly believed that the culture provides people with evidence of what is true or false in life. To assess the effects of culture, Kelly turned to his own form of personality testing.

Although Kelly made considerable use of personality testing as an aid in diagnosing problems and in assessing therapy effectiveness, he stressed that it should not be used to classify or pigeonhole the individual in any fixed way. Nor should it interfere with the ongoing therapeutic process. Thus, testing should occur early in the process—not after several months of therapy, when it might lead clients to believe the therapist was uncertain about their progress. Clients should be assured that there are no right or wrong answers to the questions and that the therapist will continue to see them as worthwhile individuals no matter what the test results show. Testing should be seen simply as a way of providing helpful information to the therapist—information that will guide the therapy in a positive direction.

The Role Construct Repertory Test

One test that proved extremely useful to Kelly in his therapeutic work was the **Role Construct Repertory Test** (RCRT), which he devised as the major diagnostic tool for assessing the personal construct systems of people in clinical settings. Clients are first asked to list the names of the important people in their social environments across the top of a matrix, or grid. (See Table 11.1.) They are then asked to sort these people by successively considering three of them at a time, making circles under their names, and marking down, in a space to the right of each row in the grid, the way in which two of them are alike but different from the third. When they have decided on the two people and the important way in which they are alike, they are asked to put an X in the two circles corresponding to the ones who are alike. This identifies the similarity part of the

TABLE 11.1 CLIENT'S REPERTORY GRID

Important People in Client's Life

Legend: ⊗ and ✓ indicate similarity; O and blanks indicate contrast.

#	Similarity Pole	Self	Mother	Father	Brother	Sister	Spouse	Ex-girlfriend	Friend	Ex-friend	Rejected person	Pitied person	Threatening person	Attractive person	Accepted teacher	Rejected teacher	Boss	Successful person	Happy person	Ethical person	Contrast Pole
1	Don't believe in God							✓			✓		✓					⊗	⊗	O	Very religious
2	Same sort of education	✓	⊗	✓	✓	✓	✓		✓		⊗		✓		⊗	⊗	O	✓			Completely different education
3	Not athletic	✓	✓	✓	✓	✓	⊗	✓				⊗		⊗	✓			✓			Athletic
4	Both girls			⊗	O	✓	✓	⊗	O										✓	✓	A boy
5	Parents	✓	⊗	⊗	O	✓	✓		✓					✓			✓	✓			Ideas different
6	Understand me better				✓	O	✓		✓						⊗	✓	✓		⊗		Don't understand me at all
7	Teach the right way				✓	✓									⊗	✓	✓		✓	✓	Teach the wrong way
8	Achieved a lot		✓	O	✓				✓		✓	✓			✓	✓		⊗	✓	✓	Hasn't achieved a lot
9	Higher education				⊗						O	✓	✓		✓	⊗	✓	✓		⊗	No education
10	Don't like other people				⊗	✓	⊗	✓			⊗	✓				O					Like other people
11	More religious	✓	✓	✓	⊗				✓			O	✓		✓	✓	✓	✓	✓	⊗	Not religious
12	Believe in higher education	✓	✓	✓	⊗	✓		O	✓	✓	✓	✓	⊗	✓	✓	✓	✓	✓	✓	✓	Don't believe in much education
13	More sociable		✓		✓		O						⊗		✓	✓	⊗	⊗	⊗		Not sociable
14	Both girls		O			✓	⊗	⊗	✓										✓		Not girls
15	More understanding	✓	✓	✓	✓	✓		O	✓	✓	✓				⊗	⊗	✓	✓	✓	✓	Less understanding
16	Both have high morals	✓	✓	✓	✓	✓			⊗		✓		✓	⊗	✓	✓	✓	✓	✓	✓	Low morals
17	Think alike	⊗		✓	✓	O	✓		✓		✓		✓	✓	✓	✓			✓	✓	Think differently
18	Same age				✓	✓	✓		✓	✓						✓	⊗	⊗	✓	O	Different ages
19	Both friends				✓		✓	⊗		✓	✓	O						✓			Not friends
20	Both appreciate music	⊗			✓	O	✓	⊗					✓			✓		✓		✓	Don't understand music

⊗ and ✓ indicate similarity; O and blanks indicate contrast.

Source: Adapted from Kelly, G.A., *The Psychology of Personal Constructs*, Vol. 1, p. 270, 1955. Reproduced by permission of Taylor & Francis Book UK.

construct. Next they are asked to write in a space to the right the way in which the third person is different from the other two. This is the contrast part of the construct.

Clients are then asked to consider all the other people listed in the grid and to place a checkmark (✔) under each person to whom the similarity of the first two people also applies. If the space is left blank, it means that the contrast part of the construct applies. Clients then proceed to sort all these people again on new dimensions. The number of constructs utilized varies from client to client: Some will be able to sort people on only a few dimensions or constructs; others will sort them on a great many dimensions.

Table 11.1 shows the cognitive matrix of one of Kelly's clients. The columns list the important individuals in this person's life; the rows represent the constructs used by the client to construe them. Construct 2, for example, can be termed an education construct. The client sees both a teacher he accepts (⊘) and one he rejects (⊗) as similar in terms of educational level. He sees his boss, in contrast, as having a different educational background (○) His brother (✔) sister (✔), friend (✔), and a successful person he knows (✔) are all similar to his teachers in educational background. The remaining figures (blanks)—himself, mother, father, spouse, ex-girlfriend, ex-friend, a rejected person, a pitied person, a threatening person, an attractive person, a happy person, and an ethical person—all have an educational background that is different from his teachers'.

Once the grid has been completed, it can be scored in a variety of ways. One simple way used by psychologist James Bieri (1955) is to compare the check patterns across the various rows. Similar patterns suggest a lack of differentiation in the person's perception of others (cognitive simplicity); highly dissimilar patterns suggest a highly differentiated view of others (cognitive complexity). In a clinical setting, the therapist can use cognitive complexity, along with other testing information, to illuminate the client's problems.

Other, more detailed interpretations can be derived from the RCRT as the therapist seeks to understand a specific client's construct system. By way of illustration, look at the client matrix shown in Table 11.1. If we look at column 1 (self) and simply note the incidents (⊘ and ✔) and voids (blanks and empty circles), we can get some idea of how this person sees himself. Remember that the incidents refer to the similarity poles, and the blanks and empty circles to the contrast poles of the constructs. The client describes himself as similar to his parents in a few respects, including being very religious. He claims that he does not understand himself; nor do his parents, wife, or ex-girlfriend understand him. He is not friends with his parents or his sister. He sees his brother as one of the few people who understand him. Although he sees his brother as having accomplished a great deal in his lifetime, the client does not think of himself as very successful. Although the client seems to admire his brother very much, he does not consider him a friend, or perhaps his brother does not see him as a friend. He sees his ex-girlfriend and his wife as friends (see construct 19) but, ironically, the person he calls his friend is not someone he regards as a real friend.

We might tentatively interpret his construct system to mean that the client sees himself as alone and isolated, even among people who are supposed to be close to him. He is convinced that his parents do not understand him. Although he believes his brother and his friend understand him, he does not really see them as his friends. The client also describes himself as not sociable. We have, then, a clinical picture of a young man who may be lonely either because his family and friends have failed to communicate with him or because he is unsociable and withdrawn. Of course, it is possible that his feelings of isolation are being produced by other factors, but his responses on the RCRT provide the clinician with clues that can be supplemented by other techniques.

Research Applications of the RCRT

Kelly's RCRT or one of its many variants has been used to study both clinical and non-clinical populations and issues. One example of the application of the RCRT to a clinical population is a study conducted by Harter, Erbes, and Hart (2004, pp. 27–43). These investigators did a content analysis of the personal constructs generated by college women who had experienced childhood sexual abuse and compared it to an analysis of the personal constructs generated by college women who had no history of childhood sexual abuse. They found that sexual abuse survivors had fewer constructs referring to emotional arousal (fewer constructs about fear, anger, and anxiety) than college women with no history of sexual abuse. They explained their findings by pointing out that survivors of sexual abuse are often pressured to keep silent about the experiences by the abusing relative. Very often perpetrators may impose their own positive constructions on the child's experience, thereby preventing him or her from validating their attempts to meaningfully construe the experience. In addition, the nonoffending parent may be inattentive to any attempts to verbalize the child's experience, either through lack of awareness of the abuse or active rejection of the child's attempts to disclose the abuse. Thus, sexually abused children may have few opportunities to develop verbal representations for emotional constructs, a problem that stunts their emotional growth and presents special difficulties for the therapist to overcome during the course of treatment. Newer research by Bell, Winter, and Bhandari (2010, pp. 102–117) suggests further that university student survivors of childhood sexual abuse do not approach very many people (e.g., female friends, male friends, doctor, teachers, grandparents) for help when they are experiencing troubles in understanding their sexuality and their boyfriend/girlfriend relationships in comparison to students who were not sexually abused as children. These researchers conjecture that their traumatic childhood experiences may lead them to become isolated from others and that, as a result, they may not open up to many people to get the help and support they need to begin overcoming their difficulties.

In nonclinical samples, The RCRT has been used to assess the level of cognitive complexity of students. Students who are cognitively complex tend to have more constructs to use in making judgments about people, situations, and issues than do students who are cognitively simple. Cognitively complex students can differentiate among many different events in the environment and are more capable of making discerning and accurate judgments than those who see many events as similar and who apply the same labels to them.

In research examining individual differences in cognitive complexity, Pancer, Hunsberger, Pratt, and Alisat (2000, pp. 38–57) have noted that that most students experience great levels of stress during the transition from high school to college. New college students must learn to adjust to the new demands of adult independence (e.g., managing their own finances and doing their own laundry), to make new friends, and to meet the challenges of their academic work, which is often more difficult than the work they did in high school. Pancer and his colleagues predicted and found that students who were cognitively complex were better able to cope successfully with these stresses than students who were cognitively simple. Cognitively complex individuals had done a great deal of thinking about the possible problems that they would encounter in the college environment before they enrolled at the school and developed strategies for coping with them once they occurred. They had long discussions with their parents, friends, and officials of the school prior to enrolling and had gathered more information about what life on the campus would be like, for example, what their classes, their professors, and their social life would be like. As a result, the cognitively complex students were able to reduce their stress and make a better adjustment to college life, for example, by keeping up-to-date with their course work and by participating in many of the social activities offered by the school.

This research also showed that cognitive complexity about college life was increased by giving students information about campus life in advance of their enrollment, and such newly generated complexity served to protect many students from some of the stresses they experience at college. Pancer and his colleagues then suggested that college officials should provide students who are about to enroll with information about what college life is like, thus increasing their readiness for college. Such programs could also prepare the students for some of the challenges they might face while attending college and give them strategies that they could use to overcome these tasks, for example, time-management strategies that would help them prioritize their activities so that their course work gets done (Pancer et al., 2000, p. 54).

Bieri (1955, pp. 263–268) also sought to test the validity of Kelly's RCRT using college students. He began by classifying students as either cognitively complex or cognitively simple on the basis of their scores on the RCRT. Using Kelly's assumptions that a basic characteristic of human beings is to move toward greater predictability of their environments and that each person has a set of constructs to use in making those predictions, Bieri hypothesized that people who are cognitively complex would be better able to predict the behavior of others than would those who are cognitively simple. His reasoning was that those who can differentiate among many different events in the environment would be more capable of making discerning and accurate judgments than would those who see many events as similar and who apply the same labels to them.

To test this hypothesis, Bieri had cognitively complex and cognitively simple study participants respond to a questionnaire depicting 12 social situations with four alternative behaviors, as in the following sample item:

You are working intently to finish a paper in the library when two people sit down across from you and distract you with their continual loud talking. Would you most likely:

a. Move to another seat?
b. Let them know how you feel by your facial expression?
c. Try to finish up in spite of their talking?
d. Ask them to stop talking?

After participants had completed the questionnaire, they were asked to guess how two of their classmates would respond in the same situations. The participants' predictive accuracy was assessed by noting the number of times their predictions matched the actual responses of their classmates. As expected, the cognitively complex students were much more accurate in their predictions than were the cognitively simple ones. It also was found that the cognitively simple, or undifferentiated, participants were more likely than were the complex participants to perceive inaccurate similarities between themselves and others; that is, they tended to assume that the predictions they made for themselves would also apply to others. In brief, cognitively simple participants tended to be egocentric.

Finally, another interesting use of the RCRT can be seen in the area of trying to map out individuals' construct systems as they relate to their work situations and to show how these systems of personal meaning guide people in making effective vocational choices. One interesting early finding in this research literature shows that people with less differentiated construct systems about work tended to make less realistic choices in their selection of an occupation than did those with more differentiated systems. An undifferentiated system would include only a few constructs (e.g., high/low salary, easy/hard), whereas a more differentiated system would include many constructs (for example, high/low salary, easy/hard work, pleasant/unpleasant work, stimulating/ boring work, upward mobility/downward mobility, high/low status, good/poor retirement plan, good/poor coworkers). The realism of the person's vocational choices was assessed by examining their aptitudes and abilities to do the job. Thus, study participants with relatively simple cognitive systems who considered only the salary associated with the job and its degree of difficulty chose jobs for which they were unsuited, whereas participants with more complex systems who considered a larger number of factors made choices that were consistent with their actual skill levels and interests.

Other research in this area shows that it is not only the level of differentiation that is important in making realistic vocational choices but also the degree of integration of the person's construct system. System integration is determined by the intercorrelations among the constructs. Systems that are integrated show high intercorrelations; systems that are fragmented show little or no correlations among the constructs. A person with a fragmented system, for example, would think of the salary and the difficulty of the work separately. Thinking about salary level would not trigger a thought about the difficulty of the job and vice versa. On the other hand, a person with an integrated or organized system would see the interconnections between the salary level of the job, its degree of difficulty, its level of stimulation or challenge, its associations with promotion and upward mobility, and other factors. People with more differentiated and integrated systems are better able to make more realistic and ultimately satisfying vocational choices (Neimeyer, G. J., 1992, pp. 93–97).

In conclusion, there are many studies based on the use of the RCRT and Kelly's theorizing; in general, the findings tend to support his formulations.

Theory's Implications for Therapy

The Role of the Therapist

In Kelly's view, the sick person is one who continues to use constructs that are invalid. Thus, the basic aim of psychotherapy is to help clients form new constructs or revise old ones so that they can deal more effectively with their environment. Therapy is concerned primarily with opening up the possibility of continual change in the client's construct system. The therapist's job is to diagnose the illness and to throw light on the paths by which clients can become well (Kelly, 1955, Vol. 2, p. 582).

The therapeutic process begins as both parties try to define their roles. Clinicians, Kelly believed, should conceptualize their role quite broadly. If a client sees therapy as involving only minor adjustments, the therapist must begin with this limited view but help the client see the need for more drastic change; the therapist listens closely to the client's complaints and uses a variety of techniques to produce change.

Techniques that produce minor change include threat, invalidation, and exhortation (Kelly, 1955, Vol. 2, pp. 583–587). By threat, Kelly meant clients' awareness of the possibility of imminent change in their construct structures. Under such conditions, Kelly believed, the therapist can take advantage of the situation by pointing out new ways for clients to construe their experiences in order to facilitate constructive growth. Change can also be produced if the therapist invalidates clients' constructs, by showing them why and how their constructs do not work. Finally, the therapist can produce minor change by admonishing clients and exhorting them to behave differently and more effectively.

For major change to occur, clients must be convinced that the therapist accepts them and is willing to help them think through their problems. Kelly's view of acceptance differs from that of other nondirective therapists, however. In the traditional view, the therapist assumes that everyone has the right to choose to become anything she or he desires. In Kelly's view, acceptance does not necessarily imply approval of the clients' characteristics, but rather a readiness to understand clients' construct systems and to use their own systems to help them get well. One implication of this stance is that therapists must have a clear and firm understanding of their own construct systems. They must be able to empathize with clients without surrendering their own viewpoint. Toward this end, therapists should try to subsume much of the client's system into their own (Kelly, 1955, Vol. 2, pp. 585–587).

Controlled elaboration is Kelly's term for the therapist-assisted process of thinking through. Its aim is to make the client's construct system internally consistent and communicable so that it can eventually be validated or invalidated by new experiences. The therapist takes an active role in this process, by suggesting that new elements be added to old constructs (for example, "Your view of your brother should also include the fact that he is highly considerate of your friends") or helping the person formulate new constructs (for example, "Your minister is a person who might help you to better understand why you doubt the existence of God"). These suggestions create anxiety in clients, because the new elements lie mostly outside the range of convenience of their construct system. This anxiety is necessary, however, as a precondition to making changes in the construct system (Kelly, 1955, Vol. 1, p. 498). In challenging the client's system in these and other ways, however, the therapist tries to avoid precipitating a catastrophe (Kelly, 1955, Vol. 2, pp. 589–590).

Another aspect of the therapist's role is to help clients use current constructs to deal with problems experienced in childhood. All too often, in Kelly's view, therapists allow their clients to dwell on the past and to recount their experiences in childish terms. Revision of these constructs, he believed, can happen only if client and therapist are willing to apply new, adult thinking to the old experiences. The therapist also helps clients to design new experiments, to test hypotheses with courage, and to weigh the evidence critically. Thus, the role of the therapist is similar to that of an experienced scientific investigator helping to initiate a beginner into the realm of science (Adams-Webber, 2001, pp. 255–262). The therapist also acts as a validator of the evidence the client accumulates.

> It is important that the therapist play his role, not only with an acceptance and a generosity possibly rare in the client's interpersonal world but always with a kind of naturalness and faithfulness to reality which will not mislead the client who uses him as a validator. In a sense, the therapist must play a part as a reasonably faithful example of natural human reactions, rather than one which is superhuman or divested of all human spontaneity. In a sense, the therapist takes the best to be found in human nature and portrays it in such a way as to enable the client to validate his constructs against it. Having identified the therapist's generalization of the acceptable values in human nature, the client may seek them out among his companions. (Kelly, 1955, Vol. 2, p. 593)

In summary, therapists must have a clear idea of their own construct systems and must be alert and sensitive to a variety of cues emanating from their clients. As scientists, they must display propositional thinking and a willingness to change their views on the basis of the evidence. They must, in brief, be flexible. They must also be courageous, according to Kelly, because psychotherapy is often a distressing experience for them as well as for their clients. Finally, therapists must be verbally skilled, creative, and energetic (Kelly, 1955, Vol. 2, pp. 595–605).

The Therapeutic Conference and Role Playing

One of Kelly's principal methods is the interview or conference. In a series of therapeutic conferences, therapists attempt not only to assess the realities of their clients' lives but also to point out directions in which they can proceed toward solution of their problems

(Kelly, 1955, Vol. 2, pp. 774–775). During these sessions, therapists encourage clients to discuss their problems by acting in a supportive, reassuring, and accepting manner. Acceptance does not mean approval of the clients' construct systems nor their views of themselves (Kelly, 1955, Vol. 2, p. 587); instead, it means that therapists are capable of understanding their clients and of anticipating events in the way that the clients anticipate them. In this nonthreatening environment, clients should feel free to experiment with new ideas or beliefs and to revise or discard existing ones without fear of suffering devastating consequences if their experiments go awry (Kelly, 1955, Vol. 2, p. 581).

A large part of this experimentation involves role playing. Role enactment provides clients with insights into their maladaptive behavior and gives them new and more satisfying ways of behaving; thus, it enables them to change their invalid construct systems. Clients are typically assigned roles by their therapists, who often engage in complementary role playing to clarify their clients' feelings about themselves and to provide them with an opportunity for self-insight. Clients are not passive, however. They may also cast their therapists into a variety of roles—for example, parent, teacher, or child. This process is similar to Freudian transference, in that clients may act toward their therapists as though they were significant authority figures from their past. Through this intellectual and emotional process, they may achieve needed insight into their own problems. However, the emphasis in Kelly's therapy is not on reliving the past; rather, the therapy aims to provide clients with new roles that will promote growth and allow them to participate more fully and effectively in current life situations.

Kelly viewed therapy as a creative process, and role playing as the major technique enabling clients to act creatively. Although playing new roles seems artificial and stultifying at first, this feeling soon dissipates and clients become more spontaneous. Role playing makes them more susceptible to change. Loosening of constructs can also be achieved, in Kelly's judgment, by use of relaxation techniques, free association, and dream analysis.

Self-Characterization Sketches and Fixed-Role Therapy

As part of the therapeutic process, the clinician may ask the client to write a **self-characterization sketch**. This technique reflects Kelly's belief in the direct approach: "If you do not know what is wrong with a person, ask him; he may tell you" (Kelly, 1955, Vol. 1, pp. 322–323). Clients are asked to imagine themselves as the principal character in a play written by a friend who knows them intimately and sympathetically. This other-person format is designed to make the task as nonthreatening as possible.

After the client writes the sketch, the therapist interprets it and then uses the interpretation to write an **enactment sketch**, which the client is asked to play. The sketch is designed to contrast sharply with the client's current self-perception, as revealed in the self-characterization sketch, and thus to produce major changes in the client (Kelly, 1955, Vol. 1, p. 370). At the same time, the enactment sketch is designed to protect the client by encouraging the belief that he or she is simply playing a fictitious character. Kelly found that, with this disclaimer, clients were willing to try out the new role and that later they began to see its implications for them and to act accordingly.

Kelly provided a clear example of how the self-characterization and **fixed-role therapy** techniques worked in the case of an actual client he called Ronald Barrett. Ronald's self-characterization sketch revealed a compulsive individual who believed dogmatically that there was a reason behind all existence and that the only way to understand the causes of his existence (that is, the causes of his behaviors and the behaviors of others) was to rely on rational thought and logic. Thus, the only way for Ronald to solve problems was to maintain control over his feelings and to rely solely on reason. Despite his attempt at maintaining strict control, however, Ronald saw himself "ready to explode" on many occasions; these feelings disturbed him, because he believed they would bring disapproval from others. Although he had no warm and friendly relationships with people, he thought that he must have their approval and that it could be gained only by keeping his emotions in check and appearing calm and restrained. His concern with restraining his feelings even extended to his relationships with women. He wrote in his self-characterization sketch:

> He [Ronald] has some ideas concerning girls that seem odd or just plain crazy to most people. He completely refrains from calling a girl "beautiful." She may be cute, pretty, attractive, or some other adjective in his mind, but he uses the word "beautiful" only [to] describe material things that have no "feeling" as humans have. Although he listens attentively to stories or general discussions about sex, he rarely enters into the conversation. One may say that he puts too much meaning and thought into kissing a girl. If he has gone out with a girl a couple of times, or even once, and doesn't continue to go out with her or to call her, he is very hesitant about asking her for a date again, say two or three months later. He is usually lost for conversation when meeting someone new, or seeing a girl he knows, but if he once "breaks the ice," he can usually talk freely. However, when he calls a girl on the telephone, no matter how well he knows her, he hates to have anyone around him or even within hearing distance. Furthermore, he doesn't like to practice anything, such as a musical instrument, any place where he can be seen or heard. (Kelly, 1955, Vol. 1, p. 328)

Kelly noted that Ronald was himself disturbed by some of his ideas about women. Pointing out that Ronald attributed feeling to women, but not to beautiful ones, Kelly drew the inference that Ronald saw women, like all feeling things, as imperfect. As a consequence, he was continually hesitant and awkward in his relationships with women. To help Ronald overcome his problems, Kelly wrote a fixed-role sketch for him to enact in his daily life. The sketch was about a man called Kenneth Norton.

> Kenneth Norton is the kind of man who, after a few minutes of conversation, somehow makes you feel that he must have known you intimately for a long time. This comes about not by any particular questions that he asks but by the understanding way in which he listens. It is as if he had a knack of seeing the world through your eyes. The things which you have come to see as being important he, too, soon seems to sense as similarly important. Thus, he catches not only your words but the punctuations of feeling with which they are formed and the little accents of meaning with which they are chosen.
>
> Girls he finds attractive for many reasons, not the least of which is the exciting opportunity they provide for his understanding the feminine point of view. Unlike some men, he does not "throw the ladies a line," but, so skillful a listener is he, soon has them throwing him one, and he is thoroughly enjoying it.
>
> With his own parents and in his own home he is somewhat more expressive of his own ideas and feelings. Thus, his parents are given an opportunity to share and supplement his new enthusiasms and accomplishments. (Kelly, 1955, Vol. 1, pp. 374–375)

According to Kelly, the sketch centered on a simple theme, namely, seeking answers in the feelings of other people rather than in argument with them (Kelly, 1955, Vol. 1, p. 375). He asked Ronald to become Kenneth Norton for two weeks. First, however, Kelly let Ronald rehearse in his office a number of times until he was thoroughly familiar with the sketch (Kelly, 1955, Vol. 1, p. 387). Of course, Kelly insisted on addressing the client as Kenneth throughout the rehearsal and enactment period. Kelly also held therapy sessions during the enactment period to assess Ronald's progress or lack of progress. Progress was uncertain at first but, by the 12th interview, Ronald reported feeling much less insecure in social situations and more willing to express his feelings. Shortly afterward, the therapist broke the client's Kenneth Norton role and told him that Kenneth Norton was, in a sense, supposed to be Ronald Barrett. Ronald accepted this view after some discussion and then thanked the therapist for all his help. Ronald returned to his everyday situation with a changed set of constructs and a more realistic assessment of his own behavior and the behavior of others (Kelly, 1955, Vol. 1, pp. 394–395).

Assessment and Treatment of Schizophrenics

Much of the research utilizing Kelly's theory has employed variants of his RCRT to study psychiatric patients who have been diagnosed as schizophrenic. Kelly (1955, Vol. 1, pp. 483–485) originally proposed that the thinking of schizophrenics involves the use of **loose constructions**, weak and unstable ideas, and networks of ideas that lead to varying predictions.

To test the assertion that schizophrenia is associated with disordered thinking, Bannister and Fransella (1966, pp. 95–102) measured the thinking of schizophrenics and compared it with the thinking of depressives, neurotics, patients with mild forms of brain damage (organics), and normal individuals. A variant of the RCRT served as the instrument to measure disordered thinking. All study participants were tested individually. Each person studied eight photos of strangers, one at a time, and then rank-ordered the photos according to how kind the person in the photo appeared to be, from 1 (most) to 8 (least). Then the eight photos were reshuffled and each subject was asked to rank-order them again along a dimension of stupidity. The photos were again reshuffled and then rank-ordered along a dimension of selfishness. This same rating procedure was used again to elicit judgments of the degree of sincerity, meanness, and honesty of the people in the photos.

After completing this task (administration 1), participants were given the same set of photos and were asked to repeat the entire procedure (administration 2); that is, participants were asked to rank-order the same eight people on the same six personality dimensions.

Correlational analyses were then conducted between the ratings of the photos on the six dimensions for each group of participants for administration 1 and 2. Separate correlations were computed for each group—schizophrenics, depressives, neurotics, organics, and normals—to determine the extent to which the various groups were consistent in their rankings from one administration to the next. Ranking a given person as most kind the first time and as most kind the second time would be consistent; ranking a person most honest the first time but low on honesty the second time would be inconsistent. The results were as follows: for normals, $r = +.80$; for depressives, $r = +.75$; for neurotics, $r = +.74$; for organics, $r = +.73$; and for schizophrenics, $r = +.18$. The high correlations for the first four groups indicate highly consistent rankings, whereas the low correlation for schizophrenics indicates a lack of consistency, even though the second set of rankings was made *immediately* after completion of the first set. These results do suggest a problem in thinking for schizophrenics. Bannister, Fransella, and Agnew (1971, pp. 144–151) showed further that not only is the structure (organization and consistency) of thinking poor in schizophrenics, but the content of their thinking (the kind of beliefs they hold) is bizarre; that is, much of their thinking is characterized by paranoid delusions and by illogical connections between constructs.

In comparison to normal individuals, schizophrenics also have been found to have very weak and simplistic perceptions of themselves; that is, they use very few traits to describe themselves. In addition, schizophrenics are not very accurate in their descriptions of other people; that is, they have stereotypic views of others (Gara, Rosenberg, & Mueller, 1989, pp. 265–266; Rosenberg, 1993, p. 231).

Schizophrenics also have difficulty categorizing people in terms of their personal qualities (abilities, motives, traits). When investigators asked schizophrenics to look at photos of people and react to them, their comments were impersonal: they observed, for example, whether the person was standing or sitting, or that there was a book in the photo. Normals, in contrast, made many more personal judgments: they reported, for example, that the person looked kind, sincere, or competitive (McPherson, Armstrong, & Heather, 1978, pp. 319–324; McPherson, Buckley, & Draffan, 1971, pp. 277–280).

Bannister, Adams-Webber, Penn, and Radley (1975, pp. 169–180) have attempted to explain the origins of loose constructions in schizophrenics. They propose that schizophrenics, like normals, utilize constructs to make predictions about how the world operates, but that their predictions do not work very well; that is, they are invalid. The consequence of being wrong is to receive punishment from others. To avoid more punishment, schizophrenics weaken the constructs themselves and the associations between them; as a consequence, they begin to live subjectively in a highly fluid and largely meaningless (for them) universe. Specifically, as children, schizophrenics may have lived in a family situation riddled with inconsistencies, in which they were treated sometimes with kindness and at other times with cruelty. For example, their parents may have rewarded them for a particular behavior at times and punished them for the same behavior at other times. Perhaps their parents also ridiculed them unexpectedly in front of peers and arbitrarily reneged on promises. As a consequence of severe and erratic treatment, schizophrenics develop highly fluid constructs about their parents and an inability or unwillingness to make definite predictions about how their parents, or people in general, will behave toward them.

On the basis of this analysis, Bannister and associates reasoned that the process of thought disorder in schizophrenics can be reversed by providing them with new experiences that are consistently accurate. If thought disorder is the long-term consequence of repeated failures to predict accurately the behavior of others and themselves, then implementing therapeutic procedures in which patients are provided with evidence that they *can* accurately predict their own behavior and the behavior of others should result in an improvement in their health and functioning. Accordingly, they recruited therapists to help schizophrenic patients, over a two-year period, identify beliefs that were weak and then strengthen them. For instance, if a patient very tentatively believed that loud-mouthed people were mean, the therapist would enlist the support of the staff (psychologists and nurses) to present themselves in a loud-mouthed way to the patient whenever she requested cigarettes or candy and to refuse to give them to her. Similarly, if a patient believed that it was manly to be aggressive, the therapist would work to convince him that this belief was faulty and that it was manly to act like a gentleman. The therapist then arranged situations in which staff members would praise the patient and call him a fine gentleman for acting in a cooperative and nonaggressive way. Although the results of this long-term project were not completely positive, they were generally supportive of the investigators' theorizing, and there was evidence of some improvement in the thinking and psychological health of the patients.

Evaluative Comments

We now examine the scientific worth of Kelly's theory.

Comprehensiveness Kelly's theory is not very comprehensive, but it has the potential to handle far more phenomena than it does currently. Its perspective has focused largely on psychopathological behavior, for example, schizophrenia, depression, eating disorders, and dysfunctional families. However, there have been attempts to redress this imbalance by focusing on more normal behaviors, such as occupational choice and decision making, and on the development of healthy personal relationships. Expansion of the scope of the theory is increasingly likely as interest in Kelly's theory among investigators grows (Neimeyer, G. J., 1992, pp. 91–120).

Precision and testability   In comparison to most of the theories reviewed in this text, Kelly's position is unusually clear and testable. The theory is housed within an explicitly stated framework, so that hypotheses can be derived and tested. In addition, the RCRT provides a precise and reliable way of measuring many of the basic ideas in the theory.

Parsimony   Kelly's position seems too economical. It has too few concepts to account for personality functioning. There are relatively few concepts used to describe the developmental process, and an independent assessment of the impact of various situations on the person's behavior is not emphasized.

Empirical validity   The experimental evidence in support of certain aspects of Kelly's theory is strong. Much of this research has been concerned with establishing the reliability and validity of the RCRT and with testing some of the basic propositions of the theory. In the clinical area, research has centered mainly on Kelly's seminal ideas about thought disorder in schizophrenia and has provided general support for Kelly's theorizing (Pierce, Sewell, & Cromwell, 1992, pp. 151–184).

Two points should be made about this empirical support, however. First, the evidence is largely correlational and paper-and-pencil in nature. There is a definite need for more sophisticated experimental work that uses behavioral criterion measures and assesses interaction effects between the individual's cognitive functioning in specific situations. There is also a need to move beyond the laboratory to test the theory in natural settings. Despite the provocative nature of Kelly's formulations, research efforts have remained at a fairly unsophisticated level. Perhaps investigators will remedy this problem in the near future, so that the worth of Kelly's theory can be assessed more adequately. Second, it should be pointed out that the RCRT is primarily a descriptive device; that is, it describes the constructs the client claims to use in articulating and ordering experiences. Interpretation of the meanings of the constructs, however, rests on the clinician's skills and sensitivity. Kelly contends that the measure can be used to help clients improve their behavior, but the evidence he offers is based on the therapist's subjective judgment that the client has improved. In this respect, Kelly's claim that his case-history materials prove the validity of his views on psychotherapy cannot be totally convincing.

Heuristic value   Kelly's theory has proven very interesting and challenging to British psychologists, who have been most active in testing various aspects of it. Some contributions to personal construct theory have also been made by researchers in the Netherlands, Canada, and Israel. Yet, given the originality and provocative nature of much of Kelly's thinking, research by U.S. psychologists has been remarkably sparse (Jankowicz, 1987, p. 481). Perhaps part of the difficulty is that the theory is sharply different from other existing positions in U.S. psychology. Nor is it clear to many U.S. psychologists that the elimination of important traditional concepts, such as motivation and reinforcement, is a move in the right direction. Advocates of personal-construct theory increasingly recognize their isolation from the mainstream of U.S. psychological thought. They think that the tendency of personal-construct researchers to disaffiliate themselves from more traditional lines of thought has resulted in an ingrown pattern of communication, thereby hindering the development of the theory (Neimeyer, R. A., 1985, pp. 111–112). In addition, some U.S. psychologists believe that the theory is too cognitive and presents a view of personality that is too one-sided and simplistic, although one prominent British advocate of the theory has sought to convince psychologists that such a view is erroneous (Bannister, 1977).

Applied value   Until recently, Kelly's theory had little effect on disciplines outside of psychology. Today, however, Kelly's ideas and measurement techniques are being utilized successfully by business managers and occupational counselors. For example, business measurement specialists have used variations of the RCRT to assess consumers' views of a variety of products. The test provides a systematic basis for discovering the criteria that consumers use in making their purchasing decisions and is helpful to business owners and managers in their efforts to make certain that their products meet the needs of their customers. In the employment counseling field, counselors have used the RCRT to help people seeking work to identify occupations they view as similar, to determine which occupations they identify as ideal, and to become aware of the implications of their thoughts (constructs) about employment (Jankowicz, 1987, pp. 481–487). Thus, although the theory is currently in its initial stages of verification, it is beginning to have a positive impact on the solution of social problems.

CRITICAL THINKING QUESTIONS

1. Do you believe that your behavior is free and not determined? In what way(s)? Give some examples, along with reasons, to justify your position.
2. How do we act as scientists in the prediction of our behavior and the behavior of others? Cite limitations to the use of this analogy as an aid in understanding behavior.
3. What is a personal construct? Why must constructs contain at least three elements?

Can you think of constructs that contain only two elements?

4. What are some of your superordinate constructs? In your view, is your social success superordinate to your academic success or vice versa? Why?
5. Make up a repertory grid that describes your own constructs in relation to the important people in your life. When you are finished, report whether the exercise provided you with any insights into your personality.

GLOSSARY

choice corollary   The proposition that people select between alternatives in dichotomized constructs in making their judgments about reality.

commonality corollary   The proposition that similar construct systems in different individuals lead to similarities in their behavior.

constellatory construct   Type of construct that allows its elements to belong to other constructs concurrently; however, once identified in a particular way, these elements are fixed. For example, an individual may have a stereotypic construct of a fat person as lazy, dirty, and slovenly. These elements or traits could also belong to some of the individual's other constructs—for

example, homeless person, coal miner; that is, the individual might also see a homeless person and a coal miner as lazy, dirty, and slovenly. However, once the individual applies the fat-person construct to a person in a particular situation, the traits (or elements) lazy, dirty, and slovenly are automatically and inflexibly attributed to that person.

constructive alternativism   Fundamental assumption that human beings are capable of changing their interpretations of events.

constructs   Ways of representing our experiences; they are abstractions that are defined in terms of the similarities and contrasts of their poles.

controlled elaboration   Therapeutic technique in which clients are encouraged to clarify and think through their problems in consultation with the therapist; this process enables them to revise or discard old constructs and to formulate new and more effective ones.

core constructs   Important beliefs that are part of the individual's personal identity.

core role constructs   Set of beliefs associated with important role relationships that constitute the person's social identity.

enactment sketch   A description of a role that clients are asked to play that provides an opportunity for them to behave in ways that contrast with the self-characterization sketch. For example, a person who characterizes herself as shy plays the role of someone who is assertive.

fixed-role therapy   Therapeutic procedure used by Kelly to produce personality changes in clients by constructing roles for them that help them overcome their weaknesses and, in the process, enable them to reconstrue themselves and their life situations.

fragmentation corollary   The proposition that an individual's personal construct subsystems may be disjointed and mutually incompatible and that the person is often unaware of the inconsistency.

individuality corollary   The proposition that people differ in their constructions of reality.

loose constructions   Beliefs that are unstable, weak, and poorly defined and that lead to erratic and often invalid predictions about how the world operates.

organization corollary   The proposition that the individual's constructs are arranged in particular ways within his or her personal system.

peripheral constructs   Beliefs that are relatively unimportant to the person and that can be changed rather easily.

permeability   The degree to which new elements will be admitted within the boundaries of a construct.

preemptive construct   Type of construct that includes only its own elements and maintains that these elements cannot apply to other constructs.

propositional construct   Type of construct that leaves all of its elements open to modification.

range of convenience   The scope of a construct; the number of other constructs to which it is related.

Role Construct Repertory Test (RCRT)   Test devised by Kelly to assess an individual's personal construct system; also known as the REP test.

self-characterization sketch   Initial step in fixed-role therapy, in which clients are asked to write a brief character outline of themselves as it might be written by an intimate and sympathetic friend.

sociality corollary   The proposition that constructive interpersonal relationships depend on mutual understanding of each other's construct systems.

subordinate constructs   Constructs that are controlled by other constructs.

superordinate construct   Construct that controls many other constructs.

SUGGESTED READINGS

Butler, R. J. (2009). *Reflections in personal construct theory.* Chichester, West Sussex, UK: John Wiley & Sons, Ltd.

Kelly, G. A. (1955). *The psychology of personal constructs* (Vols. 1 & 2). New York: Norton.

Neimeyer, R. A., & Neimeyer, G. J. (Eds.) (1992). *Advances in personal construct psychology* (Vol. 2). Greenwich, CT: JAI Press.

PART 5

Humanistic/Existential Perspectives

The theories considered in this section of the text are part of the third-force movement in contemporary psychology. (The other two movements are psychoanalysis and behaviorism.) The term was coined by Abraham Maslow (Chapter 12) to describe a position that focuses on the creative potentialities inherent in human beings and that seeks ways to help them realize their highest and most important goals. Virtually all of the humanistic theories postulate the existence of an innate growth mechanism within individuals that will move them toward realization of their potentialities if environmental conditions are right. This growth process has been variously labeled by its numerous proponents as the drive toward self-actualization, self-realization, or selfhood.

The roots of the humanistic movement can be found in the writings of Jung, Adler, Horney, Kohut, Allport, Maslow, Rogers, May, and others. These theorists all emphasize the uniqueness of individuals and believe that all individuals should be free to make their own choices about the direction they want to take in their own lives. People should be allowed to organize and control their own behavior; they should not be controlled by society. Society is generally seen as the "bad guy," the enforcer of rules and regulations that stifle personal growth. According to the humanists, a benevolent, helpful attitude toward people allows them to grow and prosper. Most societies, they believe, attempt to coerce individuals into behaving appropriately, that is, normally. The result is rather dull, conventional people who usually obey, without much question, the moral prescriptions of the majority. In other words, the result is the average, law-abiding man or woman.

The humanistic psychologists argue, instead, for allowing individuals to develop to their fullest potential. They see people as naturally striving to be creative and happy rather than mediocre and conventional. Of course, the assumption that what is conventional is mediocre is open to question, especially in a society that encourages people to strive for excellence in their pursuits. Another assumption underlying many of the humanist positions is that it is possible to specify a universal set of values that will provide people with a moral anchor so that they will be able to decide what is right or wrong and good or bad. Such a set of values, rooted in biology, would allow people to make moral decisions by looking inside themselves, instead of relying on the judgments of society. Yet there has never been clear-cut agreement among philosophers or psychologists on a universal set of human values, although numerous attempts to devise such a list have been made throughout history. Also the question of who will decide which values are universally valid has never been resolved. Is it the philosophers? The psychologists? The politicians? The artists? The theologians? As we will see in Chapter 15, B. F. Skinner thought that behavioral psychologists can best make this decision, but surely not everyone will agree with him. Finally, despite the claims of the humanists, there is little scientific evidence for the existence of an innate mechanism that would allow us to make morally correct decisions.

Instead of rejecting this aspect of the humanistic psychologists' position, however, we ought to give it a fair hearing. First, the fact that there is no agreement on a universal set of values does not mean that such a value system can never be devised. Second, although there is currently little evidence for the existence of an internal, biologically based mechanism to guide moral behavior, such evidence may be found in the future. Even if it is not found, this does not mean there is nothing of merit in the humanistic position. By raising significant questions and challenging the tenets of orthodox psychology, humanistic psychologists have forced more traditional psychologists to reconsider the directions and value of their work. In this author's view, the overall impact of the humanists has been very beneficial, although some of the more rigorous experimental psychologists would certainly disagree. After we review the two major challenges hurled by the humanists at orthodox psychology, you can make your own judgment.

The first challenge is the assertion that contemporary psychologies, including psychoanalysis and behaviorism, provide only a partial and limited view of human functioning, which is in need of drastic revision. Allport put the matter succinctly and picturesquely:

> It is especially in relation to the formation and development of human *personality* that we need to open doors. For it is precisely here that our ignorance and uncertainty are greatest. Our methods, however well suited to the study of sensory processes, animal research, and pathology, are not fully adequate; and interpretations arising from the exclusive use of these methods are stultifying. Some theories are based largely upon the behavior of sick and anxious people or upon the antics of captive and desperate rats. Fewer theories have derived from the study of healthy beings, those who strive not so much to preserve life as to make it worth living. Thus we find today many studies of criminals, few of law-abiders; many of fear, few of courage; more on hostility than on affiliation; much on the blindness in man, little on his vision; much on his past, little on his outreaching into the future. (Allport, 1955, p. 18)

In building his theory of self-actualization, Maslow also pointed out the limitations of the Freudian conception of personality. Freud devoted most of his attention to understanding the unconscious forces that determine behavior and neglected the rational, conscious forces. The Freudian world is one in which neurotic people are continually struggling to adjust to the environment and to gain a feeling of security. Maslow, in contrast, posited that human beings have a need hierarchy consisting of basic and growth urges. The need for security is one of the lower, basic needs; if gratified, it frees the individual to pursue higher goals. Most of Maslow's attention was directed to establishing a psychology of personal growth and creative striving. He set out to study the behavior of psychologically healthy people in order to learn more about the growth process. In Chapter 12, we outline his efforts and provide a review of the major characteristics of self-actualizing individuals.

In summary, the first challenge posed by Maslow and other humanistic psychologists is the need for a drastic revision of contemporary psychology so that primary attention can be paid to topics that have been relatively ignored by existing theories—among others, love, affiliation, creativity, spontaneity, joy, courage, humor, independence, and personal growth. Focusing on these should teach us about the good side of human nature and serve as a corrective to the more limited and pessimistic picture projected by Freudians and behaviorists.

The second challenge is to the prevailing view that psychology is a natural science and must therefore employ methods of study consistent with those used in physics, chemistry, physiology, and biology. The humanists claim that this attitude has led to a psychology that does not do justice to the full range of human experience and behavior. To understand the arguments of the humanists more fully, let us look briefly at the history of psychology and the reasons for its initial alliance with the natural sciences.

Psychology as a science began in 1879, when Wundt established his experimental laboratory in Leipzig, Germany. Psychologists had originally been linked with speculative philosophers, but dissatisfaction with this relationship and the desire to establish an independent, more empirically oriented discipline led them toward the natural sciences and the scientific method. The benefits of this move would be twofold: First, psychologists would have a ready-made approach to the study of behavior acceptable to members of the scientific community; second, psychology would gain status and respectability. So appealing was this prospect that psychologists adopted rather uncritically the scientific method used in the natural sciences.

The natural-science approach focuses on the accumulation of facts by means of objective and reliable measurement procedures. It avoids speculation and deduction and relies instead on induction. This tough-minded empiricism can be seen most clearly in the work of Watson and Skinner. Because of their concern with objective and precise measurement, advocates of this approach have focused only on those problems that can meet their criteria; as a result, phenomena such as jealousy, hatred of a parent, and love between mature adults have been excluded from consideration.

The natural-science approach also insists that investigators be objective in their study of problems. It tends to see the investigator as a potential source of bias, whose influence on the inquiry process must be neutralized and controlled. The implication is that science is a value-free enterprise and that the investigator should study phenomena dispassionately as well as objectively. It is this depersonalized view of science that has been rejected by the humanistic psychologists. Rogers, for example, argued that science exists only in people.

> Each scientific project has its creative inception, its process, and its tentative conclusion, in a person or persons. Knowledge, even scientific knowledge, is that which is subjectively acceptable. Scientific knowledge can be communicated only to those who are subjectively ready to receive its communication. The utilization of science also occurs only through people who are in pursuit of values which have meaning for them. (Rogers, 1965, p. 164)

Rogers wanted psychologists to develop a science of psychology that has its primary focus within the person. In Chapter 13, we review Carl Rogers's reasons for the establishment of such a science and his theory of personality. Rogers's approach is based on personal growth and respect for the worth of the individual and his or her innate potential.

Rollo May (Chapter 14) developed an orientation similar to Rogers's. In his view, we should regard science as a human endeavor and begin our inquiry by asking, "What is it in human nature that leads to the emergence of a scientific attitude?" We should not begin with an established methodology and try to fit human problems into that mold; instead, we should start with our own experiences and formulations of problems and use procedures that will allow us to obtain answers. This orientation would mean emphasizing the problem rather than the use of elegant measurement techniques and equipment for the sake of being scientific. It would make psychology a human science, rather than a natural science.

The humanists do not think the natural-science approach is meaningless; their point is that psychology should adopt an expanded set of methods to help us better understand reality. We now begin our examination of theories in the humanistic/existential tradition that reflect these hopes for change.

CHAPTER 12

Maslow's Self-Actualization Position

Archives of the History of American Psychology—The University of Akron.

Biographical Sketch

Abraham Maslow was born in Brooklyn, New York, in 1908; he was the eldest of seven children. His parents were Russian Jews who had emigrated to the United States. At 18, he entered City College of New York to study law but, despite his high IQ, he did poorly in some of his courses. He had chosen to study law only to satisfy his father's wishes and had little interest in becoming a lawyer; he found the course materials dry and boring. Even more disheartening to Maslow was the nearly total absence of moral considerations in the class discussions of legal cases, which seemed to him "to deal only with evil men, and with the sins of [humankind]" (Hoffman, 1988, p. 23). During the second semester of his first year, he quit school.

Maslow later transferred to Cornell, which he hoped would offer greater academic stimulation. While there, he enrolled in the introductory psychology course, but his high expectations for the class were quickly crushed. As he put it, the subject matter was "awful and bloodless and had nothing to do with people, so I shuddered and turned away from it" (Hoffman, 1988, p. 26). Disappointed academically, he then left Cornell and returned to his parents' home in Brooklyn, and to his friend and cousin, Bertha Goodman, who still lived in the Bronx.

Maslow was enormously attracted to Bertha and was determined to be with her; but he was also very shy with women. For several weeks, he visited Bertha at her home, but said nothing about his affection for her. Then, one day, he sat down beside her on a couch. They exchanged warm glances. As the silence grew, she gazed at him demurely and moved a bit closer. Timid and yet wanting desperately to touch her, Maslow sat there, hesitating. Bertha's sister, Anna, older and more experienced in the affairs of the heart, intervened in this slow-motion romance. Shoving him toward Bertha by the scruff of his neck, she exclaimed, "For the love of Pete, kiss her, will ya!" Startled, and almost intimidated by Anna's shove, Maslow did so. Bertha "didn't protest or fight back," he recalled. "She kissed back and then life began." (Hoffman, 1988, p. 29) Maslow always regarded that first kiss as one of the greatest moments of his life, a true peak experience.

Eventually, he matriculated at the University of Wisconsin, but his longing for Bertha continued. Although his parents opposed the marriage and all of his friends and professors at the university discouraged him because he had no money to support a family, Maslow sent Bertha a telegram announcing that they would marry over the Christmas break. He felt so certain of his decision that he did not even bother to ask Bertha for her consent. But she loved him equally and immediately agreed. They were married on December 31, 1928, and returned to Wisconsin together. They remained happily married until his death (Hoffman, 1988, pp. 36–37).

At the University of Wisconsin, he was first exposed to the scientific psychology of the Wundt/Titchener structuralism school. Advocates of the structuralist position sought to demonstrate that "mental life" could be studied in the same way as phenomena in chemistry, that is, by analyzing the various "elements" of sensation and perception and the ways in which they combined to affect behavior. Maslow found this approach boring, but his interest was piqued by the behaviorist approach being promulgated by John B. Watson. It is difficult to imagine that Maslow could be stimulated by Watson's crude stimulus-response (S-R) treatment of human behavior; later in his career, in fact, he rejected that approach. While Maslow was a student, however, Watson's method did interest him, because it seemed to imply that people could be understood and improved scientifically, a belief directly in line with Maslow's interest in helping people realize their potential.

During his Wisconsin days, Maslow worked with Harry Harlow, who later became famous for his work on curiosity and affectional motives in monkeys. Maslow was interested in the fact that monkeys would work to solve problems for long periods of time, even when they were not hungry. He observed similar behavior in pigs. The stronger and healthier pigs would explore their surroundings much more than did the weaker ones. Maslow was also aware of an early experiment showing that, if chickens are allowed to choose their own diets, some will select a healthy diet and others will not. These results suggested to Maslow that there is a fundamental drive toward health in animals. Eventually, he came to believe that a similar drive toward knowledge, power, and insight also exists in humans. Thus, his initial work in animal biology provided the groundwork for his theory of self-actualization.

Maslow received his doctorate from Wisconsin in 1934, and then worked for 18 months at Columbia University with eminent learning theorist E. L. Thorndike. As Thorndike's assistant, Maslow was required to do research designed to discover the percentage of human behavior determined by genes and the percentage controlled by culture. Maslow found the project silly because he believed that behavior was determined by both. He made his views known to Thorndike and, much to his surprise, Thorndike gave him permission to pursue his own research on dominance and sexuality in monkeys and humans. Out of this work emerged Maslow's ideas about the hierarchy of needs in human beings. His classic paper was published in *Psychological Review* in 1943, after he had left Columbia and begun teaching at Brooklyn College. During Maslow's 14 years at Brooklyn College, he had an opportunity to meet and be exposed to the ideas of such prominent psychologists, psychoanalysts, and cultural anthropologists as Max Wertheimer, Karen Horney, Alfred Adler, Erich Fromm, and Ruth Benedict. The exposure had a considerable influence on his thinking, and it was at this point that he rejected the oversimplified S-R view of human behavior and embraced instead a more holistic and dynamic view of personality functioning.

In 1951, Maslow moved to Brandeis University, where he served as department chair for many years. While at Brandeis, he produced two of his most creative works, *Motivation and Personality* (1954) and *Toward a Psychology of Being* (1962). In 1967, he was elected president of the American Psychological Association. That same year, he accepted a fellowship at the Laughlin Foundation in Menlo Park, California, to devote all his time to writing. Unfortunately, he died of a heart attack one year later, at the age of 62 (Wilson, 1972, pp. 129–202).

Concepts and Principles

Humanistic Biology and Self-Actualization

Maslow laid the groundwork for his theory of **self-actualization** by making the assumption that each of us has an intrinsic nature that is good or, at the very least, neutral

(Maslow, 1962, p. 3). Because this inner nature is good or neutral, he argued, it is best to encourage its development. Healthy development is likely, however, only in a society that "offers all [the] necessary raw materials and then gets out of the way and stands aside to let the organism itself utter its wishes and demands and make its choices" (Maslow, 1970a, p. 277). If the environment is restrictive and minimizes personal choice, the individual is likely to develop in neurotic ways, because this inner nature is weak and subject to control by environmental forces. Maslow believed that this inner tendency, though weak, remains and continuously presses toward actualization (Maslow, 1962, pp. 3–4).

The objective of Maslow's **humanistic biology** was to establish a "scientific ethics, a natural value system, a court of ultimate appeal for the determination of good and bad, of right and wrong" (Maslow, 1962, p. 4). Such an ethic would overcome the relativism inherent in traditional appeals to moral authority and provide a set of ideals to serve as guides for human conduct. If our inner natures, for example, told us that aggression against others is wrong, then no amount of preaching or exhortation by authorities that it is justified under certain circumstances would dissuade us from our inner conviction. Presumably, we would be able to cast out this evil in ourselves. Because the evidence for a natural ethic is unconvincing, however, we are left with only the word of a moral authority, Maslow, that such a set of values indeed exists.

The Hierarchy of Human Needs

According to Maslow, human beings have two basic sets of needs that are rooted in their biology: **deficiency needs** (or basic needs), and **growth needs** (or meta needs). The basic needs are more urgent than the growth needs and are arranged in a hierarchical order. Maslow acknowledged that there may be exceptions to this hierarchical arrangement. For example, he maintained that there are creative people whose drive to create is more important than any other need. There are also people whose values and ideals are so strong that they will die rather than renounce them. The meta needs, in contrast, are not arranged hierarchically. In general, they are equally powerful and can be easily substituted one for another. When any of these needs is not fulfilled, the person becomes sick. Just as we need adequate amounts of vitamin C to remain healthy, so we need love from others in sufficient quantities to function properly (Maslow, 1962, p. 21). In order to move toward self-actualization, we must have sufficiently gratified our basic needs, so that we are free to pursue fulfillment of the higher, transcending, meta needs (Maslow, 1962, p. 23).

Basic needs   From most to least powerful, the basic needs are the physiological drives, safety needs, belongingness and love needs, and esteem needs. (See Figure 12.1.) The preconditions necessary for the satisfaction of these needs include the "freedom to speak… freedom to express oneself, freedom to investigate and seek for information, freedom to defend oneself, justice, fairness, honesty, orderliness in the group" (Maslow, 1970a, p. 47). Without these freedoms, satisfaction of the basic needs is virtually impossible.

The physiological needs include, among others, hunger, thirst, and sex. People deprived of food for long periods of time, for example, would begin to focus more and more of their attention on that deficiency. They would start to think and dream about food in an obsessive way. They would become less and less concerned with other activities, such as fixing the roof, buying a car, or taking the children on camping and fishing trips. They would also become less interested in what other people thought of them and in trying to help others. In short, when hunger is not satisfied, people are less concerned with safety needs, love and belongingness, esteem needs, and movement toward self-actualization. Thus, one implication of Maslow's scheme is that few poor people are involved in the quest for self-actualization. The poor use all their energies in finding enough work to feed themselves and their families.

FIG-12.1 Maslow's
needs hierarchy.

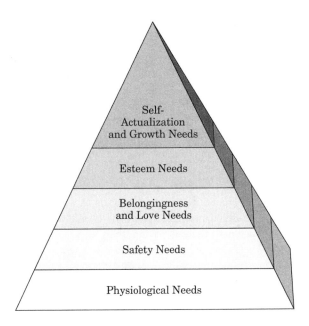

Once people's physiological needs are relatively well satisfied, however, a set of safety needs is presumed to emerge. This set includes needs for security, protection, structure, law, order, limits, and freedom from fear, anxiety, and chaos (Maslow, 1970a, p. 39). In Maslow's view, the need for security manifests itself in infants and children when their environment is disturbed. For example, they may feel threatened by loud noises, flashing lights, rough handling, and inadequate support (Maslow, 1970a, p. 39). Needs for safety may also be reflected in their preference for an environment in which reinforcers are dispensed by caregivers in a systematic and consistent manner; erratic behavior on the part of parents can be debilitating. Children also need limits on their behavior, according to Maslow. Without such limits, they function poorly. Maslow maintained that the typical child will often react with panic in unfamiliar and unmanageable situations. For example, a mother may be surprised to find her young son crying and clinging to the handrail of a stairway that leads to his classroom a few minutes after he had given her repeated assurances that he knew how to get there.

Like children, adults also have definite needs for safety, but they are more subtle and difficult to detect. A stable society frees adults from worry about adequate food supplies and housing, about being assaulted on the streets or in their homes, about military coups or civilian takeovers of the government, and the like. In a more moderate way, people act to secure tenure in their jobs and to receive old-age pensions and medical coverage in case of illness or accidents.

The needs for belongingness and love tend to emerge once the physiological and safety needs are routinely met. Maslow argued that all of us need to feel wanted and accepted by others. There is some research that supports Maslow's belief that we all need to feel wanted and accepted by others. Carvallo and Gabriel (2006, pp. 697–709) focused on undergraduate students who had a dismissing avoidant attachment style, that is, students who explicitly rejected or minimized the importance of emotional attachments to others and passively avoided close relationships. Instead they strove for self-reliance and independence from others in all situations. The investigators maintained that if the need to belong is universal like Maslow maintained, then even individuals with an avoidant attachment style who claimed not to care about social relationships should experience positive emotional reactions when accepted by other members of a group with whom they had been interacting. As expected, even avoidant attachment students who claimed not to care about others' views of them experienced positive emotions and increased self-esteem when they learned that group members had formed favorable impressions of them during the interactions in which they had taken part.

Like Maslow, modern personality psychologists maintain that the needs to belong and feel loved are very powerful and are highly adaptive from an evolutionary perspective. That is, both survival and reproduction benefit immensely by a person's being part of a group as opposed to being alone in the world (Tice & Baumeister, 2001, p. 72). Thus, Maslow believed that some of us gratify these powerful needs through our friends, others through family life, and still others through membership in groups and organizations. Without such ties, we would feel rootless and lonely.

The basic, or deficiency, need for love is a selfish concern with seeking love from others; Maslow termed it **D-love** (deficiency-love). Once this need is relatively gratified, however, we become capable of loving others. Maslow called this **B-love** (being-love), to distinguish it from the lower need to be loved. B-love, or mature love, becomes possible in Maslow's system only when the basic needs have been sufficiently gratified and the person is moving toward self-actualization.

Research by Dietch (1978) provides initial support for some of Maslow's ideas about mature love. He found that college men and women with higher scores on a test of self-actualization were more likely to have been truly in love with at least one person during the past three years than were students with lower scores. The implication is that students who were higher in self-actualization were more capable of giving affection and of intimately relating to others than those who were lower in the actualization hierarchy. Dietch also found a positive correlation between capacity for mature love and self-actualization in this sample of students. Moreover, among students who reported that their relationships had broken up those who were higher in self-actualization were less resentful toward their former lovers than were those who were less actualizing. In accordance with Maslow's theory, this finding suggests that students higher in actualization were more mature and could accept the ending of an important relationship with more grace and understanding than did those who were lower in the hierarchy.

Esteem needs are the last of the basic urges to emerge. Maslow maintained that individuals become sick when these needs are thwarted. He divided them into two sets: esteem based on respect for our own competence, independence, and accomplishments, and esteem based on others' evaluations. Esteem needs of the second type are best seen in the striving for recognition from others and in attempts to secure status, fame, dominance, importance, and appreciation (Maslow, 1970a, p. 45). He also believed that we should base our self-esteem on actual competence and adequacy at the task rather than on praise or criticism from others. Surely there is little question that acceptance of undeserved praise from others may eventually have harmful consequences for personal development. A young woman who has been continually praised by her high-school teachers and her parents for academic prowess that she does not really possess, and who consequently believes that she will excel at college, may find her first year at the university traumatic. Conversely, undeserved criticism may hinder functioning. A creative young man who writes marvelous poems may never share them with others, because of excessive reliance on the opinion of family members who continually derogate his efforts. Eventually, he might even give up poetry completely.

In these extreme cases, individuals would do better to rely on themselves and not others in making their judgments. In many instances, however, people lack the competence to make correct judgments and need to rely on the advice of others. For example, children on a picnic might do well to heed their parents' advice to avoid swimming in certain areas. Similarly, self-diagnosis and treatment of illness can have serious consequences; listening to the advice of a competent doctor may be wiser. Thus, Maslow's general prescription that we rely on ourselves and not on others in making decisions is questionable. We do not exist in a social vacuum, and we do not always know what actions are in our best interest. We cannot always rely on that "which comes naturally and easily out of one's own true inner nature, one's constitution, one's biological fate or destiny" (Maslow, 1970a, p. 46). Such a biologically based individualism can deteriorate into a kind of idiosyncratic subjectivism that assumes that each person's comprehension of reality is just as accurate as any other person's.

Meta needs Once the basic needs in Maslow's hierarchy have been sufficiently gratified, the needs for self-actualization and cognitive understanding become salient. People seek to gratify their innate curiosity about themselves and the workings of the environment, to know and understand phenomena that go beyond the gratification of basic needs, to move toward realization of their own unique potentialities. But movement in this positive direction is not automatic. Maslow believed that we often fear "our best side, our talents, our finest impulses, our creativeness" (Maslow, 1962, p. 58). Discovery of our abilities brings happiness, but it also brings fear of new responsibilities and duties, fear of the unknown. Maslow called this fear the **Jonah complex**.

For many women, Maslow argued, this fear takes the form of reluctance to make full use of their intellectual abilities, because achievement is considered unfeminine and they fear social rejection. However, while Maslow's argument may apply to some women, such fear of success is not present in *all* women: Piedmont (1988) found differences among women in terms of their fear of success. In comparison to women with a high fear of success, women with a low fear of success performed well on a masculine-oriented task.

For men, the motives underlying fear of success are different, because success is considered gender-appropriate behavior for males and does not bring with it a loss in masculinity or social rejection. Instead, fear of success in men may reflect a wish to avoid the responsibilities that continued success brings, a feeling that material success somehow will not bring emotional well-being or spiritual fulfillment, or a belief that success will not bring them enough social recognition (Hoffman, 1974, p. 356).

Crawford and Marecek (1989) have criticized the concept of fear of success in females because it implies that females have a problem; that is, fear of success is used to explain deficiencies in females' achievement strivings and performances. Females are seen as acting against their own best interest when they fail to perform as well as they can on male-oriented tasks. Thus, females are being judged in relation to male norms and values, which assume that it is good to compete against others and to strive for success (Crawford & Marecek, 1989, pp. 151–153).

As an alternative to this deficiency view, Hyland (1989) proposes that success-avoiding behavior in females occurs not because they are motivated to avoid success but because success avoidance is a compromise reflecting the desire for some other goal(s). For example, some females may avoid getting ahead so that they can make friends (Hyland, 1989, p. 668). In Hyland's view, avoiding success is not always an irrational or self-destructive behavior but may reflect a rational choice to sacrifice success for more important goals (Hyland, 1989, p. 674).

In reality, however, people do not always sacrifice one goal for another; often they have a variety of goals that they value highly and pursue simultaneously. It does not seem rational for females (or males) to enroll in college with the goal of earning good grades and achieving success by graduating, and then to jeopardize the attainment of this goal by performing poorly because they wish to avoid rejection by their peers. A more rational strategy would be to pursue academic excellence, while at the same time making and keeping close friends. These goals are not mutually exclusive. Why should females or males waste thousands of dollars in tuition and fees and all that time and effort (and pain from poor performance) to pursue only the fulfillment of their affiliative needs?

To the extent that our socialization practices teach one sex or the other values that restrict individual growth, people will have difficulty moving toward self-actualization, according to Maslow. The fears that some females have of appearing unfeminine because they are pursuing traditionally masculine goals are being reduced gradually, as their roles evolve and become less restrictive. Males, too, have been subjected to socialization practices that restrict their personal growth. As their roles evolve, men are learning that the expression of emotion and feelings of tenderness toward others makes them more fully human.

In Maslow's view, poor socialization practices also contribute to a **desacralizing attitude** among young people that hinders movement toward self-actualization. Maslow believed this attitude emerges because many adolescents have parents whom they do not respect, parents who are confused about their own values. They never punish their children or stop them from doing things that are wrong. They are terrified of their children and let them do whatever they want. As a result, the children despise them, often with good reason. Concluding that all grown-ups are like their parents, they lose their respect for adults. As adolescents, they are cynical and mistrustful of all grown-ups. Maslow believed that movement toward self-actualization is possible for such people only when they learn to resacralize their lives—that is, when they give up their cynicism and mistrust and begin to see not only the weaknesses in adults but also their virtues and strengths (Maslow, 1971, pp. 49–50).

In summary, movement toward actualization depends upon good environmental conditions (Maslow, 1970a, p. 99), including a socialization process that fosters equality and trust between people, along with respect and support of the individual's right to make his or her own decisions. In support of these contentions, research shows that students who are more self-actualizing report that their parents were more likely to use an authoritative disciplinary style to facilitate the personal growth of their sons and daughters. This **authoritative parenting style** involved parental respect for them, a willingness to encourage them to voice disagreements, and consistent and firm discipline of them, without resorting to physical or verbal abuse. Parental firmness was moderated by warmth, reason, flexibility, and verbal give-and-take. The investigators also found that a **permissive parenting style** was unrelated to movement toward self-actualizing, whereas an **authoritarian parenting style** actually inhibited personal growth. Authoritarian parents demanded unquestioned obedience to their judgments, were very upset with any disagreements or challenges to their authority, and showed a willingness to use physical punishment to ensure the compliance of their children (Dominguez & Carton, 1997, pp. 1094–1098).

B-Cognition and Actualization

Assuming that good socialization conditions are present and that people are willing and able to take risks, positive growth will occur. Individuals begin more and more to exist in a **B-cognition** state. In Maslow's scheme, **D-cognition** experiences involve judging, condemning, and approving and disapproving of ourselves and others; B-cognition experiences are nonjudgmental, self-validating, nonstriving, and temporary (Maslow, 1962, p. 68). In such states of **peak experience**, people experience phenomena in their simplicity, "oughtness," beauty, goodness, and completeness. There is a lack of strain, an effortlessness, a spontaneity about the experience that is almost overwhelming (Maslow, 1962, p. 73). Typically, the person has no consciousness of space and time and feels intense emotions such as wonder, awe, and reverence. During these intense experiences, individuals transcend their own selfishness and perceive events and objects as they truly are, without distorting them to meet their own needs or wishes (Maslow, 1970b, pp. 59–68). As examples, Maslow (1962, p. 79) cites "perceiving the beautiful person or the beautiful painting, experiencing perfect sex and/or perfect love, insight, creativeness." College students cite being in awe of the beauties of nature, experiencing ecstasy during moments of quiet reflection or when they are listening to music, engaging in physical exercise, reading a poem or novel, praying, and making sexual love with their partners (Keutzer, 1978, p. 78). Research shows that staff members of a British institution of higher education report that taking drugs did not help them trigger peak experiences (Lowis, 2003, pp. 41–53). Also, research suggests that peak experiences may occur in children as well as in adults. Since children are unable to describe well their most exalted moments, adults were asked to recall as many peak experiences as they could from their own childhoods. Such retrospective reports are, of course, subject to memory distortion and falsification effects so the results in this study should be viewed very skeptically. With that caveat in mind, these retrospective reports included unforgettable dreams, prayer, and looking at the grandeur of nature as the kinds of peak experiences that adults said they had when they were children (Hoffman, 1998, p. 115). In a related study, Shin (1993, p. 252) found that Canadian campers who had a greater appreciation of the uniqueness and beauty of the wilderness and a greater approval of its preservation were more self-actualizing than were those who were less appreciative of the wilderness. As we might expect from those who are more pro-environment, individuals who have peak experiences report being less materialistic, less status conscious, and more concerned with the welfare of others than nonpeakers (cf., Christopher, Manaster, & Campbell, 2002, pp. 35–51).

B-cognition is not a perfect state in which people live happily forever after. Although self-actualizing people are more capable than ordinary people of B-cognizing, they do not live in this state continuously (Maslow, 1962, pp. 109–110). Continual existence in such a passive and noninterfering state would prove fatal, because survival often demands action. The person who appreciates the beauty of the tiger without taking safety precautions may not survive the experience. As Maslow put it, "the demands of self-actualization may necessitate killing the tiger, even though B-cognition of the tiger is against killing the tiger" (Maslow, 1962, p. 111). In this example, self-actualization demands D-cognition, or the arousal of safety needs, as well as B-cognition. In a broader sense, the actualization process involves conflict, struggle, uncertainty, guilt, and regret, as well as bliss and pleasure (Maslow, 1962, p. 111).

Another danger associated with B-cognizing is indiscriminate acceptance of others, "because every person, seen from the viewpoint of his own Being exclusively, is seen as perfect in his own kind. Evaluation, condemnation, … criticism, comparison [with others] are all then inapplicable and beside the point" (Maslow, 1962, p. 115). Yet there are times when people can be too tolerant of others. In Maslow's view, people must also accept responsibility for fostering growth in others by setting limits for them, by disciplining them, and by deliberately being the frustrater. Parents and teachers are confronted continuously by this painful dilemma (Maslow, 1962, p. 112). A related danger is that people may misinterpret the B-cognizer's failure to evaluate and criticize as a lack of love, concern, and compassion. If, as a consequence, they come to perceive others as bad, or less deserving of their trust and respect, their growth may be retarded (Maslow, 1962, p. 113).

Characteristics of Self-Actualizing People

To discover the distinguishing characteristics of **self-actualizers**, Maslow selected the best specimens of humanity he could find from among his friends and acquaintances and from among various public and historical figures—including Abraham Lincoln in his later years, Thomas Jefferson, Albert Einstein, Eleanor Roosevelt, Jane Addams, William James, Albert Schweitzer, Aldous Huxley, and Baruch Spinoza. He selected these individuals for intensive study because they all showed an absence of neurosis, psychopathic personality, or psychosis and the presence of self-actualization tendencies. He admitted that his data were impressionistic and did not meet conventional scientific reliability, validity, and sampling standards, but he felt the problem of psychological health was so important that he was compelled to present this evidence for its heuristic value (Maslow, 1970a, pp. 149–152).

After extensive analysis of these individuals' lives, Maslow concluded that actualizers have a more efficient perception of reality than do nonactualizers. They are more capable than are nonactualizers of perceiving the truth in many different situations and of detecting dishonesty and fakery in others, and they are less guided in their judgments by stereotypes and prejudices (Maslow, 1970a, pp. 153–154). Actualizers show a greater acceptance of themselves, others, and nature than do nonactualizers. They recognize their own and others' shortcomings, but they do not feel excessively guilty or anxious about them. Instead, they tend to deal with them stoically, in the same way that we accept the workings of nature. Maslow also found that actualizers tend to be hearty in their appetites and to enjoy themselves without regret, shame, or apology (Maslow, 1970a, p. 156). They sleep well and enjoy sex without unnecessary inhibitions. They are not ashamed of their biological functioning, urination, defecation, menstruation, pregnancy, and growing older, which they accept as part of reality (Maslow, 1970a, p. 156).

Actualizing people are more problem-centered than are nonactualizers, more concerned with undertaking tasks that will benefit others, less introspective, and more task-oriented. Among elementary and high-school teachers, actualizers show less burnout (emotional exhaustion) and have higher levels of personal accomplishment on the job (Malanowski & Wood, 1984, p. 25) than nonactualizers. Nonactualizers tend to be very concerned with themselves and are characterized by feelings of inferiority (Maslow, 1970a, pp. 159–160). Actualizers tend to resist enculturation, to be "ruled by the laws of their own character rather than by the rules of society" (Maslow, 1970a, p. 174). They show neither excessive rejection nor uncritical acceptance of society's rules, but tend to be detached from the culture. They can yield to folkways perceived by them as harmless, yet react strongly against injustices. In general, they "show what might be called a calm, long-time concern with culture improvement that seems to imply an acceptance to slowness of change along with the unquestioned desirability and necessity of such change" (Maslow, 1970a, p. 172).

Actualizers, according to Maslow, possess a democratic character structure. Compared to nonactualizers, they are less likely to focus attention on race, creed, sex, religious affiliation, educational level, or social class. Although they tend to be more creative than their more average counterparts, they do not consider themselves superior in all respects. They acknowledge their own limitations and can ask for help in areas in which they lack expertise. They honestly respect others and can be genuinely humble before people who can teach them something they do not know. Although they tend to select elite individuals for their friends, that choice is made on the basis of talent and ability, not birth, race, sex, family, age, fame, or power (Maslow, 1970a, pp. 167–168).

Actualizers do have their weaknesses. They "can be boring, stubborn, [and] irritating. They are by no means free from superficial vanity, pride, partiality to their own productions, family, friends, and children. Temper outbursts are not rare" (Maslow, 1970a, p. 175). They can also show extraordinary ruthlessness; for example, they may reject a friend totally and irrevocably if they find he or she has been dishonest with them. They may show behavior and use language that is shocking and insulting. In brief, they are as capable as any other human being of displaying injurious and primitive behavior on occasion.

Personality Development

Maslow posited a universal stage-emergent theory of personal development, in which the individual must satisfy, at least to a certain extent, the lower needs before higher ones can become operative. The emergence or nonemergence of the stages depends to a considerable degree on the environment. Environments that threaten the individual and do not allow for the satisfaction of basic needs are detrimental to growth, whereas environments that are supportive and provide for the gratification of these needs promote growth toward self-actualization. In Maslow's view, environment is crucial in the early stages of development when people are struggling to gratify basic needs. The needs for safety, love, and belongingness all depend on the cooperation of other people for gratification. Later on, as the higher needs emerge, people become less dependent on the environment and on rewards or approval from others. They rely increasingly on their own inner experiences to guide behavior their inner nature, capacities, potentialities, talents, and creative impulses (Maslow, 1962, p. 32). In support for Maslow's view, Bordages (1989) has shown that self-actualizing individuals behave independently of the expectations and demands of others. They rely heavily on their own abilities and judgments in solving problems.

> The techniques of repeatedly acquiring from the outside world satisfactions of motivational deficiencies are much less needed. Associative learning [or simple conditioning] give[s] way more to perceptual learning, to the increase of insight and understanding, to knowledge of self and to the steady growth of personality. Change becomes much less an acquisition of habits or associations one by one, and much more a total change of the total person. This kind of character-change learning means changing a very complex, highly integrated, holistic organism, which in turn means that many impacts will make no change at all because more and more such impacts will be rejected as the person becomes more stable and more autonomous. (Maslow, 1962, p. 36)

With the advent of persistent perceptual learning, people are free to make their own spontaneous choices not by relying on the values and expectations of others, but by listening to their inner nature.

Self-transcendence as a separate motivational state beyond self-actualization?
Recently, Koltko-Rivera (2006, pp. 302–317) has argued that Maslow, near the end of his life, had modified his hierarchy of needs scheme and had described a new motivational stage, namely, self-transcendence, that was a step beyond self-actualization. Koltko-Rivera points out that most textbook writers on personality theory have not accurately incorporated this new motivational level into their presentations of Maslow's views. This new motivational level is one in which the individual seeks to further a cause beyond the self and to experience a communion with others and nature that goes beyond the boundaries of the self. In Koltko-Rivera's view, by placing self-actualization at the top of the hierarchy, as has been done traditionally by most scholars, there is the perpetuation of a "certain self-aggrandizing aspect" (Koltko-Rivera, 2006, p. 306) to self-actualization, where the individual's selfish needs still take precedence over the more unselfish view (self-transcendence) that puts the highest good as being oriented in favor of service to others and to a cause outside of the personal self. Unfortunately, this view does an injustice to Maslow's own evolving conceptualization of the self-actualizing individual. In his later work, he distinguished between a nontranscending self-actualizing person and a **transcending self-actualizing person**. While the nontranscending self-actualizer was healthy, the transcending self-actualizer was even more healthy. He or

she was moving toward becoming the ultimate psychologically healthy person (Maslow, 1971, pp. 270–286). This evolving view did not mean, however, that transcending self-actualizing people are never selfish, never make mistakes, or have no limitations. If so, they would be God, not human beings. Instead, Maslow thought these very healthy people had both selfish and unselfish qualities, as he had originally surmised. In this evolving view, he noted that these highly developed individuals, more than other people, worked to eliminate their selfish qualities and to develop their unselfish ones. They struggled often to reconcile the dichotomy between being selfish and unselfish, and they had evolved enough in their personal development to make it more likely they would emerge frequently on the side of the virtues. Thus, Maslow never postulated a self-transcendent stage that was orthogonal to self-actualization, as Koltko-Rivera (2006, p. 307) insists. While not saints, transcending self-actualizers are primarily concerned with working to create a world of peace and justice for all.

Assessment Techniques

Identifying Self-Actualizers

Maslow utilized a variety of research techniques in an attempt to identify self-actualizing individuals. He began by employing a selection technique called *iteration* (Maslow, 1970a, p. 151). Starting with his general belief concerning the meaning of self-actualization, he collated it with other, popularly used definitions and, by the systematic elimination of logical inconsistencies among them, arrived at a common definition. He then used this definition to divide a group of 3,000 college students into actualizers and nonactualizers. The same students were then examined in case-study fashion, using the Rorschach Test, Murray's Thematic Apperception Test, free association, and in-depth interviews, to determine whether they possessed the characteristics of actualizers.

In an ongoing effort to validate the concept of self-actualization empirically, the definition was then changed and corrected, as necessary, in light of the findings. Then the original subject pool was reselected on the basis of the new definition, and the retainees were restudied using the same clinical procedures. On the basis of these new data, the self-actualization definition was again revised, and the new definition was used to reselect study participants from the remaining participants' pool for further clinical study, and so on, until a precise identification of actualizers and nonactualizers was obtained. As you might expect, this iterative procedure greatly reduced the number of individuals who met the stringent definition of self-actualization within the original sample of 3,000. Maslow concluded that perhaps young people had not had sufficient time and experience to develop the characteristics associated with actualization and that it might be more useful to study middle-aged and older people.

As his next pool of potential actualizers, Maslow used his personal friends and acquaintances and a number of public and historical figures, among them, Lincoln, Jefferson, Eleanor Roosevelt, Einstein, Schweitzer, Spinoza, G. W. Carver, Eugene V. Debs, Pablo Casals, Adlai Stevenson, George Washington, Robert Benchley, and Camille Pissarro. Maslow turned to historical figures because he found that biographical sources provided sufficient information about them to permit meaningful conclusions, whereas it was nearly impossible to obtain such information about living figures, many of whom, when informed of the purpose of his research, "became self-conscious, froze up, laughed off the whole effort, or broke off the relationship" (Maslow, 1970a, p. 151). The results of his investigations revealed that, although more older people than college students were self-actualized, the numbers remained very small.

Maslow's assessment procedures are fraught with ambiguities and imprecisions. We are not certain, for example, how the various tests used in the interviews were administered or scored, what kinds of free associations led Maslow to conclude that his study participants were or were not actualized, or how he decided that some of his historical figures were self-actualized and others were not. Most important, since Maslow chose for study people he greatly admired, it is distinctly possible that his definition of self-actualization was simply a reflection of his own personal value system.

The Personal Orientation Inventory

Although Maslow's theory was plagued initially by methodological problems that prevented adequate research, investigation of certain aspects of the theory has been facilitated by the construction of a more reliable and valid measure of self-actualization called the **Personal Orientation Inventory (POI)** (Shostrom, 1963). The POI is a self-report questionnaire consisting of 150 forced-choice items that reflect the values and behavior of major importance in the development of a self-actualizing person. Study participants are asked to select the one statement in each of the 150 pairs that is most true of themselves. These responses are then scored by awarding a point for each response that is consistent with self-actualization, with higher scores indicative of greater actualization. Sample items are presented in Table 12.1.

Much of the early work with the POI was concerned with establishing its reliability and validity as a research instrument. Test/retest reliabilities for various samples are satisfactory (Ilardi & May, 1968, pp. 68–72). In terms of validity, a number of studies show that the measure can be used to distinguish between groups in society that we would ordinarily consider to differ in their actualization levels. For example, two studies have shown that groups of psychiatric patients scored lower (were less self-actualized) on virtually all the POI scales than were groups of people judged by experienced clinical psychologists to be self-actualized (Fox, Knapp, & Michael, 1968, pp. 565–569). In another study, all scales of the POI discriminated among groups of alcoholic wives, nonalcoholic wives, and clinically judged self-actualizers in the expected way. A group of normal study participants also scored higher on many of the POI scales than did the alcoholic wives (Zaccaria & Weir, 1967, pp. 151–157). In general, these studies and others indicate that POI is a valid discriminator between normal and abnormal groups.

A large number of studies indicate that the POI can be utilized effectively to measure changes in self-actualization following sensitivity training and encounter-group experiences. Dosamantes-Alperson and Merrill (1980, pp. 63–68), for example, administered the POI to groups of people before and after they participated in a number of group-therapy sessions. Control groups (a ballet class and a waiting-list group drawn from the same population as the therapy groups) also filled out the POI at the same time but received no therapeutic experiences. The results indicated that, in comparison to the controls, participants in the therapy sessions became more self-actualizing; that is, they became more inner-directed, spontaneous, and self-accepting. Another investigation also found changes in POI scores on the two major scales and most of the subscales in the direction of greater self-actualization following counseling that emphasized expression of feelings and the need to be sensitive to the desires of others, as compared to a variety of control groups who received no counseling (Pearson, 1966).

Despite these generally positive results, the POI does have some methodological flaws. A primary, recurring problem is that study participants can deliberately fake their responses in ways designed to elicit positive impressions from others. That is,

TABLE 12.1   ITEMS FROM SHOSTROM'S PERSONAL ORIENTATION INVENTORY*

1. a. I strive always to predict what will happen in the future.
   b. **I do not feel it necessary always to predict what will happen in the future.**
2. a. I prefer to save good things for future use.
   b. **I prefer to use good things now.**
3. a. **It is important to me how I live in the here and now.**
   b. It is of little importance to me how I live in the here and now.
4. a. I am bound by the principle of fairness.
   b. **I am not absolutely bound by the principle of fairness.**
5. a. **I often make my decisions spontaneously.**
   b. I seldom make my decisions spontaneously.
6. a. **It is possible to live life in terms of what I want to do.**
   b. It is not possible to live life in terms of what I want to do.
7. a. I live by values which are in agreement with others.
   b. **I live by values which are primarily based on my own feelings.**
8. a. It is important that others accept my point of view.
   b. **It is not necessary for others to accept my point of view.**
9. a. **I try to be sincere but I sometimes fail.**
   b. I try to be sincere and I am sincere.
10. a. **I believe that man is essentially good and can be trusted.**
    b. I believe that man is essentially evil and cannot be trusted.
11. a. **For me, work and play are the same.**
    b. For me, work and play are opposites.
12. a. **I find some people who are stupid and uninteresting.**
    b. I never find any people who are stupid and uninteresting.

*A person who answers the items by choosing the bold-faced alternatives is more self-actualizing than is a person who does not.
Source: Adapted from Shostrom, *POI*, Copyright © 1999. Reproduced by permission from EdITS Publishers, San Diego, CA. All rights reserved.

participants who are familiar with the **humanistic psychology** literature can deliberately present themselves as actualized when in fact they are not. Even though the POI has a built-in lie-detection scale to uncover such dissimulation, its usefulness as a research instrument would be weakened if it could be shown that sizable numbers of participants do indeed fake their responses. The percentage of such participants in various populations has yet to be determined, but a reasonable conclusion would be that the instrument can be used primarily with naive populations.

Another problem is that study participants generally dislike responding to forced-choice questionnaires, because such instruments do not allow them to present their feelings and opinions fully and accurately. Moreover, as with most measures of personality, the POI cannot assess people's traits in interaction with specific situations. One POI item, for example, is:

a. I can cope with the ups and downs of life.
b. I cannot cope with the ups and downs of life.

Perhaps the participant can cope with the downs (or failures) in life when they involve schoolwork but not when they involve the loss of a close friend. Maybe the person copes well with success in school but reacts poorly to praise from teachers or friends. The point is that a number of questions on the POI do not assess people's reactions in specific situations.

Research Applications of the POI

Despite its flaws, the POI has proven useful to researchers in testing some of Maslow's ideas. For example, Maslow's theory posits that actualizing individuals have gratified their basic needs for food, shelter, belonging and love, and self-esteem. Because they are no longer concerned primarily with fulfilling their basic needs, they are free to focus their attention on enhancing their own physical and mental health. Thus, self-actualizing individuals should engage in more health-promoting behavior, for example, by following a healthy diet, exercising consistently, cutting out smoking and heavy drinking. A study by Acton and Malathum (2000, p. 796) provided support for this prediction in college-educated adults. Recent research shows further that self-actualizing individuals are also more mentally healthy, that is, they are highly secure in their understanding of themselves and others, and in their ability to cope with daily demands, challenges, and pressures (Bar-On, 2010, pp. 54–62; Vaughn, Naylor, & White, Jr., 2009, pp. 2–12).

In interesting research there is a focus once again on the concepts of basic needs satisfaction and self-actualization. Kasser and his colleagues (Kasser & Ahuvia, 2002, pp. 137–146; Kasser & Ryan, 1993, pp. 410–422; Kasser & Sheldon, 2000, pp. 348–351) have maintained that people who grow up in families that have been unable to satisfy their basic needs, for example, those who have been unable to satisfy their longing for friendship, love, and self-esteem are likely to feel insecure. These feelings of insecurity give rise to an inordinate concern with power over others, wealth, popularity, and social recognition, all extrinsic values. This concern with the attainment of extrinsic goals leads these individuals to neglect the development of intrinsic values, that is, values involving self-acceptance, friendship, and feelings of community that are associated with personal growth and mental health. Kasser and his colleagues found that individuals who were insecure were more concerned with materialistic values, and that their greater materialistic orientations were associated with lower self-actualization. Even when they had attained *actual* financial success, individuals with very strong materialistic values were still unhappy and lower in self-actualization. In contrast, individuals who valued community involvement strongly were found to be higher in self-actualization.

While Carver and Baird (1998, pp. 289–292) agree, for the most part, with the basic conception and results of the Kasser studies, they maintain that Kasser and his colleagues have not pursued their analysis to its logical conclusion. Specifically, Carver and Baird note that Kasser and his colleagues have not analyzed the motivations and reasons underlying the value orientations to financial and personal success and to community involvement. Specifically, they argued that, if people high in materialistic values were pursuing their goal of financial wealth for intrinsic reasons (e.g., because success is fun, exciting, and challenging), then there should be a positive correlation between materialistic values and self-actualization. If, on the other hand, these people were pursuing materialistic goals for extrinsic reasons (e.g., for power over others and social recognition, like Kasser and his colleagues suggest), then the correlation between materialistic values and self-actualization should be negative. In terms of community involvement, Carver and Baird maintain that, if people high on this value were pursuing it for extrinsic reasons (e.g., to enhance their status in the community, to win favorable comments from church members), then the more importance they attach to community involvement, the lower their self-actualization scores would be. In contrast, they maintain that the more importance people attach to community involvement based on intrinsic reasons (e.g., to help other people in need, it's the right thing to do), then the higher their self-actualization. Carver and Baird found support for all of their predictions. These researchers conclude that, in general, it is often more important *why* a goal or value is being pursued than *what* the goal is (Carver & Baird, 1998, pp. 289–292).

Theory's Implications for Therapy

In Maslow's view, neurotics are people who have been prevented and who have prevented themselves from attaining gratification of their basic needs, and thus have been precluded from moving toward the ultimate goal of self-actualization. They feel threatened and insecure and have little self-respect or self-esteem. Because gratification of these basic needs can occur only through contact with other people, it follows that therapy must be interpersonal in nature (Maslow, 1970a, p. 242).

Maslow likened the psychotherapeutic relationship between therapist and client to a relationship between friends. The therapy situation must involve mutual frankness, trust, honesty, and lack of defensiveness. It should also allow for the expression of a healthy amount of childishness and silliness (Maslow, 1970a, p. 249). This is only possible when the relationship is nonthreatening and supportive. In such a democratic context, the therapist should provide the client with the respect, love, and feelings of belongingness he or she must have in order to grow. In other words, the therapist must act to gratify the client's basic need deficiencies. But effective therapy must go beyond this point. The therapeutic relationship should encourage not only the therapist's giving of love to the client but also the client's expression of love and affection toward the therapist and others (Maslow, 1970a, p. 250). More generally, the client should be encouraged to display those values associated with positive growth, to open up to the world and learn to understand more about its complex nature.

Maslow realized that a warm, supportive therapeutic approach was unworkable with some clients, particularly those with chronic, stabilized neuroses that involve deep mistrust and hostility toward others (Maslow, 1970a, p. 251). He believed that, under those conditions, a depth analysis in the Freudian tradition might be more useful. In such an analysis, clients would work through their problems both cognitively *and* emotionally, as a means of achieving change and self-improvement.

Evaluative Comments

We now evaluate the scientific worth of Maslow's position in terms of our six criteria.

Comprehensiveness   Maslow's theory is a pioneering and creative effort aimed at moving personality psychology away from an exclusive concern with psychopathology and toward a more positive and optimistic view of people and their potential creativeness. His theory can be considered comprehensive in the sense that it incorporates much of the Freudian model of pathology and, in addition, addresses itself to the issue of positive growth; but, technically speaking, its focus is primarily and explicitly on the latter rather than the former. In this sense, the theory is not quite as comprehensive as it appears at first. Thus, Maslow's theory is somewhat limited both in the range and diversity of phenomena it explicitly encompasses and in the explanatory system it uses to account for these events.

Precision and testability   Maslow's theory is not very precise and, as a result, is difficult to test properly. Take, for example, his hierarchical scheme of human motivation, in which the emergence of basic needs from most to least potent is presumed to follow their successive gratification. Yet some people are willing to suffer hunger and thirst, and eventually even to die, for values Maslow assumed to be less potent than physiological needs. Although he recognized this problem, his theory does not account for the exceptions.

The theory also lacks precision regarding the amount of gratification the individual must experience before the next higher need will emerge. Maslow maintained that most people's basic needs are partially satisfied and partially dissatisfied at the same time. Thus, a given need will not be completely gratified before the next one emerges. Instead, Maslow posited a gradual emergence of higher needs as lower needs become increasingly gratified. For example, if a lower need is 10% gratified, the next higher need may not emerge. But if the lower need is 25% gratified, then the higher need may emerge at 5% of potency; if the lower need is 50% gratified, there may be a 25% emergence; and so on (Maslow, 1970a, pp. 53–54).

Adequate definition of self-actualization and a number of other terms (purposefulness, inner requiredness, and good and bad situations) remains a major problem with the theory.

Parsimony   Maslow's theory fails to meet the parsimony criterion. The motivational deficiency scheme he used to account for various behaviors is too simplistic to account adequately for the phenomena within its domain. Moreover, it does not spell out precisely the situational variables that control the occurrence, maintenance, and modification of self-actualization phenomena (Lethbridge, 1986, p. 90).

Empirical validity   Without adequate measures of the major constructs in Maslow's theory, tests of its empirical validity are impossible. As we have seen, researchers have constructed an adequate measure of actualization but, when it has been used to test the theory, the research results have not been consistently supportive. For example, Mathes (1978, pp. 215–222) found no evidence for Maslow's hypothesis that self-actualizers are more creative than nonactualizers. Similarly, Ryckman, Robbins, Thornton, Gold, and Kuehnel (1985, pp. 288–298), using two independent samples of college undergraduates, could find no support for his hypothesis that actualizers tend to be physically strong, fit people. Despite these negative findings, research interest in Maslow's theory continues to grow, as evidenced by the construction of new individual-difference measures of peak experiences (Mathes & Zevon, 1982, pp. 92–108) and basic needs (Haymes & Green, 1982, pp. 179–192).

Heuristic value   Despite its many limitations, Maslow's theory has been provocative and has stimulated the thinking of many investigators in a variety of disciplines. Not only has he encouraged theorists and researchers to consider the healthy side of human nature (See Chapter 18, section on Positive Psychology), but he has also forced some of them to reconsider their own myopic view of science and its limitations for understanding human functioning. Specifically, he castigated them for their "inevitable stress on elegance, polish, technique, and apparatus [that] has, as a frequent consequence, a playing down of meaningfulness, vitality, and significance of a problem and of creativeness in general" (Maslow, 1970a, p. 11). As a result, he has persuaded some of them to think of science as an enterprise in which people ask significant questions and then adopt techniques to help answer them, rather than an enterprise in which they use sophisticated techniques to study relatively unimportant problems.

Applied value   Maslow's theory is also very strong in the applied area. His formulations have had a decided impact on pastoral and educational counseling programs. In addition, many business managers have embraced Maslow's idea that humane, enlightened companies have a responsibility to help their employees move toward self-actualization and that helping them reach that goal will also prove financially profitable. As a result, they have endorsed and implemented programs of shared decision making, mutual trust, caring, and cooperation among people at all levels of the company

(Maslow, 1987, p. 257). Finally, Maslow's theory has had a major impact on the world of education of children and adults alike, restructuring curricula to give students more choice and freedom to participate in a creative way in their own education.

CRITICAL THINKING QUESTIONS

1. Do you accept Maslow's assumption that human nature is good or, at the very least, neutral? Why or why not?
2. Is it possible, in your opinion, to create a universal set of ethical principles? What principles guide your behavior? Where did they originate?
3. Do you agree with Maslow that children need limits on their behavior? Why?
4. Have you ever experienced B-love? How could you be certain that it was not D-love?
5. Maslow maintained that we not only fear failure but often are afraid to be successful. Why did he hold such a belief? What great work are you planning in your own life? Are you satisfied with your progress toward your goals? Why or why not?

GLOSSARY

authoritarian parenting style   A disciplinary style in which parents discourage verbal give-and-take with their children and expect instead complete and unquestioning obedience to their judgments. Failure to comply can result in physical and/or verbal abuse of their children.

authoritative parenting style   A disciplinary style in which children are consulted by parents in the establishment of disciplinary rules. Once established, children are reinforced for adherence to them and punished firmly and consistently for nonadherence, but without resorting to physical and/or verbal abuse. Such parents are warm, respectful, and considerate in their treatment of their children. They listen to their children and are willing to take their disagreements into account.

B-cognition   State of experiencing that is nonjudgmental and self-validating.

B-love   A mature form of love in which the person is more concerned with giving love to benefit others than in receiving love from others to gratify his or her needs; also known as being-love.

D-cognition   State of experiencing that involves judgments of approval and disapproval.

D-love   A selfish love in which the individual is more concerned with receiving love and gratifying his or her needs than with giving love to another; also known as deficiency-love.

deficiency needs   Basic needs that must be gratified to a large extent before an individual can progress toward self-actualization.

desacralizing attitude   Tendency to be disrespectful, cynical, and mistrustful; it causes the perceiver to overlook the virtues and strengths of the perceived.

growth needs   Higher needs that may emerge once the basic needs have been satisfied; also known as meta needs.

humanistic biology   View that the basic nature of human beings is potentially good and capable of pushing people in the direction of self-realization if the right social conditions prevail.

humanistic psychology   Approach to psychology that is primarily concerned with helping individuals to reach their maximum development and that emphasizes, and tries to foster, the dignity and worth of each human being.

Jonah complex   Fear that exercising our abilities to the maximum will bring with it responsibilities and duties that we will be unable to handle; an unwillingness to sacrifice current safety and security for the unknown.

peak experience   Intense, mystical experience in which an individual exists in a temporary state of joy and wonderment.

permissive parenting style A disciplinary style in which parents make few demands on their children and use little punishment. Parents typically shower their children with affection and go along with whatever their children want to do; such parents provide little active guidance.

Personal Orientation Inventory (POI) Test designed to measure an individual's self-actualizing tendencies.

self-actualization Process whereby the healthy development of people's abilities enables them to fulfill their own true natures.

self-actualizers Individuals who have gratified their basic needs and developed their potentialities to the point that they can be considered healthy, more fully functioning human beings.

transcending self-actualizing person The most fully developed, psychologically healthy person, one who frequently has B-cognition and peak experiences and can transcend his/her own selfish concerns and work to better humankind.

SUGGESTED READINGS

Maslow, A. H. (1943). A theory of human motivation. *Psychological Review, 50,* 370–396.

Maslow, A. H. (1962). *Toward a psychology of being.* New York: Van Nostrand.

Maslow, A. H. (1971). *The farther reaches of human nature.* New York: Viking Press.

Maslow, A. H. (1987). *Motivation and personality* (3rd ed.). New York: Harper & Row.

CHAPTER 13

Rogers's Person-Centered Theory

Bettmann/Corbis.

Biographical Sketch

Carl Ransom Rogers was born in 1902 in Oak Park, Illinois, a suburb of Chicago; he was the fourth in a family of six children. His father was a successful civil engineer and contractor. Rogers was raised in a home marked by close, warm family relationships but also by strict and uncompromising religious principles. His parents controlled his behavior and would allow no alcoholic beverages, no dancing, no card playing or theatergoing, and very little contact with other people. They extolled the virtues of the Protestant ethic: hard work, responsibility for one's actions, and the importance of personal success. Rogers reported that "even carbonated beverages had a faintly sinful aroma, and I remember my slight feeling of wickedness when I had my first bottle of pop" (Rogers, 1961, p. 5). His wife, who was his childhood sweetheart, remembers him as a "shy, sensitive, and unsocial boy who preferred to live in his books and his dream world rather than encounter the rough [and] tumble of the play yard or enter into competitive sports" (Rogers, H. E., 1965, p. 94).

When he was 12, his parents bought a farm a short distance from Chicago, and Rogers spent his adolescence there. His father encouraged his sons to raise animals for profit, and Rogers reared chickens, lambs, pigs, and calves. The venture aroused an interest in scientific agriculture and the application of scientific methods to farming. In retrospect, Rogers concluded that the experience had taught him a healthy respect for science as a means of solving problems. He entered the University of Wisconsin and chose scientific agriculture as his field of study. Shortly afterward, his professional goals shifted dramatically, as a result of some emotion-laden experiences at a student religious conference. Specifically, Rogers was chosen as one of only a dozen students from the United States to attend a World Student Christian Federation conference in Peking, China. On the trip, he was forced to modify drastically his thinking about his strict, family-based religious beliefs, because of his associations with this small group of highly intelligent and creative young people. Rogers came to recognize that it was possible for other sincere and honest people to have religious beliefs that differed from his own. He wrote to his parents about his new feelings and ideas, and these letters undoubtedly deeply distressed and even scandalized them. Also, during this trip, Rogers corresponded with his childhood sweetheart, Helen, and the relationship became increasingly intimate. Upon his return to Wisconsin, Rogers bought his first car and frequently drove 25 miles over rough roads in order to see her. In time, his feelings toward her were reciprocated. Finally, the day arrived when, in his own words, "the most wonderful miracle in the world took place," when she told him she loved him too. They were married two months after his graduation from the University of Wisconsin. They piled all of their worldly possessions into a used car that Rogers bought for $450 and set out for New York City, where he had enrolled in the Union Theological Seminary (Thorne, 1992, pp. 4–6).

At the seminary, he and a group of other students decided they were being unilaterally presented with ideas by their instructors and were not being given an opportunity to explore their own personal doubts and questions. Accordingly, they petitioned the administration for a seminar without a formal instructor. To their surprise, the request was granted. Rogers found the seminar most gratifying; he later said that, as a result of the experience, he thought himself right out of religious work.

Rogers had taken some courses in psychology and enjoyed them, and he decided to enter that field. He began his studies at Columbia University, across the street from the seminary. At the end of his clinical internship, even though he had not completed his doctorate, Rogers felt he had to have a job to support his growing family. He took a position as a psychologist in the Child Study Department of the Society for the Prevention of Cruelty to Children in Rochester, New York, and completed his doctorate in 1928. For Rogers, the 12 years spent at Rochester were valuable ones. During most of that time, he was immersed in practical work, the diagnosis and treatment of delinquent and disadvantaged children. His unique nondirective, or client-centered, approach to therapy evolved during this period, which culminated in a book entitled *The Clinical Treatment of the Problem Child* (1939). In 1940, he accepted an academic position as a full professor at Ohio State University, where he began to attract capable students, to conduct research on his theory, and to achieve international recognition. *Counseling and Psychotherapy* (1942), a book designed to provide therapists with procedures he felt would engender constructive changes in their clients, was written during this time.

In 1944, Rogers was given an opportunity to establish a counseling center at the University of Chicago. He then wrote *Client-Centered Therapy* (1951), in which he laid out the theory that underlies his approach to understanding human relationships. A decade later he published *On Becoming a Person* (1961), a collection of papers on a variety of issues related to this basic approach to understanding personal growth.

In 1957, Rogers returned to the University of Wisconsin. He recalls that his experiences there were generally unpleasant, as he became aware of the restrictions under which graduate students were forced to work. Rogers called for massive reform in the graduate program; he argued that students have within themselves the potential for learning and development but that this potential can be realized only when they are provided with freedom and a supportive environment (Rogers, 1968). Shortly after he released the reasons for his disagreement with current educational policies, he resigned from the department.

In 1963, Rogers became a member of the Western Behavioral Sciences Institute in La Jolla, California. In 1968, he left the institute to help form the Center for the Studies of the Person in La Jolla.

In 1967, he wrote *Person to Person: The Problem of Being Human* in collaboration with Barry Stevens. This book was followed by *Freedom to Learn* (1969), *Carl Rogers on Encounter Groups* (1970), *Becoming Partners: Marriage and Its Alternatives* (1972), *Carl Rogers on Personal Power* (1977), *A Way of Being* (1980), and *Freedom to Learn for the 80s* (1983). In the book on personal power, Rogers attempted to illustrate the revolutionary impact of his person-centered approach on psychotherapy, family life, education, administration, and politics. He also discussed the implications of his approach for the emergence of a new type of self-empowered person, who would spearhead the revolution in human relationships that Rogers saw occurring.

Rogers received many honors and awards from his professional colleagues. He served as president of the American Psychological Association in 1946–1947. In 1956, he received the first Distinguished Scientific Contribution Award presented by the American

Psychological Association, which also honored him with its Distinguished Professional Contribution Award in 1972.

Carl Rogers died of a heart attack in La Jolla, California, on February 4, 1987, at the age of 85. His last few years were spent productively, that is, he attended numerous international workshops, at which he demonstrated to psychologists and other mental health workers, educators, and politicians how various concepts and propositions from his person-centered approach could be utilized to ease world tensions and promote peace.

Concepts and Principles

The Fundamental Perspective: The Person's Experiences as the Ultimate Authority

Rogers's psychology starts and ends with the subjective experiences of the individual. In his view, the subjective experiencing of reality serves as the basis for all the individual's judgments and behavior. It is this phenomenological, inner reality, rather than external, objective reality, that plays the key role in determining the person's behavior.

Inner experience includes everything that is occurring within the organism at a particular moment. All this experience, conscious and unconscious, is said to comprise the person's phenomenal field. Conscious experience, or awareness, is the aspect of the phenomenal field that can be symbolized, that is, verbalized or imagined. Unconscious experience, in contrast, is experience that cannot be verbalized or imagined by the person. Healthy individuals, in Rogers's view, are those who can symbolize their experiences accurately and completely; unhealthy people distort or repress their experiences and are unable to symbolize them accurately and sense them fully.

The Master Motive: Self-Actualizing Tendency

Within each of us, according to Rogers, is an innate motivation called the self-actualizing tendency, an active, controlling drive toward fulfillment of our potentials that enables us to maintain and enhance ourselves.

Rogers based this concept primarily on his varied and prolonged experience with troubled individuals in therapy. He noticed in them

> a growth tendency, a drive toward self-actualization. It is the urge which is evident in all organic and human life, to expand, extend, become autonomous, develop, mature. This tendency may become deeply buried under layer after layer of encrusted psychological defenses but it is my belief that it exists in every individual, and awaits only the proper conditions to be released and expressed. (Rogers, 1961, p. 35)

In support of this concept, he cited experiments showing that even rats prefer an environment offering more complex stimuli over one offering less complex stimuli. Human beings similarly seek new experiences and avoid environments that are lacking in stimulation. Experiments have shown that, when people are suspended weightless in a soundproof tank of water, they soon experience aversive hallucinations. To Rogers, these studies, together with his clinical experience, suggested that there is a directional tendency in each of us to grow, to seek new and varied experiences.

The actualizing tendency has both a biological and a psychological aspect. The biological aspect includes drives aimed at the satisfaction of basic survival needs, the need for water, food, and air. The psychological aspect involves the development of potentials that make us more worthwhile human beings. In Rogers's judgment, we are all basically good. The actualizing tendency is, thus, selective and directional; it is a constructive tendency. Organisms do not, according to Rogers, develop their capacity for nausea or self-destruction except under the most perverse circumstances (Rogers, 1977, p. 242). Instead, they develop their innate goodness, but only if society acts toward them in a helpful, encouraging way. Although Rogers was clearly optimistic about human nature, he was, nevertheless, keenly aware that human beings are sometimes immature and antisocial and that they sometimes act out of fear, ignorance, and defensiveness. Such behavior, however, is not in accordance with their basic natures, according to Rogers, but is the result of faulty socialization practices. Thus, society can facilitate or hinder movement toward self-actualization.

Personality Development

The Valuing Process in Infants

Rogers maintained that infants perceive their experiences as reality. They operate from an internal frame of reference, unencumbered by the evaluations of others. He also believed that infants interact with their reality in terms of their basic actualizing tendency (Rogers, 1959, p. 222); their behavior is directed toward the goal of satisfying their need for self-actualization as they perceive it. Thus, infants engage in an **organismic valuing process**, in which they use their actualization tendency as a criterion in making judgments about the worth of a given experience. Experiences that help promote actualization are good, or positively valued; experiences that hinder actualization are bad, or negatively valued. In support of this view, Rogers cited the example of an infant who values food when hungry but rejects it when satiated. According to Rogers, infants have a built-in mechanism that allows them to select the diet that, in the long run, enhances their development (Rogers, 1959, p. 210; Rogers & Stevens, 1967, p. 6); in other words, infants know instinctively which foods and experiences are good for them and which are bad.

The investigation most cited by Rogers, Maslow, and others who have attempted to build a psychology on the notion that people instinctively know what is best for them is the Davis (1928) study of infant feeding behavior. Three infants ranging in age from 8 to 10 months were given thorough physical examinations by a medical doctor, including a blood count, urinalysis, and skeletal X-rays, and then given the opportunity to select their own diets from saucers holding a variety of foods and glasses holding a variety of liquids. The choices for a typical meal are shown in Table 13.1. Nurses were present at each feeding but did not offer any food to the infants. If the infants reached or pointed to a food, the nurses were allowed to offer them a spoonful. Two infants remained on such a diet for six months, and the third for one year. At the end of this period, the infants were again given complete physical examinations. The results showed that, in general, the diets selected were optimal and the infants were healthy.

What is wrong with this study? One possible source of error revolves around the role of the nurses, who could have misjudged random arm waving and reaching as signs of the infants' wanting a particular food. Also, because the experiment lasted a relatively short time, the long-range impact on development is impossible to assess. It also should be noted that none of the foods offered to the infants was lacking in nutritive value; arguably, the available choices could only promote health. Of course, it would have been unethical to provide infants with nonnutritive food choices, but this does not negate this shortcoming. Finally, only three infants participated in the study, and so it is clearly unwarranted to generalize these results to all infants in the culture.

TABLE 13.1 TYPICAL MEAL SERVED TO TEST FOR ADEQUACY OF SELF-SELECTION DIET

Milk, grade A	Lamb, cooked	Cauliflower, cooked
Milk, lactic	Chicken, cooked	Cabbage, raw
Sea salt	Lettuce, raw	Cabbage, cooked
Rye-Krisp	Potatoes, cooked	Spinach, cooked
Bone marrow, raw	Beets, cooked	Peas, cooked
Bone marrow, cooked	Carrots, raw	Peas, raw
Beef, raw	Carrots, cooked	Cornmeal, cooked
Beef, cooked	Turnips, cooked	

Source: Adapted from Davis, 1928, p. 659.

The research literature with lower animals does not support much of the specific hungers hypothesis, that is, the idea that animals tend to select those foods that enable them to compensate for specific nutritional deficiencies. While they do select foods with sodium in them when they have a sodium deficiency because these items have a taste, they cannot select the correct foods with the vitamins and minerals they need because these nutrients have no taste. Moreover, some studies have shown that animals can be easily trained to eat sweet foods with no nutritional value and to bypass unsweetened foods with nutritional value. In fact, in order to maximize their profits, many manufacturers produce foods with the tastes human consumers prefer but with most of the essential nutrients extracted from them. Think of the sugary cereal products that many parents buy to ward off the crying and complaining of their children (Galef, 1991, pp. 218–223; Garcia, Kimeldurf, & Hunt, 1961, pp. 383–395; Pinel, 2000, pp. 255–256). Thus, we might conclude that humans would have an extremely difficult time getting in touch with their organismic wisdom mechanism (assuming that one existed) in order to make good decisions, because of interference from their learning experiences. Rogers hinted at this problem when he stated that the drive toward self-actualization may be "deeply buried under layer after layer of encrusted psychological defenses" (Rogers, 1961, p. 35). At the very least, then, the process of getting in touch with our innermost feelings would be difficult.

The Valuing Process in Adults

In adults, the valuing process is much more complex than it is in infants. At this point in the developmental process, the adult is making much more complicated judgments about a variety of experiences relating to issues in art, politics, career, ethics, personal relationships, and so forth. Value judgments in these areas often change. A painting we found satisfying last year may be abhorrent to us now. Judgments about friends, acquaintances, politicians, doctors, teachers, clergy, parents, and others do not remain constant. In addition, adults, unlike infants, are exposed to a variety of opinions and come to incorporate them into their value systems. Yet, in Rogers's view, adults, after listening to what others think, must ultimately trust the wisdom of their own bodies if they are to grow constructively. If they can trust themselves fully, he maintained, their feelings and intuitions may be wiser than their thinking or what they have learned from others (Rogers & Stevens, 1967, pp. 15–16).

The Fully Functioning Person

If people are able to utilize their organismic valuing processes fully, they will inevitably begin to experience personal growth and movement toward realization of their potentials.

In Rogers's terminology, they will be moving toward becoming **fully functioning persons**. Such individuals have the following characteristics, according to Rogers:

1. *They are open to experience.* Fully functioning people are nondefensive individuals who are open to all their feelings: fear, discouragement, pain, tenderness, courage, and awe. They are fully aware of their experiences and accept them, rather than shutting them out.

2. *They are characterized by existential living.* Fully functioning people live their experiences as they occur in the present, without trying to superimpose preconceived meaning on them. They are open and flexible, deal with the experience as it is, and discover its meaning for themselves.

3. *They trust their organisms.* Fully functioning people do what feels right. This does not mean they are inevitably right in their choices, but rather that they make their own choices, experience the consequences, and correct them if they are less than satisfying.

4. *They are creative.* Creative products and creative living emerge when individuals are open to new experiences, able to trust their own judgments, and willing to take risks if they feel good about a new venture.

5. *They live richer lives than do other people.* They live the good life, not in the sense of happiness, contentment, security, and bliss, although fully functioning people experience each of these feelings at appropriate times, but a life that is exciting, challenging, meaningful, and rewarding. Not a life for the fainthearted, it involves taking risks, experiencing pain occasionally, and facing challenges courageously (Rogers, 1961, pp. 187–196).

In his later writings, Rogers (1977) extended and amplified his view of the fully functioning person and applied it to what he called **emerging persons**: corporate executives who have given up the rat race to live a simpler life; young people who have defied many of the current cultural values and formed a counterculture; priests and nuns who have rejected the dogma of their churches to live more meaningful lives; African Americans, Mexican Americans, women, and others outside of the dominant culture who have shed their passivity and begun to live more assertive and positive lives (Rogers, 1977, p. 264). He described them as having the following characteristics:

1. *They are honest and open.* They reject the sham and hypocrisy of government, Madison Avenue advertisers, parents, teachers, and clergy. They are open about their sexual relationships and open in their dealing with others. These humanistically oriented people are opposed to highly structured, inflexible bureaucracies. They believe that institutions exist for human beings and not vice versa.

2. *They are indifferent to material comforts and rewards.* Blue jeans replace expensive clothes; sleeping bags replace Holiday Inns; and natural foods replace fine cuisine. Emerging people are not power-hungry or achievement-hungry. They are not concerned with status but prefer to relate to people in informal, egalitarian ways.

3. *They are caring persons.* They have a deep desire to help others, to contribute to society. They are suspicious of people in the helping professions: therapists, social workers, and drug counselors, for example, who earn their livelihood by offering help for pay and very frequently hide behind a professional facade. Instead, emerging people voluntarily help others in crisis. They share food and lodging without question. Their caring is gentle, subtle, and nonmoralistic. When they help others down from a bad drug trip, for example, they do not preach to them.

4. *They have a deep distrust of cognitively based science and a technology that uses that science to exploit and harm nature and people.* Emerging people have an intuitive belief that significant discoveries involve feelings. They also respect the environment and do not want to see technology used to destroy it. For example, they oppose

nuclear arms and the profound disregard for human life of political leaders who continue to advocate the construction of increasingly destructive weapons (Rogers, 1982). Emerging persons can support the use of technology, but only when it is used wisely to promote human welfare.

5. *They have a trust in their own experience and a profound distrust of all external authority.* Neither the pope nor the president nor intellectuals can convince emerging persons of anything that is not borne out by personal experience. They do not obey laws just for the sake of obeying; they obey when it feels right for them to do so. They will deliberately disobey the law and accept the consequences when the law seems unjust or immoral (Rogers, 1977, pp. 255–274).

Rogers recognized that emerging persons are a small minority of the total population. However, he believed that they have an impact on society out of proportion to their numbers and will continue to exert significant influence in the future.

The Social Self and the True Self

The **social self** is the organized set of characteristics that the individual perceives as being peculiar to himself or herself. The social self is primarily acquired through contact with others. Rogers believed that when we interact with significant people in our environment, parents, brothers, sisters, friends, teachers, we begin to develop a concept of self that is largely based on the evaluations of others; that is, we come to evaluate ourselves in terms of what others think and not in terms of what we actually feel.

The reason we rely so heavily on the evaluation of others, according to Rogers, is that we have a strong **need for positive regard**. Rogers was uncertain whether this need is innate or learned but maintained that its origins are less important than its impact on the individual. When we satisfy another's needs, we experience satisfaction of our own need for positive regard (Rogers, 1959, p. 223). As a consequence, the desire for positive regard from others may become more compelling than our own organismic valuing process (Rogers, 1959, p. 224). If, for example, we feel that aggression against others is wrong, but significant others place a positive value on it, we may ignore the validity of the feelings of our **true self** and act in terms of their expectations as a means of gaining their approval.

This need to seek approval and avoid disapproval leads to a social self-concept that is conditional on the performance of certain kinds of behavior (Rogers, 1959, p. 209). Such a self-concept carries with it **conditions of worth**. We perceive experiences and behaviors as acceptable only if they meet with approval from others; experiences and behaviors that meet with disapproval we perceive as unacceptable.

Recent research by Roth, Assor, Niemiec, Ryan, and Deci (2009, pp. 1119–1142) showed that children who had parents who withdrew their affection and approval when their children did not follow parental expectations had children who resented them, viewing them as highly controlling and punitive. Such parental training resulted in children who avoided their parents as much as they could. In contrast, children who had parents who gave them approval and affection only when they followed their expectations had children who were highly controlled in their behavior and who suppressed any negative emotions they had about their parents and their expectations of them. Such children were constricted in their views of life and less open to new learning experiences. For example, if their parents provided them with lots of praise for getting good grades, their children became primarily oriented toward only learning those materials related directly to earning good grades. Thus, their curiosity, willingness to explore alternative solutions to problems, and love of learning for its own sake became highly constrained.

The ideal condition for development of a healthy self-concept and movement toward becoming fully functioning, in Rogers's view, is **unconditional positive regard**, a deep and genuine caring by others, uncontaminated by judgments or evaluations of our thoughts, feelings, or behaviors (Rogers & Sanford, 1984, p. 1379). With unconditional positive regard, the self-concept carries no conditions of worth, there is a **congruence** between the true self and experience, and the person is psychologically healthy. Thus, parents who take the child's perspective and encourage them to express their own true feelings and to make their own choices tend to have children who grow up most psychologically healthy.

In real life, we all have conditions of worth placed on our behavior. We all learn in the course of socialization that some of our feelings and behaviors are appropriate and others are inappropriate. When these normative rules are congruent with our organismic evaluations, we can get in touch with our true self and continue our movement toward self-actualization. In such cases, our social selves and our true selves are in harmony. Rogers believed that parents and others can establish creativity-fostering environments, with rules that encourage children to be curious, self-reliant, and respectful of themselves and others. Classic research by Harrington, Block, and Block (1987, pp. 851–856) has shown that children raised in such environments are more creative later in life than are children raised in environments with overly controlling, critical parents who did not give them freedom to grow and make their own decisions.

In conclusion, Rogers believed that when we are guided by the expectations of others that run counter to our innate evaluations, problems occur. In this case, our social selves prevent our getting in touch with our true selves and actual feelings, and movement toward actualization is hindered. Congruence between the true self and organismic experiencing leads to accurate symbolization of experiences and positive growth; incongruence leads to inaccurate or distorted symbolization, psychological maladjustment, and vulnerability. Under such incongruent conditions, the person may experience a vague sense that something is wrong. The threat, in Rogers's view, may be "subceived" before it is clearly perceived; that is, the person may experience an increase in heartbeat and breathing rate and a sense of anxiety without being able to identify accurately the source of the difficulty. This anxiety triggers defense mechanisms to cope with the threat. If the incongruence between the true self and organismic experiencing is too great, the defense may be unsuccessful; the result is a profound state of disorganization that may be labeled psychotic.

Empirical Support for the Self Theory

If Rogers's theorizing about the relationship between the self and organismic experiencing is correct, we would expect persons who deny threats to their self-picture, that is, persons who are defensive, to be more maladjusted than those who are less defensive. Chodorkoff (1954) hypothesized that, the greater the agreement between a person's self-description and a description of the person by others, the less perceptual defense the person will show. This hypothesis was based on the assumption that nondefensive people are open to all their experiences, threatening or otherwise; they should be able to assimilate them into their self-concept, as long as they are organismically valid. Chodorkoff's second hypothesis was that, the greater the agreement between the personal and objective descriptions, the greater would be the individual's personal adjustment.

To test these hypotheses, clinical judges provided descriptions based on biographical information and on the results of two projective tests, the Rorschach and the Thematic Apperception Test. (The assumption was that diagnostic tests accurately reflect the individual's own assessment at an organismic level, an assumption that Rogers himself repeatedly challenged.) Scores based on the degree of agreement between the two sets of ratings were then correlated with the person's perceptual defense score, as measured by the time it took the study participant to react to tachistoscopic presentations of threatening words (for example, bitch and whore) compared with time latencies for nonthreatening words (for example, chair and table). Personal adjustment was measured by having the judges check on a list of adjectives, such as kind, confident, well-liked, all those they thought described the participant; the more adjectives they checked, the higher the personal adjustment score. Perceptual agreement scores were found to be related to defense and adjustment scores as predicted, and the hypotheses were confirmed.

Rogers's self theory also predicts that persons who are nondefensive (self-accepting) should also be more accepting of the behavior of others. "When the individual perceives and accepts into one consistent and integrated system all his sensory and visceral experiences, then he is necessarily more understanding of others and is more accepting of others as separate individuals" (Rogers, 1951, p. 520). Several studies have yielded support for Rogers's prediction (Wylie, 1979).

Finally, it is clear that Rogers believed that self-acceptance is related positively to mental health, and there are numerous studies that support his view. In an early study, Fisher and Specht (1999, pp. 457–472) found that elderly people who were aging successfully, as evidenced by their ability to cope with their present circumstances by drawing on their past experience and maintaining a positive sense of their future, were characterized by greater self-acceptance, independence, positive interactions with others, and personal growth. In a later study, Scott (2007, pp. 35–64) found that British psychology undergraduate students (average age 19) *and* British non-student adults (average age 48) characterized by higher self-acceptance were less depressed than study participants characterized by lower self-acceptance.

Assessment Techniques

Rogers believed that assessment of the individual's personality must be based on an exploration of the person's feelings and attitudes toward himself or herself and others. It is the client who subjectively interprets experiences and who provides the therapist with valid information about his or her functioning. Rogers recognized that this phenomenological extremism has its limitations. The therapist can gain only that experiential information about the client that the client is able or willing to articulate. Moreover, clients may purposely distort reports to the therapist to win approval. Despite these limitations, Rogers believed that his person-centered approach provides a meaningful way to understand the individual's personality. When the therapist provides a supportive and nonthreatening milieu for the client, distortions and evasions are minimized. The therapist also actively tries not to prejudge the client by fitting him or her into a preconceived theoretical structure. Under these conditions, the therapist can gain an accurate understanding of the unique strengths and weaknesses of the client, with the goal of enabling the client to move toward self-realization.

Although Rogers argued against the clinical use of formal assessment techniques, he was forced to rely on measurement procedures to test his theory. In the Chodorkoff study, for example, judges' ratings were used to assess the person's organismic experiencing. Rogers was also a pioneer in developing a technique for assessing the nature of the interactions between client and therapist and in showing how these data are related to the therapeutic outcome. The technique involves the use of video and audio tape recordings of the therapeutic process. These tapes provide a more accurate, comprehensive, and available set of data for analysis and interpretation than do written records of therapy sessions made by the therapist from memory.

Rogers also conducted research on the impact of person-centered therapy using the **Q-sort**, an assessment procedure pioneered by Stephenson (1953). According to Rogers, a person's self-concept should change over the course of therapy. He believed that the initial discrepancies between the way in which clients actually view themselves and the way in which they would like to view themselves are reduced by effective counseling. The Q-sort is designed to measure these discrepancies between actual and ideal selves.

On entering therapy, clients are asked to sort (arrange) a large number of self-referent statements on a 7-point continuum ranging from "not like me" (1) to "like me" (7). The list might include statements such as "I am tolerant," "I am confident," "I am intelligent," and "I am emotionally mature." After sorting these statements (usually 100 or so), clients are asked to re-sort them in terms of their ideal selves, on a 7-point continuum ranging from "unlike my ideal" (1) to "like my ideal" (7). The two sets of scores are then correlated. Correlations for clients entering therapy are generally low; this suggests that clients see their actual selves as very different from their ideal (or wanted) selves. Following therapy, however, correlations tend to be high and positive; this suggests that clients see fewer discrepancies between their actual and their ideal selves.

In practice, then, Rogers utilized a variety of assessment procedures to ascertain the validity of his theory and the efficacy of his approach to therapy. His reliance on these measures may seem to be in direct contradiction to his statements opposing the use of such techniques in therapy. But a more reasonable interpretation might be that assessment procedures, although an inevitable and necessary part of the therapeutic process, should be deemphasized. They should not be allowed to become so important that they prevent the therapist from understanding the client's own experiencing.

Theory's Implications for Therapy

Rogers not only created a theory of how the self evolves and is related to actualization; he also posited a theory of psychotherapy that focuses on the kind of relationship between the therapist and client that must be attained before positive growth is possible.

This theory had its roots in the soil of personal experience. When he first started practicing psychotherapy with children and adults at the guidance center in Rochester, he reported having very definite preconceptions about the nature of personality functioning, based on the center's Freudian orientation. In practice, however, Rogers found that the Freudian formulations were unworkable; they failed to produce constructive changes in his clients. As a consequence, he abandoned the Freudian view and adopted instead a more pragmatic orientation toward therapy. The only criterion he used to judge the validity of his work with patients was, "Does it work? Is it effective?" (Rogers, 1961, p. 10). Out of this inductive approach, Rogers established the therapeutic conditions necessary for positive growth.

Therapeutic Conditions That Facilitate Growth

In order to identify the conditions that promote growth, Rogers focused not only on his direct experiences with clients but also on the history of attempts by counselors and others to change behavior. He noted that four major techniques had been used: (1) ordering and forbidding; (2) exhortation; (3) suggestion (which includes reassurance and encouragement); and (4) advice (Rogers, 1942, pp. 20–27). Since none of these techniques had been successful, Rogers thought it was time they were abandoned. But what is wrong, for example, with reassuring clients who are experiencing doubts about their personal worth? The problem, according to Rogers, is that counselors tend to use the technique indiscriminately. The consequence of telling clients repeatedly that they are improving is denial of their problems and failure to explore clients' feelings about the problems. Under these conditions, Rogers maintained, it is impossible for clients to improve.

In a broader sense, he held that all these techniques have directive aspects; that is, the therapist acts as an authority figure who understands the nature of the client's problems and the best way or ways to solve them. In terms of the therapeutic process, counselors perceive themselves as experts who discover, diagnose, and treat other people's problems. In Rogers's nondirective, person-centered approach, the focus is on the client. Instead of asking, "How can I treat and cure this person?" Rogers asked, "How can I provide a relationship which this person may use for his own personal growth?" (Rogers, 1961, p. 32).

Rogers believed that people have the capacity for change within themselves and will change in constructive ways if the therapist creates the appropriate conditions for growth. These conditions are:

1. The client and the therapist are in psychological contact; that is, each makes an impact on the phenomenological field of the other.
2. The client is in a state of incongruence and feels anxious about it.
3. The therapist is congruent in the relationship.
4. The therapist experiences unconditional positive regard for the client.
5. The therapist experiences an empathic understanding of the client's internal frame of reference.
6. The client perceives the therapist's unconditional positive regard and the therapist's empathic understanding (Rogers, 1959, p. 213).

For growth to occur, then, the therapist must be congruent, that is, genuine. The congruent therapist is not playing a role as an authority, but displays openly the feelings that are flowing within him or her at that moment. The therapist is aware of these feelings and able to communicate them to the client if it is appropriate to do so (Rogers & Stevens, 1967, p. 87). A therapist who feels bored with a client, for example, may choose not to report this feeling immediately; but if the client continues to be boring through many sessions, the therapist may then report his or her reaction in the hope of dealing with it openly and constructively. Thus, the therapist does not impulsively blurt out every passing feeling and accusation under the guise of being real and genuine. If and when the therapist does express negative feelings, however, they are presented as his or her own personal reaction, and not as an indication of some character flaw in the client (Rogers & Stevens, 1967, p. 88). Thus, the therapist might say, "I am feeling bored," but not "You are a boring person." As Rogers saw it, the therapist is expressing an honest reaction, rather than passing judgment on the client.

The second essential ingredient in a facilitative therapeutic relationship is the therapist's empathic understanding of the client. The therapist should be able to sense accurately the client's inner world of private meanings (Rogers & Stevens, 1967, p. 89). The empathic therapist is able to sense the client's confusion, joy, anger, hostility, and tenderness and is able to communicate this information accurately. Under these conditions, the client will be more trusting and accepting of the therapist's communications even concerning experiences of which the therapist is scarcely aware (Rogers & Stevens, 1967, p. 89).

Finally, the facilitative therapist is one who feels unconditional positive regard for the client. This regard is "an outgoing, positive feeling without reservations and without evaluations. It means *not* making judgments" (Rogers & Stevens, 1967, p. 91). The therapist should not accept certain feelings in the client and reject others but should prize the client in a total rather than in a conditional way. A possible exception involves working with schizophrenics. In such cases, Rogers noted, some therapists are more effective when they appear to be highly conditional, that is, when they do *not* accept some of the clients' bizarre, psychotic behavior (Rogers & Stevens, 1967, p. 94). At the very least, however, Rogers believed that all clients must be treated with respect and dignity and be given positive support by their therapists.

If the previously stated six conditions are operative, according to Rogers, the following changes will be observed in clients:

1. Clients will increasingly express their feelings about their lives and problems.
2. They will become increasingly accurate in their assessment of the meaning of their feelings.
3. They will begin to discern the incongruity between their self-concepts and their experiences.
4. They will feel threatened by the incongruity. The experience of threat is possible only because of the continued unconditional positive regard of the therapist.
5. They will then begin to experience fully, in awareness, feelings that have in the past been denied to awareness or distorted in awareness.
6. They will then become capable of reorganizing their self-concepts by assimilating these previously threatening experiences.
7. As therapy continues, their self-concepts will become increasingly congruent with their experiences. Their self-concepts will now include experiences that previously would have been too threatening to be in awareness. Defensiveness will be decreased.
8. They will become increasingly capable of experiencing the therapist's unconditional positive regard for them.
9. They will become increasingly positive in their regard for themselves.
10. They will come to evaluate their own experiences more in terms of their organismic valuing process and less in terms of the values endorsed by other people. (Rogers, 1959, p. 216)

As a result of this process, Rogers believed, people will become what they organismically *are*, rather than what other people want them to be, and will be more psychologically healthy.

Empirical Support for the Theory of Therapy

To determine whether or not this theory of therapy had any validity, Rogers and his colleagues embarked on an ambitious research program in the 1950s. In one study, Butler and Haigh (1954) found that the average correlation between actual and ideal self for 25 clients before therapy was −.01; this indicates that there was no link between perceived actual and ideal selves. Following counseling, the correlation was +.34; this figure suggests that clients had changed their view of themselves by moving toward their ideal self-picture. A control group of 16 normal individuals who did not undergo therapy, but who did the Q-sorts in the same periods as the counseling group, had correlations of +.58 in the first test and +.59 in the second test. These correlations indicate that normals tend to see less discrepancy between their actual and ideal selves and that this relationship remains stable over time. Unfortunately, this study has a number of methodological flaws (Eysenck, 1961). For instance, the investigators failed to equate the control and treatment groups in terms of their initial psychological adjustment, and consequently it was impossible to assess the effectiveness of the person-centered therapy in producing changes in self-concept among the clients.

In a case study not subject to such methodological criticisms, Rogers (1954, pp. 259–348) analyzed the case of a patient known as Mrs. Oak, a dependent, inarticulate, passive person who had experienced rejection by others both at home and in social groups, as revealed by her self-sort responses before therapy. Repeated self-sorts during the course of therapy were correlated with this pretherapy baseline, with the following results: after the 7th therapeutic session, +.50; after the 25th session, +.42; at the end of therapy, +.39; and 12 months after therapy, +.30. These declining correlations indicate that during the course of therapy, and in the months thereafter, Mrs. Oak became increasingly unlike the person she described herself as being before therapy. Following therapy, she perceived herself to be much more secure, confident, emotionally mature, and expressive, warmer in relationships, and less afraid than she was before therapy began (Rogers, 1954, pp. 274–276). Although not every person who undergoes Rogerian therapy shows such improvement, Rogers concluded that her case did indicate that positive changes *can* be achieved when utilizing this type of psychotherapy (Rogers, 1954, p. 343).

If person-centered therapy is indeed effective in some cases, why does it work? The key, in Rogers's theory, is the facilitative therapist, one who is accurately empathic, genuine, respectful, and unconditionally supportive. Rogers believed that, if the therapist could create these facilitative conditions in therapy, constructive growth was inevitable. While contemporary research has not supported Rogers's extreme belief in the inevitability of constructive growth if these facilitative conditions are met, a host of research studies do indicate that these qualities tend to be very helpful in promoting positive personality changes in clients and successful therapeutic outcomes (Hill & Nakayama, 2000, pp. 869–870; Kirschenbaum & Jourdan, 2005, pp. 37–51; Sexton and Whiston, 1994, pp. 11–15; Wong & Ng, 2008, pp. 58–76). However, this research also shows that successful therapy depends not only on the presence of the facilitative conditions, but on the qualities that the clients bring to the therapeutic relationship. Clients have their own unique personalities, motives, symptoms, and backgrounds, and these factors all enter into the therapeutic process and influence the outcomes. For example, a study found that, in comparison to highly involved clients, those who were relatively uninvolved in the therapeutic process, for instance, clients who disclosed personal information at low and superficial levels, saw their therapists as less helpful if the therapists asked them many open-ended questions (for example, "Would you tell me more about your life?") Such questions tended to scare clients who were having difficulty talking about themselves, to make them feel inadequate, and to create the impression that the therapist was being unsupportive. Knowledge of client characteristics is considered crucial if therapists are going to be able to create the facilitating conditions that will help promote psychological health. Unfortunately, many Rogerian practitioners and also researchers tend to overemphasize the qualities of the therapist needed for therapeutic success, while deemphasizing the characteristics of clients (Gelso & Carter, 1985, pp. 155–243; Hill et al., 1988, pp. 222–233).

While research generally suggests that facilitative therapists can promote some constructive growth in many clients, there are several problems associated with many of these investigations. In most of the studies, the measurement of successful therapeutic change is based only on clients' or therapists' verbalizations or clients' self-reports and not on clients' actual *behavior*. There is also a lack of long-term follow-up studies; that is, most studies of treatment effectiveness assess only immediate changes in clients' functioning, without attempting to assess their permanence. Finally, there is a lack of agreement among researchers on the meaning of various key concepts. For example, Bachelor (1988) found that the term *empathy* has at least four separate meanings to people in therapy: First, it refers to the therapist's accurate, cognitive understanding of the client's subjective state at any particular time; second, it means that the therapist is experiencing the same feelings as the client; third, it refers to the client's feeling that he or she has experiences in common with the therapist; and, fourth, it refers to the therapist's nurturant attitude toward the client, that is, the therapist's supportive or totally attentive presence. Fuzzy concepts lead to the construction of inadequate measures and consequently to poor tests of the theory.

Despite these difficulties, there is still considerable research support for the effectiveness of Rogers's person-centered therapy. The facilitative therapeutic conditions promulgated by Rogers as essential in helping to promote constructive growth in clients are still accepted as the bedrock of many contemporary counseling training programs today (Mason, 2009, pp. 357–362). In addition, even cognitive-behavioral therapists now recognize the need to establish a good therapeutic relationship with clients through the therapist's creation of a warm, empathic, supportive atmosphere before trying to effect behavioral change.

Theory's Implications for Education

Rogers believed his theory to be applicable to many areas besides therapy, including family life, marriage, group leadership, politics, and education. We will look more closely at two of these areas: education and marriage.

In Rogers's view, current educational practices at the elementary, secondary, and college and university levels are basically authoritarian and coercive. Teachers are perceived as possessors of knowledge and students as its recipients, with lectures as the means of transmitting information from teachers to students. Rogers also believed that too much emphasis is placed on the acquisition of cognitive skills (the learning of facts and problem-solving skills) and not enough on the development of affective skills (learning how to be a sensitive and loving person). Moreover, too little attention is devoted to issues of importance to students, for example, sexual relationships and friendship. Educational settings are typically impersonal, with too much emphasis on performance and its evaluation through testing and grading.

According to Rogers, the educational establishment bases its program on a number of faulty assumptions (Rogers, 1968, 1969, 1983):

Students cannot be trusted to pursue their own educational goals   In Rogers' view, teachers exhibit their mistrust of students by constantly supervising and checking on them and their work. If students were allowed to make their own choices concerning their educational goals, he believed, there would be no need to monitor their behavior so closely because they would be positively motivated to study and learn. Surveillance is necessary to ensure compliance only when teachers set goals that are irrelevant or radically at variance with student concerns and interests.

Rogers maintained that students should be allowed to make their own educational choices and set their own goals, because they are the ones who know best what is right for them. This assumption seems dubious, in view of the continual shifting of goals experienced by many students in the course of their educational careers. However, even if they could choose the goals that are right for them, students exist in a society that may not recognize the worth and usefulness of their aims. People have the right to pursue whatever goals they wish, but society also has the right to express its priorities and reward those it considers worthy.

Creative people develop from passive learners   Rogers objected strongly to what he considered the primary emphasis in education, students as passive learners. University students, for example, are typically given information by professors and are expected to regurgitate that information on examinations. Rogers believed that such an emphasis stifles the development of original and creative ideas. Students are taught to conform, to defer coming to grips with their own ideas, and to accept unquestioningly the ideas of their professors. He argued that, in an atmosphere of trust, mutual respect, and freedom from constraints, students would be free to test their own ideas and become creative individuals.

Not everyone agrees with Rogers on this point. Brown and Tedeschi (1972, pp. 1–15), for example, argued that many creative individuals throughout history have been impatient with the constraints of institutions but that their complaints "are interesting not because they tell us anything about the development of genius but because they tell us of [the geniuses'] reactions to the formalities of the learning environment" (Brown & Tedeschi, 1972, p. 5). They observed that child prodigies such as John Stuart Mill, Charles Sanders Pierce, and Ludwig van Beethoven all learned under extremely demanding circumstances, yet their creative impulses were not stifled.

It is clear both from the evidence and from history that the mere absence of constraint or evaluation is not a necessary condition for the development of creative persons. Great ideas are not gathered while sitting under a banyan tree waiting for them to drop. Edison once said that creativity was 99% perspiration and 1% inspiration. What was meant is that the individual must gather a great deal of information that may be relevant for solving a problem. This assimilation process can be quite tedious and tests the motivational intensity of the individual's interest in the problem. Hence, there are times when the work takes on the form of sheer drudgery and there are times when the work is intensely exciting and exhilarating (Brown & Tedeschi, 1972, p. 6).

By way of rebuttal, Rogers argued that self-discipline is one of the most demanding and fruitful of all constraints and is present in almost every creative experience. Conformity, he maintained, does not breed self-discipline; to the contrary, it breeds undisciplined people dependent on the evaluations of others (Rogers, 1972b, pp. 17–18).

Evaluation is education: Education is evaluation Rogers argued forcefully that "examinations have become the beginning and the end of education" (Rogers, 1968, p. 691). Students face endless quizzes and final examinations in their courses. Such obstacles prevent them from doing the real independent learning necessary to a creative life. Thus, they are, in Rogers's view, stultifying to the student. Rogers's point is well taken that students would lack sufficient time to pursue their own interests under such grueling schedules. A more reasonable approach might be to ensure that students have the basic concepts that are a prerequisite of creative activity by testing them as early as possible in their course and careers, and then to provide them with the latitude Rogers advocates.

In summary, Rogers believed that the educational system was in desperate need of reform. He saw it as too authoritarian and coercive and as not ministering to the needs of students. In his view, there is a need for more participation by students in the decisions that affect their academic and social development and a need for better communication and cooperation among faculty, students, and administrators. Students should be able to choose their own goals and to pursue them with the help and encouragement of faculty (Rogers, 1970, p. 154).

Theory's Implications for Marriage

Rogers saw marriage as a failing institution. He attributed its decline to the fact that couples can now prevent conception, so that women need no longer be fully occupied with pregnancy, nursing, and child-rearing. They are now as free as men to explore relationships outside of marriage and to choose between family and career. For the first time in history, women are physically free agents, liberated from their subjugated role. The women's movement has also played a part, by encouraging women to make their own choices and not to stay in unsatisfactory marriages that stifle their growth. Finally, increased life expectancies mean that flaws in a relationship that might have been endured in previous times, when life expectancies were lower, will no longer be tolerated in a relationship that is expected to endure for 50 years or more.

Rogers believed that people, especially young people, are searching for meaningful alternatives, hence the upsurge in cohabitation without legal ties, communal lifestyles, and the like. Another meaningful alternative, in Rogers's view, is a new kind of marriage that is radically different from the traditional version, in which the husband is the sole provider and the ultimate authority and the wife occupies a more subservient role. Rogers did not oppose marriage per se, but only the kind of marriage that is not egalitarian, enriching, satisfying, and a growth experience for both partners. He also opposed marriages that are consummated only to please parents or to resolve a crisis in the relationship as when one person threatens to break up the relationship if the other does not agree to marry (Rogers, 1972a, p. 39). Rogers observed that marriages in which couples make the following kinds of statements may experience difficulties:

1. "I am more concerned for you than I am for myself." Although a loving relationship certainly involves a deep concern for the other person's welfare, an uncritical willingness to submerge one's own identity to please the other person can prove lethal to the relationship.
2. "We pledge ourselves to each other until death do us part." Again, the sentiment is fine but, if the cost is too great, the parties are likely to demean or destroy themselves or each other or to "break the bonds" (Rogers, 1972a, p. 200).

As Rogers saw it, marriage is a free-flowing, changing process, rather than a contract with a list of unalterable stipulations. It does not involve a rigid commitment at any cost, but a dedication on the part of both people to try to enhance and enrich the relationship. An appropriate statement, in his view, would be: "We each commit ourselves to working together on the changing process of our present relationship, because that relationship is currently enriching our love and our life and we wish it to grow" (Rogers, 1972a, p. 201).

In such a relationship the following kinds of events are likely to occur:

1. *Difficulties always present in the partnership are brought into the open.* The parties are willing to take risks and explore the differences between them, thereby (usually) deepening the bonds of partnership.
2. *Communication is more open and more real, with mutual listening.* Trust is evident, and the parties are willing to listen to each other rather than attack and accuse.
3. *The partners will come to recognize the value of separateness.* The partners begin to recognize that each one has separate needs and desires and that they do not have to pursue the same activities and goals together to be happy.
4. *Women's growing independence is recognized as valuable in the relationship.* Wives are able to discuss their needs with their husbands, instead of submerging their resentments. As a result, husbands have more respect for their wives, and the relationship is more mutually satisfying.
5. *Roles and role expectations tend to drop away and are replaced by people choosing their own way of behaving.* The expectations inherent in the traditional marriage relationship are given up. Men no longer see themselves as superior to their wives and as controlling all activities, including sexual ones. Women no longer see themselves as subordinate and submissive to their husbands. The resulting role flexibility leads to behavior that is sometimes in line with role expectations, sometimes not. At no time, however, is behavior governed totally by the role the person is expected to play.
6. *Either partner may form satellite relationships, which will often cause great pain but enrich growth.* **Satellite relationships** are close secondary relationships outside the marriage that may or may not involve sexual intercourse but are valued for themselves. According to Rogers, when two people learn to see each other as separate

persons, with separate as well as mutual needs and interests, they are likely to discover that outside relationships are among those needs. Thus, married people may feel the need to date or become sexually intimate with others.

Although Rogers saw satellite relationships as a legitimate part of healthy marriages, others would disagree strongly, and would condemn them as immoral, illegal, and grounds for divorce. They would say that such relationships are adulterous, plain and simple, and no fancy term can alter that fact. Rogers considered this view old-fashioned and ridiculous (Rogers, 1972a, p. 241); he argued that any partnership entered into by mutually consenting adults is legal, as long as it does no injury to others. Even if we accept his position on theoretical grounds (though, of course, many people would not), it seems to be a disaster in practice: Partners who agree to such arrangements very often wind up in divorce court. Rogers's response was that in these cases, although both parties consented to the arrangement intellectually, emotionally they were not ready for it. As a result, they were jealous and hurt when their partner had a sexual relationship with someone else (Rogers, 1977, p. 53). It was his hope that couples of the future would be more sophisticated and able to accept these experiences both intellectually and emotionally. They would then be motivated to enhance each other and to promote mutually positive growth by allowing the other to satisfy his or her needs outside the relationship.

Evaluative Comments

Let us now examine Rogers's theory in terms of how well it meets the criteria outlined in Chapter 1 for acceptance of scientific theories.

Comprehensiveness   Initially, Rogers's theory was restricted in scope; it was concerned primarily with explaining the origins of pathological behavior and the means of treating it in therapy. Later he extended his theory to explain a number of other phenomena, including problems of marriage, family life, education, race relations, and politics, and to suggest ways of overcoming these difficulties. As a result, his theory is now more comprehensive than it was originally.

Precision and testability   To Rogers's credit, he made a tremendous effort to construct a precise and testable theory. However, there are still some serious problems associated with measuring key concepts such as empathy, genuineness, and unconditional positive regard. Nonetheless, Rogers did make significant strides toward the creation of a theory with explicitly stated concepts and hypotheses capable of being tested.

Parsimony   Rogers's theory fails to meet the parsimony criterion. Although the phenomena he chose to examine are complex, he relied on only a few concepts and assumptions to account for them. Thus, the explanatory base of Rogers's theory is restricted in scope and clearly reductionistic in nature.

For example, Rogers's proposed solutions to help minimize racial and international conflict, hostility, and aggression rely primarily on a psychological analysis of the problems and application of the same principles utilized in his work with troubled individuals in therapy. Thus, he proposed reducing these tensions by having the concerned parties communicate with each other under facilitative group conditions (Rogers, 1977). Although the proposal is provocative and would likely help promote better relations between antagonists, it ignores the complex set of historical, political, economic, and cultural factors that serve to preserve the status quo. A psychological analysis of such problems is useful but clearly limited if not coupled with social, economic, and political analyses.

Empirical validity   Numerous tests of Rogers's theory to date have produced generally positive results; this provides some encouragement for investigators to continue their explorations and testing.

Heuristic value   Rogers's views have been highly controversial and have provoked continued, vigorous debate. Some therapists have argued that it is impossible for a therapist to be consistently nondirective as Rogers insisted because their own theoretical and personal biases inevitably intrude. They would prefer an approach to therapy where the therapist could offer at times their own interpretations tentatively (and with an acknowledgement that they may be fallible) to guide the client's thinking (Kahn, 1999, p. 94; 2002, pp. 88–89). But other therapists strongly disagree, arguing in accordance with Rogers that such interpretations have a directive aspect that robs the client of their dignity and freedom to make their own judgments and hinders their movement toward self-realization (e.g., Bozarth, 2002, p. 81). These important issues await resolution through future research.

In any event, all person-centered therapists agree that Rogers's strong stand on the sanctity of the person has had a positive influence. His humanistic concern for the integrity and uniqueness of the individual has inspired such therapists and many researchers to question views of human beings as automatons reacting uncritically to environmental forces.

Applied value   Rogers's theory is also very strong in the applied area. Aspects of it have been applied fruitfully to such diverse areas as education, race relations, politics, family relationships, administration, leadership, and counseling. His views on therapy have had tremendous impact on the counseling and community mental health movement.

Today there are nearly 200 organizations and training centers worldwide that teach the principles of person-centered therapy (Kirschenbaum & Jourdan, 2005, pp. 35–51).

CRITICAL THINKING QUESTIONS

1. Discuss Rogers's concept of the organismic valuing process and how it is related to the development of the person. Do you believe that you have a biological mechanism that allows you to distinguish right from wrong? Is there any scientific evidence to support Rogers's hypothesis of organismic wisdom?

2. What are some of the conditions of worth that your parents have attached to your behavior? What conditions of worth have you placed on your parents?

3. Why did Rogers feel that many educators are doing an ineffective job in educating people? Do you agree with him? Can you cite additional problems with the current educational system? What are some of its strengths?

4. Do you believe it is possible to be creative without first learning the basic concepts in a discipline? Why or why not?

5. What is your opinion about Rogers's view that sexual relationships outside marriage can be healthy if both partners agree?

GLOSSARY

conditions of worth   Stipulations upon which our sense of self-worth depends; they are associated with the belief that we are only worthwhile if we perform behaviors that others think are good and refrain from actions that others think are bad.

congruence   State of harmony that exists when there is no discrepancy between the person's experiencing and his or her self-concept.

emerging persons   People of the future whose interpersonal relationships are characterized by honesty, cooperation, and concern for others; who avoid sham, facades, and hypocrisy; and who welcome change and opt for growth even when it is painful to do so.

fully functioning persons   Individuals who are utilizing their potentials to the maximum degree. In other words, these individuals are engaged in self-realization or self-actualization.

need for positive regard   Learned or innate tendency to seek and need approval from others.

organismic valuing process   An innate bodily mechanism for evaluating which experiences are right or wrong for the person. People experience satisfaction in those behaviors that maintain and enhance them and aversion to those behaviors that do not.

Q-sort   Self-report assessment procedure designed to measure the discrepancy between a person's actual and ideal selves.

satellite relationships   Relationships formed outside the marriage that may or may not involve sexual intimacy.

social self   A self-concept based largely on the expectations of others. It has a powerful influence on us because we want to please others and win their positive regard. When the social self is incongruent with the person's true self, we are likely to distort our true feelings by repressing, denying, or distorting them. Under these conditions, progress toward self-realization is hindered. However, when the social self is congruent with the true self, we have no need to repress, deny, or distort our actual feelings. Under such conditions, we can assimilate our actual experiences into the true self and move toward self-realization.

true self   A self-concept that is based on our actual feelings about our experiences. Under conditions of unconditional positive regard (or where the social self is congruent with the true self), we have no need to repress, deny, or distort our actual experiences. These experiences can be adequately symbolized (conceptualized or thought about) and assimilated into our true self. When this occurs, we make progress toward self-realization.

unconditional positive regard   A total caring or prizing of the person for what he or she is, without any reservations or conditions of worth; in therapy, the therapist's complete acceptance of the client's expression of negative as well as positive feelings.

SUGGESTED READINGS

Rogers, C. R. (1959). A theory of therapy, personality, and interpersonal relationships, as developed in the client-centered framework. In S. Koch (Ed.), *Psychology: A study of a science* (Vol. 3, pp. 184–256). New York: McGraw-Hill.

Rogers, C. R. (1961). *On becoming a person*. Boston: Houghton Mifflin.

Peter Vandermark/Stock Boston, LLC.

CHAPTER 14

May's Existential-Analytic Position

Biographical Sketch

Rollo May was born in Ada, Ohio, in 1909, into a family characterized by intense marital conflicts. His mother was a lonely and depressed person who fumed at her husband's abandonment when he was away on business and who fought with him continually when he was home. She essentially had to raise six children by herself, and this fact contributed to her having severe mental problems. May described his parents as austere disciplinarians and anti-intellectuals. Despite this authoritarian home life, May's parents were religious and instilled in him the high ideal of Christian service to others. Also, May was the oldest child and was seen and treated most favorably by his parents. He was seen as having a special destiny and was encouraged to realize it by his parents (Abzug, 1996, pp. 18–19; deCarvalho, 1996, p. 8). He earned a bachelor of arts degree from Oberlin College in Ohio in 1930. After graduation, he pursued an early interest in art by touring Poland with a group of artists and painting pictures of its citizens (Reeves, 1977, p. 252). He then traveled extensively through Europe, taught at a college in Greece, and attended summer classes led by Alfred Adler.

When May returned to the United States in 1934, he served as an advisor to students at Michigan State University. Later he enrolled at Union Theological Seminary in New York, not to become a preacher, but rather to ask fundamental questions about human existence (Reeves, 1977, p. 252). At the seminary he was exposed to the existentialism of Kierkegaard and Heidegger in classes led by theologian Paul Tillich, who greatly influenced his thinking. He earned his bachelor of divinity degree cum laude in 1938.

May served as a counselor to students at City College of New York and studied psychoanalysis at the William Alanson White Institute of Psychiatry, Psychoanalysis, and Psychology in New York. In 1946 he opened a private practice, and in 1948 he became a member of the faculty at the White Institute (Reeves, 1977, p. 256). In 1949 he submitted his dissertation on anxiety to Columbia University and was awarded the university's first Ph.D. in clinical psychology. The dissertation was published in modified form in 1950 as *The Meaning of Anxiety*.

During this period of his life, May contracted tuberculosis and lived for a few years at a sanitarium in upstate New York. This was a particularly terrifying and depressing time for May; several times he was close to death. During his illness, he studied Kierkegaard's and Freud's views on anxiety and came to the conclusion that, although Freud had brilliantly analyzed the reactions of the individual made anxious by threat, it was Kierkegaard who had seen most clearly that anxiety is ultimately the threat of becoming nothing (Reeves, 1977, p. 257).

Following his recovery, May continued to write, teach, and practice therapy. He served as a faculty member at the New School for Social Research, New York University,

Harvard, Yale, and Princeton. He also published a number of books, including *Man's Search for Himself* (1953), *Psychology and the Human Dilemma* (1967), *Love and Will* (1969), *Power and Innocence* (1972), *Paulus: Reminiscences of a Friendship* (1973), *The Courage to Create* (1975), *Freedom and Destiny* (1981), *The Discovery of Being: Writings in Existential Psychology* (1983), *My Quest for Beauty* (1985), *The Cry for Myth* (1991), and his last major work, published posthumously, *The Psychology of Existence: An Integrative, Clinical Experience* (1995), coauthored with Kirk Schneider.

Professor May was honored with numerous awards for his outstanding achievements in psychology. He was a fellow of the American Psychological Association, emeritus fellow and faculty member at the White Institute, and a fellow of Brantford College, Yale University, and the National Council of Religion in Higher Education (Reeves, 1977, p. 263). He received the Dr. Martin Luther King Award from the New York Society of Clinical Psychology and the Psychological Professional Gold Medal from the American Psychological Association for his outstanding contributions to professional research.

In poor health for the last two years of his life, Professor May died from congestive heart failure on October 22, 1994, at his home in Tiburon, California.

Concepts and Principles

What Is Existentialism?

The term **existentialism** has become popular in academic and literary circles and is used in so many different ways by philosophers, psychologists, theologians, novelists, actors, and others that it has almost lost its meaning. In the popular mind, it is often equated with gloom and despair, not to mention suicide and death. For some, it suggests that the world is an absurd place with no meaning, and they self-righteously invoke it when any misfortune befalls them. Because the concept is so central to an understanding of May's position, we will begin by tracing its use historically.

Existentialism has its roots in the 19th-century writings of the Danish philosopher, Soren Kierkegaard. In his attempts to understand human functioning, Kierkegaard rejected Hegel's monumental effort to comprehend reality by identifying it with abstract thought and logic (May, 1973, p. 263). Kierkegaard, and later Friedrich Nietzsche, sought to correct the one-sidedness of Hegel's arguments by starting with the basic realities of people's existence, or **Dasein**. Thus, existentialism is concerned with **ontology**, or the study of the nature of **being**. But what precisely did May mean by the term *being*? First, May said that existentialists' use of this term is unfortunate, because it connotes a substance that is static and unchanging; he preferred the term *becoming*. (Compare Allport's views, described in Chapter 8.) Being (becoming) is a process in which we ourselves are the source of change, as we struggle as individuals to realize our potential— that is, as we try to become what we truly are. Being (or becoming) is not given once and for all; it does not unfold automatically. Instead, we each must become aware of what our unique potentialities are and then take responsibility for realizing them (May, 1983, p. 97). To achieve self-realization, we must focus directly on our personal experiences and avoid analyzing our circumstances by means of logical systems of thought that are abstract and impersonal.

Proponents of this philosophy, and especially Kierkegaard, argued that truth cannot be regarded as something detached from human experience. According to Kierkegaard, truth can only be known by starting with the person's perception of it as it relates to natural phenomena. May argued that Kierkegaard's insight changed our way of thinking about truth, and his radical stance has had tremendous implications for all scientific endeavors, including psychology. Kierkegaard gave us the concept of relational truth, forerunner of the notion of relativity; he showed us that "the subject, man, can never be separated from the object which he observes" (May, 1958b, p. 26). May thus defines existentialism as "the endeavor to understand man by cutting below the cleavage between subject and object which has bedeviled Western thought and science since shortly after the Renaissance" (May, 1958b, p. 11).

A major existentialist criticism of Western science is that it treats people as objects. Scientists tend to view human beings in an impersonal way and to restrict themselves to detached and objective measurement of human behavior. According to the existentialists, this value-free approach is incorrect; we are human beings first, and the scientific approach should emerge from that fundamental fact.

> Man may seek the meaning of science by approaching it as a typically human endeavor and asking: What is it in human nature that leads to the emergence of the scientific attitude? Once I have the answer to this question I may begin to grasp what science really means. From that moment on, I may be able to trace back to man's existence all forms, aims, and methods of science and to demonstrate that they are manifestations of his nature. (Van Kaam, 1969, p. 15)

What the existentialists are advocating, in effect, is that we bring the *subject*, our own inner world of experiences, into our view of science. Yet they do not dismiss the object side of the reality equation. Rather, they believe that we should focus first on our own subjective experiences in the formulation of problems and then proceed to study them as objectively as possible. Thus, scientists should adapt their methods of study to meaningful human problems and not tailor their problems to a restricted methodology borrowed from physics or physiology (Van Kaam, 1969, p. 26). May presented this view in the form of a parable:

> A psychologist, any psychologist, or all of us, arrives at the heavenly gates at the end of his long and productive life. He is brought up before St. Peter for the customary accounting. An angel assistant in a white jacket drops a manila folder on the table which St. Peter opens and looks at it, frowning. St. Peter's frown deepens. He drums with his fingers on the table and grunts a few nondirective "uhm-uhms" as he fixes the candidate with his Mosaic eyes.
>
> The silence is discomfiting. Finally, the psychologist opens his briefcase and cries, "Here! The reprints of my hundred and thirty-two papers."
>
> St. Peter slowly shakes his head. At last [he] speaks, "I'm aware, my good man, [of] how industrious you were. It's not sloth you're accused of. [Then he] slaps his hand resoundingly down on the table, and his tone is like Moses breaking the news of the Ten Commandments. "You are charged with *Nimis simplicandum* [oversimplifying]! You have spent your life making molehills out of mountains, that's what you're guilty of. When man was tragic, you made him trivial. When he suffered passively, you described him as simpering; and when he drummed up enough courage to act, you called it stimulus and response. You made man over into the image of your childhood Erector Set or Sunday School Maxims, both equally horrendous." (May, 1967, pp. 3–4)

In May's story, there is no ending. There is only the implication that eternal damnation awaits psychologists and others who continue to dissect the human experience and who, by so doing, tend to trivialize it. He also took issue with those who utilize only the subjective or objective view of reality in their formulations (May, 1967, pp. 15–20). As examples, he mentioned Rogers and Skinner. He criticized Rogers for overemphasizing the subjective side. Rogers was also guilty, in May's view, of assuming that people are "inherently good" and "exquisitely rational" and will always make the right choices if given an opportunity; Rogers ignored the evil and irrational side of human nature. May

(1982) believed that all human beings have the capacity for both good and evil. Skinner, in contrast, placed too much emphasis on the objective side of human behavior. He was concerned almost exclusively with the ways in which the manipulation of precisely defined environmental variables determine behavior, and totally ignored the subjective side of human functioning.

May believed that both views of human nature are necessary for a science of psychology and for meaningful living, and contemporary researchers in this area agree (Silvia & O'Brien, 2004, pp. 475–489). Both views of human nature are necessary for healthy living because we are all faced with the dilemma of living in both worlds at once. "The human dilemma is that which arises out of a man's capacity to experience himself as both subject and object at the same time" (May, 1967, p. 8). A major aspect of this dilemma is knowing that we are subject to illness, death, limitations of intelligence and experience, and other deterministic forces, but at the same time realizing that we have the subjective freedom to choose how we relate to these objective and deterministic forces. We alone can assign meaning to them; we are responsible for our own destinies. Of course, strict determinists such as Skinner would disagree; they maintain that all our behavior is determined, even our belief that we are free to make our own decisions, because we consider only those options determined by our past experiences and by current stimulation from the external environment.

Besides the subject/object dichotomy, a number of other interesting ideas have been put forth by prominent existentialists, among them, philosophers Martin Heidegger, Karl Jaspers, Maurice Merleau-Ponty, Paul Tillich, Albert Camus, and Jean-Paul Sartre and psychotherapists Ludwig Binswanger, Medard Boss, Viktor Frankl, and May. Although existentialism cannot be called a systematic and unified philosophy, its adherents do share certain views.

First, existentialists all take the *person* as the starting point in their analyses of human existence. They all ask fundamental questions about existence: Who am I? What is the meaning of life? Is there a meaning to life? Is life worth living? How do I realize my potentialities? How do I become an individual?

Second, they consider *free will* a central concept in understanding human functioning and development. To be human means to exercise free will, to consider goals, to make choices that we hope will promote our development. It is our freedom to make these choices that gives us a sense of significance and our feelings of dignity and worth (May, 1981, p. 9).

Third, in order to move toward answers, existentialists focus on our *immediate experience* as we exist from day to day—on what they often call our being-in-the-world. We view the world of natural phenomena from a subjective perspective. We face a world filled with uncertainties, a world that, in many respects, is absurd. The greatest absurdity from the existentialists' viewpoint is that we each realize we are finite and must die. Death is the great equalizer. All accomplishments, all hopes and dreams, will inevitably be blasted into oblivion at some point. The key question for the person under these circumstances is: What should I do? Should I retreat into nothingness or should I, in Tillich's words, have the courage to be? It is up to the person to make a choice and take action. As Kierkegaard said, "Truth exists only as the individual himself produces it in action" (May, 1958b, p. 12). Individuals must choose their own goals and then commit themselves to pursue them.

Thus, the person assumes almost godlike status in the existential design. We must assign meaning to our existence and act in terms of that meaning. We must exercise our freedom and act authentically. We act inauthentically when we let other people define our goals and tell us how we should behave. To be authentic, we must be who we are.

The ultimate form of nothingness is suicide. But nothingness, or nonbeing, can be seen in less extreme forms. We may choose not to exercise our freedom to be; we may avoid commitment to goals and responsibilities; we may decide to follow the moral dictates of the crowd. Indeed, choosing these options is easier than facing our responsibilities. The exercise of freedom is costly. In many instances, it creates severe anxiety, and an immediate and easier way for us to cope is to lose ourselves by accepting the moral values dictated by society. Such acceptance of values at variance with our being leads to self-alienation, apathy, and despair. The similarity between the existentialists and Rogers and Maslow is apparent here. Human existence is seen as a continuous struggle, as we try to deal with the problems of life and to move toward the realization of our potentialities.

Existentialism and Psychoanalysis

The major applications of existentialism to personality and psychotherapy have come from the work of people trained in classical psychoanalysis. To better understand May's **existential-analytic perspective**, which is an integration of the Freudian and existentialist positions, let us look at some of the similarities and differences between these two approaches to the study of human behavior.

Both psychoanalysis and existentialism ask fundamental questions about human existence. Although Freud was distrustful of mere speculation unsubstantiated by data, he nevertheless frankly acknowledged at an early point in his career that he was vitally concerned with the great problems of human existence and with understanding human nature. (See Chapter 2.) Both positions also focus on the irrational as well as the rational side of our natures. The existentialists talk about the inevitability of death and nothingness and the varied ways in which we try to cope with it. Freud, too, recognized the overwhelming importance of death in the human psyche and incorporated it into his theory in terms of a self-destructive urge he called the death instinct. Freud was also rather pessimistic about our long-range chances for survival as a species, because he believed that we have within us the seeds for our own destruction.

Although the existentialists have generally been reproved for being overly concerned with death and unduly pessimistic, a careful reading of their work suggests that the criticism is not entirely justified. It is true that death is given a high priority in their formulations, but they would argue that in fact death is experientially important because it touches us all. Their focus may be seen as morbid, because many of us have an unrealistic view of death and have been taught from a very early age to avoid thinking about it. Accordingly, they would argue that we are the ones with the unhealthy attitude, not they. As one existentialist has observed

> throughout the ages men have shunned the sight of death and the mention of death, and they have devised innumerable ways of assuring themselves, when the reality of death inevitably confronts them, that death does not really change anything and that after death it will be business as usual. In contemporary America the attempts to deprive death of its reality are just as frantic at they ever were in any culture, the embalming of bodies, the expensive caskets designed to delay as long as possible decay and decomposition, soft music piped into tombs. Then there is the deep-freezing of bodies, in the hope that one day medicine will have discovered a cure for the victim's disease, and there can take place a joyous (?) resurrection.
>
> It is, of course, natural to fear death or to be anxious in the face of death. But this is very different from constructing a vast cultural illusion (to say nothing of a highly profitable industry) to help us forget about death or to persuade ourselves that it is unreal. (Macquarrie, 1972, pp. 154–155)

Furthermore, not all existentialists treat death in the same way; some are more optimistic than others. For example, Sartre sees death as the final absurdity, but Heidegger maintains that an honest acceptance of death can help us to live more authentically and happily (Macquarrie, 1972, p. 155).

The next point of agreement between Freudians and existentialists lies in their concern with the alleviation of human suffering. Both positions address the ways in which conflict and anxiety disrupt functioning. Some existentialists focus on the positive features of anxiety, on anxiety as a prerequisite of self-affirmation. Both groups also assume that people often deal with severe anxiety by avoiding responsibilities. According to the existentialists, people deny what they really are (Boss, 1963, p. 68). Freudians talk about the avoidance of responsibility through the repression of impulses that are an integral part of human nature.

Both positions blame society, to a large extent, for not allowing people to be true to their natures. In the Freudian scheme, society works through superego mechanisms to restrain the expression of uncivilized impulses. In the existential design, society often waylays individuals by inducing them to behave in inauthentic and self-alienating ways. Advocates of both positions are deeply concerned with understanding human nature. Freud, like the existentialists, sought to free people from illusions about themselves and to get them to recognize who they really are (Boss, 1963, p. 62).

Despite these commonalities, there are a number of interesting and provocative differences between the two positions. As should be apparent from our discussion of the subject/object dichotomy, the existentialists disapprove strongly of Freud's attempts to fashion a science of human nature by relying on an abstract and logical system of thought. The existentialists want to avoid creating lofty theories removed from human experience. As Kierkegaard proclaimed, "away from Speculation, away from the System, and back to reality" (May, 1958b, p. 25). By reality, he meant experience as it is immediately given to us. This phenomenological stance, so characteristic of existential thought, is quite different from Freud's attempts to objectify experience, to measure and calculate it precisely.

In the existential view, Freudian theorizing also leads to a reductionism that violates the unity of experience. Reductionism means lessening an entity by changing it from one state to another. The existentialists accuse Freud of changing complex human experience into a few hypothetical components that he called id, ego, and superego. They accuse him of intellectualizing and analyzing the interplay of these three components in a structure he called the psyche. Such a reductionism, they contend, destroyed his primary understanding of our being-in-the-world.

Three Modes of Being-in-the-World

Existential analysts recognize three modes of being-in-the-world. There is the **Umwelt**, or biological environment. This is the natural environment for animals and humans. It is the world that includes biological needs, drives, and instincts—a world that would still exist if we had no self-consciousness. This is primarily what Freud investigated. But this is only one world, according to May, and to focus only on understanding this realm would be highly limiting.

The second mode of being-in-the-world is **Mitwelt**. This is the world of interrelationships. It includes the meanings of things that we share with others. Thus, love can never be totally understood by focusing only on its connections with the biological world of lust and sex. It also depends upon such Mitwelt factors as personal decision and commitment to the other person.

The final mode of being-in-the-world is **Eigenwelt**, our own world; it is the self in relation to itself. Eigenwelt involves self-awareness and self-relatedness. It occurs when I become aware of the impact that another person has on me, or aware of what a flower means to me. Without Eigenwelt, the world would be intellectually arid and impersonal.

According to May, human beings live in all three worlds simultaneously. Any complete understanding of the personality of the individual would have to examine all three modes of being-in-the-world (May, 1983, pp. 126–132). Existentialists seek to understand the unique problems of human beings without fragmenting their humanity (May, 1958b, p. 36).

Values Disintegration in Modern Society and the Loss of Our Moral Compass

May pointed out that we live in an age of transition, in which our values and goals are continually being called into question. A central value of the 19th century, he suggested, was a **healthy individualism** that consisted of self-reliance, competitiveness, and assertiveness. These qualities helped clear the frontier, ensure economic growth, and maximize the prosperity of all. However, May believed that there was another kind of individualism—**unhealthy individualism**—that creates serious mental health problems for people because it leaves them with no sense of community (May, 1991, p. 109). As he saw it, many of us today have acquired an exploitative competitiveness (hypercompetitiveness) that "makes every [person] the potential enemy of his neighbor, generates much interpersonal hostility and resentment and increases our anxiety and isolation from each other" (May, 1953, p. 48). Support for May's contention is seen in research by Ryckman, Libby, van den Borne, Gold, and Lindner (1997, pp. 271–283). These investigators found that hypercompetitives showed a lack of concern for others. Instead they were primarily concerned with establishing power and control over others as a means of enhancing feelings of their own superiority.

May also believed that the unhealthy individualism that characterizes so much of our society and many other societies today incorporate an extreme self-reliance which keeps many of them from asking for help and support when they need it most. Furthermore, this corrupted individualism is manifested in the behavior of many citizens as they relentlessly pursue personal success and material possessions. Making money is the highest goal for many people. Surveys have shown that many students in our country and abroad are overwhelmingly materialistic and are so competitive that they condone cheating and lying to achieve their personal goals. Their aspirations are extremely narcissistic rather than social and humanitarian (Karabati & Cemalcilar, 2010, pp. 624–633; May, 1991, p. 56).

And why shouldn't many students have these attitudes, given the things they see around them? May contended that many parents provide poor examples for their children and are unworthy of emulation, and this contention is echoed by many social critics (e.g., Hwang, 1995, pp. 484–490). Many parents make more money than they can possibly spend and yet give their children only 5% of their time (May, 1991, p. 60). Parents may justify their behavior by talking about quality time, but their children are not fooled. Other parents give little of their time because they are forced by economic circumstances to work in order to provide the basics of life. While such parents cannot be blamed, unfortunately the result is often the same. Specifically, their children grow up with little or no guidance. Divorce rates are high, some parents are into drugs, and many are concerned primarily with their own narcissistic self-fulfillment (Hwang, 1995, pp. 484–490). As a result, their children turn to unhealthy alternatives like gangs, cults, drugs, and excessive drinking to cope with their own feelings of powerlessness and alienation. Research by Knee and Neighbors (2002, pp. 536–539), for example, showed that university students who felt inadequate and powerless were more susceptible to peer pressures to drink to excess (i.e., five or more drinks at one sitting), and the results for some of them were not pretty, for example, doing damage to property, being absent from classes, and getting failing grades. On the plus side, these results suggest that students who feel powerful (good sense of self-determination and responsibility) were able to ward off peer pressure and control their drinking behavior.

May also contended that in a world filled with violence, crime, and corruption, students do not have enough genuine heroes to imitate. Instead, society today gives us film "heroes" who kill, athletes who are more interested in the almighty dollar than in the game or its fans, and reality show "stars" with minimal talents who are glamorized by the media for their perpetual night-clubbing and indiscriminant attempts at "hooking-up." In the political and business realms, young people see corruption, greed, and scandals surrounding various politicians and corporate leaders. Witness the current "Occupy Wall Street" protests. In the religious area, they grow nauseous as they watch some unctuous clergy exploit their congregations monetarily (May, 1991, p. 56). Recently, too, they learned about the corruption in the Catholic church as some clergy were sentenced to jail for sexually abusing their young parishioners. Finally, in the sports arena, they see revered basketball coaches at prestigious universities who have sexually abused boys under their care and guidance.

Besides losing a healthy individualism and adopting an unhealthy one, a second value we have lost is our sense of self-worth and dignity (May, 1953, p. 55). In May's view, this loss is partially due to people's feeling that they are powerless to change the operations of government and business, which are seen as huge, impersonal enterprises unresponsive to the needs of society. Feelings of powerlessness accrue in a worsening economy in which the jobs of thousands of workers are terminated with little or no warning. In such a threatening and uncertain world, many people feel the situation is beyond their control—that they are pawns in a terrifying game, in which a few mediocre people make moves that affect their destinies.

Next, May contended that many of us have lost not only our sense of identity but also our sense of relatedness to nature (May, 1953, p. 68). In Western society, we have been too concerned with the development of techniques to master nature and not concerned enough with understanding our relationship to it. The romantic back-to-the-land movement in this country can be seen as a reaction to an indiscriminate emphasis on technology. Because of our anxiety and emptiness, we have lost our feelings for and sense of awe about nature (May, 1953, p. 69). Our task, as May saw it, is to fill the impersonality of nature with our own aliveness and awareness. We must confront the power and vastness of nature and relate to nature creatively (May, 1953, p. 75).

Finally, May (1969) maintained that many of us have lost our ability to relate to others in a mature, loving way. We have confused sex with love. The media have contributed to this confusion by glorifying sex and by suggesting that people who do not engage in continual sexual affairs are unhealthy. Thus, people are pressured to have innumerable temporary liaisons. In May's opinion, sex is used as a narcotic to dull the senses and to keep individuals from becoming fully aware of their essential separateness from others. Despite the threats from AIDS and STDs, many people still regard the ability to perform the sexual act with many different partners as an indication of their worth and adequacy as human beings. Unfortunately, this production-line mentality is not ultimately satisfying, and people who are tied to it feel dissatisfied and lonely. In May's view, mature relationships are difficult to achieve and take time to develop. They involve a commitment to, and concern for, the welfare of the other person. Sex is the natural expression of affection and caring between people in an evolving, deepening relationship; it is not an experience that should be forced on individuals before they are ready for it. In a world fraught with troubles and anxiety, however, this lesson is difficult to learn, according to May. Although sex decreases anxiety, its effects are temporary. The eventual result is increased feelings of alienation, worthlessness, and loneliness (May, 1991, p. 214). Research supports May's arguments, showing that university students with strong, unfulfilled needs to belong and to establish meaningful social connections experienced greater loneliness than students who felt more fulfilled in their current relationships (Lee & Robbins, 2000, pp. 484–491). Similar results were found by Mellor, Stokes, Firth, Hayashi, and Cummins (2008, pp. 213–218) among Australian male and female adults (mean age of 59 years). These lonely adults also experienced less satisfaction with their lives.

Emptiness and Loneliness

The primary result of the confusion that comes from the disintegration of our values is that we feel empty inside and isolated from others. The vastness and complexity of the problems that confront us contribute to these feelings. According to May, however, feelings of emptiness should not be taken to mean that we are literally empty or without potential for feeling (May, 1953, p. 24). Instead, the experience of emptiness comes from feelings of powerlessness in which events seem beyond our control. We seem unable to direct our own lives, to influence others, or to change the world around us. As a result, we feel a deep sense of despair and futility. Eventually, if we see that our actions make no difference, we give up wanting and feeling; we become apathetic. In May's opinion, the greatest danger at this point is that the attempt to defend ourselves against despair will lead to painful anxiety. If the situation goes uncorrected, the result is the restriction of our potential to grow as human beings or our surrender to some destructive form of hostility, violence, and/or authoritarianism (May, 1953, pp. 25–26). Cowan and Mills (2004, pp. 67–78) found that males who feel powerless and inadequate are likely to have very hostile and mistrustful attitudes toward women.

May believed that there is a close association between emptiness and loneliness. We adopt an **unhealthy communal orientation** when we do not know what we want or feel and when we stand in the midst of a general upheaval and confusion about ourselves and our values (May, 1953, p. 27). We may then turn to others in a mindless attempt to overcome our sense of separateness from others. Yet, paradoxically, the more we attempt to reach out to others to ease our feelings of loneliness, the more lonely and desperate we become. Many of us mistakenly believe that we need to be in a relationship all the time in order to feel safe and secure. We tend to cling to partners we really do not like or respect. We are afraid that others will think less of us if we are single. As a result, we suffer in silence and try to make the best of a bad situation. We learn to adjust to the person and to stifle our own individuality in order to protect the status quo. We yearn for security and yet are constrained by it.

Part of the syndrome also involves seeking invitations to parties, dinners, night-clubs, or other outings with people. Often, we do not especially want to go but feel compelled to as a means of proving to ourselves that we are not alone and that we are acceptable to others. We "think" we have made it if we are continually sought after and if we are never alone. We must be accepted in order to consider ourselves alive. This compulsive need for acceptance may manifest itself among college students in excessive partying and drinking, in the adoption of uniform clothing styles and uniform opinions, or in striving to be academically average. It feels safe to be average and anti-intellectual. But such conformity is illusory and, in the final analysis, harmful to human growth. It is temporarily comforting, but the eventual price is that we give up our separate identities. We avoid relying on ourselves and renounce a major thing that would help us overcome our loneliness in the long run, the development of a **healthy communal orientation**—an attitude encompassing a strong and sincere concern with the welfare of others.

The Emergence of Anxiety

According to May, feelings of anxiety stem from loneliness and emptiness. Like Freud, he believed that anxiety signals an internal conflict, but May's theorizing about the nature and source of the conflict differs from Freud's. For Freud, the conflict was nearly always sexual in nature; to reduce the unpleasant feelings that it generated, the person banned the conflict from consciousness. For May, anxiety is not simply an unpleasant feeling; it is "the human being's basic reaction to a danger to his existence, or to some value he identifies with his anxiety" (May, 1953, p. 40). Since ontological anxiety is a threat to values, no one can escape anxiety, for no values are unassailable (May, 1967, p. 79).

According to May, the conflict that generates ontological anxiety is between being and nonbeing. Anxiety occurs as the individual attempts to realize his or her potentialities. If, for example, a man's overtures at friendship have been rejected, he faces a fundamental conflict between being and nonbeing: He can try to understand the reasons for the rejection by questioning the other person, or he can avoid asking questions that may prove embarrassing. He is thus faced with a fundamental choice, a choice that generates anxiety. He has the freedom to move forward or backward, and it makes him anxious. Kierkegaard describes this feeling of anxiety as the "dizziness of freedom" (May, 1958a, p. 52). If the man decides to assume responsibility and question the other person, he is using the experience of ontological anxiety constructively. If he fails to ask the pertinent questions, he is denying his responsibility and blocking the realization of his potentialities. In this case, May would say he is guilty. Like anxiety, then, guilt is also an ontological characteristic of human existence (May, 1967, p. 52). But ontological guilt does not occur because the person fails to act in terms of cultural prohibitions, as Freud thought. It occurs because an individual who can choose fails to do so (May, 1958a, p. 55). Such a person fails to act in terms of his central need in life—the fulfillment of his potentialities (May, 1953, p. 93).

May clarified the meaning of ontological anxiety further by dividing it into two components: **normal anxiety** and **neurotic anxiety**. Normal anxiety is anxiety that is proportionate to the threat to our values. It does not involve repression and can be confronted constructively on the conscious level. Neurotic anxiety, in contrast, is a reaction that is disproportionate to the threat and involves repression. Neurotic anxiety develops when we are unable to address the normal anxiety arising at the time of the actual crisis in our growth and the threat to our values (May, 1967, p. 80). For example, normal anxiety occurs for many of us when we first move out of our parents' home. We experience a threat to our family security. Yet if we confront this threat directly we are usually able to live through it successfully and to emerge from the crisis as a more independent and self-reliant person. We experience a healthy transformation of values. In contrast, if we feel threatened when we first move away from home and repress our feelings of anxiety about it, we may find ourselves calling and writing home almost daily and rushing home during every school recess throughout our college career. Such behavior may keep us overly dependent on our parents for support, help, and advice, hinders formation of close friendships with other students, and prevents us from solving our own problems.

For May, the goal in helping people to maximize their mental health is not to free the person from all anxiety. It is rather to help free them from neurotic anxiety, so that they can confront normal anxiety constructively. Normal anxiety is an integral part of growth and creativity.

The Expansion of Consciousness

In May's theory, individuals cannot fulfill their potentialities if these capabilities are largely unconscious. The unconscious involves "those potentialities for knowing and experiencing which ... individual[s] cannot or will not actualize" (May, 1983, p. 18). Thus, May believed that, the more conscious of our being we are, the more spontaneous and creative we will be, and the more capable we will be of choosing our plans and reaching our goals (May, 1953, pp. 94–104). Our objective, then, should clearly be an increase in consciousness. According to May, severe anxiety (neurotic anxiety) tends to restrict our consciousness, as we try to defend ourselves from pain through a variety of defense mechanisms, including those first postulated by Freud. These defenses help us avoid coping with our own being and are thus detrimental to growth.

In May's view, the sense of being that needs to be uncovered is the capacity to see ourselves as beings-in-the-world who can deal with the problems of our existence. This fundamental sense of being is not the same as the ego. The Freudian ego, according to May, is weak and passive, buffeted by id impulses and admonishments from the super-ego; it has little of the vitality and aliveness associated with a sense of being. Movement toward realization begins with awareness of our potentialities as we journey toward becoming fully human (May, 1958a, pp. 46–47). This awareness makes it possible for our potentialities to unfold; it also involves an increasing awareness of our links to others. By seeing that we are all mortal, on the planet for only small segments of time, and part of a world community where we depend on each other for survival, we all become brothers and sisters, in the same family at last (May, 1991, p. 302). Thus, according to May, our mental health depends on the integration of a healthy individualism and a healthy communal orientation. We need to rely on our own inner resources, for example, our own skills and feelings of efficacy and sense of moral responsibility, to initiate actions, which contribute to our own growth and to the betterment of others around us and to the community. Research tends to support some of May's interesting arguments (Horvath, 1998, pp. 137–154; Sato, 2001, pp. 89–127).

Personality Development

May's discussion of the development process centers on the physical and psychological ties between us and our parents and parental substitutes—teachers, friends, clergy. He pointed out our physical dependence on our mothers, which begins when we are fed as fetuses through the umbilical cord. This tie is severed at birth, but physical dependency remains. As we grow older, physical dependence tends to subside, but psychological dependence often does not. This to May is a major problem, and the way in which we handle it will determine in large degree whether we will move toward maturity and personal growth. We must make a decision to assume responsibility for our actions or to let others make our decisions for us. Thus, "the conflict is between every human being's need to struggle toward enlarged self-awareness, maturity, freedom and responsibility, and his tendency to remain a child and cling to the protection of parents or parental substitutes" (May, 1953, p. 193).

This dependency struggle is May's reinterpretation of the classic Oedipal conflict postulated by Freud. Whereas Freud believed the conflict was sexual in nature, May sees it as a power confrontation. The struggle revolves around the attempt to establish autonomy and identity in our relationships with people who are very powerful. In this battle for freedom, we progress through several stages of consciousness (May, 1953, pp. 138–139). The first stage is simply our innocence as infants with no consciousness of self. The second stage is rebellion, whereby we seek to establish our inner strength. This struggle typically takes place at age 2 or 3 and again during adolescence. Although rebellion is a necessary step in the evolution of consciousness, it should not be confused with freedom. Rebellion is defiance, an active rejection of parental and societal rules. Such behavior is automatic, rigid, and reflexive. True freedom, in contrast, involves "openness, a readiness to grow; it means being flexible, ready to change for the sake of greater human values" (May, 1953, p. 159).

The third stage is ordinary consciousness of self. At this point, we are capable of understanding some of our errors and of recognizing some of our prejudices. We are also capable of learning from our mistakes and assuming responsibility for our actions. Many people identify this state of ordinary consciousness with being, maturity, and health. But, according to May, there is still another stage, a fourth stage of consciousness that, if attained, actually signifies maturity. He calls this stage the creative consciousness of self. Transcending the usual limits of consciousness, we are able to see the truth without distortion. These moments of insight are joyous ones and occur only occasionally. Note that May's concept of creative consciousness is closely akin to Maslow's peak experiences.

We attain maturity and move close to self-realization when we experience these joyous moments. We are able to make choices, confront our problems, and take responsibility for our actions. We are not pushed along by deterministic forces. We are not bound by the past, by our role training, or by the standards we have been taught by others, including our parents. We are conscious of these forces but are able to choose freely whether or not to act in accordance with them. "Consciousness of self gives us the power to stand outside the rigid chain of stimulus and response, to pause, and by this pause to throw some weight on either side, to cast some decision about what the response will be" (May, 1953, p. 161). Recent research by Morton and Markey (2009, pp. 912–916) shows that college students who discuss openly their emerging goals (e.g., their academic, career, social, and moral goals) with their parents are less likely to experience distress and unhappiness in their relationships with them. These results suggest further that such college students are more likely to be moving toward an independent maturity.

Critics might question whether our behavior can really be determined by something as vague as consciousness of self. But May's position is that, although behavior is often determined by other events, we still have the freedom to make choices. When our consciousness is restricted or stifled, we move away from self-realization and maturity. Such a lessening of consciousness results from threats to our sense of being. May saw neurosis and psychosis as attempts to adjust to these threats—ways of accepting nonbeing so that some aspect of being can be preserved (May, 1967, p. 117). To cope with the threats to our being, we repress or distort our experiences through defensive maneuvers. The overwhelming threats then recede into unconsciousness. But through these maneuvers we deny our own freedom to make choices. We shrink from our responsibilities and reject our own potentialities (May, 1958a).

Assessment Techniques

Like Rogers, May was not primarily concerned with technique in his attempts to understand human functioning. His main focus in the therapeutic relationship was on the dynamic encounter between the two participants. In fact, May believed that a premature emphasis on technique may actually hinder understanding:

> Existential analysis is a way of understanding human existence, and its representatives believe that one of the chief (if not the chief) blocks to the understanding of human beings in Western culture is precisely the overemphasis on technique, an overemphasis which goes along with the tendency to see the human being as an object to be calculated, managed, "analyzed." Our Western tendency has been to believe that understanding follows technique; if we get the right technique, then we can penetrate the riddle of the patient. The existential approach holds the exact opposite; namely, that technique follows understanding. (May, 1958a, pp. 76–77)

May maintained that existential analysis is an *attitude* rather than a set of psychotherapeutic techniques. It involves a stress on understanding the special meanings of the person's existence. In the pursuit of this understanding, the therapist may derive new techniques or utilize existing ones. Thus, the therapist may employ dream analysis, free association, and transference, as do the Freudians, or personality measures, as do the Rogerians. But the therapist seeks to interpret dreams and symbols to ferret out their meaning for the patient's existence now and their implications for his or her future (May, 1958a, p. 77).

Thus, May's approach to understanding patients was characterized by flexibility and versatility; techniques vary from patient to patient and from time to time during the therapeutic process (May, 1958a, p. 78). His orientation was eclectic, but made systematic use of each selected procedure to shed light on the person's unique potentialities and existence.

Theory's Implications for Therapy

The Goal of Therapy

The primary task of the therapist, according to May, is to make empty and lonely people more aware of themselves and their potential for growth through the expansion of their consciousness and experience (May, 1967, p. 126). To accomplish these goals, the therapist must seek to understand patients as human beings and as beings-in-the-world (May, 1958a, p. 77). The focus is not on a detailed analysis of the patients' problems, but on how past experiences and aspirations shed light on where they are at the moment and where they are headed. "The context is the patient not as a set of psychic dynamisms or mechanisms but as a human being who is choosing, committing, and pointing himself toward something right now; the context is dynamic, immediately real, and present" (May, 1958a, p. 77). In short, the focus is on the ontological basis of the person's problems. These problems can be understood only when there is a real relationship between patient and therapist. The therapist, if he or she is to be successful, must relate to the person as "one existence communicating with another" (May, 1958a, p. 81).

Under such conditions, May believed, patients can experience their existence as real. They can become aware of their potentialities and develop the courage to act on the basis of them (May, 1958a, p. 45). The patients are cured, according to May, not when they come to accept the standards of the culture but when they become oriented toward the fulfillment of their own unique existence (May, 1958a, p. 87).

The Case of Mrs. Hutchens

May (1983) provided an actual case study to illustrate some of the assumptions and principles that guided him in therapy. The patient, known as Mrs. Hutchens, was a suburban woman in her mid-30s who suffered from a hysterical tenseness of the larynx, with the result that she spoke with a perpetual hoarseness.

As May's analysis revealed, the woman felt that, if she said what she really believed, especially to her parents, she would be rejected; therefore, she concluded, it was safer to be quiet. May believed that he understood the childhood origins of her problem—her need to protect herself against authoritarian criticism and belittling by her mother and grandmother—but to him this analysis and interpretation was not the most important part of the therapy. The most important part was the person now "existing, becoming, emerging … in the room with [him]" (May, 1983, p. 25). Focusing on his patient, May realized that this person, like every human being, was centered in herself; that is, she was attempting to preserve her existence by speaking in a hoarse voice. She also protected herself by being too controlled and proper in her behavior.

In the course of analysis, the patient revealed a dream in which she was searching room by room for a baby in an unfinished house near an airport. When she found the baby, she placed it in a pocket of her robe and then was seized by anxiety that it would be smothered. Much to her joy, she found that the baby was still alive. She then had a terrifying thought: "Shall I kill it?"

Analysis revealed that the airport was where, at age 20, she had learned to fly solo, an act that asserted her independence from her parents. The baby was her youngest son, whom she regularly identified with herself; the baby, therefore, was herself. The baby was also a symbol of her growing consciousness; in her dream, she considered killing that consciousness.

Approximately six years before entering therapy, Mrs. Hutchens had left her parents' religious faith and joined a church whose denomination she dared not tell her authoritarian parents. During therapy she considered telling them but, whenever May brought up the topic, she became faint. She would report feeling empty inside and would have to lie down on the couch for a few minutes. Finally, she wrote her parents informing them of her change in religious faith and telling them it would accomplish nothing if they tried to change her mind. In the next therapeutic session, she told May that she felt tremendous anxiety and wondered if she might become psychotic. May assured her that he thought this outcome was highly unlikely.

May interpreted her fainting and her anxiety attacks as attempts to kill her emerging consciousness. She was struggling to accept her hatred of her mother and her mother's hatred of her, to free herself from her mother's painful dominance, and to accept responsibility for her own actions and choices, even though they might not always have the best consequences. In brief, Mrs. Hutchens was actively confronting herself in these areas. The result was the opportunity for fuller independence, positive growth, and the development of a healthier lifestyle.

Evaluative Comments

We now evaluate May's theory in terms of our six criteria.

Comprehensiveness   Like the other humanistic psychologists, May's primary concern was to develop a model of positive growth as a means of alleviating human suffering. Thus, he focused principally on understanding abnormal behavior and changing it. His position is more comprehensive than those of Rogers and Maslow, however, because he integrated psychoanalytic and existential principles more thoroughly into his theory and presented a more detailed treatment of the developmental process. In addition, May sought a compromise with American behaviorism and its assumptions. In some of his earlier work, he attempted to utilize learning principles and experiments to increase our understanding of the meaning of anxiety, although he saw this approach as limited. Thus, May's system is relatively comprehensive, especially when compared with the other major humanistic positions.

Precision and testability   May's theory is quite imprecise and difficult to test. Terms such as being, potentiality, and ontological guilt are vague and nearly impossible to define accurately. In addition, the theory consists of a series of disjointed and unconnected propositions that do not lend themselves readily to scientific inquiry.

May's position retains close ties to philosophy. This is not a weakness in itself, as some psychologists seem to think, but it does hinder any attempt to convince investigators of his theory's scientific status. At this point, because its deficiencies in terms of precision and testability are so apparent, May's theory will probably not even get a fair hearing from members of the scientific establishment. This is unfortunate, because it includes many interesting and provocative ideas, especially regarding the need for change in our ideas about science. At best, May will be seen as a philosophical gadfly to be endured, but the full impact of his message about the need for a humanistic science of psychology will go unheeded. It is a message that deserves a better fate.

Parsimony   While overall judgments about the parsimony of May's position are difficult to make, it does seem to have an excess of concepts. For example, there is considerable redundancy in the terms awareness, consciousness, self-awareness, self-consciousness, and self-relatedness (Reeves, 1977, p. 269). Also, he described the person who has achieved healthy self-expression as being spontaneous, original, and genuine, explaining each of these characteristics in the same way (Reeves, 1977, p. 36).

Empirical validity   Empirical support for the theory is limited. Much of the evidence is based on clinical observation in therapy sessions and is largely unsystematic and retrospective. Research on May's position is still in an exploratory stage.

Heuristic value   May's position has proved highly stimulating to investigators in the humanistic psychology movement and to members of the public but, for the most part, his efforts have been ignored by traditional scientific investigators within psychology.

Applied value   May's theory has been fruitfully applied to problems in areas such as education, pastoral counseling, family life, and religion.

CRITICAL THINKING QUESTIONS

1. Do you agree with May that many psychologists study human behavior and experience in abstract and oversimplified terms? Give reasons for your judgment.
2. Do you agree with May that many people have lost their moral compass? Why or why not?
3. Is there too much emphasis in our culture on technology and gadgets and mastery of the environment? Do we have a good understanding of our relationship to the environment? Have you seen any progress recently in our attempts to preserve the environment?
4. Do people really endure unsatisfying relationships because they are afraid of loneliness?
5. Do you think that many students are struggling to become independent of parental control? If you are a nontraditional student, do you still have issues concerning parental control? Do you agree with May that one of the basic struggles in life involves our attempts to accept ultimate responsibility for our actions? Is dependency always harmful to the person?

GLOSSARY

being   Developmental process whereby the individual seeks to realize his or her unique set of potentials.

Dasein   A term derived from the German words *sein* (being) and *da* (there). Dasein indicates that a person exists in a particular place at a particular time. Thus, the individual can be conscious of, and responsible for, his or her existence, and can therefore choose the direction his or her life will take.

eigenwelt   The unique presence in human beings of self-awareness and self-relatedness.

existential-analytic perspective   Theoretical approach to understanding human personality that combines elements of existential philosophy with Freudian concepts. Both positions, for example, focus on how people cope with the anxieties that result from the inability to love others and the inevitability of death.

existentialism   Philosophy that focuses on people's attempts to make sense of their existence by assigning meaning to it and then taking responsibility for their own actions as they try to live in accordance with their chosen values and principles.

healthy communal orientation   A view that other people should be treated with dignity and respect and helped when they are in need.

healthy individualism   A set of personal characteristics that fosters the ability to initiate action by confronting problems constructively without hurting others.

mitwelt   The world of interrelationships. The experiences and meanings we share with others through our relationships.

neurotic anxiety   Painful feeling that is produced by an excessive reaction to a threat to our values. It involves a failure to make a choice that could lead to further growth.

normal anxiety   Painful feeling that emanates from a realistic threat to our established values. It is healthy to confront this threat, by making choices that lead to further growth. A child decides to walk and leaves the security of his playpen; an adolescent decides to establish a romantic relationship with another person; an adult decides to marry and have children of her own.

ontology   Branch of philosophy that seeks to understand the nature of being.

unhealthy communal orientation   The view that others should be used to further one's own ends and to satisfy only one's personal goals.

unhealthy individualism   A set of personal characteristics that drives people to see themselves as separate from others, that is, to believe that they are superior to others and must exercise control over them.

umwelt   The biological or natural environment in which human beings exist. A world of biological needs and drives, it consists of natural cycles, of sleep and waking, of being born and dying, of desire and relief.

SUGGESTED READINGS

May, R. (1950). *The meaning of anxiety.* New York: Ronald Press.

May, R. (1953). *Man's search for himself.* New York: Norton.

May, R. (1969). *Love and will.* New York: Norton.

PART 6

Social-Behavioristic Perspectives

Historically, two major lines of thought and investigation have shaped the course of personality psychology. One grew out of clinical practice, beginning with the work of the French physicians Charcot and Janet, and culminating in the efforts of Freud and his disciples. These investigators were medical practitioners concerned primarily with understanding the etiology of their patients' abnormal behavior in order to help them overcome their problems. Thus, they emphasized behavior change. They also focused on some of the most interesting, important, and complicated phenomena in human functioning: love, hate, death, sexual behavior, and aggressiveness.

In contrast to this medical orientation, the other major line of investigation had its roots in the experimental laboratory. Theorists in this tradition were primarily concerned with the scientific understanding of the learning process. They assumed that most of our behavior was acquired and that the task of the psychologist was to specify the environmental conditions responsible for producing behavior. Proponents of a simple stimulus-response (S-R) psychology, they sought to understand how given stimuli became linked to given responses.

The most important proponent of the S-R model in psychology was John B. Watson. Watson was originally educated at the University of Chicago as a functionalist. The functionalists explained behavior in terms of *mental functions*. Borrowing from Darwin's evolutionary theory, they maintained that human beings, like animals lower in the phylogenetic scale, were engaged in a constant struggle to survive. To survive, they had to learn to adjust their behavior. Such adjustment was possible because human beings possessed minds that encompassed the ability to reason and helped them solve problems presented by the environment.

Watson rejected this approach because, in his view, it did little to advance psychology as a science. He believed that terms such as mind, spirit, and soul were useless because the private events to which they referred could not be measured objectively and reliably. Psychology would advance only if it got rid of such mentalism and focused on public events that could be objectively validated. As a result, Watson proclaimed that psychology was the study of observable behavior and that references to all private events were unscientific and unworthy of scientific investigation.

Watson's pronouncements had a significant effect on psychology during his lifetime, and vestiges of his viewpoint can be seen in the work of the various contemporary social-behavioristic theorists discussed in this part of the text. Watson's influence is especially evident in the work of B. F. Skinner (Chapter 15), but it is also apparent to some extent in the positions taken by Julian Rotter and Albert Bandura (Chapters 16 and 17).

Like Watson, Skinner had a basic aversion to the study of private events. He concluded reluctantly that only those private events that could be measured objectively and reliably were worthy of scientific study. His primary focus was on observable behavior that could be recorded objectively. Like Watson, he was primarily concerned with trying to understand how environmental stimuli influence behavior, in the hope of generating fundamental laws. This goal could be achieved, Skinner believed, only through systematic observation and experimentation under controlled conditions. Such control could be exercised most readily in laboratory studies of animals lower in the evolutionary scale. Because the behaviors most amenable to control are simple ones, Skinner believed that the investigator should proceed from the simple to the complex.

Such a position means that his followers concern themselves primarily with a restricted set of phenomena and do not usually engage actively in attempts to explain phenomena such as love and hate. Skinner thought that his approach paid off handsomely, as principles of behavior painstakingly discovered in laboratory work with lower animals have been successfully applied to people in therapeutic and educational settings. In his later years, Skinner concentrated his attention directly on the study of human behavior; thus, he shifted from a simple behaviorism focused exclusively on lower animals to a more complex social behaviorism that addresses itself to important human issues and problems.

In Chapter 15, we review Skinner's arguments about the need for a scientific technology of behavior and the dangers of mentalistic explanations that seem to help us understand behavior but, in fact, impede our understanding. "He was kind to you because he has a pure soul," and "She scored an A on her chemistry exam because she has a good mind" are examples of mentalistic explanations that lack scientific explanatory power; they are invoked on a post hoc basis (See Chapter 1 glossary) and are meaningless from a scientific standpoint. Skinner distinguished mentalism from cognition, which he considered a legitimate object of study. Although both terms refer to private events, *mentalism* describes events that cannot be studied scientifically, whereas *cognition* refers to events that can be objectively and reliably recorded and communicated clearly among scientists. Cognitive events are studied primarily by means of verbal reports, and Skinner accepted their use.

In Chapter 15, we also present the major terms and principles in Skinner's operant analysis of personality. Of particular importance is his study of various kinds of reinforcers and reinforcement schedules and their effects on the acquisition and modification of behavior. Skinner is frequently lambasted by critics as advocating the use of punishment to control behavior, but this accusation is simply not true. As we shall see, Skinner did not consider punishment an effective means of altering behavior. We also discuss the development of normal and abnormal personalities within Skinner's unique framework and the ways in which operant principles can be applied in therapeutic and educational settings.

The work of Rotter and Bandura also shares a number of features with the psychology advocated by Watson. Both Rotter and Bandura believe that most of our behavior is learned. They also believe that the advancement of psychology as a science depends on the establishment of precise measurement procedures and the systematic observation of behavior under controlled conditions. Yet their theories rely heavily on the use of cognitive constructs, in defiance of Watson's dictum that the study of such events has no place in psychology. Thus, their positions go far beyond Watson's simple, mechanistic model of human functioning. Whereas Watson leaned heavily on Pavlov's classical-conditioning paradigm to explain the acquisition of behavior, Rotter and Bandura expand this view by incorporating the role of organismic variables into their formulas. Their neobehavioristic position includes such cognitive constructs as expectancy, imitation, covert rehearsal of events, self-efficacy, value, memory, and habits. These stimulus-organism-response (S-O-R) models attempt to deal with more complex phenomena than those studied by Watson and, to a considerable extent, by Skinner. At the same time, however, Rotter and Bandura insist on accurate and objective measurement of these complex phenomena.

The positions of Rotter and Bandura are a more direct outgrowth of learning theories propounded after Watson. Rotter himself traces the origins of his position to the work of learning theorists Thorndike, Tolman, and Hull. From Thorndike, Rotter adopted the view that behavior is subject to modification by its consequences. In other words, Rotter, like Skinner, accepts the concept of instrumental or operant conditioning. From Tolman and Hull, Rotter borrowed the notion that behavior is purposive—that we are guided by our motives to attain certain goals. Rotter's thinking is particularly close to Hull's in this regard. To predict the probability that a behavior would occur, Hull proposed the formula

$$E = H \times D$$

where E refers to the excitatory potential (probability) of the behavior, H refers to habit strength, and D refers to drive strength. Thus, in Hull's formulation, the probability of a given response, or movement toward a goal, is a function of the animal's drive strength (motive) multiplied by its habit strength. In Rotter's scheme, excitatory potential becomes behavior potential; habit strength is roughly translated as expectancy of the occurrence of reinforcement; and drive strength is reinterpreted as the value of the reinforcement. Therefore, the probability that a given behavior will occur is a function of the expectancies or habits that a person has acquired—primarily as a result of previous experiences—and the importance of the reinforcer that will affect the person's drive level.

In Chapter 16, we review these and other concepts in Rotter's theory. We focus on one construct of particular importance in his social-learning position—internal/external control of reinforcement—and provide a sampling of recent research findings based on the measurement of individual differences in locus of control.

Bandura's work, like Rotter's, places heavy emphasis on the role played by cognition in the acquisition, retention, regulation, maintenance, and modification of behavior. He does not reject the concept of reinforcement; he simply utilizes it differently in his theorizing and research. Whereas Skinner believed that reinforcement automatically strengthens or weakens responses, Bandura's view is that reinforcement provides people with information—information concerning the kinds of behaviors they must perform in order to gain beneficial outcomes and avoid punishing ones. Within this framework, learning from response consequences is largely a cognitive process. According to Bandura, observational learning plays a primary role in the acquisition, maintenance, and modification of behavior.

As he rightly notes, the study of imitation learning has been relatively ignored by traditional learning theorists. Historically, the concept can be traced to the work of Lloyd Morgan in 1896, Gabriel Tarde in 1903, and William McDougall in 1908. All these theorists believed that imitation was an innate tendency in human beings. As the popularity of Watsonian behaviorism drove the instinct doctrine into disrepute, a few learning theorists, including Humphrey, Allport, and Holt, tried to account for imitation in terms of Pavlovian conditioning. According to this learning paradigm, imitative responses were the simple result of a person's matching his or her behavior to the behavior of another. In other terms, imitation involved contiguous associations between social stimuli. Soon, however, the behaviorist focus shifted from classical conditioning to instrumental, or operant, learning. This new view was advocated primarily by Miller and Dollard in their classic text *Social Learning and Imitation* (1941). In essence, their position was that imitation learning occurred when a motivated person was positively reinforced for matching the behavior of a model during a sequence of random trial-and-error responses.

Bandura's main objection to both the classical- and instrumental-conditioning explanations of imitation is that they fail to account for the acquisition of new responses through observation. Bandura believes that operant conditioning, the notion that the person makes a long series of random responses that are eventually shaped through reinforcement until they match the behavior of the model, is simply too cumbersome to account for the many responses we learn in the course of our lives. He suggests instead that imitative learning often occurs in the absence of external reinforcement. We acquire behavior without performing it overtly and without being reinforced for it. We simply watch the behavior of others, represent it cognitively (that is, symbolically), and then perform it under the appropriate conditions.

In Chapter 17, we discuss the major assumptions underlying Bandura's social-cognitive position and then present the basic concepts and principles of his theory. The focus is on the ways in which behavior is learned when the person is exposed to single and multiple models with varying personality characteristics. As we shall see, the impact of multiple models on children's behavior is often complicated and difficult to assess, because the models often show contradictory behaviors. We also discuss the role of self-control processes in the acquisition of behavior and examine some applications of modeling principles and research to two major social problems: violence in the media and problem behaviors, particularly phobias in children. In examining Bandura's treatment of the developmental process, we discuss his use of the concepts of imitation, successive approximation, and schedule of reinforcement. Finally, we present Bandura's more recent theorizing about self-efficacy and its role in the development and change of pathological behavior, along with supporting empirical evidence.

Topham/The Image Works.

CHAPTER **15**

Skinner's Operant Analysis

Biographical Sketch

Burrhus Frederick Skinner was born in Susquehanna, Pennsylvania, in 1904. In his autobiography (Skinner, 1976), he reported that his home life was warm and stable. He was never physically punished by his lawyer father and only once by his mother, when she washed his mouth with soap and water after he said a word that did not meet with her approval. He liked school and acquired a strong background in English, literature, mathematics, and the sciences from a few fine teachers. As a boy, he was always building and creating things. He built roller-skate scooters, wagons, sleds, seesaws, merry-go-rounds, slingshots, blowguns, kites, and model airplanes. This fascination with mechanical objects can be seen in his invention and use of various devices in his experimental work. These devices include the Skinner box, an apparatus designed to help investigators study the effects of different reinforcement schedules on animal behavior; the cumulative recorder, a device to assess the rate of responding of organisms; and the teaching machine, an instrument designed to facilitate learning in students.

Skinner enrolled at Hamilton College in New York State as an English major. He never really adjusted to student life, however. He joined a fraternity but knew little about fraternity life; he was inept at sports; and he complained bitterly about unnecessary curriculum requirements. By his senior year, he was in open revolt. He participated in activities designed to humiliate faculty members whom the students thought pompous and arrogant. One of these incidents is particularly noteworthy. In order to deflate a name-dropping English professor, Skinner and another student printed posters that read, in part: "Charles Chaplin, the famous cinema comedian, will deliver his lecture 'Moving Pictures as a Career' in the Hamilton College Chapel on Friday, October 9." The lecture was reported to be under the professor's auspices. After plastering posters all over town, they returned to the campus and went to bed. The next morning, the other student called the local newspaper and told reporters that the college president wanted the lecture publicly announced. By noon, the situation was completely out of hand. Swarms of children were taken by their parents to the railway station to greet the famous actor. In spite of police roadblocks, approximately 400 cars got through to the campus. Other escapades were followed by threats of expulsion, but Skinner was finally permitted to graduate.

After college, Skinner pursued a career as a writer. As a senior, he had met the famous poet Robert Frost, who requested that Skinner send him samples of his work. Skinner sent the poet three short stories and received encouraging comments in reply. He spent the next two years living in Greenwich Village in New York City and in Europe. Eventually he realized he would not be successful as a writer, presumably because he had nothing important to say. To explore his interest in human behavior, he then entered graduate school at Harvard in 1928 to study psychology.

Skinner found the intellectual atmosphere at Harvard stimulating and challenging. In order to improve his skills in a new field, he set up a rigorous study schedule and adhered to it for almost two years; he read nothing that did not pertain to psychology and physiology. Among his academic mentors were historian E. G. Boring, clinician Henry Murray, and physiologist W. J. Crozier. The writings of J. B. Watson, Ivan Pavlov, and E. L. Thorndike also had a considerable impact on the young psychologist. He was particularly impressed by Watson's concern with devising a technology of behavior. In one fell swoop, Watson had thrown out all mentalistic concepts, including mind, spirit, and consciousness, and proclaimed instead that psychology was the scientific study of observable behavior. Skinner, too, maintained that psychologists should focus on behavior that is observable and verifiable but, unlike Watson, he believed that psychologists must also account for internal or private events, as long as such events can be measured objectively and reliably.

Skinner was also greatly influenced by the work of the Russian physiologist Ivan Pavlov on the conditioned reflex. Pavlov was originally interested in the process of digestion in lower animals and the conditions under which digestive juices were secreted. In the course of his work, he discovered that animals salivated not only when food was actually in their mouths but also when it was shown to them by the experimenter. He called this phenomenon a "psychic secretion." His next step was to control the conditions under which such secretions occurred. As virtually every psychology student knows, Pavlov designed a room that minimized the intrusion of extraneous stimuli and was eventually able to demonstrate, through a precise series of maneuvers, that salivation could be brought under the control of specific stimuli such as a light or a bell. Previously neutral stimuli acquired the power to evoke responses originally evoked by other stimuli. The animals were classically conditioned. Besides the fact that such respondent conditioning can account for a variety of behaviors, Skinner was impressed by the procedure Pavlov used to bring the behavior under control. He reported that, then and throughout his career, he fully accepted Pavlov's dictum, "Control your conditions and you will see order."

Although some of our behavior is learned via classical conditioning, most of it is learned after we behave voluntarily and find that our actions are followed by positive or negative experiences. Skinner's interest in operant behavior, that is, behavior that operates on the environment, was piqued by animal experiments conducted by learning theorist E. L. Thorndike. Typically, cats were deprived of food, and then placed in problem boxes and left there until they accidentally moved a mechanism that opened a door and allowed them to escape. The animals usually made a variety of responses before making the correct one. Thorndike explained this trial-and-error learning by maintaining that an association was established between the animals' responses and the reinforcing consequences. Responses that resulted in pleasurable sensations Thorndike considered to be "stamped in," whereas he considered responses followed by an annoying state of affairs to be "stamped out." Skinner adopted a modification of this **law of effect** to explain the acquisition of behavior; he recast the law in terms of the changes in the probability of responding produced by the application of reinforcers or punishers.

After three years in the psychology graduate program, Skinner received his Ph.D. from Harvard in 1931, and then spent five postdoctoral years working in Crozier's laboratory. In 1936, he accepted his first academic position, at the University of Minnesota; two years later, he wrote his first book, *The Behavior of Organisms*, which presented his initial formulations for an **operant analysis** of behavior. While at Minnesota, Skinner also found the time to begin a novel entitled *Walden Two*, a story about a miniature utopian society based on reinforcement principles. *Walden Two* was eventually published in 1948.

After a brief stint as chair of the psychology department at Indiana University, he returned to Harvard in 1948. Skinner was accorded many honors by his fellow psychologists and was also one of the few behavioral scientists to win the President's Medal of Science. He was a prolific writer; his books include *Science and Human Behavior* (1953), *Verbal Behavior* (1957), *Schedules of Reinforcement* (with C. B. Ferster, 1957), *Cumulative Record* (1961), *The Technology of Teaching* (1968), *Contingencies of Reinforcement* (1969), *Beyond Freedom and Dignity* (1971), *About Behaviorism* (1974), *Particulars of My Life* (1976), *Reflections on Behaviorism and Society* (1978), *The Shaping of a Behaviorist* (1979), *A Matter of Consequences* (1983), *Enjoy Old Age* (with M. E. Vaughan, 1983), and *Upon Further Reflection* (1987). In his book on old age, Skinner offered advice to the elderly on how to manage their environments so as to maximize their enjoyment of old age despite declines in physical prowess and health (Skinner, 1970, pp. 1–21).

On August 10, 1990, Professor Skinner was awarded a Citation for Outstanding Lifetime Contribution to Psychology by the American Psychological Association. He died of complications from leukemia on August 18, 1990, in Cambridge, Massachusetts.

Concepts and Principles

Scientific Behaviorism

Like virtually all of us, Skinner believed we are faced with problems that threaten our very existence. He argued that, although we often misuse the products of our technology, we can utilize the same technological prowess to solve our problems. We have even taken a few small steps in that direction, for example, in population control, pollution control, improved methods of crop production, and disease control (Skinner, 1971, p. 1). Yet in each of these areas we have only scratched the surface. Why is this so? In Skinner's view, it is because the solutions to these problems lie not in the application of our physical and biological knowledge but in an understanding of human behavior. Birth-control methods are useless if people do not use them; pollution-control devices accomplish nothing if people continue to ignore or resist them. Thus, what we need are drastic changes in our behavior (Skinner, 1971, p. 4).

Why, then, have we not made more progress in understanding human behavior? The answer, Skinner believed, lies in our refusal to give up mentalistic explanations of behavior that give the *appearance* of helping us understand our actions, but in fact hinder us in our quest.

> We are told that to control the number of people in the world we need to change *attitudes* toward children, overcome *pride* in size of family or in sexual potency, build some *sense of responsibility* toward offspring, and reduce the role played by a large family in allaying *concern* for old age. To work for peace we must deal with the *will to power* or the *paranoid delusions* of leaders; we must remember that wars begin in the *minds* of men, that there is something suicidal in man, *a death instinct* perhaps, which leads to war, and that man is aggressive by *nature*. To solve the problems of the poor we must inspire *self-respect,* encourage *initiative*, and reduce *frustration*. This is staple fare. Almost no one questions it. Yet there is nothing like it in modern physics or most of biology, and that fact may well explain why a science and a technology of behavior have been so long delayed. (Skinner, 1971, pp. 9–10)

Such explanations are post hoc in nature, according to Skinner (See Glossary in Chapter 1). They seem to provide answers to questions, but they do not. Further, such

mentalism brings curiosity to an end (Skinner, 1971, p. 12). The problem seems to be solved, and we are lulled into a false sense of security. For example, if a student is asked why John physically assaulted Bill, and he replies "Because John's aggressive," many people would be satisfied with that answer and would be lured into a false sense of security that a satisfactory explanation had been given. But Skinner would maintain that a scientific approach to the study of human behavior would force us to give up such a comforting inner "explanation" and to search instead for the precise antecedent event(s) that actually produced the behavior (Skinner, 1987, p. 785). In other words, Skinner would say that we must look for the environmental event(s) prior to the behavior that caused it. We might find upon doing an environmental analysis that Bill had gotten into an argument with John's girlfriend at a nightclub, called her a slut and shoved her, and that John had then retaliated by waiting for Bill until he came out of the nightclub and had attacked him, punching him and breaking his nose. The name-calling and shoving by Bill of John's girlfriend was the antecedent event that caused John to commit the criminal act of physically assaulting Bill, eventuating in his arrest by the police.

In any event, Skinner did not categorically reject the study of all private events. In his book *About Behaviorism*, he took pains to point out that Watson, in his zeal to establish psychology as a science, made an exaggerated and incorrect commitment to the elimination of the study of introspective life (Skinner, 1974, p. 5). Skinner believed, albeit halfheartedly, that psychologists must provide adequate explanations of private events. He insisted, however, that the events studied must be capable of being reliably and objectively recorded. Verbal reports could provide acceptable data for Skinner and his followers if scientific criteria were met (Skinner, 1974, p. 31). But because other people have difficulty teaching us the appropriate labels for our private experiences, we must be cautious in accepting such reports at face value. Thus, contrary to popular belief, Skinner did not simply accept Watson's simplistic S-R formulation. Skinner maintained that such an approach was obsolete and claimed to recognize the complexity of human behavior. Those who continued to criticize him for treating human beings as robots, he suggested, should "stop beating a dead horse."

An example may help clarify what Skinner would find scientifically objectionable or acceptable. Imagine a person sitting down at a table in a restaurant and eating a meal consisting of fettuccini Alfredo, Beaujolais, spumoni, and coffee. Why did he eat? The typical answer is that he ate *because* he was hungry. Skinner would reject this explanation as mentalistic. The term *hunger* would have to be explained by linking it to antecedent events in the environment, for example, the number of hours since the previous meal. Hunger did not *cause* the person to eat; rather, food deprivation, along with a host of other environmental variables (the decor of the restaurant, the price and attractiveness of the food), contributed to the probability that he would eat that meal at that particular time.

A behaviorist analysis would force us to focus on those events in the environment, past or current, that help produce the behavior. This information, coupled with data about our genetic endowments, where it is pertinent to the explanation of a given behavior, helps us in prediction. For example, if the diner had been allergic to the starches in the fettuccini, he might have decided not to eat at all or to eat different food. Thus, inner events, that is, our prior histories, which are based on transactions with the environment, and our unique genetic heritages, contribute to the prediction of behavior. Although Skinner recognized the legitimacy of such inner events for a behavioral psychology, he nevertheless de-emphasized them in his own analysis. He accorded the same legitimacy to physiological events, but again paid little actual attention to them in experimental analysis. Besides the difficulty of reliable measurement, the scientist cannot often systematically manipulate physiological events and observe their effects on behavior. Skinner believed that major advances will occur only when psychologists focus on the ways in which behavior and external environmental variables are causally related. What is needed, in brief, is a **functional analysis** of behavior.

Free Will versus Determinism

According to Skinner, this search for order among events is offensive to many people because, once these relationships are specified, scientists can begin to anticipate and determine our actions (Skinner, 1953, p. 6). They can start to exercise control over our behavior. Such an idea runs counter to a long tradition of viewing ourselves as free agents. We do not like to believe that our actions are the product of specifiable antecedent conditions; we prefer to believe we are free and capable of spontaneous inner change (Skinner, 1953, p. 7). As members of a democratically oriented society, we also resist anyone who says he or she wants to control our behavior. According to Skinner, this belief in our own autonomy has a number of unfortunate implications.

Acceptance of this belief may mean that we do not see the powerful role played by the environment in causing our behavior. Instead we believe that we alone are responsible for our own actions, and thus we should be rewarded for behaving well and punished when we behave badly. For example, some of us are convinced that people living in poverty are responsible for their own situation. We shouldn't feel sorry for them because "They should show some initiative and work like we do." As to juvenile delinquents, "Well, they got themselves into it; let them get themselves out of it!" In making such judgments, we have lost sight of the part played by oppressive environments. The focus on the inner man or woman prevents us from seeing clearly the external factors that contribute to their behavior (Skinner, 1971, pp. 19–20). Interestingly, although some of Skinner's critics called him a fascist, a reactionary, and a Machiavellian because of his stand on determinism, in this regard he emerges as a super liberal.

A science of behavior that questions our autonomy threatens beliefs about personal worth and dignity. A scientific analysis shifts both the credit and the blame for our actions to the environment (Skinner, 1971, p. 21). We may not object to an analysis that absolves us of blame, but we do object to one that deprives us of a chance to be admired and loved (Skinner, 1971, p. 75). Typically, the amount of credit we give someone for a performance, Skinner observed, is inversely proportional to the conspicuousness of the causes of the behavior: "We stand in awe of the inexplicable, and it is therefore not surprising that we are likely to admire behavior more as we understand it less" (Skinner, 1971, p. 53). For example, we may be more impressed by the performance of a young figure skater if we do not know that she has practiced six hours a day every day for the past 11 years to attain her current level of skill. We are probably more impressed with a brilliant new novelist if we do not know that he began writing at age 19 and received 45 rejection slips from publishers before they decided to publish one of his manuscripts when he was in his forties.

Denying that we are autonomous beings is also threatening because it implies that we are not free to do what we want (Carpenter, 1974, p. 87). But our wants, Skinner maintained, are conditioned by external events. For instance, if you buy a computer, it's not because you simply and freely want one; it's because your old one has broken down, or you see a new model advertised, or your friends or colleagues have been pressuring you to upgrade. Whatever the reason or reasons, your behavior is determined by events in your past or current environment.

Many of us have been taught to believe that all external control is bad (Carpenter, 1974, p. 89). But numerous instances in which our behavior is controlled are perfectly acceptable to us. Parents restrain small children from diving into the 12-foot end of a swimming pool. Society controls driving behavior with elaborate rules and regulations. State governments require auto safety inspections. Compulsory vaccinations protect us against disease. Doctors exercise control when they operate on people. The list is endless. Some of Skinner's critics continue to insist that a particular form of control, coercion, is bad because it involves the exploitation of one party by another. In fact, Skinner agreed wholeheartedly with them; he, too, opposed control of this sort.

What, then, are the critics' objections to his position? There seem to be two main points: (1) that Skinner sought to manipulate people without their being aware of it; and (2) that Skinner sought to set himself up as the arbiter of good and evil (Carpenter, 1974, p. 90). Skinner answered by pointing out that all of our behavior is determined, whether we are aware of it or not. As to good and bad, his position was that we already have a general consensus. Virtually everyone is against disease, poverty, war, and indiscriminate destruction of the environment. Nearly all of us prefer politeness to rudeness, generosity to greed, love to selfishness. Why quarrel over the obvious?

Despite the cogency of Skinner's arguments for a thoroughgoing determinism, the fact remains that the determinist viewpoint is an assumption on his part, even though there is considerable evidence to support it. Most of the evidence is based on studies with lower animals in which it is possible to control conditions and observe systematic changes in behavior. For human beings, the problem is much more complicated. The scientist usually does not have control over previous environments and thus, in contrast to experiments with lower animals, cannot observe changes in behavior as a function of the manipulation of events in the current environment. In short, there is too much "noise" in the human system for us to argue conclusively that determinism is scientifically proven. Nevertheless, it appears to be a reasonable working assumption; it continues to lead to the accumulation of data that advance our understanding of human behavior.

Personality from the Perspective of a Radical Behaviorist

Now that we have considered some of the major arguments underlying Skinner's scientific approach to behavior and some of its provocative philosophical implications, we come to an important question: What about the study of personality? Is it lost in Skinner's strict emphasis on a cause-and-effect analysis of behavior? Skinner considered the study of personality legitimate, but only if established scientific criteria are met. He would not, for example, accept the idea of a personality or self that guides or directs behavior. He regarded that as a vestige of animism, a doctrine that presupposed the existence of spirits as an animating force within the body (Skinner, 1974, p. 167). Nor, as we have seen, was he satisfied with dead-end mentalistic explanations of behavior.

Skinner believed that the study of personality involves a systematic examination of the idiosyncratic learning history and unique genetic background of the individual.

> In a behavioral analysis, a person is an organism which has acquired a repertoire of behavior. [He] is not an originating agent; he is a locus, a point at which many genetic and environmental conditions come together in a joint effect. As such, he remains unquestionably unique. No one else (unless he has an identical twin) has his genetic endowment, and without exception no one else has his personal history. Hence no one else will behave in precisely the same way. (Skinner, 1974, pp. 167–168)

The study of personality, then, involves the discovery of the unique set of relationships between the behavior of an organism and its reinforcing or punishing consequences. Of course, such an analysis would have to be consistent with the organism's genetic capacity to respond to events in the environment.

Operant Conditioning

All behavior takes place in situations and produces outcomes. In terms of Skinner's system, we operate on the environment to generate consequences (Skinner, 1953, p. 65). Operant behavior includes talking to people, reading, walking, writing, kissing, dressing, singing a song, criticizing a teacher, and countless other activities. If we are deprived of water and then drink, we are reinforced. Turning the house thermostat from 55 to 70 degrees on a winter morning is reinforcing. If, by accident, we turn the thermostat from 70 to 50 degrees that same morning, the consequences would be punishing. The establishment of an association between behavior and its consequences is called **operant conditioning**. Through operant conditioning, the occurrence of behavior is made more or less probable.

The three-term contingency   A **contingency** is a rule stating that some event (B) will occur if and only if another event (A) occurs (Mazur, 1986, p. 131). For example, during an early afternoon play session at home, 6-year-old Matthew shares his toy truck (event A) with his 5-year-old brother, Leo, and receives a kiss (event B) from his mother for his cooperative behavior. After dinner, however, Matthew and Leo are watching television when Leo decides he does not like the program and arbitrarily changes the channel. Matthew becomes very upset and hits his brother (event A). Their mother then sends Matthew to bed early (event B) as punishment. Skinner would say that Matthew has learned that a kiss from his mother in a play situation is contingent, or dependent, on his cooperative behavior. The boy has also learned, in Skinner's view, that being sent to bed early when he is watching television is contingent on his aggressive behavior.

Thus, there are three important components in an operant-conditioning contingency: (1) the environmental or situational event in which a response or behavior occurs (that is, the event that precedes the behavior); (2) the behavior itself; and (3) the environmental stimuli (consequences) that follow the behavior (Skinner, 1953, pp. 108–109).

Discrimination   The stimuli preceding the behavior are important because they provide the occasion under which reinforcement is likely to occur if the behavior is performed. Thus, people learn a **discrimination**. They learn that, in the presence of certain stimuli (or in some situations), their behavior is likely to be reinforced, whereas the same behavior in the presence of other stimuli (or in other situations) is not likely to be reinforced. Or they learn the discrimination that their behavior is likely to be punished in certain situations, whereas the same behavior under different circumstances is unlikely to be punished. Traffic lights, for example, act as discriminative stimuli. We learn that a red light is a cue for us to bring our car to a halt, whereas a green light indicates that we can proceed. Failure to make this simple discrimination can lead to arrest by the police or sometimes to serious injury or death. Obviously, we do not have to learn this discrimination through direct experience. We can and do learn the appropriate behavior through oral or written instructions, through observation of what other drivers do in actual situations, or through films. Driver-education courses typically use films of accidents to show license applicants the tragic consequences of a failure to obey various traffic rules, including the failure to make an appropriate discrimination between green and red lights.

When our responses are differentially controlled by antecedent stimuli or situations, they are considered to be under **stimulus control**. Much of our behavior is under the control of stimuli. In social interactions, for example, we learn that we are likely to be reinforced when we approach people who are smiling, whereas we are likely to be punished when we approach people who are scowling. We also learn to be careful about the kinds of food we eat. The smells and colors of the foods influence our behavior. We quickly learn to avoid eating rancid meat, rotting tomatoes, and moldy bread. Instead, we purchase and eat fresh bread, firm tomatoes, and red meats. In our environmentally conscious society, we learn to react appropriately to various cues in our physical environment. For example, as we leave a classroom at the end of a session, we turn off the lights when we see instructions to "Please turn off the lights to conserve energy." We throw our litter into trash cans when we see instructions asking us to do so. We also avoid another person's property when we see ominous "No Trespassing" or "Beware of the Dog" signs.

Instructions, directions, examples, and models are all used to facilitate the development of responses. Such stimuli are called **prompts**, antecedent events that help initiate responses. Thus, if a parent tells a child to return home immediately after school and hugs and kisses her for complying, the prompt (instruction) becomes a discriminative stimulus. It signals the child that reinforcement is likely to follow when the behavior is performed. In general, when a prompt consistently precedes reinforcement of a behavior, it becomes a **discriminative stimulus** and can effectively control behavior. Prompts often take on the value of events (consequences) that follow them. Thus, the child is likely to look forward to hearing her parent instruct her to come home immediately after school.

Prompts can also become aversive if they are associated often enough with punishing consequences. If parents continually remind their son to clean his room or face a loss of privileges, it takes little time for such prompts to become aversive in their own right. The boy may try to terminate the aversive prompt by cleaning his room, leaving the house, or arguing with his parents (Kazdin, 1989, pp. 42–43).

A good research example of the effectiveness of prompts is seen in a recent study by Clayton and Helms (2009, pp. 161–164). In a baseline or control condition, they had a student hold up a large sign that simply said "Have a Nice Day" and another student (observer) simply recorded the number of student drivers who saw the sign and buckled up their seat belts upon leaving a campus parking lot. Seventy-two percent of the students in this control condition were observed with their seat belts buckled. In two other, separate conditions, a student either held up a sign that read, "Please buckle up-I Care" or a sign that read "Click it or Ticket." (There were no police actually present in the area in this latter condition.) In each condition, a student observer recorded the number of drivers who buckled up after seeing the sign. In the "Please Buckle up-I care" condition, 86% of the drivers buckled up, and in the "Click it or Ticket" condition, 92%. Compared to the baseline condition, significantly more students buckled up in each of the two experimental conditions. Since other data from the National Highway Safety Administration indicate that the use of seat belts reduces the risk of fatal injuries to drivers, the prompts used in this study could translate into lives saved and injuries prevented.

Generalization   A response that is repeatedly reinforced in a particular situation is likely to be repeated in that situation. Situations, however, consist of complex sets of stimuli that often share common properties. In Skinner's view, the control exerted by a given stimulus is shared by other stimuli that are similar to it (Skinner, 1953, p. 132). **Stimulus generalization** occurs if a behavior that is reinforced in one situation also increases in other situations, even though it is not reinforced in those situations (Kazdin, 1989, p. 46).

Generalization is the opposite of discrimination. When people discriminate between two situations, it means that their response has failed to generalize from one situation to the other. When their response does generalize across two situations, it means that they have failed to discriminate between the two situations and make the same response in both situations. These two phenomena have highly important implications for the psychological health and well-being of humans. For example, if a man fails to discriminate between people who can be trusted and those who cannot be trusted, his generalized mistrust may result in his being highly suspicious of others and even paranoid. The teenager who is rewarded by her peers' smiles and laughter for swearing in a playground situation may face punishing consequences if she repeats the behavior in front of her date's parents and relatives at the dinner table in his home. Skinner would say that she failed to learn an appropriate discrimination. Stimulus generalization can operate in a beneficial way when the information learned in your college classes transfers to a job setting after you graduate.

Reinforcement and punishment terminology

Behavior is controlled not only by antecedent stimuli, but also by its consequences. Skinner spoke of these consequences as involving the presentation or removal of either pleasant or unpleasant stimuli following a behavior. He termed the presentation of a stimulus as positive and the removal of a stimulus as negative, so you should not think stereotypically of the term "good" when you see the term "positive," nor should you think of the term "bad" when you see the term "negative." Instead simply think of the term "presentation" when you see the term "positive" and of the term "removal" when you see the term "negative."

Reinforcement

The principle of **positive reinforcement** refers to an increase in the frequency of a behavior when that behavior is followed by the presentation of pleasant stimuli or **positive reinforcers**. There are two types of positive reinforcers: **primary,** or unconditioned, **reinforcers** are automatically or naturally reinforcing, for example, food, water, and sex; **secondary,** or conditioned, **reinforcers** acquire their reinforcing properties through association with primary reinforcers or with other conditioned reinforcers. Examples of secondary reinforcers are praise, attention, money, and good grades. Giving a boy a candy bar for having cleaned his room strengthens his room-cleaning behavior. Awarding an A to a student for having written a highly creative essay encourages this behavior.

Negative reinforcement refers to the removal of an aversive or unpleasant stimulus following a response, thereby increasing the rate of occurrence of that response. The removal of an aversive stimulus (**negative reinforcer**) following a response increases the probability of that behavior occurring in the future under the same or similar circumstances. Taking medicine that removes your stomachache (aversive stimulus) is a good example of negative reinforcement. Medicine-taking behavior is strengthened when it is followed by the elimination or removal of an aversive stimulus. Another example is the child who learns to apologize for undesirable behavior because it terminates or removes parental criticism. Apologizing by the child is strengthened when it is followed by the termination of parental criticism.

In summary, the principle of **reinforcement** is that a behavior will increase in frequency when it is followed either by the presentation of a positive reinforcer (pleasant stimulus) or by the removal of a negative reinforcer (unpleasant stimulus).

Punishment

The principle of **punishment** refers to a decrease in the frequency of a response when that response is followed immediately by certain consequences. Aversive events, or punishers, can be applied to behavior to make its occurrence less probable. The presentation of an aversive stimulus following a behavior is called **positive punishment**. **Primary,** or unconditioned, **punishers** are stimuli that are inherently aversive or unpleasant, for example, spankings, being hit by a rock, and falling down and breaking a leg. **Secondary,** or conditioned, **punishers** acquire their aversive properties by being paired with primary punishers or other conditioned punishers. Examples of conditioned punishers are poor grades, criticism, ridicule, and sarcasm. Fining a person for speeding is intended to discourage the behavior. A teacher's reprimand to "Stop talking" is intended to decrease talking by students. The command "No" also serves as a conditioned punisher for many people. The word may acquire its punitive value by being paired originally with physical pain (for example, spanking a child for misbehavior while telling him or her "No") or loss of privileges (for instance, taking the keys to the family car away from a teenager who loves to drive).

The removal of a desirable or pleasant stimulus (positive reinforcer) following a behavior also decreases its occurrence and is called **negative punishment**. Taking a toy away from a child for lying is a form of negative punishment called **response cost**. Response cost involves a penalty of some kind, for example, a fine for a traffic violation or fees for late filing of income tax or late registration for classes (Kazdin, 1989, p. 153).

Another form of negative punishment is **time-out from reinforcement**, the removal of all pleasant stimuli (positive reinforcers) for a certain period of time. Telling a child who misbehaves to stop watching television and go to his or her room is a good example of time-out, if the child's room offers no opportunities for reinforcing activities such as playing music or text messaging his or her friends while in the room. Table 15.1 summarizes these operant principles, in terms of the various combinations of consequences that follow a response, presentation or removal of a positive or negative stimulus.

Skinner's view of punishment   Skinner observed that punishment is the most common technique of control in modern life.

> If a man does not behave as you wish, knock him down; if a child misbehaves, spank him; if the people of a country misbehave, bomb them. Legal and police systems are based upon such punishments as fines incarceration and hard labor. Religious control is exerted through penances, threats of excommunication, and consignment to hell-fire.
>
>   Education has not wholly abandoned the birch rod. In everyday personal contact we control through censure, snubbing, disapproval, or banishment. All of this is done with the intention of reducing tendencies to behave in certain ways. (Skinner, 1953, p. 182)

Why is punishment so pervasive? It is easy to apply, and it has immediate, observable, and satisfying effects for the punisher. In addition, the technique is easily learned, whereas alternative, positive techniques are more difficult to acquire. Punishment also has the ostensible support of history (Skinner, 1971, p. 80). For all these reasons, many of us resort to it.

Does punishment work? Certainly in the short run it seems to be effective: It stops the undesired behavior. Skinner maintained that this effect may be misleading, however, because the reduction in strength of the behavior may not be permanent (Skinner, 1953, p. 183). As evidence, he cited a study in which he trained rats of the same sex, age, and genetic strain to press a lever in a Skinner box as a means of obtaining food

TABLE 15.1   SUMMARY OF OPERANT CONDITIONING PRINCIPLES

	Positive Stimulus	*Negative (Aversive) Stimulus*
Presentation (contingent on response)	Positive reinforcement	Positive punishment
Removal (contingent on response)	Negative punishment	Negative reinforcement

pellets (Skinner, 1938, pp. 151–160). After establishing the bar-pressing response, Skinner withheld the reinforcers from these animals in order to bring about **extinction** of the behavior. Skinner let some of the animals in a control group continue to press the bar without punishment until they stopped responding completely. In the experimental group, each time the animals pressed the lever, they were punished by a mechanically administered slap on the paws. This punishment continued for the first 10 minutes of the extinction period and then was terminated. Skinner found an initial decrease in the rate of response for the animals while they were being punished. When the punishment was ended, however, the experimental group began to respond again. Eventually, this group produced as many responses as the controls. Skinner concluded that punishment temporarily suppresses behavior, but the behavior is likely to reappear when the punishing contingencies are withdrawn.

Punishment, according to Skinner, has two other undesirable effects. It may give rise to emotional responses that are incompatible with appropriate behavior (Skinner, 1953, pp. 186–187). For example, a man who, as an adolescent, is severely punished for masturbating while looking at pictures of naked women may later experience strong feelings of guilt in a situation where sexual behavior with an actual woman (e.g., his wife) is appropriate. Or a child who has been beaten by her parents for reading poorly may later experience considerable resentment toward teachers who are trying to help her improve her reading skills; as a result, she may refuse to read and thereby perpetuate her reading difficulties.

Punishment may create strong conflict in people (Skinner, 1953, p. 190). In Skinnerian terms, such conflict would not be an inner struggle, but rather an incompatibility between responses, one of which is positively reinforcing and the other potentially punishing. The male student who has been rejected by a number of female students but who continues to seek relationships with women on campus would be a pertinent example. In traditional personality terms, such a person might be labeled as awkward, indecisive, and timid.

For all these reasons, Skinner believed we should shun the use of punishment to control behavior, but should focus instead on the use of positive reinforcers. (The use of positive reinforcers in education will be discussed later in this chapter.) Skinner's views on punishment make sense to many people on ethical grounds. Moreover, there is substantial research evidence that the use of physical punishment by parents in disciplining their children has deleterious consequences. Corporal punishment (e.g., slapping, grabbing and shaking, whipping, and paddling) is associated with an increased subsequent probability of aggressive and delinquent behavior in their children. Interestingly, parents who are seen by their children as loving and supportive even though they are spanked by them later show antisocial behavior in school (Gamez-Guadix, Straus, Carrobles, Munoz-Rivas, & Almendros, 2010, pp. 529–536).

While Skinner's views on punishment may make sense to many people on ethical grounds, his dictum that physical punishment should never be used, because it doesn't work, is not acceptable to many scientific researchers. That is, these scholars note that there are many studies which have shown that punishment can effectively stop undesired behavior when it is properly applied (Kazdin, 1989; Matson & LoVullo, 2009; Walters & Grusec, 1977). (The effective use of aversive techniques, including physical punishment, to stop self-injurious behavior in patients so that positive reinforcers can be implemented to encourage constructive behavior will be discussed later in this chapter.) We will also see that nonphysical punishment techniques that involve removing positive reinforcers from people following an undesirable behavior work well (e.g., Reynolds & Kelley, 1997, pp. 216–230).

Operant extinction   As we saw in Skinner's rat study, failure to reinforce a response reduces the probability that the response will occur. In traditional terms,

> [a] person is said to suffer a loss of confidence, certainty, or sense of power. [He] is said to be unable to go to work because he is discouraged or depressed, although his not going, together with what he feels [discouragement and depression], is due to a lack of reinforcement, either in his work or in some other part of his life. (Skinner, 1974, p. 58)

We control the behavior of others by withholding reinforcement. To eliminate behavior we consider undesirable, for example, we ignore it. If our roommate acts in obnoxious ways, we may simply pay no attention to him or her. If a child has a temper tantrum, her parents may ignore her by reading the newspaper or turning on the television set. Such a procedure seems to make sense, but unfortunately is often unworkable in practice. If the undesirable behavior has been reinforced many times in the past, it is highly resistant to extinction. The mother who tries to eliminate temper tantrums by ignoring her child's behavior is likely to give in eventually by listening to her child, comforting her, and giving her what she wants. These actions positively reinforce the child's behavior and ensure that it will continue. An alternate strategy in this situation might be to send the child to her room for a brief period (time-out) until she stops whining and complaining, and then to show her a more constructive way of solving her problem and to reinforce her for using it.

Shaping   Sometimes it is impossible to develop new behavior by reinforcing the response when it occurs. The target behavior may not be in the repertoire of the individual because it is too complex. For example, the use of language in children is a complicated activity that can be developed only slowly, with the help of a shaping procedure. **Shaping** means teaching a new behavior by reinforcing responses that approximate it. **Successive approximations**, behaviors increasingly similar to the final goal, are reinforced, until eventually the goal is achieved. For example, when parents want to teach their child to say *mommy* and *daddy,* they first reinforce sounds like *ma* and *da* by giving effusive praise when the child utters them. At the same time, they ignore other sounds (*bo, go*) that do not resemble the terminal words. Over time they continue to reinforce sounds that come closer to the words *mommy* and *daddy* until eventually the child says them and receives strong reinforcement from the elated parents (Kazdin, 1989, p. 38).

Schedules of reinforcement   All of us are exposed to different environments and to different schedules or arrangements of reinforcement in our daily lives. Some parents, for example, consistently reinforce their children's behavior; others supply only intermittent reinforcers. These schedules have a tremendous impact on our responses. Numerous studies with lower animals, for example, have shown that behavior learned on a **continuous reinforcement** schedule, that is, a schedule in which each performance is followed by a reinforce, produces higher rates of response than behavior reinforced only intermittently. Behavior learned on a schedule of **intermittent** (or partial) **reinforcement**, however, is much more resistant to extinction than behavior acquired on a continuous schedule (Skinner, 1953, p. 99). Animals trained on a continuous reinforcement schedule also show greater signs of emotional reaction or low frustration tolerance when their behaviors are subjected to extinction than do animals trained on intermittent schedules.

The implications for human functioning are quite straightforward. Affluent parents who raise their children on continuous reinforcement schedules should not be surprised that their offspring do not show behaviors that could be labeled persistent, hardworking, ambitious, and competitive. These behaviors are more likely to be found in children who have been subjected to partial or intermittent schedules of reinforcement (Carpenter, 1974, pp. 27–28).

Intermittent reinforcement can take many forms. Two of the most common are the fixed-ratio schedule and the fixed-interval schedule. In a **fixed-ratio schedule**, an absolute number of behaviors is required before reinforcement is applied (Ferster & Perrott, 1968, p. 525). For example, a student may have to complete two class projects before receiving a grade in the course. Or a worker may be placed on a fixed-ratio schedule, commonly known as piecework pay. In a **fixed-interval schedule**, the first performance that occurs after an absolute amount of time has elapsed is reinforced (Ferster & Perrott, 1968, p. 526). There are many examples of the operation of such schedules in our daily lives. We eat at certain times of the day; we go to bed and get up at a regular time. Sometimes we get paid by the hour. An interesting feature of behavior regulated on fixed-interval schedules is that the rate of responding tends to be low just after reinforcement but increases rapidly as the time for reinforcement approaches.

Self-control processes   Skinner was interested not only in the ways in which schedules of reinforcement determine behavior but also in the role of **self-control processes**. For him, studying self-control involves an analysis of "how the individual acts to alter the variables of which other parts of his behavior are functions" (Skinner, 1953, p. 229). Individuals are said to exercise self-control when they actively change those variables or factors that determine their behavior. For example, we may find that we cannot study when there is a TV blaring music. We get up and shut it off. We have actively changed the nature of the variable (loud music) that affected our behavior. Another example might be an obese person who exercises control over his behavior by buying and eating only low-calorie foods. He can also politely refuse to eat high-calorie foods when they are offered to him by others.

Skinner outlined a number of the techniques that we use to control our behavior (Skinner, 1953, pp. 231–241); many of these have subsequently been studied by social-cognitive theorists interested in modeling and behavior modification. (See Chapter 17.)

Physical restraints   Sometimes we control our behavior through the use of physical restraints. For instance, some of us clap our hands over our mouths to avoid laughing at someone else's mistakes. Others put their hands in their pockets to keep from biting their fingernails. In unusual cases, people who feel strongly tempted to commit criminal or psychotic acts may present themselves at the door of an institution for incarceration.

Another form of physical restraint is simply to move out of situations in which the behavior to be controlled takes place. We walk away from someone who has insulted us, lest we lose control and physically attack him. Parents often prevent the occurrence of undesirable behavior (for example, fights, ridicule, criticism, or taunts) between their children by physically separating them. They may order one child to go outside to play and the other to stay inside and watch or play video games.

Physical aids   Physical aids can also be used to control behavior. Some truckers take stimulants to avoid falling asleep at the wheel. Students often drink large amounts of coffee after all-night study sessions in an effort to remain alert during early morning exams. **Physical aids** can also be used to facilitate certain behavior, as when people with vision problems put on eyeglasses or the hearing impaired make use of hearing aids.

Changing the stimulus conditions   Another technique we use to control our behavior is to change the stimuli responsible for it. Overweight people put a box of candy out of sight so that they can restrain themselves. Some alcoholics avoid temptation by giving their liquor supply away. Some student athletes put their athletic equipment out of sight when they sit down to study. Other students draw the curtains in their rooms to avoid being lured out of doors on a bright spring day.

Smokers sometimes try to reduce their smoking behavior by destroying their cigarettes. Other smokers adopt more moderate strategies (Williams & Long, 1979,

p. 117). If they ordinarily carry their pack of cigarettes in their right-hand shirt pocket, they shift it to their left-hand pocket or to their coat so that it is more difficult to find. Sometimes they deliberately neglect to carry matches or a lighter; as a result, they must ask someone for a light each time they want to smoke. The object of these strategies, of course, is to disrupt the smokers' habits and consequently to limit the unhealthy behavior.

Another way to reduce smoking frequency is to reduce the range of stimuli associated with it. Smokers typically have favorite times and situations in which they smoke, for example, while studying, working, eating, partying, or watching television. Various studies have shown that, if they can break these associations, they can reduce their smoking drastically (Williams & Long, 1979, p. 118).

In each of these examples, people are removing a discriminative stimulus that induces unwanted behavior. Not only do we remove certain stimuli in given situations, however, we also present stimuli in order to make certain behaviors more probable. For example, we may use a mirror to master a difficult dance step or listen to our voice on tape in an attempt to improve our diction.

Manipulating emotional conditions   We sometimes induce emotional changes in ourselves for purposes of control. Some people employ meditation techniques to alleviate stress. Similarly, we may work ourselves into a good mood before a stressful meeting in order to increase our likelihood of performing well. When athletes psych themselves up before an important game, they are using this method of control.

Performing alternative responses   We often keep ourselves from engaging in behavior that leads to punishment by energetically engaging in something else. The overweight person may turn to an intensive jogging regimen to burn off excess calories and to keep from excessive eating. The recently bereaved may be advised by friends to keep very busy as a means of avoiding depressing thoughts. To avoid talking about taboo topics—for example, telling Catholic nuns about a woman's right to abortion—we may talk to these nuns about the less threatening subject of how to play a good game of bridge.

Positive self-reinforcement   We also control behavior by positive self-reinforcement: We reward ourselves for commendable behavior. A student may reward himself for studying hard and doing well on an exam by going to see an interesting film. An athlete may promise herself an expensive meal at a favorite restaurant if she surpasses her old record in the 100-meter dash.

Self-punishment   Individuals also punish themselves for failure to reach self-generated goals. As punishment for failing to do well on an exam, a student may give away valuable concert tickets. College football players often voluntarily jog extra laps around the track Monday morning as punishment for failure to perform adequately during a game on Saturday afternoon.

Personality Development

A Schedule-of-Reinforcement Approach

In seeking to explain changes in the individual's personality over time, Skinner looked to unique environmental schedules of reinforcement rather than the emergence of maturational stages. Although he acknowledged some predictive value in theories such as Freud's and Piaget's, Skinner generally opposed them because they do not allow for the control or manipulation of events, a procedure he considered crucial for a science of behavior (Skinner, 1974, p. 12). Such theories tend to be descriptive rather than explanatory and, as Skinner saw it, the primary goal of science is the prediction and control of events (Skinner, 1953, p. 6).

In Piaget's stage theory, for example, children in stage 1 (from birth to about 3 years of age) are observed to play games without any attempt to adapt to social rules. In stage 2, children between the ages of 3 and 5 imitate the rule-regulated behavior of adults and regard the rules of a game as sacred and immutable. In stage 3, children who range in age from 7 to adolescence play games with a mutually agreed upon set of rules, but understand that the rules can always be changed with the approval of the other players (Flavell, 1963, pp. 291–292). With these descriptions of behavior at the various age levels, we can predict the kind of behavior children will exhibit if we know their age. But we do not have an adequate explanation for their behavior; that is, we do not know *why* they behave as they do. We have descriptive information of limited usefulness, not causal information. To ascertain why children behave as they do, we must be able to control and manipulate events that have an effect on their game-playing behavior.

For these reasons, Skinner preferred to study personality by focusing on the learning of a multitude of behaviors that allow the individual to survive and prosper in his or her transactions with the environment. In rough terms, people learn throughout life which contingencies provide satisfaction and which produce pain in given situations. The child learns to discriminate between stimuli or situations that are occasions for the reinforcement of specific behaviors and those that do not lead to reinforcement of the same behaviors. These learned behaviors are said to be under stimulus control. A student may quickly learn, for example, that studying in a library and not in a noisy dormitory leads to passing grades. Simple skills are learned at first; later on, more and more complex behaviors are acquired and utilized. But Skinner did not see people as passive organisms who simply respond automatically to reinforcement cues. Instead, they exercise self-control over their environments by actively selecting and changing environmental variables in order to satisfy their own needs.

The Development of Normal and Abnormal Personalities

Some people have had a unique set of transactions with the environment that results in the acquisition of a **repertoire** we might label normal. Others have had a set of experiences that result in the acquisition of unique response patterns we might label abnormal. In Skinner's view, there is no qualitative difference between the so-called normal and abnormal individuals; the same set of reinforcement principles can account for the behavior of all individuals, irrespective of the labels we might use in describing their actions. According to him, we should focus more on the environmental determinants of behavior than on inner determinants. He would eliminate all references to a mental apparatus such as Freud employed. Such theorizing, in his view, is imprecise and ambiguous, and leads to pseudoexplanations of behavior.

Skinner believed, however, that Freud contributed much to our understanding of behavior and that many of his ideas can profitably be translated into terms amenable to scientific inquiry. For example, the various ego defense mechanisms Freud postulated can be examined in terms of people's attempts to avoid or escape punishment. In Skinner's view, punishment makes the stimuli associated with punished behavior aversive. As a consequence, any behavior that reduces or eliminates that stimulation becomes positively reinforcing. In repression, therefore, behavior which is punished becomes aversive, and by not engaging in it or by not 'seeing' it, a person avoids conditioned aversive stimulation (Skinner, 1974, p. 155). There is no need to postulate an inner process in which id impulses incapable of fulfillment are kept lurking in the unconscious. Another example is sublimation. In Freudian terms, sublimation is the "discharge of instinctual energy and especially that associated with pregenital impulses through socially approved activities" (Skinner, 1974, p. 156). In Skinnerian terms, if two forms of behavior are positively reinforcing, but one of them is punished, the other is more likely to occur. Again, for Freud, conversion is "the transformation of an unconscious conflict into a symbolically equivalent somatic symptom" (Skinner, 1974, p. 156). Such mental events are presumed to have the power to produce physical illness. Inner-directed rage, for example, is said to produce ulcers. Skinner maintained that "the condition felt as rage is medically related to the ulcer, and that a complex social situation causes both" (Skinner, 1974, pp. 156–157). Of course, the complex social situation would have to be precisely and adequately defined. Hypothetically, however, it might include a punishing boss, a nagging spouse, whiny kids, loss of a loved one, and so on. Skinner's central point is that many traditional clinical concepts can be translated into terms that make them amenable to scientific investigation.

Assessment Techniques

Skinner was primarily interested in the experimental analysis of behavior. He sought to identify those environmental variables that control the emission of behavior, namely, situational factors and reinforcement schedules. As the functional analysis of behavior is a complicated matter that involves the interplay of a multitude of variables, Skinner proceeded by focusing on specific behaviors and those environmental events considered to be controlling influences. In short, Skinner sought to discover a cause-and-effect relationship between events. To accomplish this goal, Skinner first focused on simple, observable behaviors that could be readily and reliably quantified and on those environmental stimuli thought to control the emission of these behaviors. Other variables thought to be irrelevant he eliminated or held constant.

Skinner believed that his approach could be implemented best by focusing on the behavior of nonhuman species, because their environments are relatively easy to control and many of their behaviors are simple and readily quantifiable. The environment usually used for study purposes is the so-called Skinner box, a small, soundproof chamber usually containing a lever or bar that an animal such as a rat can depress to obtain food reinforcers. For work with pigeons, translucent disks are used: When the pigeon pecks at the right disk, that is, a disk of a particular color chosen by the experimenter as correct, food is delivered via a feeding disk. Behavior is quantified through the use of a cumulative recorder wired to the apparatus, which precisely and automatically records the frequency of response and displays it by means of a stylus or pen that moves along paper attached to a revolving drum.

Skinner maintained that the use of lower animals, such as rats and pigeons, to establish the principles of behavior is a good strategy and that these principles are generalizable to the behavior of human beings. In his view, a single set of principles can account for much, though not all, of the behavior of both nonhuman and human organisms.

Theory's Implications for Therapy

Psychopathology and Behavior Modification

Behavior modification is an attempt to change undesirable behavior by the application of learning principles derived primarily from laboratory experiments (Krasner, 1970, p. 89). These principles are based on research in classical conditioning and observational learning as well as in operant conditioning. Because Skinner's work focused mainly on operant conditioning, however, we will examine the use of operant conditioning principles to increase the performance of certain desirable behaviors or to reduce or eliminate a variety of problem behaviors. Specifically, investigators have demonstrated that, by employing a variety of therapeutic procedures, it is possible to increase the school performances of children with attention deficit/hyperactivity disorders, to increase the social skills of those with mental retardation, to develop appropriate speech in such individuals, to lessen the amount of aggressive and disruptive behavior of youngsters and delinquents with various behavioral disorders, to enable obese individuals to lose weight, to curtail smoking in cigarette smokers, to reduce stuttering in children and adults, and to control the undesirable behavior of people experiencing difficulties in their lives.

Reinforcement Contingencies

The use of reinforcers dependent on the expression of various desirable behaviors has been used by researchers to improve various performances of children with attention deficit/ hyperactivity disorder (AD/HD). Children with this problem are inattentive, hyperactive, and impulsive. Their motivation to perform various tasks is poor, and they show little initiative. Since reinforcement is highly associated with motivation, reinforcers have been used to increase their motivation to perform, thereby normalizing their behavior and improving the quality of their performances. A review of the research literature has shown that children with AD/HD, in comparison to normal children, perform best when the level of the reinforcers is high, reinforcers are delivered immediately after performance, and continuous rather than intermittent reinforcement is given.

Intermittent reinforcement tends to be frustrating to them and results in poorer performances. When these kinds of reinforcement contingencies (high levels of reinforcers, immediate reinforcement, and continuous reinforcement) are used, various behaviors in school, sports, and home settings are normalized and improved (Luman, Osterlaan, & Sergeant, 2005, pp. 183–213).

Another study shows how positive reinforcers can be used to reduce undesirable behaviors in children (Putnam, Handler, Ramirez-Platt, & Luiselli, 2003, pp. 583–590). The study focused on trying to improve the bus-riding behavior of students attending an urban public elementary school (kindergarten through grade 5). Disruptive behavior by students such as roughhousing, getting out of their seats, and yelling posed a threat to safe travel by distracting the driver and needed to be eliminated. Accordingly, the researchers met with school officials where disruptive behavior on the buses was very high and devised a plan in cooperation with the officials and bus drivers whereby a list of safe bus-riding rules was generated and explained to the students. The bus drivers then were taught how to monitor the students' behavior more effectively during transportation and to provide them with "caught being good" cards when they adhered to the rules. The cards included the name of the student, his or her grade (e.g., 4th grade), identified the positive behavior, gave a date on which the card was given, and the name of the bus driver. Completed cards were collected each day by teachers and entered into a weekly lottery. Lottery winners received small prizes (primarily toys) donated by local businesses and by the school. After the plan was implemented, the number of office referrals for disruptive behaviors reported by the bus drivers to the school principal decreased dramatically and remained low over a three-year period.

Discrimination training   Many obese individuals report that their eating occurs in a wide variety of situations and at many different times of the day. They may eat snacks while reading a book or magazine, talking on the phone, watching television, or arguing with their families, for example. These situations exert control over the person's behavior and act as cues that facilitate the occurrence of the eating behavior. A classic study by Penick, Filion, Fox, and Stunkard (1971, pp. 49–55) demonstrated that it is possible to encourage such overweight individuals to make appropriate discriminations by teaching them to confine their eating to one place only, namely, a dining-room table with a distinctively colored place mat and napkin. In this study, patients were asked to keep written accounts of the amount, time, and situations in which they ate food over a three-month period. This record-keeping device helped make patients aware of the situations that stimulated their eating, so that it became easier to dissociate the situations from their eating of food. If they behaved appropriately, that is, if they ate only at the dining-room table, patients were awarded points that could subsequently be exchanged for money. They lost points (and therefore money) for failure to exercise control over their behavior, that is, for eating while reading or watching television. Patients also received points for decreasing the speed of their eating, chewing their food slowly, and counting each mouthful of food eaten, and lost points for failure to perform these behaviors.

The amount of weight loss achieved by patients using these behavior-modification techniques (approximately 18 pounds) exceeded the amount lost by a control group who received traditional counseling to encourage weight loss (approximately 14 pounds). What the authors found even more significant was the difference in the percentage of patients who lost 40 pounds or more in the course of treatment. Of the patients in the behavior-modification program, 27% achieved this level of weight loss, whereas only 12% of the control patients did so. It should be noted that the number of patients in the study was very small (15 in the behavior-modification program and 17 in the control program), so that the results are unlikely to be highly reliable. More recent research, however, indicates that even larger losses in weight can be achieved by establishing programs that last more than three months and by coupling these longer programs with exercise.

After leaving the program, most people regain some, if not all, of the weight they have lost. To deal with this problem, leading researchers are now suggesting that therapists reconceptualize the problem of obesity and regard it as a chronic condition, similar to hypertension or diabetes, rather than an acute condition. As such, it requires long-term treatment. In such a program, eating and exercise behavior would be monitored on an ongoing basis. Threshold levels would be set for weight gain or relapse. When these thresholds were exceeded, treatment would emphasize identifying likely situations in which relapses occur (for example, the loss of a boyfriend/girlfriend), so that preventive action (for example, development of new hobbies, interests, or friends) could be taken (Brownell & Jeffery, 1987, pp. 353–374).

Time-out from reinforcement   According to Porterfield, Herbert-Jackson, and Risley (1976, pp. 55–64), a major problem in day-care programs for young children (1–2 years of age) is the child's immaturity in the development of appropriate play behavior. Some children engage in behavior that disrupts the activities of others, including aggressive behavior (hitting, pushing, biting, kicking), destructive use of toys (pounding a toy against the wall or on a piece of furniture), creating a situation dangerous to themselves or others (standing on a bench, throwing hard toys), or having temper tantrums. Parents and teachers are often counseled by media experts to respond to such behavior by describing its inappropriateness to the child and then redirecting him or her to an alternative toy or activity. If a child took a toy from another child, for example, the caregiver would say, "No, don't take toys. Come over here and listen to a story." Unfortunately, this **redirection procedure** is not very effective in reducing disruptive behavior, because young children learn that, if they behave inappropriately, they will be reinforced with an attractive toy or a pleasurable alternative activity. Another technique, time-out by seclusion (isolating the child), is considered too harsh a penalty for disruptive behavior and does not allow the child to observe appropriate social behavior.

Porterfield and associates conducted a study in a toddler day-care program in which they tested a different technique. Caregivers used each instance of disruptive behavior to instruct the child in appropriate alternative behavior, and then had the child sit on the periphery of the group and observe the appropriate social behavior of the other children. After a sit-and-watch period (usually less than a minute), the child was asked whether he or she understood how to play appropriately and, after a positive response, was invited to return to the group. For example, if a child took a toy from another child, the caregiver would say, "No, don't take toys from other children. Ask me for the toy you want." The caregiver then moved the child to the periphery of the group, sat him or her on the floor without play materials, and said, "Sit here and watch how the other children ask for the toys they want." When the child had watched quietly for a brief period of time, the caregiver would inquire, "Do you know how to ask for the toys you want?" Upon indicating, by a nod or a word, that he or she was ready to rejoin the group, the child was allowed to do so. If the child did not respond or responded negatively, the caregiver said, "Sit here and watch the children until you think you can ask for the toy you want." When the child finally expressed readiness to rejoin the group (usually 30 seconds to 1 minute), he or she was allowed to do so. When the child returned to the group, the caregiver took the first opportunity that presented itself to give positive reinforcement for the correct behavior by saying, "Good! You asked for the toy you wanted." This **contingent observation procedure** was highly effective in reducing disruptive behavior in the group, as compared to the redirection procedure described earlier. Furthermore, the investigators reported that caregivers and parents found this observational time-out method easy to administer, effective, and humane (Porterfield, Herbert-Jackson, & Risley, 1976, pp. 55–64).

Response-cost procedure Hyperactive children are known for their impulsivity, attentional problems, and poor classroom performance. The most common form of treatment is the prescription of medication, usually methylphenidate (Ritalin). Rapport, Murphy, and Bailey (1982, pp. 205–216) conducted a study in which they demonstrated that the use of a response-cost procedure was more effective than Ritalin in reducing the attentional problems of two hyperactive boys, ages 7 and 8.

The two children were required to solve various problems in arithmetic and reading. Two observers recorded the amount of time they spent on task (paying attention to the materials and solving the problems) and off task (not paying attention to the materials) during two daily sessions of 20 minutes each. Baseline data were collected for one week before any treatment procedures were implemented. Then the boys were given Ritalin for several weeks. Finally, the medication was discontinued and the experimental response-cost procedure was implemented. The boys were told they could earn points by paying attention and working hard on the problems and could subsequently exchange these points for up to 20 minutes of free time (for play). They were also told that failure to pay attention would cost them points. Although the use of Ritalin resulted in some improvement in comparison to the baseline, the data showed clearly that the greatest improvement in on-task behavior and academic performance occurred during the days when the response-cost procedure was used.

Differential Reinforcement of Other Behavior (DRO)

In order to reduce aggressive behavior, another technique in the arsenal of operant conditioners may be used. **Differential Reinforcement of Other Behavior** involves reinforcing, not the aggressive behavior of people, but their nonaggressive behavior. Specifically, Hegel and Ferguson (2000, pp. 94–101) focused on reducing the aggressive behavior of a 28-year-old man who had been severely brain damaged as a result of a car accident. He was living in a rehabilitation facility, confined to a wheelchair, and showed significant speech apraxia (loss of the ability to coordinate his breath and vocal cords so that he could not use language to communicate). This man often grabbed at passersby, and kicked and screamed at them. His aggressive behavior was negatively reinforced because it terminated an aversive state of boredom and provided him with the attention he strongly desired. However, this behavior interfered with his recovery and had to be brought under control to help him get better. First, his caregivers on the day shift determined that he liked to eat yogurt in a medicine cup, to tour outside the facility for short periods of time, and to play card games with staff members. He was told in order to earn any of these rewards (points) he would have to sit quietly (for increasing lengths of time) without acting aggressively in order to obtain positive reinforcers. A staff member placed a timer in clear view of the patient and set it for 15 minutes. If the patient showed no aggressive behavior for this time period, that is, until the timer buzzer sounded, the patient received his points and later could exchange them for an activity or food that he found reinforcing. In contrast, if he showed aggressive behavior, he was given no points and was instead reprimanded briefly, and the timer reset and started. After successfully controlling his behavior for two additional 15-minute periods and receiving his rewards, the time interval was stretched to an hour and eventually to two hours. There was a dramatic reduction of 74% in the patient's aggressive behavior during the day shift. Interestingly, the patient reverted to aggressive behavior during the night shift, until the DRO procedure was implemented. Reductions in aggressive behavior occurred immediately following the implementation. This suggested to the investigators that the patient's aggressive behavior was under the control of specific environmental stimuli and was not a spontaneous central nervous system activity due to brain damage. Often patients, even those with severe brain damage, can exercise control over their behavior under the right environmental conditions.

Self-Management Strategies

While the use of time-out, response-cost, and DRO procedures have been shown to be highly effective in reducing disruptive and aggressive behavior in both normal and abnormal children and adults, these techniques have certain drawbacks. For example, in school settings, they require an external agent like the teacher to implement and monitor them to deter the undesirable behavior and to reinforce the child's positive behavior. This creates an extra burden upon teachers and detracts from time spent on instructional activities. The implementation of **self-management procedures** remedies these problems. In a study by DuPaul and Hoff (1998, pp. 290–303), for example, elementary school children who were highly disruptive in their classes (e.g., acting aggressively, being noisy and defiant, and violating other classroom rules) were first taught the appropriate rules required of them (no fighting, hitting, slapping, biting, pushing, no leaving their seats without raising their hands, no talking while the teacher was speaking to the class, and so forth). They were then told that if they obeyed the rules they would receive points which could be exchanged at the end of the school day for positive reinforcers of their own choosing (e.g., extra computer time, free homework pass, and new pencils). The students were asked to rate their own behavior at the end of the day on a scale from 1 (poor—broke one or more rules) to 5 (excellent—followed all the classroom rules). Then, at the end of the day the students compared their ratings to those the teachers had made independently using the same rating scale. If the teachers and students agreed perfectly (or nearly perfectly) that the students' behavior had been excellent, then the students would receive their points. If teachers and students disagreed strongly on their ratings, no points were given. Eventually, the rules were learned so well that no comparison between the students' ratings and the teachers' ratings were necessary. The students simply kept accurate records on their own (without teacher monitoring) and were awarded bonus points for their desirable behavior. Their disruptive behavior was reduced dramatically.

Habit reversal Behavioral therapists have created a very simple yet highly useful procedure to reduce stuttering. Oral and laryngeal muscle tension increases during a stuttering episode. As stutterers start to speak, the tension in their vocal musculature leads to airflow problems. This tension is reduced by stuttering. The therapy involves training clients to make a response that is incompatible with stuttering behavior. One obvious incompatible reaction to stuttering is to discontinue speaking. Since speaking requires exhalation of air and inhalation is incompatible with speaking, children with stuttering difficulties were trained to stop speaking following the anticipation or start of a stuttered word, to take a deep diaphragmatic breath by exhaling the remaining air in their lungs and then inhaling slowly to consciously relax their chest and throat muscles. As they inhaled, they were asked to formulate mentally the words to be spoken, to start speaking shortly after they began exhaling, and to exhale slowly and smoothly. As they spoke, they were to emphasize the initial part of a statement, and to speak for short durations. As their speech became more fluent, they gradually increased the duration of speech. This regulated breathing procedure was practiced during a two-hour counseling session. The therapist modeled the procedure for each client by placing his or her finger-tips in front of the therapist's mouth to demonstrate what a slight exhalation of air felt like. Clients then practiced the procedure by placing their fingers in front of their mouths until they could speak without stuttering. This training dramatically reduced stuttering in the clients (Wagaman, Miltenberger, & Arndorfer, 1993, p. 53). Moreover, a follow-up study conducted three and one-half years later showed that none of the clients who continued using the procedure had any problem with stuttering. The two clients who reported not using the procedure during the follow-up period reverted to high levels of stuttering (Wagaman, Miltenberger, & Woods, 1995, pp. 233–234).

The token economy To alter the behavior of psychotics within institutions, investigators have designed special environments in which patients can earn tokens for performing socially appropriate tasks and then exchange them for goods and activities that are positively reinforcing. Such an incentive system is commonly known as a **token economy**.

Ayllon and Azrin (1965, pp. 357–383) conducted the classical attempt to design such an environment within a mental hospital as a means of strengthening key desirable behaviors in psychotics. They pointed out that the most important limitation in trying to develop a technology of behavior is lack of standardization in observing and recording behavior and in administering reinforcers. Different attendants may define the target behaviors differently; for example, they may be stricter or more lenient in their assessment of good grooming. In addition, it is difficult to record and reinforce desired behaviors on a ward of approximately 45 patients, all of whom engage in a variety of activities at the same time. Research has shown that reinforcers are most effective if they are applied immediately following the desired response. If different attendants reinforce patients at varying time intervals following responses, the impact on behavior will be lessened or even nonexistent. In short, if the attendants do not know which behaviors to reinforce, how much to reinforce, or when to reinforce, it seems unlikely that there will be much improvement. Accordingly, the investigators spent 18 months developing their program in order to eliminate these and other problems. The final program included a standard list of behaviors to be changed, as well as a list of reinforcers. The behaviors to be strengthened differed from patient to patient, but included: helping serve meals to the other patients; washing dishes; cleaning tables; typing letters; answering the telephone and calling hospital personnel to the phone; washing sheets, pillow cases, and towels in the laundry; and so on. A list of the reinforcers to be given in exchange for tokens is shown in Table 15.2.

TABLE 15.2   LIST OF REINFORCERS AVAILABLE TO PATIENTS FOR TOKENS

Reinforcer	Number of Tokens Daily
I. Privacy	
Selection of room 1	0
Selection of room 2	4
Selection of room 3	8
Selection of room 4	15
Selection of room 5	30
Personal chair	1
Screen (room divider)	1
Choice of bedspreads	1
Coat rack	1
II. Leave from the ward	
Twenty-minute walk on hospital grounds (with escort)	2
Thirty-minute grounds pass	10
Trip to town (with escort)	100
III. Social interaction with staff	
Private audience with ward psychologist	20
Private audience with social worker	100
IV. Devotional opportunities	
Extra religious services on ward	1
Extra religious services off ward	10
V. Recreational opportunities	
Movie on ward	1
Exclusive use of a radio	1
Television (choice of program)	3
VI. Commissary items	
Candy, milk, cigarettes, coffee, and sandwich	1–5
Toilet articles such as toothpaste, comb, lipstick, and talcum powder	1–10
Clothing such as gloves, scarf, and skirt	12–400
Reading and writing materials such as pen, greeting card, newspaper, and magazine	2–5
Miscellaneous items such as ashtray, potted plant, picture holder, and stuffed animals	1–50

Source: Adapted from Ayllon, T. and Azrin, N. H., "The measurement and reinforcement of behavior of psychotics" in *Journal of the Experimental Analysis of Behavior*, Vol. 8, pp. 357–383. Copyright © 1965 by the Society for the Experimental Analysis of Behavior, Inc. Used with permission.

In general, the results of the program showed significant improvement in patient behaviors over a 42-day period. In another experiment within the same program, the investigators found that, when the tokens were withdrawn, the behavior of the patients deteriorated. When the system was reinstated, performance levels rose again. This shift in performance shows the powerful impact of the tokens in changing behavior.

This study and other experiments with token economies, though generally successful (Kazdin, 1989), have raised a number of questions. First, what is so wonderful about getting patients to comb their hair or wash some dishes? The answer is that, although major problem behaviors remain untouched, the behaviors that were strengthened represent a significant shift in functioning for these patients. At the beginning of the experiments, some patients refused to wash or groom themselves. A few of them lay in their own excrement. Some refused to utter a word. The application of operant techniques changed this state of affairs and was the first step toward recovery. It also increased the patients' freedom, in the sense that it provided them with an opportunity to perform a variety of activities for positive payoffs rather than simply sitting all day doing nothing. The changes in appearance are also beneficial because staff members tend to treat patients better. "If you can't tell the patient from the staff without a score card, you will most likely react to him (or her) as if he (or she) were normal just like you" (Krasner, 1970, p. 97). The effort to implement some method of treatment is monumentally preferable to providing no treatment at all, which is the alternative all too often adopted in mental institutions. Behavior modification is not the only therapeutic method that can be employed to overcome this impasse, but it does work.

Second, do the new behaviors learned in the token-economy program generalize to other settings once the patients leave the institution? In fact, removal of the contingencies learned in the program usually results in a decline in performance of the behaviors in other settings. In the past several years, however, tremendous progress has been made in elaborating the principles whereby the behaviors will transfer to new settings. One obvious procedure for ensuring that the behaviors will be maintained is to bring them under the control of consequences that ordinarily occur in the new settings. For example, the treatment of a withdrawn patient in a hospital setting might involve having staff members give attention and an expression of interest whenever the patient socializes with them or with other patients. Later, in a home setting, the patient's parents and relatives can continue to reinforce the person's social interactions through the use of praise, smiles, displays of affection, and expressions of interest. However, researchers have found that, in the home setting, family members do not necessarily use the required reinforcers; in other words, some people do not ordinarily give much praise and attention to others. Instead, they tend to ignore attempts at showing social behaviors, or to reinforce the wrong behaviors. This problem can usually be overcome by training family members to reinforce appropriate behaviors (Kazdin, 1989, pp. 264–269).

Aversive techniques   Behavior modification also raises some serious ethical questions, especially with regard to aversive techniques. Is it morally acceptable to use punishment, for example, to change behavior? Experts in the area of behavior modification agree that the use of physical punishment should generally be avoided, because it has undesirable side effects and interferes with the learning of socially appropriate behavior, as Skinner suggested. However, it can be used effectively to stop extremely undesirable behavior if other procedures based on positive reinforcement have been tried and failed (Kazdin, 1989, pp. 142–148).

Let us examine an actual case history in which aversive control techniques were used, so that you can decide for yourself whether or not the use of punishment can be justified under certain circumstances. The case involved self-destructive behavior in a severely retarded 7-year-old boy who was nonverbal and who functioned like a 2-year-old (Kushner, 1970, pp. 42–44). The self-destructive behavior consisted of hand-biting severe enough to cause bleeding and infection. Hospital personnel tried to prevent the behavior by placing boxing gloves on the boy's hands but, when they were removed, he simply went back to biting his hands. The child also tried to prevent the behavior by sitting on his hands or by holding onto his nurse's hand. This strategy worked only temporarily, and he continued to bite his hands when they were free. Observation by the investigator indicated that the nurses' reaction to his crying following the hand-biting was to become very solicitous, to pick him up, and to give him a great deal of attention and affection. Discussion with the nurses about the reinforcing properties of their behavior met with great resistance. It was obvious that the nurses could not be convinced of the necessity to ignore the behavior and, in any case, the extinction process would be so slow that much more damage would be inflicted. Therefore, the investigator decided to use electric shock to prevent the behavior. Electrodes were placed on the child's thigh and shock was administered following any hand-biting behavior. After the initial application of shock, the mother was brought into the room and was asked to say "No" at the same time that the shock was being administered. The decline in hand-biting was rapid and dramatic. Later the nurses were instructed to say "No" whenever the child moved his hand to his mouth and to say "Good boy" when he moved his hand away. Other behavioral methods were then applied to maintain the low rate of hand-biting.

Would you condone the use of punishment in this case? It is a very difficult judgment to make. If all other possibilities have been tried and found wanting, perhaps aversive control can be justified in certain instances. There are no easy answers in this situation, but no progress in helping people is made by denying the efficacy of punishment in producing behavioral change.

In the past, there have been some abuses of patients' rights in programs using behavior-modification techniques. Occasionally, investigators have administered cruel and unusual punishment; in one study, for example, patients were shocked without their consent and deprived of meals for a number of days. Even in the Ayllon and Azrin (1965) study reviewed in this chapter, there is a question of the abuse of patients' rights. A reexamination of Table 15.2, which shows the kinds of reinforcers that could be bought with earned tokens, indicates that, theoretically at least, attendance at extra religious services could be prohibited by the investigators if the patient had not earned any tokens. This kind of prohibition comes very close to an abridgment of the patient's constitutional rights concerning freedom of religion. This is not to say, however, that denial of patient rights or the administration of cruel and unusual punishment is pervasive and, therefore, that behavior modification procedures should be abandoned. Abuses are relatively few, and the benefits to thousands and thousands of people have been tremendous. Instead, investigators must work to eliminate abusive practices and uphold, to the best of their abilities, the ethical ideals of the profession.

Shaping   Jackson and Wallace (1974, pp. 461–471) used shaping to develop appropriate speech in a 15-year-old girl named Alice who was diagnosed as "severely disturbed, withdrawn, and mildly retarded" by the school diagnostician. Her teacher reported that Alice participated only rarely in group activities and almost never spoke at an audible level. The goal was to shape the loudness of her voice until it reached a normal level.

Wearing a microphone to detect the volume of her speech, Alice sat in a private booth, and read to the experimenter single words taken from her classroom reading books. When her voice achieved a specified volume, a token was automatically delivered. At first, only slight increases in volume were required for the delivery of a token. Eventually, however, Alice had to speak louder to activate the relay attached to the microphone sound system that triggered delivery of the tokens. Alice underwent 20 shaping sessions. After each session, she was required to read from a book to the experimenter for 10 minutes. The tokens Alice earned could be exchanged for several items she wanted, including books, beauty aids, and a photo album.

Once Alice spoke at a normal level, the experimenter attempted to generalize Alice's new behavior to her classroom. To promote generalization, the experimenter rearranged the laboratory setting so that it resembled her actual classroom and continued her training. For example, the side of Alice's booth was swung out at a 45-degree angle, greatly reducing her privacy. Five students and her teacher conducted a study period in the room during the shaping period. Eventually, following intense training, Alice was returned to her regular classroom, where she began to behave in a more appropriate way. Her teacher reported that, although she was a long way from being a typical teenager, she had made considerable improvement both in voice loudness and in other social behaviors such as smiling, playing with others, and initiating verbal interactions with her peers.

Theory's Implications for Education

According to Skinner, teachers and administrators in this country and in many others tend to rely on many different aversive practices to control the behavior of students, and he was opposed to such educational efforts. But a recent survey of all the research literature starting in the 1970s and continuing to the present day showed that Skinner was wrong, at least about the use of punishment to control children's *academic* behavior. This investigation found in hundreds of classes primarily at the elementary school level in many countries, including the United States, New Zealand, Australia, Canada, and Great Britain that teachers are increasingly using more praise and approval (positive reinforcement) to encourage appropriate academic behavior (e.g., praise for solving problems, writing good book reports, getting high grades on tests). These findings are consistent with Skinner's continual plea that authority figures teach people by using positive reinforcement. However, the same massive literature review showed that Skinner was right in regard to attempts to control children's undesirable *social* behavior. Teachers in nearly all of these studies persistently used punishment and disapproval to discipline students (e.g., by criticizing them, threatening them, making hostile remarks to them, forcing them to stay after school, giving them extra homework) when they misbehaved in class. These techniques are clearly still used as the primary form of discipline for social behavior in the classroom (Beaman & Wheldall, 2000, pp. 431–446), even though Skinner was adamantly opposed to them. According to Skinner, such techniques are painful for large numbers of students and generate many unwanted by-products (Skinner, 1968, p. 97). For example, the student may try to escape from the punishing situation by being tardy, or may eventually drop out of school altogether. Students who commit suicide are often those who have experienced difficulties in school. Subtler forms of escape include chronic daydreaming and restlessness. A student who cannot sit still for a few minutes in class can spend hours playing in the neighborhood park or watching television. Another serious result of aversive control, in Skinner's view, is that students may attempt to attack their controllers, by becoming defiant, rude, or impudent, using obscene language, and even physically assaulting their teachers. For Skinner, vandalism is another indirect manifestation of students' attempts to weaken the control of powerful others.

The detrimental nature of such practices has prompted many well-intentioned and concerned teachers to seek alternatives. But their suggestions, according to Skinner, are also fundamentally flawed. For example, one major alternative to such aversive practices accepted by such is permissiveness. Permissiveness has a number of seeming advantages; one of these is that the practitioners are spared the labor of supervision and the enforcement of standards. But "permissiveness is not a policy; it is the abandonment of policy; and its apparent advantages are illusory. To refuse to control is to leave control not to the person himself but to other parts of the social and nonsocial environments" (Skinner, 1968, p. 84).

Skinner also opposed another major alternative, related in many respects to permissiveness, namely, guidance. Its effects on the educational process are usually described with a horticultural metaphor: Students are said to grow like a flower or tree if their experiences occur in the right soil; behavior can be cultivated but only under the right conditions; behavior is developed until maturity (Skinner, 1968, p. 87). In Chapters 12 and 13 on Maslow and Rogers, we saw good examples of the guidance position. Skinner noted some convenient advantages for its practitioners:

> One who merely guides a natural development cannot easily be accused of trying to control it. Growth remains an achievement of the individual, testifying to his freedom and worth, his "hidden propensities," and as the gardener is not responsible for the ultimate form of what he grows, so one who merely guides is exonerated when things go wrong. (Skinner, 1968, pp. 87–88)

In Skinner's view, the primary disadvantage of this position is that it obscures the reinforcements actually responsible for the changes in behavior by attributing them to "the unfolding of some predetermined pattern" (Skinner, 1968, p. 88). Skinner himself opted for a detailed examination of the environmental determinants of behavior. In his view, education involves "the arrangement of [the] contingencies of reinforcement under which students learn" (Skinner, 1968, p. 64). These contingencies can be effectively arranged through the use of teaching machines, computer-assisted instruction, and other programmed techniques. Complex subject matter is presented to the student in a series of small, easy-to-learn steps. In one form of programmed learning, a question is presented and the students write their answer in a space provided by the program. Then they lift a lever that moves the answer under a transparent cover and simultaneously exposes the correct answer. If the two answers match, the students punch a hole in the paper near their response to indicate that they have answered correctly. This procedure instructs the machine to allow the next question to appear. Following the same procedure, the students answer all the questions. They then start the series again and attempt to answer correctly those questions they answered incorrectly at first. The process is repeated until they have mastered the program materials (Skinner, 1968, p. 162).

Skinner maintained that such a format has many advantages over the traditional system. It is more efficient than traditional instructional procedures. It is a labor-saving device, because it can bring many students into contact with one programmer (Skinner, 1968, p. 162). Although programming may suggest mass production to some people, in reality it acts almost like a private tutor for the student. Unlike lectures and films, there is a continual interplay between the student and the materials. Programming does not eliminate the need for the teacher. The teacher is the key person who arranges the contingencies of reinforcement for the student but now he or she can make these arrangements pay off in effective learning. In addition, the teacher still has the tremendous responsibility of weaning students from the machine and showing them how the facts and principles they have learned can be related to other areas of life.

The teaching machine is programmed to ensure that the student thoroughly understands a point before he or she can proceed. One of the tragedies of traditional educational practices is that, all too often, the teacher is faced with the task of educating large numbers of students simultaneously. Under such conditions, it is impossible for even the best teacher to give each student the amount of attention he or she needs to learn the materials well. Still another advantage is that the machine reinforces the student sufficiently for each response and does it immediately (Skinner, 1968, p. 39). Very often, the teacher in the traditional setting knows the value of immediate and adequate reinforcement but cannot provide it. Finally, the programmed-learning approach recognizes the importance of individual differences. Skinner (1968, p. 242) maintained that failure to account for these differences is the greatest single inefficiency in education today.

For all these reasons, Skinner strongly advocated the adoption of his programmed-learning approach. But, although he was hopeful of eventual change in our educational system, he realized that his innovations might be resisted by educators.

> Many of these charged with the improvement of education are unaware that technical help is available, and many are afraid of it when it is pointed out. They resist any new practice which does not have the familiar and reassuring character of day-to-day communication. They continue to discuss learning and teaching in the language of the layman. (Skinner, 1968, p. 259)

Thus, Skinner recommended the application of a scientific analysis of behavior to educational practices. It seems that his approach is gaining support among some educators, as evidenced by the large number of academic institutions that now use the programmed-learning format to help educate students.

Theory's Implications for Society

In his book *Walden Two*, Skinner (1948) makes an effort to apply operant principles not only to education and psychopathology but to the extremely complicated problem of creating an ideal society. Skinner envisages Walden Two as a behaviorally engineered utopia. It is portrayed as a rural community with cooperative housing and dining systems for its nearly 1,000 members. Such a communal arrangement avoids the unnecessary duplication of facilities and the great expense associated with building separate houses. Because of the relatively small size of the living quarters, it is possible to interconnect all of the bedrooms with common lounge areas, dining rooms, a theater, and a library. Thus, for the most part, members can avoid going out in bad weather. These protected arrangements are consistent with Skinner's emphasis on changing the environment to meet individual needs; they permit more control of undesirable weather conditions, so that community members are masters of their own situation rather than the victims of it.

An additional benefit of living in such a small, largely self-contained community is that there is no long-distance commuting to work along congested and polluted highways, a nerve-wracking practice that continues to plague many contemporary workers (Freedman, 1972, chap. 2, p. 3). A few trucks simply ferry some of the workers back and forth over the short distance from the living quarters to the workshops (where, for example, furniture is made and repaired), gardens, and livestock areas.

Skinner insisted that his utopia was not founded on the simplistic and romanticized return-to-the-farm philosophy of the 1800s, nor did it spring from a rejection of modern life. For example, the farming to meet food and clothing needs relies on the best equipment available, bought from the larger, outside community. Also, the power to run these machines (including the trucks) is supplied by the larger community. The emphasis in Walden Two is on minimizing uncreative and uninteresting work for its members. This orientation demands the best that technology can offer.

Although necessary at times for transactions with the larger community, money is not needed or used within Walden Two. Money earned by members as a result of work done for outsiders is placed in a community fund to be used for future purchases from outsiders. Within Walden Two, food, clothing, shelter, recreation, and medical services are provided, and so there is no need for money. To keep the system operating, however, members are required to contribute 1,200 labor credits a year (or four credits for each of 300 workdays) in return for the goods and services provided to them. In general, one credit is given for each hour of work; thus, the average workday lasts four hours, so that residents have ample time for recreational activities and other diversions (for instance, games, theatrical plays, reading, writing, art, science, hobbies). To ensure that unpleasant jobs get done and to avoid resentment over aversive types of work, the apportionment of the labor credits is adjusted to make all kinds of work equally attractive. For example, cleaning sewers earns 1.5 credits per hour, whereas working in the community flower garden earns only 0.7 or 0.8 credits per hour (Skinner, 1948, p. 52). Even though each member works an average of only 20 hours per week, such an economy is viable, for several reasons. Thus, there is little unnecessary duplication of goods; for example, there are community automobiles but not everyone owns one. Unnecessary services are eliminated; for instance, there are no bars or taverns, because Skinner believed that the satisfied people of his utopia would have no need to drink (Freedman, 1972, chap. 2, p. 3). Because community members are not bombarded daily by fashion advertisers, clothing styles change more slowly in Walden Two, and members do not throw away clothes in good condition (Skinner, 1948, p. 35). And because there is no unemployment, the bureaucratic burden and cost of administering benefits to the unemployed are eliminated.

Walden Two also makes efficient use of all of its citizens, including women. Skinner was unequivocally egalitarian in his views on the relationships and roles of men and women. There is no sexual division of labor in Walden Two. Because all community members, irrespective of gender, share the labor of preparing and serving food, cleaning the living quarters, and educating the young, women are able to participate equally with men in every area of communal life. Child care is also shared by members of the community of both sexes.

Child care was of particular concern to Skinner, and he devoted considerable attention to it. Children in Walden Two do not live with their natural parents, nor are they raised by them. Instead, group members share the responsibility of raising children. In the nursery, infants are raised by community experts, both male and female. They live in a controlled environment so that they never know fear, frustration, or anxiety. After the first year of life, they are placed in dormitory quarters, and annoyances are introduced on a gradual basis in order to develop tolerance for a certain degree of frustration. For example, Skinner describes a situation in which, tired and hungry, a group of children come home after a long walk. Instead of being allowed to eat immediately, they must stand for five minutes in front of steaming bowls of soup (Skinner, 1948, p. 109). Children are encouraged to have a sense of humor and not to take annoyances too seriously. These lessons in self-control are taught so that children can handle any unhappiness they might experience later in life. Whereas in our culture children may meet with uncontrolled frustration and subsequent defeat, in Walden Two the degree of frustration is carefully controlled so that success can be assured (Freedman, 1972, chap. 3, p. 3).

Group care of children weakens the relationship between parent and child; this state of affairs is encouraged in Walden Two. Skinner believed that, in the typical home, parents do not know how to raise their children properly. This job is best left in the hands of experts. Children regard all adult members of Walden Two as their parents, which provides several benefits. Children are discouraged from being too dependent on their biological parents. Foster children and stepchildren are loved as dearly as one's own. If the biological parents divorce, children are not embarrassed by severe changes in their lifestyles. It is also easier to discourage people who are unfit or unwell from seeking parenthood, because no stigma attaches to being childless and the childless have others to love. Finally, children grow up more secure, because they receive affection and help from hundreds of adults (Skinner, 1948, pp. 142–145).

Walden Two is governed by a board of six planners, three of whom are usually women. The planners are chosen by the board members themselves, from names supplied by the managers. Planners may serve for a period of up to 10 years but no more. They are responsible for policy making and for the supervision of the managers.

The managers are responsible for providing adequate goods and services to community members; for example, there are managers of food, health, dentistry, play, arts, nursery school, and dairy. They are specialists who have been carefully trained and selected for the job through apprenticeship procedures (Skinner, 1948, p. 55).

The only other group besides the workers, managers, and planners is the scientists. The community supports research aimed at the improvement of the economy and the psychological well-being of its members. Experiments are often done in plant and animal breeding to improve the economy, and psychological experiments are performed to increase knowledge of the impact of the environment on behavior, so that the environment can be effectively manipulated to increase community members' happiness.

In Walden Two, the workers do not elect the planners, managers, or scientists. Skinner maintained that the average citizen (worker) is unable to make such selections intelligently (Skinner, 1948, p. 267). These decisions are best left in the hands of specialists, who, he believed, would wield their power for the good of others. Should they take any steps that reduced the total happiness of the community, they would begin to experience a reduction in their power. Skinner was convinced that this potential reduction in power would serve as a check against misuse of authority (Skinner, 1948, p. 264).

It could be argued that Skinner's view is naive and that concentration of power in the hands of a few people is likely to lead to misuse of that power, irrespective of the level of unhappiness of community members. This criticism assumes that power is a means to personal gain: Dictators exploit citizens to enhance their own feelings of esteem and to accrue wealth and possessions. In Skinner's utopia, however, a person's self-esteem is based on contributing to the betterment of the community and not on personal gain. Possessions and wealth are shared, and so there is no incentive to accumulate goods. A loss in power would signify to leaders that community members are less accepting of their efforts to help them; consequently, the leaders would be unhappy. Also, the socialization process in Walden Two ensures that members do not see punishment as a primary means of controlling behavior; rather, the emphasis is on positive reinforcement and cooperative behavior (Skinner, 1948, p. 272). Finally, if the planners did abuse their authority, they could be replaced, under the code adopted by community members to govern behavior. Despite all these assurances, Walden Two is clearly a dictatorship, albeit a benevolent one, and as such is unsettling to most democratically oriented Americans.

Even more unsettling is Skinner's harsh indictment of democracy. He argued that democracy is really despotism, because the minority is at the mercy of the majority (Freedman, 1972, chap. 3, p. 7). Skinner saw little point in national elections, especially presidential elections; with so little difference between the parties and their political platforms, the election of either candidate makes no appreciable difference in the lives of the electorate. Instead of striving to improve democracy, he would simply abandon it (Freedman, 1972, chap. 3, p. 7).

In Skinner's version of the ideal society, people would be in a position to tell the experts (planners, managers, and scientists) directly what they like or dislike about the life they are leading. Thus, protests would be legitimate and would be taken "as seriously as the pilot of an airplane takes a sputtering engine" (Skinner, 1948, p. 269). If current practices were unsatisfactory, they would be changed, because Skinner's utopia is an experimenting society, where the aim is maximization of the happiness of every community member.

In conclusion, while there were small groups of people in the United States who attempted to create communities based on the Walden II model in the 1970s, in present day America there appear to be no on-going attempts to establish and maintain such socially engineered living groups. Instead Skinner's work is mentioned by social planners and architects as an example of a utopian society in discussions that seek to use the marvels of new technology to help people live more effective lives.

Evaluative Comments

An evaluation of the scientific worth of Skinner's theory in terms of our six criteria is now in order.

Comprehensiveness   Skinner constructed a theory of behavior that initially focused almost exclusively on the functioning of lower animals. His primary concern was to generate a set of learning principles for certain types of simple, nonsocial performance. Thus, the range of topics actually covered by Skinner in his initial theorizing was highly limited, and he was severely criticized for this narrow focus. His principal rebuttal was that, in all sciences, advances occur as investigators focus first on the simple and then progress to the more complex. The focus on simple behaviors allows scientists to control current situational conditions better, to record behavior over longer periods of time, and to control genetic and environmental-history variables (Skinner, 1953, p. 38). Once the basic processes are understood in lower animals, this information can be utilized in the study of the more diverse and complicated behavior of human beings.

This research strategy has had major payoff value in terms of the important findings about behavior it has generated. Yet there is a kind of conservatism about it that may seem unnecessarily stultifying to some investigators of human behavior. Science is a human enterprise and should, at least occasionally, be fun. Part of the enjoyment is based on taking risks, on testing hunches that are not firmly grounded in data. Nonetheless, Skinner's allegiance to the strict simple-to-complex principle is generally cogent.

In his later writings, Skinner argued that the imbalance in his work had been corrected, because much of the current work in behavior modification focuses exclusively on human behavior. On this basis, Skinner's theory can now be considered much more comprehensive.

Precision and testability   The terms of Skinner's theory are precisely defined, and the various relational statements are capable of experimental verification. The concern with rigor and precision in the study of behavioral phenomena is one of the impressive strengths of the work of Skinner and his operant colleagues.

Parsimony   Skinner's theory is relatively economical, especially when compared with some of the psychodynamic positions. It is not burdened by excess concepts and assumptions. In fact, it can be argued that the theory lacks a number of concepts that could help to explain various social-learning phenomena. Skinner himself recognized that additional concepts may be needed in a theory that attempts to account for complex and cognitively based human learning.

Empirical validity   Skinner's position, in sharp contrast to the psychodynamic positions, is firmly grounded in laboratory data. Despite strong empirical support for many aspects of his learning theory, however, critics argue that Skinner's claim to a technology of behavior that can solve complex social problems is unsupported, that he made sweeping and unwarranted generalizations on the basis of limited empirical evidence (Black, 1973, p. 129). Skinner acknowledged that he was indeed offering interpretations about the functioning of society from limited data but argued that this is perfectly legitimate and is done by scientists in other fields without attracting much attention. He maintained that "when phenomena are out of reach in time or space, or too large or small to be directly manipulated, we must talk about them with less than a complete account of relevant conditions" (Skinner, 1973, p. 261). This is true, but it is also easy to confuse speculation with fact, and Skinner's arguments about the efficacy of his approach in solving major social problems like poverty and overpopulation are as yet unconfirmed.

Heuristic value Skinner's theory has had tremendous impact on the thinking and research activities of investigators in many disciplines. He was a controversial figure, whose position has been severely criticized by a variety of critics, including humanistic psychologists, psychiatrists, politicians, philosophers, theologians, biologists, novelists, and journalists. Some people have taken these attacks as proof that Skinner was a revolutionary thinker whose position will eventually force a major shift in the way we view ourselves and others (Platt, 1973, p. 23). Be that as it may, it is clear that Skinner's theory ranks high in heuristic value.

Applied value Skinner's position has far-reaching implications for the functioning of society. Beginning with experiments on the behavior of lower animals, he derived, over approximately a 60-year period, a set of simple and precise reinforcement principles that have been applied to a number of significant problems faced by human beings. The theory's tremendous applied value can perhaps be seen most clearly in the areas of psychopathology and education.

CRITICAL THINKING QUESTIONS

1. Is there really a need for a scientific technology of behavior, as Skinner suggested? Give reasons for your answer.
2. Do you ever use mentalistic explanations to account for your behavior? If so, cite some recent instances and try to reanalyze them in terms of possible environmental variables that were salient at the time.
3. Is all control of behavior bad? In what ways does control yield positive or negative outcomes for people? Why do many people dislike those who control the outcomes of others?
4. Do you agree with Skinner that punishment is the most common technique of control in modern life? What are the limitations of punishment as a control technique? Is its use ever effective and desirable?
5. What is behavior modification? What are its strengths and weaknesses? Do you think that token economies are useless, sterile, and unethical ways of changing undesirable behavior? What do you propose as an alternative?

GLOSSARY

behavior modification Series of procedures that seek to change behavior through reliance on reinforcement principles or, less often, by reliance on punishment principles.

contingency Relationship between a behavior and its consequences. In some cases, events that precede the behavior are also specified by a contingency.

contingent observation procedure Technique in which children who have behaved disruptively in a play situation are required to sit on the periphery of the group and watch the other children playing appropriately. A return to the group is dependent on the child's acknowledgment that he or she understands the correct behavior to be exhibited in the play situation.

continuous reinforcement Schedule of reinforcement in which each response is followed by a reinforcer.

differential reinforcement of other behavior (DRO) A schedule of reinforcement in which reinforcement is delivered at the end of a time interval during which no instances of unacceptable behavior occurred, i.e., no fighting, biting, screaming or kicking.

discrimination Responding differently in the presence of different situational events.

discriminative stimulus Stimulus whose presence signals an individual to respond because he or she has learned previously that its presence leads to reinforcing consequences.

extinction   Reduction in behavior that occurs as a result of the failure to reinforce previously reinforced behavior.

fixed-interval schedule   Schedule of reinforcement in which the first response that occurs after a fixed amount of time has elapsed is reinforced.

fixed-ratio schedule   Schedule of reinforcement in which a fixed number of responses is required before a reinforcer is applied.

functional analysis   Attempt to understand behavior by identifying the environmental conditions that determine its occurrence or nonoccurrence. A functional analysis says that behavior is caused by the operation of environmental factors.

intermittent reinforcement   Schedule of reinforcement in which responses produce reinforcers only occasionally or intermittently.

law of effect   For Thorndike, the principle that behavior is determined by its consequences. In his view, behavior followed by reward was "stamped in," whereas behavior followed by punishment was "stamped out." In current operant-conditioning theory, the principle is that a behavior becomes more probable when it is followed by a positive reinforcer and less probable when it is followed by a punisher.

mentalism   Pejorative term used by some learning theorists to indicate their dissatisfaction with the use of concepts that cannot be objectively assessed or validated as explanatory devices in attempts to account for behavior. These concepts are supposed to have explanatory power, but in reality do not.

negative punishment   Removal of a positive reinforcer following a response, with the result that the rate of that response decreases.

negative reinforcement   The removal of an aversive or unpleasant stimulus following a response, with the result that the rate of that response increases.

negative reinforcer   Aversive or unpleasant stimulus, for example, electric shock, an extremely loud noise, an extremely bright light, and physical assault whose removal following a response strengthens the occurrence of that response. An aversive stimulus is a punisher whose removal following a response or behavior strengthens the occurrence of that response or behavior.

operant analysis   Study of the ways in which behavior is acquired, maintained, or modified by its reinforcing or punishing consequences.

operant conditioning   Establishment of the linkage or association between a behavior and its consequences.

physical aids   Tools used to facilitate certain behaviors, for example eyeglasses used by people with vision problems to facilitate sight, hearing aids used by the hearing impaired to facilitate hearing.

positive punishment   Presentation of an aversive stimulus following a response, with the result that the rate of that response decreases.

positive reinforcement   The presentation of a positive reinforcer following a response, with the result that the rate of that response increases.

positive reinforcers   Stimuli that, when they follow behavior, increase the frequency of the behavior.

primary punishers   Stimuli that are innately aversive. They do not need to be paired with other aversive stimuli to achieve their aversive properties.

primary reinforcers   Stimuli that are innately reinforcing. They do not depend on learning to achieve their reinforcing properties.

prompts   Antecedent stimuli that help initiate behaviors.

punishment   Presentation of an aversive stimulus or removal of a positive reinforcer following a behavior, with the result that the performance of that behavior decreases.

redirection procedure   A technique in which children who are acting inappropriately are removed from the situation and their attention is directed to an alternative activity.

reinforcement   Presentation of a positive reinforcer or removal of a punisher following a behavior, with the result that the frequency of that behavior increases.

repertoire   Unique set of acquired behavior patterns.

response cost   A punishment procedure in which, contingent on undesirable behavior, a positive reinforcer is removed or lost.

secondary punishers   Stimuli that become aversive by being paired with other stimuli (primary or conditioned) that are already punishing.

secondary reinforcers   Stimuli that become reinforcing by being paired with other stimuli (primary or conditioned) that are already reinforcing.

self-control processes   Actions instigated by a person to alter the conditions that influence his or her behavior.

self-management procedures   Techniques used by authorities with which institutional members learn to manage or control their own behavior. In educational settings, for example, teachers use a procedure with which children learn to manage or control their own disruptive behavior so that teachers can spend time on instructional activities. Children first learn the appropriate rules (no pushing, hitting, and so forth). Obedience to the rules during the school day results in rewards being given to them by their teachers at the end of the day. Inappropriate behavior (pushing, hitting, fighting) means that no rewards are given.

shaping   Teaching a new behavior by reinforcing responses that successively approximate it.

stimulus control   The process in which a person's response is determined by particular stimuli. If a person has been reinforced for a given behavior in the presence of certain stimuli and not in the presence of others, he or she learns to respond only in the presence of those stimuli that provide the opportunity for reinforcement. Behavior is then said to be under the control of those stimuli.

stimulus generalization   The process by which responses made in the presence of a particular stimulus come to be made in the presence of other, similar stimuli.

successive approximations   A procedure whereby responses that more and more closely resemble a terminal response are reinforced.

time-out from reinforcement   A punishment procedure in which, contingent on undesirable behavior, access to positive reinforcers is withdrawn for a brief period.

token economy   A behavior modification procedure in which patients earn tokens (or chips or points) for performing behaviors that the hospital staff judges are necessary if the patients are to live effectively. The tokens are conditioned reinforcers that can be exchanged for experiences and/or goods desired by the patients.

SUGGESTED READINGS

Skinner, B. F. (1948). *Walden two*. New York: Macmillan.

Skinner, B. F. (1953). *Science and human behavior*. New York: Macmillan.

Skinner, B. F. (1971). *Beyond freedom and dignity*. New York: Knopf.

Skinner, B. F. (1974). *About behaviorism*. New York: Knopf.

CHAPTER 16

Rotter's Expectancy-Reinforcement Value Model

Courtesy of Dr. Julian R. Rotter.

Biographical Sketch

Julian Rotter was born in Brooklyn, New York, in 1916. He received his B.A. from Brooklyn College in 1937, his M.A. from the University of Iowa in 1938, and his Ph.D. in psychology from Indiana University in 1941. During his undergraduate and graduate days he was greatly influenced by neoanalyst Alfred Adler and by Kurt Lewin, a prominent social psychologist. Rotter attended a series of Adler's clinics, demonstrations, and university seminars and also met informally with Adler at his home (Mosher, 1968, pp. 33–45). He credits Adler with focusing his attention on the goal-directedness of behavior and on the unity of personality. Many of the concepts in Rotter's position, as we shall see, can be traced directly to Adler's influence.

Rotter was also influenced by Lewin's field-theory approach, which emphasizes the interrelatedness of behavior and postulates that multiple factors are responsible for the occurrence of any behavior. Rotter accepted these assumptions, as well as the view that behavior must be described from the perspective of the person whose behavior is under scrutiny (Rotter & Hochreich, 1975, p. 97). In addition to Adler and Lewin, Rotter reports being influenced by the writings of a number of learning theorists, including Thorndike, Tolman, and Hull. In general terms, his social-learning position is an attempt to integrate two major trends embodied in the work of these theorists: a reinforcement approach and cognitive or **field theory** (Rotter, Chance, & Phares, 1972, p. 1).

After serving as a psychologist and personnel consultant to the U.S. Army during World War II, Rotter accepted a position at Ohio State University, where he eventually became director of the psychological clinic. During his stay at Ohio State, he published *Social Learning and Clinical Psychology* (1954), in which he presented an extended treatment of his social-learning theory of personality. He also attracted a number of capable students, who worked with him to test various predictions derived from the theory. Some of these students have since become leading proponents of the social-learning view in contemporary psychology.

In 1963, Rotter left Ohio State and accepted a position as a full professor in the department of psychology at the University of Connecticut, where he also served as director of the clinical-psychology training program. Rotter is a diplomate in clinical psychology of the American Board of Examiners in Professional Psychology. He coauthored *Applications of a Social Learning Theory of Personality* (1972), with two former students, J. E. Chance and E. J. Phares, and *Personality* (1975) with colleague Dorothy Hochreich. In 1982, Rotter published *The Development and Application of Social Learning Theory*, a compilation of his most important theoretical and research papers. In 1976–1977 he served as president of the Eastern Psychological Association, and in 1988 the American

Psychological Association honored him with an award for Distinguished Scientific Contributions to Psychology. Although Professor Rotter retired in 1987, he continues to be actively engaged in writing and research work in the social-learning area.

Concepts and Principles

Rotter has constructed a theory of personality based on learning concepts and principles. The basic assumptions are that most of our behavior is learned and that it is acquired through our experiences with other people (Rotter et al., 1972, p. 4). Such a social-learning view also makes use of a historical approach to the study of personality, in which the antecedent events in people's lives are investigated to understand their present behavior. Unlike the Freudians, however, Rotter does not believe it necessary to probe the individual's past experiences in great depth in order to predict behavior adequately. Instead, he argues that we should focus on past events only to the extent that they help us to meet our predictive goals (Rotter et al., 1972, p. 5). For example, there may be no need to inquire into a student's traumatic experiences during the oral stage of infancy in order to predict his failure to attain a college degree; an examination of his relatively poor high school grades and low college-board scores may be sufficient.

Rotter emphasizes the unity or interdependence of personality (Rotter et al., 1972, p. 7), in which a person's experiences and interactions continually influence one another. Past experiences influence current experiences, and current experiences change the things learned in the past. For example, a student may reject potentially helpful advice from the college counselor because he or she has consistently been given poor advice by other counselors in the past. If he or she can be induced to accept the advice of this counselor, however, and it proves helpful, his or her general attitude toward counselors may become more positive. Thus, personality is seen as both changing, because the individual is continuously exposed to new experiences, and stable, because previous experiences affect new learning (Rotter & Hochreich, 1975, p. 94).

Another aspect of unity or interdependence is that different behaviors are functionally related (Katkovsky, 1968, p. 215). For example, you may succeed in having your name added to the class list for a popular course by getting up very early and registering online, by asking a friend to register for you, by speaking directly to the instructor, by getting approval from the college dean, and so on. Each of these behaviors is functionally related; that is, they all operate to secure the same outcome. Reinforcements can also become functionally related (Rotter et al., 1972, p. 19). For example, a star hockey player may learn that leading his team to the coveted Stanley Cup means not only a healthy increase in his annual salary but praise from teammates, the coach, and members of the media and also lucrative advertising contracts with major manufacturers.

Motivation

Rotter assumes that much of our behavior is goal-directed. This directionality is inferred from the effect of reinforcing conditions (Rotter et al., 1972, p. 8). In other words, Rotter considers human behavior to be motivated. People strive to maximize rewards and to minimize or avoid punishment. Thus Rotter, like Skinner, endorses the empirical law of effect. In his formulation, "any stimulus complex has reinforcing properties to the extent that it influences movement toward or away from a goal" (Rotter et al., 1972, p. 9). Some investigators have objected to this principle, because it seems circular: There is no attempt to define a reinforcer independently of behavior. Rotter argues that this criticism might be valid if we were unable to identify reinforcers until after they had occurred, but that in fact it is possible to identify reinforcing events that have known effects both for groups and for individuals (Rotter et al., 1972, p. 9). This knowledge can then be used to make predictions about the effects of reinforcers on behavior.

Two other aspects of motivation should be mentioned at this point. First, when investigators using social-learning theory focus on the environmental conditions that determine the direction of behavior, they speak in terms of goals or reinforcements; when they focus on the person determining the direction of behavior, they speak of needs. For Rotter, the distinction between needs and goals is a semantic one used merely for convenience (Rotter et al., 1972, p. 10).

Second, social-learning theory assumes that early goals are learned within a family setting. We are born with certain physiological needs that are satisfied by parents and parental surrogates. The association of our parents with the satisfaction or frustration of our basic, unlearned needs provides the basis, in Rotter's judgment, for our later reliance on them and others for affection, love, praise, recognition, status, and dependency (Rotter et al., 1972, p. 10).

This view, however, creates theoretical difficulties. It assumes that all reinforcers are reinforcing because they have become associated with drive reduction. For example, a mother's praise of her son's performance in school is positively reinforcing to him because it is associated with earlier feeding experiences that reduced his hunger drive. Such a drive-reduction view of reinforcement may be adequate when we are dealing with simple behaviors, but it becomes difficult to defend when we begin to consider complex social behavior (Rotter et al., 1972, p. 9). For example, how can we show that an athlete with a high need for achievement has experienced reduction of an unlearned drive (such as hunger) by winning the mile run in a track meet? To overcome this difficulty, social-learning theory relies instead on an empirical law of effect: Reinforcement is judged to have occurred if changes in behavior are observed following the introduction or removal of stimulating events. Thus, social-learning theory assumes that the initial learning of goals occurs within a drive-reduction framework, but that the later acquisition of highly complex behaviors is better explained by using a reinforcement concept based on the empirical law of effect.

Social-Learning Concepts

The social-learning approach is based on four major concepts: behavior potential, expectancy, reinforcement value, and the psychological situation. In its simplest form, the formula for behavior is that "the potential for a behavior to occur in any specific situation is a function of the expectancy that the behavior will lead to a particular reinforcement in that situation and the value of that reinforcement" (Rotter, 1975, p. 57). Let us examine each of these concepts in turn.

Behavior potential   In Rotter's formulation, **behavior potential** is "the potentiality of any behavior's occurring in any situation or situations as calculated in relation to any single reinforcement or set of reinforcements" (Rotter et al., 1972, p. 12). Like Skinner, Rotter is talking about the probability of the individual's responding when certain environmental conditions are present. Rotter's view, however, places more emphasis on the role of cognitive factors than does Skinner's, because Rotter makes active use of people's subjective interpretations of the events that confront them. For example, he assumes that the potential for behavior is affected by people's perception of the other behaviors available to them in a given situation. Thus, a complex set of internal, or cognitive, factors is typically involved in the prediction of behavior. Finally, it should be noted that Rotter's definition of behavior is quite broad:

> Behavior may be that which is directly observed but also that which is indirect or implicit. This notion includes a broad spectrum of possibilities, swearing, running,

crying, fighting, smiling, choosing, and so on are all included. These are all observable behaviors, but implicit behavior that can only be measured indirectly, such as rationalizing, repressing, considering alternatives, planning, and reclassifying, would also be included. The objective study of cognitive activity is a difficult but important aspect of social learning theory. Principles governing the occurrence of such cognitive activities are not considered different from those that might apply to any observable behavior. (Rotter et al., 1972, p. 12)

Expectancy Rotter defines **expectancy** as a cognition or belief about the property of some object or event (Rotter, 1982, p. 13). Expectancies can vary in magnitude from 0% to 100% and are subject to modification by experience. For example, a person might believe initially that a woman could never be elected President of the United States (an expectancy of 0%) but, as a result of media coverage of the number of women who have entered politics and been elected to high government offices, like Secretary of State Hillary Rodham Clinton and United States Senators Susan Collins and Olympia Snowe, this expectancy could change radically and even approach absolute certainty (100%).

Social-learning theory postulates three different kinds of expectancy (Rotter, 1982, p. 4): (1) simple cognitions or labeling of stimuli ("I think that is a painting by Picasso"); (2) expectancies for behavior-reinforcement outcomes ("If I wear my Tommy Hilfiger jacket, my friends will compliment me"); and (3) expectancies for reinforcement sequences ("If I graduate from a top-rated medical school, I will probably get a high-paying job and become wealthy and respected").

In social-learning theory, any behavior that has been associated with a reinforcement gives rise to an expectancy. Thus, each expectancy is based on past experience (Rotter & Hochreich, 1975, p. 96). According to Rotter, simply knowing how important a goal or reinforcement is to a person is no guarantee that we can predict the person's behavior. A student may want to obtain an A in a history course very badly, but his previous experiences in other courses lead him to expect that he will fail no matter how much effort he expends. It is virtually certain he will not study and will, as a consequence, fail.

Expectancies vary in terms of their generality; that is, we may acquire generalized expectancies or expectancies specific to a given situation (Rotter & Hochreich, 1975, p. 97). Generalized expectancies operate across a variety of situations. For example, a student may acquire a generalized expectancy for academic success: Having obtained As in a variety of courses or situations, he or she always expects to do well. Another student may have learned a specific expectancy in his or her academic career: Having earned As in mathematics but struggled for Cs in literature and philosophy, he or she expects to do well only in mathematics courses.

Later in this chapter, we will focus on another generalized expectancy called internal/external control of reinforcement, a construct that has generated a considerable amount of interesting research.

Reinforcement value Rotter defines **reinforcement value** as "the degree of preference for any one of a group of reinforcements to occur, if the probabilities of all occurring were equal" (Rotter et al., 1972, p. 21). In the simplest terms, reinforcement value refers to the importance we attach to different activities. For some of us, attending a symphony concert is highly rewarding; others would find it dreadfully dull. Some of us like to play tennis; others do not. In addition to these differences among people, we can arrange our own activities in order of preference. Given the option, we may attach more importance to reading a novel by Leo Tolstoy than to playing a game of basketball or riding a bicycle. Like expectancies, the values associated with different reinforcers are based on our past experiences.

Psychological situation The fourth major concept utilized in the prediction of behavior is the **psychological situation**—that is, the situation as it is defined from the individual's personal perspective. In Rotter's view, this concept plays an extremely important part in the determination of behavior. Traditional theories tend to focus almost exclusively on an inner core of personality, within which certain motives or traits are considered to control behavior, irrespective of the operation of situational demands (Rotter et al., 1972, p. 37). For example, a person may have a strong need for aggression (i.e., an aggressive trait or disposition) that causes him or her to erupt into fighting, irrespective of the situation. At the other end of the spectrum, approaches such as Skinner's emphasize the importance of situational influences and minimize, at least in research practice, individual differences based on idiosyncratic learning histories. Social-learning theory recognizes the importance of *both* dispositional and situational influences. In other words, it pays attention to the ways in which behavior is influenced by the unique past experiences of the person *and* by current situational cues. For example, a person who has strong aggressive tendencies based on prior learning experiences may nevertheless not act aggressively in a given situation if such behavior is likely to lead to punishment by others.

Rotter believes that, on the basis of the complex cues in a particular situation, the person develops expectancies for behavior-reinforcement outcomes and also for reinforcement-reinforcement sequences (Rotter, 1981, p. 3). For example, a college student about to give a speech to her communications class might believe (or expect) that she will do poorly and will therefore receive a low grade from her instructor and ridicule from her classmates. As a result, we might expect her to drop the course or to take other action designed to prevent the anticipated humiliating outcome.

Freedom of movement and minimal goal Two other concepts, freedom of movement and minimal goal, play a lesser but nevertheless important role in Rotter's theory.

Freedom of movement is defined as the "mean expectancy of obtaining positive satisfactions as a result of a set of related behaviors directed toward obtaining a group of functionally related reinforcements" (Rotter et al., 1972, p. 34). For example, students usually acquire general expectancies as to how well they will do in various academic courses and situations. Some students have high general expectations for success; others have very low ones. Thus, we could say that the former students have high freedom of movement, whereas the latter are hindered by low freedom of movement.

Minimal goal is defined as "the lowest goal in a continuum of potential reinforcements for some life situation or situations which will be perceived as a satisfaction" (Rotter, 1954, p. 213). In other words, a minimal goal is the dividing point, on some dimension, between those outcomes that are positively reinforcing and those that are punishing. If we consider course grades on a continuum, one student may find a grade of B punishing, whereas another would be happy with it. The first student would be said to have a higher minimal goal than the second.

These concepts can be combined and used in the prediction of behavior. Thus, students who are adjusted in terms of academic achievement are those who have high freedom of movement in their academic expectations and who do not set exceedingly high minimal goals for themselves in that area. On the basis of many successful experiences in a variety of courses, they have come to expect success; at the same time, they do not set their goals for positive reinforcement so high that they are bound to experience disappointment. Thus, they do not set a minimal goal of A in every course. Such indiscriminate goal striving is unrealistic for most people. Conversely, students can be considered maladjusted if they have low freedom of movement in terms of academic achievement but continue to set high minimal goals for themselves. If, on the basis of past experiences, they expect to fail in virtually all their courses, yet feel they must attain all As, they are engaging in unproductive behavior. A study by Catanzaro (1991, pp. 243–261) provides empirical support for these ideas.

Finally, Rotter's conception of the maladjusted person who sets unattainable minimal goals is clearly reminiscent of Adler's conception of the neurotic person who sets fictional goals that cannot be attained; similarly, Rotter's low freedom of movement echoes Adler's feelings of inferiority.

Personality Development

Rotter believes that personality development hinges largely on the range, diversity, and quality of the individual's experiences with other people. Early in life, these important figures are usually, and quite obviously, our parents. The individual's early goals arise out of certain physiological needs that are then satisfied by the parents or parent substitutes. As a result of their association with need reduction, parents become reinforcing stimuli in their own right. The child comes to rely on them for affection, love, praise, recognition, and other reinforcers. Rotter assumes that **stimulus generalization** occurs, so that other people who resemble the parents are perceived and evaluated in the same or similar ways. Rotter assumes that, once parents and others (teachers, clergy, other adults) acquire value as conditioned reinforcers, the child will work to secure their approval and avoid their disapproval, irrespective of whether their behavior toward the child results in primary-drive reduction.

In Rotter's view, language acquisition also plays a critical role in the child's development. Words serve as cues in directing people's behavior. Parents issue instructions that often help children solve problems in a few trials rather than the hundreds of trials it would take by unassisted trial and error. Parents thus direct their children to the relevant cues in given situations and show them how to avoid the irrelevant ones. Parents also use words as verbal reinforcers, in statements of recognition, love, rejection, and shame, to shape their children's behavior (Rotter, 1954, p. 218). In this way, children learn different expectancies for success and failure in many different situations.

These expectancies are also subject to modification through the use of verbalizations. People can build up or tear down children's expectancies, and the value of their reinforcers, for that matter, by directing their attention to new and previously neglected consequences of performing given behaviors. Or parents can change their children's expectancies by analyzing the children's previous experiences and showing them how they are responding to the wrong cues and how to rectify the situation (Rotter, 1954, pp. 219–220). Language can be used not only to help children make appropriate discriminations between events, but also to increase generalization.

> Since the effect of language is to classify, to categorize, or to abstract similarity in events, it serves, therefore, to determine and enhance the nature of generalization. If an event is symbolized, it will increase generalization to other events that are similarly abstracted. Not only does language determine generalization on the basis of the subject's implicit categorizing, the language of others may be used by the observer as a stimulus to determine, control, or enhance generalization. (Rotter, 1954, p. 220)

Thus, the developmental process involves the acquisition and modification of expectancies and reinforcement values through contact with various socialization agents. These socialization agents include not only adult authority figures but also peers (Rotter, 1954, p. 414). Rotter believes that development is contingent on the standards, mores, goals, and techniques communicated to children by classmates as well as by parents. Next to the home, the school has the greatest influence on development, according to Rotter (1954, p. 416). He contends that the origins of healthy or unhealthy behavior are in the home, and later transfer to the school situation. Health is promoted by parents who encourage the development and maintenance of behavior that leads to acceptance, love, and identification with others. Such behavior is most likely to occur in homes in which the parents themselves show affection and concern for the welfare and development of their offspring. In homes where parents do not provide such reinforcement, children are unlikely to learn the kinds of behaviors that will permit them to adjust to the larger society (Rotter, 1954, pp. 406–407). Such individuals are likely to develop in an antisocial way and to show selfish behaviors that produce hostility in others.

Not only do neglect and rejection lead to maladjustment, Rotter believes, but over-indulgence and overprotection can create problems, too. For overindulged children, school may be a traumatic experience. In contrast to the home, school may seem to be a place where they are unwanted, unloved, and unprotected (Rotter, 1954, p. 418). Generally speaking, the rejected child is likely to enter school with low expectations for success, whereas the overindulged one will likely have expectations that are too high. Both attitudes are unrealistic. According to Rotter, the main role of the school is to correct these views and help children achieve a feeling of security and a realistic set of expectations for success that will serve them well when they assume adult responsibilities (Rotter, 1954, p. 419). To help children grow into effective citizens, then, Rotter believes that parents, teachers, and others should be warm, accepting, good-natured, democratic, and consistent in their disciplinary practices.

Assessment Techniques

Rotter relies on a variety of measurement procedures in his attempts to assess personality. In his early efforts to test hypotheses derived from social-learning theory, he utilized the experimental method to good advantage. His central question was whether people learn tasks and perform differently in situations in which they perceive reinforcing outcomes to be related or unrelated to their behavior. In other words, he wanted to determine whether learning and performance were different for people under skill and chance conditions. After a series of experimental studies, he concluded that there were significant differences in behavior in the two situations. People who perceived a task as controlled by chance relied less on past experiences in guiding current behavior, learned less, and performed less well than did people who perceived the task as skill-determined (Rotter, 1966). These results suggested that reinforcement effects do not have a direct impact on behavior but are mediated by the person's perception of the relationship (or lack of it) between behavior and application of the reinforcer.

Rotter notes the potential usefulness of five major techniques for the clinical measurement of personality: (1) the interview, (2) projective tests, (3) controlled behavioral tests, (4) behavioral observation methods, and (5) the questionnaire (Rotter, 1954, p. 250). Each of these techniques has limitations as well as strengths.

The interview is useful for the assessment of personality traits and for counseling and therapeutic purposes. In terms of social-learning theory, it can be used to assess an individual's need potentials, freedom of movement, and need value (Rotter, 1954, p. 252).

Projective tests such as the Rorschach, Thematic Apperception Test (TAT), and his own Incomplete Sentences Blank, Rotter believes, can be used to advantage in clinical diagnostic work. While he finds the Rorschach of relatively little use in measuring social-learning concepts (Rotter, 1954, p. 289), the TAT can be used to advantage, because the social-learning position is concerned with the individual's reactions to stimuli such as mother and father. The incomplete-sentences method can also be used to measure freedom of movement. In this technique, people are asked to finish sentences after the investigator provides the first few words, for example, "I like…", "I suffer…," "I wish…," "My father…," "Sometimes I feel…." Responses are assumed to indicate underlying conflicts that determine expectancy levels of failure in given situations (Rotter, 1954, pp. 302–304).

In controlled behavioral tests, people are placed in actual situations and their behavior is assessed in reaction to stimulus changes engineered by the investigator (Rotter, 1954, p. 311). For example, suppose that a clinician wants to know how clients react to stress. Instead of simply asking the clients to report how they might behave, the clinician can place them under actual conditions of stress and watch their reactions. Such measures have been used to test hypotheses derived from social-learning theory, most notably in the area of expectancy changes following experiences of success or failure. The behavioral-observation technique, in contrast to the controlled behavioral test, involves the relatively informal assessment of behavior by observers in natural settings (Rotter, 1954, p. 326). This technique, Rotter believes, should be used to assess the generality of experimental findings to real-life situations.

Finally, Rotter believes that questionnaires can be employed to test social-learning hypotheses. Rotter's own I-E Scale is one such questionnaire; we turn now to a consideration of this test and some of its personality and behavioral correlates.

Internal/External Control and the I-E Scale

One of the key constructs in social-learning theory is called **internal/external control of reinforcement** or **locus of control of reinforcement**. According to Rotter, people acquire generalized expectancies to perceive reinforcing events either as dependent on their own behavior or as beyond their control (Rotter, 1966, p. 1). Internally oriented people tend to believe that reinforcers are subject to their own control and occur when they display their skills. Externals, in contrast, see little or no connection between their behavior and various reinforcers; they perceive the occurrence of the reinforcers as determined primarily by fate, luck, or powerful others. Constructs such as competence, powerlessness, helplessness, hopelessness, mastery, and alienation have been used by other investigators in psychology and sociology to describe the degree to which people feel they can control important events in their lives. Rotter's construct of internal/external control, however, has the advantage of being an integral part of a formal theory from which relatively precise predictions can be made.

Although there are many different measures of control orientation for use with children and adults, the **I-E Scale** constructed by Rotter has most often been used by investigators in the area. It is a forced-choice scale consisting of 23 items. (See Table 16.1 for some examples.) Scores are obtained by assigning one point for each external alternative endorsed by the subject and summing across all items. Thus, scores can range from 0 to 23; higher scores indicate greater externality. In research using the measure,

---

TABLE 16.1   SAMPLE ITEMS FROM ROTTER'S I-E SCALE

1. a. I have often found that what is going to happen will happen. (E)
    b. Trusting to fate has never turned out as well for me as making a decision to take a definite course of action. (I)
2. a. Becoming a success is a matter of hard work; luck has little or nothing to do with it. (I)
    b. Getting a good job depends mainly on being in the right place at the right time. (E)
3. a. In the long run, people get the respect they deserve in this world. (I)
    b. Unfortunately, an individual's worth often passes unrecognized no matter how hard he tries. (E)

Source: Adapted from Rotter, J. B., "Generalized expectancies for internal versus external control of reinforcement," in *Psychological Monographs: General and Applied,* 80 (Whole no. 609), pp. 11–12. Copyright © 1966 by the American Psychological Association. Used with permission.

the distribution of scores is usually divided at the median or mean, the study participants are classified correspondingly as either internals or externals, and then these test responses are correlated with other personality variables and behavior. This split into two categories is not meant to imply a typology, but is done for research convenience. Rotter conceptualized people as being more or less internal or external, but not as falling into one category or the other (Rotter, 1975, p. 57).

Research on I-E

Origins of I-E orientations   The bulk of the research literature indicates that parents of internal children tend to be internally oriented themselves. Such parents are consistent in their disciplinary practices, thereby encouraging the development of a belief in internal control in their children during early childhood. In other words, parents of internal children consistently reward appropriate behavior and punish inappropriate behavior. They do not change the rules continually or administer punishments that are much more severe than the offense. Such parents are also warm and supportive of their children, encourage them to succeed, and praise them for their accomplishments. They also do not try to exercise excessive control over them. In comparison to externals, internally oriented students from third grade to college report that their parents were warmer, more emotionally supportive, accepting, and nurturant. Under such conditions, young people typically learn to accept blame for failure as well as credit for success.

In contrast, parents of external children tend to be externally oriented themselves. They are inconsistent in their disciplinary practices. They continually change the rules and administer punishment that is excessive. Such parents also tend to be overprotective and overly controlling. As a result, their children have difficulty learning to perceive themselves as competent and as being able to solve their own problems (Spokas & Heimberg, 2009, pp. 543–551). Also, these parents typically maintain an emotional distance from their children, being either neglectful or rejecting. Research indicates further that families characterized by continual conflict tend to have children who are externally controlled. Also, families where the father is absent due to divorce or death have children who are more externally controlled. Furthermore, college students who reported that their parents had divorced when they were very young were more externally controlled than were their peers from intact families (Carton & Nowicki, 1994, pp. 38–41; Morton, 1997, pp. 222–223; Trusty & Lampe, 1997, p. 375).

Changes in I-E over the lifespan   There is some evidence that people tend to become more internally oriented as they grow older, at least up until middle age (Lefcourt, 1982, pp. 150–151). People at college age are generally more internal than high school students, and high school students are more internal than elementary school kids. As people move from young adulthood into the work force and pursue a career, they also become more internally oriented. During middle age, the internal locus of control of individuals tends to stabilize until old age when, generally speaking, individuals start to suffer losses in their physical abilities and start to become more external in their orientations. Yet it would be stereotypical to conclude that all elderly people are externally oriented. Many of them are very internal, despite experiencing losses in physical resources. How do these individuals maintain an internal locus of control orientation?

The role of education   A study by Mirowsky (1995, pp. 31–43) suggests that whether or not elderly maintain their internal orientations depends upon their educational level. He maintains that education develops people's abilities to be flexible and to solve a wide variety of problems, and these abilities increase control over events and outcomes in life. He collected data from a large national sample of elderly ranging in ages from 65 through their 80s and found that, whereas uneducated elderly are externally oriented, more highly educated elderly are quite internally oriented, despite physical impairments that include trouble in seeing, hearing, walking, lifting, and climbing stairs. Moreover, a study by Brandtstadter and Rothermund (1994, pp. 265–273) indicates that many highly educated elderly people maintain their internal orientations by being flexible; that is, they change the value that they assign to goals that they can no longer attain. For example, elderly people whose physical health has become impaired might adapt to their new health status by reducing the importance of their goal of excelling in competitive sports; they adjust their goal to make it commensurate with the reality of their physical situation. For example, if their physician diagnoses severe arthritis in their hands, they may give up competitive tennis or racquetball and turn to power walking or jogging to keep physically fit. Elderly who are characterized by even greater physical impairments, such as severe lung disease, may give virtually no importance to the attainment of physical sports goals and may begin instead to place more value on goals of intellectual competence and to pursue these with greater intensity. In this way, many elderly individuals can maintain, or perhaps even enhance, general perceptions of personal control over their lives and outcomes.

The role of religion   While education can play a role in helping many elderly people maintain an internal orientation, a belief in God also may be personally empowering. Many religions teach their followers that they are not powerless in the face of life's difficulties, but rather that they can solve their problems with God's encouragement. In other words, such believers rely on **God-mediated control** to solve their problems. While it might appear as though such individuals are externally oriented, in reality they are not. They do not believe that God is solving their problems for them. Instead they believe that God's support and encouragement provides them with the strength to persist and work harder to achieve their personal goals. Such beliefs provide individuals with a vicarious type of internal control (Schieman, Pudrovska, & Milkie, 2005, p. 169). Research by Krause (2005, pp. 136–164) with a nationally representative sample of elderly found that those with a stronger sense of God-mediated control continued to be successful at various tasks, tended to have greater life satisfaction, more optimism, a higher sense of self-worth, and lower levels of death anxiety.

I-E and attribution of responsibility   It should be clear that a person's willingness to strive for excellence in performance is clearly related to how the person accounts for success and failure. A great variety of studies, with only a few exceptions, have shown that, in contrast to externals, internals tend to attribute success to internal factors (ability and effort) rather than to external factors (luck or task difficulty). In other words, internals attribute their success to ability and hard work, whereas externals attribute it to good luck or an easy task. Thus, internals experience more pride in their achievements and a greater willingness to persist at tasks than do externals.

Research has also shown that internals attribute their failures internally, that is, to a lack of ability and/or effort. Thus, when they suffer defeat, internals experience more shame and guilt than do externals. Externals rely more on external attributions in trying to explain their failures. They may claim, for example, that the test was too difficult or that they simply had bad luck (Phares, 1976, pp. 113–115). Moreover, Basgall and Snyder (1988, pp. 656–657) found that externals were more likely to use the following excuses to justify their poor performances on a test: (1) "It doesn't matter how I did on this test because I am doing very well in my other classes"; and (2) "I just had a bad day." The implication in this second excuse is that on some other day the excuse maker's performance would have been better.

Externals also tend to use other excuses for failure. Thus, they devalue tests that they fail, in a classic example of sour grapes. After failing tests that they strongly wanted to pass, externals claimed that success on these tests was not so important (Phares, 1971, pp. 386–390; 1979, pp. 195–208).

Phares and Lamiell (1974, pp. 872–878) found that externals employ defensive strategies *prior* to task performance as well as after it. These investigators gave internals and externals the choice of taking one of four tests. Two of the tests contained built-in rationalizations for subsequent failure; for example, on the task instructions for one test, the experimenter wrote, "Some of the symbols on this sheet did not print out very well. I hope it won't affect your performance too much, but there is always that possibility." The other two did not contain such rationalizations. Externals, more than internals, chose to take the tests that contained the excuses for failure already built in.

Research indicates that internals not only take responsibility for their own actions but also assume that others are responsible for theirs. Externals, in contrast, assume that others' behavior as well as their own is controlled by outside forces (Phares, 1976, pp. 102–104). Given the opportunity, internals are thus more likely than externals to mete out more severe punishment to rule violators in a variety of situations. Thus, they may be more punitive and less sympathetic than are externals in their judgments and behavior toward wrongdoers (Kauffman & Ryckman, 1979, 340–343).

I-E and academic performance

A study by S. Suh and J. Suh (2006, pp. 11–20) with a nationally representative sample of American high-school students showed that internally oriented students were more likely to get their high-school diplomas and less likely to drop out of the educational process during their high-school years than were externally oriented students.

Several investigations show that internally oriented, White college students outperform externals in terms of test scores on exams and final course grades. (Cassidy, 2000, pp. 307–322; Kalechstein & Nowicki, 1997, pp.29–56; Mooney, Sherman, & Lo Presto, 1991, pp.445–448). There are several possible explanations for these findings. As compared to externals, internals are more focused on the task, persistent, cognitively active and flexible, and efficient in learning the rules necessary for problem solving. They have also been found to gather more information about their situations, which helps them devise strategies to cope with and control outcomes. A study by Smith and Hopkins (2004, pp. 312–321) showed that internally oriented Black college students with a strong sense of cultural identity performed more effectively on several academic tests than did Black students with an external orientation. Internally oriented Black students with a poor sense of cultural identity did not fare well on the tests. These investigators noted that, because the internally oriented Black students with strong cultural identity took pride in their own culture, they did not succumb to the negative stereotypes about Black students as being incapable of performing well on tests standardized using samples of White students. As a result, such students performed well.

I-E and career development and status

At some point in our lives, each of us has to make a decision about which career to pursue. This decision is very difficult for most of us to make, and research indicates that it is particularly difficult for externally oriented people. In comparison to internals, externals believe that the career they eventually pursue will be a matter of luck or timing. Lease (2004, pp. 239–254) found that, as a result, external college students show little motivation to engage in the decision-making process. In comparison to internals, they are unfocused and do not actively seek out information about the kinds of occupations available to them or try to find out what the jobs entail.

Internals report growing up in homes where their parents/guardians worked, thereby providing them with good work role models (Strauser, Ketz, & Keim, 2002, pp. 20–26). Accordingly, it is not very surprising that they show a stronger tendency than do their external counterparts to take responsibility for their own actions and to work hard to achieve long-range goals when they reach college age.

Consistent with this research, Luzzo and Ward (1995, pp. 307–317) found that internal students were more likely than were external students to take the time and make the effort necessary to obtain part-time employment experiences that were congruent with their long-term, career aspirations. Some examples include: (1) internal students with career interests in business obtained part-time jobs in retail sales rather than as mechanics; (2) internals with interests in public administration and city management secured part-time jobs in municipal government rather than as housepainters; and (3) internal students with interests in athletic careers secured part-time jobs in the athletic programs of local Young Men's Christian Associations (YMCAs) rather than as bartenders. Employment in congruent part-time jobs may help to facilitate career development and eventual occupational success. Luzzo (1993, pp. 271–275) also found that internal students were more task-oriented and serious in their attitudes toward work and their careers.

Several studies have shown that internally oriented people have the characteristics that help promote and maintain occupational success. In comparison to externals, internals have a greater tendency to budget and save their money in the hopes these savings can be put to good use in helping them to live successfully (Lim, Thompson, & Loo, 2003, pp. 411–429). Internals also are assertive, independent, dominant, efficient, competent, and confident. Swedish workers with an internal orientation tend to be more satisfied with their jobs, to report less stress, and fewer symptoms of illness (Muhonen & Torkelson, 2004, pp. 21–28). Internals from America and Germany also report perceiving themselves as having more autonomy and control on the job and to being on the job longer without thinking of quitting (Kirkcaldy, Shepard, & Furnham, 2002, pp. 1361–1371; Spector, 1988, pp. 335–340; Spector & O'Connell, 1994, pp. 1–12). As a result, they perform more effectively on the job than externals (Hattrup, O'Connell, & Labrador, 2005, pp. 461–481). Also, they are highly successful in a variety of high-status occupations that demand strong leadership qualities (Kapalka & Lachenmeyer, 1988, pp. 418–419).

I-E and physical health   Many investigations indicate that internally oriented individuals engage in more health-promoting behavior and are consequently more physically healthy than are externally oriented individuals (Burker, Evon, Galanko, & Egan, 2005, pp. 695–704; Johnson, 2002, pp. 777–789; Steptoe & Wardle, 2001, pp. 659–672; K. A. Wallston & B. S. Wallston, 1981, pp. 189–243). These studies, surveying students from 18 European countries and also the United States, show that college students with an internal orientation have more knowledge about proper nutrition and diet, including the need to avoid eating large amounts of salt and foods that are highly fatty. They also understand the need for exercise to maintain or enhance health, and the hazards of smoking and excessive drinking than do external students (Quadrel & Lau, 1989, p. 1505). Not only do they have more information about the direct link between exercise and physical health, internal students also engage in more exercise than do external students (Burk, 1994, pp. 14–23). Other research has shown that internals take more precautionary measures to protect their psychological and physical health than do externals. Internal male and female adolescents report having used contraceptives at time of first intercourse to prevent unwanted pregnancy (Gueye, Castle, & Konate, 2001, pp. 56–62). Internal high-school students report greater use of seat belts when driving than do externals. They also report going to the dentist for checkups and maintenance more often than do externals, even when their teeth or gums are not sore or hurting. Several studies have shown that it is less likely for internals to smoke than externals. Of the relatively few who do smoke, internals are more likely to reduce or quit smoking when exposed to persuasive messages showing the harmful consequences of their behavior to their health (M. Booth-Butterfield, Anderson, & S. Booth-Butterfield, 2000, pp. 137–148; Chen, Percy, & Horner, 2001, pp. 167–175; K. A. Wallston & B. S. Wallston, 1982, p. 78).

Of those individuals who quit smoking, internals also are less likely to begin smoking again (Segall & Wynd, 1990, pp. 338–344). Finally, research using American war veterans showed that internals were more likely than externals to adhere to their medications to help control their hypertension (Hong, Oddone, Dudley, & Bosworth, 2006, pp. 20–28).

It is clear, therefore, that an internal locus of control is associated generally with preventive health care, good health, and better coping with harmful behavior when it does occur.

I-E and psychological health   Virtually all of the research investigating the association between I-E and mental health indicates that internals are psychologically healthier than externals (Bostic & Ptacek, 2001, pp. 357–358; Cooper, Okamura, & McNeil, 1995, p. 410; Cvengros, Christensen, & Lawton, 2005, pp. 677–686; Kelley & Stack, 2000, p. 531; Liu et al., 2000, p. 1565). Several studies have shown that depressives, schizophrenics, and neurotics are more likely to be external than internal. Drug addicts also are higher in externality and report less control over their aggressive impulses than do nondrug users (De Moya, 1997, p. 41). Externals who are heavy drinkers and who are convicted for driving under the influence (DUI) are not very receptive to counseling designed to curb their excessive drinking because they believe that their accidents and convictions were just due to bad luck or unfortunate circumstances. Thus, they are at risk of being repeat offenders (Cavaiola & Strohmetz, 2010, pp. 52–62). University students who are externally oriented report that they feel powerless and, as a result, engage in compulsive shopping and the misuse of credit cards (Watson, 2009, pp. 268–275). Externals are also more likely to be Machiavellian; that is, they are more likely to lie, cheat, and manipulate others to get what they want. They are also dogmatic and low in self-esteem, and they have high levels of debilitating anxiety (Holder & Levi, 1988, pp. 753–755; Keltikangas-Jarvinen & Raikkonen, 1990, pp. 1–18; Lefcourt, 1982, pp. 119–124; Morrison, 1997, p. 264; Mudrack, 1990, pp. 125–126; Schmitt & Kurdek, 1984, pp. 403–409). Debilitating anxiety is reflected in items on the I-E scale such as: "During exams, I block on questions to which I know the answers, even though I might remember them as soon as the exam is over" and "I am so tired from worrying about an exam that I find I almost don't care how well I do by the time I start the test." Conversely, internals tend to have more facilitating anxiety than do externals; they endorse items such as: "I work most effectively under pressure, as when the task is very important"; and "Nervousness while taking a test helps me do well" (Lefcourt, 1982, p. 122).

Finally, research has indicated that internals are better able to cope successfully with stress in a variety of situations. For example, Liu et al. (2000, pp. 1565–1577) noted that, among adolescents, there are many stresses associated with winning acceptance into top-flight universities. There is ample peer competition for the few openings available, difficult, qualifying exam pressures, and high parental and teachers' expectations for excellent school performance. These stressors produce many negative psychological symptoms, for example, anxiety, depression, fears about failing, conflicts with teachers and parents. Liu and his colleagues maintained that having an internal locus of control serves a protective function by leading internals to believe that they could control the outcomes of negative events. This belief, in turn, would reduce the negative impact of such stressful events. Also, Liu et al. (2000) thought that internals would be more likely to use effective coping strategies, for example, turning to friends for support and allocating more time for studying, to handle the stress than externals. In a sample of approximately 1,300 adolescents, Liu et al. found support for his theorizing.

Not only are internals better able to cope with the stresses associated with academic life, they are better able to handle the stresses associated with divorce and bereavement than are externals. For example, Barnet (1990, pp. 93–109) found that, while internal divorced women reported experiencing more predecision stress than did externals, they experienced far less stress during the divorce proper, less postdivorce stress, and less social maladjustment following the divorce (Barnet, 1990, p. 107). Investigators have found that, in coping with stress following the death of their spouse, internal Israeli widows were more able to cope with monetary, house maintenance, and transportation concerns and to engage in meaningful social activities than were externals; that is, internally oriented widows were more likely to ask their parents, grown-up children, relatives, and friends for help in solving these problems than were externally oriented widows (Lowenstein & Rosen, 1995, pp. 114–115).

Limitations of the Current View of Locus of Control

Finally, virtually all of the studies examining differences in personality characteristics and behavior between internals and externals have painted a rosy picture of internals as people who possess all positive characteristics, in comparison to externals who are seen as possessing characteristics that are negative. This one-sided view of internals and externals is overly simplistic.

Negative qualities in internals   There are a few studies in the research literature which suggest that internals may have some negative qualities. For example, compulsive individuals, with their excessive concern for order and control, are likely to score very high on internal locus of control (Smith, Magaro, & Pederson, 1983, p. 499). In addition, **emetophobics** (individuals with extreme fears of vomiting) have an exaggerated sense of internal control (Davidson, Boyle, & Lauchlan, 2008, pp. 30–39). Because of their excessively strong need to control, they greatly fear the loss of control that happens during vomiting. As a consequence, they sometimes have to leave work early for fear of vomiting, skip classes if they are enrolled in school, avoid travel in buses and planes, avoid trying new medicines, and eat only from a restricted list of "safe foods." In addition, almost half of all female emetophobics avoid or delay becoming pregnant because of their fear of "morning sickness" (Lipsitz, Fyer, Paterniti, & Klein, 2001, pp. 149–152). Also, because of their very strong tendencies to attribute events internally, many individuals with extreme internal orientations may also indiscriminately blame themselves for failure even when it is not their fault. As a result, they may be needlessly hard on themselves at times.

Finally, it is possible for people with moderately internal orientations to show less psychologically healthy behavior under some conditions. For example, while they ordinarily have strong inhibitions against committing illegal and violent acts, these inhibitions can be lost under the right circumstances, as shown in a recent study by Gallagher and Parrott (2010, pp. 299–306). In this investigation, internally oriented adult men with a low history of alcohol consumption reported a low history of physical assault and sexual coercion against women partners who had provoked them. Under these conditions, these men obeyed inhibitory cues that they had learned earlier in the socialization process that it was wrong to show such aggressive behavior against others. Interestingly, internally oriented men with a high history of heavy drinking reported high levels of aggression toward partners who had argued with them. Under these circumstances, the men's attention under the influence of alcohol shifted from strong inhibitory cues to strong instigator cues (stopping the partners' argumentative behavior), and the result was undesirable behavior. Externally oriented men who reported either a low or high history of alcohol consumption acted aggressively against their partners, apparently in an attempt to rid themselves of anxious feelings of powerlessness by asserting control over their antagonists under both conditions.

Positive qualities of externals   Researchers have also argued that the adoption of an external view may well be very healthy under certain circumstances (cf. Burish et al., 1984, pp. 326–332). There are numerous situations that are largely beyond our control so that it may be maladaptive to continue to act on the belief that such situations are subject to our control. For example, internal patients scheduled to undergo major heart surgery may first work to ensure that they will have the best surgeon for the operation, the hospital with the best facilities, and the best nursing staff for support following the operation. At some point, however, they must relinquish control to the surgeon finally chosen and assume that he or she will do the job effectively. It is not helpful to continue to distress themselves with thoughts about a negative outcome or to cancel the operation at the last minute because they fantasize that the surgeon is incompetent and uncaring. Externals, who believe that these situations are essentially not under their control, may benefit from their control orientation in such a situation by accepting the direction of their physician and their nurses, thereby experiencing much less distress and worry than internally oriented patients.

Matching health messages to patients' locus of control orientation   There are some initial reports in the healthcare literature that show that the medical community is starting slowly to recognize the benefits to patients of tailoring their health recommendations to their patients' control orientations. It makes little sense to try and change personality dispositions that are strongly rooted in the learning histories of individuals than it does to adapt health recommendations to the locus of control orientations of patients. In one particularly interesting study, researchers focused on matching their health messages to the locus of control orientations of women patients in an effort to promote mammography screening. Breast cancer is the second leading cause of cancer death (following lung cancer) among American women. Yet only 67% of women 40 years of age and older in the United States undergo mammography screening, a procedure that can save lives by detecting the presence of cancer early in the disease process so it can be treated, often with positive results.

Women with an internal or external control orientation were assigned randomly to receive either an internally or an externally oriented brochure encouraging them to have a mammogram. The internally oriented brochure was entitled "The Best Thing *You* Can Do for Your Health-Mammography," and it underscored the woman's personal responsibility for her health and the need for her to initiate action. The externally oriented brochure was entitled "The Best Thing Medical Science Has to Offer for Your Health," and emphasized that the responsibility for maintaining health is in a women's partnership with her healthcare provider. This message was consistent with the external's belief that doctors and other health professionals determine her health outcomes.

As expected, the results indicated that a higher percentage of internals than externals responded positively to the internally oriented health message by going for a mammograph, when checked against medical records during 6- and 12-month follow-ups. Also consistent with predictions, a higher percentage of externals than internals responded positively to the externally oriented message by having a mammograph, as assessed during the same time periods (Williams-Piehota, Schneider, Pizarro, Mowad, & Salovey, 2004, pp. 407–423). The researchers suggest that healthcare providers do some personality testing of their patients when patients first enter their practices and then subsequently utilize the test data in formulating and guiding their patients' treatments.

The Ideal Person: A Blend of Internal and External Orientations

While it may be fruitful and practical to tailor one's messages to the control orientations of patients given the fact that most people learn predominantly either an internal or an external orientation, researchers are beginning to rethink the relationship between locus of control and physical and psychological health, seeing ideally healthy people, not as those who are either internal *or* external, but as those who would be raised within the culture to learn both internal *and* external orientations and to show either an internal or external orientation depending on the kind of situation that confronts them. Such individuals would learn to respond flexibly in situations and to display behaviors which are compatible with an internal or an external view depending on circumstances. Such individuals would understand that it is unrealistic to try to control all aspects of their environments and yet it would be equally maladaptive to relinquish control in all situations. Instead they would adopt the view that they should make personal efforts to solve problems that are solvable and to accept what cannot be changed. Such psychologically healthy people would be those who act flexibly and adaptively by assessing the nature of the situation before making their judgments and then would proceed to act in accordance with an internal or external orientation.

In conclusion, research with the I-E construct has proven highly informative, and there is little doubt that it will continue to be a popular area of investigation for personality psychologists, as they continue to explore more sophisticated ways of thinking about the role of locus of control in people's lives.

Theory's Implications for Therapy

In Rotter's view, psychotherapy is a learning process. Thus, the same learning principles applied to change the behavior of people in everyday situations can also be utilized to advantage in a therapeutic setting (Rotter, 1954, p. 335). Rotter sees the problems of maladjusted people as originating not in their heads but in their relationships with other people (Rotter & Hochreich, 1975, p. 109). In general, adjusted individuals experience satisfactions growing out of the performance of behaviors that are seen as constructive by society; maladjusted people, in contrast, are perpetually dissatisfied with themselves and behave in ways that precipitate punishing responses from society. Furthermore, Rotter believes that maladjusted people are often characterized by low freedom of movement and high need value (Rotter & Hochreich, 1975, p. 106). Such individuals are convinced that they are unable to obtain the gratification they desire. As a result, instead of learning how to achieve their goals, they learn how to avoid or defend themselves against actual or anticipated failure.

Rotter and other social-learning theorists accept the defense mechanisms postulated by Freud but reconceptualize them as avoidance or escape behaviors. Projection, for example, involves blaming others for one's own mistakes in order to avoid anticipated punishment. Rationalization is the construction of elaborate excuses for one's own inadequate behavior in an effort to stave off punishment. One of the unfortunate results of such maneuvering is that maladjusted people fail to learn new behaviors. They simply continue to gain temporary relief by avoiding the punishment, criticism, failure, or rejection they believe will follow if they attempt to perform behaviors for which they have low expectations for success. In the long run, however, such defensive maneuvers are maladaptive.

Maladjusted people often inappropriately apply their low expectations for success in one area (for example, the workplace) to other areas (for example, home life), so that they come to perceive themselves as generally worthless. Clinicians have found that maladjusted people also tend to place too much importance on the gratification of one need (Katkovsky, 1968, p. 228). For example, people with a strong need to dominate others may distort what others say in order to act in an aggressive manner when it is totally inappropriate (Katkovsky, 1968, p. 228). Such individuals will often be dissatisfied, because their need to dominate will bring them into repeated conflicts with others.

Maladjusted individuals tend to engage in behaviors that lead to immediate rewards but are punishing in the long run (Katkovsky, 1968, pp. 229–230). Compulsive gamblers find gambling exciting but usually learn that their behavior has severe negative consequences for themselves and their families. In order to pursue their passion, they may cut into the food budget, sell household property, and even steal from other family members. Maladjusted people not only engage in behavior that others consider undesirable; they often also fail to show behaviors that others consider desirable (Katkovsky, 1968, p. 230). Society encourages its members to communicate with one another, for example, but maladjusted people lack the necessary verbal and social skills.

In order to change the behavior of such individuals, Rotter believes, therapists need to be flexible. Because clients come into the therapeutic setting with different problems arising from unique life experiences and motives, the environmental conditions that promote optimal change will vary from person to person. In some cases, treatment strategies may include recommendations for changes in the client's job, academic situation, or home life. For other clients, various behavior therapies, direct or indirect suggestions, or support and reassurance may be appropriate. All these procedures and others can be used singly or in combination to help clients (Rotter & Hochreich, 1975, p. 109).

In general, Rotter believes that therapy should be an evolving relationship between client and therapist in which clients are helped to discover how their present needs, attitudes, and behaviors developed, which ones are appropriate or inappropriate for effective living, and what alternatives are available. Clients must take responsibility for change, be motivated to change, and be willing to try out new behaviors (Rotter, 1954, p. 353). Therapeutic goals may include teaching clients to discriminate between situations in which behaviors are likely to lead to failure and those likely to produce success, helping them to lower unrealistically high expectations for punishment, and encouraging them to assess the importance of their goals more critically and appropriately.

In order to encourage discrimination between situations, the therapist may analyze and contrast a client's past life situation with his present situation and show him that his previous experiences of failure are unlikely to transfer into the present. For example, the therapist might encourage a first-year student to minimize past experiences of failure in elementary school and to believe instead that he can and will be successful in college on the basis of outstanding aptitude test scores. In this case, the therapist's job is to teach the person to differentiate between two situations and to raise his expectations for success on the basis of solid evidence. Another client may have inordinately high expectations for success that need lowering. We all know of people who brag about abilities they do not in fact possess. This bragging may bring temporary gratification and a bolstering of self-esteem, but the long-range consequences of such behavior are likely to be punishing. Therapy in such a case may call for a lowering of the person's expectations.

Therapy may also require changes in the importance a person attaches to certain goals. For example, a woman who has learned to value winning above everything else because it brought acceptance and love from her parents may be encouraged to de-emphasize that goal. The therapist might point out that her indiscriminate attempts to prove herself better than others, even in a friendly game of Ping-Pong, serve only to alienate people. She could be shown that her feeling of being disliked by everyone stems from indiscriminate pursuit of her goal and that a change in behavior is therefore necessary.

Rotter advocates a therapy that focuses not only on the elimination of undesirable and inadequate behaviors but also on the acquisition of desirable ones. The person is taught methods of analyzing problems as a means of finding better solutions and encouraged to try out new behaviors. It is not enough, in Rotter's view, for therapists to help clients understand the sources of their problems; clients must be shown how to perform new behaviors designed to overcome them (Rotter, 1954, p. 398).

Evaluative Comments

We now examine the scientific worth of Rotter's theory in terms of our six criteria.

Comprehensiveness   Rotter's theory has its roots in both the clinical setting and the experimental laboratory. It covers a wide range of phenomena, including parental attitudes and behaviors, academic achievement, defensive behavior, interpersonal trust, social activism, alcoholism, maladjustment, mental retardation, and a host of psychopathological behaviors. As such, it is quite comprehensive.

Precision and testability   Compared to most of the other theories covered in the text, Rotter's is characterized by concepts that are well-defined and hypotheses that are capable of being tested.

Parsimony   Rotter's position seems fairly parsimonious, at least in its attempts to account for performances by individuals who differ in their locus of control orientations. The picture is unsettled, however, when we consider the theory's treatment of abnormal and therapeutic phenomena. Rotter seems undecided about whether to retain, modify, or reject some of the psychoanalytic concepts, for example. As a result, it is difficult to assess the parsimony of his views on abnormal phenomena.

Empirical validity   Most of the research based on Rotter's theory has focused on his I-E concept. Empirical support for this aspect of the theory is very strong. However, this work has not been balanced by research on the rest of Rotter's theory, which, unfortunately, remains largely fallow.

Heuristic value   The I-E concept has stimulated research in many areas, including learning theory, psychopathology, psychotherapy, personality development, and social psychology. Also, whereas Rotter's scale assesses the tendency for people to be more internal or external across a variety of situations, a more recent development has been the creation of a number of situation-specific scales (e.g., the Work Locus of Control Scale, the Drinking-Related Locus of Control Scale, and the Health Locus of Control Scale). Researchers working in particular areas often prefer these scales because they typically lead to more accurate predictions of behaviors than is the case when a generalized I-E scale is used.

Thus, the heuristic value of Rotter's ideas regarding I-E differences is clear.

Applied value   Rotter's theory has strong applied value. It has been used, for example, by clinical psychologists in their diagnoses of the origins of a variety of deviant behaviors, including alcoholism, depression, anxiety reaction, and shyness. The theory has also proved useful to clinical psychologists in their efforts to devise effective strategies for treating different types of patients. Studies by C. V. Abramowitz, S. I. Abramowitz, Roback, and Jackson (1974, pp. 849–853) and Trice (1990, pp. 233–234), for example, have shown that therapists who use treatment strategies that are congruent with their patients' control expectancies are likely to be more successful in helping their patients than are therapists who use procedures that are incongruent with their patients' expectancies. Specifically, they found that nondirective or unstructured therapies work better with internals, whereas more directive or structured techniques work better with externals. Also, in the area of physical health, treatments tailored to patients' control expectancies have proved useful in maximizing weight loss in the obese and in reducing cigarette smoking in smokers (Strickland, 1978, 1979).

CRITICAL THINKING QUESTIONS

1. Describe the four basic concepts of Rotter's social-learning theory. Give some personal examples of how the concepts could be combined to predict a given behavior of one of your friends.

2. What is a minimal goal? What is your minimal goal for academic grades? Do you think that it is realistic in terms of your abilities and motivation as a student?

3. What are some of the determinants of a person's locus of control? Are the elderly primarily external in their orientations?

4. Can internally oriented people show maladaptive behaviors in some situations? If so, give some examples from your own life.

5. What are some of the strengths and weaknesses of the social-learning approach to the study of abnormal behavior?

GLOSSARY

behavior potential   Probability that a particular behavior will occur, as a function of the person's unique expectancies and the perceived value of the reinforcer secured by the behavior in a given situation.

emetophobics   Intensely anxious individuals with very strong internal control orientations who fear vomiting because they would lose control.

expectancy   A cognition or belief—held with a higher or lower degree of certainty—about the property of some object or event.

field theory   The idea that behavior is determined by a complex interplay between cognitive and environmental variables.

freedom of movement   The individual's expectancy that his or her behaviors will generally lead to success (high freedom of movement) or failure (low freedom of movement) in a given life area.

God-mediated control   An indirect form of internal control in which individuals work collaboratively with God to achieve their personal goals.

I-E scale   Test designed by Rotter to measure the individual's belief that forces are or are not beyond his or her control. Internals (Is) are people who believe that events

are under their own control; externals (Es) are people who believe that outcomes are controlled by outside forces such as luck, fate, God, or powerful others.

internal/external control of reinforcement   The individual's belief that his or her behavior is self-determined (internal control) or determined by outside factors (external control).

locus of control of reinforcement   Term that refers to people's beliefs about the location (internal/external) of controlling forces in their lives.

minimal goal   Dividing point between those outcomes that produce feelings of satisfaction and those that produce dissatisfaction.

psychological situation   The meaning of the situation as it is defined by the person.

reinforcement value   The importance of a given reinforcer to an individual in relation to other reinforcers if the probabilities of attaining all of them are equal.

stimulus generalization   The process in which responses made in the presence of an original stimulus come to be made in the presence of other, similar stimuli.

SUGGESTED READINGS

Rotter, J. B. (1954). *Social learning and clinical psychology*. Englewood Cliffs, NJ: Prentice-Hall.

Rotter, J. B. (1966). Generalized expectancies for internal versus external control of reinforcement. *Psychological Monographs, 80* (Whole No. 609).

Linda A. Cicero/Stanford News Service.

CHAPTER 17

Bandura's Social-Cognitive Theory

Biographical Sketch

Albert Bandura was born on December 4, 1925, to a family of wheat farmers of Polish heritage. He grew up in the small town of Mundare in northern Alberta, Canada, and attended a high school that had only two teachers and 20 students. Upon graduation from high school, Bandura spent the summer before entering college near Whitehorse, in the Yukon, filling holes in the Alaskan highway. He found himself in the midst of an unusual collection of characters, most of whom had fled creditors, alimony, or probation officers. This experience gave him an appreciation for the psychopathology of everyday life.

In search of an intellectually stimulating environment, Bandura enrolled in the University of British Columbia in Vancouver, where he graduated three years later, in 1949. He then earned an M.A. and Ph.D. in psychology from the University of Iowa in 1951 and 1952, respectively. After serving a year's clinical internship at the Wichita Guidance Center, he accepted a position in the department of psychology at Stanford University, where he has remained ever since. He became a full professor in 1964, and in 1974 was awarded an endowed chair, the David Starr Jordan Professor of Social Science in Psychology.

During his tenure at Stanford, Bandura has been actively engaged in the development of a social-cognitive approach to the understanding of human behavior. He has also been a highly productive scholar, publishing several influential books and countless research articles in scientific journals. His early books, *Adolescent Aggression* (1952) and *Social Learning and Personality Development* (1963), were written in collaboration with Richard H. Walters. His *Principles of Behavior Modification* (1969) is an extensive review and summary of the social-psychological principles that govern behavior; *Social Learning Theory* (1971) is an abbreviated treatment of these principles in pamphlet form. In 1973, he published *Aggression*, a review of current theory and research on the determinants of aggressive behavior. In 1977, Bandura greatly expanded his pamphlet coverage of the social-psychological principles that control behavior in his book *Social Learning Theory*. *Social Foundations of Thought and Action* (1986) presents more recent theoretical and research developments in his position. In 1995, Bandura edited *Self-Efficacy in Changing Societies*, in which he and other colleagues examined the ways in which strong feelings of self-efficacy in people can help them to create beneficial familial, academic, occupational, and medical environments in a rapidly changing world. His most recent book is *Self-efficacy: The Exercise of Control*, published in 1997.

In recognition of his many contributions to psychology, Bandura has received numerous awards and honors. In 1969–1970, he was a fellow at the Center for Advanced Study in the Behavioral Sciences. In 1972, he received a Guggenheim Fellowship and was awarded the Distinguished Scientist Award in Clinical Psychology by the American Psychological Association. The California Psychological Association honored him with its Distinguished Scientific Achievement Award in 1973, and in 1974 he served as president of the American Psychological Association. He received the James McKeen Cattell Award in 1977 and an honorary Doctor of Science degree from the University of British Columbia in 1979. In 1980, he was honored with a Distinguished Contribution Award from the International Society for Research on Aggression, the Distinguished Scientific Contributions Award from the American Psychological Association, and election to fellow status in the American Academy of Arts and Sciences.

Concepts and Principles

Assumptions of the Social-Cognitive Approach

According to Bandura, behavior is not caused solely by either inner forces or environmental influences. Like Rotter, Bandura believes that behavior occurs as a result of a complex interplay between inner processes and environmental influences (Bandura, 1971, p. 2). In his formulation, these internal processes, based largely on the previous experiences of the individual, are measurable and manipulable covert events. "These mediating events are extensively controlled by external stimulus events and in turn regulate overt responsiveness" (Bandura, 1969, p. 10). Unlike Skinner, who acknowledged that stimulus-response covariations are mediated by internal events but proceeded to neglect them in favor of causal explanations couched in terms of external manipulatively events, Bandura places special emphasis on the role of the cognitive determinants of behavior, seeing them as not mere epiphenomena, but as actual causes of behavior (Bandura, 1996, p. 325).

Bandura postulates a **triadic reciprocal determinism**, in which cognitive and other personal factors, behavior, and environmental influences all operate interactively as determinants of one another (Bandura, 1986, pp. 23–24). Thus, people do not simply react to environmental events; they actively create their own environments and act to change them. Cognitive events determine which environmental events will be perceived and how they will be interpreted, organized, and acted on (Bandura, 1978, p. 345). Positive or negative feedback from behavior, in turn, influences people's thinking (cognitions) and the ways in which they act to change the environment (Bandura, 1986, p. 24).

> Television viewing provides a good example of the interdependencies among cognition, behavior, and the environment. Personal preferences (in the form of thoughts or cognitions) influence when and which programs, from among available alternatives, individuals will choose to watch. Their actual viewing behavior then partly reshapes their preferences concerning which programs to watch in the future and determines to some extent the programming that television executives will provide. The kind of programming subsequently offered by the networks will then shape people's viewing behavior and their preferences for particular shows. Thus, all three factors—viewer preferences, viewing behavior, and televised offerings—mutually affect one another. (Bandura, 1986, p. 24)

According to Bandura, we typically represent external events symbolically and later use both **verbal representation** and **imaginal representation** to guide our behavior. Thus, we can solve problems symbolically without having to resort to actual, overt trial-and-error behavior; we foresee the probable consequences of our behavior and modify our actions accordingly. The higher mental processes of human beings allow us to perform both insightful and foresightful behavior (Bandura, 1971, pp. 2–3).

Although Bandura places great emphasis on cognitive processes in his analysis of behavior, he does not ignore the effects of reinforcement. On the contrary, he assigns the reinforcement construct a major role in his theory, but its role is compatible with a cognitive orientation, and goes far beyond the view offered by many traditional learning theorists. Skinner, for example, focused on the changes in behavior that result from our direct experiences of the rewarding and punishing consequences of our actions: Responses that are rewarded tend to be repeated; those that are punished tend to be inhibited. Bandura, in contrast, believes that reinforcers and punishers do not provide automatic strengthening or weakening of behavior, nor do they fully account for the ways in which our behavior is acquired, maintained, or altered (Bandura, 1971, p. 3).

In Bandura's view, most of our behavior is not controlled by immediate external reinforcement. As a result of earlier experiences, we tend to expect that certain kinds of behavior will have effects we desire, that others will produce unwanted outcomes, and that still others will have little significant impact. Our behavior is therefore regulated to a large extent by **anticipated outcomes** (Bandura, 1971, p. 3). For example, we do not wait until we have a car accident to buy insurance. Instead, in deciding to purchase it, we rely on information from others about the potentially disastrous consequences of not owning insurance. We do not wait until we are caught in a blinding snowstorm to decide what to wear in extremely cold weather; we can imagine the consequences of being poorly prepared and take the proper precautionary steps. In countless ways, we make decisions based on the anticipation of consequences. This notion of anticipation is similar to Rotter's concept of expectancy.

Bandura also maintains that behavior can be acquired without the administration of **external reinforcement**. We learn much of the behavior we eventually display by example: We simply watch what others do and then repeat their actions. Technically, we acquire the behavior through **observational learning**. According to Bandura, **modeling** plays a prominent role in our lives, for several reasons. Because the environment is loaded with potentially lethal consequences, trial-and-error behavior is too costly. We do not rely on trial and error in learning to swim, drive a car, or pilot an airplane; some explanation and instruction must be provided before the direct experience can be safely attempted. Furthermore, it would be too cumbersome to try to socialize people by selective reinforcement of their random activities. Imagine trying to teach children language and the many rules and customs of the culture in this way. The acquisition process can be shortened considerably through the use of appropriate models (Bandura, 1971, p. 5). Although the first cohort of learning theorists tended to neglect the role of observational learning in their attempts to understand human behavior, Bandura and other proponents of the social-cognitive approach have rectified this shortcoming and shed much more light on the ways in which we acquire, maintain, and modify our behavior through emulation of models.

Modeling Theory

At first glance, the modeling process seems simple and straightforward. We have an observer and a model, and the primary question is: Will the observer imitate the actions of the model? But the answer is far from simple, because it depends on a host of factors.

First, the personality characteristics of the observer play an important role. People develop preconceptions of performance capabilities during the socialization process. For example, whether the model's behavior is imitated may be determined, in part, by the gender of the observer and, correspondingly, by the gender of the model. Males tend generally to imitate male models, whereas females are more likely to emulate the behavior of female models. Boys, for example, tend to show more aggressive behavior after watching an aggressive male model than a female one, whereas girls tend to imitate the aggressive actions of a female model more often than those of a male model (Bandura, 1997; Bandura, Ross, & Ross, 1963a, pp. 3–11; Bussey & Bandura, 1984, pp. 1292–1302). Other research has shown that people who lack self-esteem or are incompetent, as well as those who have been rewarded in the past for imitative behavior, are more likely than others to follow the behavior of a successful model (Bandura & Walters, 1963, p. 85).

Along with the characteristics and prior experiences of the observer, the characteristics of the model also play a significant role. Observers imitate the behavior of a competent model more rapidly than the behavior of an incompetent one (Rosenbaum & Tucker, 1952, pp. 183–190). Models who are similar in personal background and physical appearance to the observers tend to have a greater influence on them (Rosenkrans, 1967, pp. 307–355). Observers also tend to learn more of a model's behaviors when the model is highly nurturant or rewarding and when the model has control over the future resources of the observer (Grusec & Mischel, 1966, pp. 211–215).

Rewards and punishments associated with the model's behavior can also affect the imitative behavior of observers. We learn by observing the behavior of others and the occasions on which they are reinforced for their actions, and we alter our behavior accordingly. To test the effect of such **vicarious reinforcement**, Bandura exposed nursery school children to a five-minute film in which an adult model behaved aggressively toward a large plastic doll:

The film began with a scene in which a model walked up to an adult-size plastic Bobo doll and ordered him to clear the way. After glaring for a moment at the noncompliant antagonist the model, exhibited four novel aggressive responses each accompanied by a distinctive verbalization.

First, the model laid the Bobo doll on its side, sat on it, and punched it in the nose while remarking, "Pow, right on the nose, boom, boom." The model then raised the doll and pommelled it on the head with a mallet. Each response was followed by the verbalization, "Sockeroo, stay down." Following the mallet aggression, the model kicked the doll about the room, and these responses were interspersed with the comment, "Fly away." Finally, the model threw rubber balls at the Bobo doll, each strike punctuated with "Bang." This sequence of physically and verbally aggressive behavior was repeated twice. (Bandura, 1965, pp. 590–591)

Children in the control condition saw only this film and observed no consequences to the model for his aggressive actions. Other children, however, saw a second film sequence in which the model was rewarded or punished for his behavior. In the reward condition, a second adult praised the model for his aggressive behavior and rewarded him with soda pop and candy. In the punishment condition, the second adult spoke disparagingly to the aggressive model, and accused him of being a coward and a bully. The punishing adult also spanked the model with a rolled-up newspaper and threatened him with a beating if he was caught being aggressive again.

The independent variable in this study was the nature of the reinforcement administered to the model for aggressive actions. The dependent measure was the amount of aggression exhibited by children in each of the three conditions when given an opportunity to display the behavior they had seen modeled. The children were escorted to a separate room that contained a Bobo doll, three balls, a mallet and pegboard, and an assortment of other toys. A wide variety of toys was presented so that the children had full opportunity to engage in either imitative or nonimitative behaviors. The experimenter left the room, presumably to fetch other toys, and the children were left alone to play. Observers then recorded the children's responses after watching their behavior through a one-way mirror. As expected, children exposed to the model who had been punished for his aggression showed significantly less aggression in the free-play situation than did children who observed the rewarded model or the one who had incurred no consequences for his behavior. Thus, the first phase of this study showed clearly that differential reinforcements administered to a model can indeed have a profound impact on the performance of observers.

But a question with practical social implications still remained. Although we know that the children in the various reinforcement conditions *performed* differently, did they all actually *acquire* the model's behavior? In other words, is it possible that all the children learned the model's behavior but that only those who saw him rewarded or go unpunished decided to imitate him? In the second phase of the study, Bandura showed that this was indeed the case. After their performances in phase one were measured, all the children were offered attractive prizes contingent on their reproducing the model's aggressive responses. The introduction of these attractive incentives completely washed out the previously observed differences in performance, and the researchers concluded that an equivalent amount of learning had taken place in the model-rewarded, model-punished, and no-consequences conditions. These findings suggest that people may *learn* a variety of behaviors but actively decide whether or not to *perform* them on the basis of their estimate of the consequences. Why is this acquisition/performance distinction so important? Bandura believes that it counters the argument that showing crime in the mass media is not harmful to young observers because the criminal is always punished. These results suggest that punishment of the model (the criminal) does not prevent the acquisition of immoral and illegal behaviors, which may surface later under the appropriate circumstances—for example, under conditions in which peers reward the person for such behaviors.

Bandura has conducted many other studies in which he applied modeling and reinforcement principles and research to the problem of violence in the media and its harmful effects on viewers. We now provide some illustrations of aggression and violence in the media, and then review Bandura's theorizing about aggression and violence, along with supportive data, in this important area.

Aggression and Violence in Films, Television, and Video Games

As virtually all of us recognize, violence and aggressive acts permeate our society. We read in the newspapers every day about inhumane actions on the local, national, and international levels. We cannot help but notice the violence in the cartoons and dramas that children watch on television. By the time the average child graduates from elementary school, he or she will have witnessed more than 8,000 murders and approximately 100,000 other acts of violence on television (Bushman, 1998, p. 537).

In the evenings, we watch the news (preferably not while we're eating) and listen as commentators document for us the latest kill counts of faceless people who live in obscure foreign lands where political factions vie for power.

We watch with horror as suicide bombers drive cars loaded with explosives into buildings or marketplaces in Baghdad, Iraq, or Kabul, Afghanistan, thus slaughtering scores of innocent people. On MTV, we watch programs in which some reality show "stars" senselessly break things, or hit one another, and sometimes some of the male "heroes" commit acts of violence against women. On the law-and-order shows, the good guys and bad guys sometimes resolve their problems by systematically blowing holes in one another with a wide assortment of weapons. Many of the films we watch provide an even more gruesome catalogue of aggression. The old John Wayne shoot-'em-ups, though laden with aggression, are tame fare indeed in comparison to the films shown today (e.g., today we see people being dissected with chainsaws).

Finally, if we get bored with mindless films and TV programming, we can purchase violent video games for entertainment (e.g., Grand Theft Auto, God of War III,) to play on our TV screens, or we can play such video games by accessing them on the Internet.

The problem is that we are often exposed to the same fare that we see in films and TV programming. That is, many of these videos contain senseless acts of violence and murder as we try to "win" the game by destroying people who oppose us. For example, in one violent video game called Grand Theft Auto, San Andreas, the player, is a young man working with gangs to gain respect. He can steal money from prostitutes and then beat them to death with only temporary punitive consequences.

In another violent video game, God of War III, a warrior gores, dismembers, and eviscerates his opponents, and their bodies float in a river of blood. Increasingly, these games are often not played in solitary fashion as much, but rather in terms of teams of actual people coming together on the Internet as players who are then pitted against each other in a virtual world (Sherry, 2001, p. 410).

Granted that we are exposed to a steady diet of violence in the media, does such exposure lead inevitably to aggression? Many critics claim that any impact it may have is minimal and relatively innocuous. Bandura, however, believes that media portrayal of violence can have serious and harmful effects on behavior. While acknowledging that media portrayal of violence is neither a sufficient nor a necessary cause of aggression, he argues vigorously that such exposure can, under the right circumstances and in the right types of people (e.g., those low in impulse control and/or high in hypermasculinity), facilitate aggression (Bandura, 1973, p. 267; Scharrer, 2001, p. 159).

Another argument used by critics is that exposure to violence only affects disturbed individuals. Bandura counters by pointing to research in which models were able to convince so-called normal people to act aggressively against others under the right circumstances (Milgram, 1963, pp. 371–378). By countering these and other arguments with an impressive mass of research evidence, Bandura has tried to make all of us aware of the potential danger inherent in the unabated portrayal of violence in the media. Let us examine some of these findings, to see how both personal and situational variables can act to facilitate or inhibit aggressive behavior.

Research Evidence for Aggression and Violence in Our Society

We have already learned that observers who watch models being rewarded for certain behaviors tend to repeat them, whereas observers who watch models being punished for their actions tend not to repeat those actions. Moreover, we have also seen that, when models are punished for their actions, observers still have learned the disapproved behaviors and can repeat them if given strong incentives. Bandura also has conducted research which shows that, when aggressive models receive no punishment for their behavior, viewers are more likely to imitate their actions (Bandura, 1986, p. 291). In a study which examined more than 5,000 hours of programming on television, violence went unpunished 73% of the time (Bushman, 1998, p. 537).

Another study has shown that, even though young observers reported they disliked a model who had been rewarded for aggression, they still imitated him and reported wanting to be like him. It seems as though they knew aggression was wrong but also believed that it was fun. This finding suggested to the investigators an analogous situation in many television programs, in which the bad guy is rewarded throughout an episode for his wrongdoing and punished only at the very end (Bandura, Ross, & Ross, 1963b, pp. 601–607). Viewers may know he is guilty of wrongdoing and has been punished for it, but may admire him, nevertheless, for performing exciting and rewarding feats they themselves would love to perform. In other words, all the positive reinforcement he has received for his actions may easily override and outweigh the single punishment suffered at the end.

There is also a serious question about the advisability of using violence to punish wrongdoers. Although it is true that witnessing such punishment will inhibit imitative behavior, at least temporarily, we have already seen that viewers may learn the behavior anyway and show it under more favorable circumstances. More importantly, by giving viewers the impression that the use of violence is both justifiable and a ready solution for problems, this approach hinders their consideration of alternative, nonviolent strategies. An early experiment by Berkowitz (1962) found that, when people view acts of violence that seem justified, their inhibitions are lowered and aggressive responding is facilitated; when they witness violence they consider inappropriate, their aggressive responding is inhibited.

These findings suggest that typical film and television presentations in which the hero appears justified in annihilating the villain by violent means may actually lead to an increase in aggressive behavior among viewers. The motto of such angry viewers may well be: "Give it to him! He deserves it!" This primitive eye-for-an-eye and tooth-for-a-tooth philosophy, which still governs the behavior of many people, may well add to the problem of aggression in our culture.

Research also has shown that viewers are more apt to behave aggressively if they are low on impulse control. They also behave more aggressively if they identify with the victor, as in the case of moviegoers who imagine themselves to be the winners of fights in the films that they see (Turner & Berkowitz, 1972, pp. 256–264). Observers are also more apt to be aggressive if they can dehumanize the victim, or when the injuries suffered by the victim are minimized or sanitized. Sanitized violence is violence which appears to be good, clean fun where no one really gets hurt. Think of the bar room fights in the old westerns as a good example. Amidst laughter, people are hit over the head with a bottle or tossed through windows; yet they recover miraculously with no injuries (or minor injuries at best) (Bandura, 1986, p. 291). Thus, it is clear that a number of factors, both personal and situational, can serve to instigate and facilitate aggressive actions.

While much of the research supporting Bandura's theorizing which we have just reviewed is based on studies done in the 1960s and 1970s, hundreds of research studies since that time have produced overwhelming evidence for Bandura's contention that exposure to violent TV or films causes significant increases in aggression, that repeated exposure of children to media violence increases their aggressiveness as young adults and that media violence is a significant risk factor in youth violence which is increasing steadily in our culture (Anderson & Bushman, 2001, p. 354; Anderson et al., 2010, pp. 151–173).

Interestingly, the introduction of violent video games into the culture in the late 1970s has introduced a new source of youth aggressiveness (Vessey & Lee, 2000, p. 607). People opposed to these games point out that, in the three towns (Paducah, Kentucky, Jonesboro, Arkansas, and Littleton, Colorado) that have experienced multiple school killings, the shooters were students who habitually played violent video games. Eric Harris and Dylan Klebold, the Columbine High School students who murdered 13 people and wounded 23 in Littleton, before killing themselves, enjoyed playing the bloody video game Doom. Of course, the fact that some highly publicized school killings were committed by people who habitually played violent video games is suggestive but not strong evidence that violent video games increase aggression. However, scientific evidence of a more experimental nature is increasing since the mid-1980s, indicating that there may well be truth to the critics' claim. Let us now review some of this research.

Violent video games and aggression

In a study by Bartholow and Anderson (2002, pp. 283–290), college students were randomly assigned to play either a violent video game (Mortal Kombat) or a nonviolent video game (Golf Tournament) before competing on a computerized "game" in which each participant was led to believe that he or she was competing with another person over several trials to see who could respond most quickly on each trial to an auditory tone by clicking a mouse button. The students were told that they would be punished by their opponent if the opponent responded more quickly to the auditory tone and that they could punish their opponent if they responded more quickly than the opponent. The punishment was a noise delivered via earphones, which could vary from 0 (0 decibels) to 10 (100 decibels). Students who played the violent video game were more likely to deliver very intense levels of punishment to their opponent than those who had played the nonviolent video game, despite the fact that the experimenter had arranged the punishment levels and frequencies delivered by their opponent to them to be equal in both the violent and nonviolent video game conditions. Other studies with young children have shown that those who played violent video games showed increases in short-term aggressiveness, with the children tending to imitate those behaviors portrayed in the theme of the game (such as a martial arts master or a jungle hero) (Vessey & Lee, 2000, pp. 607–610). Still other research showed that children who played violent video games during school time were more aggressive in their behavior during free play (e.g., hitting, pushing other kids) than children who had not played these video games prior to free play (Sherry, 2001, p. 414). Thus, there is substantial evidence (hundreds of studies) indicating that playing violent video games can increase subsequent aggressive thoughts, feelings, and behaviors and lead to decreases in empathy and pro-social behavior in many males and females of varying ages in several different countries (Anderson, Gentile, & Buckley, 2007; Anderson et al., 2010, pp. 151–173; Barlett, Anderson, Swing, 2009, pp. 377–403).

Recommendations   There are two major recommendations made by Bandura and other psychologists to modify and control media representations of aggressive and violent behavior. First, media executives need to be encouraged by members of the public to create more constructive shows and video games. Films, TV, and video games all have the potential to foster creativity and promote prosocial behaviors, such as helping and caring (Vessey & Lee, 2000, pp. 607–610). Encouraging the creation of shows and video games that are interesting, informative, and nonviolent would probably lead to greater progress than simply condemning the shows and video games that are saturated with violence. One example is the children's show *Sesame Street*, which was designed with the help of psychologists. It is informative and entertaining and has demonstrated that it can attract large audiences of children. In contrast to many of the morning cartoon shows, *Sesame Street* does not rely on violence, but it has proven highly successful. Also, animated features like *Toy Story 3* and *Shrek: The Final Chapter* have been huge successes (hundreds of millions dollars in worldwide gross box office receipts), despite the fact that they are not filled with gore and brutality. Second, parents need to limit their children's exposure to media violence by monitoring the content of programs in advance, modeling nonaggressive behavior for their children, and rewarding nonviolent behavior. It is unfortunate that many parents have adopted a permissive attitude toward the programming their children watch and the video games they play. For example, teens in grades 8 through 12 report that 90% of their parents never check the ratings of video games before allowing their purchase, and only 1% of the teens' parents had ever prevented a purchase based on its rating. Also, 89% of these kids reported that their parents never limited the time they could spend playing video games (Anderson & Bushman, 2001, p. 354). More parental guidance is needed.

Efficacy Expectations

Bandura has come to place the cognitive mechanism of self-efficacy in a primary position in his theory as he tries to account for personality functioning and change. Modeling, while still retaining an important role in the theory, is now seen more as a procedure that can help instill in people the level of self-efficacy necessary for effective behavior (Bandura, 1977, pp. 191–215; Bandura, 1982b, pp. 122–147). In Bandura's view, people who perform effectively have acquired high (but realistic) efficacy expectations that guide their actions, whereas people who are unable to perform adequately in a variety of situations typically have acquired low and often unrealistic expectations that adversely influence their performances. **Efficacy expectations** are beliefs or convictions on the part of individuals that they can produce certain behaviors. They are not to be equated with people's actual skills. Bandura points out that individuals who know what to do in a situation and have the skills required to do it will not necessarily perform well, if they have serious self-doubts about their capabilities. Thus, different people with the same skills, or the same person on different occasions, may perform poorly, adequately, or extraordinarily. Competent functioning requires not only skills but the judgments of self-efficacy to permit their effective use. Furthermore, even when people possess the needed skills and a strong sense of efficacy, they may not choose to perform the activities if they have no incentive to do so (Bandura, 1986, p. 391).

According to Bandura, efficacy expectations influence people's choices of activities and environmental settings. Judgments of self-efficacy also determine how much effort people will expend on activities and how long they will persist on challenging tasks and in the face of aversive experiences.

People with low efficacy expectations are likely to avoid threatening situations that they believe exceed their coping skills. If, for some reason, they have to perform in threatening situations, their low efficacy expectations lead them to expend little effort and give up after a short time. As a result, they are unlikely to gain corrective experiences that would enhance their sense of efficacy, and they remain defensive and fearful. Thus, for example, shy people may avoid social situations. If they must attend social functions, they expend little effort in trying to meet and converse with people; they usually end up as wallflowers. Such people are wracked by self-doubts and persistently engage in debilitating self-criticism about their incompetence, which, in turn, leads to poor performances in a variety of social situations. These poor performances serve to reinforce low expectations of efficacy and to prevent the learning of new, assertive behaviors.

People with high efficacy expectations, in contrast, opt for challenging tasks where they have an opportunity to develop new skills. In such challenging situations, they are likely to expend maximum effort, to persist in the pursuit of their goals despite obstacles, and to engage in a minimum of debilitating self-criticism; as a result, they increase the probability of eventual success. This probability can be further enhanced by the setting of proximal goals, subgoals that can be attained along the way to final, distal goals. Proximal goals help focus people's attention and provide them with feedback that sustains efforts. Breaking a task into a number of small steps also increases their initial perceptions of self-efficacy by making the task seem more manageable. Subgoal attainment then provides an indicator of progress that is likely to further boost perceptions of self-efficacy and to enhance their chances of attaining the final goal (Stock & Cervone, 1990, pp. 483–489). In one study, for example, obese individuals who adopted daily subgoal limits for how much they ate achieved substantial continuing reductions in their weight. In contrast, individuals who pursued distal weekly goals rarely attained them and shed no weight (Bandura, 1986, p. 474).

According to Bandura (1977, 1986), the acquisition of high or low efficacy expectations has four major sources: performance accomplishments, vicarious experiences, verbal persuasion, and states of physiological (emotional) arousal.

Performance accomplishments

Bandura believes that efficacy expectations are rooted primarily in personal mastery experiences. Success experiences tend to create high expectations, whereas failure experiences tend to generate low expectations. Once strong high-efficacy expectations have been created, however, occasional failures are unlikely to have much impact on people's judgments of their capabilities. Conversely, once low expectations have been instilled by repeated failure, occasional successes are not very effective in changing people's judgments of their capabilities. However, low expectations can be changed by repeated and frequent successes fueled by determined effort on the part of individuals. Through such efforts, people can eventually overcome and master the most difficult obstacles (Bandura, 1981, p. 203).

Vicarious experiences   Performance accomplishments are the most influential source of efficacy expectations, because they are based on actual mastery experiences, but vicarious experiences can also influence the acquisition of efficacy expectations. In other words, seeing or visualizing other people performing successfully can instill high self-perceptions of efficacy in observers, who come to believe that they too possess the capabilities to master comparable activities (Bandura, 1982a, p. 27). Watching others of similar competence fail despite high efforts, conversely, lowers observers' judgments of their own capabilities and undermines their efforts.

Verbal persuasion   Verbal persuasion is used very often to convince people that they have the necessary capabilities to accomplish their goals. Many parents, for example, encourage their children to believe that they can succeed in different life spheres. To the extent that such encouragement persuades the children to try hard enough to succeed, it may promote development of skills and a sense of personal efficacy. This encouragement must be kept within realistic bounds, however, because unsuccessful attempts to accomplish goals following persuasion are likely to create low efficacy expectations and lessen the credibility of the source (Bandura, 1977, p. 198). Conversely, parents who continually discourage mastery attempts by their children through ridicule, criticism, and belittling are likely to generate low efficacy expectations in their offspring.

Emotional arousal   Stressful and difficult situations tend to generate high states of arousal in most individuals, and they use this arousal information to judge their capabilities. Because high arousal usually debilitates performance, individuals are more likely to expect failure—that is, to experience low efficacy expectations, when they feel that they are tense and physiologically aroused. Conversely, they are more likely to expect success—to experience high efficacy expectations when they perceive that they are relaxed and not highly aroused in the face of challenge or obstacles.

Research on Self-Efficacy

The study of individual differences in self-efficacy as they relate to performances in clinical and nonclinical areas has mushroomed since Bandura first introduced the concept into his theory. There are three major areas where self-efficacy theory has produced research, which has increased our understanding of important phenomena: academic development and achievement, career choices and job performance, and physical and mental health.

Academic development and achievement   Students develop perceptions of self-efficacy in various academic areas from a variety of sources. Foremost among these sources are their parents. Parents with a strong sense of personal efficacy themselves are able to appraise problems faced by their children as challenges rather than threats and to encourage them to develop the confidence and skills necessary to solve them. Thus, parents high in self-efficacy tend to raise children with a strong sense of personal efficacy (Jackson, Choi, & Bentler, 2009, pp. 1339–1355; Suzuki, Holloway, Yamamoto, & Mindnich, 2009, pp. 1339–1355). Also, research has shown that the quality of students' social relationships with their classmates and teachers can affect their perceptions of their academic self-efficacy and their subsequent performances on tests. That is, students who feel accepted and encouraged by their peers and teachers are likely to turn to them for help with their school work, thereby increasing their perceptions of their academic abilities and their performances on tests (Jackson, 2002, p. 243; Patrick, Hicks, & Ryan, 1997, pp. 109–111). Also, students often compare themselves with classmates who attempt similar tasks and make judgments about their own academic competence as a result. Outperforming other students is likely to boost self-efficacy levels. By far the strongest source of efficacy information, however, comes from the actual levels of prior accomplishments and mastery of tasks. Once established, self-efficacy beliefs influence what students do by determining the kinds of strategies they will use to achieve success. Students with higher efficacy use more rehearsal strategies (e.g., "When I read material for a science class, I say the words over and over again to myself to help me remember"), elaboration strategies (e.g., "When I study for this English class, I put important ideas into my own words"), and organizational strategies (e.g., "I outline the chapters in my book to help me study"). The use of these strategies results in superior performances (Pintrich & De Groot, 1990, pp. 35–37). Their extreme focus on mastering the materials and performing at superior levels on exams typically leads to less disruptive behavior. Students with lower efficacy expectations, in contrast, lack confidence in their abilities to perform well and, as a result, engage in more disruptive behavior in class to protect their feelings of self-worth. Anticipating failure on academic exams, they also tend to use self-handicapping strategies such as delaying studying for a test to the last minute. When they fail, they have a ready excuse for the failure, namely, they did not care about test results and only studied briefly at the last minute (Kaplan, Gheen, & Midgley, 2002, p. 1993). As mentioned earlier, self-efficacy beliefs also direct the amount of effort people will expend and the level of persistence they will show in the face of the adversity and anxiety they experience. Research by Pajares and Valiante (1997, pp. 353–359) showed that fifth-grade students who were higher in writing self-efficacy reported lower levels of writing anxiety and higher levels of writing performance. This finding implies that students who are very anxious about their writing are low in self-efficacy and can be helped by teachers to the degree that they can increase their students' confidence (or sense of self-efficacy) in their writing ability. Other research on reading and writing achievements in fourth, seventh, and tenth graders shows that there are increases in self-efficacy from the lower to the higher grades along with corresponding increases in reading and writing abilities. Such a trend is consistent with Bandura's argument that increases in perceived self-efficacy are associated directly with improvement in actual cognitive and behavioral skills (Shell, Colvin, & Bruning, 1995, p. 395).

Finally, there is some research with traditional and nontraditional cultural minority and majority college students and non-college adults which shows that self-efficacy beliefs are linked positively with achievement strivings and accomplishments (Bandura, 1986, pp. 430–431; Zajacova, Lynch, & Espenshade, 2005, p. 696).

Career choices and job performance   The self-efficacy concept has also been used to increase our understanding of career-relevant behaviors, such as vocational choice and job satisfaction and performance. For example, an early study by Betz and Hackett (1981, pp. 399–410) found that male and female college students differed in their beliefs about whether they could successfully complete the educational or training requirements for various occupations. In general, men perceived themselves as efficacious in preparing for traditionally masculine occupations (accountant, engineer, highway patrol officer, mathematician) and, to some extent, for traditionally feminine occupations (art teacher, medical technician, social worker, X-ray technician). Females, in contrast, perceived themselves as much more efficacious in preparing for traditionally feminine than for traditionally masculine occupations, with two exceptions (physician and lawyer). Perhaps the women's movement has helped increase women's confidence concerning these two occupations. In any event, females who believed that they could not successfully complete the required training or education in the traditionally masculine occupations also reported that they were unwilling to consider careers in those areas. These results were obtained even though both the male and female study participants had the same levels of verbal and mathematical skills. Thus, low self-efficacy perceptions may be an important factor in females' decisions to eliminate certain career choices. Lent, Brown, and Larkin (1986, pp. 265–269) showed further that female participants with lower perceived self-efficacy in completing the training requirements for traditionally masculine occupations in the sciences received lower grades in science and technical courses than did students with higher levels of perceived self-efficacy.

More recent research, however, has shown that therapeutic interventions based on Bandura's modeling theory can be used to increase females' poor perceptions of their efficacy toward traditionally masculine occupations such as engineering. While women have achieved increasing inclusion and success in professions that were formerly occupied primarily by men (e.g., medicine and the law), they remain underrepresented in the field of engineering. Thus, only 8.5% of all professional engineers are women, although women constitute 56.8% of the total work force. To change these poor perceptions and negative beliefs, Rosenberg-Kima, Baylor, Plant, and Doerr (2008, pp. 2741–2756) randomly assigned females with low levels of self-confidence toward engineering and negative stereotypes about the occupation to either an animated female film model who was similar to themselves (attractive, young, and "cool") or an animated female film model who was dissimilar to themselves (unattractive, old, and "uncool"). The "cool" model wore popular clothing and a fashionable hairstyle, whereas the "uncool" model wore outdated clothing and an unfashionable hairstyle. The "cool" and "uncool" models presented the same 20-minute filmed talk on the benefits of engineering as a career to all participants. Afterward, participants exposed to the similar models were found to have much higher levels of self-efficacy and more positive attitudes toward engineering than participants exposed to the dissimilar model, as predicted by modeling theory, as mentioned earlier in the chapter. Such interventions could well broaden career options for females and improve their grades in this academic discipline.

Physical and mental health   Numerous studies have indicated that people with lower self-efficacy expectations are less likely to be physically and mentally healthy, whereas those with higher efficacy expectations are more likely to be physically and mentally healthy. When people have low efficacy expectations, they are unable to cope with stress, which leads to an activation of their neuroendocrine, catecholamine, and opioid systems and impairs the functioning of their immune systems, thereby making them susceptible to infection and disease. On the other hand, high efficacy expectations produce an ability to cope with stress and produce no adverse physical effects (Bandura, 1997, pp. 262–272). Moreover, lower efficacy expectations are associated with poor mental health, whereas higher efficacy expectations are linked to good mental health. For example, three studies found that higher levels of self-efficacy in university students were associated with greater courage in facing stressful academic experiences and turning them into opportunities for positive growth. Such students also reported lower levels of depression, anxiety, neuroticism, and physical complaints and higher levels of life satisfaction and personal achievement (Maddi, Harvey, Khoshaba, Fazel, & Resurreccion, 2009, pp. 292–305; Muris, 2002, p. 337; Schweizer & Koch, 2001, p. 569). In addition, Resnick (2001, pp. 83–92) found that increases in self-efficacy are related to increases in exercise which, in turn, are associated with both physical and mental health benefits. People with higher efficacy expectations are also more likely to seek early treatment for various physical and mental health problems than are those with lower efficacy expectations. Furthermore, in contrast to low self-efficacy people, individuals with higher efficacy expectations are more likely to be able to control a harmful behavior (for example, to control their obesity through diet and exercise), to cope successfully with their hypertension through the use of relaxation procedures, to stop a self-destructive behavior (for example, to give up smoking or excessive drinking or binge eating), or to increase a desirable behavior (for example, to have safer sex by using condoms) (Bandura, 1986, pp. 179–181; Bardone-Cone, Abramson, Heatherton, & Joiner, 2006, pp. 27–42; Engels, Hale, Noom, & De Vries, 2005, p. 1886). Increases in self-efficacy stemming from patients' personality dispositions such as optimism about the future, high self-esteem and an internal locus of control helped women who had abortions cope more successfully with their feelings of guilt and depression (Cozzarelli, 1993, p. 1232).

Other investigations have shown that, after self-efficacy expectations are strengthened through exercise activities, patients gain greater control over their physical illness. For example, chronic back pain patients were placed on an exercise regimen during their hospital stay to increase their perceptions of their physical self-efficacy. Four months later, patients who had acquired higher perceptions of self-efficacy through the initial exercise program reported having an increased ability to cope with their pain, having less pain, and feeling more comfortable when standing or sitting than they were before undergoing the exercise activities.

Other procedures used to strengthen self-efficacy include graded mastery experiences, verbal persuasion, or vicarious modeling experiences. These techniques have been utilized to help reduce depression and phobias in people who initially lacked confidence in their abilities to overcome these disorders (Bandura, 1997, p. 288; Bryan, Aiken, & West, 1997, p. 473; Grembowski et al., 1993, pp. 89–104; Kores, Murphy, Rosenthal, Elias, & North, 1990, pp. 165–169; O'Leary, 1992, pp. 229–245).

Personality Development

In Bandura's theory, social-cognitive experiences play a crucial role in the development and modification of behavior. Obviously, parents can have a positive or negative impact on their children's development. On the plus side, imitation of parents' behaviors often meets with reward. Rewarded behavior tends to be repeated and, when performed in the presence of other people, is reinforced positively. As a result, children learn at an early age to match the behavior of successful models. On the minus side, parents who abuse their children by severely punishing them or by being cold and impersonal in their treatment of them are likely to have children with an assortment of behavioral problems by the time they go to school (e.g., they act out aggressively and/or have temper tantrums). The parents' severe physical discipline simply provides the children with poor role models. They learn that violence is the way to respond to behavior that is disliked in others (Herrenkohl & Russo, 2001, pp. 3–16; Onyskiw & Hayduk, 2001, pp. 376–385).

The acquisition of many complex forms of behavior is not always so simple and direct, however. Children are often exposed to multiple models, who present conflicting behaviors. One parent might reward them for speaking in the presence of guests, for example, whereas the other might punish them for the same behavior. Even when both parents are in agreement, teachers or other social agents may disagree and communicate that information to the children. Peers may try to indoctrinate the children in still other ways. Thus, the reinforcers for given behaviors are not always applied consistently.

Another complication is that behavior is not always imitated accurately or completely and must be shaped by the socializing agents through the application of the successive-approximation principles pioneered by Skinner. The establishment of proper table manners in children provides a clear example of the need to apply reinforcers in a subtle manner to a variety of behaviors that initially bear little resemblance to the complicated set of behaviors that eventually emerges.

In addition to imitation and successive approximation, Bandura believes, the maintenance and extinction of behaviors in the person's repertoire depends on the application of various schedules of reinforcement. In particular, he proposes that behavior is maintained through the application of combined schedules. He cites, as a prime example, attention-seeking behavior in children.

> In the training of children, the use of combined schedules certainly predominates. Let us take the example of attention-seeking behavior. Most young children attempt many times in the day to elicit a nurturant response from their mothers. Sometimes the mother will respond immediately, but more often she is busy. At varying intervals she will reward the child with interest and attention. Many mothers are inclined to ignore mild forms of attention-seeking behavior and to respond only when this behavior is frequent or intense. It can be predicted, on the basis of laboratory studies ... that these mothers should have children who show persistent attention-seeking behavior occurring at the rates and intensities that have previously brought reward. One may suspect that most "troublesome" behavior has been rewarded on a combined schedule by which undesirable responses of high magnitude and frequency are unwittingly reinforced. The behavior is thus persistent, difficult to extinguish, and baffling for the parents. Perhaps the genesis of much aggressive behavior is to be found in the use of schedules which reward *only* responses of high magnitude; these could be attention-seeking, food-seeking, and other so-called "dependency" responses, as well as responses of the kind more usually regarded as "aggressive." (Bandura & Walters, 1963, p. 7)

Thus, reinforcers appear to be dispensed in complicated ways by various socializing agents. Also, very importantly, children gradually learn in the course of their development to apply reinforcers to their own behavior. Standards for self-reward and self-punishment can be acquired in a variety of ways. Children may be taught rules of behavior by their parents and others and be rewarded for following them and punished for violating them. Children may also learn these standards through exposure to books, newspapers, films, television, radio, and video games. And, as you might expect, they may also learn them through modeling procedures.

In one early study, two groups of children participated in a miniature bowling game with adult models (Bandura & Kupers, 1964, pp. 1–9). In one condition, the children watched a model reward himself with candies only for excellent performances. In another condition, they watched a model reward himself even for poor performances. After exposure to the models, the children were left alone to play the game with no models present. The results indicated that the children tended to match the behavior of the model to whom they had been exposed. Although both groups of children had access to a generous supply of candy, those who were exposed to a high-performance standard rewarded themselves sparingly and only when they had matched or exceeded the criterion, whereas those who were exposed to the low-standard model rewarded themselves quite often, even for poor performances.

In an extension of this work, two investigators sought to determine **multiple modeling effects** on imitative behavior (McMains & Liebert, 1968, pp. 166–171). Using the bowling game just described, adults in phase one imposed either a stringent criterion for self-reward (that is, they rewarded themselves only for attaining a certain score and told the children to do likewise) or a lenient standard for self-reward (that is, they rewarded themselves for attaining either of two scores). In phase two of the investigation, the children who had seen the model impose a stringent standard were introduced to a second adult model, who either adhered to the stringent criterion set by the first model or violated it by rewarding himself for attaining the lenient standard. The investigators found that children who had initially been trained on the stringent criterion and then saw the second model adhere to the same standard deviated very little from the standard; that is, they rewarded themselves only when they met the stringent criterion. Children who had been trained on the stringent standard but then saw a second adult violate that standard were the least likely to hold to the stringent standard in the absence of the models; they rewarded themselves for attaining a variety of scores. These findings suggest that parents and others who impose severe restrictions on children but do not follow through by example are likely to be quite ineffective in training children to adopt their rules. It is not adequate, it seems, to use the old saw, "Do as I say, not as I do," to instill desired behaviors in children. Rather, the motto should probably be, "Do as I say *and* do."

One speculation associated with this study concerns the relationship between the learning of standards and feelings of well-being. If people learn to accept standards that are too high or that can be attained only rarely, they may experience stress. As a result, they may feel anxious, guilty, and depressed. Part of the tragedy here is that many people who adopt such standards are relatively competent, but live in continual agony because they rarely consider their best efforts to be good enough. Approval—the application of rewards and praise—by others may not be acceptable to such people; that is, external reinforcement may have little impact on their behavior. This notion of self-reward contingent on the attainment of extremely high standards is similar to Rotter's concept of high minimal goals and Adler's concept of the unrealistic pursuit of fictional goals. Thus, Bandura clearly recognizes the need to account for the impact of self-determined reinforcement, as well as external reinforcement, on behavior (Bandura, 1969, p. 39).

Although Bandura places great emphasis on observational and instrumental learning and on self-reinforcement, he does not ignore the biological determinants of behavior. He recognizes that constitutional factors inevitably influence the nature of the individual's social-learning history.

Social manipulations can have relatively little influence on some biologically determined characteristics, such as the body type or facial features of an individual. Yet within a society that sets high value on the possession of certain physical attributes, the frequency with which social reinforcers are dispensed is partly dependent on the extent to which these cultural ideals are met. In North American society, where prestige and social rewards are bestowed for athletic ability and physique, boys who are small, lack muscular strength or dexterity, or who are obese and possess feminine-like physiques, are relatively unsuccessful in obtaining positive reinforcement from peers. Similarly, a female who does not match the standards of beauty within her society evokes far fewer positive responses, especially from males, than one who possesses these socially esteemed characteristics. The slender, petite female has been highly admired in North American culture; she may, however, be the recipient of relatively few positive reinforcers and considerable aversive treatment if she lacks these qualities and is instead heavy set (Bandura & Walters, 1963, pp. 26–27).

Assessment Techniques

Bandura does not use dream analysis, free association, transference, or any of the other techniques utilized by practitioners in the psychodynamic tradition. Nor does he seem particularly interested in using personality questionnaires as assessment devices, although his position does not preclude the use of reliable and valid questionnaires, as long as they are situation-specific. His case for the use of situation-specific measures in preference to global assessment techniques rests on the fact that situation-specific measures allow for more accurate prediction of behavior than do measures that claim to assess generalized traits across situations (Bandura, 1997, pp. 48–49).

For the most part, Bandura relies on experimental methods to assess personality functioning and change. He believes that the most stringent tests of a theory are provided by anchoring a hypothesized mediator (for example, a cognitive event) in an independently measurable indicant and then confirming that external factors are linked to the indicant and that the indicant is linked to overt behavior (Bandura, 1982b, p. 123). In other words, Bandura is interested in demonstrating that experimental manipulations of antecedent events influence cognitive functioning, which, in turn, influences subsequent responses. If the problem area is complex and uncharted, however, Bandura thinks it is advantageous to begin by conducting field studies that are essentially correlational in nature (Bandura & Walters, 1963, p. 391).

Theory's Implications for Therapy

Modeling of Others as a Therapeutic Technique

Modeling of others has been employed successfully in the treatment of language deficiencies in autistic children (Lovaas, 1967, pp. 108–159). Such children are typically not very responsive to environmental influences; before employing modeling procedures, the therapist must first gain their attention. To accomplish this goal, the therapist sits directly in front of the children, so that they cannot ignore him or her. The therapist also rewards them for maintaining eye contact and physically restrains any effort by the children to move away. Having established attentional control, the therapist proceeds to model sounds, words, and phrases of speech and to administer rewards for appropriate responding. Under such training procedures, it has been possible to develop some language skills in autistic children. Modeling has also been used to increase communication skills in asocial psychiatric patients (Gutride, Goldstein, & Hunter, 1973, pp. 408–415).

Modeling has been used to reduce a variety of fears in children. In one particularly interesting study, Bandura and Menlove (1968, pp. 99–108) showed that avoidance behaviors could be eliminated through observation of modeled approach responses. Specifically, the investigators were able to eliminate a fear of dogs in nursery school children by having them watch another person approach, pet, and handle the animals without being bitten. Bandura and Menlove began by administering a standardized test of avoidance behavior in order to identify those children who were fearful of dogs. The test consisted of a graded series of 14 tasks, in which the children were required to participate in increasingly intimate interactions with a dog. The tasks included: walking up to a playpen containing a dog and looking down at it; touching and petting it; opening the enclosure; walking the dog; and eventually getting into the playpen with the dog and petting it. Following the identification procedure, the dog-phobic children were assigned randomly to one of three conditions. In one condition, children observed a single model who displayed progressively bolder approach responses to a cocker spaniel. In a second, multiple-model condition, other children observed the same sequence of events and, in addition, watched other models of various ages playing with a wide variety of dogs, both small and large. In the control condition, still other children saw movies of Disneyland and Marineland but no modeled interactions with dogs. Following the administration of these procedures, all the children were retested using the same standardized test. Approximately one month after the posttest, they were tested again, to determine the stability of

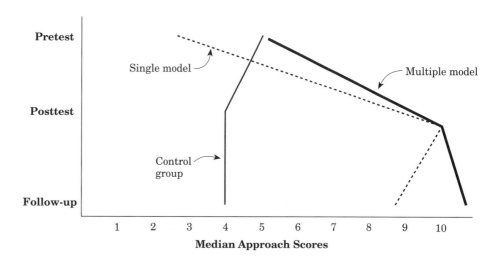

FIG-17.1 Median approach scores obtained by children under the various conditions of the experiment. (Adapted with permission from Bandura & Monlove, *Journal of Personality and Social Psychology* Vol. 8 (p. 102). Copyright © 1968 American Psychological Association. Used with permission.)

the modeling effects. The results (Figure 17.1) showed clearly that the modeling procedures were instrumental in reducing and sustaining a reduction in the children's fears. Similar modeling procedures have been used to reduce fear of snakes in adolescents and adults (Bandura, Blanchard, & Ritter, 1969, pp. 173–199).

Research has shown that test-anxious college students tend to perform poorly because they spend much of their time paying attention to irrelevant cues. Such students tend to be self-centered and overly concerned with questions about their intellectual competence and the reaction of others to their performances. Sarason (1975, pp. 148–153) conducted an investigation to determine whether models' disclosures about their own anxieties in evaluation situations and the strategies they had devised to cope with these interfering cues could improve the task performances of highly anxious students. All study participants filled out a personality questionnaire to determine their characteristic levels of test anxiety. Then groups of study participants who were classified as either high or low in test anxiety were exposed to a variety of models. In one condition, they were exposed to an anxious coping model, who mentioned that she became anxious during testing situations and that she attempted to cope with her anxiety by (1) reminding herself periodically to stop thinking about herself and to concentrate on the task; (2) thinking about interesting aspects of the task; (3) not allowing herself to get flustered by errors; and (4) forcing herself not to think about the reactions of other people. In the second condition, a noncoping anxious model simply mentioned that she became very anxious during testing, had difficulty concentrating on the task, and was continually worried about what others would think of her if she failed. In a third condition, a neutral model did not mention testing or grading and talked instead about activities, programs, and issues on the campus.

All study participants then performed a task that involved learning a series of nonsense syllables. As expected, the model who not only mentioned that testing situations caused her anxiety but provided information on how she coped with it had the greatest positive impact on the students with high test anxiety. (See Figure 17.2.) Apparently, the self-disclosures provided them with modeled information about ways to improve their performances, and they utilized it.

An intriguing study by Downs, Rosenthal, and Lichstein (1988, pp. 359–368) demonstrated the powerful therapeutic effects of modeling in changing the undesirable behavior of elderly (average age 75) residents of a care facility. Many of these elderly patients are required by their physicians to take whirlpool baths, as a means of promoting healthy

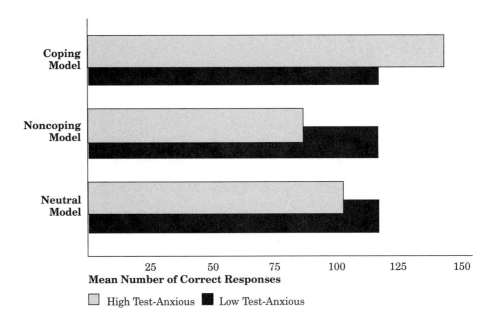

FIG-17.2 Mean number of correct responses on serial learning task for students with low and high test anxiety under different modeling conditions. (Adapted with permission from Sarason, *Journal of Consulting and Clinical Psychology* Vol. 43 (p. 150). Copyright © 1975 American Psychological Association.)

skin tissue and relieving pain associated with arthritis, bursitis, or limb amputation. The bath-time procedure is very stressful for these patients. They cannot enter or depart the bath independently, because the tub walls are approximately three feet high. Instead, the patient is strapped into a chair, which is then raised by a mechanical lift over the edge of the tub and then lowered into the water up to the patient's waist. After the bath, the lifting procedure is reversed. Even though you might expect bath-time to be a refreshing highlight of the patient's routine, many dislike it and resist strongly. Some patients resist entering the bathroom or sitting down in the chair. Some express fear and aggravation, shout verbal insults or obscenities at the staff, or struggle to avoid being strapped into the chair.

In this study, patients who were highly avoidant of bathing were randomly assigned to one of three conditions. In the in vivo (actual situation) **guided participation modeling** condition, a therapist model guided patients through the bath-time procedure by modeling the desired behavior and then showing them how to perform the activity themselves; the therapist also provided physical support and verbal encouragement. In the filmed modeling condition, patients watched two peers who were initially afraid of the bath-time procedure successfully cope with their fears after being guided through the activity by a therapist. In the third condition, a control group received no exposure to models.

Initially, the results in the in vivo guided participation modeling condition were not in accordance with what the investigators expected on the basis of Bandura's modeling theory; that is, very few of the patients made any positive progress in overcoming their fears. The reason, however, was obvious. When the therapist was modeling the bathing procedure for a group of four patients, one became extremely anxious and disruptive; the other patients then became very afraid and were unable to make much progress during subsequent sessions. In a second experiment, this problem was corrected by having patients undergo treatment by the therapist individually. Under these conditions, the patients showed substantial progress. After several training sessions, they were much more comfortable in the bath situation, showed little resistance, and successfully completed the bathing activity. Almost as much progress was made in the filmed modeling condition; and both groups performed better than the control participants, who continued to be disruptive and avoidant in the bath situation. On the basis of these findings, the investigators recommended that the modeling film be used to introduce new patients to the bathing situation, and then followed up with in vivo modeling by a therapist to ensure that patients would be comfortable with the bathing procedure.

Self-Modeling as a Therapeutic Technique

Self-modeling also has been used to help people with physical and mental difficulties. Bandura maintains that self-monitoring increases self-efficacy and performance. Students with serious emotional disturbance typically engage in a variety of disruptive classroom behaviors (e.g., hitting, pushing, defiance, making noise, talking out-of-turn, inattention). In one of the self-modeling studies, students, ages 10–13, were videotaped for 25 minutes while in their classes. Then the videotapes were edited, removing all of their disruptive behaviors. These new tapes were approximately 12 minutes along and contained only exemplary behavior. Each child was shown the edited version of his own behavior on five or six occasions over a two-week period of time. Disruptive behavior was reduced, on average, from 47% to 11% after a six-week follow-up. Bandura believes that viewing their own appropriate behavior was rewarding, increased their self-efficacy, and led to less disruptive behavior. This procedure is very helpful to teachers. Ordinarily, attempts by teachers to control disruptive behaviors are very frustrating, tedious, and unsuccessful. To date, there have been over 150 studies in the research literature showing that self-modeling can be effective in the treatment of a variety of problem behaviors (Kehle, Bray, Margiano, Theodore, & Zhou, 2002, pp. 203–207).

In conclusion, countless studies in the modeling-others and self-modeling literature demonstrate convincingly the positive impact that modeling can have in changing undesirable behavior. Modeling is thus a viable alternative to traditional psychodynamic approaches that seek to give people insights into their behavior through protracted and costly analysis but provide little guidance as to specific courses of action they can take to help themselves. Its continued usage as an aid in therapeutic settings seems assured.

Efficacy Expectations and Fear Reduction

Most of Bandura's recent research focuses on attempts to eliminate a variety of fears in people by raising efficacy expectations. In effect, the factors that contribute to the acquisition of efficacy expectations can be manipulated experimentally to reduce pathological behavior by raising clients' perceptions of their own efficacy.

In a variety of studies, Bandura (1986, 1997) has employed clinical treatments involving performance accomplishments to reduce and eliminate snake phobias. Snake phobics are guided by models to engage in progressively more threatening interactions with boa constrictors or corn snakes, including: (1) approaching a glass cage containing the snake; (2) looking down at it; (3) holding it with gloved and bare hands; (4) letting it loose in the room and returning it to the cage; (5) holding it within 12 centimeters of their faces; and (6) tolerating the snake crawling in their laps while they held their hands passively at their sides. Bandura found that, before the guided modeling occurred, the phobics' efficacy expectation for completing these tasks was very low, but after the treatment achievement of mastery was high, and so were the phobics' efficacy expectations. Control participants who did not receive the guided participation modeling had lower levels of expectations throughout the experiment and did not achieve mastery.

In other experiments, Bandura has demonstrated that vicarious-experience treatments— in which snake phobics simply watch models successfully engage in the increasingly threatening activities (without guided participation) and then independently try to imitate the behavior of the models—result in higher efficacy expectations, lower physiological arousal (that is, reductions in heart rate and blood pressure), and more effective performances than are found in phobic participants not exposed to models at all (Bandura, 1977, p. 206; Bandura, Reese, & Adams, 1982, pp. 14–21). It should be noted, however, that exposure to models under vicarious conditions is not as effective in reducing phobics' fearful behavior as having the phobics engage directly in mastery experiences under guided participation conditions.

Bandura and his colleagues also have demonstrated that these therapeutic treatments work not only with study participants who are immobilized by fears of animals but also with people who are afraid of public places (agoraphobics) (Bandura, Adams, Hardy, & Howells, 1980, pp. 39–66). Many agoraphobics cannot shop in stores and supermarkets, because they find the crowds and checkout lines too threatening. Similarly, theaters, restaurants, buses, subways, and even riding as a passenger in cars arouse highly negative emotions in many of them. If untreated, most of these individuals are eventually unable to venture out at all into public settings and become virtual prisoners in their own homes.

To help these clients, Bandura and his associates utilized a number of therapeutic treatments simultaneously. They began with group sessions in which clients were taught how to identify the situations that aroused varying levels of fear. They also learned how to identify self-debilitating thoughts and how to cope with them through the use of body relaxation procedures and through the substitution of more positive, emboldening thoughts. But the primary treatment consisted of experiences of mastery in the field. The emphasis in this treatment was on successful experiences with the feared objects and settings, because successes tend to raise mastery expectations. Exposure to these highly intimidating situations was undertaken gradually, by using graded subtasks and by carefully and slowly lengthening the time spent in the settings. For example, agoraphobics who feared automobile travel first rode in residential areas, then on busier streets, and eventually on freeways. Clients who shunned supermarkets and department stores made shopping trips first to small, uncrowded stores and then to progressively larger stores. Those who feared restaurants gradually extended the amount of time they spent in them.

These performance accomplishments were generally aided by treatments that employed modeling by therapists and by ex-agoraphobics using guided performance and encouragement. Whenever clients became unduly distressed, they were encouraged to retreat momentarily and then to move forward again with proper guidance and support. As clients developed their ability to cope, however, the field therapists gradually reduced their support and their guided participation. Clients were assigned progressively more challenging tasks to perform alone while the therapists remained in the vicinity. Using these multiple techniques, Bandura and his associates were able to reduce substantially the fears of these clients and to restore mastery behavior.

Ozer and Bandura (1990, pp. 472–486) also conducted a study designed to raise the efficacy expectations of women who were very fearful of a sexual assault. Initially, these women were convinced that there was nothing they could do to overcome a sexual assault, and this belief resulted in restriction in their life styles. That is, these women tended to avoid dating, going out at night to events such as films, lectures, plays, or concerts, and working late hours. They were highly fearful and had many negative thoughts about being powerless if a sexual assault occurred. The women were then provided with an opportunity to learn the physical skills necessary to protect them against assault by watching an expert model disable an assailant quickly by delivering powerful blows to vital areas of the body, for example, the eyes, throat, knees, and groin. The women then practiced these power blows and received corrective feedback from the expert until they had mastered all of the physical defense skills. The entire course took 5 sessions of 4 and

1/2 hours each. During this mastery training, the women also were taught verbal techniques for halting coercive and potentially assaultive encounters in their incipient stages.

The mastery training had very positive effects. Women who had undergone the training reported higher levels of self-efficacy than they did prior to the self-defense training. They became much more confident of their ability to defend themselves successfully if they were attacked. Their fearfulness was greatly diminished as were the number of negative thoughts they had about being powerless. Importantly, the newly empowered women also expanded their activities and began to attend evening cultural and educational events and to participate in various social activities (Ozer & Bandura, 1990, pp. 472–486).

Finally, Bandura has conducted research in which he assesses the impact of various stressors on the bodies of individuals high and low in perceived self-efficacy. He thinks that perceived self-efficacy affects a wide range of biological processes that mediate human health and disease. In several studies, he shows that, as phobic individuals gain control over their fears and anxiety by increasing their perceptions of self-efficacy through guided participation modeling procedures, the biological stresses on their bodies are lessened dramatically, and their immune system resistance is increased. This process results in stronger, healthier and more capable individuals. In contrast, people who perceive themselves as inefficacious are unable to cope with the stresses and thus continue to experience elevated blood pressure and accelerated heart rates which can weaken their immune systems, possibly resulting in more physical disease if the stresses are chronic in nature (Bandura, 1992, pp. 356–361; Bandura, 1997, pp. 141–143).

Evaluative Comments

We now evaluate the scientific worth of Bandura's theory in terms of our six criteria.

Comprehensiveness Although it still does not encompass the range and diversity of phenomena explored by Freud's theory, Bandura's position is nevertheless quite comprehensive. It provides a thorough analysis of the social-cognitive variables responsible for the acquisition, maintenance, and modification of disordered behavior, thereby contributing to our understanding of alcoholism, academic and occupational anxieties and performance, frigidity, impotence, exhibitionism, insomnia, nightmares, obsessive-compulsive problems, phobias, and physical illnesses. In addition, Bandura and his associates have focused a great deal of attention on the variables responsible for the acquisition and modification of aggressive behavior. More generally, social-cognitive research has increased our knowledge of the ways in which childhood training practices influence personality development, how language is acquired and honed, and how self-reinforcement can be utilized in the acquisition, maintenance, and modification of behavior. This last area seems especially promising and exciting to investigators, as evidenced by the amount of research conducted on such phenomena in recent years.

Precision and testability Many of the cognitive variables in Bandura's theory are complex and difficult to define precisely, but Bandura has made strong efforts to define and measure them objectively and reliably. To a substantial degree, these efforts have been successful, and he has been able to incorporate the cognitive variables into experimental tests of his theory and to demonstrate the theory's predictive accuracy.

Parsimony Social-cognitive theory is based on relatively few assumptions, but those it does make are broadly stated and designed to encourage investigation of the ways in which social and cultural phenomena affect behavior and thought. The theory encompasses not only the concepts traditionally associated with learning positions (reinforcement, discrimination, generalization, extinction) but also a variety of new and different cognitive concepts. Although Skinner believed that Bandura invented needless constructs to account for behavior, it is this author's judgment that these constructs are necessary for the development of an adequate theory of personality and that Bandura's theory is, in most respects, commensurate with the complexity of the phenomena it seeks to explain. Thus, it is a parsimonious theory.

Empirical validity   The evidence in support of Bandura's position is impressive. There have been countless empirical tests of the theory, and the results have been highly supportive. For example, studies of observational learning have yielded evidence showing the importance of modeling in helping to mold, maintain, and vary behavior. Much of this research has demonstrated clearly that modeling can be used to eliminate fears, anxieties, and disordered behaviors. Modeling principles have been applied to the study of nonneurotic behaviors as well. Much of the newer research testing Bandura's theory has focused on the self-efficacy concept. Hundreds of studies have shown that increases in the person's efficacy levels produce increases in coping skills and have consequences for physical and mental functioning in a wide variety of situations. In general, then, Bandura's position has a high degree of empirical validity.

Heuristic value   Bandura's position has had considerable impact on the work of psychologists, especially in the areas of clinical psychology, social psychology, health psychology, and vocational counseling. It has also had a positive impact on the work of researchers in business, education, and medicine. Nevertheless, it has not had the interdisciplinary impact of Freud's theory. Still, its promise remains strong, and in the future we should see even a greater increase in its heuristic value for professionals in other disciplines.

Applied value   The applied value of social-cognitive theory is very high in the area of education. His work has enabled educators to develop strategies to enhance the self-efficacy of their students and their subsequent performances. It also has been used very successfully to understand and modify the psychopathology of many individuals. A variety of behavioral therapy techniques derived from social-cognitive theory have been successfully utilized in the treatment of an assortment of phobias and other problems. In addition, Bandura's pioneering research in the area of aggression has increased greatly our understanding of the origins of such behavior and has provided insights into the ways it can be modified and controlled. As such, his work in a variety of areas has made significant contributions to our culture.

CRITICAL THINKING QUESTIONS

1. What is triadic reciprocal determinism? Give several personal examples of how cognitive, behavior, and environmental factors all interact.

2. If positive reinforcers are such a potent determinant of behavior, why don't we praise and reinforce each other more often?

3. In what ways does violence in the media influence the behavior of many people? Has it ever had an adverse effect on you or any of your friends?

4. What are some of the primary personal and situational determinants of aggressive behavior? What suggestions would you make for reducing such destructive behavior in our culture?

5. How anxious do you get before taking an examination? Does this anxiety interfere with your performance? What do you do to reduce the interference?

GLOSSARY

anticipated outcomes   A person's expectancy that the performance of certain behaviors will secure certain reinforcers.

efficacy expectations   Individuals' convictions or beliefs that they can execute the behaviors required to produce certain response consequences.

external reinforcement   A reinforcing environmental stimulus that controls the occurrence of behavior; it might be food, money, praise, approval from others, a pat on the back, or a smile.

guided participation modeling   Phobia-reduction procedure in which models first show study participants how to successfully tolerate increasingly threatening interactions with dreaded objects, and then guide the participants through these threatening activities until they are finally able to master their fears.

imaginal representation   An image called up by a person that resembles an object in the environment. For example, the person can picture, or imagine, a professor who exists in the environment.

modeling   Type of learning in which individuals learn new behavior by observing others.

multiple modeling effects   Impact on a person's imitative behavior of being exposed to a variety of models.

observational learning   Type of learning in which new responses are made as a result of watching the performance of others; also called imitative learning.

self-modeling   Type of learning in which individuals watch themselves behave in a situationally appropriate manner via videotape and then show the same behaviors later on.

triadic reciprocal determinism   The belief that cognition, behavior, and the environment operate interactively as determinants of one another.

verbal representation   A word that signifies an object in the environment. For example, the word *dog* is a verbal representation of a barking quadruped that exists in the environment.

vicarious reinforcement   Willingness to imitate the behavior of a model after observing that the model was reinforced for the behavior.

SUGGESTED READINGS

Bandura, A. (1986). *Social foundations of thought and action: A social cognitive theory.* Englewood Cliffs, NJ: Prentice-Hall.

Bandura, A. (1997). *Self-efficacy: The exercise of control.* New York: W.H. Freeman.

PART 7

The Role of the Grand Personality Theories in Contemporary Personality Psychology

While it is true that many investigators prominent in personality psychology today are currently using more circumscribed theoretical models that focus on fewer phenomena in their research programs, this does not mean that the **grand theories of personality** that we have covered in this text are dead and not worth studying except in an historical sense. A mistake made by some people is to assume simplistically that if a theorist is deceased, then the theory is dead too and that it is obsolete and not worth testing. Yet, as we have seen, most of the grand theories are not lying dormant and untested.

On the contrary, many of these more comprehensive theories are still being tested actively by researchers. For example, consider the wealth of data currently being gathered to test the validity of different aspects of the theories of Freud, Jung, Horney, Kohut, Erikson, Kelly, Cattell, Eysenck, Rogers, and Skinner. Thus, in terms of their current status, many of these theories are alive and well. Besides generating new data, most of the theories continue to serve a vital heuristic function in the discipline, as they motivate, challenge, provoke, and influence personality psychologists in their own theorizing and research.

In the last chapter of the book, we highlight the critical importance of the grand theories as they continue to stimulate and inspire contemporary personality psychologists to create new theory and to do new research, activities which increase our understanding of personality development and functioning even more.

CHAPTER 18

Theory and Research in Contemporary Personality Psychology

Heuristic Value of the Grand Theories in Five Important Areas

We have now completed a long and complicated, yet hopefully interesting and enlightening journey through the major theoretical perspectives on human personality. It should be apparent that none of these theories ranks at the highest level on all the criteria used by investigators in judging the scientific worth of a theory. Despite that fact, all of them have considerable strengths that have contributed to our understanding of personality development and functioning.

Contemporary personality psychologists also have been stimulated, provoked, and influenced by the current theories to challenge, revise, and/or extend them by developing new ideas and hypotheses for empirical testing. In this chapter, we will examine five important areas in contemporary personality theory and research and the role often played by the current theories we have covered in the course in generating interest in them. These areas include (1) a focus by investigators on the special impact of biological factors on human personality development and functioning, (2) the necessity of incorporating a multicultural perspective into personality theory and research and psychotherapy, (3) the use of a trait taxonomy to increase our understanding of the role of traits within personality, (4) the role of positive psychology in promoting the study of human strengths and virtues in personality development and functioning, and (5) the emergence of the study of personality differences as they relate differentially to the kinds of activities such individuals select for use on the Internet, the frequency of their use, and their consequences for personality development and functioning.

Area 1: A Focus on Biological Contributions to Personality

Although various personality theorists—especially Freud, Cattell, and Eysenck—have sought to explain personality development largely in biological terms, for much of personality psychology's history, most theorists and researchers had not paid much attention to biological explanations; instead they favored environmental explanations. In the past two decades or so, however, there has been an increasing recognition of the importance of the biology of personality, and more specifically there has been a growing research interest in the genetic underpinnings of personality. Major advances have occurred in **behavioral genetics**, the scientific study of the complex genetic and environmental conditions that together contribute to the expression of behavior in human personality.

A major part of behavioral genetics involves the study of **quantitative genetics**. Essentially all human traits (e.g., intelligence, competitiveness, depression, altruism, extraversion) show some variations between individuals within a population as well as between specific populations, and these variations can be quantified. For example, while males are more competitive, on average, than females in our culture, within both sexes there are substantial individual differences in competitiveness. Understanding the nature of these individual genetic differences, and the relative importance of genetic versus environmental factors in the expression of variations in behavior, is the task undertaken by quantitative behavioral geneticists. These scientists have developed assessment procedures to help them complete the task based to a considerable extent on the pioneering work of Cattell and Eysenck. For example, they credit Cattell with development of a multimethod approach, multiple abstract variance analysis (MAVA), that is highly useful in assessing the relative quantitative contributions of genes and environmental influences to personality functioning (Plomin, Chipuer, & Loehlin, 1990, p. 234). MAVA allows them to assess family, twin, and adoption data from several studies in the same analysis (see Chapter 9). With the development of these procedures and others, personality psychology began to shift away from an extreme environmentalism that was used as the sole explanation of behavior (Plomin, 2000, pp. 30–34).

Many studies in quantitative genetics have demonstrated that people's genes (as well as their environments) influence the expression of many behaviors. Investigations to identify the influence of genes on behavior on the most general level use twin, adoption, and family procedures. For example, in twin studies, the correlation between identical twins on a given behavior (even those raised in radically different environments) for a behavior based entirely on heredity should theoretically be +1.00. (In reality, the correlation will be slightly lower because of errors in measurement; the test will not be perfectly reliable.) In contrast, since fraternal twins have only 50% of their genes in common, the correlation for a behavior that is totally genetically determined would be lower for fraternal than for identical twins. This judgment is based on the principle that, for a genetically based behavior, the further away we get from genetic similarity, the smaller the correlations should be. Based on this reasoning, research shows that there is a substantial genetic influence on various behaviors. For example, in schizophrenia the concordance rate (percentage of twin pairs that both have schizophrenia) for identical twins is about 48%, whereas the concordance rate for fraternal twins is only about 17%, suggesting a genetic base for the disorder (Plomin, DeFries, McClearn, & McGuffin, 2008, p. 198). Using the same procedure (comparing the difference in the sizes of the correlations between identical and fraternal twins), studies have shown that genetics has some influence on general intelligence, neuroticism, Alzheimer's disease, autism, panic disorder, antisocial behavior, alcohol and drug misuse, depression, and suicide (Plomin, Owen, & McGuffin, 1994, pp. 1733–1739; Voracek & Loibl, 2007, pp. 463–475).

You should not get the impression that because there is a genetic component to the aforementioned behaviors that genes cause them directly. Instead, genetic influences may interact with environmental factors to eventually produce the behavior. (Workman & Reader, 2008, pp. 26–27). For individuals who abuse alcohol and drugs, for example, the misuse is not caused directly by their genes; rather, their genes predispose them (put them at risk) to perform the destructive behaviors. Under the right environmental conditions, they may show the unhealthy behaviors. For example, research has shown that adults with genetic susceptibilities to alcohol and drug misuse are more likely to show the behaviors if they live in family environments that are filled with conflict and poor moral and religious training (Jang, Vernon, Livesley, Stein, & Wolf, 2001, pp. 1307–1318).

Finally, even though behaviors are determined within a general interactional framework, the nature of that interaction is often quite complex. For example, the genetic basis of **temperament** (e.g., characteristics such as anger and fear) may influence the formation of personality structures which, in turn, influence environmental interactions, and eventually produce behavior. Specifically, Finch and Graziano (2001, pp. 27–55), investigating depression, found that the temperamental characteristics of anger and fear served as the basis for the development of neurotic personality characteristics (irritability and moodiness) which, in turn, lowered the amount of environmentally based, social support they received from others when they were under stress (Who can like and support people who are continually irritable and moody?), which then led to depression. They also found that individuals low on fearfulness and anger were more likely to develop a personality trait of agreeableness (pleasantness and charm), and that this trait was associated positively with the amount of social support they received from others during times of stress, leading to lower levels of depression. While this example is complex enough, very often several or more genes, a number of hormones, several different personality characteristics, and a host of environmental factors may all jointly influence the expression of a given behavior. It is clear, then, that a given behavior is seldom adequately explained by an exclusive emphasis on a single gene (Beckworth & Alper, 2002, pp. 317–318).

Behavioral genetics not only encompasses quantitative genetics but also **molecular genetics**. The scientists working in this important domain study how specific genes influence behavior. Molecular genetics seeks to understand how genes at the **DNA** (deoxyribonucleic acid) level encode for the various sequences of the 20 amino acids that form the thousands of specific enzymes and proteins of which human beings are made (Plomin, DeFries, et al., 2008, p. 42). Proteins create the skeletal system, muscles, the endocrine system, the immune system, the digestive system, and most importantly for behavior, the nervous system. Genes do not code for individual differences in behavior directly, as mentioned earlier, but rather it is DNA variations that create differences in these physiological systems that can, in turn, affect personality functioning and behavior (Plomin, DeFries et al., 2008, p. 46). For example, when mutations or changes in the DNA sequence of a gene occur, the result may affect neuronal functioning in the brain and produce impairments in intellectual functioning and behavior. Many single-gene disorders that involve genetic mutations have already been discovered through the work of genetic scientists, for example, sickle-cell anemia, cystic fibrosis, and muscular dystrophy (Bethell, 2005, pp. 157–159).

Finally, genetic scientists have been working in the **Human Genome Project** to identify the number of genes in the human body. Thus far, they have identified roughly 20,000 human protein-coding genes (Nilius, 2010, pp. 221–222). Many scientists working in the project believe that the task is now one of spelling out more precisely the mechanisms by which these genes operate at the DNA level to influence behavior. In addition, they believe the quest is to find, not just a single gene and how it operates for a trait, but the multiple genes (and how they operate) that affect the expression of a trait in a probabilistic rather than predetermined manner (Hall, 2010, pp. 60–67; Plomin, DeFries et al., 2008, p. 355). Some of these scientists maintain that the primary advantage of successfully completing this monumental task lies in the ability of scientists to identify people with specific genetic risks and to generate interventions that might prevent them from occurring (Plomin, DeFries et al., 2008, p. 46). Other scientists argue further that, once the sequencings of the genes have been determined, it will be possible to replace dysfunctional segments of DNA with new segments that work, and that this "gene therapy" will cure major diseases that have already been caused by genetic defects, that is, by dysfunctional genetic mutations. Unfortunately, progress in achieving this latter goal has proven highly elusive, and some critics have argued strongly that they doubt geneticists can ever deliver the cures they originally promised (Bethell, 2005, pp. 147–163; Lewontin, 2000, p. 177). While the outcome of this debate is still in doubt, many believers in the potential benefits of "gene therapy" push doggedly on, while the doubters of the efficacy of this approach are beginning to search for a new theoretical and empirical approach that may eventually prove more viable.

Evolutionary theory   Besides the research in behavioral genetics, another outgrowth of the increased interest in biological contributions to personality is the development of various forms of **evolutionary theory** as it relates to psychology (Buss, D. M., 1999; Caporael, 2001). Evolutionary theory points out that humans are mammals—specifically, primates—and, as such, are biologically similar to the three great apes: orangutans, gorillas, and chimpanzees. Although it is clear that we differ from the great apes in important ways—for instance, our language, imagery, and thought processes are far more advanced than theirs—we do share the same sense organs, many ways of perceiving and learning, many facial expressions, and various behaviors.

Like other primates, we follow a circadian rhythm of activity, which typically reaches a low point at night and peaks during the day, especially before feeding; we also exhibit intense bursts of energy in aggressive, escape, and sexual behavior, or in rollicking play. We are curious and move around to investigate our environments, just as they do. In the process we (and they) may meet strangers and become wary and shy. Thus, shyness may be one component of fear. Despite differences in the way in which we and the other primates express fear, activation of the sympathetic nervous system triggers a common set of reactions, including an increased rate of breathing, higher blood pressure, and the shunting of blood from the digestive system to the skeletal muscles in preparation for fight or flight (Buss, A. H., 1988, pp. 1–4). According to A. H. Buss, (1988, p. 10; 1995, p. 50), these diverse behaviors are expressions of underlying, broad-based temperaments that we share with other primates. The definitions of these temperaments are as follows:

1. *Emotionality* involves high physiological arousal and generalized negative affect such as irritability and moodiness. It is the tendency to become aroused easily and intensely, to become easily frustrated and distressed.
2. *Fearfulness* involves the tendency to be wary, run away, or cower, as well as the accompanying physiological arousal.
3. *Activity* refers to total energy output, as expressed in vigor or tempo.
4. *Nurturance* is the tendency to help others; it includes altruism.
5. *Sociability* is a preference for being with others rather than remaining alone.
6. *Impulsivity* is the tendency to act on the spur of the moment without pause or reflection.
7. *Aggressiveness* consists of attacking or threatening.
8. *Dominance* refers to seeking and maintaining superior status over others.

Each of these temperaments has a genetic component. They have evolved because they have adaptive value; that is, they help ensure survival and reproduction. A closer examination suggests that moderate levels of these traits are more likely to be adaptive than extreme levels (Zuckerman, 1990, p. 315). For example, moderate levels of fear and activity would keep the organism wary and able to physically respond to the threat, and thus, to survive, whereas extreme fearfulness and a complete lack of activity would probably result in severe injury or death in dangerous situations.

Although these temperament traits have a biological basis, it is clear that the environment also plays a determining role in each of them (Buss, A. H., 1988, p. 20; Strelau, 2008, p. 82). Just like the behavior geneticists, evolutionary theorists assume that both biology and environment influence behavior. They endorse an **interactional temperament model**, which states that environment and temperament traits mutually influence each other. At this point, let us look in more detail at how one of these eight traits, emotionality, interacts with the environment to influence the expression of certain behaviors.

Consider that there are individual differences among infants in their emotionality. Some babies are "easy," meaning that they are adaptable and easily soothed and generally cheerful, whereas others are "difficult," meaning that they are highly reactive to frustration and are fearful, moody, and fussy. Some mothers are able to respond sensitively and warmly to their babies' needs, whereas others are easily overwhelmed by the environmental stresses associated with infant care. In one study, investigators found that infants with difficult temperaments were not able to form secure attachment relationships with their mothers where the mothers were highly reactive to stress and felt alienated from their infants. In contrast, when mothers were low in their reactivity to stress and felt warmth toward their babies, the infants were able to form secure attachments. Secure attachments are ones in which the infants reached out to the mother when she approached and showed no resistance to her following a brief separation. Insecure attachments are ones in which the infants actively resist (stiffening their bodies and crying) being touched and held by the mother. The development of insecure attachments apparently occurs because difficult infants require extra care and frustrate their mothers. The mothers, in turn, interpret the complaints and fears of their infants as evidence of rejection or as signs of their own incompetence. Insensitive handling and insecure attachment tend to follow (Ipsa, Fine, & Thornburg, 2002, pp. 130–144).

More recent research by Stright, Gallagher, and Kelley (2008, pp. 186–200) shows further that mothers who demonstrated high quality parenting skills (i.e., mothers who encouraged autonomy and were warm and sensitive) were able to influence the development of their emotionally difficult infants in a positive direction as indicated by the fact that these infants showed better adjustment to school when they reached first grade. The children of such parents were more cooperative with their teachers (i.e., paid more attention to their teachers' instructions and put away materials properly) and peers (i.e., volunteered to help them with tasks and controlled their tempers when they had an occasional argument). Mothers with low quality parenting skills and difficult infants raised children who showed poorer adjustment to school when they reached first grade. A. H. Buss also believes that the broad temperament traits we inherit become more differentiated into specific components as we mature. Aggressiveness, for example, may become differentiated as physical aggression, verbal aggression, irritability, and passive-aggression. Passive-aggressive people try to hurt or get back at their antagonists by indirect means: For example, they may give their antagonists the silent treatment, respond excruciatingly slowly to requests from others, or do the opposite of what they are asked to do (Buss, A. H., 1988, pp. 177–178). An individual may use one or more of these forms of aggression, depending on the demands of the situation.

The temperament traits can also combine to produce unique behaviors (Kristal, 2005, pp. 23–25). For example, people who are sociable *and* dominant tend to seek social status through sharing and working with others. In contrast, people who are low in sociability *and* high in dominance are likely to seek social status through aggression. Sociable people who are altruistic will feel empathy for others and try to be helpful not only to friends and relatives but also to strangers in distress. Unsociable people who are altruistic will tend to help others, not out of empathy, but because of a moral code or a sense of responsibility (Buss, A. H., 1995, pp. 174–175).

Finally, evolutionary theorists argue that there are biologically rooted sex differences in humans and in other primates for most of these traits. Primate males tend to be larger and stronger than are females, which may account for males' more aggressive and dominant behavior. Primate males also have more testosterone than females, and this hormone has been implicated in the aggressiveness and dominance of mammalian males. Primate males are more active than are females and tend to explore their environments more. In contrast, females tend to be more fearful, more sociable, and more nurturant than are males. The male-oriented traits all emphasize moving out into the environment with great energy. The female-oriented traits emphasize safety. In brief, primate males tend to poke, pry, and stir things up, whereas females tend to act as a conservative, quieting, and nurturant force in primate groups (Buss, A. H., 1988, pp. 24–25).

Evolutionary theorists also maintain that primate males are more likely to compete among themselves for access to females, whereas females are more likely to exercise selectivity in their choice of mates. This difference is explained in terms of a **differential parental investment hypothesis** (Buss, D. M. & Schmitt, 1993, p. 206); that is, females are thought to make a greater investment in each offspring because they must endure a nine-month pregnancy, whereas men can produce that same child with as little as a few minutes of investment (Buss, D. M., 1999, p. 103).

In addition, females must nurse the infant and nurture its growth, and, in contrast to the male, are limited in the number of offspring they can produce. Because of their different levels of investment in each offspring, males and females are likely to engage in different mating strategies. Specifically, females will be attracted to males who show characteristics associated with dominance, including an ability to protect them and to provide the resources necessary for their survival and the survival of their offspring. Thus, females also generally prefer to mate with males who are a few years older than themselves, because the males' age provides an important cue about their access to resources; that is, income usually increases with age in many cultures. Females also believe that older males are likely to be more mature, more stable, and more reliable in their provision of support and protection (Buss, D. M., 1994, p. 28; Ellis, 1998, pp. 383–442). Males, in contrast, tend to be more concerned with the females physical attractiveness, according to evolutionary psychologists. In evolutionary history, males who preferred to mate with females marked by physical signs of old age and disease (wrinkled skin, gray hair, open sores) produced few or no children. In contrast, males who preferred to mate with females possessing physical cues linked to youth and health (smooth, clear skin, lustrous hair, full lips, absence of lesions) experienced greater reproductive success. Because females' reproductive capacity is strongly correlated with age, and because physical appearance historically provided the most reliable cues to age, males have evolved powerful mate preferences for females who are young and physically attractive (Buss, D. M. & Dedden, 1990, pp. 399–400). Also, considerable research has shown that males gain in social status by their associations with attractive females. Unattractive males are thought to have high status if they can interest stunning females, presumably because attractive females are known to have high value as mates and therefore to be able usually to get what they want in a mate (Buss, D. M., 1994, pp. 59–60). Also, since males are oriented to pass on their genes by having offspring, they can only be certain that this is the case if they are unequivocally the father of the offspring. So sexual fidelity in a mate is a primary consideration for males. Infidelity by their mates produces intense jealousy in males and can sometimes lead to violence. For females, the primary task is also having children. In addition, they must also spend long periods of time raising and nurturing them. Female rivals for their mates' affection threaten mothers because it suggests that their mates will not be as supportive and will not provide the resources that are needed to ensure the mothers' survival and the survival of their offspring. Thus, males are concerned primarily with sexual infidelity and females with emotional infidelity (Buss, D. M., 2000, pp. 51–52).

Research on humans based on some of these speculations has been generally supportive. A study of university students found that, in comparison to males, females were much more concerned with a possible mate's earning capacity, wealth, and social status. Females, more than males, also wanted their mates to be powerful, ambitious, and intelligent. In couples who were dating exclusively, females were more concerned that their partners wanted children following marriage, whereas males were more concerned that their prospective marriage partners be physically attractive (Kenrick, Sadalla, Groth, & Trost, 1990, pp. 97–116). D. M. Buss (1989) has reported confirmatory findings in 37 cultures, suggesting a biological basis for these concerns.

Although the results in the two studies mentioned previously are supportive of the evolutionary perspective, they are also consistent with a social-learning or socialization approach to sex differences; that is, it can be argued that these differences between the sexes are learned in the course of the socialization process. For example, males traditionally have been expected to pursue careers that will eventually provide them with social status and the resources necessary to support and protect their mates and offspring. Females, in contrast, are trained traditionally to be nurturant and supportive of others and to believe that their physical attractiveness is their chief marketable asset and that it can and should be used to entice males into long-term relationships. Thus, the evolutionary and socialization views are compatible, even though the etiology of the viewpoints differs.

Research by Eagly and Wood (1999, pp. 408–423) has provided some support for the socialization position. They reanalyzed the data that D. M. Buss (1989) reported in support of the biological position in 37 cultures. Eagly and Wood assessed the degree of gender equality among partners in these 37 countries (which had not been done by D. M. Buss) and found that, as the power between the partners became more equal, there was a decrease in females seeking male partners who were older and wealthy who could support and protect them and their children. Also, as the partners shared power more equally, men placed less emphasis on wanting a younger woman (although this was a weak effect statistically) and a mate with domestic skills, results that Eagly and Wood maintain are inconsistent with the biological position. Furthermore, they argue that their findings suggest that social and cultural factors play a large role in mate selection.

Finally, in the most recent development in this interesting and important area, evolutionary psychologists like D. M. Buss argue that the fact that evolutionists like himself maintain that females are predisposed biologically to prefer mates with status and financial resources does not mean that all females *today* will necessarily prefer mates with such resources. He maintains that evolutionary psychologists do not embrace a strict biological determinism and do recognize that social and cultural factors (like those cited by Eagly and Wood in the socialization hypothesis) may operate so that the biological predisposition may be overridden under certain environmental conditions. Thus, contemporary females, although predisposed ancestrally to favor mates with resources, may not seek out such mates if they (the females) already have such resources themselves (e.g., if they have high-paying jobs and are self-sufficient). The senior author of the socialization paper, Alice Eagly, now accepts this more differentiated, interactional position offered by the evolutionists (cf. Workman & Reader, 2008, pp. 94–95).

Area 2: The Need for a Multicultural Perspective on Personality

The development of personality characteristics is highly dependent on the meanings and practices that people learn as a result of immersion in their cultures. People develop their personalities over time as they actively participate in various cultural situations. A cultural psychological perspective assumes that different cultures, as well as subcultures within a given culture, have special differential effects on the personality development and functioning of their citizens (Markus & Kitayama, 1998, pp. 66–67). In some instances, these impacts produce shared similarities among individuals, and in other instances differences in personal characteristics and qualities are generated. For example, in the United States and in several other Western countries, people generally grow up in highly individualistic cultures which place heavy emphasis on inculcating the traits of independence, self-reliance, ambition, determination, aggression, competition, and the achievement of personal success in its members. Thus, these cultures produce members who generally have many similar personality characteristics. In other non-Western cultures—for example, in much of Africa, Asia, and Latin America—the primary orientation is collectivistic. Collectivistic cultures teach their members to be more harmoniously interdependent, to share resources, to see success as depending on help from others, and to focus largely on trying to fit in with the group and to place the needs of the group above their own needs (Triandis, 2001, p. 908). Thus, peoples in these cultures have many shared personality characteristics such as nurturance, cooperation, and altruism.

When individuals in Western and non-Western cultures are compared, they generally possess different motives, interests, attitudes, behavior, values, and ideas of mental health and psychopathology. For example, in Western cultures people explain their own successes in terms of their own internal and relatively stable attributes, such as ability or talent, while discounting their failures by attributing them to external factors (e.g., blaming others). In non-Western cultures, individuals explain their successes in terms of effort or luck and their failures as caused by deficiencies in ability or talent. Thus, individuals in Western cultures tend to strive toward self-enhancement, whereas the members of non-Western societies are oriented toward self-criticism. The emphasis on self-criticism in non-Western cultures should not be seen as an indicator of pathology, however. Rather it should be perceived as a willingness by individuals to acknowledge that they have fallen short of meeting the standards of excellence shared by their cultural group. Self-criticism is used to improve their behavior, thus affirming their belongingness to the group (Kitayama, Markus, Matsumoto, & Norasakkunkit, 1997, pp. 1245–1267).

Most of what we know about human personality in Western cultures is based on our view of individuals as independent, self-contained, autonomous beings whose unique configurations of traits, abilities, values, and motives influence their behavior. As a result, personality psychologists' views of human personality are unnecessarily limited (Markus & Kitayama, 1991, p. 224). For example, our models of psychological health, especially those of Rogers and Maslow, tend to emphasize self-realization, self-fulfillment, fulfilling individual potential, and so forth. These models, in many respects, mirror the individualistic bias of our culture. Although they do point out that self-actualizing people care about others and are socially responsible, the primary emphasis appears to be on the glorification of the individual. Models that emphasize the role played in the development of optimal psychological health by harmonious interdependence, sharing resources, and caring about the welfare of others are relatively rare in Western cultures, although a good case could be made for the social interest model created by Adler. Even if we acknowledge that many subcultures within the United States value interdependence and that various religious denominations emphasize love and caring for others (Markus & Kitayama, 1991, p. 228), the fact remains that the overall cultural emphasis is on independence, personal success, and self-fulfillment. Within that context, it appears clear that personality psychologists need to expand their views, inquiries, and analyses beyond their own cultural perspective if they are to continue making progress toward an adequate theory of human personality. Fortunately, personality psychologists are paying increasing attention to cross-cultural and sub-cultural perspectives in their theorizing and research, especially in the areas of gender, race/ethnicity, and religion.

Gender differences   These differences are shaped to a large extent by cultural socialization processes. Interest in these differences (and in the many similarities between males and females) is skyrocketing among investigators in the discipline. Feminist scholars, for example, have examined a variety of theories of personality and pointed out their limitations in explaining females' development. They point out that many of the basic concepts in these theories are based on a male perspective of life, which depicts males as embodying values which the culture strongly endorses and females learning a set of values which the culture devalues. As mentioned earlier, the predominant cultural philosophy in the United States centers around individualism and personal success. To achieve personal success, it is believed that individuals must be strong, self-reliant, powerful, determined, independent, rational, logical, unemotional, aggressive, and highly competitive. These traits are associated with an idealized masculine role. In contrast, to meet the standards of the ideal feminine role, it is believed that females must be warm, dependent, deferent, passive, emotional, sensitive, caring, and nurturant, thus acquiring traits that would generally hinder the attainment of personal success in a high-powered, highly competitive society like ours. Within this male-dominated, cultural framework, males and females actually do internalize and acquire the traits associated with their respective gender roles during the socialization process (Feingold, 1994, p. 449). Thus, it is easy to see why females are often seen as inadequate and inferior to males. Females are not socialized traditionally to acquire traits that would help facilitate personal success in occupations that a male-dominated society values most highly. Instead, females are often judged, and often judge themselves, as being unable to live up to the standards embodied in an individualistic society (Chodorow, 1989, p. 23).

Feminist scholars have continually challenged these biased views. They have developed models of psychological health based upon feminine values that emphasize relationship and nurturance rather than on masculine values that emphasize independence and self-determination. In an early writing, Chodorow (1978) maintained, for example, that Freudian theory can be challenged for its one-sided, derogatory view of women. Freud believed that males were superior and females inferior. Male superiority was seen as an outgrowth of conflicts within the family during the phallic stage. Boys, according to Freud, develop a longing for sexual contact with the mother. In the most general sense, they seek affection and love from her. At the same time, however, male children are increasingly aware that there is a sexual relationship between their parents and that their fathers are their rivals. But their fathers are bigger and stronger physically, and boys are fearful that they will be punished for their desires—specifically, that their penis will be cut off. Boys alleviate this castration anxiety by identifying with their fathers. By identifying in this way, their sexual desires are shunted into more socially acceptable channels. The superego is an outgrowth of the resolution of this complex, as boys take on the values of their fathers and their attitudes toward society. These values are ones strongly endorsed by society so boys feel superior, especially in relation to girls.

Freud believed that females discover early in life that they do not have a penis and then think that they have been castrated and are inferior. Females experience penis envy and begin to love their father because he possesses the desired object. Girls eventually are forced to identify with a mother they resent and blame for their lack of a penis in order to vicariously obtain the desired object. In brief, by identifying with their mothers and becoming like them, they experience indirectly the love, affection, and praise that the father gives to his wife. Their active sexuality now becomes passive as they identify with the traditional feminine role and its values. Since society generally devalues these characteristics, many girls perceive themselves as inferior.

Chodorow reformulated Freud's thinking in this matter. She stated that, while both boys and girls see their mothers initially as primary sex objects, girls form a more intense attachment to their mothers than do boys. Girls form longer-lasting bonds with their mothers because they are the same gender and because they have more experiences in common with them (Chodorow, 1978, p. 109). Thus, they identify more strongly with them and are more accepting of their values and characteristics. Influenced by their mothers, they adopt the role of their mothers and are more likely to develop motherly qualities, that is, stronger feelings of empathy, caring, nurturance, and sensitivity to the needs of others than do boys. Interestingly, Chodorow maintained that girls do not turn away from their mothers to their fathers in their search for a love object, but instead start to focus on the father as an additional person in the family whose needs and interests have to be considered and met (Chodorow, 1978, pp. 92–93). Thus, they always maintain strong emotional ties to their mothers, even as they are beginning to become attached to opposite-gendered objects. But how do they become committed to males as heterosexual love objects (i.e., their fathers and later other men)? Chodorow speculated that girls' sexual focus on males as appropriate erotic objects may be partially the result of seductive behavior on the part of their fathers and/or other male relatives and/or from learning of the appropriate sexual role as communicated by their parents, siblings, relatives, teachers, peers, and the media (Chodorow, 1978, pp. 167–168).

According to Chodorow, the identification process in boys is different. Mothers experience their sons as opposite-gendered, and they are not as close emotionally to them. When boys identify with their fathers, it is typically not based on strong affectional ties to them. Given the fact that fathers most often work outside the home and are not present to teach their sons and/or because they have difficulty in expressing their emotions as a consequence of their own immersion in the masculine role, boys are taught the masculine role and its requirements primarily by their mothers and to a lesser extent by their fathers. In the process of identifying with the same sex parent, boys deny identification with and relationship to their mothers and later to other females. They come to perceive women as inferior. Thus, masculine identification stresses separation from others (independence), denial of the importance of emotion-based relationships, and rejection of all that is feminine (Chodorow, 1978, p. 176). Masculine identification stresses independence and self-determination and actively rejects the importance of relationship and connection to others. Feminine identification, on the other hand, sees a primary value in relationships and interdependence.

In conclusion, Chodorow rejected the Freudian idea of male superiority and female inferiority and concluded simply that the sexes develop differently with their own unique values, interests, attitudes, motives, behaviors, and goals. Both genders have strengths and weaknesses. For males, independence may be an asset when it contributes to problem-solving, but in its extreme, it deteriorates into implacability and rigidity. For females, connection to others brings several positive results. For example, mutual empathy in a relationship creates greater trust and a greater willingness to disclose intimate information to the other, leading oftentimes to personal growth for both. Connection can also energize both parties, and both feel an increased sense of worth (Miller, 1994, pp. 85–86). Furthermore, a willingness to listen to the concerns of others who are experiencing difficulties in their relationships at home or at work without being judgmental can be helpful. However, the downside of this orientation is that it may lead to a willingness to be overly dependent on the judgments of others rather than to develop and utilize one's own skills and intellect (Chodorow, 1978, p. 169).

Like Chodorow, Gilligan (1982) maintained that males and females respond to their experiences in "different voices." That is, males and females interpret their experiences differently, with females emphasizing relationships and connection to others and males emphasizing separation from others and individuation. Then she noted that several theories of personality development (e.g., Erikson, 1950; Maslow, 1987; Rogers, 1961) have perspectives that assume the moral superiority of the male orientation. Maslow, for example, notes that self-actualizing people are relatively independent of their physical and social environments. Because they are propelled by growth motives rather than by deficiency motives, self-actualizing people are not dependent on other people or the culture for help and support (Maslow, 1987, pp. 135–136). A major deficiency motive within Maslow's scheme is the need for esteem from others, that is, the need for support, recognition, and appreciation by others. Thus, many women are probably operating on a deficiency level as a result of being socialized to be concerned primarily with connections and relationships. In contrast, men are generally socialized to value separation from others and individuation. Thus on logical grounds, they are more likely to make steady progress toward actualization than women because men are not very dependent on relationships with others, that is, they are operating on a level that is well-beyond the deficiency level. Instead they are concerned primarily with their own self-actualization (individuation), irrespective of the expectations and needs of others. Thus, women are placed by implication in a secondary position in terms of their personal growth and moral development in comparison to men. Women, of course, could move more readily toward self-actualization within this male-oriented, Western scheme if they adopted a masculine gender-role orientation. Alternatively, if women were part of a more communally oriented society that fostered interdependence, cooperation, affiliation, caring, and support, they would be placed in a primary position in terms of their personal growth and moral development in comparison to men. Men would be seen as healthier within an interdependent, caring, and affiliative framework only if they adopted a more feminine gender-role orientation.

Sensitivity to gender differences in therapy   These provocative, early criticisms by feminists of some traditional personality theories have changed the ways in which many therapists see and treat their male and female clients. Before these criticisms became known, some males and females suffered at the hands of some of these professionals because these therapists had focused on the negative side of the feminine role and then acted in ways that were harmful to their clients. For example, between 5% and 12% of male therapists had mirrored the general cultural view of women as inferior and exploited them sexually. These violations had a tremendous detrimental effect on these women's self-esteem. Also, some of these therapists were guilty of having a benevolent patriarchal attitude, which may have prevented them from sharing their knowledge with their female clients and allowing them to participate in the decision making about their own treatment (Philpot, Brooks, Lusterman, & Nutt, 1997, p. 16).

In regard to men, some of these therapists were insensitive to the male perspective. Men who embraced a strong, traditional masculine role generally feared self-disclosure, were less aware of their feelings, and expressed less affect (emotions and feelings) in therapy than women did. Because many therapies were based on the idea that disclosure and open expression of emotions were necessary for therapeutic progress, these therapists were likely to view the restricted emotional expressiveness of their male clients negatively and as hindrances to cure. In general, such strongly traditional males were also more likely to be intensely competitive and homophobic, and these attitudes may have interfered with their capacity to establish effective relationships with male therapists (Philot, Brooks, Lusterman, & Nutt, 1997, p. 18).

Some family therapists also were criticized by the early feminists for fostering traditional roles in therapy and for not trying to alleviate the oppression of women. Some therapists, for example, ignored the power inequities between traditional men and women in their families and tended to reinforce the status quo, thereby hampering the personal growth of both partners (Philpot, Brooks, Lusterman, & Nutt, 1997, p. 26).

On the plus side, many contemporary family therapists have responded positively to these early (and to current) feminist criticisms and have now evolved new ways of conducting therapy with clients, which involve confronting traditional gender role orientations which tend to foster unequal power and control arrangements. Clients in such relationships are now replacing them with an egalitarian outlook. Such positive change is fostered when both parties are made aware of how traditional gender role orientations cripple intimacy in their relationships. With such awareness, couples then begin to evolve beyond traditional gender roles and stereotypes by challenging gender entitlement. They start to develop new competencies that involve a process of sharing responsibilities and tasks based on mutual respect for the abilities and values of both parties. Such change results in more healthy and satisfying couple relationships (Knudson-Martin & Mahoney, 2009, pp. 63–78).

Racial/ethnic differences   Intermarriage among various racial/ethnic groups in the United States has tripled since the early 1970s (McGoldrick & Giordano, 1996, p. 19). This mixing of groups has made it difficult to assess precisely the racial backgrounds of many individuals. Given this ambiguity, some researchers prefer dropping the term race. They think that genetic isolation among racial groups has been relaxed because of inter-marriage so that it is unwise to continue acting as though one could identify pure racial groups. Still, most investigators argue that distinctions based on race should be main-tained. They maintain that it is indisputable that generations of geographic separation have given rise to racial subdivisions, traceable by different biological lineages. Thus, they believe that we can talk about racial differences based on physical appearance in a meaningful way and insist that we continue to use the term in our theorizing and research, while recognizing the problems associated with the term. For example, it is meaningful to examine the harmful impact of the negative attitudes and beliefs associ-ated with racial color and to conduct research which seeks ways to reduce or eliminate such prejudices (Rowe, Vazsonyi, & Flannery, 1994, pp. 396–397).

Ethnicity refers to shared culture and background. This common background includes language, religion, customs, and national or political identification. Ethnicity is also increasingly being used to denote all distinctions based on birth or ancestry. Since race can be linked to ancestry, that is, to birth-ascribed characteristics, many investigators see race as an important component of ethnicity, so they use the hyphenated term, racial/ethnicity, in their professional work (Bahr, Chadwick, & Stauss, 1979, pp. 4–6). Accord-ingly, we have adopted this convention.

As mentioned earlier in Chapter 6 on the topic of ethnic identity, the study of racial/ethnic differences is highly important as the country's population becomes increasingly diverse. Let's focus on the three largest racial/ethnic **minority groups**: African Americans or Blacks, Asian Americans, and Hispanics. African Americans have experienced an increase in population from nearly 35 million members in 2000 to approximately 37 million in 2008. Asian Americans increased from more than 10 million members in 2000 to 13 million members in 2008. Hispanics went from a little over 35 million according to census popula-tion estimates in 2000 to a whopping 46 million people in 2008. There were over 211 million White, majority group people in 2000, and 198 million in 2008 (World Almanac, 2010, pp. 612–650). It is estimated that by the year 2050, the representative face of Americans will still be White, but barely so. These changes will result from higher birth rates in com-munities of color and from the increasing numbers of immigrants who are people of color. Psychologists have begun to awaken to these changes and are now in the process of creating a more inclusive psychology as they seek to promote an appreciation for **multiculturalism** in our society. Along with this awakening we see a mushrooming of theory and research dealing with cultural diversity issues.

Operating from an egalitarian perspective, multiculturalists maintain that racial/ethnic minority groups are treated unfairly by the **majority group** and that change toward a more just society is needed. Minority group members are still discriminated against in many areas of their lives, for example, in education, job hiring, health care, housing, and by the criminal justice system (Derous, Nguyen, & Ryan, 2009; Roscigno, Karafin, & Tester, 2009, pp. 49–69). An emphasis on multiculturalism makes it clear that many of the differences between all groups in society, majority and minority, should be celebrated and not automatically feared and rejected. Negative stereotyping, prejudice, and discrimination toward any group, majority or minority, are rejected by individuals with a multiculturalist orientation. Instead multiculturalist individuals maintain that all people, regardless of their group status, should be treated with respect and as equals. Treatment as equals does not mean that all of these groups have ideas for solving problems in society that are equally valid. It does mean that minority voices (and majority voices as well) should be recognized, respected, heard, and accepted if their suggestions are to contribute to the solutions of problems.

Sensitivity to racial/ethnic differences in therapy   All of the personality theorists whose works are covered in the text are White. Of the theorists who practiced psychotherapy, their clients were virtually always White. Thus, their theories of psychotherapy were unduly restrictive and generally ignored the ways in which racial/ethnic differences influence client treatment and cure. Contemporary clinical and counseling psychology have begun to redress this imbalance, hoping to create more inclusive therapies that are sensitive to the various cultural life experiences of clients. While many professional therapists are sensitive to the racial/ethnic identity of their clients, the ones who are insensitive often do considerable harm (Chang & Berk, 2009, pp. 521–536). Several examples from different racial/ethnic groups provide examples of therapist insensitivity and its negative impact on the mental health of minorities.

In Native American culture, for instance, listening is valued highly. Silence may connote respect, that the client is forming his or her thoughts, or is waiting for signs that it is the right time to speak. However, long periods of silence may be highly uncomfortable for some non-Indian therapists. Such therapists may interpret silence as resistance, when they actually represent forms of communication (Sutton & Broken Nose, 1996, p. 37).

For Asians, the primary identity is collectivistic. They feel most comfortable sharing their problems with their family and friends. When they first arrive in America, many Asians experience culture shock as they encounter unfamiliar values, behaviors, and norms, resulting in anxiety and depression. Therapists with an individualistic orientation often ignore their Asian clients' ideology and do not attempt to incorporate social support networks (family and friends) into their counseling sessions. The result may be a lack of progress toward psychological health (Yeh & Inose, 2002, pp. 69–82).

For African Americans with collectivistic orientations who identify strongly with other Blacks who have suffered for centuries from racism in our country, well-meaning individualistic White therapists may make a mistake when they try to be encouraging to their clients by saying, "You're a credit to your race, if only more of your people were like you" or "I think your success shows that racism can't stop a person if he or she works hard." Such comments, meant to be flattering, might well be seen as insulting (Helms & Cook, 1999, p. 137). Therapists should work hard to explore their own feelings about their own race, as well as their feelings about other people's racial heritage and experiences as a means of becoming more comfortable interacting with patients who have backgrounds different from their own (Adams, 2000, p. 51).

Misunderstandings also can arise based on the normative distancing behaviors of clients and therapists. For example, Hispanics tend to converse and feel comfortable at much closer distances than do Whites. Thus, if White therapists step back or away from their Hispanic clients, the clients may interpret their therapists' behavior as being cold, aloof, or not wanting to communicate. Therapists, on the other hand, may interpret their clients' closeness as being inappropriately intimate (Gonzalez, 1995, p. 702).

Finally, other misunderstandings can hinder the personal growth of clients. For example, Puerto Rican women are taught to lower their eyes and to avoid eye contact, which some White therapists may interpret as an inability to relate interpersonally. Irish families may not give affection or praise to their children during a family counseling session for fear of giving them a "swelled head," which some therapists may misinterpret as a lack of caring (McGoldrick & Giordano, 1996, pp. 1–27).

Religious differences   More and more personality psychologists are beginning to take an active interest in the role played by religious factors in personality development and functioning. Like Jung, they believe that the psychologically healthy life is more than the accumulation of material goods. Moreover, they think that it is crucial to address questions of ultimate concern and purpose embodied by religiosity and spirituality if we are ever to achieve an understanding of the person's attempts to resolve his or her conflicts and achieve mental health.

Thus, they think there is a need to incorporate and study people's religiosity if we are ever going to arrive at a fuller understanding of human personality. This surge in interest runs contrary to the negative attitudes that many psychologists have shown toward religion throughout the history of the discipline. (Delaney, Miller, & Bisono, 2007, p. 538; Sedikides, 2010, p. 3).

There are two major reasons for this antipathy on the part of many psychologists. First, religion is seen by many of them as unscientific. Its study is dotted with concepts that empirically oriented psychologists find hopelessly unscientific, for example, God, the devil, angels, heaven and hell, soul, salvation. Second, psychologists who are non-believers often see psychologists who are believers as biased in their theoretical and research orientations. (Incidentally, believing psychologists could make the same argument about the theorizing and research of non-believing psychologists.) In any event, non-believing psychologists claim that the research findings of the believers are subjective and unreliable (Wulff, 1991, p. 33).

Theorists like Jung, Erikson, Allport, Maslow, and Rollo May disagree strongly with these negative attitudes. Instead they have argued cogently that the role of religion in personality development can be studied scientifically and objectively and that it is short-sighted to exclude it from our theories of mental health. These grand personality theorists are, in fact, right, as there is today a substantial body of scientific research involving religious issues in personality (e.g., Kay, Gaucher, McGregor, & Nash, 2010; Spilka, Hood, Hunsberger, & Gorsuch, 2003). Also, these personality theorists all agree that religion can *either* be a source of personal growth or an impediment to it. On the constructive side, they believe that religion may provide people with a set of principles, values, and beliefs that help them to cope successfully with stresses and crises. Thus, religion can be a source of comfort in times of stress and uncertainty. It also may provide individuals with a sense of dignity and worth, may foster the development of an ethical awareness and sense of personal responsibility and caring for others, and give people's lives purpose and meaning. Witness the caring for others that occurs on a daily basis in communities large and small across this country (and in many others) at countless food pantries and homeless shelters affiliated with religious organizations where the needs of people who are less fortunate are attended to and met. Or consider the many members of religious organizations in countless international communities that provided food, clothing, and medical care for the victims of massive earthquakes like those that occurred in 2011 in Japan and in 2010 in Haiti.

On the dark side, many of the grand theorists have argued that religion may enhance prejudice, discrimination, and violence against outsiders. Literal belief in religious doctrines limits choice and personal freedom and may make adherents overly dependent on more powerful forces. This possibility could limit their acceptance of personal responsibility for their actions and lead them to follow authority figures blindly (Kay et al., 2010, p. 37;

Wulff, 1991, p. 620). One major consequence of this indiscriminant conformity and zealotry is the slaughter of non-believers. Throughout history, religion has been one of the major contributing factors to conflicts that have resulted in the deaths of millions of people (e.g., the Crusades, French Wars of Religion, Islamic Conquests). This figure is mind-numbing. Tragically, such atrocities continue to occur in the world today in parts of Asia and in many countries in the Middle East, in Africa, and in the United States. Some examples include the facts that over 1.3 million Christians in the Sudan in Africa have been killed by Muslims associated with the National Islamic Front since 1989; that an estimated 10,000 Muslims and Christians in Nigeria have been killed in religious warfare; that tens of thousands of Muslims have been killed by Orthodox Christian Serbs during the Bosnian War; that thousands of Muslims and Hindus have perished in riots in India; that Christians have been persecuted and many killed by Islamic extremists in Iraq; that most suicide bomber terrorists in Iraq and Pakistan are following religious leadership; that Jews and Palestinians continue slaughtering one another at a depressing rate in the Middle East based to a large extent on differences in religious beliefs; and that thousands of civilians perished at the World Trade Center in New York City on September 11th, 2001, in a terrorist attack upon the United States by members of the Muslim Al-Qaeda organization (e.g., Jost, 1997, pp. 1011–1018; Silberman, 2005, pp. 529–530; Stone, 2008, pp. 1–118; van der Veer, 1994, p. 7).

Whether religion has positive or negative aspects to it, there is little doubt that it has effects on human personality and behavior and is worthy of being studied. Thus, many of the grand personality theorists have been a primary source of inspiration for personality psychologists who conduct research in this complicated research area. Also, perhaps it is not surprising that there is a resurgence of interest in such investigations, given the many contemporary ecological, social, political, and religious crises now confronting all of us.

While there are some inconsistent findings in the research literature, the majority of the research in this area suggests that religious beliefs are related to some aspects of mental health. **Mature religious orientations** are linked to greater positive moods and feelings, higher self-efficacy, higher self-esteem, greater life satisfaction, and greater longevity (Harris, Thoresen, McCullough, & Larson, 1999, p. 427; Saroglou, 2002, pp. 20–21). Such religious views are also correlated with lower levels of alcohol abuse, depression, criminal behavior, and suicide. Mature religiosity also is associated positively with physical health, helping to reduce high blood pressure in patients as well as the possibility of stroke and heart attack (Gartner, 1996, pp. 189–190). Possible explanations for these findings include the idea that religious teachings emphasize respect for the body as temples of God. Such teachings might well encourage believers to see physicians immediately upon detection of some illness, thereby helping to ensure receiving prompt and adequate treatment. Religious commitment may also discourage risky sexual behavior, drinking, smoking, and overeating, activities which can adversely affect health. Also, mature religious orientations may enhance the establishment of friendships, especially within the religious community. These friendships can provide patients with the social support they need to cope successfully with stress and serious illness (Koenig, 1997, pp. 53–90).

Finally, there is some evidence in the empirical literature that people who have **immature religious orientations** tend to be less psychologically healthy, that is, more authoritarian, neurotic, rigid, and prejudiced (Gartner, 1996, pp. 198–199; Saroglou, 2002, p. 21). For example, rigid adherence to religious doctrine can lead clients to cling to a patriarchal gender bias that rejects or minimizes the needs of other family members and precludes the possibility of open discussion about family planning, divorce and remarriage.

Sensitivity to religious differences in therapy

Given the fact that many therapists find religion relatively unimportant in their own lives, it is not surprising that they have typically failed to meet the needs of their religious clients (Delaney et al., 2007, pp. 538–546). Their lack of familiarity with and insensitivity to the religious needs of their clients can readily result in misunderstandings, conflicts, and resistance, thereby hindering progress toward cure. For example, members of a religious family in counseling said that their son was experiencing difficulties because he stopped attending church. As they began to explore the important role played by religion in their family, the therapist interrupted them. Instead of agreeing to explore the family's religious beliefs and how they influenced the mental health of family members, the therapist closed the door immediately, saying "We don't deal with the religious or spiritual aspects (of people's experiences).... [W]e are a mental health center and our orientation is psychological and psychiatric, not the spiritual, not the religious." The family left treatment and did not return (Boyd-Franklin, 1989, p. 88).

On the plus side, therapists who do become familiar with the religious background of their clients can often incorporate the clients' beliefs into the therapeutic process in a way that promotes personal growth. In a case study, a counselor reports seeing a middle-aged female who was seeking counseling because she was lonely and spending long periods of time crying. She was extremely afraid of social contacts, and any type of mild social criticism was devastating to her. She refused to take even mild risks to meet people and to establish relationships. She had made the assumption that it was always better to avoid pain by withdrawing from stressful situations The therapist then asked her if Jesus made the same assumption. She answered no, declaring that Jesus had taken many great risks in his lifetime to confront injustice and even chose to give up his life to save humanity. Since she loved Jesus, and he was a great risk-taker, she decided to emulate his behavior by confronting her fears and pain. Before therapy even ended, she was able to establish a romantic relationship. Although she found such a relationship initially threatening, she ventured into the relationship with the thought that ... "following Jesus means I will risk the pain of a possible rejection" (Propst, 1996, pp. 402–403).

Conclusions regarding the study of gender, racial/ethnic, and religious differences Finally, it is clear to many investigators in personality psychology and in other psychological specialty areas that there is a need to take gender, racial/ethnic, and religious differences into account in their theorizing and research.

For example, substantial changes in traditional graduate programs which train individuals to be clinical psychologists or counselors are being implemented. Such cultural diversity training is designed to familiarize these professional aspirants with the cultural backgrounds of their clients, to train them to be open to these backgrounds, and to instill in them an appreciation and respect for their clients, even if they and the clients often hold very different values and goals (Negy, 2004, p. 18). The leaders of such programs are required now to pay increased attention to multicultural issues in their training programs if they are to achieve accreditation by their primary professional organization (American Psychological Association, 2005, pp. 10–26). While only a relatively few studies in clinical psychology have focused on the therapeutic treatment of minority clients at the present time, we can expect the field to place more emphasis on meeting the needs of an increasingly diverse clientele in the future (Iwamasa, 2002, pp. 931–944). Outside of clinical psychology, we also expect that investigators in many different specialty areas within psychology (e.g., social psychology, developmental psychology) will continue making efforts to do research which incorporates the cross- and sub-cultural experiences of people.

Area 3: The Use of the Big Five Super-Traits to Increase Our Understanding of Personality

Allport's (1937) provocative theory of traits raised an important question about the number of traits required to describe human personality adequately. Within personality, traits are arranged hierarchically; those higher in the hierarchy are broader and more abstract than those lower in the hierarchy. Knowledge of the broad traits, or factors, higher in the hierarchy would help us define, organize, and understand the narrower sets of traits lower in the hierarchy that are associated with each broad factor. Such a taxonomy (structural framework) would help reduce the current confusion generated by simply compiling long lists of traits on an intuitive and unsystematic basis. It would also reduce the redundancy that results from measuring the same construct under different names (McCrae & John, 1992, p. 177). Furthermore, a generally accepted taxonomy would promote cooperative research and facilitate the communication of empirical findings among investigators by providing a standard set of trait terms (John, 1990, p. 66). Finally, a comprehensive taxonomy would assure personality psychologists that they had not inadvertently omitted consideration of an important trait in their study of some problem (McCrae & Costa, 1990, p. 32).

In their early, provocative research, Allport and Odbert (1936) took the natural language of personality description as the starting point for construction of this taxonomy. They made the reasonable assumption that the most important individual differences in human transactions will come to be encoded as single trait terms in language. Accordingly, they began by extracting all personality-relevant terms from an unabridged dictionary. The final list totaled nearly 18,000 words, of which approximately 4,500 described personality traits.

Cattell (1943) later utilized this list in his own pioneering work and eventually reduced it to 35 variables, by developing bipolar clusters of related traits. Stimulated by his innovative work, other researchers examined simplified descriptions of these traits with a variety of populations and ultimately were able to derive five relatively strong factors (Borgatta, 1964; Digman & Takemoto-Chock, 1981; Goldberg, 1981, 1990; Norman, 1963, 1967; Tupes & Christal, 1961). Goldberg (1990), for example, administered a list of 339 trait adjectives to university students and asked them to describe themselves on each trait in terms of a 9-point scale, where 1 denoted "extremely inaccurate as a self-description," 5 denoted "I'm uncertain" or "the meaning of the term is unclear," and 9 denoted "extremely accurate as a self-description." The data were then factor analyzed, and five factors emerged. These **Big Five factors**, with some of their representative traits, are listed in Table 18.1.

Do these five factors—Surgency, Agreeableness, Conscientiousness, Emotional Stability, and Intellect—represent a comprehensive taxonomy of personality traits? Unfortunately not. The basic criticisms are twofold. First, the factor analyses in the various studies designed to discover the underlying broad factors have not been based on a comprehensive list of personality traits. Goldberg acknowledges that the list used in his analysis, though more comprehensive than any previously employed, is still not quite complete (Goldberg, 1990, pp. 1217–1223). Second, researchers do not agree on the factor labels (Briggs, 1989, p. 248; John, 1989, p. 262; John & Srivastava, 1999, pp. 113–114). For example, some researchers label Factor I Extraversion rather than Surgency. A perusal of the traits associated with Factor I in Table 18.1 show clearly that some of these traits (extraverted, gregarious, sociable) are associated with extraversion, whereas others (active, energetic, vigorous) are more clearly linked to Surgency. Factor II, Agreeableness, is ambiguous because it refers both to a person's being pleasing (genial, pleasant, friendly) to others and to the tendency to agree with others (accommodating, cooperative). Factor III, Conscientiousness, has been interpreted variously as Dependability, Conformity, Prudence, Task Interest, and the Will to Achieve. Factor IV, Emotional Stability (versus Neuroticism on the negative pole) has almost universal acceptance. Finally, Factor V, Intellect, has also been labeled Culture and Openness to Experience (John, 1990, p. 95). Openness to Experience refers to a person's receptiveness to new ideas, approaches, and experiences. People who are closed to experience are not necessarily defensive, nor are they necessarily narrow-minded in the sense of being intolerant and judgmental. Rather,

TABLE 18.1   THE BIG FIVE FACTORS AND THEIR ASSOCIATED TRAITS

Factor I: Surgency

Positive Factor Pole/Cluster	**Trait Terms Included**
Gregariousness	Extraverted, gregarious, sociable
Expressiveness	Communicative, expressive, verbal
Spontaneity	Carefree, happy-go-lucky, spontaneous
Energy level	Active, energetic, vigorous
Talkativeness	Talkative, verbose, wordy
Negative Factor Pole/Cluster	
Aloofness	Seclusive, unsociable, withdrawn
Silence	Quiet, silent, untalkative
Reserve	Detached, reserved, secretive
Shyness	Bashful, shy, timid
Inhibition	Inhibited, restrained

Factor II: Agreeableness

Positive Factor Pole	
Cooperation	Accommodating, agreeable, cooperative, helpful, patient, peaceful, reasonable
Amiability	Amiable, cordial, friendly, genial, pleasant
Empathy	Considerate, kind, sympathetic, trustful, understanding
Leniency	Lenient, uncritical, undemanding
Courtesy	Courteous, diplomatic, polite, respectful, tactful
Negative Factor Pole	
Belligerence	Antagonistic, argumentative, combative, quarrelsome
Overcriticalness	Faultfinding, harsh, unforgiving, unsympathetic
Bossiness	Bossy, demanding, domineering, manipulative
Rudeness	Abusive, disrespectful, impolite, impudent, rude, scornful
Cruelty	Cruel, ruthless, vindictive

Factor III: Conscientiousness

Positive Factor Pole	
Organization	Orderly, organized, systematic
Efficiency	Concise, exacting, efficient, fastidious, self-disciplined
Dependability	Dependable, reliable, responsible
Precision	Meticulous, perfectionist, precise
Persistence	Industrious, persistent, tenacious, thorough
Negative Factor Pole	
Disorganization	Disorganized, haphazard, inefficient, scatterbrained, sloppy, unsystematic
Negligence	Careless, negligent, undependable, unconscientious, unreliable
Inconsistency	Erratic, inconsistent, unpredictable
Forgetfulness	Forgetful, absentminded
Recklessness	Foolhardy, rash, reckless

TABLE 18.1   THE BIG FIVE FACTORS AND THEIR ASSOCIATED TRAITS (CONTINUED)

Factor IV: Emotional Stability

Positive Factor Pole

Placidity	Passionless, unexcitable, unemotional
Independence	Autonomous, independent, individualistic

Negative Factor Pole

Insecurity	Defensive, fretful, insecure, negativistic, self-critical, self-pitying
Fear	Anxious, fearful, nervous
Instability	Temperamental, touchy, unstable
Emotionality	Emotional, excitable
Envy	Envious, jealous

Factor V: Intellect

Positive Factor Pole

Intellectuality	Contemplative, intellectual, introspective, meditative, philosophical
Depth	Complex, deep
Insight	Foresighted, insightful, perceptive
Intelligence	Bright, intelligent, smart
Creativity	Artistic, creative, imaginative, innovative, inventive

Negative Factor Pole

Shallowness	Shallow, unintellectual, unreflective
Unimaginativeness	Uncreative, unimaginative
Imperceptiveness	Imperceptive, unobservant
Stupidity	Dull, ignorant, unintelligent

Source: Adapted from Goldberg, L.R., "An alternative 'description of personality': The Big Five factor structure," *Journal of Personality and Social Psychology*, 59, pp. 1224–1225. Copyright © 1990 by the American Psychological Association. Used with permission from the American Psychological Association.

they are characterized by a preference for the familiar, practical, and concrete and show a lack of interest in experience for its own sake (McCrae & Costa, 1990, pp. 41–42).

There have been other problems with measures of the Big Five besides the differential interpretations of the factors. The original measures (see Table 18.1 for an example) were simply too lengthy. Scales which are too long are boring and fatiguing so that study participants either give up or resort to quick, stereotype responding in an effort to finish (John & Srivastava, 1999, p. 114). Thus, investigators have worked hard to develop briefer measures. There are now a number of shorter, yet reliable, and valid measures of the Big Five in existence, created by Goldberg (1992), John, Donahue, and Kentle (1991) and Costa and McCrae (1992).

In addition to these problems, some investigators state that there are other basic personality dimensions beyond those summarized in the Big Five factors. For example, Paunonen and Jackson (2000, pp. 828–830) reanalyzed the lexical data of English person-descriptive adjectives collected by Saucier and Goldberg (1998). Whereas Saucier and Goldberg identified only the usual Big Five super traits on the basis of their data analysis, Paunonen and Jackson identified an additional 10 factors! These ten factors consisted of (1) religiosity, (2) manipulativeness, (3) honesty, (4) sexuality, (5) frugality, (6) traditionality, (7) masculinity (femininity), (8) conceitedness, (9) humor, and (10) risk-taking.

Advocates of the five-factor model concede that there well might be more than five factors, but they maintain that some version of the Big Five factors is at least *necessary* for an adequate description of personality (McCrae & John, 1992, p. 177). Research to clarify the meaning of the five factors and to determine whether or not factors beyond the Big Five factors are needed to help describe human personality adequately is currently under way. In the meantime, convinced that, even with its limitations, the current five-factor model is an important breakthrough in the study of personality, researchers have proceeded to generate some interesting research utilizing the five basic dimensions of personality, which they now label as Extraversion, Agreeableness, Conscientiousness, Neuroticism, and Openness to Experience.

Research with the Big Five   As we all know, television plays a great role in our educational development. Although television can be a useful tool for the education and socialization of children, extensive research has shown that it often has a negative impact on them. For example, violence viewed on television is associated with subsequent aggressive behavior in children (Paik & Comstock, 1994). Also, heavy television watching by children is related in various ways to the Big Five variables in ways that suggest negative personality and behavioral effects (Persegani et al., 2002, pp. 977–990). These investigators showed that Italian schoolchildren of elementary school age who watched TV heavily (two hours or more) each day were found to be higher in Neuroticism and lower in Agreeableness, Conscientiousness, and Openness to Experience than children who watched TV for less than an hour daily. (There was no difference in the Extraversion scores of the children who hardly watched TV and those who watched 2 hours or more daily.)

The results suggested further that the lower scores on Openness to Experience by the children in the heavy TV watching category was related to lower creativity, while the lower scores on the Conscientiousness factor by this same grouping of children was associated with a deterioration in their reading abilities. These findings do not augur well for the personal and academic development of these children as they move through the educational system.

On the other hand, these research findings suggest that children who are low in Neuroticism and high in Agreeableness, Openness to Experience, and Conscientiousness will do well in their personal and academic development. For example, there are many research studies showing that the broad trait, Conscientiousness, is related positively and consistently to excellent performance in a variety of academic courses at the high school, undergraduate, and graduate school levels. The fathers and mothers of such students tend to have an authoritative parenting style which means that they are firm in their demands on their children, yet they are not overly restrictive. Such parents combine firmness of treatment with rationality and warmth (see the glossary in the Maslow chapter). They encourage their children to work hard and to take responsibility for their actions (Heaven & Ciarrochi, 2008, p. 452). As a result, conscientious students learn to be careful, thorough, responsible, achievement-oriented, diligent, and persevering, and much more self-motivated to reach their goals than students who are lower in conscientiousness. Such responsible students are capable of prioritizing and delaying gratification (studying before exams instead of partying), following classroom norms and rules, and planning and organizing for tests. Not unexpectedly, therefore, they are better adjusted to school and achieve higher grades in their courses and have higher grade point averages (GPAs) than their less conscientious classmates (Nguyen, Allen, & Fraccastoro, 2005, pp. 105–116; Noftle & Robins, 2007, pp. 116–130).

In contrast, adolescent males who are low in Conscientiousness have major adjustment problems and perform poorly in school. In particular, studies have shown that such males committed several kinds of antisocial behavior, for example, fire setting with major damage, theft of a car, driving unsafely, selling of drugs, gang fighting, and breaking and entering (Hong & Paunonen, 2009, pp. 675–696; John, Caspi, Robins, Moffitt, & Stouthamer-Loeber, 1994, pp. 160–178). Lower scores on the Conscientiousness dimension meant that such delinquents set lower standards for themselves, were not motivated to get things done, were unreliable, and did not think of the consequences of their behavior before they acted. Not only were they lower in Conscientiousness, but they were also lower in Agreeableness and Openness to Experience than adolescents who had committed no delinquent acts. The lower scores in Agreeableness meant that these delinquents were more stubborn and bossy, selfish, antagonistic, inconsiderate of the feelings of others, and manipulative. Lower scores in Openness to Experience meant that the delinquents were not very curious, creative, imaginative, or intelligent.

Newer research suggested that the Agreeableness dimension is probably the most important of the Big Five traits in predicting adjustment in school. Students who are low in Agreeableness tend to show much anger toward their peers and to act in antisocial ways (e.g., fighting, stealing, vandalizing property). They also report substance abuse (excessive alcohol use, marijuana smoking, and the use of psychedelics) and risky sexual behavior (having many sexual partners and not using condoms) (Miller, Lynam, & Jones, 2008, p. 160). Students high in Agreeableness, in contrast, have developed a personality which allows them to control their negative emotions. They work hard to suppress their anger, show a willingness to suspend their personal interests (put their own goals aside), and to work cooperatively on tasks. Agreeable people tend to like others, tend to express their liking for others openly, and, as a consequence, are well-liked. Their cheerfulness attracts people to them, and they tend to avoid the bullying and aggressiveness of other children. It's hard, even for bullies, to attack those people who like them. Agreeable students are not only better adjusted than many others in school, but they attain higher grades (Jensen-Campbell et al., 2002, pp. 224–251).

While the preceding studies concentrated on the application of the five-factor model to the adjustment and performance of adolescents in a school context, other research by D. M. Buss (1992) sought to show how the super traits in married couples were linked to various manipulation tactics used by each partner to get his or her own way when there was a dispute. D. M. Buss found that men high in Extraversion (those who were very active, energetic, talkative, wordy) used coercion tactics to get their own way during an argument; that is, such men made demands and criticized and yelled at their wives to get them to comply. Wives did not use such tactics. Both husband and wives low in Extraversion (those who were quiet, withdrawn, and shy) tended to use debasement tactics to get their own way. Specifically, such spouses reported that they lowered or devalued themselves by saying that they were not as competent or intelligent as their partner.

D. M. Buss reported further that both spouses high on Agreeableness (those who are cooperative, helpful, friendly, respectful, and considerate) or on Openness to Experience (those who are creative, imaginative, and intelligent) used two kinds of tactics: pleasure induction and reason. In other words, these spouses tried to convince their partners that they would have fun if they engaged in the contested behavior. For example, a husband might try to convince his wife to take a ride on his motorcycle by telling her that she would enjoy herself immensely. A wife might try to convince her husband to take dance lessons by telling him how much fun he would have. Spouses high in Agreeableness and in Openness to Experience and also those high in Conscientiousness (those who are self-disciplined, dependable, and responsible) also tried to use reason to get their partners to do something. They would explain to their partners why they should do it and point out all the good things that would come from it. Those spouses low in Agreeableness (those who were antagonistic, argumentative, faultfinding, domineering, and disrespectful) tended to use coercion tactics and the silent treatment; in other words, they would ignore the spouse until she or he agreed to do it.

D. M. Buss also found that spouses high in Neuroticism (those who are fearful, anxious, touchy, and unstable) used the tactics of regression and hardball. Regression tactics—sulking, pouting, and whining—were used primarily by wives. Hardball, which was used primarily by husbands, involved hitting the spouse or threatening to leave if she did not comply.

Finally, some interesting research suggests that people's personality characteristics shape the display of their own physical environments. Observers can then use such environmental information to draw inferences about the personalities of these individuals, with particular reference to the Big Five traits. In this research, observers examined the dorm rooms of students and then used the cues in the rooms to form personality impressions of them. For example, if an observer looked into a student's room and noticed that he had a snowboard and a ski pass and posters of males hang-gliding and parachuting from an airplane, he might conclude that the occupant of the room was probably high in sensation-seeking. Alternatively, if an observer noticed that a student had wall posters in her room of Luciano Pavarotti, prints by Marc Chagall and Picasso, and tickets to the local community theater to see Phantom of the Opera, she might conclude that the student was probably high in artistic appreciation.

A study by Gosling, Ko, and Mannarelli (2002, pp. 379–398) showed convincingly that student observers could examine the dorm rooms of student strangers, assess their contents, and form accurate impressions of the strangers' personalities. They found that observers who noted that various students' rooms were more neat, tidy, clean, organized, and uncluttered concluded that they were higher in Conscientiousness; and, in fact, their judgments agreed with the occupants' own assessments of their personalities, based on their scores on a measure of the Big Five traits. Specifically, the higher the observers' ratings of Conscientiousness, the higher the occupants' own scores of Conscientiousness. In addition, observers examined the rooms of other students, rated the rooms as being more or less distinctive and varied (many different kinds of books and CDs) and concluded that where the rooms were more distinctive and varied, the occupants were probably high in Openness to Experience; and they were right. Also, students whose rooms were rated as more cheery, comfortable, and colorful were judged to be higher in Agreeableness, and they were. Finally, there were no distinguishing characteristics that observers associated with the rooms of students who were high or low in Extraversion and Neuroticism, except that students higher in Extraversion lived in a house that was rated by observers as noisier (not their individual rooms) and those higher in Neuroticism had rooms that were assessed by observers as more dimly lit.

In conclusion, it is clear that the Big Five trait taxonomy within the discipline is helping to coordinate and guide research investigations that increase our understanding of personality functioning. However, the five-factor model is useful primarily for descriptive and general predictive purposes. Thus, ties to explanatory theoretical frameworks are needed. A good start has been made in this direction, because two of the three dimensions used by Eysenck in his powerful explanatory biological theory of personality— Extraversion and Neuroticism—are inherent in the five-factor model. In regard to their predictive utility, the Big Five factors are able to predict various behaviors primarily at a low level of accuracy, so they are of limited usefulness. Low predictive accuracy occurs where the traits being assessed are broad in scope (like the Big Five traits) and the behavior being predicted is very specific (Paunonen & Ashton, 2001, pp. 78–90). For example, the broad trait of Conscientiousness consists of traits that are more limited in scope like Achievement Striving, Dutifulness, and Order. Achievement striving involves working hard to achieve one's goals; Dutifulness means adhering to one's moral principles; and Order involves keeping things in their proper place. Whereas the need for Order would be strongly correlated with the neatness and organization of a student's room, the generalized trait of Conscientiousness would be only moderately correlated with neatness and organization of the room. Using the broad trait of Conscientiousness means that only one (Order) of the three specific traits that comprise it predicts neatness and organization; the other two do not, so the broad, composite measure (the three traits together) leads to poorer accuracy of prediction than just using the Order specific trait alone.

Also, the use of broad personality traits typically means that the impact of cultural and situational contexts on the expression of behavior is ignored (McAdams, 1992, pp. 342–343). Thus, while research shows that factors similar to the Big Five have been found in many Western cultures, in several Eastern cultures, including China, analyses based on language do not cleanly yield the Big Five factors (John & Srivastava, 1999, p. 106–109). Accuracy of prediction could be increased if researchers took into account the unique contributions of the language in their cross-cultural research, instead of simply assuming that the same Big Five factors are found in every culture. Also, researchers can often better understand personality functioning if they focus more on how the expression of personality traits might be modified by the demands of given situations. For example, a person high in the broad trait of aggressiveness will not behave aggressively in all situations, but rather will likely modify his expression of aggressiveness depending on the situation. He may, for example, behave aggressively when confronted by another student in school over a disputed seat in the high school cafeteria at lunchtime, but not when attending a Sunday service at his church or eating dinner with his family during the Christmas holidays (Thorne, 1989, p. 149; Wright & Mischel, 1987, p. 1175).

Area 4: The Role of Positive Psychology in Promoting Strengths and Virtues in Personality

A little more than a decade ago, Seligman and Csikszentmihalyi (2000, pp. 5–14) sought to encourage psychologists to implement a "positive psychology" which would be designed to help all of humankind. They maintained that such a psychology would be a science of positive emotions, positive individual traits, and positive institutions that would attempt to improve the quality of life for everyone. It would be a science that seeks to promote human strengths and virtues. These human strengths would include, for example, courage, humility, gratitude, loyalty, altruism, compassion, hope, social responsibility, politeness, forgiveness, and self-control. Seligman and Csikszentmihalyi stated further that psychology can play a significant role in our personal lives by articulating a vision of the good life that is empirically grounded, while being understandable and attractive. It can show what actions lead to greater happiness and well-being, to more virtuous and creative human beings, and to thriving communities. According to these investigators, psychologists should be able to show, through their research, the kinds of families in which children flourish, what work settings support the greatest satisfactions in workers, what political policies result in the best communities, and how people's lives can be most worth living, for example, how they can be encouraged to be more loyal, courageous, generous, altruistic, compassionate, hopeful, polite, and forgiving.

Seligman and Csikszentmihalyi maintained in their original argument that such a development is long overdue. They believed strongly that psychology has been preoccupied during much of its history with understanding weaknesses, deficiencies, pathology, and damage in human beings. Think about Freud's focus in therapy on understanding repressed unpleasant memories, unresolved Oedipal complexes, and traumatic sexual experiences. Or recall Cattell's therapeutic focus on identifying the pathological traits of neurotics and psychotics before implementing treatment and measuring reductive changes in these traits over the course of therapy to demonstrate that the therapy has been effective. Seligman and Csikszentmihalyi maintained that this preoccupation with pathology is too one-sided. They believed that clinical treatments are not just about fixing what is broken. It is not only about counseling people who are depressed or violent to correct their weaknesses. While these treatments may be very helpful, they do not focus enough on encouraging people to be virtuous, happy, joyful, optimistic, and creative. What was needed, according to Seligman and Csikszentmihalyi, was more research by psychologists which shows how social environments and institutions that nurture friendship, caring, and empathy can be developed to prevent pathological disorders in the first place.

But haven't humanistic psychologists like Rogers, Maslow, and May made the same arguments as Seligman and Csikszentmihalyi? Of course they have. Maslow, for example, maintained that humanistic psychology was an attempt to add to and supplement viewpoints like Freud's that focused primarily on the pathological. Maslow's humanistic position emphasized instead the need to study empirically in a replicable, cumulative, and objective way the psychological health and creativity of people and to help give all of them more possibilities for controlling and improving their lives and making them better people (Maslow, 1968, p. 5).

Seligman and Csikszentmihalyi have acknowledged the many significant contributions of the humanistic psychologists to the positive psychology viewpoint they are espousing. But they have maintained that the humanistic psychology movement has never been accepted by academic psychologists as part of mainstream academic psychology because leaders subsequent to Maslow and Rogers in the humanistic psychology movement emphasized far too often research that was often not replicable, cumulative, objective, and empirical.

Some humanistic psychologists have taken strong offense at the statements of Seligman and Csikszentmihalyi, maintaining that humanistic psychology does have a strong, replicable, cumulative, objective, and empirical base. They note that the *Journal of Humanistic Psychology* has published over 100 research articles on a variety of topics and that considerable research has been done and continues to be done on humanistic therapies in high quality, clinical psychology journals (Bohart & Greening, 2001, pp. 81–82).

Although Seligman and Csikszentmihalyi's words were probably ill-chosen, their next argument was more telling. They maintained that humanistic psychology has never been part of the academic mainstream in psychology, and that this fact has made it very difficult for the humanistic movement to make much progress in understanding the best in human personality and behavior. In the academic mainstream in psychology, research by faculty and students is rewarded with grants, prizes, supportive colleagues, and jobs. Such rewards increase greatly the number of people willing to do research that identifies the phenomena of daily living that are worthwhile, the social and cultural conditions that make their occurrence more probable, leading the discipline to expand and grow. They maintained that the net result of doing such research by mainstream academic psychologists would be the generation of much more new knowledge that improves the quality of life for everyone. So, Seligman and Csikszentmihalyi argued that the new term, "positive psychology," is needed to usher in a movement that is more in line with mainstream academic psychology and that has the infrastructure (grants, prizes, supportive colleagues, and jobs) to encourage its growth. In their view, positive psychology does not replace humanistic psychology but is a supplement to and an extension of it (Seligman, 2002, pp. 266–267).

In the five years since Seligman and Csikszentmihalyi made their original plea for the implementation of a positive psychology, the discipline has emerged and begun to flourish (Seligman, Steen, Park, & Peterson, 2005, pp. 410–421). There is evidence that, although positive psychology is a relatively new area, some students are being attracted to graduate work in psychology in the positive psychology specialty area, grants are being offered, and scientific conferences in the area are being held, and more and more mainstream researchers are doing research under its umbrella. Intriguing studies on human strengths by researchers in positive psychology have been conducted and more are forthcoming. Let us examine some of the theorizing and research on just two of these strengths: forgiveness and self-control.

The strength of forgiveness   Positive psychologists believe that forgiveness in human beings generally has a beneficial impact on people's behaviors and performances. Forgiveness is a human strength which is defined as a letting go of anger, hostility, and resentment, as well as thoughts of revenge, against a wrongdoer. Forgiveness does not mean that the injured party must reconcile with the harmdoer. It does not mean that he or she must forget or condone what the harmdoer did. It does not mean excusing the harmdoer's behavior (Luskin, 2002, pp. 68–76). Rather, forgiveness is about the injured party making a choice to take back control of his or her life, to stop dwelling on the painful past, and to start acting in an alternative and constructive manner in order to become more mentally and physically healthy. As you undoubtedly know, it is very difficult to forgive someone who has harmed you, and for most people forgiveness is a long and painful process; and unfortunately because of the seriousness of the trauma that some people experience, they may never recover completely. Such individuals should not be seen as inadequate or as "failures" because their level of forgiveness does not reach an ideal state. Instead many researchers think they deserve credit for trying to overcome the injury. Researchers maintain that it is important that people make the best effort they can to forgive those who have injured them because there is now mounting research evidence that people who are more forgiving experience physical and psychological benefits (Bono, McCullough, & Root, 2008, pp. 182–195).

For example, adult patients who were more forgiving had fewer physical illness symptoms, used less medication, slept better, and had less fatigue and few of death than patients who were less forgiving (cf. Recine, A., Werner, & Recine, L., 2009, pp. 115–123). Also, college students who reported greater tendencies to forgive others who had harmed them were found to have less vengeful rumination, depression, anger, and hostility and increases in self-esteem, empathy, hope, and higher levels of life satisfaction than students who were less forgiving (Berry, Worthington, O'Connor, Pattott, & Wade, 2005, p. 183; Brown & Phillips, 2005, pp. 627–638; Kachadourian, Fincham, & Davila, 2004, p. 373). Finally, Harrar (2002, pp. 38–39) asked people to relive a bad experience with a wrongdoer who they still had not forgiven. In reliving the experience they expressed considerable anger as they told the experimenter about the grudge they still felt against him. These individuals had heart rates and blood pressure levels that were two and a half times higher than the levels experienced by other study participants who relived similar experiences but had forgiven the wrongdoer.

A lack of forgiveness also has negative consequences for the mental health of individuals. For example, many college students are wronged by their romantic partners. Transgressions include infidelity, date rape, hitting, verbal abuse, and arbitrary breaking-up of the relationship. As a result, many of the wronged individuals feel anger and hostility toward the wrongdoer. While anger can have immediate adaptive consequences, such as helping victims disengage from such relationships and enhancing feelings of control, in the long-term the continuation of these negative feelings and emotions can take a devastating toll on the mental health of the injured party. Rye and Pargament (2002, pp. 419–441) assigned college students who had broken up with their romantic partners to either a forgiveness intervention condition or to a control condition in which no forgiveness intervention had occurred. Participants in the forgiveness condition were encouraged by group discussion leaders to share their feelings of anger and hostility toward their ex-partners and to discuss how their feelings were preventing them from getting on with their lives. For example, some students reported pessimistically that they would never be able to trust another man (woman) again and would never be able to start a new relationship. They were also asked to discuss events in their own lives in which they had hurt others in the hopes of providing them with greater understanding of the failings of all individuals, including the wrongdoer. Participants also were given support by the other group members throughout several, one-hour sessions, and eventually were encouraged to let go of their pain and bitterness. The participants in the no-forgiveness condition did not participate in a discussion group. The results indicated that students in the forgiveness condition showed significant reductions in anger, hostility, and resentment and increases in forgiveness of the wrongdoer and hopefulness for the future as a result of undergoing the discussion process, whereas the participants in the no-forgiveness condition remained angry, hostile, and depressed, and pessimistic about the future.

Finally, while forgiveness tends to facilitate psychological and physical well-being, researchers are becoming aware that forgiveness may not be universally a positive thing. For example, research indicates that people who are more willing to forgive their partners are also more likely to stay in the abusive relationship (McCullough, 2000, p. 51). This decision can have devastating consequences. Recent research by McNulty (2011, pp. 770–783) shows that individuals who forgive their spouses repeatedly for their transgressions (e.g., verbal and physical abuse) and stay in the relationship leads their transgressors to feel free to offend again because there are no known consequences for his or her harmful actions. It is, therefore, critical for therapists to stress the point with abused clients that forgiveness does not mean that the injured party who forgives must remain in the abusive relationship. Forgiveness, as mentioned earlier, is a choice that people make to regain some control over their lives and to increase their feelings of calm and happiness. Thus, forgiveness may result in the injured party leaving a relationship where abuse occurs continually and seeking other avenues for living that are more healthy. In general, forgiveness can have positive consequences for the individual and for society as it can reduce personal pain and bitterness and increase social cohesion.

The strength of self-control   Another human strength that is increasingly being studied by personality psychologists who embrace positive psychology, as well as by psychologists in other specialty areas, is self-control. Many of the current professionals who work in this area were inspired by the work of Bandura (1977; 1986). Self-control refers to people's ability to alter their own cognitive processes, feelings, and behavior to achieve healthier functioning. It frees individuals from being driven by external stimuli and automatic, impulsive, or instinctual processes.

The origins of individual differences in self-control have been traced by researchers to childhood. In particular, parents and other caregivers are largely responsible for whether or not children learn how to regulate their emotions and behavior. There are three parenting styles that have been identified: authoritative, permissive, and authoritarian (Baumrind, 1991, pp. 746–758). Parents who maintain moderate control over their children's behavior, set limits for them, were nurturing (warm and encouraging), and used positive reinforcement more than punishment were classified as authoritative. Those who exercise extreme control, were highly restrictive and punishing, and show little affection and support were classified as authoritarian. Finally, permissive parents make few demands on their children, set few limits, and provide little supervision. Children of authoritarian and permissive parents tend to lack self-control and do not learn how to control their impulses. They tend to show more antisocial behavior and poorer academic behavior. Children of authoritative parents, in stark contrast, learn to delay gratification of their needs, show better problem-solving skills, better academic performance, better peer relations, and less antisocial behavior (Chipman, Olsen, Klein, Hart, & Robinson, 2000, pp. 5–11). Researchers in this area conclude that parents should regard the inculcation of self-control as the premier goal in child-rearing, (Baumeister, Heatherton, & Tice, 1994, p. 259).

There is also research on self-control using adolescents and young adults as study participants and this work shows the many benefits of having self-control skills and the negative consequences of lacking these skills. For example, university students with high levels of self-control have fewer drinking problems and, for females in particular, fewer problems with binging and purging. A recent study shows further that adolescents with higher levels of self-control are less willing to use cigarettes and alcohol after watching favorite actors in movies do so than are adolescents with low self-control (Wills et al., 2010, pp. 539–549). High self-control people also have more harmonious personal relationships, refraining from saying rude and inappropriate things to others on impulse (DeBono, Shmueli, & Muraven, 2011, pp. 136–146). They also are better able to resist angry outbursts and even aggressive behavior when offended by others. They also have an ability to move beyond interpersonal slights by forgiving others, in comparison to those with low self-control. In terms of their academic performance, high self-control students were able to achieve higher grades because they were better able to get tasks done on time (e.g., term papers, reading assignments) and to use their study time more effectively, thereby preventing leisure activities from interfering with their academic work (Tangney, Baumeister, & Boone, 2004, pp. 271–322).

A lack of self-control also results in major problems, not only among university students, but among members of the general population as well (e.g., alcoholism, other drug addictions, physical assaults, and other acts of violence). Adolescents and adults in the general population who lack self-control may act impulsively, lashing out at others when they are frustrated (cf. Stucke & Baumeister, 2006, pp. 1–13). Teens and adults who experience major stressors in their lives may become addicted to cigarettes, alcohol, and other drugs. People who lack the discipline to exercise may eat to relieve boredom or to make themselves feel temporarily happy. Many of these underdisciplined people practically live at the malls, and shop and impulsively buy things ("I just had to have it") they don't need and can't afford. Such behavior may be amusing to some people, but it ceases to be fun when monies are no longer available and such individuals engage in credit card fraud ("Used someone else's credit card without their permission") and/or in shoplifting (Holtfreter, Reisig, Piquero, N., & Piquero, A., 2010, pp. 188–203).

Studies in this research literature show that there are three causes for such self-control failure (cf. Baumeister et al., 1994, pp. 3–34). First, people who are unclear about the goals or standards they are pursuing are more likely to experience control failures. For example, overweight people are less likely to be successful if they pursue the vague goal of "trying to lose some weight" than if they are trying to attain a more specific goal of "losing 20 pounds." Second, when people pursue conflicting goals and standards, the result is more likely to be indecisiveness, muddled responses, rumination about the proper course of action, and a failure at self-management. For example, a student who "loves partying," but who also wants to "excel academically" may experience conflict on a night when his friends want to party, but he has an exam the next day and knows that he must study most of the night so that he can earn a high grade. Failure at self-control is more likely in such a situation than it would be if the student had only one over-riding and clear goal and that was to be an "excellent student."

A second cause for lack of control is the failure to keep track of (monitor) of one's own behavior. For self-control efforts to succeed, people must set clear goals or standards and then frequently evaluate themselves against the relevant standards to see how well they are measuring up. For example, students who decide that it is desirable to "get some exercise" would probably not get as many health benefits from jogging as those who decide to "jog 45 minutes a day" and then check a stop-watch to determine when the 45 minutes was up. Better yet, they could record their performance times in a log book so they would have a clear idea of the number of days in the week they have run and the amount of time they have spent exercising each day. Thus, people can generally benefit themselves greatly if they watch what they're doing. Increases in monitoring often result in increases in self-control in a variety of areas, for example, eating, drinking, spending money, studying, or exercising. In contrast, decreases in monitoring produce lapses in self-control. For example, when people drink heavily, they tend to stop monitoring their behavior. Drunken people find it difficult to keep track of their spending, exercising, smoking, paying their bills, and even their drinking behavior itself (Baumeister & Mick, 2002, pp. 670–676).

The third cause of lack of control is strength failure. In an important sense, self-regulation or self-control is a contest between the power of impulses against the power of the self-regulatory mechanism to interrupt and prevent the impulsive response (Baumeister et al., 1994, pp. 17–20). Thus, it takes effort to initiate and maintain self-control. Like a muscle, making such efforts results in fatigue. Experiencing stressors like preparing for final examinations, breaking up a relationship, trying to meet mounting bills and/or changing cars or apartments can all work to deplete the amount of energy people have to exercise self-control. Accordingly, people's capacity for self-regulation needs to be managed like any other limited resource. For example, it might be better to try and exercise self-control during times when most major pressures are off. For instance, it will probably be easier to quit smoking during summer vacation when all the pressures directly related to school are over rather than during the school year, especially around exam time.

In conclusion, high self-control contributes greatly to the diversity and flexibility of human behavior and has strong implications for successful and healthy functioning of individuals in society (Muraven, Baumeister, & Tice, 1999, pp. 446–457).

Area 5: Increasing Understanding of Personality Differences Through Analyses of Internet Use

The number of Internet users has exploded—approximately 1.1 billion people worldwide now make frequent use of the medium (Internet World Stats, 2007). In America, 75% of adults report they are on online, and an even more whopping percentage (93%) of adolescents use the Internet (Correa, Hinsley, & Gil de Zuniga, 2010, pp. 247–253). Thus, the majority of Americans are making use of this wondrous technology, and most of them use it appropriately and moderately. They use it as a learning tool, drawing upon the vast amounts of information on it on countless topics. They also use it for social networking purposes (Facebook, MySpace, Twitter). Recently, we have seen the stupendous power of these social networking sites to mobilize and organize protests against corrupt dictators in North Africa which, in turn, have led to the toppling of regimes in Tunisia, Egypt, and Libya. On a less political note, social network sites are used to form friendships, to communicate with people locally, nationally, and even internationally, to chat with friends and virtual friends, to receive and give emotional support to others, to play games, to seek information about health, and for a host of other reasons. Furthermore, research has indicated that some of these networking sites that are primarily aimed at young people can be used by instructors to help them clarify and improve their critical thinking skills through discussions in chat rooms, thereby making them less prejudiced toward members of other racial and ethnic groups (Tynes, 2007, pp. 575–584).

But the Internet also has a dark side. Hackers can and do invade people's privacy by lifting information from their Facebook and Twitter accounts and then use it to steal their identities. The result has been the misappropriated use of the victims' credit and debit cards.

In addition, many students (and nonstudents) use the Internet excessively and inappropriately. Researchers have labeled the phenomenon **Internet addiction** and say that people caught up in it tend to report less likelihood of engaging in health-promoting activities such as exercising and seeking medical care when ill, suffer disruptions in their sleep patterns, nervousness, and obsessive thinking about what is happening on the Net. This can result in heavy users being overweight and can lead to depression, impairments of a person's academic and/or work productivity, and deterioration of their family life, and personal and love relationships (Armstrong, Phillips, & Saling, 2000, pp. 537–550; Cheng & Peng, 2008, pp. 467–469; Kim et al., 2010, pp. 215–220).

Potentially destructive behaviors also can be reinforced quickly online. Although most websites are clearly opposed to the adoption of the psychologically harmful behaviors about to be discussed, there are nevertheless *some* websites that do encourage their adoption. For example, these potentially destructive sites encourage people with radical political views to make bombs ("We can teach you how to make a bomb in five easy steps"). Other sites teach suicidal people how to accomplish their goal ("Here are some fun and interesting ways to kill yourself"). Women with perpetual concerns about their body image are encouraged by people at certain websites to believe that their extreme, compulsive dieting is a voluntary and healthy act ("**Anorexia** is not a disorder, but rather a lifestyle choice"). People with gambling proclivities are encouraged to believe that such activities are fun and harmless ("Make lots of money and have an exciting time by joining our online casino club"). People with desires to binge drink are told at these sites to view their excessive drinking as harmless fun ("Drinking beer and whiskey shots until the room begins to swim and my legs seem to be on backwards is great fun. In the morning I love chatting with my friends about our wild behavior the night before"). And finally, some sites seek to encourage individuals with **self-cutting** desires to injure themselves by slicing themselves with knives or other sharp objects ("I love cutting myself; it takes away my pain." "I also like to show-off my scars to my friends.").

Personality psychology researchers have begun to do studies on the role of personality differences as they relate differentially to Internet use. This research depends heavily on the pioneering work of theorists of many of the grand theorists. At this point, let us sample some of the ways in which people with different personality characteristics use the Internet and its impact on them.

Internals versus externals   In Rotter's view, internals are individuals who believe that events are under their control, whereas externals are people who believe that events are controlled by outside forces, such as luck, fate, God, or powerful others. In terms of Internet addiction, research by Chak and Leung (2004, pp. 559–570) has shown that internals are less addicted to the Internet than externals. Internals believed that they had control over their Internet use and could cut back or stop their participation at will. As a result, internals did not have the withdrawal symptoms associated with Internet addiction, that is, fatigue, irritability, and depression. They continued to maintain their relationships with male and female peers and to perform well academically and/or occupationally. Externals, in contrast, believed that they were not in control of their Internet use so they often stayed online longer than they intended. Thus, they experienced fatigue, irritability, and moodiness when they finally did withdraw each day, which then jeopardized their real-life relationships with their peers and their academic and/or job performances.

Since externals are more compulsive about Internet use than internals, we would expect externals to log-on to the Internet even in situations when it is inappropriate to do so, for example, when they are at work. In addition to their impulsive and indiscriminant tendencies to use the Internet, Blanchard and Henle (2008, pp. 1067–1084) argued that externals also would engage in such inappropriate behavior at work because they believe that what they do or what happens to them in any situation including work is beyond their control and is a chance occurrence. If they slacked off at work by using the Internet and got caught by their employers, they would claim it was simply bad luck and if they slacked off and did not get caught, it was simply good luck. Internals, in contrast, believed that their behavior was under their own control and that they were responsible for their behavior and had to live with the consequences of their actions. Thus, these investigators predicted that externals would act more irresponsibly by engaging in more **cyber loafing** on the job than internals. Some cyber loafing is minor, for example, sending and receiving personal e-mail and/or making personal phone calls using company phones while on the job and some slacking off is major, for example, online shopping, online gambling, visiting pornographic sites. All of these activities cost the employers money through decreases in productivity. Also, some of these activities can subject the employers to legal action (e.g., when employees download music without paying music publishers or when they send threatening mail to others). The data indicated that external university students who were employed while attending school did engage in more minor and major cyber loafing than internals.

Finally, Blanchard and Henle argued that to decrease such slacking off in their employees, supervisors should not simply post organizational policies in the work place. Such a procedure would not work with external employees because they remain convinced that getting caught is random. Instead, supervisors should post policies along with a set of enforcement mechanisms. Employees should be informed that employers have installed software to monitor e-mail and Internet activities and that any violations of company policies would then be followed up by disciplinary actions, thereby showing employees that getting caught is not random and has real consequences.

Introverts versus extraverts   In Eysenck's view, introverts are individuals who are reserved, quiet, and submissive, whereas extraverts are those who are cheerful, sociable, and active. Valkenburg, Schouten, and Peter (2005, pp. 383–402) found that older introverted Dutch adolescent students used the Internet more heavily than extraverted students to experiment with their emerging identities. Introverts have more trouble in forming friendships in real-life situations so online interactions provide a more anonymous environment where they can find out how others react to them. It also offers a safe environment to overcome the shyness they often feel. While such a strategy provides an environment that is more comfortable and disinhibiting and thus helps them to clarify and hone their identities, Mottram and Fleming (2009, pp. 319–321) have found that unfortunately introverts more than extraverts may become addicted to its use with many negative consequences. For example, the long hours they spend on the Internet daily can interfere with their sleep patterns. They also experience feelings of irritability when they are unable to access the Internet when they wish. These facts can lead to depressive feelings and eventually to impairments in their academic performances and in their personal and love relationships (Armstrong et al., 2000, pp. 537–550; Cheng & Peng, 2008, pp. 467–469).

Nonneurotics versus neurotics   The construct of neurosis has a long history in personality psychology starting with Freud and the neo-Freudians, progressing through humanistic/existentialist theorists like Maslow and Rollo May, and culminating in the work of trait theorists like Cattell and Eysenck. Nonneurotics are emotionally stable individuals who are secure, calm, unfearful, and nondefensive, whereas neurotics are emotionally unstable individuals who are highly anxious, insecure, temperamental, insecure, and defensive.

In terms of academic performance, research has shown that neurotic students tend to have poorer academic performance than nonneurotic students. This lower performance is explained as being caused by their high fear of failure and their continual worrying prior to exams and their feeling of being pressured during exams (cf. Kappe & van der Flier, 2010, pp. 142–145). Given their poor academic performance, it should not be surprising that recent research by Karim, Zamuri, and Nor (2009, pp. 86–93) shows that students higher in neuroticism are more likely to use the Internet to resort to plagiarism. More specifically, these researchers report that neurotics more than nonneurotics use the Internet to (1) copy others' work to meet a classroom deadline without the authors' permission; and (2) use other people's complete works for personal assignments without acknowledging the author(s).

There are also some interesting findings for neurotics and nonneurotics in regard to their use of the Internet for social networking and for leisure and entertainment purposes (Amichai-Hamburger, 2002, pp. 1–10; Amichai-Hamburger & Ben-Artzi, 2003, pp. 71–80; Guadagno, Okdie, & Eno, 2008, pp. 1993–2004). These studies have shown that neurotic men more than neurotic women tend to use the Internet for leisure and entertainment purposes (e.g., playing games, visiting pornographic sites). Neurotic women, but not neurotic men, engage primarily in a variety of social networking activities on the Internet (e.g., chat rooms, discussion groups, e-mailing, blogging). Blogging is one of the newest forms of self-presentation and self-expression on the Internet and many neurotic women, but not neurotic men, use it to assuage their loneliness. They discuss personal relationships, daily experiences, and their own personalities. In using **blogs**, many women higher in neuroticism than those lower in neuroticism discuss very revealing personal information and often display personal photos, sometimes in provocative poses. While the Internet does often afford people relative anonymity, many times neurotic women bloggers give identifying personal information. For example, in a study by Guadagno et al. (2008, pp. 1993–2004), the majority of women bloggers used their real names in their blogs. It is possible that such information could be used by unscrupulous people in unwanted ways. For example, such people could try to extort money from these women by threatening to post their photos on other websites for millions of strangers to see.

The Future of Personality Psychology

In conclusion, personality psychology is currently a thriving and exciting discipline. Much of its foundation continues to rest on the wisdom embedded in many of the current grand theories of personality. Personality psychology also has borrowed knowledge, principles, and procedures from other disciplines within psychology, including cognitive psychology, social psychology, developmental psychology, clinical psychology, and biological psychology. By drawing on these sources, personality psychologists have gained a much-needed infusion of energy and enthusiasm and have expanded the range of ideas, issues, and phenomena that they study. This expansion has created many challenges for personality psychologists in their quest for a fuller understanding of personality development and functioning. For example, most researchers in personality psychology use primarily self-report data to study personality because it is convenient and economical.

Most of this self-report data is collected from university student samples. While the data collected using such a procedure are very valuable, the method is nevertheless limited because the sample population is restricted and the self-report technique is not always trustworthy. Participants do not always describe themselves or their relationships with others accurately. There is a need to use other actual life-outcome techniques to gather individual difference data (e.g., health records, job performance evaluations, criminal records, peer reports, **life story techniques**, diaries, and direct behavioral observations) to supplement self-report data. These methods will help personality psychologists know better what people actually do, think, or feel in various situations in their lives (Funder, 2001, p. 213). Personality psychologists have begun to tackle this challenge as they use life-outcome techniques to obtain a broader and more valid understanding of human personality (McAdams, 2001).

In addition, the most exciting development in this area in the last decade or so involves the use of the Internet as a research instrument. This amazing technological tool provides easy access to and the collection of data from large groups of people nationally and internationally from a variety of ages and diverse cultural backgrounds (Suarez-Balcazar, Balcazar, & Taylor-Ritzler, 2009, pp. 96–104).

Within this framework, personality psychologists are using a variety of data collection techniques ranging from self-reports to life-outcome techniques to increase our understanding of personality development and functioning. Given the many exciting conceptual and methodological developments and tremendous research activity in the discipline in the past few years, the future of personality psychology in the 21st century looks promising indeed.

CRITICAL THINKING QUESTIONS

1. Do you agree or disagree with the evolutionary viewpoint that females prefer males as mates who are a few years older than themselves, whereas males prefer females as mates who are younger than themselves? State the reasons for your agreement or disagreement.

2. In your opinion, why is it so important for therapists to be aware of and knowledgeable about the racial/ethnic and religious backgrounds of their clients in treating them? On a related note, why is it important for you to be aware of and knowledgeable about the racial/ethnic and religious backgrounds of other people?

3. What are the strengths and weaknesses of utilizing the Big Five model for theorizing and research? Can you think of any other traits that have been overlooked by psychologists who have adopted the Big Five taxonomy? Why are they important to incorporate into this taxonomy?

4. Why do many psychologists call the "positive psychology" approach to the study of personality uplifting and liberating? Since virtues are ideals, which ones (e.g., patience, honesty, politeness, generosity, forgiveness) do you think you need to work at strengthening in your own personality? Why?

5. In thinking about your own personal use of the Internet, what kind of impact has it had on your own life? Give concrete examples of its benefits and costs to you.

GLOSSARY

anorexia   Eating disorder in which there is an intense fear of gaining weight or becoming fat, even though such individuals are underweight, coupled with a denial of the implications of their current low body weight for their physical health and survival.

behavioral genetics   Scientific discipline that seeks to document the relative influences of heredity and environment on behavioral differences observed among individuals. It includes quantitative genetics (twin, adoption, and family studies) and molecular genetics (DNA studies).

Big Five factors   Five major, broad dimensions of personality which have been derived largely from analyses of the language people use to describe themselves and others.

blogs   Regularly updated and personalized web pages that allow people to express themselves on a variety of topics and issues.

cyber loafing   Employees' non-work related use of company-provided e-mail, mobile cell phones, and the Internet while working.

differential parental investment hypothesis   From an evolutionary perspective, the conjecture that males and females will employ different mating strategies because of their differential investments in parenting.

DNA   Genetic material whose sequencing specifies how and when to build proteins, the essential constituents of all living cells.

evolutionary theory   A theory that seeks to understand the development of human behavioral tendencies by focusing primarily on our animal heritage.

grand theories of personality   Theories that cover a broad range of phenomena and seek to explain virtually all individual differences in behavior.

healthy dependence   A manifestation of dependence that occurs in some contexts but not others and in ways that are situationally appropriate.

Human Genome Project   An international scientific effort to map all of the genes in the human body and to understand how and when genes at the DNA level code for sequences of amino acids that form the thousands of proteins that are the building blocks of human life. Eventually, it is hoped that this massive effort will help us understand the genetic basis of physical diseases and mental disorders so scientists can work more effectively to reduce and eliminate them. The additional hope is that this effort will help us gain greater insights into human evolution and behavior.

immature religious orientations   The use of religion as a means to an end. People with such orientations use religion primarily for self-serving purposes which include the enhancement of their own comfort and status.

interactional temperament model   The theory that temperament (traits) and environment affect each other.

Internet addiction   Preoccupation with the Internet (i.e., thoughts about previous online activities or anticipation of next online session). Increasing amount of time spent on Internet. Repeated efforts to control, cut back, or stop using the Internet which results in feelings of restlessness, irritability, or depression when unsuccessful. Persistent and indiscriminant use of Internet to escape from problems.

life story techniques   Attempts to understand the lives of individuals by analyzing the life narratives they create to help them make sense of their lives, to give themselves a sense of identity, and a purpose and direction for their lives.

mature religious orientations   The use of religion as an end in itself. People with such orientations do not bargain with God or use God to satisfy their own selfish motives. Rather they embrace a set of religious beliefs and use them to organize and guide their lives.

multiculturalism   Perspective that values the diverse experiences that people develop and maintain based on their racial, ethnic, gender, sexual orientation, religious, and social class identities. Personality psychology researchers attempt to examine and understand the impact of these diverse cultural and sub-cultural identities on human personality development and functioning.

majority group   The most dominant and powerful group in a society whose members typically enjoy more privilege and advantages than members of minority groups.

minority groups   Stigmatized groups of people who face negative stereotyping, prejudice, and discrimination by members of the larger society because of their physical or cultural characteristics.

molecular genetics   The field of biology which studies the structure and functions of genes at a molecular level. Findings in this discipline may directly impact theorizing and research in personality psychology.

quantitative genetics   The study of the individual variations in traits through procedures that allow for the assessment of the relative contributions of genetic and environmental factors.

self-cutting   Maladaptive technique in which individuals cut themselves to experience short-term relief from a host of strongly negative feelings, including anxiety, hostility, and anger. The behavior often provides a temporary sense of control, reaffirms the presence of one's body and identity, and converts unbearable emotional pain into manageable physical pain.

temperament   Biologically based individual differences that influence children's unique behavioral styles and the ways in which they experience and react to the environment.

SUGGESTED READINGS

Boyle, G. J., Matthews, G. & Saklofske, D. H. (Eds.) (2008). *The Sage Handbook of Personality Theory and Assessment. Vol. 1 Personality Theories and Models. Vol 2. Personality Measurement and Testing.* Thousand Oaks, CA. Sage Publications, Inc.

Seligman, M. E. P. (2011). *Flourish: A visionary new understanding of happiness and well-being.* New York: Free Press.

References

Abraham, A., Windmann, S., Daum, I., & Gunturkun, O. (2005). Conceptual expansion and creative imagery as a function of psychoticism. *Consciousness and Cognition, 14*, 520–534.

Abramowitz, C. V., Abramowitz, S. I., Roback, H. B., & Jackson, C. (1974). Differential effectiveness of directive and nondirective group therapies as a function of client internal-external control. *Journal of Consulting and Clinical Psychology, 42*, 84–853.

Abzug, R. H. (1996). Rollo May as friend to man. *Journal of Humanistic Psychology, 36*, 17–22.

Acton, G. J., & Malathum, P. (2000). Basic need status and health-promoting self-care behavior in adults. *Western Journal of Nursing Research, 22*, 796–811.

Adams-Webber, J.R. (2001). Fixed role therapy. In R. Corsini (Ed.), *Handbook of innovative therapy* (2nd ed.) (pp. 255–262). New York: John Wiley & Sons.

Adams, G. R., & Fitch, S. A. (1982). Ego stage and identity status development: A cross-sequential analysis. *Journal of Personality and Social Psychology, 43*, 574–583.

Adams, G. R., & Fitch, S. A. (1983). Psychological environments of university departments: Effects on college students' identity status and ego stage development. *Journal of Personality and Social Psychology, 44*, 1266–1275.

Adams, G. R., Berzonsky, M. D., & Keating, L. (2006). Psychosocial resources in first-year university students: The role of identity processes and social relationships. *Journal of Youth and Adolescence, 35*, 81–91.

Adams, G. R., Ryan, B. A., & Keating, L. (2000). Family relationships, academic environments, and psychosocial development during the university experience: A longitudinal investigation. *Journal of Adolescent Research, 15*, 99–122.

Adams, J. M. (2000). Individual and group psychotherapy with African American women: Understanding the identity and context of the therapist and patient. In L. C. Jackson and B. Greene (Eds.), *Psychotherapy with African American women: Innovations in psychodynamic perspectives and practice* (pp. 33–61). New York: Guilford Press.

Adler, A. (1927). *Understanding human nature.* Garden City, NY: Doubleday Anchor.

Adler, A. (1930a). *The education of children.* South Bend, IN: Gateway.

Adler, A. (1930b). *The pattern of life.* New York: Cosmopolitan Book Corporation.

Adler, A. (1937). Position in family constellation influences life style. *International Journal of Individual Psychology, 3*, 211–227.

Adler, A. (1969). *The science of living.* Garden City, NY: Doubleday Anchor. (Original work published 1929)

Adler, A. (1973a). Advantages and disadvantages of the inferiority feeling. In H. L. Ansbacher & R. R. Ansbacher (Eds.), *Superiority and social interest* (pp. 50–58). New York: Viking.

Adler, A. (1973b). Complex compulsion as part of personality and neurosis. In H. L. Ansbacher & R. R. Ansbacher (Eds.), *Superiority and social interest* (pp. 71–80). New York: Viking.

Adler, A. (1973c). On the origins of the striving for superiority and of social interest. In H. L. Ansbacher & R. R. Ansbacher (Eds.), *Superiority and social interest* (pp. 29–40). New York: Viking.

Adler, A. (1973d). Technique of treatment. In H. L. Ansbacher & R. R. Ansbacher (Eds.), *Superiority and social interest* (pp. 191–201). New York: Viking.

Adler, A. (1978). *Cooperation between the sexes: Writings on women, love & marriage, sexuality & its disorders* (Edited and translated by H. L. Ansbacher and R. R. Ansbacher). Garden City, NY: Anchor Books.

Akhtar, S. (1989). Kohut and Kernberg: A critical comparison. In D. W. Detrick and S. P. Detrick (Eds.), *Self psychology: Comparisons and contrasts* (pp. 329–362). Hillsdale, NJ: Analytic Press.

Allen, J., & Brock, S.A. (2000). *Health care communication using personality type.* London: Routledge.

Allport, G. W. (1937). *Personality: A psychological interpretation.* New York: Holt.

Allport, G. W. (1950). *The individual and his religion: A psychological interpretation.* New York: Macmillan.

Allport, G. W. (1955). *Becoming: Basic considerations for a psychology of personality.* New Haven, CT: Yale University Press.

Allport, G. W. (1961). *Pattern and growth in personality.* New York: Holt, Rinehart & Winston.

Allport, G. W. (1965). *Letters from Jenny.* New York: Harcourt, Brace & World.

Allport, G. W. (1968). An autobiography. In G. W. Allport (Ed.), *The person in psychology: Selected essays.* Boston: Beacon Press.

Allport, G. W., & Odbert, H. S. (1936). Trait names: A psycholexical study. *Psychological Monographs, 47* (Whole No. 211).

Allport, G. W., & Odbert, H. S. (1936). Trait names: A psycholexical study. *Psychological Monographs, 47,* 171–220.

Allport, G. W., & Ross, J. M. (1967). Personal religious orientation and prejudice. *Journal of Personality and Social Psychology, 5,* 432–443.

Allport, G. W., Vernon, P. E., & Lindzey, G. (1960). *A study of values* (3rd ed.). Boston: Houghton Mifflin.

American Psychiatric Association. (2000). *Diagnostic and statistical manual of mental disorders* (4th ed., text rev.). Washington, DC.

Amerikaner, M. Monks, G., Wolfe, P., & Thomas, S. (1994). Family interaction and individual psychological health. *Journal of Counseling and Development, 72,* 614–623.

Amichai-Hamburger, Y. (2002). Internet and personality. *Computers in Human Behavior, 18,* 1–10.

Amichai-Hamburger, Y., Ben-Artzi, E. (2003). Loneliness and internet use. *Computers in Human Behavior, 19,* 71–80.

Anderson, C. A., & Bushman, B. J. (2001). Effects of violent video games on aggressive behavior, aggressive cognition, aggressive affect, physiological arousal, and prosocial behavior: A meta-analytic review of the scientific literature. *Psychological Science, 12,* 353–359.

Anderson, C. A., Gentile, D. A., & Buckley, K. E. (2007). *Violent video game effects in children and adolescents.* New York: Oxford University Press.

Anderson, C. A., Shibuya, A., Ihori, N., Swing, E. L., Bushman, B. J., Sakamoto, A., Rothstein, H. R., & Saleem, M. (2010). Violent video game effects on aggression, empathy, and pro-social behavior in Eastern and Western countries: A meta-analytic review. *Psychological Bulletin, 136,* 151–173.

Ansbacher, H. L. (1990). Alfred Adler's influence on the three leading cofounders of humanistic psychology. *Journal of Humanistic Psychology, 30,* 45–53.

Ansbacher, H. L., & Ansbacher, R. R. (Eds.). (1956). *The individual psychology of Alfred Adler.* New York: Basic Books.

Ansbacher, H. L., & Ansbacher, R. R. (Eds.). (1973). *Superiority and social interest: A collection of later writings.* New York: Viking.

Ardelt, M. (2000). Antecedents and effects of wisdom in old age. *Research on Aging, 22,* 360–394.

Armstrong, L., Phillips, J. G., & Saling, L. L. (2000). Potential determinants of heavier internet usage. *International Journal of Human-Computer Studies, 53,* 537–550.

Arseth, A. K., Kroger, J., Martinussen, M., & Marcia, J. E. (2009). *Identity, 9,* 1–32.

Austin, E. J., Hofer, S. M., Deary, I. J., & Eber, H.W. (2000). Interactions between intelligence and personality: Results from two large samples. *Personality and Individual Differences, 29,* 405–427.

Ayllon, T., & Azrin, N. H. (1965). The measurement and reinforcement of behavior of psychotics. *Journal of the Experimental Analysis of Behavior, 8,* 357–383.

Baars, B. J., Cohen, J., Bower, G. H., & Berry, J. W. (1992). Some caveats on testing the Freudian slip hypothesis. In B. J. Baars (Eds.), *Experimental slips and human error: Exploring the architecture of volition* (pp. 289–313). New York: Plenum Press.

Bachelor, A. (1988). How clients perceive therapist empathy: A content analysis of "received" empathy. *Psychotherapy, 25,* 227–240.

Bahr, H. M., Chadwick, B. A., & Stauss, J. H. (1979). *American ethnicity.* Lexington, MA: D.C. Heath.

Bair, D. (2003). *Jung: A biography.* Boston: Little, Brown and Company.

Baker, H. S., & Baker, M. N. (1987). Heinz Kohut's self psychology: An overview. *American Journal of Psychiatry, 144,* 1–9.

Bandura, A. (1965). Influence of models' reinforcement contingencies on the acquisition of imitative responses. *Journal of Personality and Social Psychology, 1,* 589–595.

Bandura, A. (1969). *Principles of behavior modification.* New York: Holt, Rinehart & Winston.

Bandura, A. (1971). *Social learning theory.* Morristown, NJ: General Learning Press.

Bandura, A. (1973). *Aggression: A social learning analysis.* Englewood Cliffs, NJ: Prentice-Hall.

Bandura, A. (1977). Self-efficacy: Toward a unifying theory of behavioral change. *Psychological Review, 84,* 191–215.

Bandura, A. (1978). The self system in reciprocal determinism. *American Psychologist, 33,* 344–358.

Bandura, A. (1981). Self-referent thought: A developmental analysis of self-efficacy. In J. H. Flavell & L. Ross (Eds.), *Social cognitive development: Frontiers and possible futures* (pp. 200–239). Cambridge, England: Cambridge University Press.

Bandura, A. (1982a). The self and mechanisms of agency. In J. Suls (Ed.), *Psychological perspectives on the self* (Vol. 1, pp. 3–39). Hillsdale, NJ: Erlbaum.

Bandura, A. (1982b). Self-efficacy mechanism in human agency. *American Psychologist, 37*, 122–147.

Bandura, A. (1986). *Social foundations of thought and action: A social cognitive theory*. Englewood Cliffs, NJ: Prentice-Hall.

Bandura, A. (1992). Self-efficacy mechanism in psycho-biologic functioning. In R. Schwarzer (Ed.), *Self-efficacy: Thought control of action* (pp. 354–394). Philadelphia: Hemisphere Publishing Corporation.

Bandura, A. (1996). Ontological and epistemological terrains revisited. *Journal of Behavior Therapy and Experimental Psychiatry, 27*, 323–345.

Bandura, A. (1997). *Self-efficacy: The exercise of control*. New York: W.H. Freeman.

Bandura, A., & Kupers, C. J. (1964). The transmission of patterns of self-reinforcement through modeling. *Journal of Abnormal and Social Psychology, 69*, 1–9.

Bandura, A., & Menlove, F. L. (1968). Factors determining vicarious extinction of avoidance behavior through symbolic modeling. *Journal of Personality and Social Psychology, 8*, 99–108.

Bandura, A., & Walters, R. H. (1963). *Social learning and personality development*. New York: Holt, Rinehart & Winston.

Bandura, A., Adams, N. E., Hardy, A. B., & Howells, G. N. (1980). Tests of the generality of self-efficacy theory. *Cognitive Therapy and Research, 4*, 39–66.

Bandura, A., Blanchard, B., & Ritter, B. (1969). Relative efficiency of desensitization and modeling approaches for inducing behavioral, affective, and attitudinal changes. *Journal of Personality and Social Psychology, 13*, 173–199.

Bandura, A., Reese, L., & Adams, N. E. (1982). Microanalysis of action and fear arousal as a function of differential levels of perceived self-efficacy. *Journal of Personality and Social Psychology, 43*, 5–21.

Bandura, A., Ross, D., & Ross, S. A. (1963a). Imitation of film-mediated aggressive models. *Journal of Abnormal and Social Psychology, 66*, 3–11.

Bandura, A., Ross, D., & Ross, S. A. (1963b). Vicarious reinforcement and imitative learning. *Journal of Abnormal and Social Psychology, 67*, 601–607.

Bannister, D. (Ed.). (1977). *New perspectives in personal construct theory*. New York: Academic Press.

Bannister, D., & Fransella, F. (1966). A grid test of schizophrenic thought disorder. *British Journal of Social and Clinical Psychology, 5*, 95–102.

Bannister, D., Adams-Webber, J. R., Penn, W. L., & Radley, A. R. (1975). Reversing the process of thought disorder: A serial validation experiment. *British Journal of Social and Clinical Psychology, 14*, 169–180.

Bannister, D., Fransella, F., & Agnew, J. (1971). Characteristics and validity of the grid test of thought disorder. *British Journal of Social and Clinical Psychology, 10*, 144–151.

Bar-On, R. (2010). Emotional intelligence: An integral part of positive psychology. *Psychological Society of South Africa, 40*, 54–62.

Bardone-Cone, A. M., Abramson, L. Y., Heatherton, T. F., & Joiner, T. E., Jr. (2006). Predicting bulimic symptoms: An interactive model of self-efficacy, perfectionism, and perceived weight status. *Behaviour Research and Therapy, 44*, 27–42.

Barlett, C. P., Anderson, C. A., & Swing, E. L. (2009). Video game effects-confirmed, suspected, and speculative: A review of the evidence. *Simulation & Gaming, 40*, 377–403.

Barnet, H. S. (1990). Divorce stress and adjustment model: Locus of control and demographic predictors. *Journal of Divorce, 13*, 93–109.

Barry, H., III, & Blane, H. T. (1977). Birth order of alcoholics. *Journal of Individual Psychology, 33*, 62–79.

Bartholow, B. D., & Anderson, C. A. (2002). Effects of violent video games on aggressive behavior: Potential sex differences. *Journal of Experimental Social Psychology, 38*, 283–290.

Basch, M. F. (1989). A comparison of Freud and Kohut: Apostasy or synergy? In D. W. Detrick and S. P. Detrick (Eds.), *Self psychology: Comparisons and contrasts* (pp. 3–22). Hillsdale, NJ: Analytic Press.

Basgall, J., & Snyder, C. R. (1988). Excuses in waiting: External locus of control and reactions to success-failure feedback. *Journal of Personality and Social Psychology, 54*, 656–662.

Baumeister, R. F., & Mick, D. G. (2002). Yielding to temptation: Self-control failure, impulsive purchasing, and consumer behavior. *Journal of Consumer Research, 28*, 670–676.

Baumeister, R. F., Dale, K., & Sommer, K. L. (1998). Freudian defense mechanisms and empirical findings in modern social psyhology: Reaction formation, projection, displacement, undoing, isolation, sublimation, and denial. *Journal of Personality, 66*, 1081–1124.

Baumeister, R. F., Heatherton, T. F., & Tice, D. M. (1994). *Losing control: How and why people fail at self-regulation.* San Diego, CA: Academic Press.

Baumrind, D. (1991). Parenting styles and adolescent development. In R. M. Lerner, A. C. Petersen, and J. Brooks-Gunn (Eds.), *Encyclopedia of adolescence: Vol. 2* (pp. 746–758). New York: Garland Publishing.

Beaman, R., & Wheldall, K. (2000). Teachers' use of approval and disapproval in the classroom. *Educational Psychology, 20*, 431–446.

Beckworth, J., & Alper, J. S. (2002). Genetics of human personality: Social and ethical implications. In J. Benjamin, R. P. Ebstein, and R. H. Belmaker (Eds.) *Molecular genetics and the human personality* (pp. 315–331). Washington, D.C.: American Psychiatric Publishing.

Bell, R. C., Winter, D., & Bhandari, S. (2010). Hierarchical relationships in dependency grids: Explorations in survivors of childhood sexual abuse. *Journal of Constructivist Psychology, 23*, 102–117.

Belmont, L., & Marolla, F. A. (1973). Birth order, family size, and intelligence. *Science, 182*, 1096–1101.

Berglund, E., Eriksson, M., & Westerlund, M. (2005). Communicative skills in relation to gender, birth order, childcare and socioeconomic status in 18-month-old children. *Scandinavian Journal of Psychology, 46*, 485–491.

Berkowitz, L. (1962). *Aggression: A social psychological analysis.* New York: McGraw-Hill.

Berry, J. W., Worthington, E. L., O'Connor, L. E., Parrott, L., & Wade, N.G. (2005). Forgivingness, vengeful rumination, and affective traits. *Journal of Personality, 73*, 183–228.

Berzonsky, M. D. (1992). Identity style and coping strategies. *Journal of Personality, 60*, 771–788.

Berzonsky, M. D., & Neimeyer, G. J. (1988). Identity status and personal construct systems. *Journal of Adolescence, 11*, 195–204.

Bethell, T. (2005). *The politically incorrect guide to science.* Washington, DC: Regnery Publishing.

Betz, N. E., & Hackett, G. (1981). The relationship of career-related self-efficacy expectations to perceived career options in women and men. *Journal of Counseling Psychology, 28*, 399–410.

Beutler, L. E., Moleiro, C., & Talebi, H. (2002). Resistance in psychotherapy: What conclusions are supported by research. *Journal of Clinical Psychology, 58*, 207–217.

Beyers, W., & Seiffge-Krenke, I. (2010). Does identity precede intimacy? Testing Erikson's theory on romantic development in emerging adults of the 21st century. *Journal of Adolescent Research, 25*, 387–415.

Bieri, J. (1955). Cognitive complexity-simplicity and predictive behavior. *Journal of Abnormal and Social Psychology, 51*, 263–268.

Bing, M. N. (1999). Hypercompetitiveness in academia: Achieving criterion-related validity from item context specificity. *Journal of Personality Assessment, 73*, 80–99.

Bishop, D. I., Weisgram, E. S., Holleque, K. M., Lund, K. E., & Wheeler-Anderson, J.R. (2005). Identity development and alcohol consumption: Current and retrospective self-reports by college students. *Journal of Adolescence, 28*, 523–533.

Black, M. (1973). Some aversive responses to a would-be reinforcer. In H. Wheeler (Ed.), *Beyond the punitive society* (pp. 125–134). San Francisco: W. H. Freeman.

Blaine, B., & Crocker, J. (1995). Religiousness, race, and psychological well-being: Exploring social psychological mediators. *Personality and Social Psychology Bulletin, 21*, 1031–1041.

Blake, J. (1989). *Family size and achievement.* Berkeley: University of California Press.

Blanchard, A. L., & Henle, C. A. (2008). Correlates of different forms of cyberloafing: The role of norms and external locus of control. *Computers in Human Behavior, 24*, 1067–1084.

Blanton, P. W. (2000). The Adlerian perspective in the context of contemporary marriages. *Journal of Individual Psychology, 56*, 411–418.

Blum, G. S. (1953). *Psychoanalytic theories of personality.* New York: McGraw-Hill.

Blustein, D. L., & Phillips, S. D. (1990). Relation between ego identity statuses and decision-making styles. *Journal of Counseling Psychology, 37*, 160–168.

Bohart, A. C., & Greening, T. (2001). Humanistic psychology and positive psychology. *American Psychologist, 56*, 81–82.

Bono, G., McCullough, M. E., & Root, L. M. (2008). Forgiveness, feeling connected to others, and well-being: Two longitudinal studies. *Personality and Social Psychology Bulletin, 34*, 182–195.

Boomsma, D. I., van Beijsterveld, T. C. E. M., Beem, A. L., Hoekstra, R. A., Polderman, T. J. C., & Bartels, M. (2008). Intelligence and birth order in boys and girls. *Intelligence, 36*, 630–634.

Booth-Butterfield, M., Anderson, R.H., & Booth-Butterfield, S. (2000). Adolescents' use of tobacco, health locus of control, and self-monitoring. *Health Communication, 12,* 137–148.

Bordages, J. W. (1989). Self-actualization and personal autonomy. *Psychological Reports, 64,* 1263–1266.

Borgatta, E. F. (1964). The structure of personality characteristics. *Behavioral Science, 9,* 8–17.

Bornstein, R. F. (1992). The dependent personality: Developmental, social, and clinical perspectives. *Psychological Bulletin, 112,* 3–23.

Bornstein, R. F. (1993). Dependency and patienthood. *Journal of Clinical Psychology, 49,* 397–406.

Bornstein, R. F. (1994). Adaptive and maladaptive aspects of dependency: An integrative review. *American Journal of Orthopsychiatry, 64,* 622–635.

Bornstein, R. F. (1998). Dependency in the personality disorders: Intensity, insight, expression, and defense. *Journal of Clinical Psychology, 54,* 175–189.

Bornstein, R. F. (1999). Objectivity and subjectivity in psychological science: Embracing and transcending psychology's positivist tradition. *Journal of Mind and Behavior, 20,* 1–16.

Bornstein, R. F. (2010). Psychoanalytic theory as a unifying framework for 21st century personality assessment. *Psycho-Analytic Psychology, 27,* 133–152.

Bornstein, R. F., & Cecero, J. J. (2000). Deconstructing dependency in a five-factor world: A meta-analytic review. *Journal of Personality Assessment, 74,* 324–343.

Bornstein, R. F., & Gold, S. H. (2008). Comorbidity of personality disorders and somatization disorder: A meta-analytic review. *Journal of Psychopathology and Behavioral Assessment, 30,* 154–161.

Bornstein, R. F., & O'Neill, R. M. (2000). Dependency and suicidality in psychiatric patients. *Journal of Clinical Psychology, 56,* 463–473.

Bornstein, R. F., Ng, H. M., Gallagher, H. A., Kloss, D. M., & Regier, N. G. (2005). Contrasting effects of self-schema priming on lexical decisions and interpersonal Stroop task performance: Evidence for a cognitive/interactionist model of interpersonal dependency. *Journal of Personality, 73,* 731–762.

Bornstein, R. F., Riggs, J. M., Hill, E. L., & Calabrese, C. (1996). Activity, passivity, self-denigration, and self-promotion: Toward an interactional model of interpersonal dependency. *Journal of Personality, 64,* 637–673.

Bornstein, R. F. (2001). A meta-analysis of the dependency-eating-disorders relationship: Strength, specificity, and temporal stability. *Journal of*

Psychopathology and Behavioral Assessment, 23, 151–162.

Bornstein, R. F. (2005a). *The dependent patient: A practitioner's guide.* Washington, DC: American Psychological Association.

Bornstein, R. F. (2005b). The dependent patient: Diagnosis, assessment, and treatment. *Professional Psychology: Research and Practice, 36,* 82–89.

Bornstein, R. F. (2010). Psychoanalytic theory as a unifying framework for 21st century personality assessment. *Psychoanalytic Psychology, 27,* 133–152.

Boss, M. (1963). *Psychoanalysis and daseinanalysis.* New York: Basic Books.

Bostic, T. J., & Ptacek, J. T. (2001). Personality factors and the short-term variability in subjective well-being. *Journal of Happiness Studies, 2,* 355–373.

Bourne, E. (1978). The state of research on ego identity: A review and appraisal: Part 1. *Journal of Youth and Adolescence, 7,* 223–251.

Boyd-Franklin, N. (1989). *Black families in therapy: A multisystems approach.* New York: Guilford Press.

Bozarth, J. D. (2002). Nondirectivity in the person-centered approach: Critique of Kahn's critique. *Journal of Humanistic Psychology, 42,* 78–83.

Bradley, C. L., & Marcia, J. E. (1998). Generativity-stagnation: A five-category model. *Journal of Personality, 66,* 39–64.

Brandtstadter, J., & Rothermund, K. (1994). Self-percepts of control in middle and later adulthood: Buffering losses by rescaling goals. *Psychology and Aging, 9,* 265–273.

Breland, H. M. (1974). Birth order, family configuration, and verbal achievement. *Child Development, 45,* 1011–1019.

Brennan, J. F. (1969). Autoeroticism or social feeling as basis of human development. *Journal of Individual Psychology, 25,* 3–18.

Brezo, J., Paris, J., & Turecki, G. (2006). Personality traits as correlates of suicidal ideation, suicide attempts, and suicide completions: A systematic review. *Acta Psychiatrica Scandinavica, 113,* 180–206.

Briggs, K. C., & Myers, I. B. (1943, 1944, 1957, 1976). *Myers-Briggs type indicator.* Palo Alto, CA: Consulting Psychologists Press.

Briggs, S. R. (1989). The optimal level of measurement for personality constructs. In D. M. Buss & N. Cantor (Eds.), *Personality psychology: Recent trends and emerging directions* (pp. 246–260). New York: Springer-Verlag.

Brown, R. C., & Tedeschi, J. T. (1972). Graduate education and psychology: A comment on Rogers' passionate statement. *Journal of Humanistic Psychology, 12,* 1–15.

Brown, R. J., & Donderi, D. C. (1986). Dream content and self-reported well-being among recurrent dreamers, past-recurrent dreamers, and non-recurrent dreamers. *Journal of Personality and Social Psychology, 50,* 612–623.

Brown, R. P., & Phillips, A. (2005). Letting bygones be bygones: Further evidence for the validity of the tendency to Forgive Scale. *Personality and Individual Differences, 38,* 627–638.

Brownell, K. D., & Jeffery, R. W. (1987). Improving long-term weight loss: Pushing the limits of treatment. *Behavior Therapy, 18,* 353–374.

Bruinius, H. (2006). *Better for all the world: The secret history of forced sterilization and America's quest for racial purity.* New York: Alfred A. Knopf.

Bryan, A. D., Aiken, L. S., & West, S. G. (1997). Young women's condom use: The influence of acceptance of sexuality, control over the sexual encounter, and perceived susceptibility to common STDs. *Health Psychology, 16,* 468–479.

Bullock, W. A., & Gilliland, K. (1993). Eysenck's arousal theory of introversion-extraversion: A converging measures investigation. *Journal of Personality and Social Psychology, 64,* 113–123.

Burish, T., Carey, M., Wallston, K., Stein, M., Jamison, R., & Lyles, J. (1984). Health locus of control and chronic disease: An external orientation may be advantageous. *Journal of Social and Clinical Psychology, 2,* 326–332.

Burk, C. (1994). Examining the relationship among locus of control, value, and exercise. *The Journal of Health Behavior, Education, & Promotion, 18,* 14–23.

Burker, E. J., Evon, D. M., Galanko, J., & Egan, T. (2005). Health locus of control predicts survival after lung transplant. *Journal of Health Psychology, 10,* 695–704.

Bushman, B. J. (1998). Priming effects of media violence on the accessibility of aggressive constructs in memory. *Personality and Social Psychology Bulletin, 24,* 537–545.

Buss, A. H. (1988). *Personality: Evolutionary heritage and human distinctiveness.* Hillsdale, NJ: Erlbaum.

Buss, A. H. (1995). *Personality: Temperament, social behavior, and the self.* Boston: Allyn & Bacon.

Buss, D. M. (1989). Sex differences in human mate preferences: Evolutionary hypotheses tested in 37 cultures. *Behavioral and Brain Sciences, 12,* 1–49.

Buss, D. M. (1992). Manipulation in close relationships: Five personality factors in interactional context. *Journal of Personality, 60,* 477–499.

Buss, D. M. (1994). *The evolution of desire: Strategies of human mating.* New York: Basic Books.

Buss, D. M. (1999). *Evolutionary psychology.* Boston: Allyn & Bacon.

Buss, D. M. (2000). *The dangerous passion: Why jealousy is as necessary as love and sex.* New York: Free Press.

Buss, D. M., & Dedden, L. A. (1990). Derogation of competitors. *Journal of Social and Personal Relationships, 7,* 395–422.

Buss, D. M., & Schmitt, D. P. (1993). Sexual strategies theory: An evolutionary perspective on human mating. *Psychological Review, 100,* 204–232.

Bussey, K., & Bandura, A. (1984). Gender constancy, social power, and sex-linked modeling. *Journal of Personality and Social Psychology, 47,* 1292–1302.

Butler, J. M., & Haigh, G. V. (1954). Changes in the relation between self-concepts and ideal concepts consequent upon client-centered counseling. In C. R. Rogers & R. F. Dymond (Eds.), *Psychotherapy and personality change* (pp. 55–75). Chicago: University of Chicago Press.

Buttsworth, L. M., & Smith, G. A. (1995). Personality of Australian performing musicians by gender and by instrument. *Personality and Individual Differences, 18,* 595–603.

Campbell-Sills, L., Cohan, S. L., & Stein, M. B. (2006). Relationship of resilience to personality, coping, and psychiatric symptoms in young adults. *Behaviour Research & Therapy, 44,* 585–599.

Campbell, A., & Rushton, J. P. (1978). Bodily communication and personality. *British Journal of Social and Clinical Psychology, 17,* 31–36.

Campbell, J. B., & Hawley, C. W. (1982). Study habits and Eysenck's theory of extraversion-introversion. *Journal of Research in Personality, 16,* 139–146.

Campbell, J. F. (1991). The primary personality factors of Hawaiian middle adolescents. *Psychological Reports, 68,* 3–26.

Campbell, W. K., & Foster, C. A. (2002). Narcissism and commitment in romantic relationships: An investment model analysis. *Personality and Social Psychology Bulletin, 28,* 484–495.

Cann, D. R., & Donderi, D. C. (1986). Jungian personality typology and the recall of everyday and archetypal dreams. *Journal of Personality and Social Psychology, 50,* 1021–1030.

Capaldi, E. J., & Proctor, R. W. (2000). Laudan's normative naturalism: A useful philosophy of science for psychology. *American Journal of Psychology, 113*, 430–454.

Caporael, L. R. (2001). Evolutionary psychology: Toward a unifying theory and a hybrid science. *Annual Review of Psychology, 52*, 607–628.

Capron, E. W. (2004). Types of pampering and the narcissistic personality trait. *Journal of Individual Psychology, 60*, 76–93.

Carpenter, F. (1974). *The Skinner primer.* New York: Free Press.

Carton, J. S., & Nowicki, S., Jr. (1994). Antecedents of individual differences in locus of control of reinforcement: A critical review. *Genetic, Social, and General Psychology Monographs, 120*, 33–81.

Carvallo, M., & Gabriel, S. (2006). No man is an island: The need to belong and dismissing avoidant attachment style. *Personality and Social Psychology Bulletin, 32*, 697–709.

Carver, C. S., & Baird, E. (1998). The American dream revisited: Is it what you want or why you want it that matters? *Psychological Science, 9*, 289–292.

Cassidy, S. (2000). Learning style, academic belief systems, self-report student proficiency and academic achievement in higher education. *Educational Psychology, 20*, 307–322.

Catanzaro, S. J. (1991). Adjustment, depression, and minimal goal setting: The moderating effect of performance feedback. *Journal of Personality, 59*, 243–261.

Cattell, H. E. P. (2001). The Sixteen Personality Factor (16PF) Questionnaire. In W. I. Dorfman and M. Hersen (Eds), *Understanding Psychological Assessment* (pp. 187–215). New York: Kluwer Academic Press.

Cattell, H. E. P., & Mead, A. D. (2008). The Sixteen Personality Factor Questionnaire (16PF). In G. J. Boyle, G. Matthews, and D. H. Saklofske (Eds.), *The Sage Handbook of Personality Theory and Assessment: Vol. 2. Personality Measurement and Testing* (pp. 135–159). Thousand Oaks, CA: Sage Publications.

Cattell, H. E. P., & Schuerger, J. M. (2003). *Essentials of 16PF Assessment.* Hoboken, New Jersey: Wiley & Sons.

Cattell, R. B. (1943). The description of personality: Basic traits resolved into clusters. *Journal of Abnormal and Social Psychology, 38*, 476–506.

Cattell, R. B. (1950). *Personality: A systematic theoretical and factual study.* New York: McGraw-Hill.

Cattell, R. B. (1957). *Personality and motivation: Structure and measurement.* New York: Harcourt, Brace & World.

Cattell, R. B. (1961). *The meaning and measurement of neuroticism and anxiety.* New York: Ronald.

Cattell, R. B. (1965). *The scientific analysis of personality.* Baltimore, MD: Penguin.

Cattell, R. B. (1972). *A new morality from science: Beyondism.* New York: Pergamon Press.

Cattell, R. B. (1974). Raymond B. Cattell. In G. Lindzey (Ed.), *A history of psychology in autobiography* (Vol. VI, pp. 59–100). Englewood Cliffs, NJ: Prentice-Hall.

Cattell, R. B. (1979). *Personality and learning theory: Vol. 1. The structure of personality in its environment.* New York: Springer.

Cattell, R. B. (1980). *Personality and learning theory: Vol. 2. A systems theory of maturation and structured learning.* New York: Springer.

Cattell, R. B. (1982). *The inheritance of personality and ability.* New York: Academic Press.

Cattell, R. B. (1987). *Beyondism: Religion from science.* New York: Praeger.

Cattell, R. B., & Kline, P. (1977). *The scientific analysis of personality and motivation.* New York: Academic Press.

Cavaiola, A. A., & Strohmetz, D. B. (2010). Perception of risk for subsequent drinking and driving related offenses and locus of control among first-time DUI offenders. *Alcoholism Treatment Quarterly, 28*, 52–62.

Center, D., & Kemp, D. (2003). Temperament and personality as potential factors in the development and treatment of conduct disorders. *Education and Treatment of Children, 26*, 75–88.

Chak, K., & Leung, L. (2004). Shyness and locus of control as predictors of internet addiction and internet use. *CyberPsychology and Behavior, 7*, 559–570.

Chang, D. F., & Berk, A. (2009). Making cross-racial therapy work: A phenomenological study of clients' experiences of cross-racial therapy. *Journal of Counseling Psychology, 56*, 521–536.

Chang, E. C., & Bridewell, W. B. (1998). Irrational beliefs, optimism, pessimism, and psychological distress: A preliminary examination of differential effects in a college population. *Journal of Clinical Psychology, 54*, 137–142.

Chaplin, M. P., & Orlofsky, J. L. (1991). Personality characteristics of male alcoholics as revealed through their early recollections. *Individual Psychology, 47*, 356–371.

Chen, H. S., Percy, M. S., & Horner, S. D. (2001). Cigarettes: A growing problem for Taiwanese adolescents. *Journal of Community Health Nursing, 18*, 167–175.

Cheng, Y.-F., & Peng, S. S. (2008). University students' internet use and its relationships with academic performance, interpersonal relationships, psychosocial adjustment, and self-evaluation. *CyberPsychology and Behavior, 11*, 467–469.

Chermahini, S. A., & Hommel, B. (2010). The (b)link between creativity and dopamine: Spontaneous eye blink rates predict and dissociate divergent and convergent thinking. *Cognition, 115*, 458–465.

Chipman, S., Olsen, S. F., Klein, S., Hart, C. H., & Robinson, C. C. (2000). Differences in retrospective perceptions of parenting of male and female inmates and noninmates. *Family Relations, 49*, 5–11.

Chodorkoff, B. (1954). Self-perception, perceptual defense, and adjustment. *Journal of Abnormal and Social Psychology, 49*, 508–512.

Chodorow, N. (1978). *The reproduction of mothering: Psycho-analysis and the sociology of gender.* Berkeley, CA: University of California Press.

Chodorow, N. (1989). *Feminism and psychoanalytic theory.* New Haven, CT: Yale University Press.

Christopher, J. C., Manaster, G. J., & Campbell, R. L. (2002). Peak experiences, social interest, and moral reasoning: An exploratory study. *Journal of Individual Psychology, 58*, 35–51.

Clack, G.B., Allen, J., Cooper, D., & Head, J.O. (2004). Personality differences between doctors and their patients: Implications for the teaching of communication skills. *Medical Education, 38*, 177–186.

Clayton, M.C., & Helms, B.P. (2009). Increasing seat belt use on a college campus: An evaluation of two prompting prompting procedures. *Journal of Applied Behavior Analysis, 42*, 161–164.

Cofer, C. N., & Appley, M. H. (1964). *Motivation: Theory and research.* New York: Wiley.

Cohen, A. B., & Hill, P. C. (2007). Religion as culture: Religious individualism and collectivism among American Catholics, Jews, and Protestants. *Journal of Personality, 75*, 709–742.

Cohen, A. B., Hall, D. E., Koenig, H. G., & Meador, K. G. (2005). Social versus individual motivation: Implications for normative definitions of religious orientations. *Personality and Social Psychology Review, 9*, 48–61.

Coles, R. (1970). *Erik H. Erikson: The growth of his work.* Boston: Little, Brown.

Collier, S. A., Ryckman, R. M., Thornton, B., & Gold, J. A. (2010). Competitive personality attitudes and

forgiveness of others. *Journal of Psychology, 144*, 535–543.

Colzato, L. S., Slagter, H. A., van den Wildenberg, W. P. M., & Hommel, B. (2009). Closing one's eyes to reality: Evidence for a dopaminergic basis of psychoticism from spontaneous eye blink rates. *Personality and Individual Differences, 46*, 377–380.

Coolidge, F. L., Moor, C. J., Yamazaki, T. G., Stewart, S. E., & Segal, D. L. (2001). On the relationship between Karen Horney's tripartite neurotic type theory and personality disorder features. *Personality and Individual Differences, 30*, 1387–1400.

Cooper, H., Okamura, L., & McNeil, P. (1995). Situation and personality correlates of psychological well-being, social activity, and personal control. *Journal of Research in Personality, 29*, 395–417.

Corbitt, E. M. (1994). Narcissism from the perspective of the five-factor model. In P.T. Costa and T.A. Widiger (Eds.), *Personality disorders and the five-factor model of personality* (pp. 199–203). Washington, D.C.: American Psychological Association.

Correa, T., Hinsley, A. W., & Gil de Zuniga, H. (2010). American Psychological Association (2005). *Accreditation Operating Procedures of the Committee on Accreditation.* Washington, DC: Author.

Costa, P. T., & McCrae, R. R. (1992). *NEO PI-R Professional Manual.* Odessa, FL: Psychological Assessment Resources.

Cote, J. E., & Levine, C. (1983). Marcia and Erikson: The relationships among ego identity status, neuroticism, dogmatism, and purpose in life. *Journal of Youth and Adolescence, 12*, 43–53.

Cowan, G., & Mills, R. D. (2004). Personal inadequacy and intimacy predictors of men's hostility toward women. *Sex Roles, 51*, 67–78.

Cox-Fuenzalida, L.-E., Angie, A., Holloway, S., & Sohl, L. (2006). Extraversion and task performance: A fresh look through the workload history lens. *Journal of Research in Personality, 40*, 432–439.

Cozzarelli, C. (1993). Personality and self-efficacy as predictors of coping with abortion. *Journal of Personality and Social Psychology, 65*, 1224–1236.

Cramer, P. (1991). *The development of defense mechanisms: Theory, research, and assessment.* New York: Springer-Verlag.

Cramer, P. (1998). Freshman to senior year: A follow-up study of identity, narcissism, and defense mechanisms. *Journal of Research in Personality, 32*, 156–172.

Cramer, P. (2000). Development of identity: Gender makes a difference. *Journal of Research in Personality, 34*, 42–72.

Cramer, P. (2002). Defense mechanisms, behavior, and affect in young adulthood. *Journal of Personality, 70,* 103–126

Cramer, P. (2004). Identity change in adulthood: The contribution of defense mechanisms and life experiences. *Journal of Research in Personality, 38,* 280–316.

Cramer, P. (2006). *Protecting the self: Defense mechanisms in action.* New York: Guilford Press.

Cramer, P. & Kelly, F.D. (2010). Attachment style and defense mechanisms in parents who abuse their children. *Journal of Nervous and Mental Disease, 198,* 619–627.

Crandall, J. E. (1975). A scale for social interest. *Journal of Individual Psychology, 31,* 187–195.

Crandall, J. E. (1980). Adler's concept of social interest: Theory, measurement, and implications for adjustment. *Journal of Personality and Social Psychology, 39,* 481–495.

Crawford, M., & Marecek, J. (1989). Psychology reconstructs the female: 1968–1988. *Psychology of Women Quarterly, 13,* 147–165.

Cresswell, J. D., Welch, W. T., Taylor, S. E., Sherman, D. K., Gruenewald, T. L., & Mann, T. (2005). Affirmation of personal values buffers neuroendocrine and psychological stress responses. *Psychological Science, 16,* 846–851.

Cross, M., & Epting, F. (2005). Self-obliteration, self-definition, self-integration: Claiming a homosexual identity. *Journal of Constructivist Psychology, 18,* 53–63.

Curlette, W. L., & Kern, R. M. (2010). The importance of Meeting the need to belong. *Journal of Individual Psychology, 66,* 30–42.

Cvengros, J. A., Christensen, A. J., & Lawton, W. J. (2005). Health locus of control and depression in chronic kidney disease: A dynamic perspective. *Journal of Health Psychology, 10,* 677–686.

Daugherty, D. A., Murphy, M. J., & Paugh, J. (2001). An examination of the Adlerian construct of social interest with criminal offenders. *Journal of Counseling and Development, 79,* 465–471.

Davidson, A. L., Boyle, C., & Lauchlan, F. (2008). Scared to lose control? General and health locus of control in females with a fear of vomiting. *Journal of Clinical Psychology, 64,* 30–39.

Davies, D. R., & Parasuraman, R. (1982). *The psychology of vigilance.* London: Academic Press.

Davis, C. M. (1928). Self-selection of diet by newly weaned infants. *American Journal of Diseases of Children, 36,* 651–679.

De Haan, M. (2010). Birth order, family size and educational attainment. *Economics of Education Review, 29,* 576–588.

De Moya, C. A. (1997). Scores on locus of control and aggression for drug addicts, users, and controls. *Psychological Reports, 80,* 40–42.

DeBono, A., Shmueli, D., & Muraven, M. (2011). Rude and inappropriate: The role of self-control in following social norms. *Personality and Social Psychology Bulletin, 37,* 136–146.

deCarvalho, R. J. (1996). Rollo R. May (1909–1994). *Journal of Humanistic Psychology, 36,* 8–16.

Delaney, H. D., Miller, W. R., & Bisono, A. M. (2007). Religiosity and spirituality among psychologists: A survey of clinician members of the American Psychological Association. *Professional Psychology: Research and Practice, 35,* 538–546.

Derous, E., Nguyen, H.-H., & Ryan, A. M. (2009). Hiring discrimination against Arab minorities: Interactions between prejudice and job characteristics. *Human Performance, 22,* 297–320.

Dezutter, J., Soenens, B., & Hutsebaut, D. (2006). Religiosity and mental health: A further exploration of the relative importance of religious behaviors vs. religious attitudes. *Personality and Individual Differences, 40,* 807–818.

Dietch, J. (1978). Love, sex roles, and psychological health. *Journal of Personality Assessment, 42,* 626–634.

Digman, J. M., & Takemoto-Chock, N. K. (1981). Factors in the natural language of personality: Reanalysis and comparison of six major studies. *Multivariate Behavioral Research, 16,* 149–170.

Dominguez, M. M., & Carton, J. S. (1997). The relationship between self-actualization and parenting style. *Journal of Social Behavior and Personality, 12,* 1093–1100.

Domino, G. (1976). Compensatory aspects of dreams: An empirical test of Jung's theory. *Journal of Personality and Social Psychology, 34,* 658–662.

Donahue, M. J. (1985). Intrinsic and extrinsic religiousness: Review and meta-analysis. *Journal of Personality and Social Psychology, 48,* 400–419.

Dosamantes-Alperson, E., & Merrill, N. (1980). Growth effects of experiential movement psychotherapy. *Psychotherapy: Theory, Research and Practice, 17,* 63–68.

Downs, A. F. D., Rosenthal, T. L., & Lichstein, K. L. (1988). Modeling therapies reduce avoidance of bath-time by the institutionalized elderly. *Behavior Therapy, 19,* 359–368.

Dry, A. M. (1961). *The psychology of Jung.* New York: Wiley.

Duina, F. (2011). Winning: Reflections on an American Obsession. Princeton, NJ: Princeton University Press.

Dunkel, C. S., & Papini, D. R. (2005). The role of ego-identity status in mating preferences. *Adolescence, 40,* 489–501.

DuPaul, G. J., & Hoff, K. E. (1998). Reducing disruptive behavior in general education classrooms: The use of self-management strategies. *School Psychology Review, 27,* 290–303.

Duster, T. (1990). *Backdoor to eugenics.* New York: Routledge.

Eagle, M. N. (1984). *Recent developments in psychoanalysis.* New York: McGraw-Hill.

Eagly, A. H., & Wood, W. (1999). The origins of sex differences in human behavior: Evolved dispositions versus social roles. *American Psychologist, 54,* 408–423.

Edmundson, M. (2007). *The death of Sigmund Freud: The legacy of his last days.* New York: Bloomsbury, USA.

Eidelson, R. J., & Epstein, N. (1982). Cognition and relationship maladjustment: Development of a measure of dysfunctional relationships beliefs. *Journal of Consulting and Clinical Psychology, 50,* 715–720.

Ellis, A. (1973). *Humanistic psychotherapy.* New York: McGraw-Hill.

Ellis, A. (1987). A sadly neglected cognitive element in depression. *Cognitive Therapy and Research, 11,* 121–145.

Ellis, A. (1995). Rational emotive behavior therapy. In R. J. Corsini and D. Wedding (Eds.), *Current psychotherapies* (5th ed.), pp. 162–196. Itasca, Illinois: F.E. Peacock Publishers.

Ellis, B. J. (1998). The Partner-specific Investment Inventory: An evolutionary approach to individual differences in investment. *Journal of Personality, 66,* 383–442.

Emmons, R. A. (1984). Factor analysis and construct validity of the Narcissistic Personality Inventory. *Journal of Personality Assessment, 48,* 291–300.

Engels, R. C. M. E., Hale III, W. W., Noom, M., & De Vries, H. (2005). Self-efficacy and emotional adjustment as precursors of smoking in early adolescence. *Substance Use & Misuse, 40,* 1883–1893.

Erdelyi, M. H. (1985). *Psychoanalysis: Freud's cognitive psychology.* New York: W. H. Freeman.

Erikson, E. (1950). *Childhood and society.* New York: W. W. Norton.

Erikson, E. H. (1963). *Childhood and society* (2nd ed.). New York: Norton.

Erikson, E. H. (1964). *Insight and responsibility.* New York: Norton.

Erikson, E. H. (1968a). Identity and identity diffusion. In C. Gordon & K. J. Gergen (Eds.), *The self in social interaction* (pp. 197–205). New York: Wiley.

Erikson, E. H. (1968b). *Identity: Youth and crisis.* New York: Norton.

Erikson, E. H. (1974). *Dimensions of a new identity: The 1973 Jefferson lectures in the humanities.* New York: Norton.

Erikson, E. H. (1975). *Life history and the historical moment.* New York: Norton.

Erikson, E. H. (1977). *Toys and reasons: Stages in the ritualization of experience.* New York: Norton.

Erikson, E. H., Erikson, J. M., & Kivnick, H. Q. (1986). *Vital involvement in old age.* New York: W. W. Norton.

Erwin, E. (1980). Psychoanalytic therapy: The Eysenck argument. *American Psychologist, 35,* 435–443.

Esterson, A. (2001). The mythologizing of psychoanalytic history: Deception and self-deception in Freud's accounts of the seduction theory episode. *History of Psychiatry, 12,* 329–352.

Evans, R. (1967). *Dialogue with Erik Erikson.* New York: Harper & Row.

Evans, R. I. (1970). *Gordon Allport: The man and his ideas.* New York: Dutton.

Eysenck, H. J. (1947). *Dimensions of personality.* London: Routledge & Kegan Paul.

Eysenck, H. J. (1952). The effects of psychotherapy: An evaluation. *Journal of Consulting Psychology, 16,* 319–324.

Eysenck, H. J. (1961). The effects of psychotherapy. In H. J. Eysenck (Ed.), *Handbook of abnormal psychology: An experimental approach* (pp. 697–725). New York: Basic Books.

Eysenck, H. J. (1965). *Fact and fiction in psychology.* Baltimore, MD: Penguin Books.

Eysenck, H. J. (1967). *The biological basis of personality.* Springfield, IL: Charles C Thomas.

Eysenck, H. J. (1970). *The structure of human personality* (3rd ed.). London: Methuen.

Eysenck, H. J. (1975). *The inequality of man.* San Diego: EdITS.

Eysenck, H. J. (1976). *The measurement of personality.* Lancaster: Medical & Technical Publishers.

Eysenck, H. J. (1980). Hans Jurgen Eysenck. In G. Lindzey (Ed.), *A history of psychology in autobiography* (Vol. *7*, pp. 153–187). San Francisco: W. H. Freeman.

Eysenck, H. J. (1982). Development of a theory. In H. J. Eysenck (Ed.), *Personality, genetics, and behavior: Selected papers* (pp. 1–48). New York: Praeger.

Eysenck, H. J. (1990). Biological dimensions of personality. In L. A. Pervin (Ed.), *Handbook of personality: Theory and research* (pp. 244–276). New York: Guilford Press.

Eysenck, H. J. (1993). Creativity and personality: Suggestions for a theory. *Psychological Inquiry, 4,* 147–178.

Eysenck, H. J. (1995). *Genius: The natural history of creativity.* New York: Cambridge University Press.

Eysenck, H. J. (1997a). Personality and experimental psychology: The unification of psychology and the possibility of a paradigm. *Journal of Personality and Social Psychology, 73,* 1224–1237.

Eysenck, H. J. (1997b). *Rebel with a cause: The autobiography of Hans Eysenck.* (Revised and expanded edition). New Brunswick, NJ: Transaction Publishers.

Eysenck, H. J., & Eysenck, M. W. (1985). *Personality and individual differences: A natural science approach.* New York: Plenum Press.

Eysenck, H. J., & Eysenck, S. B. G. (1975). *Manual of the Eysenck Personality Questionnaire.* San Diego: EdITS.

Eysenck, H. J., & Gudjonsson, G. H. (1989). *The causes and cures of criminality.* New York: Plenum Press.

Eysenck, H. J., & Kamin, L. (1981). *The intelligence controversy: H. J. Eysenck versus Kamin.* New York: John Wiley.

Eysenck, S. B. G. (1965). *Manual of the Junior Eysenck Personality Inventory.* London: Hodder & Stoughton.

Eysenck, S. B. G., Eysenck, H. J., & Barrett, P. (1985). A revised version of the psychoticism scale. *Personality and Individual Differences, 6,* 21–29.

Falbo, T. (1977). The only child: A review. *Journal of Individual Psychology, 33,* 47–61.

Falbo, T., & Cooper, C. R. (1980). Young children's time and intellectual ability. *Journal of Genetic Psychology, 173,* 299–300.

Falbo, T., & Polit, D. F. (1986). Quantitative review of the only child literature: Research evidence and theory development. *Psychological Bulletin, 100,* 176–189.

Falbo, T., & Poston, D. L., Jr. (1993). The academic, personality, and physical outcomes of only children in China. *Child Development, 64,* 18–35.

Feingold, A. (1994). Gender differences in personality: A meta-analysis. *Psychological Bulletin, 116,* 429–456.

Fenichel, O. (1945). *The psychoanalytic theory of neurosis.* New York: Norton.

Ferster, C. B., & Perrott, M. C. (1968). *Behavior principles.* New York: Appleton-Century-Crofts.

Fiebert, M. S. (1997). In and out of Freud's shadow: A chronology of Adler's relationship with Freud. *Individual Psychology, 53,* 241–269.

Field, D., & Millsap, R. E. (1991). Personality in advanced old age: Continuity or change? *Journal of Gerontology, 46,* 299–308.

Finch, J. F., & Graziano, W. G. (2001). Predicting depression from temperament, personality, and patterns of social relations. *Journal of Personality, 69,* 27–55.

Fischer, R. E., & Juni, S. (1982). The anal personality: Self-disclosure, negativism, self-esteem, and superego severity. *Journal of Personality Assessment, 46,* 50–58.

Fisher, B. J. (1995). Successful aging, life satisfaction, and generativity in later life. *International Journal of Aging and Human Development, 41,* 239–250.

Fisher, B.J., & Specht, D. K. (1999). Successful aging and creativity in later life. *Journal of Aging Studies, 13,* 457–472.

Flavell, J. H. (1963). *The developmental psychology of Jean Piaget.* New York: Van Nostrand.

Fletcher, T. D., & Nusbaum, D. N. (2008). Trait competitiveness as a composite variable: Linkages with facets of the big-five. *Personality and Individual Differences, 45,* 312–317.

Fordham, F. (1966). *An introduction to Jung's psychology.* Middlesex, England: Penguin Books.

Forer, L. K. (1977). The use of birth order information in psychotherapy. *Journal of Individual Psychology, 33,* 105–113.

Fox, J., Knapp, R. R., & Michael, W. B. (1968). Assessment of self-actualization of psychiatric patients: Validity of the Personal Orientation Inventory. *Educational and Psychological Measurement, 28,* 565–569.

Francis, L. J., Robbins, M., Kaldor, K., & Castle, K. (2009). Psychological type and work-related Psychological health among clergy in Australia, England, and New Zealand. *Journal of Psychology and Christianity, 28,* 200–212.

Franks, C. M., Wilson, G. T., Kendall, P. C., & Foreyt, J. P. (1990). *Review of behavior theory: Theory and practice* (Vol. 12). New York: Guilford Press.

Fransella, F. (1995). *George Kelly.* London: Sage Publications.

Fransella, F., & Dalton, P. (1990). *Personal construct counseling in action*. Newbury Park, CA: Sage.

Freedman, A. E. (1972). *The planned society: An analysis of Skinner's proposals*. Kalamazoo, MI: Behaviordelia.

Freeman, A., & Oster, C. (1998). Treatment of couples with relationship difficulty: A cognitive-behavioral perspective. In J. Carlson and L. Sperry (Eds.), *The disordered couple* (pp. 97–119). Bristol, PA: Brunner/Mazel.

Freud, A. (1946). *The ego and the mechanisms of defense* (C. Baines, Trans.). New York: International Universities Press.

Freud, S. (1937). Analysis terminable and interminable. In J. Strachey (Ed.), *Standard edition of the complete psychological works of Sigmund Freud* (Vol. 23, pp. 216–237). London: Hogarth Press.

Freud, S. (1938a). The history of the psychoanalytic movement. In A. A. Brill (Ed.), *The basic writings of Sigmund Freud* (pp. 931–977). New York: Random House.

Freud, S. (1938b). The interpretation of dreams. In A. A. Brill (Ed.), *The basic writings of Sigmund Freud* (pp. 179–549). New York: Random House.

Freud, S. (1938c). Totem and taboo. In A. A. Brill (Ed.), *The basic writings of Sigmund Freud* (pp. 807–930). New York: Random House.

Freud, S. (1938d). Three contributions to the theory of sex. In A. A. Brill (Ed.), *The basic writings of Sigmund Freud* (pp. 553–603). New York: Random House.

Freud, S. (1947). *Leonardo Da Vinci: A study in psychosexuality* (A. A. Brill, trans.). New York: Random House.

Freud, S. (1950). *Totem and taboo* (J. Strachey, Trans.). New York: Norton.

Freud, S. (1952a). Civilization and its discontents. In R. M. Hutchins (Ed.), *Great books of the Western world* (pp. 767–802). Chicago: Encyclopaedia Britannica.

Freud, S. (1952b). Beyond the pleasure principle. In R. M. Hutchins (Ed.), *Great books of the Western world* (pp. 639–663). Chicago: Encyclopaedia Britannica.

Freud, S. (1957). *A general introduction to psychoanalysis* (rev. ed.; J. Riviere, Trans.). New York: Permabooks.

Freud, S. (1958). Observations on transference-love. In J. Strachey (Ed.), *Standard edition of the complete psychological works of Sigmund Freud* (Vol. 12, pp. 159–171). London: Hogarth Press.

Freud, S. (1960a). *The ego and the id* (J. Riviere, Trans.; J. Strachey, Ed.). New York: Norton.

Freud, S. (1960b). *The psychopathology of everyday life* (A. Tyson, Trans.; J. Strachey, Ed.). New York: Norton.

Freud, S. (1969). *An outline of psychoanalysis* (J. Strachey, Trans. & Ed.). New York: Norton.

Fulton, A. S. (1997). Identity status, religious orientation, and prejudice. *Journal of Youth and Adolescence, 26*, 1–11.

Funder, D. C. (1991). Global traits: A neo-Allportian approach to personality. *Psychological Science, 2*, 31–39.

Funder, D. C. (2001). Personality. *Annual Review of Psychology, 52*, 197–221.

Furnham, A., & Bradley, A. (1997). Music while you work: The differential distraction of background music on the cognitive test performance of introverts and extraverts. *Applied Cognitive Psychology, 11*, 445–455.

Furnham, A., Gunter, B., & Peterson, E. (1994). Television distraction and the performance of introverts and extraverts. *Applied Cognitive Psychology, 8*, 705–711.

Furtmuller, C. (1973). Alfred Adler: A biographical essay. In H. L. Ansbacher & R. R. Ansbacher (Eds.), *Superiority and social interest* (pp. 330–394). New York: Viking.

Gabriel, M. T., Critelli, J. W., & Ee, J. S. (1994). Narcissistic illusions in self-evaluations of intelligence and attractiveness. *Journal of Personality, 62*, 143–155.

Galef, B. G., Jr. (1991). A contrarian view of the wisdom of the body as it relates to dietary self-selection. *Psychological Review, 98*, 218–223.

Gallagher, K. E., & Parrott, D. J. (2010). Influence of heavy episodic drinking on the relation between men's locus of control and aggression toward intimate partners. *Journal of Studies on Alcohol and Drugs, 71*, 299–306.

Gamez-Guadix, M., Straus, M.A., Carrobles, J.A., Munoz-Rivas, M.J., & Almendros, C. (2010). Corporal punishment and long-term behavior problems: The moderating role of positive parenting and psychological aggression. *Psicothema, 22*, 529–536.

Gara, M. A., Rosenberg, S., & Mueller, D. R. (1989). Perception of self and other in schizophrenia. *International Journal of Personal Construct Psychology, 2*, 253–270.

Garcia, J., Kimeldurf, D. J., & Hunt, E. L. (1961). The use of ionizing radiation as a motivating stimulus. *Psychological Review, 68*, 383–395.

Gartner, J. (1996). Religious commitment, mental health, and prosocial behavior: A review of the empirical literature. In E. P. Shafranske (Ed.), *Religion and the clinical practice of psychology* (pp. 187–214). Washington, D.C.: American Psychological Association.

Gelso, C. J., & Carter, J. A. (1985). The relationship in counseling and psychotherapy: Components, consequences, and theoretical antecedents. *The Counseling Psychologist, 13*, 155–243.

Gilligan, C. (1982). *In a different voice: Psychological theory and women's development*. Cambridge, MA: Harvard University Press.

Gilman, R. (2001). The relationship between life satisfaction, social interest, and frequency of extracurricular activities among adolescent students. *Journal of Youth and Adolescence, 30*, 749–767.

Goggin, J. E., and Goggin, E. B. (2001). *Death of a "Jewish science": Psychoanalysis in the Third Reich.* West Lafayette, Indiana: Purdue University Press.

Goldberg, A. I. (1980). Introductory remarks. In A. Goldberg (Ed.), *Advances in self psychology* (pp. 1–21). New York: International Universities Press.

Goldberg, A. I. (1982). Obituary: Heinz Kohut (1913–1981). *International Journal of Psychoanalysis, 63*, 257–258.

Goldberg, A. I. (1988). *A fresh look at psychoanalysis: The view from self psychology*. Hillsdale, NJ: Analytic Press.

Goldberg, C. (1980). *In defense of narcissism*. New York: Gardner Press.

Goldberg, L. R. (1981). Language and individual differences: The search for universals in personality lexicons. In L. Wheeler (Ed.), *Review of personality and social psychology* (Vol. 2, pp. 141–165). Beverly Hills, CA: Sage.

Goldberg, L. R. (1990). An alternative Adescription of personality: The Big Five factor structure. *Journal of Personality and Social Psychology, 59*, 1216–1229.

Goldberg, L. R. (1992). The development of markers for the Big-Five factor structure. *Psychological Assessment, 4*, 26–42.

Gonzalez, F. (1995). Working with Mexican-American clients. *Psychotherapy, 32*, 696–706.

Goodwin, R., & Gaines, Jr., S.O. (2004). Relationship beliefs and relationship quality across cultures: Country as a moderator of dysfunctional beliefs and relationship quality in three former Communist societies. *Personal Relationships, 11*, 267–279.

Gorsuch, R. L. (1984). R.B. Cattell: An integration of psychology and ethics. *Multivariate Behavioral Research, 19*, 209–220.

Gosling, S. D., Ko, S. J., Mannarelli T., & Morris, M. E. (2002). A room with a cue: Personality judgments based on offices and bedrooms. *Journal of Personality and Social Psychology, 82*, 379–398.

Grant, V. J. (2005). Dominance, testosterone and psychological sex differences. In J.W. Lee (Ed.), *Psychology of gender identity* (pp. 1–28). New York: Nova Science Publishers.

Greever, K. B., Tseng, M. S., & Friedland, B. U. (1973). Development of the social interest index. *Journal of Consulting and Clinical Psychology, 41*, 454–458.

Grembowski, D., Patrick, D., Diehr, P., Durham, M., Beresford, S., Kay, E., & Hecht, J. (1993). Self-efficacy and health behavior among older adults. *Journal of Health and Social Behavior, 34*, 89–104.

Grossarth-Maticek, R., & Eysenck, H. J. (1990). Prophylactic effects of psychoanalysis on cancer-prone and coronary heart disease-prone probands, as compared with control groups and behaviour therapy. *Journal of Behavior Therapy and Experimental Psychiatry, 21*, 91–99.

Grusec, J., & Mischel, W. (1966). Model's characteristics as determinants of social learning. *Journal of Personality and Social Psychology, 4*, 211–215.

Guadagno, R. E., Okdie, B. M., & Eno, C. A. (2008). Who blogs? Personality predictors of blogging. *Computers in Human Behavior, 24*, 1993–2004.

Gueye, M., Castle, S., & Konate, M. K. (2001). Timing of first intercourse among Malian adolescents: Implications for contraceptive use. *International Family Planning Perspectives, 27*, 56–62.

Gutride, M. E., Goldstein, A. P., & Hunter, G. F. (1973). The use of modeling to increase social interaction among asocial psychiatric patients. *Journal of Consulting and Clinical Psychology, 40*, 408–415.

Halamandaris, K. F., & Power, K. G. (1997). Individual differences, dysfunctional attitudes, and social support: A study of the psychosocial adjustment to university life of home students. *Personality and Individual Differences, 22*, 93–104.

Halbertal, T. H., & Koren, I. (2006). *Between "being" and "doing": Conflict and coherence in the identity formation of gay and lesbian orthodox jews*. In D. P. McAdams, R. Josselson, & A. Lieblich (Eds.), *Identity and story: Creating self in narrative* (pp. 37–61). Washington, DC: American Psychological Association.

Hall, D. L., Matz, D. C., & Wood, W. (2010). Why don't we practice what we preach? A meta-analytic review of religious racism. *Personality and Social Psychology Review, 14,* 126–139.

Hall, S. S. (2010). Revolution postponed. *Scientific American, 303,* 60–67.

Harakeh, Scholte, R. H. J., deVries, H., & Engels, R. (2006). Association between personality and adolescent smoking. *Addictive Behaviors, 31,* 232–245.

Hardigan, P. C., Cohen, S. R., & Carvajal, M. J. (2001). Linking job satisfaction and career choice with personality styles: An exploratory study of practicing pharmacists. *Journal of Psychological Types, 57,* 30–35.

Harrar, S. (2002). How grudges hurt you. *Prevention, 54,* 38–39.

Harrington, D. M., Block, J. H., & Block, J. (1987). Testing aspects of Carl Rogers's theory of creative environments: Child-rearing antecedents of creative potential in young adolescents. *Journal of Personality and Social Psychology, 52,* 851–856.

Harris, A. H. S., Thoresen, M. E., McCullough, M. E., & Larson, D. B. (1999). Spiritually and religiously oriented health interventions. *Journal of Health Psychology, 4,* 413–433.

Harter, S. L., Erbes, C. R., & Hart, C. C. (2004). Content analysis of the personal constructs of female sexual abuse survivors elicited through repertory grid technique. *Journal of Constructivist Psychology, 17,* 27–43.

Hattrup, K., O'Connell, M. S., & Labrador, J. R. (2005). Incremental validity of locus of control after controlling for cognitive ability and conscientiousness. *Journal of Business & Psychology, 19,* 461–481.

Haviland, W. A. (1994). *Anthropology* (7th ed.). New York: Harcourt Brace.

Haymes, M., & Green, L. (1982). The assessment of motivation within Maslow's framework. *Journal of Research in Personality, 16,* 179–192.

Heaven, P. C. L., & Ciarrochi, J. (2008). Parental styles, conscientiousness, and academic performance in high school: A three-wave longitudinal study. *Personality and Social Psychology Bulletin, 34,* 451–461.

Hecker, J. E., & Thorpe, G. L. (1987). Fear reduction processes in imaginal and in vivo flooding: A comment on James' review. *Behavioural Psychotherapy, 15,* 215–223.

Hegel, M. T., & Ferguson, R. J. (2000). Differential reinforcement of other behavior (DRO) to reduce aggressive behavior following trumatic brain injury. *Behavior Modification, 24,* 94–101.

Helms, J. E., & Cook, D. A. (1999). *Using race and culture in counseling and psychotherapy: Theory and process.* Boston, MA: Allyn and Bacon.

Hempel, C. (1966). *Philosophy of natural science.* Englewood Cliffs, NJ: Prentice Hall.

Herrenkohl, R. C., & Russo, M. J. (2001). Abusive early child rearing and early childhood aggression. *Child Maltreatment, 6,* 3–16.

Hill, C. E., & Nakayama, E.Y. (2000). Client-centered therapy: Where has it been and where is it going? A comment on Hathaway. *Journal of Clinical Psychology, 56,* 861–875.

Hill, C. E., Helms, J. E., Tichenor, V., Spiegel, S. B., O'Grady, K. E., & Perry, E. S. (1988). Effects of therapist response modes in brief psychotherapy. *Journal of Counseling Psychology, 35,* 222–233.

Hill, P. C., & Pargament, K. I. (2003). Advances in the conceptualization and measurement of religion and spirituality: Implications for physical and mental health research. *American Psychologist, 58,* 64–74.

Hoffman, E. (1988). *The right to be human: A biography of Abraham Maslow.* New York: St. Martin's Press.

Hoffman, E. (1994). The drive for self: Alfred Adler and the founding of Individual Psychology. Reading, MA: Addison-Wesley Publishing.

Hoffman, E. (1998). Peak experiences in childhood: An exploratory study. *Journal of Humanistic Psychology, 38,* 109–120.

Hoffman, L. W. (1974). Fear of success in males and females: 1965–1971. *Journal of Consulting and Clinical Psychology, 24,* 353–358.

Holder, E. E., & Levi, D. J. (1988). Mental health and locus of control: SCL-90-R and Levenson's IPC scales. *Journal of Clinical Psychology, 44,* 753–755.

Holt, R. R. (1962). Individuality and generalization in the psychology of personality. *Journal of Personality, 30,* 377–402.

Holtfreter, K., Reisig, M. D., Piquero, N. L., & Piquero, A. R. (2010). Low self-control and fraud: Offending, victimization, and their overlap. *Criminal Justice and Behavior, 37,* 188–203.

Hong, R. Y., & Paunonen, S. V. (2009). Personality traits and and health-risk behaviours in university students. *European Journal of Personality, 23,* 675–696.

Hong, T. B., Oddone, E. Z., Dudley, T. K., & Bosworth, H. B. (2006). Medication barriers and anti-hypertensive medication adherence: The moderating role of locus of control. *Psychology, Health & Medicine, 11*, 20–28.

Horney, K. (1937). *The neurotic personality of our time.* New York: Norton.

Horney, K. (1939). *New ways in psychoanalysis.* New York: Norton.

Horney, K. (1942). *Self-analysis.* New York: Norton.

Horney, K. (1945). *Our inner conflicts.* New York: Norton.

Horney, K. (1950). *Neurosis and human growth.* New York: Norton.

Horney, K. (1967). *Feminine psychology.* New York: Norton

Horvath, P. (1998). Agency and social adaptation. *Applied Behavioral Science Review, 6,* 137–154.

Houston, J. M., Harris, P. B., & Norman, M. (2003). The Aggressive Driving Behavior Scale: Developing a self-report measure of unsafe driving practices. *North American Journal of Psychology, 5,* 269–278.

Howard, J. A., Blumstein, P., & Schwartz, P. (1986). Sex, power, and influence tactics in intimate relationships. *Journal of Personality and Social Psychology, 51,* 102–109.

Hudson, V. M. (1990). Birth order of world leaders: An exploratory analysis of effects on personality and behavior. *Political Psychology, 11,* 583–601.

Hui, K. V., & Fung, H. H. (2009). Mortality anxiety as a function of intrinsic religiosity and perceived purpose in life. *Death Studies, 33,* 30–50.

Hull, C. L. (1951). *Essentials of behavior.* New Haven, CT: Yale University Press.

Huprich, S. K., Clancy, C., Bornstein, R. F., & Nelson-Gray, R. O. (2004). Do dependency and social skills combine to predict depression? Linking two diatheses in mood disorders research. *Individual Differences Research, 2,* 2–16.

Hwang, Y. G. (1995). Student apathy, lack of self-responsibility and false self-esteem are failing American schools. *Education, 115,* 484–490.

Hyland, M. E. (1989). There is no motive to avoid success: The compromise explanation for success-avoiding behavior. *Journal of Personality, 57,* 665–693.

Ilardi, R. L., & May, W. T. (1968). A reliability study of Shostrom's Personal Orientation Inventory. *Journal of Humanistic Psychology, 8,* 68–72.

Ingersoll-Dayton, B., & Krause, N. (2005). Self-forgiveness: A component of mental health in later life. *Research on Aging, 27,* 267–289.

Internet World Stats (2007). *World internet users and population statistics data accessed.* March 21, 2007. http://www.Internetworldstats.com/stats.htm.

Ipsa, J. M., Fine, M. A., & Thornburg, K. R. (2002). Maternal personality as a moderator of relations between difficult infant temperament and attachment security in low-income families. *Infant Mental Health Journal, 23,* 130–144.

Iwamasa, G. Y., Sorocco, K. H., & Koonce, D. A. (2002). Ethnicity and clinical psychology: A content analysis of the literature. *Clinical Psychology Review, 22,* 931–944.

Jacka, B. (1991). Personality variables and attitudes toward dream experiences. *Journal of Psychology, 125,* 27–31.

Jackson, D. A., & Wallace, R. F. (1974). The modification and generalization of voice loudness in a fifteen-year-old retarded girl. *Journal of Applied Behavior Analysis, 7,* 461–471.

Jackson, J. W. (2002). Enhancing self-efficacy and learning performance. *Journal of Experimental Education, 70,* 243–254.

Jackson, A. P., Choi, J. K., & Bentler, P. M. (2009). Parenting efficacy and the early school adjustment of poor and near-poor black children. *Journal of Family Issues, 30,* 1399–1455.

Jacobi, J. (1962). *The Psychology of C. G. Jung.* New Haven, CT: Yale University Press.

Jahoda, M. (1989). A helping hand to evolution? *Contemporary Psychology, 34,* 816–817.

Jang, K. L., Vernon, P. A., Livesley, W. J., Stein, M. B., & Wolf, H. (2001). Intra- and extra-familial influences on alcohol and drug misuse: A twin study of gene-environment correlation. *Addiction, 96,* 1307–1318.

Jankowicz, A. D. (1987). Whatever became of George Kelly? *American Psychologist, 42,* 481–487.

Jensen-Campbell, L. A., Adams, R., Perry, D. G., Workman, K. A., Furdella, J. Q., & Egan, S. K. (2002). Agreeableness, extraversion, and peer relations in early adolescence: Winning friends and deflecting aggression. *Journal of Research in Personality, 36,* 224–251.

John, O. P. (1989). Towards a taxonomy of personality descriptors. In D. M. Buss & N. Cantor (Eds.), *Personality psychology: Recent trends and emerging directions* (pp. 261–271). New York: Springer-Verlag.

John, O. P. (1990). The "Big Five" factor taxonomy: Dimensions of personality in the natural language and in questionnaires. In L. A. Pervin (Ed.), *Handbook of personality: Theory and research* (pp. 66–100). New York: Guilford Press.

John, O. P., & Srivastava, S. (1999). The Big Five trait taxonomy: History, measurement, and theoretical perspectives. In L. A. Pervin and O. P. John (Eds.) *Handbook of Personality: Theory and research* (2nd ed.) (pp. 102–138). New York: Guilford Press.

John, O. P., Caspi, A., Robins, R. W., Moffitt, T. E., & Stouthamer-Loeber, M. (1994). The "Little Five": Exploring the nomological network of the five-factor model of personality in adolescent boys. *Child Development, 65*, 160–178.

John, O. P., Donahue, E. M., & Kentle, R. L. (1991). *The Big Five Inventory 4a and 54*. Berkeley, CA: University of California, Berkeley, Institute of Personality and Social Research.

Johnson, M. (2002). The importance of self-attitudes for type A-B, internality-externality and health status. *Personality and Individual Differences, 33*, 777–789.

Johnson, P., Smith, A. J., & Nelson, M. D. (2003). Predictors of social interest in young adults. *Journal of Individual Psychology, 59*, 281–292.

Jones, E. (1963). *The life and work of Sigmund Freud* (L. Trilling & S. Marcus, Eds.). Garden City, NY: Anchor Books.

Jones, M. C. (1924). A laboratory study of fear: The case of Peter. *Pedagogical Seminar, 31*, 308–315.

Jost, K. (1997). Religious persecution, *CQ Researcher, 7*, 1011–1031.

Jung, C. G. (1923). *Psychological types*. New York: Harcourt.

Jung, C. G. (1954). The practice of psychotherapy. In *The collected works of C. G. Jung* (Vol. 16). London: Routledge & Kegan Paul.

Jung, C. G. (1958a). Commentary on secret of the golden flower. In V. S. de Laszlo (Ed.), *Psyche and symbol* (pp. 302–351). Garden City, NY: Doubleday Anchor.

Jung, C. G. (1958b). The special phenomenology of the child archetype. In V. S. de Laszlo (Ed.), *Psyche and symbol* (pp. 132–147). Garden City, NY: Doubleday Anchor.

Jung, C. G. (1958c). The psychology of the child archetype. In V. S. de Laszlo (Ed.), *Psyche and symbol* (pp. 113–131). Garden City, NY: Doubleday Anchor.

Jung, C. G. (1959). The relations between the ego and the unconscious. In V. S. de Laszlo (Ed.), *The basic writings of C. G. Jung* (pp. 105–182). New York: Modern Library.

Jung, C. G. (1961). *Two essays on analytical psychology*. New York: Meridian.

Jung, C. G. (1963). *Memories, dreams, reflections*. New York: Pantheon.

Jung, C. G. (1964). *Man and his symbols*. Garden City, New York: Doubleday and Company.

Jung, C. G. (1969). *The structure and dynamics of the psyche* (2nd ed.). Princeton, NJ: Princeton University Press.

Juni, S., & Rubenstein, V. (1982). Anality and routine. *Journal of Personality Assessment, 46*, 142.

Juni, S., Masling, J., & Brannon, R. (1979). Interpersonal touching and orality. *Journal of Personality Assessment, 43*, 235–237.

Kachadourian, L. K., Fincham, F., & Davila, J. (2004). The tendency to forgive in dating and married couples: The role of attachment and relationship satisfaction. *Personal Relationships, 11*, 373–393.

Kaczor, L. M., Ryckman, R. M., Thornton, B., & Kuehnel, R. H. (1991). Observer hypercompetitiveness and victim precipitation of rape. *Journal of Social Psychology, 131*, 131–134.

Kahn, E. (1999). A critique of nondirectivity in the person-centered approach. *Journal of Humanistic Psychology, 39*, 94–110.

Kahn, E. (2002). A way to help people by holding theory lightly: A response to Bozarth, Merry and Brodley, and Sommerbeck. *Journal of Humanistic Psychology, 42*, 88–96.

Kalechstein, A. D., & Nowicki, S., Jr. (1997). A meta-analytic examination of the relationship between control expectancies and academic achievement: A 11-year follow-up to Findley and Cooper. *Genetic, Social, and General Psychology Monographs, 123*, 29–56.

Kalkan, M. (2009). Adlerian Social Interest Scale-Romantic Relationship form (ASIS-RR): Scale development and psychometric properties. *Individual Differences Research, 7*, 40–48.

Kannarkat, J. P., & Bayton, J. A. (1979). Validity of Adler's active-constructive, active-destructive, passive-constructive, and passive-destructive typology. *Journal of Research in Personality, 13*, 351–360.

Kapalka, G. M., & Lachenmeyer, J. R. (1988). Sex-role flexibility, locus of control, and occupational status. *Sex Roles, 19*, 417–427.

Kaplan, A., Gheen, M., & Midgley, C. (2002). Classroom goal structure and student disruptive behaviour. *British Journal of Educational Psychology, 72*, 191–211.

Kappe, R., & van der Flier, H. (2010). Using multiple and specific criteria to assess the predictive validity of the Big Five personality factors on academic performance. *Journal of Research in personality, 44*, 142–145.

Karabati, S., & Cemalcilar, Z. (2010). Values, materialism, and well-being: A study with Turkish university students. *Journal of Economic Psychology, 31*, 624–633.

Karim, N. S. A., Zamzuri, N. H. A., & Nor, Y. M. (2009). Exploring the relationship between internet ethics in university students and the big five model of personality. *Computers & Education, 53,* 86–93.

Kasser, T., & Ahuvia, A. (2002). Materialistic values and well-being in business students. *European Journal of Social Psychology, 32,* 137–146.

Kasser, T., & Ryan, R. M. (1993). A dark side of the American dream: Correlates of financial success as a central life aspiration. *Journal of Personality and Social Psychology, 65,* 410–422.

Kasser, T., & Sheldon, K. M. (2000). Of wealth and death: Materialism, mortality salience, and consumption behavior. *Psychological Science, 11,* 348–351.

Katkovsky, W. (1968). Social-learning theory and maladjustment. In L. Gorlow & W. Katkovsky (Eds.), *Readings in the psychology of adjustment* (2nd ed.) (pp. 213–232). New York: McGraw-Hill.

Katz, E., Fromme, K., & D'Amico, E. (2000). Effects of outcome expectancies and personality on young adults' illicit drug use, heavy drinking, and risky sexual behavior. *Cognitive Therapy and Research, 24,* 1–22.

Kauffman, R. A., & Ryckman, R. M. (1979). Effects of locus-of-control, outcome severity, and attitudinal similarity of defendant on attributions of criminal responsibility. *Personality and Social Psychology Bulletin, 5,* 340–343.

Kay, A. C., Gaucher, D., McGregor, & Nash, K. (2010). *Religious belief as compensatory control. Personality and Social Psychology Review, 14,* 37–48.

Kazdin, A. E. (1989). *Behavior modification in applied settings* (4th ed.). Pacific Grove, CA: Brooks/Cole.

Kehle, T. J., Bray, M. A., Margiano, S. G., Theodore, L. A., & Zhou, Z. (2002). Self-modeling as an effective intervention for students with serious emotional disturbance: Are we modifying children's memories? *Psychology in the Schools, 39,* 203–207.

Kelley, T. M., & Stack, S. A. (2000). Thought recognition, locus of control, and adolescent well-being. *Adolescence, 35,* 531–550.

Kelly, G. A. (1955). *The psychology of personal constructs* (Vols. 1 & 2). New York: Norton.

Keltikangas-Jarvinen, L., & Raikkonen, K. (1990). Healthy and maladjusted Type A behavior in adolescents. *Journal of Youth and Adolescence, 19,* 1–18.

Kenrick, D. T., Sadalla, E. K., Groth, G., & Trost, M. R. (1990). Evolution, traits, and the stages of human courtship: Qualifying the parental investment model. *Journal of Personality, 58,* 97–116.

Keutzer, C. S. (1978). Whatever turns you on: Triggers to transcendent experiences. *Journal of Humanistic Psychology, 18,* 77–80.

Kevles, D. J. (1985). *In the name of eugenics.* New York: Knopf.

Kim, J. H., Lau, C. H., Cheuk, K.-K., Kan, P., Hui, H. L. C., & Griffiths, S. M. (2010). Brief report: Predictors of heavy Internet use and associations with health-promoting and health Risk behaviors among Hong Kong university students. *Journal of Adolescence, 33,* 215–220.

Kirkcaldy, B. D., Shephard, R. J., & Furnham, A. F. (2002). The influence of type A behaviour and locus of control upon job satisfaction and occupational health. *Personality and Individual Differences, 33,* 1361–1371.

Kirschenbaum, H., & Jourdan, A. (2005). The current status of Carl Rogers and the person-centered approach. *Psychotherapy: Theory, Research, Practice, Training, 42,* 37–51.

Kitayama, S., Markus, H. R., Matsumoto, H., & Norasakkunkit, V. (1997). Individual and collective processes in the construction of the self: Self-enhancement in the United States and self-criticism in Japan. *Journal of Personality and Social Psychology, 72,* 1245–1267.

Kline, P. (1972). *Fact and fantasy in Freudian theory.* London: Methuen.

Knee, C. R., & Neighbors, C. (2002). Self-determination, perception of peer pressure, and drinking among college students. *Journal of Applied Social Psychology, 32,* 522–543.

Knudson-Martin, C., & Mahoney, A. R. (2009). Beyond gender: The processes of relationship equality. In C. Knudson-Martin and A.R. Mahoney (Eds.) *Couples, gender, and power: Creating change in intimate relationships.* New York: Springer Publishing.

Koenig, H. G. (1997). *Is religion good for your health? The effects of religion on physical and mental health.* New York: Haworth Press.

Kohut, H. (1959). Introspection, empathy and psychoanalysis. In P. Ornstein (Ed.), *The search for the self* (Vol. 1, pp. 205–232). New York: International Universities Press.

Kohut, H. (1966). Forms and transformations of narcissism. *Journal of the American Psychoanalytic Association, 14,* 243–272.

Kohut, H. (1971). *The analysis of the self.* New York: International Universities Press.

Kohut, H. (1977). *The restoration of the self.* New York: International Universities Press.

Kohut, H. (1980). Reflections on advances in self psychology. In A. Goldberg (Ed.), *Advances in self psychology* (pp. 473–554).

Kohut, H. (1984). *How does analysis cure?* Chicago: The University of Chicago Press.

Kohut, H. (1985). *Self psychology and the humanities: Reflections on a new psychoanalytic approach*. New York: W. W. Norton.

Kohut, H., & Seitz, P. F. D. (1963). Concepts and theories of psychoanalysis. In J. M. Wepman and R. W. Heine (Eds.), *Concepts of personality* (pp. 113–141). Chicago, IL: Aldine.

Kohut, H., & Wolf, E. (1978). The disorders of the self and their treatment: An outline. *International Journal of Psychoanalysis, 59*, 413–426.

Koltko-Rivera, M. E. (2006). Rediscovering the later Version of Maslow's hierarchy of needs: Self-transcendence and opportunities for theory, research, and unification. *Review of General Psychology, 10*, 302–317.

Kores, R. C., Murphy, W. D., Rosenthal, T. L., Elias, D. B., & North, W. C. (1990). Predicting outcome of chronic pain treatment via a modified self-efficacy scale. *Behaviour Research and Therapy, 28*, 165–169.

Kowalski, H. S., Wyver, S. R., Masselos, G., & DeLacey, P. (2004). Toddlers' emerging symbolic play: a first-born advantage? *Early Child Development & Care, 174*, 389–400.

Kowaz, A. M., & Marcia, J. E. (1991). Development and validation of a measure of Eriksonian industry. *Journal of Personality and Social Psychology, 60*, 390–397.

Krasner, L. (1970). Behavior modification, token economies, and training in clinical psychology. In C. Neuringer & J. L. Michael (Eds.), *Behavior modification in clinical psychology* pp. 86–104). New York: Appleton-Century-Crofts.

Krause, N. (2005). God-mediated control and psychological well-being in later life. *Research on Aging, 27*, 136–164.

Kristal, J. (2005). *The temperament perspective: Working with children's behavioral styles*. New York: Paul H. Brookes Publishing Co.

Kroger, J. (1989). *Identity in adolescence: The balance between self and other*. London: Routledge.

Kroger, J. (2007). *Identity development: Adolescence to adulthood (2nd edition)*. Thousand Oaks, CA: Sage Publications.

Kuhn, T. S. (1996). *The structure of scientific revolutions* (3rd ed.). Chicago: University of Chicago Press.

Kushner, M. (1970). Faradic aversive controls in clinical practice. In C. Neuringer & J. L. Michael (Eds.), *Behavior modification in clinical psychology* (pp. 26–51). New York: Appleton-Century-Crofts.

Lamontagne, Y., Boyer, R., Hetu, C., Lacerte-Lamontagne, C. (2000). Anxiety, significant losses, depression, and irrational beliefs in first-offense shoplifters. *Canadian Journal of Psychiatry, 45*, 63–65.

Landrum, R. E. (1992). College students' use of caffeine and its relationship to personality. *College Student Journal, 26*, 151–155.

Langelaan, L., Bakker, A. B., van Doornen, L. J. P., & Schaufeli, W. B. (2006). Burnout and work engagement: Do individual differences make a difference? *Personality and Individual Differences, 40*, 521–532.

Lapsley, D. K., & Aalsma, M. C. (2006). An empirical typology of narcissism and mental health in late adolescence. *Journal of Adolescence, 29*, 53–71.

Lawson, E. D. (1971). Hair color, personality and the observer. *Psychological Reports, 28*, 311–322.

Leak, G. K., & Gardner, L. E. (1990). Sexual attitudes, love attitudes, and social interest. *Individual Psychology, 46*, 55–60.

Leak, G. K., & Williams, D. E. (1991). Relationship between social interest and perceived family environment. *Journal of Individual Psychology, 47*, 159–165.

Leak, G. K., Millard, R. J., Perry, N. W., & Williams, D. E. (1985). An investigation of the nomological network of social interest. *Journal of Research in Personality, 19*, 197–207.

Lease, S. H. (2004). Effect of locus of control, work knowledge, and mentoring on career decision-making difficulties: Testing the role of race and academic institution. *Journal of Career Assessment, 12*, 239–254.

Lee, R. M., & Robbins, S. B. (2000). Understanding social connectedness in college women and men. *Journal of Counseling & Development, 78*, 484–491.

Lee, R. M., Dean, B. L., & Jung, K. R. (2008). Social connectedness, extraversion, and subjective well-being. *Personality and Individual Differences, 45*, 414–419.

Lefcourt, H. M. (1982). *Locus of control: Current trends in theory and research* (2nd ed.). Hillsdale, NJ: Erlbaum.

Leider, R. J. (1995). The psychology of the self. In E. Nersessian and R. Kopff (Eds.), *The textbook of psychoanalysis*. Washington, DC: American Psychiatric Association Press.

Lent, R. W., Brown, S. D., & Larkin, K. C. (1986). Self-efficacy in the prediction of academic performance and perceived career options. *Journal of Counseling Psychology, 33,* 265–269.

Lesniak, K. T., Rudman, W., Rector, M. B., & Elkin, D. (2006). Psychological distress, stressful life events, and religiosity in younger African American adults. *Mental Health, Religion and Culture, 9,* 15–28.

Lethbridge, D. (1986). A Marxist theory of self-actualization. *Journal of Humanistic Psychology, 26,* 84–153.

Levitz-Jones, E. M., & Orlofsky, J. L. (1985). Separation-individuation and intimacy capacity in college women. *Journal of Personality and Social Psychology, 49,* 156–169.

Lewis, M., & Feiring, C. (1982). Some American families at dinner. In L. M. Laosa & I. E. Sigel (Eds.), *Families as learning environments for children* (pp. 115–145). New York: Plenum.

Lewontin, R. (2000). *It ain't necessarily so: The dream of the human genome and other illusions.* New York: New York Review Books.

Lichtenberg, J. D. (1991). *Psychoanalysis and infant research.* Hillsdale, NJ: Analytic Press.

Lim, V. K. G., Thompson, S. H. T., & Loo, G. L. (2003). Sex, financial hardship and locus of control: An empirical study of attitudes towards money among Singaporean Chinese. *Personality and Individual Differences, 34,* 411–429.

Lipsitz, J. D., Fyer, A. J., Paterniti, A., & Klein, D. F. (2001). Emetophobia: Preliminary results of an internet survey. *Depression and Anxiety, 14,* 149–152.

Liu, X., Kurita, H., Uchiyama, M., Okawa, M., Liu, L., & Ma, D. (2000). Life events, locus of control, and behavioral problems among Chinese adolescents. *Journal of Clinical Psychology, 56,* 1565–1577.

Lovaas, O. I. (1967). A behavior therapy approach to the treatment of childhood schizophrenia. In J. P. Hill (Ed.), *Minnesota symposia on child psychology* (Vol. 1, pp. 108–159). Minneapolis: University of Minnesota Press.

Lowenstein, A., & Rosen, A. (1995). The relation of locus of control and social support to life-cycle related needs of widows. *International Journal of Aging and Human Development, 40,* 103–123.

Lowis, M. J. (2003). Peak emotional experiences and their antecedents: A survey of staff at a British university college. *Korean Journal of Thinking & Problem Solving, 13,* 41–53.

Lubinski, D., Schmidt, D. B., & Benbow, C. P. (1996). A 20-year stability analysis of the study of values for intellectually gifted individuals from adolescence to adult-hood. *Journal of Applied Psychology, 81,* 443–451.

Luman, M., Oosterlaan, J., & Sergeant, J.A. (2005). The impact of reinforcement contingencies on AD/HD: A review and theoretical appraisal. *Clinical Psychology Review, 25,* 183–213.

Luskin, F. (2002). *Forgive for good: A proven prescription for health and happiness.* New York: HarperCollins Publishers.

Luyckx, K., Duriez, B., Klimstra, T. A., & De Witte, H. (2010). Identity statuses in young adult employees: Prospective relations with work engagement and burnout. *Journal of Vocational Behavior, 77,* 339–349.

Luzzo, D. A. (1993). Predicting the career maturity of undergraduates: A comparison of personal, educational, and psychological factors. *Journal of College Student Development, 34,* 271–275.

Luzzo, D. A., & Ward, B. E. (1995). The relative contributions of self-efficacy and locus of control to the prediction of vocational congruence. *Journal of Career Development, 21,* 307–317.

Macavei, B. (2005). The role of irrational beliefs in the rational emotive behavior theory of depression. *Journal of Cognitive and Behavioral Psychotherapies, 5,* 73–81.

Macquarrie, J. (1972). *Existentialism.* Baltimore: Penguin Books.

Maddi, S. R. (1996). *Personality theories: A comparative analysis* (6th ed.). Pacific Grove, CA: Brooks/Cole.

Maddi, S. R., Harvey, R. H., Khoshaba, D. M., Fazel, M., & Resurreccion, N. (2009). The personality construct of hardiness, IV: Expressed in positive cognitions and emotions concerning oneself and developmentally relevant activities. *Journal of Humanistic Psychology, 49,* 292–305.

Mairet, P. (Ed.). (1964). *Alfred Adler: Problems of neurosis: A book of case studies.* New York: Harper & Row.

Malanowski, J. R., & Wood, P. H. (1984). Burnout and self-actualization in public school teachers. *Journal of Psychology, 117,* 23–26.

Maltby, J. Macaskill, A., Day, L., & Garner, I. (1999). Social interest and Eysenck's personality dimensions. *Psychological Reports, 85,* 197–200.

Maltby, J., & Day, L. (2000). Religious orientation and death obsession. *Journal of Genetic Psychology, 161,* 122–124.

Marcia, J. E. (1966). Development and validation of ego-identity status. *Journal of Personality and Social Psychology, 3,* 551–558.

Marcia, J. E. (1993). The status of the statuses: Research review. In J. E. Marcia, A. S. Waterman, D. R. Matteson, S. L. Archer, & J. L. Orlofsky (Eds.), *Ego identity: A handbook for psychosocial research* (pp. 22–41). New York: Springer-Verlag.

Marcia, J. E. (1994). Ego identity and object relations. In J. M. Masling and R. F. Bornstein (Eds.), *Empirical perspectives on object relations theory* (pp. 59–103). Washington, DC: American Psychological Association.

Markus, H. R., & Kitayama, S. (1998). The cultural psychology of personality. *Journal of Cross-cultural Psychology, 29,* 63–87.

Markus, H., & Kitayama, S. (1991). Culture and the self: Implications for cognition, emotion, and motivation. *Psychological Review, 98,* 224–253.

Marshall, W. L. (1985). The effects of variable exposure in flooding therapy. *Behavior Therapy, 16,* 117–135.

Martsh, C. T., & Miller, W. R. (1997). Extraversion predicts heaving drinking in college students. *Personality and Individual Differences, 23,* 153–155.

Marx, M. H. (1964). The general nature of theory construction. In M. H. Marx (Ed.), *Theories in contemporary psychology* (pp. 4–46). New York: Macmillan.

Masling, J. (1986). Orality, pathology and interpersonal behavior. In J. Masling (Ed.), *Empirical studies of psychoanalytic theories* (Vol. 1, pp. 73–106). Hillsdale, NJ: Erlbaum.

Masling, J. (1992). What does it all mean? In R. F. Bornstein and T. S. Pittman (Eds.), *Perception without awareness* (pp. 259–276). New York: Guilford Press.

Masling, J., O'Neill, R., & Katkin, E. S. (1982). Autonomic arousal, interpersonal climate, and orality. *Journal of Personality and Social Psychology, 42,* 529–534.

Masling, J., Price, J., Goldband, S., & Katkin, E. S. (1981). Oral imagery and autonomic arousal in social isolation. *Journal of Personality and Social Psychology, 40,* 395–400.

Maslow, A. H. (1962). *Toward a psychology of being.* New York: Van Nostrand.

Maslow, A. H. (1968). *Toward a psychology of being* (2nd ed.). Princeton, NJ: D. Van Nostrand.

Maslow, A. H. (1970a). *Motivation and personality* (2nd ed.). New York: Harper & Row.

Maslow, A. H. (1970b). *Religions, values, and peak-experiences.* New York: Viking Press.

Maslow, A. H. (1971). *The farther reaches of human nature.* New York: Viking Press.

Maslow, A. H. (1987). *Motivation and personality* (3rd ed.), New York: Harper & Row.

Mason, M.J. (2009). Rogers redux: Relevance and outcomes of motivational interviewing across behavioral problems. *Journal of Counseling & Development, 87,* 357–362.

Mathes, E. W. (1978). Self-actualization, metavalues, and creativity. *Psychological Reports, 43,* 215–222.

Mathes, E. W., & Zevon, M. A. (1982). Peak experience tendencies: Scale development and theory testing. *Journal of Humanistic Psychology, 22,* 92–108.

Matson, J.L., & LoVullo, S.V. (2009). A review of behavioral treatments for self-injurious behaviors of persons with autism spectrum disorders. *Behavior Modification, 32,* 61–76.

May, R. (1953). *Man's search for himself.* New York: Norton.

May, R. (1958a). Contributions of existential psychotherapy. In R. May, E. Angel, & H. F. Ellenberger (Eds.), *Existence: A new dimension in psychiatry and psychology* (pp. 37–91). New York: Basic Books.

May, R. (1958b). The origins and significance of the existential movement in psychology. In R. May, E. Angel, & H. F. Ellenberger (Eds.), *Existence: A new dimension in psychiatry and psychology* (pp. 3–36). New York: Basic Books.

May, R. (1967). *Psychology and the human dilemma.* New York: Van Nostrand.

May, R. (1969). *Love and will.* New York: Norton.

May, R. (1973). Existential psychology. In T. Millon (Ed.), *Theories of psychopathology and personality* (pp. 263–271). Philadelphia: Saunders.

May, R. (1981). *Freedom and destiny.* New York: Norton.

May, R. (1982). The problem of evil: An open letter to Carl Rogers. *Journal of Humanistic Psychology, 22,* 10–21.

May, R. (1983). *The discovery of being: Writings in existential psychology.* New York: Norton.

May, R. (1991). *The cry for myth.* New York: Norton.

May, R., & Schneider, K. (1995). *The psychology of existence: An integrative, clinical perspective.* New York: McGraw-Hill.

Mayr, E. (1994). The advance of science and scientific revolutions. *Journal of the History of the Behavioral Sciences, 30,* 328–334.

Mazur, J. E. (1986). *Learning and behavior.* Englewood Cliffs, NJ: Prentice-Hall.

McAdams, D. P. (1992). The five-factor model in personality: A critical appraisal. *Journal of Personality, 60,* 329–361.

McAdams, D. P. (2001). The psychology of life stories. *Review of General Psychology, 5,* 100–123.

McAdams, D. P., de St. Aubin, E., & Logan, R. L. (1993). Generativity among young, midlife, and older adults. *Psychology and Aging, 8,* 221–230.

McAdams, D. P., Hart, H. M., &: Maruna, S. (1998). The anatomy of generativity. In D. P. McAdams and E. de St. Aubin (Eds.). *Generativity and adult development: How and why we care for the next generation* (pp. 7–43). Washington, D.C.: American Psychological Association.

McCrae, R. R., & Costa, P. T., Jr. (1990). *Personality in adulthood.* New York: Guilford Press.

McCrae, R. R., & John, O. P. (1992). An introduction to the Five-Factor Model and its applications. In R. R. McCrae (Ed.), The Five-Factor Model: Issues and applications. *Journal of Personality, 60,* 175–215.

McCullough, M. E. (2000). Forgiveness as human strength: Theory, measurement, and links to well-being. *Journal of Social and Clinical Psychology, 19,* 43–55.

McFarland, S. G. (1989). Religious orientations and the targets of discrimination. *Journal for the Scientific Study of Religion, 28,* 324–336.

McGee, M. G., & Wilson, D. W. (1984). *Psychology: Science and application.* New York: West.

McGoldrick, M., & Giordano, J. (1996). Overview: Ethnicity and family therapy. In McGoldrick, J. Giordano, and J. K. Pearce (Eds.), *Ethnicity and family therapy* (2nd ed., pp. 1–27). New York: Guilford Press.

McGreevy, M. H., Neubauer, J. F., & Carich, M. S. (2001). Comparison of lifestyle profiles of incarcerated sexual offenders with those of persons incarcerated for other crimes. *Journal of Individual Psychology, 57,* 67–77.

McKenzie, J., & DaCosta, C. (1999). 'Openness-to-experience' as a descriptor of the student actress personality. *Research in Drama Education, 4,* 215–225.

McMains, M. J., & Liebert, R. M. (1968). The influence of discrepancies between successively modeled self-reward criteria on the adoption of a self-imposed standard. *Journal of Personality and Social Psychology, 8,* 166–171.

McNulty, J. K. (2011). The dark side of forgiveness: The tendency to forgive predicts continued psychological and physical aggression in marriage. *Personality and Social Psychology Bulletin, 37,* 770–783.

McPherson, F. M., Armstrong, J., & Heather, B. B. (1978). Psychological construing and thought disorder: Another test of the "difficulty" hypothesis. *British Journal of Medical Psychology, 51,* 319–324.

McPherson, F. M., Buckley, F., & Draffan, J. (1971). "Psychological" constructs and delusions of persecution and "nonintegration" in schizophrenia. *British Journal of Medical Psychology, 44,* 277–280.

Melillo, D. (1983). Birth order, perceived birth order, and family position of academic women. *Individual Psychology, 39,* 57–62.

Mellor, D., Stokes, M., Firth, L., Hayashi, Y., & Cummins, R. (2008). Need for belong, relationship satisfaction, loneliness, and life satisfaction. *Personality and Individual Differences, 45,* 213–218.

Meyer, R. G. (1993). *The clinician's handbook* (3rd ed.). Boston, MA: Allyn and Bacon.

Michels, R. (1988). The future of psychoanalysis. *Psychoanalytic Quarterly, 57,* 167–185.

Milgram, S. (1963). Behavioral study of obedience. *Journal of Abnormal and Social Psychology, 67,* 371–378.

Miller, J. B. (1994). Women's psychological development: Connections, disconnections, and violations. In M. M. Berger (Ed.), *Women beyond Freud: New concepts of feminine psychology* (pp. 79–97). New York: Brunner/Mazel Publishers.

Miller, J. D., Lynam, D. R., & Jones, S. (2008). Externalizing behavior through the lens of the five-factor model: A focus on agreeableness and conscientiousness. *Journal of Personality Assessment, 90,* 158–164.

Miller, P. H. (1993). *Theories of developmental psychology* (3rd ed.). New York: W. H. Freeman.

Miranda, A. O., & Fiorello, K. J. (2002). The connection between social interest and the characteristics of sexual abuse perpetrated by male pedophiles. *Journal of Individual Psychology, 58,* 62–75.

Mirowsky, J. (1995). Age and the sense of control. *Social Psychology Quarterly, 58,* 31–43.

Mitchell, C. W., & Shuff, I. M. (1995). Personality characteristics of hospice volunteers as measured by Myers-Briggs Type Indicator. *Journal of Personality Assessment, 65,* 521–532.

Moller, A. T., Rabe, H. M., & Nortje, C. (2001). Dysfunctional beliefs and marital conflict in distressed and non-distressed married individuals. *Journal of Rational-Emotive & Cognitive Behavior Therapy, 19,* 259–270.

Mooney, S. P., Sherman, M. F., & Lo Presto, C. T. (1991). Academic locus of control, self-esteem, and perceived distance from home as predictors of college adjustment. *Journal of Counseling & Development, 69*, 445–448.

Morf, C. C., & Rhodewalt, F. (1993). Narcissism and self-evaluation maintenance: Explorations in object relations. *Personality and Social Psychology Bulletin, 19*, 668–676.

Morris, C. G. (1982). *Psychology: An introduction* (4th ed.). Englewood Cliffs, NJ: Prentice-Hall.

Morrison, K. A. (1997). Personality correlates of the five-factor model for a sample of business owners/managers: Associations with scores on self-monitoring, Type A behavior, locus of control, and subjective well-being. *Psychological Reports, 80*, 255–272.

Morton, L. C., & Markey, P. M. (2009). Goal agreement and relationship quality among college students and their parents. *Personality and Individual Differences, 47*, 912–916.

Morton, T. L. (1997). The relationship between parental locus of control and children's perceptions of control. *Journal of Genetic Psychology, 158*, 216–225.

Mosak, H. H. (1977). *On purpose: Collected papers of Harold H. Mosak.* Chicago: Alfred Adler Institute.

Moschetta, P. V., & Moschetta, E. F. (1993). Encouraging Social interest between married partners. *Individual Psychology, 49*, 399–405.

Mosher, D. L. (1968). The influence of Adler on Rotter's social learning theory of personality. *Journal of Individual Psychology, 24*, 33–45.

Mottram, A. J., & Fleming, M. J. (2009). Extraversion, impulsivity, and online group membership as predictors of Problematic internet use. *Cyberpsychology & Behavior, 12*, 319–321.

Mudrack, P. E. (1990). Machiavellianism and locus of control: A meta-analytic review. *Journal of Social Psychology, 130*, 125–126.

Muhonen, T., & Torkelson, E. (2004). Work locus of control and its relationship to health and job satisfaction from a gender perspective. *Stress and Health, 20*, 21–28.

Muraven, M., Baumeister, R. F., & Tice, D. M. (1999). Longitudinal improvement of self-regulation through practice: Building self-control strength through repeated exercise. *Journal of Social Psychology, 139*, 446–457.

Muris, P. (2002). Relationships between self-efficacy and symptoms of anxiety disorders and depression in a normal adolescent sample. *Personality and Individual Differences, 32*, 337–348.

Myers, I. B., & McCaulley, M. H. (1985). *A guide to the development and use of the Myers-Briggs Type Indicator.* Palo Alto, CA: Consulting Psychologists Press.

Narayan, R., Shams, G. K., Jain, R., & Gupta, B. S. (1997). Personality characteristics of persons addicted to heroin. *Journal of Psychology, 131*, 125–127.

Negy, C. (2004). Therapy with dissimilar clients: Issues to consider along this road more traveled. In C. Negy (Ed.), *Cross-cultural psychotherapy: Toward a critical understanding of diverse clients.* Brentworth Way, Reno, NV: Bent Tree Press.

Neimeyer, G. J. (1992). Personal constructs and vocational structure. In R. A. Neimeyer and G. J. Neimeyer (Eds.), *Advances in personal construct psychology* (Vol. 2, pp. 91–120). Greenwich, CT: JAI Press.

Neimeyer, G. J., & Hall, A. G. (1988). Personal identity in disturbed marital relationships. In F. Fransella & L. Thomas (Eds.), *Experimenting with personal construct theory* (pp. 297–307). London: Routledge & Kegan Paul.

Neimeyer, R. A. (1985). *The development of personal construct psychology.* Lincoln: University of Nebraska Press.

Nesselroade, J. R., & Cattell, R. B. (Eds.). (1988). *Handbook of multivariate experimental psychology* (2nd ed.). New York: Plenum.

Newman, J., & Taylor, A. (1994). Family training for political leadership: Birth order of United States state governors and Australian prime ministers. *Political Psychology, 15*, 435–442.

Nguyen, N. T., Allen, L. C., & Fraccastoro, K. (2005). Personality predicts academic performance: Exploring the moderating role of gender. *Journal of Higher Education Policy & Management, 27*, 105–116.

Nilius, B. (2010). Editorial: A special issue on channelopathies. *European Journal of Physiology, 460*, 221–222.

Noftle, E. E., & Robins, R. W. (2007). Personality predictors of academic outcomes: Big-Five correlates of GPA and SAT scores. *Journal of Personality and Social Psychology, 93*, 116–130.

Noll, R. (1997). *The Aryan Christ.* New York: Random House.

Norman, W. T. (1963). Toward an adequate taxonomy of personality attributes: Replicated factor structure in peer nomination personality ratings. *Journal of Abnormal and Social Psychology, 66*, 574–583.

Norman, W. T. (1967). *2800 personality trait descriptors: Normative operating characteristics for a university population*. Ann Arbor: University of Michigan, Department of Psychology.

O'Leary, A. (1992). Self-efficacy and health: Behavioral and stress-physiological mediation. *Cognitive Therapy and Research, 16*, 229–245.

O'Leary, K. D., & Wilson, G. T. (1987). *Behavior therapy: Application and outcome* (2nd ed.). Englewood Cliffs, NJ: Prentice-Hall.

O'Neill, R. M. (1984). Anality and Type A coronary-prone behavior pattern. *Journal of Personality Assessment, 48*, 627–628.

O'Neill, R. M., & Bornstein, R. F. (2001). The dependent patient in a psychiatric inpatient setting: Relationship of interpersonal dependency to consultation and medication frequencies. *Journal of Clinical Psychology, 57*, 289–298.

Okun, B. F. (1992). Object relations and self psychology: Overview and feminist perspective. In L. S. Brown & M. Ballou (Eds.), *Personality and psychopathology: Feminist Reappraisals* (pp. 20–45). New York: Guilford Press.

Olatunji, B. O., Deacon, B. J., & Abramowitz, J. S. (2009). The cruelest cure? Ethical issues in the implementation of exposure-based treatments. *Cognitive and Behavioral Practice, 16*, 172–180.

Onyskiw, J. E., & Hayduk, L. A. (2001). Processes underlying children's adjustment in families characterized by physical aggression. *Family Relations, 50*, 376–385.

Orgler, H. (1963). *Alfred Adler: The man and his work*. New York: Liveright.

Orlofsky, J. L. (1976). Intimacy status: Relationship to interpersonal perception. *Journal of Youth and Adolescence, 5*, 73–88.

Orlofsky, J. L. (1978). The relationship between intimacy and antecedent personality components. *Adolescence, 8*, 420–441.

Orlofsky, J. L. (1993). Intimacy status: Theory and research. In J. E. Marcia, A. S. Waterman, D. R. Matteson, S. L. Archer, & J. L. Orlofsky (Eds.), *Ego identity: A handbook for psychosocial research* (pp. 111–133). New York: Springer-Verlag.

Orlofsky, J. L., Marcia, J. E., & Lesser, I. (1973). Ego identity status and the intimacy versus isolation crisis of young adulthood. *Journal of Personality and Social Psychology, 27*, 211–219.

Otway, L. J., & Vignoles, V. L. (2006). Narcissism and childhood recollections: A quantitative test of psychoanalytic predictions. *Personality and Social Psychology Bulletin, 32*, 104–116.

Ozer, E. M., & Bandura, A. (1990). Mechanisms governing empowerment effects: A self-efficacy analysis. *Journal of Personality and Social Psychology, 58*, 472–486.

Paik, H., & Comstock, G. (1994). The effects of television violence on antisocial behavior: A meta-analysis. *Communication Research, 21*, 516–546.

Pajares, F., & Valiante, G. (1997). Influence of self-efficacy on elementary students' writing. *Journal of Educational Research, 90*, 353–360.

Pancer, S. M., Hunsberger, B., Pratt, M. W., & Alisat, S. (2000). Cognitive complexity of expectations and adjustment to university in the first year. *Journal of Adolescent Research, 15*, 38–57.

Papazova, E., & Pencheva, E. (2008). Adolescent self-esteem and psychological type. *Journal of Psychological Type, 68*, 1–10.

Paris, B. (1994). *Karen Horney: A psychoanalyst's search for self-understanding*. New Haven, CT: Yale University Press.

Park, C. L., Cohen, L. H., & Murch, R. L. (1996). Assessment and prediction of stress-related growth. *Journal of Personality, 64*, 71–105.

Parker, G., & Lipscombe, P. (1980). The relevance of early parental experiences to adult dependency, hypochondriasis, and utilization of primary physicians. *British Journal of Medical Psychology, 53*, 355–363.

Passmore, J., Holloway, M., & Rawle-Cope, M. (2010). Using MBTI type to explore differences and implications for practice for therapists andcoaches: Are executive coaches really likecounselors? *Counseling Psychology Quarterly, 23*, 1–16.

Patrick, H., Hicks, L., & Ryan, A. M. (1997). Relations of perceived social efficacy and social goal pursuit to self-efficacy for academic work. *Journal of Early Adolescence, 17*, 109–128.

Paul, A. M. (2004). *The cult of personality*. New York: Free Press.

Paul, H. A. (1989). Karen Horney's theory of self. In D. W. Detrick and S. P. Detrick (Eds.), *Self psychology: Comparisons and contrasts* (pp. 111–127). Hillsdale, NJ: Analytic Press.

Paunonen, S. V., & Ashton, M. C. (2001). Big Five predictors of academic achievement. *Journal of Research in Personality, 35*, 78–90.

Paunonen, S. V., & Jackson, D. N. (2000). What is beyond the Big Five? Plenty! *Journal of Personality, 68*, 821–835.

Pavlov, I. P. (1927). *Conditioned reflexes: An investigation into the physiological activity of the cortex.* New York: Dover.

Pearson, O. (1966). *Effects of group guidance upon college adjustment.* Unpublished doctoral dissertation, University of Kentucky, Lexington.

Penick, S. B., Filion, R., Fox, S., & Stunkard, A. J. (1971). Behavior modification in the treatment of obesity. *Psychosomatic Medicine, 33,* 49–55.

Perosa, S. L., & Perosa, L. (1997). Intergenerational family theory and Kohut's self-psychology constructs applied to college females. *Journal of College Student Development, 38,* 143–156.

Perry, J., Silvera, D., & Rosenvinge, J. H. (2002). Are oral, obsessive, and hysterical personality traits related to disturbed eating patterns? A general population study of 6,313 men and women. *Journal of Personality Assessment, 78,* 405–416.

Persegani, C., Russo, P. Carucci, C., Nicolini, M., Papeschi, L. L., & Trimarchi, M. (2002). Television viewing and personality structure in children. *Personality and Individual Differences, 32,* 977–990.

Phares, E. J. (1971). Internal-external control and the reduction of reinforcement value after failure. *Journal of Consulting and Clinical Psychology, 37,* 386–390.

Phares, E. J. (1976). *Locus of control in personality.* Morristown, NJ: General Learning Press.

Phares, E. J. (1979). Defensiveness and perceived control. In L. C. Perlmutter & R. A. Monty (Eds.), *Choice and perceived control* (pp. 195–208). Hillsdale, NJ: Erlbaum.

Phares, E. J., & Lamiell, J. T. (1974). Relationship of internal-external control to defensive preferences. *Journal of Consulting and Clinical Psychology, 42,* 872–878.

Philpot, C. L., Brooks, G. R., Lusterman, D. D., & Nutt, R. A. (1997). *Bridging separate gender worlds.* Washington, DC: American Psychological Association.

Phinney, J.S. (1990). Ethnic identity in adolescents and adults: Review of research. *Psychological Bulletin, 108,* 499–514.

Piedmont, R. L. (1988). An interactional model of achievement motivation and fear of success. *Sex Roles, 19,* 467–490.

Pierce, D. L., Sewell, K. W., & Cromwell, R. L. (1992). Schizophrenia and depression: Construing and constructing empirical research. In R. A. Neimeyer and G. J. Neimeyer Eds.), *Advances in personal construct psychology* (Vol. *2,* pp. 151–184). Greenwich, CT: JAI Press.

Pincus, A. L., & Wilson, K. R. (2001). Interpersonal variability in dependent personality. *Journal of Personality, 69,* 223–251.

Pinel, J. P. J. (2000). *Biopsychology.* (4th ed.). Boston, MA: Allyn and Bacon.

Pintrich, P. R., & De Groot, E. V. (1990). Motivational and self-regulated learning components of classroom academic performance. *Journal of Educational Psychology, 82,* 33–40.

Platt, J. R. (1973). The Skinnerian revolution. In H. Wheeler (Ed.), *Beyond the punitive society* (pp. 22–56). San Francisco: W. H. Freeman.

Plomin, R. (2000). Behavioural genetics in the 21st century. *International Journal of Behavioral Development, 24,* 30–34.

Plomin, R., Chipuer, H. M., & Loehlin, J. C. (1990). Behavioral genetics and personality. In L. A. Pervin (Ed.), *Handbook of personality: Theory and research* (pp. 225–243). New York: Guilford Press.

Plomin, R., DeFries, J. C., McClearn, G. E., & McGuffin, P. (2008). *Behavioral genetics* (5th ed.). New York: Worth Publishers.

Plomin, R., Owen, M. J., & McGuffin, P. (1994). The genetic basis of complex human behaviors. *Science, 264,* 1733–1739.

Pollak, J. M. (1979). Obsessive-compulsive personality: A review. *Psychological Bulletin, 86,* 225–241.

Ponton, M. O., & Gorsuch, R. L. (1988). Prejudice and religion revisted: A cross-cultural investigation with a Venezuelan sample. *Journal for the Scientific Study of Religion, 27,* 260–271.

Porterfield, J. K., Herbert-Jackson, E., & Risley, T. R. (1976). Contingent observation: An effective and acceptable procedure for reducing disruptive behavior of young children in a group setting. *Journal of Applied Behavior Analysis, 9,* 55–64.

Prager, K. J. (1986). Intimacy status: Its relationship to locus of control, self-disclosure, and anxiety in adults. *Personality and Social Psychology Bulletin, 12,* 91–109.

Prager, K. J. (1989). Intimacy status and couple communication. *Journal of Social and Personal Relationships, 6,* 435–449.

Progoff, I. (1953). *Jung's psychology and its social meaning.* London: Routledge & Kegan Paul.

Propst, L. R. (1996). Cognitive-behavioral therapy and the religious person. In E. P. Shafranske (Ed.), *Religion and the clinical practice of psychology* (pp. 391–407). Washington, D.C.: American Psychological Association.

Puner, H. W. (1947). *Freud: His life and his mind.* New York: Dell.

Putnam, R. F., Handler, M. W., Ramirez-Platt, C. M., & Luiselli, J. K. (2003). Improving student bus-riding behavior through a whole-school intervention. *Journal of Applied Behavior Analysis, 36,* 583–590.

Quadrel, M. J., & Lau, R. R. (1989). Health promotion, health locus of control, and health behavior: Two field experiments. *Journal of Applied Social Psychology, 19,* 1497–1521.

Rachman, S. (1969). Extraversion and neuroticism in childhood. In H. J. Eysenck & S. B. G. Eysenck (Eds.), *Personality structure and measurement* (pp. 253–264). London: Routledge & Kegan Paul.

Rapport, M. D., Murphy, H. A., & Bailey, J. S. (1982). Ritalin vs. response cost in the control of hyperactive children: A within-subject comparison. *Journal of Applied Behavior Analysis, 15,* 205–216.

Raskin, R., Novacek, J., & Hogan, R. (1991). Narcissism, self-esteem, and defensive self-enhancement. *Journal of Personality, 59,* 19–38.

Read, D., Adams, G. R., & Dobson, W. R. (1984). Ego identity, personality, and social influence style. *Journal of Personality and Social Psychology, 46,* 169–177.

Recine, A. C., Werner, J. S., & L. Recine (2009). Health promotion through forgiveness intervention *Journal of Holistic Nursing, 27,* 115–123.

Record, R. G., McKeown, T., & Edwards, J. H. (1970). The relation of measured intelligence to birth order and maternal age. *Annals of Human Genetics, 34,* 61–69.

Redd, W. H. (1980). In vivo desensitization in the treatment of chronic emesis following gastrointestinal surgery. *Behavior Therapy, 11,* 421–427.

Reeves, C. (1977). *The psychology of Rollo May.* San Francisco: Jossey-Bass.

Resnick, B. (2001). Testing a model of exercise behavior in older adults. *Research in Nursing & Health, 24,* 83–92.

Retherford, R. D., & Sewell, W. H. (1991). Birth order and intelligence: Further tests of the confluence model. *American Sociological Review, 56,* 141–158.

Reynolds, L. K., & Kelley, M. L. (1997). The efficacy of a response cost-based treatment package for managing aggressive behavior in preschoolers. *Behavior Modification, 21,* 216–230.

Richards, S. (1987). *Philosophy and sociology of science: An introduction* (2nd ed.). Oxford: Basil Blackwell.

Rietveld, G. (2004). Similarities between Jewish philosophical thought and Adler's Individual Psychology. *Journal of Individual Psychology, 60,* 209–218.

Roazen, P. (1976). *Erik H. Erikson: The power and limits of a vision.* New York: Free Press.

Roberts, L. C., & Blanton, P. W. (2001). "I always knew mom and dad loved me best": Experiences of only children. *Journal of Individual Psychology, 57,* 125–140.

Rodd, J. (1994). Social interest, psychological well-being, and maternal stress. *Individual Psychology, 50,* 58–68.

Rodgers, J. L., Cleveland, H. H., van den Oord, E., & Rowe, D. C. (2000). Resolving the debate over birth order, family size, and intelligence. *American Psychologist, 55,* 599–612.

Rodgers, J. L., Cleveland, H. H., van den Oord, E., & Rowe, D. C. (2001). Birth order and intelligence: Together again for the last time. *American Psychologist, 56,* 523–524.

Rogers, C. R. (1942). *Counseling and psychotherapy: Newer concepts in practice.* Boston: Houghton Mifflin.

Rogers, C. R. (1951). *Client-centered therapy: Its current practice, implications, and theory.* Boston: Houghton Mifflin.

Rogers, C. R. (1954). The case of Mrs. Oak: A research analysis. In C. R. Rogers & R. F. Dymond (Eds.), *Psychotherapy and personality change* (pp. 259–348). Chicago: University of Chicago Press.

Rogers, C. R. (1959). A theory of therapy, personality, and interpersonal relationships, as developed in the client-centered framework. In S. Koch (Ed.), *Psychology: A study of a science* (Vol. 3, pp. 184–256). New York: McGraw-Hill.

Rogers, C. R. (1961). *On becoming a person.* Boston: Houghton Mifflin.

Rogers, C. R. (1968). Graduate education in psychology: A passionate statement. In W. G. Bennis, E. H. Schein, F. I. Steele, & D. E. Berlew (Eds.), *Interpersonal dynamics* (2nd ed., pp. 687–703). Homewood, IL: Dorsey Press.

Rogers, C. R. (1969). *Freedom to learn.* Columbus, OH: Merrill.

Rogers, C. R. (1970). *Carl Rogers on encounter groups.* New York: Harper & Row.

Rogers, C. R. (1972a). *Becoming partners: Marriage and its alternatives.* New York: Delacorte Press.

Rogers, C. R. (1972b). Comments on Brown and Tedeschi's article. *Journal of Humanistic Psychology, 12,* 16–21.

Rogers, C. R. (1977). *Carl Rogers on personal power.* New York: Delacorte Press.

Rogers, C. R. (1982). A psychologist looks at nuclear war: Its threat, its possible prevention. *Journal of Humanistic Psychology, 22,* 9–20.

Rogers, C. R. (1983). *Freedom to learn for the 80s.* Columbus, OH: Merrill.

Rogers, C. R., & Sanford, R. C. (1984). Client-centered psychotherapy. In H. I. Kaplan & B. J. Sadock (Eds.), *Comprehensive textbook of psychiatry* (Vol. 4, pp. 1374–1388). Baltimore: Williams & Wilkins.

Rogers, C. R., & Stevens, B. (1967). *Person to person: The problem of being human.* New York: Simon & Schuster.

Rogers, H. E. (1965). A wife's view of Carl Rogers. *Voices, 1,* 93–98.

Romero, E., Villar, P., Luengo, M. A., & Gomez-Fraguela, J. A. (2009). Traits, personal strivings, and well-being. *Journal of Research in Personality, 43,* 535–546.

Roscigno, V. J., Karafin, D. L., & Tester, G. (2009). The complexities and processes of racial housing discrimination. *Social Problems, 56,* 49–69.

Rosenbaum, M. E., & Tucker, I. F. (1952). Competence of the model and the learning of imitation and nonimitation. *Journal of Experimental Psychology, 63,* 183–190.

Rosenberg-Kima, R. B., Baylor, A. L., Plant, E. A., & Doerr, C. E. (2008). Interface agents as social models for female students: The effects of agent visual presence and appearance on female students' attitudes and beliefs. *Computers in Human Behavior, 24,* 2741–2756.

Rosenberg, S. (1993). Social self and the schizophrenic process: Theory and research. In R. L. Cromwell and C. R. Snyder (Eds.), *Schizophrenia: Origins, processes, treatment, and outcome* (pp. 223–240). New York: Oxford University Press.

Rosenkrans, M. A. (1967). Imitation in children as a function of perceived similarity to a social model and vicarious reinforcement. *Journal of Personality and Social Psychology, 7,* 307–355.

Rosenthal, D. A., Gurney, R. M., & Moore, S. M. (1981). From trust to intimacy: A new inventory for examining Erikson's stages of psychosocial development. *Journal of Youth and Adolescence, 9,* 87–99.

Ross, S. R., Rausch, M. K., & Canada, K. (2003). Competition and cooperation in the five-factor model: Individual differences in achievement orientation. *Journal of Psychology, 137,* 323–337.

Ross, S. R., & Rausch, M. K. (2001). Psychopathic attributes and achievement dispositions in a college sample. *Personality and Individual Differences, 30,* 471–480.

Ross, S. R., Rausch, M. K., & Canada, K. E. (2003). Competition and cooperation in the five-factor model: Individual differences in achievement orientation. *Journal of Psychology, 137,* 323–337.

Ross, S. R., Stewart, J., Mugge, M., & Fultz, B. (2001). The imposter phenomenon, achievement, dispositions, and the five factor model. *Personality and Individual Differences, 31,* 1347–1355.

Roth, G., Assor, A., Niemiec, C. P., Ryan, R. M., & Deci, E. L. (2009). The emotional and academic consequences of parental conditional regard: Comparing conditional positive regard, conditional negative regard, and autonomy support as parenting practices. *Developmental Psychology, 45,* 1119–1142.

Rotter, J. B. (1954). *Social learning and clinical psychology.* Englewood Cliffs, NJ: Prentice-Hall.

Rotter, J. B. (1966). Generalized expectancies for internal versus external control of reinforcement. *Psychological Monographs, 80* (Whole No. 609).

Rotter, J. B. (1975). Some problems and misconceptions related to the construct of internal versus external control of reinforcement. *Journal of Consulting and Clinical Psychology, 43,* 56–67.

Rotter, J. B. (1981). The psychological situation in social learning theory. In D. Magnusson (Ed.), *Toward a psychology of situations: An interactional perspective* (pp. 169–178). Hillsdale, NJ: Erlbaum.

Rotter, J. B. (1982). Social learning theory. In N. T. Feather (Ed.), *Expectations and actions: Expectancy-value models in psychology* (pp. 241–260). Hillsdale, NJ: Erlbaum.

Rotter, J. B., & Hochreich, D. J. (1975). *Personality.* Glenview, IL: Scott, Foresman.

Rotter, J. B., Chance, J. E., & Phares, E. J. (1972). *Applications of a social learning theory of personality.* New York: Holt, Rinehart & Winston.

Rowe, D. C., Vazsonyi, A. T., & Flannery, D. J. (1994). No more than skin deep: Ethnic and racial similarity in developmental process. *Psychological Review, 101,* 396–413. Academic Press.

Rowe, I., & Marcia, J. E. (1980). Ego identity status, formal operations, and moral development. *Journal of Youth and Adolescence, 9,* 87–99.

Rubins, J. L. (1978). *Karen Horney: Gentle rebel of psychoanalysis.* New York: Dial.

Runyan, W. (1982). In defense of the case study method. *American Journal of Orthopsychiatry, 52,* 440–446.

Ryckman, R. M., Hammer, M., Kaczor, L. M., & Gold, J. A. (1996), Construction of a personal development competitive attitude scale. *Journal of Personality Assessment, 66,* 374–385.

Ryckman, R. M., Hammer, M., Kaczor, L. M., & Gold, J. A. (1990). Construction of a hypercompetitive attitude scale. *Journal of Personality Assessment, 55,* 630–639.

Ryckman, R. M., Libby, C. R., van den Borne, B., Gold, J. A., & Lindner, M. A. (1997). Values of hypercompetitive and personal development competitive individuals. *Journal of Personality Assessment, 69,* 271–283.

Ryckman, R. M., Robbins, M. A., Thornton, B., Gold, J. A., & Kuehnel, R. H. (1985). Physical self-efficacy and actualization. *Journal of Research in Personality, 19,* 288–298.

Ryckman, R. M., Thornton, B., & Butler, J. C. (1994). Personality correlates of the hypercompetitive attitude scale: Validity tests of Horney's theory of neurosis. *Journal of Personality Assessment, 62,* 84–94.

Ryckman, R. M., Thornton, B., & Gold, J. A. (2009). Assessing competition avoidance as a basic personality dimension. *Journal of Psychology, 143*(2), 175–192.

Ryckman, R. M., Thornton, B., Gold, J. A., & Burckle, M. A. (2002). Romantic relationships of hypercompetitive individuals. *Journal of Social and Clinical Psychology, 21,* 517–530.

Ryckman, R. M., Hammer, M., Kaczor, L. M., & Gold, J. A. (1996), 375

Rye, M. S., & Pargament, K. I. (2002). Forgiveness and romantic relationships in college: Can it heal the wounded heart? *Journal of Clinical Psychology, 58,* 419–441.

Ryska, T. A. (2002). Perceived purposes of sport among recreational participants: The role of competitive dispositions. *Journal of Sport Behavior, 25,* 91–112.

Sak, U. (2004). A synthesis of research on psychological types of gifted adolescents. *Journal of Secondary Gifted Education, 15,* 70–79.

Sandow, P. L., Jones, A. C., & Moody, R. A. (2000). Psychological type and dentistry. *Journal of Psychological Types, 55,* 26–34.

Santor, D. A., & Zuroff, D. C. (1994). Depressive symptoms: Effects of negative affectivity and failing to accept the past. *Journal of Personality Assessment, 63,* 294–312.

Sarason, I. G. (1975). Test anxiety and the self-disclosing coping model. *Journal of Consulting and Clinical Psychology, 43,* 148–153.

Saroglou, V. (2002). Religion and the five factors of personality: A meta-analytic review. *Personality and Individual Differences, 32,* 15–25.

Sato, T. (2001). Autonomy and relatedness in psychopathology and treatment: A cross-cultural formulation. *Genetic, Social & General Psychology Monographs, 127,* 89–127.

Saucier, G., & Goldberg, L. R. (1998). What is beyond the Big Five? *Journal of Personality, 66,* 495–524.

Scharrer, E. (2001). Men, muscles, and machismo: The relationship between television violence exposure and aggression and hostility in the presence of hypermasculinity. *Media Psychology, 3,* 159–188.

Schieman, S., Pudrovska, T., & Milkie, M. A. (2005). The sense of divine control and the self-concept. *Research on Aging, 27,* 165–196.

Schmidt, D. B., Lubinski, D., & Benbow, C. P. (1998). Validity of assessing educational-vocational preference dimensions among intellectually talented 13-year-olds. *Journal of Counseling Psychology, 45,* 436–453.

Schmitt, J. P., & Kurdek, L. A. (1984). Correlates of social anxiety in college students and homosexuals. *Journal of Personality Assessment, 48,* 403–409.

Schuerger, J. M. (1992). The Sixteen Personality Factor Questionnaire and its junior versions. *Journal of Counseling and Development, 71,* 231–244.

Schwartz, S. J. (2001). The evolution of Eriksonian and neo-Eriksonian identity theory and research: A review and integration. *Identity: An International Journal of Theory and Research, 1,* 7–58.

Schwartz, S. J. (2004). Brief report: Construct validity of two identity status measures: the EIPQ and the EOM-EIS-II. *Journal of Adolescence, 27,* 477–483.

Schwartz, S. J. (2005). A new identity for identity research: Recommendations for expanding and refocusing the identity literature. *Journal of Adolescent Research, 20,* 293–308.

Schwartz, S. J., Adamson, L., Ferrer-Wreden, L., Dillon, F. R., & Berman, S. L. (2006). Identity status measurement across contexts: Variations in measurement structure and mean levels among White American, Hispanic American, and Swedish emerging adults. *Journal of Personality Assessment, 86,* 61–76.

Schweizer, K., & Koch, W. (2001). The assessment of components of optimism by POSO-E. *Personality and Individual Differences, 31,* 563–574.

Scott, J. (2007). The effect of perfectionism and unconditional self-acceptance on depression. *Journal of Rational-Emotive and Cognitive-Behavior, 25,* 35–64.

Sedikides, C. (2010). Why does religiosity persist? *Personality and Social Psychology Review, 14,* 3–6.

Segall, M. E., & Wynd, C. A. (1990). Health conception, health locus of control, and power as predictors of smoking behavior change. *American Journal of Health Promotion, 4*, 338–344.

Seligman, M. E. P. (2002). *Authentic happiness: Using the new positive psychology to realize your potential for lasting fulfillment.* New York: Free Press.

Seligman, M., & Csikszentmihalyi, M. (2000). Positive psychology: An introduction. *American Psychologist, 55*, 5–14.

Seligman, M., Steen, T. A., Park, N., & Peterson, C. (2005). Positive psychology progress. *American Psychologist, 60*, 410–421.

Sexton, T. L., & Whiston, S. C. (1994). The status of the counseling relationship: An empirical review, theoretical implications, and research directions. *The Counseling Psychologist, 22*, 6–78.

Shanahan, M. J., & Pychyl, T. A. (2007). An ego identity perspective on volitional action: Identity status, agency, and procrastination. *Personality and Individual Differences, 43*, 901–911.

Shaver, P. R., & Mikulincer, M. (2005). Attachment theory and research: Resurrection of the psychodynamic approach to personality. *Journal of Research in Personality, 39*, 22–45.

Shell, D. F., Bruning, R. H., & Colvin, C. (1995). Self-efficacy, attribution, and outcome expectancy mechanisms in reading and writing achievement: Grade-level and achievement-level differences. *Journal of Educational Psychology, 87*, 386–398.

Sherry, J. L. (2001). The effects of violent video games on aggression: A meta-analysis. *Human Communication Research, 27*, 409–431.

Shilkret, C. J., & Masling, J. M. (1981). Oral dependence and dependent behavior. *Journal of Personality Assessment, 45*, 125–129.

Shin, W. S. (1993). Self-actualization and wilderness attitudes: A replication. *Journal of Social Behavior and Personality, 8*, 241–256.

Shostrom, E. L. (1963). *Personal Orientation Inventory.* San Diego: EdITS/Educational and Industrial Testing Service.

Shrake, E. K., & Rhee, S. (2004). Ethnic identity as a predictor of problem behavior among Korean American adolescents. *Adolescence, 39*, 601–622.

Silberman, I. (2005). Religious violence, terrorism, and peace. In R. F. Paloutzian and C.L. Park (Eds)., *Handbook of the psychology of religion and spirituality* (pp. 529–549). New York: Guilford Press.

Silverman, D. K. (1986). Some proposed modifications of psychoanalytic theories of early childhood development. In J. Masling (Ed.), *Empirical studies of psychoanalytic theories* (pp. 49–72). Hillsdale, NJ: Erlbaum.

Silverman, L. H. (1976). Psychoanalytic theory: The reports of my death are greatly exaggerated. *American Psychologist, 31*, 621–637.

Silvia, P. J., & O'Brien, M. E. (2004). Self-awareness and constructive functioning: Revisiting "The human dilemma." *Journal of Social and Clinical Psychology, 23*, 475–489.

Simonton, D. K. (1994). *Greatness: Who makes history and why.* New York: Guilford Press.

Skinner, B. F. (1938). *The behavior of organisms.* New York: Appleton-Century-Crofts.

Skinner, B. F. (1948). *Walden Two.* New York: Macmillan.

Skinner, B. F. (1950). Are theories of learning necessary? *Psychological Review, 57*, 193–216.

Skinner, B. F. (1953). *Science and human behavior.* New York: Macmillan.

Skinner, B. F. (1968). *The technology of teaching.* New York: Appleton-Century-Crofts.

Skinner, B. F. (1969). *Contingencies of reinforcement.* New York: Appleton-Century-Crofts.

Skinner, B. F. (1970). An autobiography. In P. B. Dews (Ed.), *Festschrift for B. F. Skinner* (pp. 1–21). New York: Appleton-Century-Crofts.

Skinner, B. F. (1971). *Beyond freedom and dignity.* New York: Knopf.

Skinner, B. F. (1973). Answers for my critics. In H. Wheeler (Ed.), *Beyond the punitive society* (pp. 256–266). San Francisco: W. H. Freeman.

Skinner, B. F. (1974). *About behaviorism.* New York: Knopf.

Skinner, B. F. (1976). *Particulars of my life.* New York: Knopf.

Skinner, B. F. (1987). Whatever happened to psychology as the science of behavior? *American Psychologist, 42*, 780–786.

Slugoski, B. R., Marcia, J. E., & Koopman, R. F. (1984). Cognitive and social interactional characteristics of ego identity statuses in college. *Journal of Personality and Social Psychology, 47*, 646–661.

Smalley, R. L., & Stake, J.E. (1996). Evaluating sources of ego-threatening feedback: Self-esteem and narcissism effects. *Journal of Research in Personality, 30*, 483–495.

Smith, C. E., & Hopkins, R. (2004). Mitigating the impact of stereotypes on academic performance: The effects of cultural identity and attributions for success among African-American college students. *Western Journal of Black studies, 28*, 312–321.

Smith, P., Magaro, P., & Pederson, S. (1983). Clinical types in a normal population: Concurrent and construct validity. *Journal of Clinical Psychology*, *39*, 498–506.

Snarey, J. (1993). *How fathers care for the next generation: A four-decade study*. Cambridge, MA: Harvard University Press.

Snarey, J., Son, L., Kuehne, V. S., Hauser, S., & Vaillant, G. (1987). The role of parenting in men's psychosocial development: A longitudinal study of early adulthood infertility and midlife generativity. *Developmental Psychology*, *23*, 593–603.

Spector, P. E. (1988). Development of the Work Locus of Control Scale. *Journal of Occupational Psychology*, *61*, 335–340.

Spector, P. E., & O'Connell, B. J. (1994). The contribution of personality traits, negative affectivity, locus of control. and type A to the subsequent reports of job stressors and job strains. *Journal of Occupational and Organizational Psychology*, *67*, 1–12.

Spilka, B., Hood, R. W., Hunsberger, B., & Gorsuch, R. (2003). *The psychology of religion: An empirical approach*. (3rd ed.) New York: Guilford Press.

Spokas, M., & Heimberg, R. G. (2009). Overprotective parenting, social anxiety, and external locus of control: Cross-sectional and longitudinal relationships. *Cognitive Therapy and Research*, *33*, 543–551.

Sprohge, E., Handler, L., Plant, D. D., & Wicker, D. (2002). A Rorschach study of oral dependence in alcoholics and depressives. *Journal of Personality Assessment*, *79*, 142–160.

Sprouse, D. S., Ogletree, S. L., Comsudes, M. M., Granville, H. G., & Kern, R. M. (2005). An Adlerian model for alliance building. *Journal of Individual Psychology*, *61*, 137–148.

Srivastava, S., Angelo, K. M., & Vallereux, S. R. (2008). Extraversion and positive affect: A day reconstruction study of person-environment transactions. *Journal of Research in Personality*, *42*, 1613–1618.

Steele, C. M. (1988). The psychology of self-affirmation: Sustaining the integrity of the self. In L. Berkowitz (Ed.), *Advances in experimental social psychology* (Vol. 21, pp. 261–302). New York: Academic Press.

Steelman, L. C. (1985). A tale of two variables: A review of the intellectual consequences of sibship size and birth order. *Review of Educational Research*, *55*, 353–386.

Steelman, L. C. (1986). The tale retold: A response to Zajonc. *Review of Educational Research*, *56*, 373–377.

Steffen, P. R., & Masters, K. S. (2005). Does compassion mediate the intrinsic religion-health relationship? *Annals of Behavioral Medicine*, *30*, 217–224.

Stein, J. A., & Newcomb, M. D. (1999). Adult outcomes of adolescent conventional and agentic orientations: A 20-year longitudinal study. *Journal of Early Adolescence*, *19*, 39–65.

Steinberg, B. S. (2001). The making of female presidents and prime ministers: The impact of birth order, sex of siblings, and father-daughter dynamics. *Political Psychology*, *22*, 89–110.

Stelmack, R. M. (1990). Biological bases of extraversion: Psychophysiological evidence. *Journal of Personality*, *58*, 293–311.

Stephenson, W. (1953). *The study of behavior*. Chicago: University of Chicago Press.

Steptoe, A., & Wardle, J. (2001). Locus of control and health behaviour revisited: A multivariate analysis of young adults from 18 countries. *British Journal of Psychology*, *92*, 659–672.

Stewart, A. E. (2010). Explorations in the meanings of excellence and its importance for counselors: The culture of excellence in the United States. *Journal of Counseling & Development*, *88*, 189–195.

Stiles, K., & Wilborn, B. (1992). A life-style instrument for children. *Individual Psychology*, *48*, 96–106.

Stilwell, N. A., & Wallick, M. M. (2000). Myers-Briggstype and medical specialty choice: A new look at an old question. *Teaching & Learning in Medicine*, *12*, 14–20.

Stock, J., & Cervone, D. (1990). Proximal goal-setting and self-regulatory processes. *Cognitive Therapy and Research*, *14*, 483–489.

Stone, R. H. (2008). *Moral reflections on foreign policy in a religious war*. Plymouth, UK: Lexington Books.

Storr, A. (1991). *Jung*. New York: Routledge.

Strano, D. A., & Petrocelli, J. V. (2005). A preliminary examination of the role of inferiority feelings in the academic achievement of college students. *Journal of Individual Psychology*, *61*, 80–89.

Strauser, D. R., & Ketz, K., & Keim, J. (2002). The relationship between self-efficacy, locus of control and work personality. *Journal of Rehabilitation*, *68*, 20–26.

Strelau, J. (2008). *Temperament as a regulator of Behavior: After fifty years of research*. Clinton Corners, New York: Eliot Werner Publications.

Strickland, B. R. (1978). Internal-external expectancies and health-related behaviors. *Journal of Consulting and Clinical Psychology*, *46*, 1192–1211.

Strickland, B. R. (1979). Internal-external expectancies and cardiovascular functioning. In L. C. Perlmutter

& R.A. Monty (Eds.), *Choice and perceived control* (pp. 221–231). Hillsdale, NJ: Erlbaum.

Stright, A. D., Gallagher, K. C., & Kelley, K. (2008). Infant temperament moderates relations between maternal parenting in early childhood and children's adjustment in first grade. *Child Development, 79,* 186–200.

Strozier, C. B. (1985). Glimpses of a life: Heinz Kohut (1913–1981). In A. Goldberg (Ed.). *Progress in self psychology* (Vol. 1, pp. 3–12). New York: Guilford Press.

Stucke, T. S., & Baumeister, R. F. (2006). Ego depletion and aggressive behavior: Is the inhibition of aggression a limited resource? *European Journal of Social Psychology, 36,* 1–13.

Stunkard, A. J. (1991). Review of Schwartz, H. J. (Eds.), *Bulimia: Psychoanalytic treatment and theory* (Madison, CT: International Universities Press, 1988). *Psychiatric Annals, 19,* 279.

Suarez-Balcazar, Y., Balcazar, F. E., & Taylor-Ritzler, T. (2009). Using the internet to conduct research with culturally diverse populations: Challenges and opportunities. *Cultural Diversity and Ethnic Minority Psychology, 15,* 96–104.

Suh, S., & Suh, J. (2006). Educational engagement and degree attainment among high school dropouts. *Educational Research Quarterly, 29,* 11–20.

Sutton, C. T., & Broken Nose, M. A. (1996). American Indian families: An overview. In M. Goldrick, J. Giordano, and J. K. Pearce (Eds.), *Ethnicity and family therapy* (2nd ed., pp. 31–43). New York: Guilford Press.

Suzuki, S., Holloway, S. D., Yamamoto, Y., & Mindnich, J. D. (2009). Parenting self-efficacy and social support in Japan and the United States. *Journal of Family Issues, 30,* 1505–1526.

Taber, B. J., Hartung, P. J., & Borges, N. J. (2011). Personality and values as predictors of medical specialty choice. *Journal of Vocational Behavior, 78,* 202–209.

Taft, L. B., & Nehrke, M. F. (1990). Reminiscence, life review, and ego integrity in nursing home residents. *International Journal of Aging and Human Development, 30,* 189–196.

Tangney, J. P., Baumeister, R. F., & Boone, A. L. (2004). High self-control predicts good adjustment, less pathology, better grades, and interpersonal success. *Journal of Personality, 72,* 271–322.

Taylor, S. E., Peplau, L. A., & Sears, D. O. (2000). *Social psychology* (10th ed.). Upper Saddle River, NJ: Prentice Hall.

Teplov, B. M. (1964). The historical development of Pavlov's theory of typological differences in the dog. In J. A. Gray (Ed.), *Pavlov's typology* (pp. 3–153). New York: Macmillan.

Thorndike, E. L. (1913). *Educational psychology.* New York: Teachers College, Columbia University.

Thorne, A. (1989). Conditional patterns, transference, and the coherence of personality across time. In D. M. Buss and N. Cantor (Eds.), *Personality psychology: Recent trends and emerging directions* (pp.149–159). New York: Springer-Verlag.

Thorne, B. (1992). *Carl Rogers.* Newbury Park, CA: Sage Publications.

Tice, D. M., & Baumeister, R. F. (2001). The primacy of the interpersonal self. In C. Sedikides and M.B. Brewer (Eds.) *Individual self, relational self, collective self* (pp.71–88). Ann Arbor, MI: Sheridan Books.

Tolpin, P. (1980). The borderline personality: Its makeup and analyzability. In A. Goldberg (Ed.), *Advances in self psychology* (pp. 299–316). New York: International Universities Press.

Triandis, H. C. (2001). *Individualism-collectivism and personality. Journal of Personality, 69,* 907–923.

Tribich, D., & Messer, S. (1974). Psychoanalytic character type and status of authority as determiners of suggestibility. *Journal of Consulting and Clinical Psychology, 42,* 842–848.

Trice, A. D. (1990). Adolescents' locus of control and compliance with contingency contracting and counseling interventions. *Psychological Reports, 67,* 233–234.

Trumpeter, N. N., Watson, P. J., O'Leary, B. J., & Weathington, B. L. (2008). Self-functioning and perceived parenting: Relations of parental empathy and love inconsistency with narcissism, depression, and self-esteem. *Journal of Genetic Psychology, 169,* 51–71.

Trusty, J., & Lampe, R. E. (1997). Relationship of highschool seniors' perceptions of parental involvement and control to seniors' locus of control. *Journal of Counseling & Development, 75,* 375–384.

Tupes, E. C., & Christal, R. C. (1961). *Recurrent personality factors based on trait ratings* (Tech. Rep. No. ASDTR61–97). Lackland Air Force Base, TX: U.S. Air Force.

Turner, C., & Berkowitz, L. (1972). Identification with film aggression (covert role taking) and reactions to film violence. *Journal of Personality and Social Psychology, 21,* 256–264.

Tynes, B. M. (2007). Internet safety gone wild?: Sacrificing the educational and psychosocial benefits of online social environments. *Journal of Adolescent Research, 22,* 575–584.

Valkenburg, P. M., Schouten, A. P., & Peter, J. (2005). Adolescents' identity experiments on the internet. *New Media & Society, 7,* 383–402.

van der Veer, P. (1994). *Religious nationalism: Hindus and Muslims in India.* Berkeley, CA: University of California Press.

Van Kaam, A. (1969). *Existential foundations of psychology.* Garden City, NY: Image Books.

Vandewater, D. A., & McAdams, D. P. (1989). Generativity and Erikson's "Belief in the species." *Journal of Research in Personality, 23,* 435–449.

Vaughn, L. M., Naylor, S., & White, Jr., S. (2009). Relationship of attachment style and ethnic identity to self-actualization in college students. *Journal of College & Character, 10,* 2–12.

Ventis, W. L. (1995). The relationships between religion and mental health. *Journal of Social Issues, 51,* 33–48.

Vessey, J. A., & Lee, J. E. (2000). Violent video games affecting our children. *Pediatric Nursing, 26,* 607–610.

Violato, C., & Holden, W. B. (1988). A confirmatory factor analysis of a four-factor model of adolescent concerns. *Journal of Youth and Adolescence, 17,* 101–113.

Voracek, M., & Loibl, L. M. (2007). Genetics of suicide: A systematic review of twin studies. *Wiener Klinische Wochenschrift, 119,* 463–475.

W., Bill (1988). *The language of the heart: Bill W's Grapevine writings.* New York: The AA Grapevine, Inc.

Wagaman, J. R., Miltenberger, R. G., & Arndorfer, R. E. (1993). Analysis of a simplified treatment for stuttering in children. *Journal of Applied Behavior Analysis, 26,* 53–61.

Wagaman, J. R., Miltenberger, R. G., & Woods, D. (1995). Long-term follow-up of a behavioral treatment for stuttering in children. *Journal of Applied Behavior Analysis, 28,* 233–234.

Wagner, M. E., & Schubert, H. J. P. (1977). Sibship variables and United States presidents. *Journal of Individual Psychology, 33,* 78–85.

Wakefield, J. C. (1992). Freud and cognitive psychology: The conceptual interface. In J. W. Barron, M. N. Eagle, and D. L. Wolitzky (Eds.), *Interface of psychoanalysis and psychology* (pp. 77–98). Washington, DC: American Psychological Association.

Walaskay, M., Whitbourne, S. K., & Nehrke, M. F. (1983/1984). Construction and validation of an ego integrity interview. *International Journal of Aging and Human Development, 18,* 61–72.

Wallerstein, R. S. (1995). Obituary: Erik Erikson (1902-1994). *International Journal of Psychoanalysis, 76,* 173–175.

Wallston, K. A., & Wallston, B. S. (1981). Health locus of control scales. In H. M. Lefcourt (Ed.), *Research with the locus of control construct: Vol. 1. Assessment methods* (pp. 189–243). New York: Academic Press.

Wallston, K. A., & Wallston, B. S. (1982). Who is responsible for your health? The construct of health locus of control. In G. Sanders & J. Suls (Eds.), *Social psychology of health and illness* (pp. 65–95). Hillsdale, NJ: Erlbaum.

Walters, G. C., & Grusec, J. E. (1977). *Punishment.* San Francisco: W. H. Freeman.

Waterman, A. S. (1982). Identity development from adolescence to adulthood: An extension of theory and a review of research. *Developmental Psychology, 18,* 341–358.

Waterman, A. S. (1985). Identity in the context of adolescent psychology. In A. S. Waterman (Ed.), *Identity in adolescence: Processes and contents* (pp. 5–24). San Francisco: Jossey-Bass.

Waterman, A. S. (1993). Developmental perspectives on identity formation: From adolescence to adulthood. In J. E. Marcia, A. S. Waterman, D. R. Matteson, S. L. Archer, & J. L. Orlofsky (Eds.), *Ego identity: A handbook for psychosocial research* (pp. 42–68). New York: Springer-Verlag.

Waterman, A. S., Geary, P. S., & Waterman, C. K. (1974). Longitudinal study of changes in ego identity status from the freshman to the senior year at college. *Developmental Psychology, 10,* 387–392.

Watkins, C. E., Jr. (1992). Birth order research and Adler's theory: A critical review. *Individual Psychology, 48,* 357–368.

Watkins, C. E., Jr. (1994). Measuring social interest. *Individual Psychology, 50,* 69–96.

Watkins, C. E., Jr., & St. John, C. (1994). Validity of the Sulliman scale of social interest. *Individual Psychology, 50,* 166–169.

Watson, J. B., & Rayner, R. (1920). Conditioned emotional reactions. *Journal of Experimental Psychology, 3,* 1–14.

Watson, P. J., Biderman, M. D., & Sawrie, S. M. (1994). Empathy, sex role orientation, and narcissism. *Sex Roles, 30,* 701–723.

Watson, P. J., Morris, R. J., & Miller, L. (2001). Irrational beliefs, attitudes about competition, and splitting. *Journal of Clinical Psychology, 57,* 343–354.

Watson, S. (2009). Credit card misuse, money attitudes, and compulsive buying behaviors: A comparison of internal and external locus of control (LOC) consumers. *College Student Journal, 43*, 268–275.

Watts, R. E., & Holden, J. M. (1994). Why continue to use "fictional finalism"? *Individual Psychology, 50*, 161–163.

Watzlawik, M. (2004). Experiencing same-sex attraction: A comparison between American and German adolescents. *Identity, 4*, 171–186.

Westen, D., Gabbard, G.O., & Ortigo, K.M. (2008). Psychoanalytic approaches to personality. In O. P. John, R.W. Robins, and L.A. Pervin (Eds.) *Handbook of personality: Theory and research* (3rd ed.) (pp. 61–113). New York: Guilford Press.

Westphal, K., & Wagner, S. (1993). Differences in irrational beliefs of pregnant and never pregnant adolescents. *Journal of Rational-Emotive & Cognitive Behavior Therapy, 11*, 151–158.

Wheeler, M. S., Kern, R. M., & Curlette, W. L. (1986). Factor analytic scales designed to measure Adlerian life style themes. *Individual Psychology, 42*, 1–16.

Wichman, A. L., Rodgers, J. L., & MacCallum, R. C. (2006). A multilevel approach to the relationship between birth order and intelligence. *Personality and Social Psychology Bulletin, 32*, 117–127.

Williams-Piehota, P., Schneider, T. R., Pizarro, J., Mowad, L., & Salovey, P. (2004). Matching health messages to health locus of control beliefs for promoting mammography utilization. *Psychology and Health, 19*, 407–423.

Williams, R. L., & Long, J. D. (1979). *Toward a self-managed life style.* Boston: Houghton Mifflin.

Wills, T. A., Gibbons, F. X., Sargent, J. D., Gerrard, M., Lee, H.-R., & Dal Cin, S. (2010). Good self-control moderates the effect of mass media on adolescent tobacco and alcohol use: Tests with children and adolescents. *Health Psychology, 29*, 539–549.

Wilson, C. (1972). *New pathways in psychology.* London: Gollancz.

Winefield, H., & Air, T. (2010). Grandparenting: Diversity in grandparent experiences and needs for healthcare and support. *International Journal of Evidence-based Healthcare, 8*, 277–283.

Wink, P. (1991). Self- and object-directedness in adult women. *Journal of Personality, 59*, 769–785.

Wink, P. (1992). Three types of narcissism in women from college to mid-life. *Journal of Personality, 60*, 7–30.

Wink, P. (1996). Transition from the early 40s to the early 50s in self-directed women. *Journal of Personality, 64*, 49–69.

Wolf, E. S. (1988). *Treating the self.* New York: Guilford Press.

Wong, S. S., & Ng, V. (2008). A qualitative and quantitative Study of psychotherapists' congruence in Singapore. *Psychotherapy Research, 18*, 58–76.

Workman, L., & Reader, W. (2008). *Evolutionary psychology: An introduction.* (2nd ed.). Cambridge, UK: Cambridge University Press.

World Almanac and Book of Facts 2010. (2010). United States Population (pp. 612–650). New York: World Almanac Books.

Wright, J. C., & Mischel, W. (1987). A conditional approach to dispositional constructs: The local predictability of social behavior. *Journal of Personality and Social Psychology, 53*, 1159–1177.

Wulff, D. M. (1991). *Psychology of religion: Classic and contemporary views.* New York: Wiley.

Wylie, R. C. (1979). *The self concept* (Vol. 2). Lincoln: University of Nebraska.

Yang, C. K., Choe, B. M., Baity, M., Lee, J. H., & Cho, J. S. (2005). SCL-90-R and 16PF profiles of senior high school students with excessive internet use. *Canadian Journal of Psychiatry, 50*, 407–414.

Yeh, C., & Inose, M. (2002). Difficulties and coping strategies of Chinese, Japanese, and Korean immigrant students. *Adolescence, 37*, 69–82.

Yusko, D. A., Buckman, J. F., White, H. R., & Pandina, R. J. (2008). Risk for excessive alcohol use and drinking-related problems in college student athletes. *Addictive Behaviors, 33*, 1546–1556.

Zaccaria, J. S., & Weir, W. R. (1967). A comparison of alcoholics and selected samples of nonalcoholics in terms of a positive concept of mental health. *Journal of Social Psychology, 71*, 151–157.

Zadra, A. L., O'Brien, S. A., & Donderi, D. C. (1997–1998). Dream content, dream recurrence, and well-being: A replication with a younger sample. *Imagination, Cognition, & Personality, 17*, 293–311.

Zajacova, A., Lynch, S. M., & Espenshade, T. J. (2005). Self-efficacy, stress, and academic success in college. *Research in Higher Education, 46*, 677–706.

Zajonc, R. B. (1976). Family configuration and intelligence. *Science, 192*, 227–236.

Zajonc, R. B. (1983). Validating the confluence model. *Psychological Bulletin, 93*, 457–480.

Zajonc, R. B. (1986). Family factors and intellectual test performance: A reply to Steelman. *Review of Educational Research, 56*, 365–371.

Zajonc, R. B. (2001). The family dynamics of intellectual development. *American Psychologist, 56*, 490–496.

Zajonc, R. B., & Bargh, J. (1980). The confluence model: Parameter estimation in six divergent data sets on family factors and intelligence. *Intelligence, 4,* 349–361.

Zajonc, R. B., & Markus, G. B. (1975). Birth order and intellectual development. *Psychological Review, 82,* 74–88.

Zajonc, R. B., & Mullally, P. R. (1997). Birth order: Reconciling conflicting effects. *American Psychologist, 52,* 685–699.

Zamostny, K. P., Slyter, S. L., & Rios, P. (1993). Narcissistic injury and its relationship to early trauma, early resources, and adjustment to college. *Journal of Counseling Psychology, 40,* 501–510.

Zuckerman, M. (1990). The psychophysiology of sensation-seeking. *Journal of Personality, 58,* 313–345.

Zweigenhaft, R. L. (1975). Birth order, approval seeking, and membership in Congress. *Journal of Individual Psychology, 31,* 205–210.

Name Index

Note Page references followed by "*f*" and "*t*" denote figures and tables, respectively.

Subject Index